AZ SUPER SCAL
GREAT BRITAIN
NORTHERN IRELAND

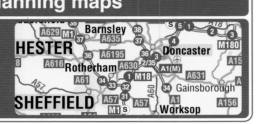

EDITION 30 2021
Copyright © Geographers' A-Z Map Company Ltd.

registered trade marks of
Geographers' A-Z Map Company Ltd

www./az.co.uk

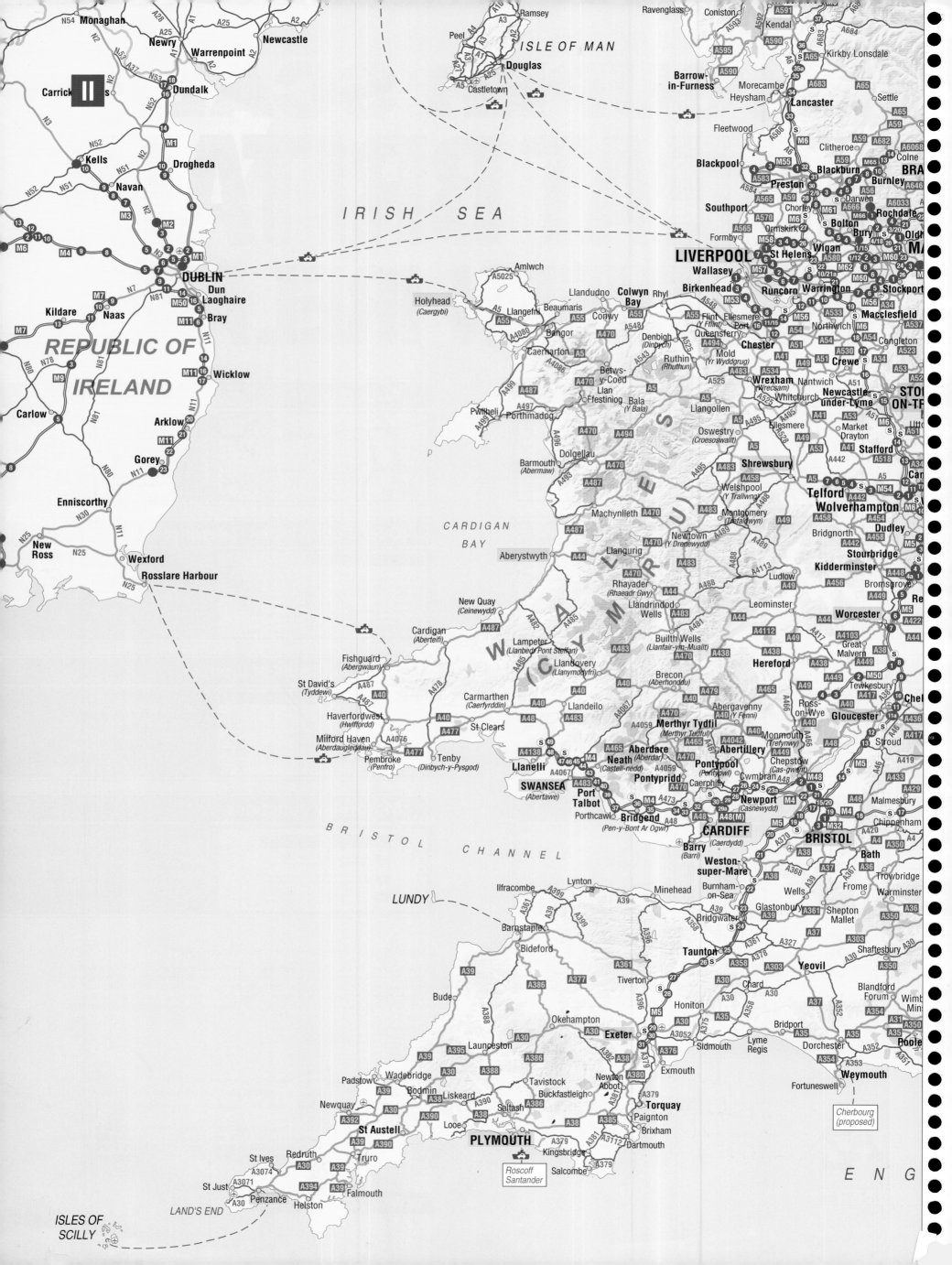

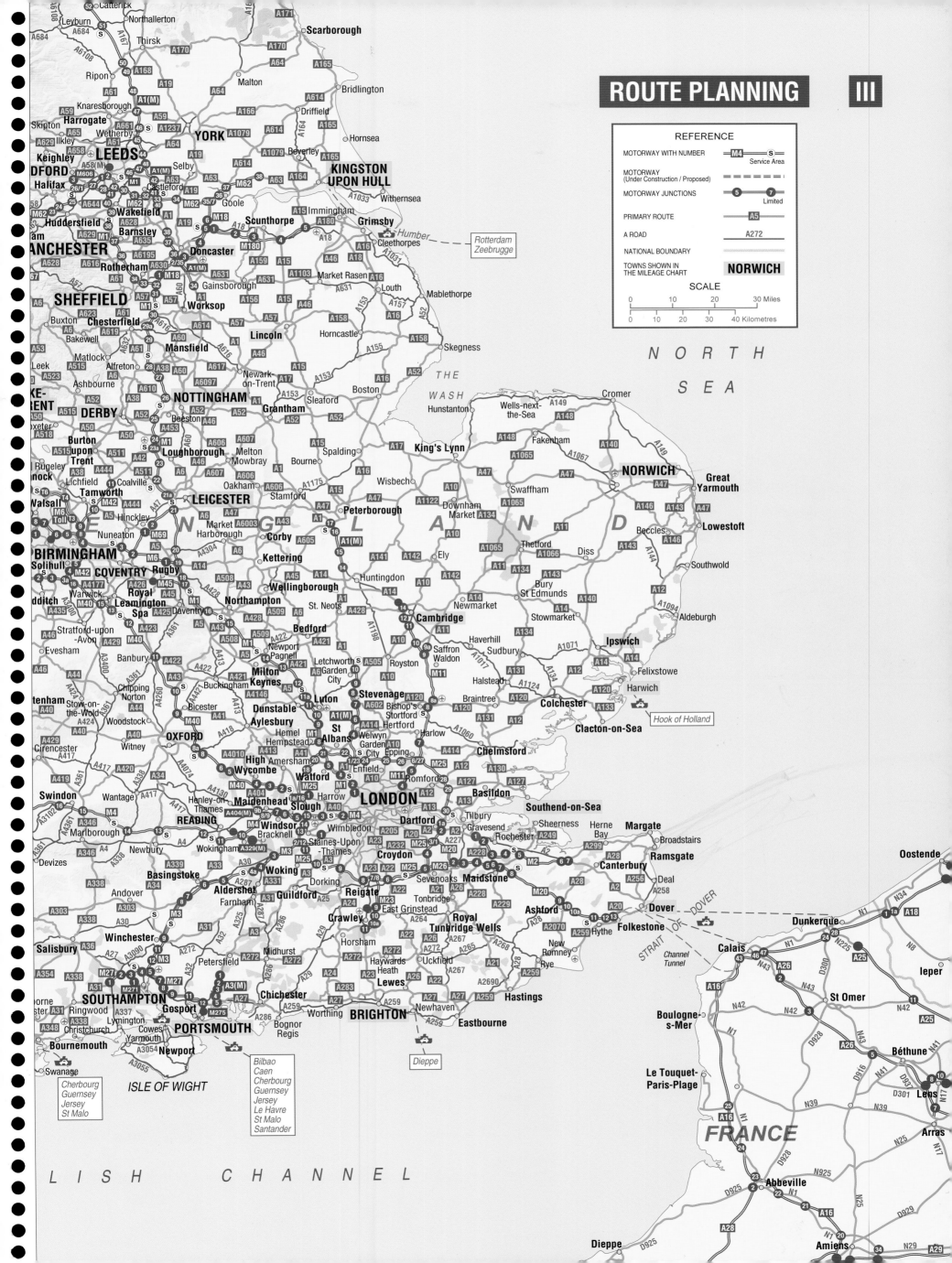

REFERENCE

MOTORWAY WITH NUMBER	M4 — s — Service Area
MOTORWAY (Under Construction / Proposed)	- - - - - - -
MOTORWAY JUNCTIONS	5 — 7 Limited
PRIMARY ROUTE	A5
A ROAD	A272
NATIONAL BOUNDARY	
TOWNS SHOWN IN THE MILEAGE CHART	**NORWICH**

SCALE

0   10   20   30 Miles
0   10   20   30   40 Kilometres

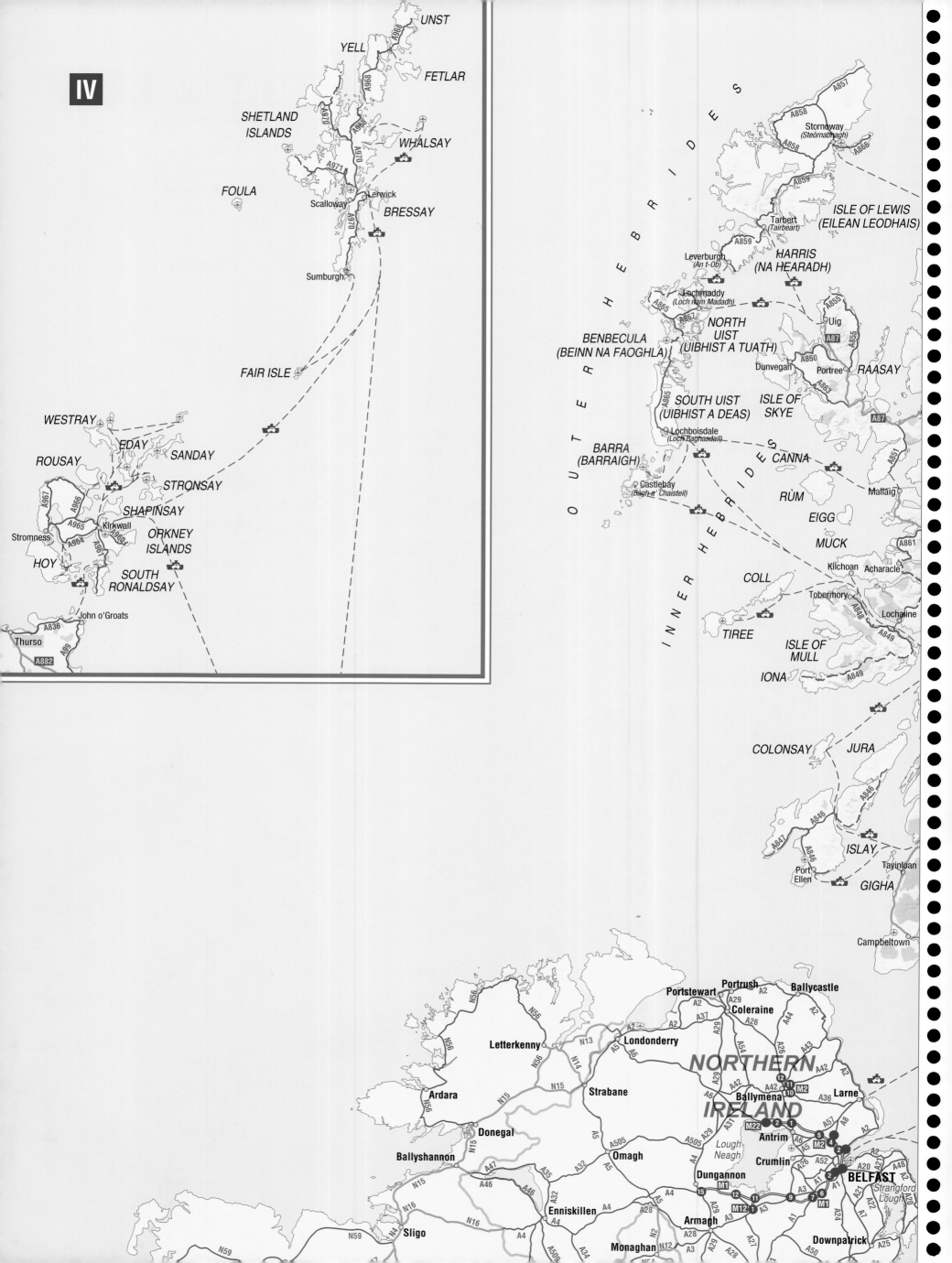

IV

V

NORTH SEA

SCOTLAND

Stromness
Scrabster
John o'Groats
Thurso
Tongue
Wick
Scourie
Helmsdale
Lochinver
Lairg
Bonar Bridge
Tain
Ullapool
Cromarty
Lossiemouth
Fraserburgh
Kinlochewe
Dingwall
Nairn
Elgin
Banff
Peterhead
Achnasheen
Keith
Shieldaig
Strathcarron
Inverness
Dufftown
Huntly
Oldmeldrum
Kyle of Lochalsh
(Caol Loch Ailse)
Loch Ness
Grantown-on-Spey
Inverurie
Invermoriston
Aviemore
Peterculter
ABERDEEN
Invergarry
Newtonmore
Spean Bridge
Braemar
Ballater
Banchory
Stonehaven
Fort William
Glencoe
Pitlochry
Brechin
Montrose
Oban
Crianlarich
Crieff
Blairgowrie
Forfar
Dunkeld
Arbroath
Perth
Dundee
Carnoustie
Inveraray
Doune
Dunblane
Kinross
St Andrews
Loch Lomond
Stirling
Glenrothes
Pittenweem
Lochgilphead
Dunfermline
Cowdenbeath
Kirkcaldy
North Berwick
Dunoon
GLASGOW
Falkirk
EDINBURGH
Dunbar
Greenock
Clydebank
Airdrie
Musselburgh
Eyemouth
Paisley
Motherwell
Livingston
Dalkeith
Largs
Hamilton
East Kilbride
Penicuik
Duns
Berwick-upon-Tweed
Ardrossan
Lauder
Irvine
Kilmarnock
Biggar
Peebles
Galashiels
Coldstream
Brodick
Troon
Selkirk
Kelso
Wooler
Prestwick
Jedburgh
Ayr
Cumnock
Hawick
Alnwick
Girvan
Sanquhar
Moffat
Amble
New Galloway
Ashington
Morpeth
Blyth
Newton Stewart
Lockerbie
Whitley Bay
Amsterdam
Dumfries
NEWCASTLE UPON TYNE
Tynemouth
Stranraer
Annan
Brampton
South Shields
Castle Douglas
Dalbeattie
Hexham
Corbridge
Gateshead
SUNDERLAND
Whithorn
Kirkcudbright
Carlisle
Consett
Washington
Seaham
Workington
Alston
Durham
Peterlee
Cockermouth
Penrith
Bishop Auckland
HARTLEPOOL
Whitehaven
Keswick
Brough
STOCKTON-ON-TEES
Egremont
Barnard Castle
Darlington
MIDDLESBROUGH
Whitby
Ambleside
Windermere
Richmond
Catterick
Ravenglass
Coniston
Northallerton
Ramsey

Légende / Zeichenerklärung

Motorway Autoroute / Autobahn	≡ M1
Motorway Under Construction Autoroute en construction / Autobahn im Bau	
Motorway Proposed Autoroute prévue / Geplante Autobahn	= = = =
Motorway Junctions with Numbers Unlimited Interchange — 4 Limited Interchange — 5 Autoroute échangeur numéroté Echangeur complet Echangeur partiel Autobahnanschlußstelle mit Nummer Unbeschränkter Fahrtrichtungswechsel Beschränkter Fahrtrichtungswechsel	4 5
Motorway Service Area (with fuel station) with access from one carriageway only Aire de services d'autoroute (avec station service) accessible d'un seul côté Rastplatz oder Raststätte (mit tankstelle) Einbahn	S S
Major Road Service Area (with fuel station) with 24 hour facilities Primary Route — S Class A Road — S Aire de services sur route prioritaire (avec station service) Ouverte 24h sur 24 Route à grande circulation Route de type A Raststätte (mit tankstelle) Durchgehend geöffnet Hauptverkehrsstraße A- Straße	S S
Major Road Junctions Detailed / Détaillé / Ausführlich Jonctions grands routiers Hauptverkehrsstraße Kreuzungen Other Autre Andere	4 ●●
Truckstop (selection of) Sélection d'aire pour poids lourds Auswahl von Fernfahrerrastplatz	T
Primary Route Route à grande circulation / Hauptverkehrsstraße	A41
Primary Route Junction with Number Echangeur numéroté Hauptverkehrsstraßenkreuzung mit Nummer	5
Primary Route Destination Route prioritaire, direction Hauptverkehrsstraße Richtung	**DOVER**

Dual Carriageways (A & B roads) Route à double chaussées séparées (route A & B) Zweispurige Schnellstraße (A- und B- Straßen)	
Class A Road Route de type A / A-Straße	A129
Class B Road Route de type B / B-Straße	B177
Narrow Major Road (passing places) Route prioritaire étroite (possibilité de dépassement) Schmale Hauptverkehrsstaße (mit Überholmöglichkeit)	
Major Roads Under Construction Route prioritaire en construction Hauptverkehrsstaße im Bau	
Major Roads Proposed Route prioritaire prévue Geplante Hauptverkehrsstraße	
Gradient 1:7 (14%) **& steeper** (descent in direction of arrow) Pente égale ou supérieure à 14% (dans le sens de la descente) 14% Steigung und steiler (in Pfeilrichtung)	≫ ≫
Toll Barrière de péage / Gebührenpflichtig	Toll
Dart Charge www.gov.uk/pay-dartford-crossing-charge	C
Park & Ride Parking avec Service Navette / Parken und Reisen	P+R
Mileage between markers Distence en miles entre les flèches Strecke zwischen Markierungen in Meilen	8
Airport Aéroport / Flughafen	✈
Airfield Terrain d'aviation / Flugplatz	+
Heliport Héliport / Hubschrauberlandeplatz	H
Ferry (vehicular, sea) (vehicular, river) (foot only) Bac (véhicules, mer) (véhicules, rivière) (piétons) Fähre (auto, meer) (auto, fluß) (nur für Personen)	⛴ ⛴ 🚶

Railway and Station Voie ferrée et gare / Eisenbahnlinie und Bahnhof	—●—
Level Crossing and Tunnel Passage à niveau et tunnel / Bahnübergang und Tunnel	
River or Canal Rivière ou canal / Fluß oder Kanal	
County or Unitary Authority Boundary Limite de comté ou de division administrative Grafschafts- oder Verwaltungsbezirksgrenze	
National Boundary Frontière nationale / Landesgrenze	+ — +
Built-up Area Agglomération / Geschlossene Ortschaft	
Town, Village or Hamlet Ville, Village ou hameau / Stadt, Dorf oder Weiler	○
Wooded Area Zone boisée / Waldgebiet	
Spot Height in Feet Altitude (en pieds) / Höhe in Fuß	·813
Relief above 400' (122m) Relief par estompage au-dessus de 400' (122m) Reliefschattierung über 400' (122m)	
National Grid Reference (kilometres) Coordonnées géographiques nationales (Kilomètres) Nationale geographische Koordinaten (Kilometer)	100
Page Continuation Suite à la page indiquée / Seitenfortsetzung	48
Area covered by Main Route map Repartition des cartes des principaux axes routiers Von Karten mit Hauptverkehrsstrecken	MAIN ROUTE 180
Area covered by Town Plan Ville ayant un plan à la page indiquée Von Karten mit Stadtplänen erfaßter Bereich	PAGE 194

Information / Touristeninformationen — Tourist Information ℹ

Abbey, Church, Friary, Priory Abbaye, église, monastère, prieuré Abtei, Kirche, Mönchskloster, Kloster	†
Animal Collection Ménagerie / Tiersammlung	
Aquarium Aquarium / Aquarium	
Arboretum, Botanical Garden Jardin Botanique / Botanischer Garten	♣
Aviary, Bird Garden Volière / Voliere	
Battle Site and Date Champ de bataille et date / Schlachtfeld und Datum	⚔ 1066
Blue Flag Beach Plage Pavillon Bleu / Blaue Flagge Strand	
Bridge Pont / Brücke	
Butterfly Farm Ferme aux Papillons / Schmetterlingsfarm	
Castle (open to public) Château (ouvert au public) Schloß / Burg (für die Öffentlichkeit zugänglich)	
Castle with Garden (open to public) Château avec parc (ouvert au public) Schloß mit Garten (für die Öffentlichkeit zugänglich)	
Cathedral Cathédrale / Kathedrale	✝
Cidermaker Cidrerie (fabrication) / Apfelwein Hersteller	
Country Park Parc régional / Landschaftspark	
Distillery Distillerie / Brennerei	
Farm Park, Open Farm Park Animalier / Bauernhof Park	

Fortress, Hill Fort Château Fort / Festung	※
Garden (open to public) Jardin (ouvert au public) Garten (für die Öffentlichkeit zugänglich)	❋
Golf Course Terrain de golf / Golfplatz	⚑
Historic Building (open to public) Monument historique (ouvert au public) Historisches Gebäude (für die Öffentlichkeit zugänglich)	🏛
Historic Building with Garden (open to public) Monument historique avec jardin (ouvert au public) Historisches Gebäude mit Garten (für die Öffentlichkeit zugänglich)	
Horse Racecourse Hippodrome / Pferderennbahn	
Industrial Monument Monument Industrielle / Industriedenkmal	✹
Leisure Park, Leisure Pool Parc d'Attraction, Loisirs Piscine Freizeitpark, Freizeit pool	
Lighthouse Phare / Leuchtturm	
Mine, Cave Mine, Grotte / Bergwerk, Höhle	
Monument Monument / Denkmal	
Motor Racing Circuit Circuit Automobile / Automobilrennbahn	
Museum, Art Gallery Musée / Museum, Galerie	M
National Park Parc national / Nationalpark	
National Trail Sentier national / Nationaler Weg	
National Trust Property National Trust Property / National Trust- Eigentum	

Natural Attraction Attraction Naturelle / Natürliche Anziehung	★
Nature Reserve or Bird Sanctuary Réserve naturelle botanique ou ornithologique Natur- oder Vogelschutzgebiet	
Nature Trail or Forest Walk Chemin forestier, piste verte Naturpfad oder Waldweg	
Picnic Site Lieu pour pique-nique / Picknickplatz	⊼
Place of Interest Site, curiosité / Sehenswürdigkeit	Craft Centre ●
Prehistoric Monument Monument Préhistorique / Prähistorische Denkmal	
Railway, Steam or Narrow Gauge Chemin de fer, à vapeur ou à voie étroite Eisenbahn, Dampf- oder Schmalspurbahn	
Roman Remains Vestiges Romains / Römischen Ruinen	
Theme Park Centre de loisirs / Vergnügungspark	
Tourist Information Centre Office de Tourisme / Touristeninformationen	🅸
Viewpoint (360 degrees) (360 degrés) (360 Grade) Vue panoramique (180 degrees) (180 degrés) (180 Grade) Aussichtspunkt	
Vineyard Vignoble / Weinberg	
Visitor Information Centre Centre d'information touristique / Besucherzentrum	V
Wildlife Park Réserve de faune / Wildpark	
Windmill Moulin à vent / Windmühle	
Zoo or Safari Park Parc ou réserve zoologique / Zoo oder Safari-Park	

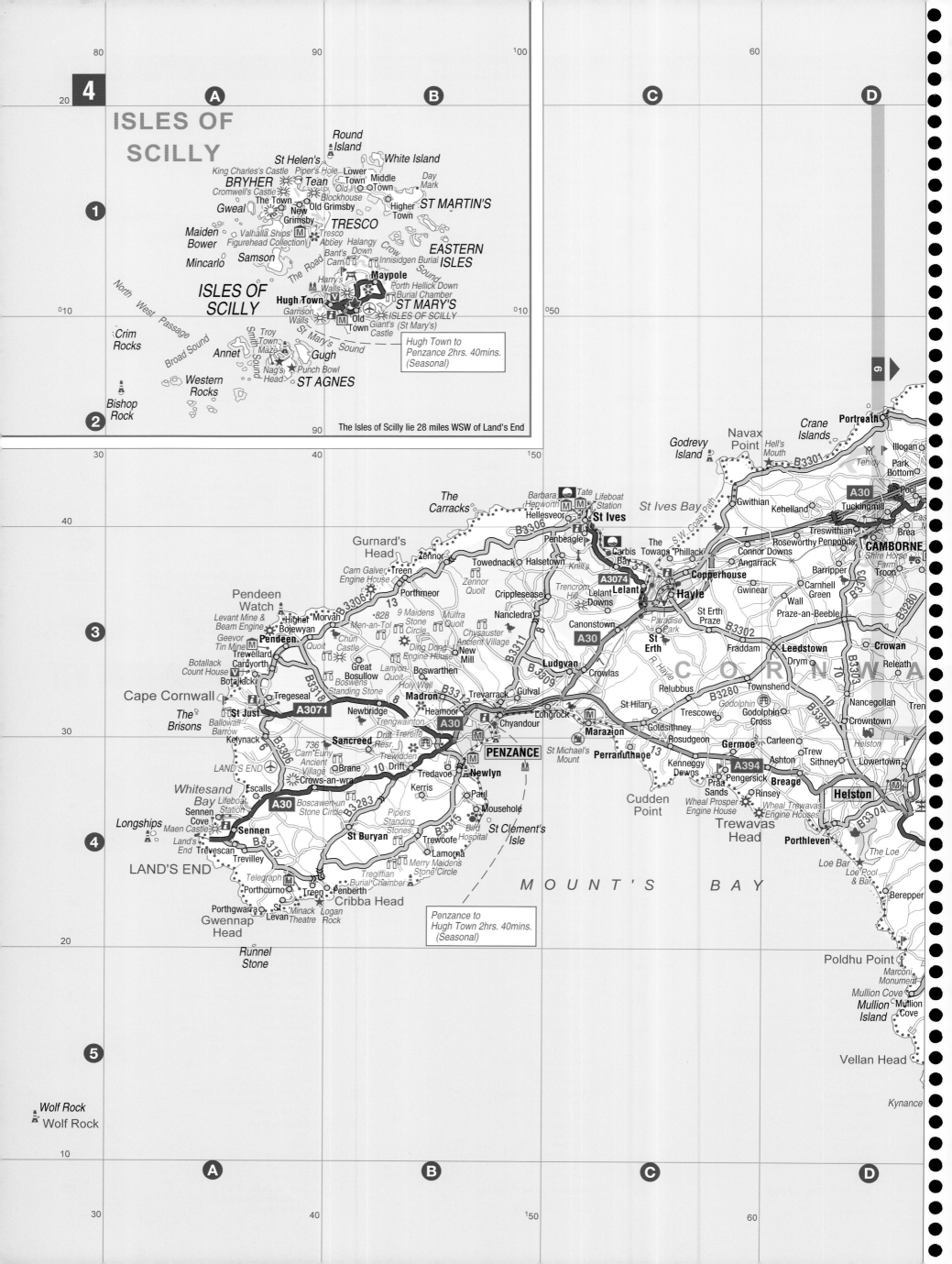

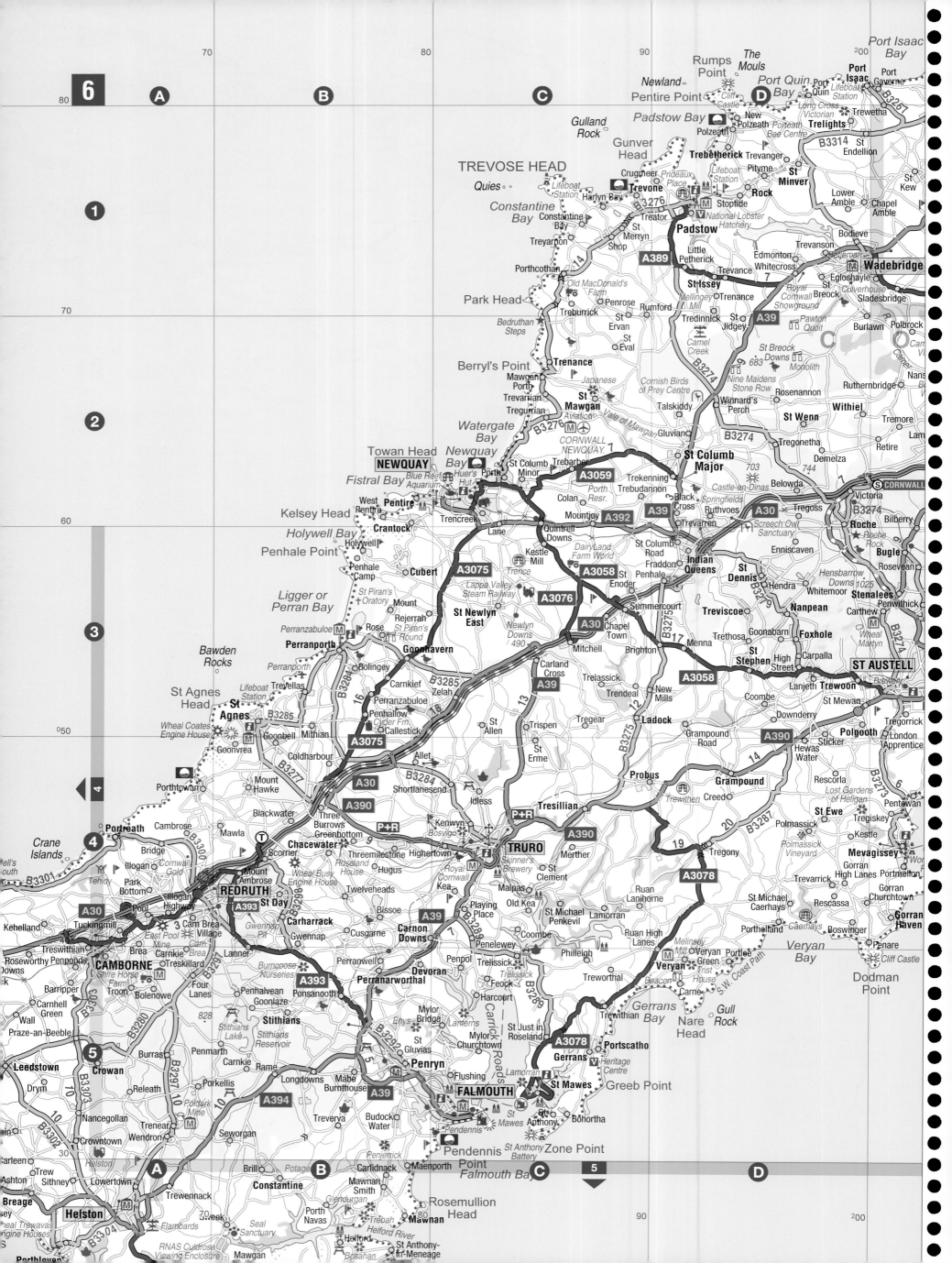

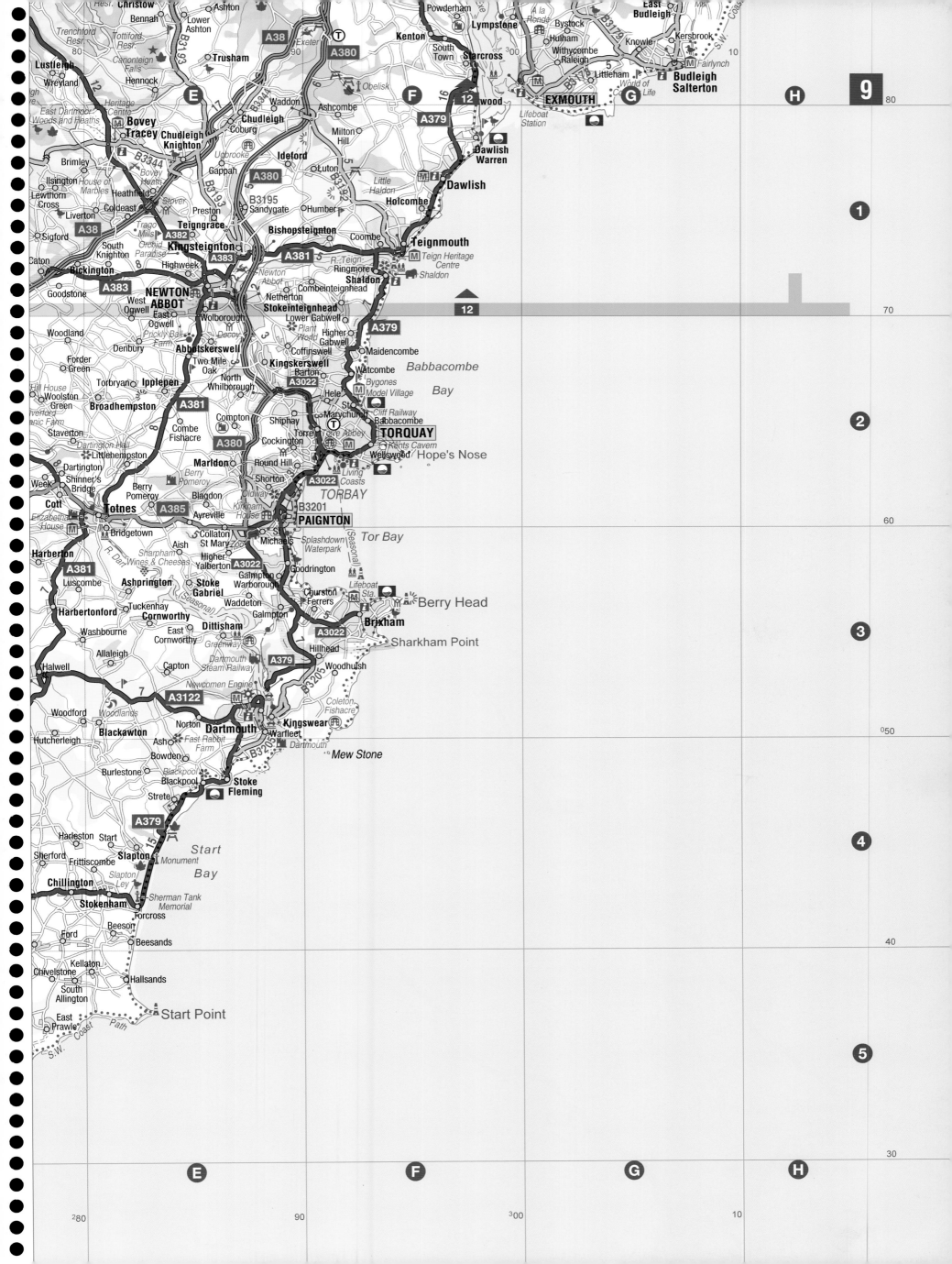

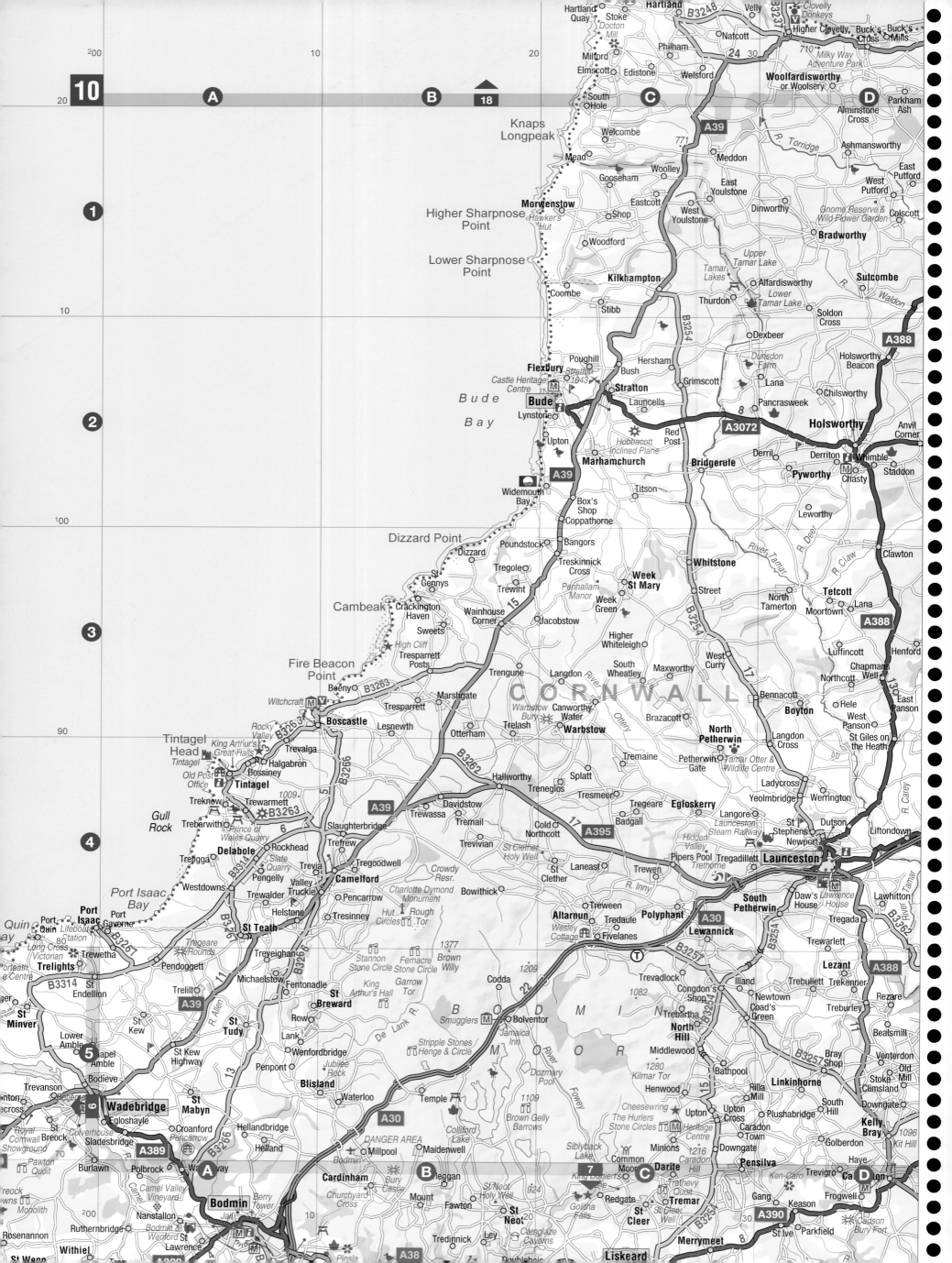

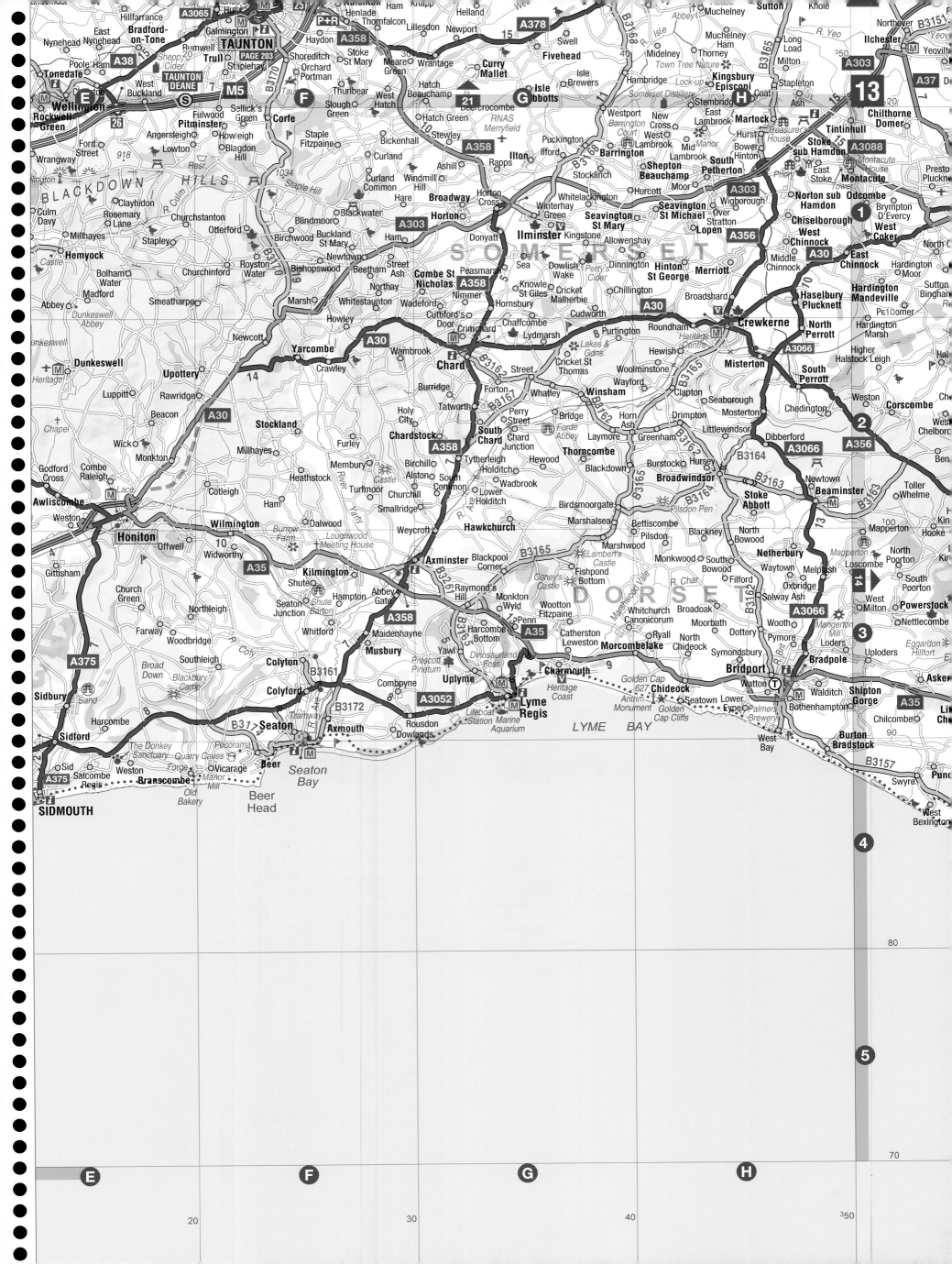

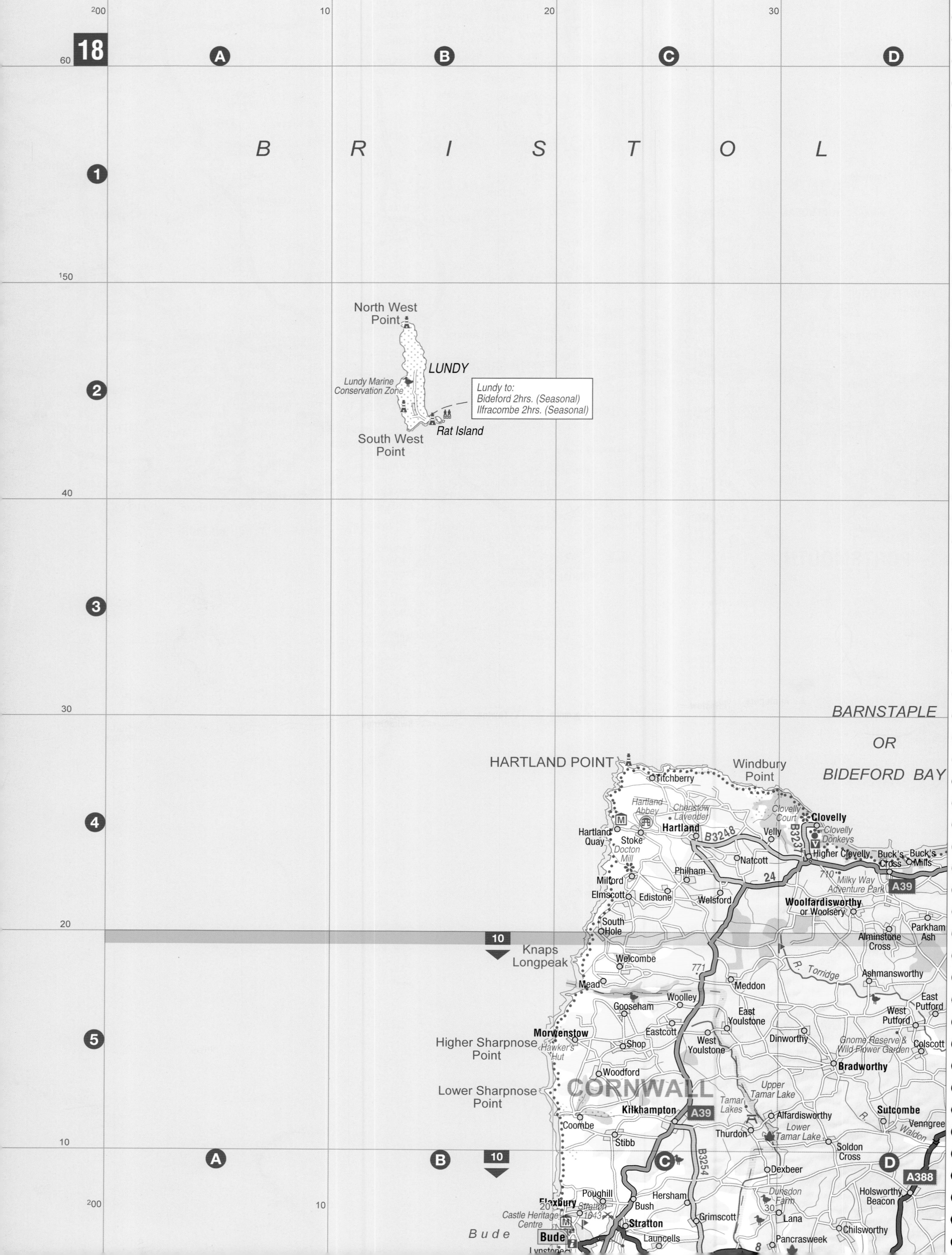

200   10   20   30

60

B   R   I   S   T   O   L

1

150

North West
Point

LUNDY

Lundy Marine
Conservation Zone

Lundy to:
Bideford 2hrs. (Seasonal)
Ilfracombe 2hrs. (Seasonal)

2

Rat Island

South West
Point

40

3

30

BARNSTAPLE

OR

HARTLAND POINT   Windbury
                          Point

BIDEFORD BAY

○Titchberry

*Hartland
Abbey*   *Cheristow
                Lavender*   ○Clovelly
                                Court   **Clovelly**

4   Ⓜ   🅿   **Hartland**   B3248   *Clovelly
Hartland   Donkeys*
Quay   Stoke   Velly   🆅 Higher Clovelly   Buck's   Buck's
        Docton   Cross   Mills
         Mill   ○Natcott   710 *Milky Way
Milford   Adventure Park* A39
Elmscott ○Edistone   Welsford   24
                                          Woolfardisworthy
                                          or Woolsery

20   Alminstone   Parkham
        ○South   Cross   Ash
         Hole

10▼ Knaps   *R. Torridge*   Ashmansworthy
         Longpeak   ○Welcombe
                                    Meddon   East
         ○Mead   ○Woolley   Putford
                                          East
              ○Gooseham   ○Woolley   Youlstone   West
                                                          Putford
5 **Morwenstow**   ○Eastcott   West   Dinworthy *Gnome Reserve &*
Higher Sharpnose *Hawker's*   Youlstone   *Wild Flower Garden* ○Colscott
     Point   *Hut*   ○Shop   Venngree
                ○Woodford   **Bradworthy**
Lower Sharpnose   *CORNWALL*   *Upper
     Point   *Tamar* *Tamar Lake*   **Sutcombe**
                          Kilkhampton A39 *Lakes*   ○Alfardisworthy Venngree
         ○Coombe   *Lower   Thurdon   Soldon *Waldon*
              ○Stibb   Tamar Lake*   Cross

10   **C**   B3254   ○Dexbeer   **D** A388

200   10

         Flexbury *Stratton*   ○Hersham
         Castle Heritage ○Bush   *Dunsdon*   **Holsworthy
         Centre Ⓜ   *Farm*   Beacon**
              Stratton   Grimscott   30 Lana Chilsworthy
    Bude   Launcells   Pancrasweek
         Bude

This chart shows the distance in miles and journey time between two cities or towns in Great Britain. Each route has been calculated using a combination of motorways, primary routes and other major roads. This is normally the quickest, though not always the shortest route.

Average journey times are calculated whilst driving at the maximum speed limit. These times are approximate and do not include traffic congestion or convenience breaks.

To find the distance and journey time between two cities or towns, follow a horizontal line and vertical column until they meet each other.

For example, the 285 mile journey from London to Penzance is approximately 4 hours and 59 minutes.

Northern Ireland

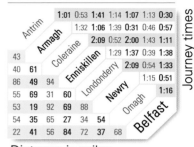

Distance in miles

Belfast to London = 440m / 9:46h (excluding ferry)
Belfast to Glasgow = 104m / 4:46h (excluding ferry)

Britain

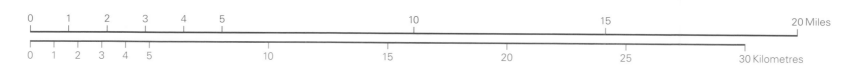

Distance in miles

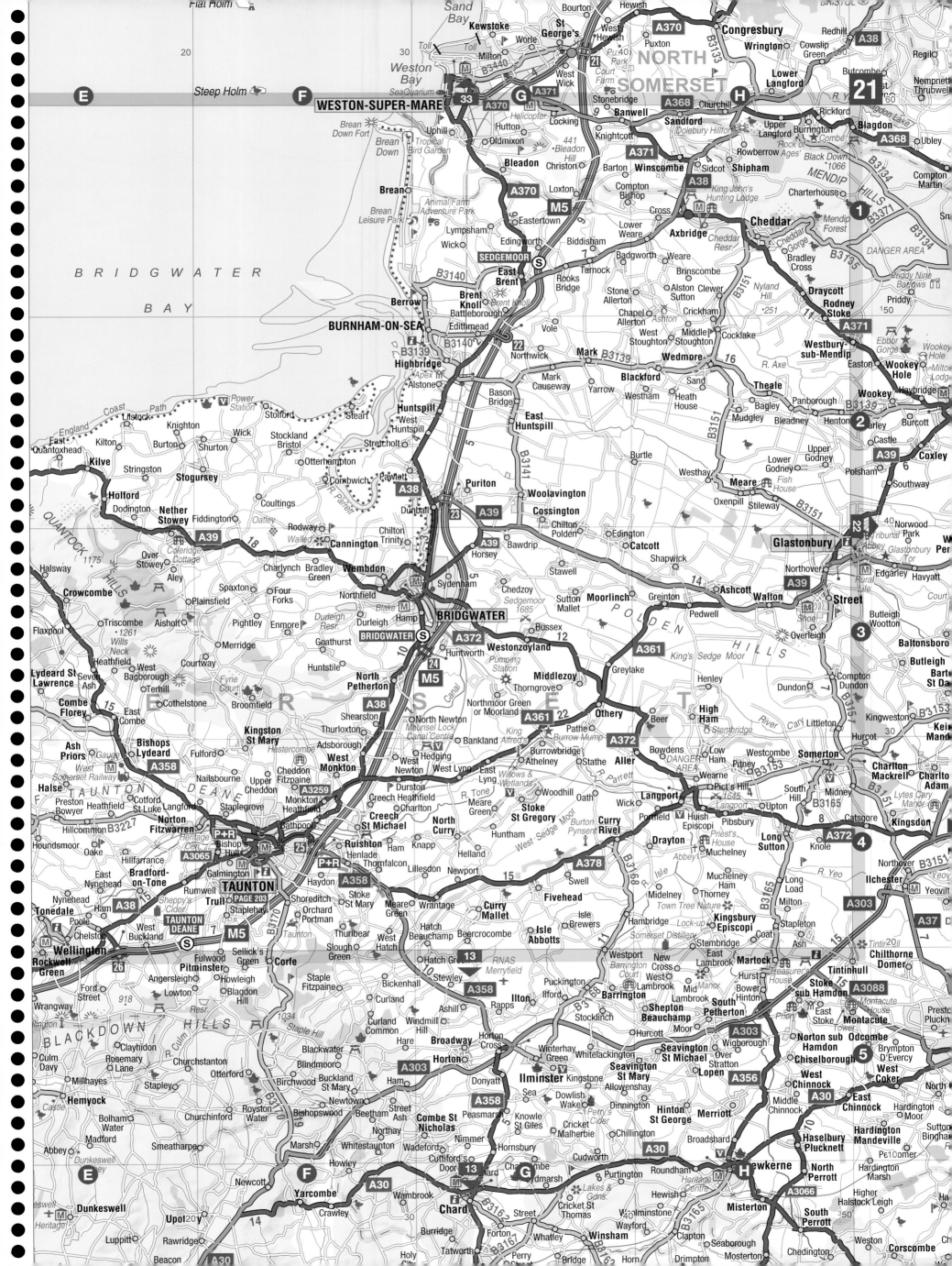

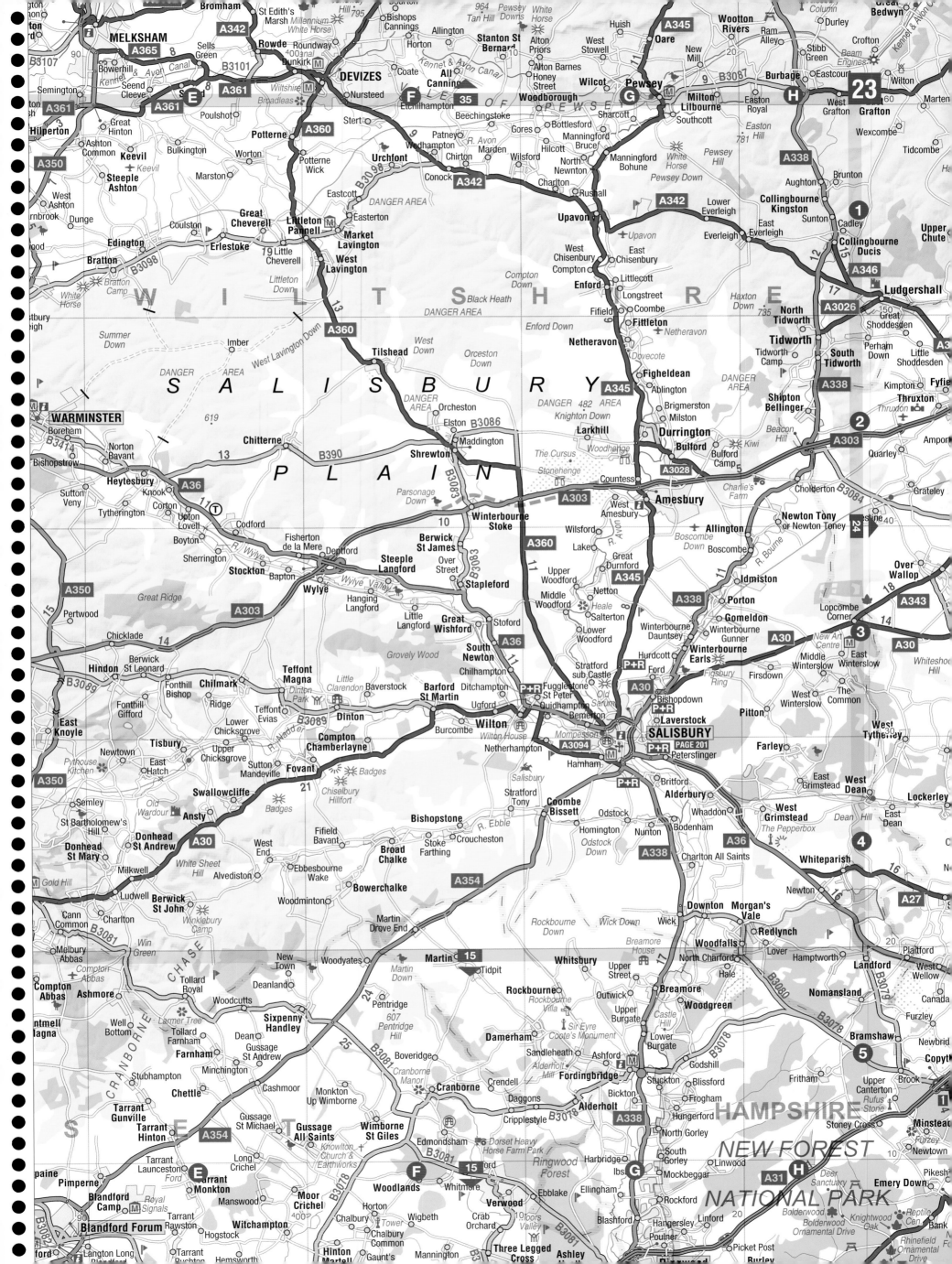

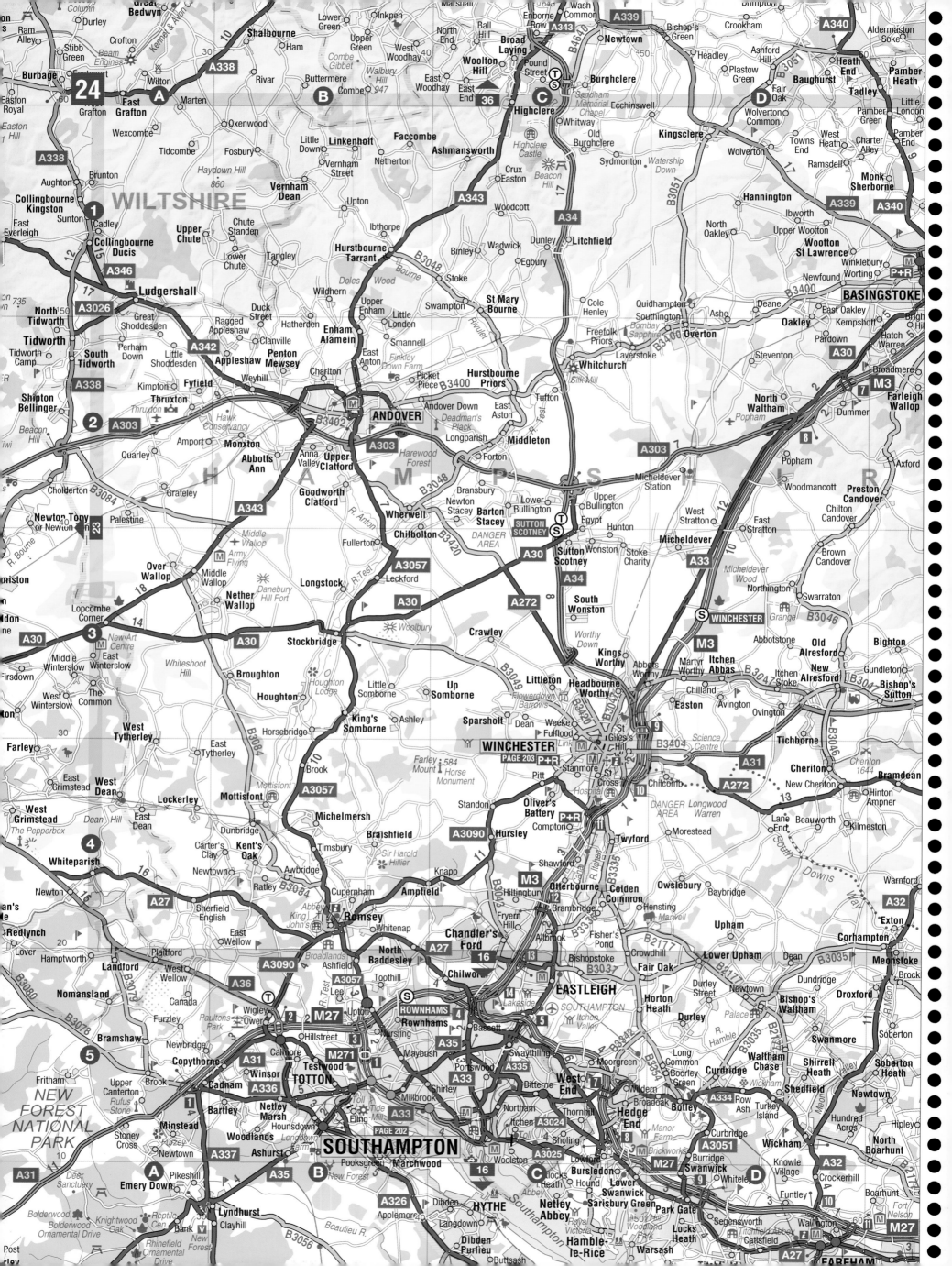

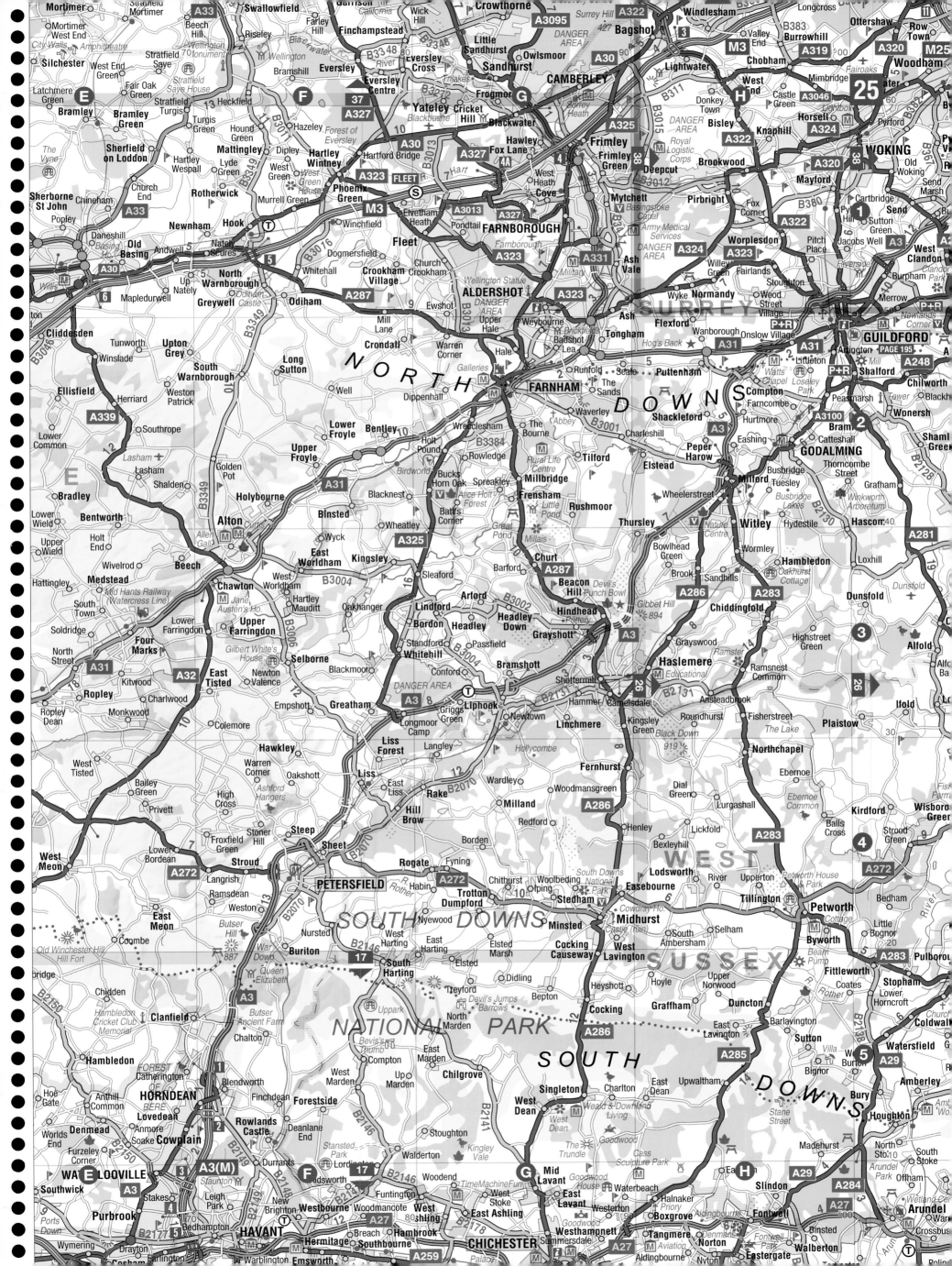

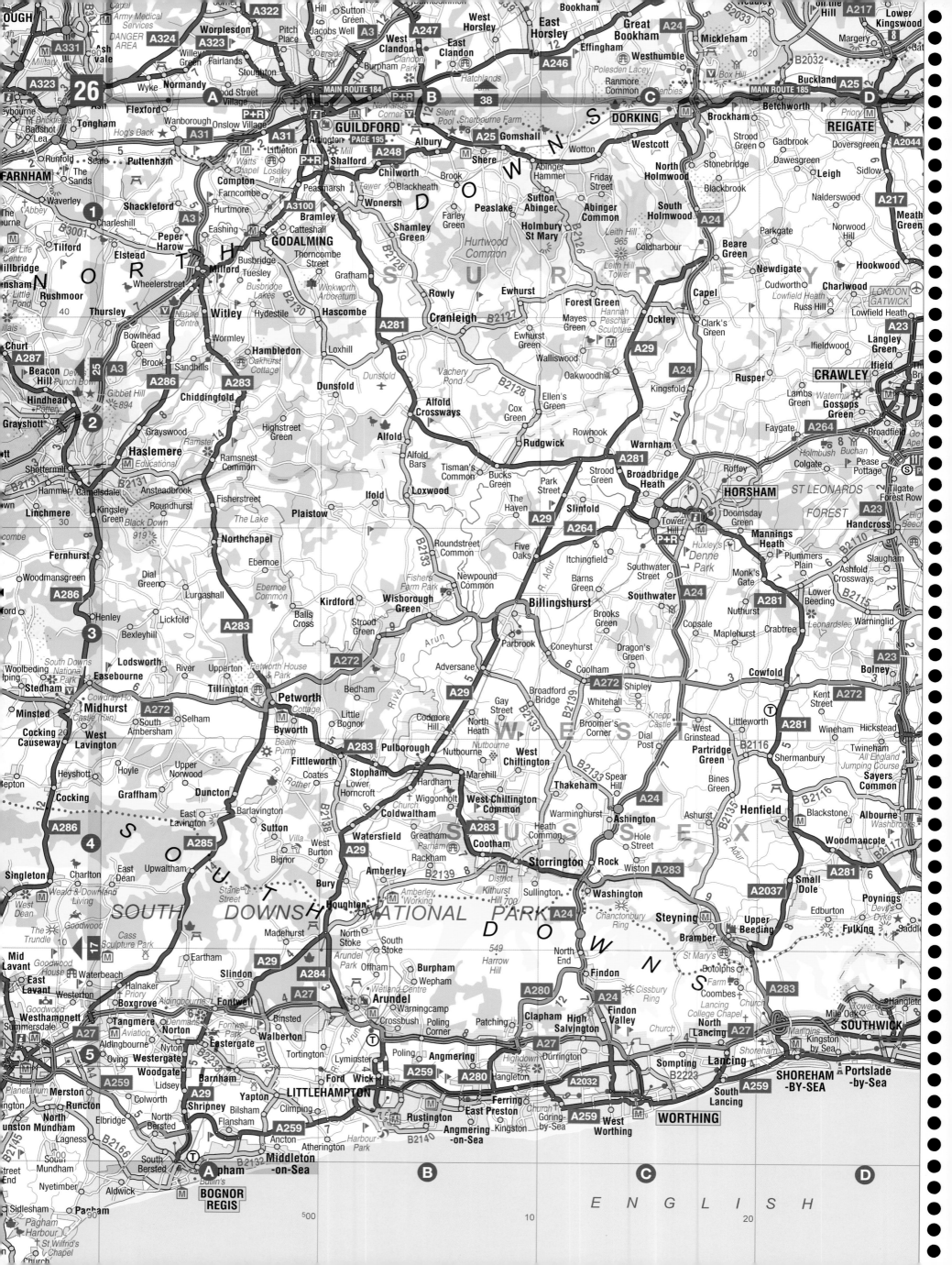

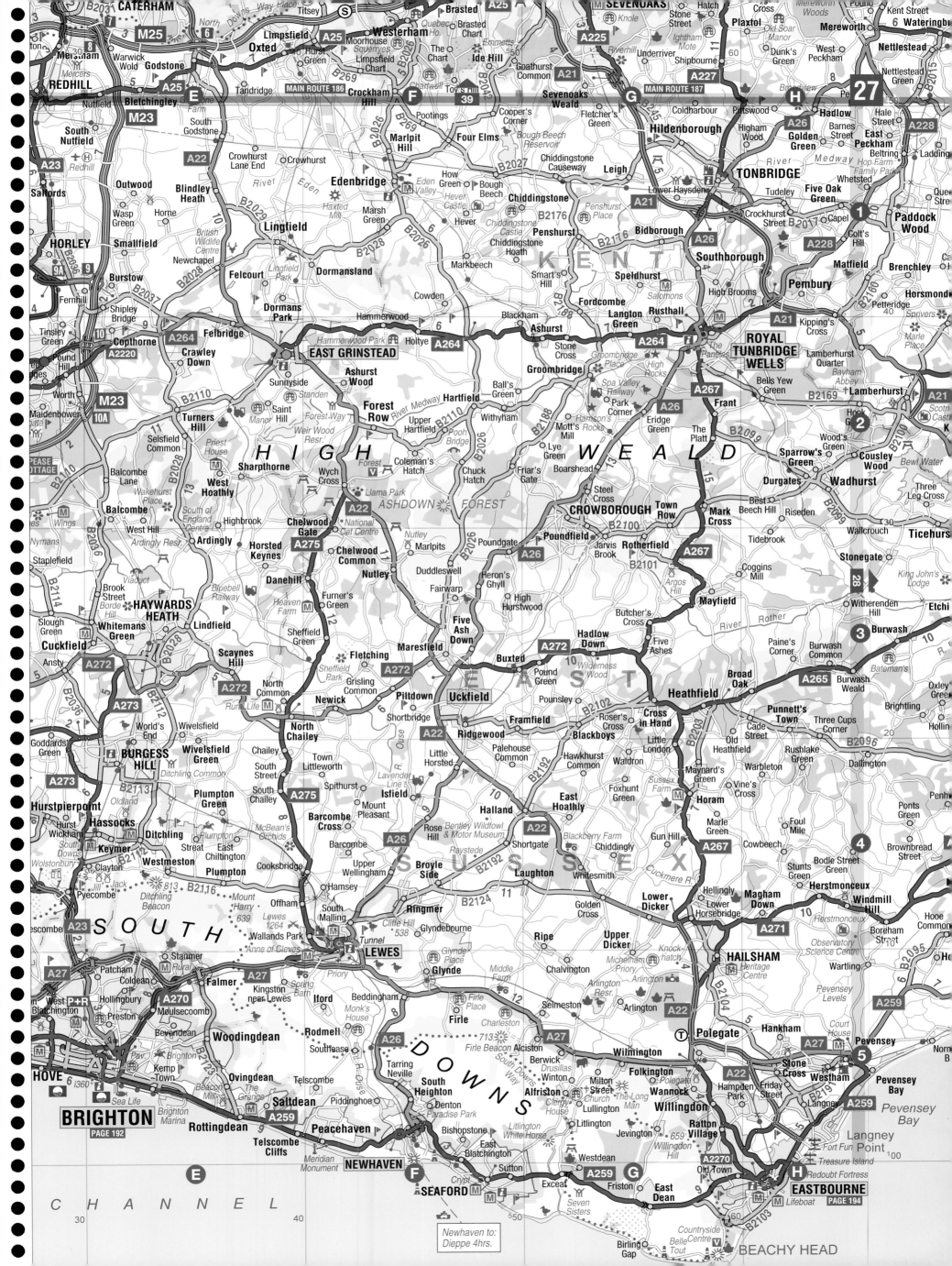

CHANNEL TUNNEL

EUROTUNNEL
(Vehicles only)
Continent by car
Drive on - Drive off
Folkestone to Coquelles 35mins.
Bookings : 08443 353535
www.eurotunnel.com

EUROSTAR
(Passengers only)
Passenger Services
St. Pancras International
Ebbsfleet International &
Ashford International to:
Paris, Brussels and Lille.
Bookings : 03432 186186
www.eurostar.com

FOLKESTONE CHANNEL TUNNEL TERMINAL
— Loading — Unloading

EUROTUNNEL
(Vehicles only)
UK by car
Drive on - Drive off
Coquelles to Folkestone 35mins.
Bookings : 0810 63 03 04
www.eurotunnel.com

CALAIS CHANNEL TUNNEL TERMINAL
— Loading — Unloading

Dover to:
Calais 1hr. 30mins.
Dunkirk 2hrs.

CHANNEL TUNNEL
Folkestone to
Calais 35mins.

DOVER
PAGE 194

FOLKESTONE
PAGE 195

The Downs
29

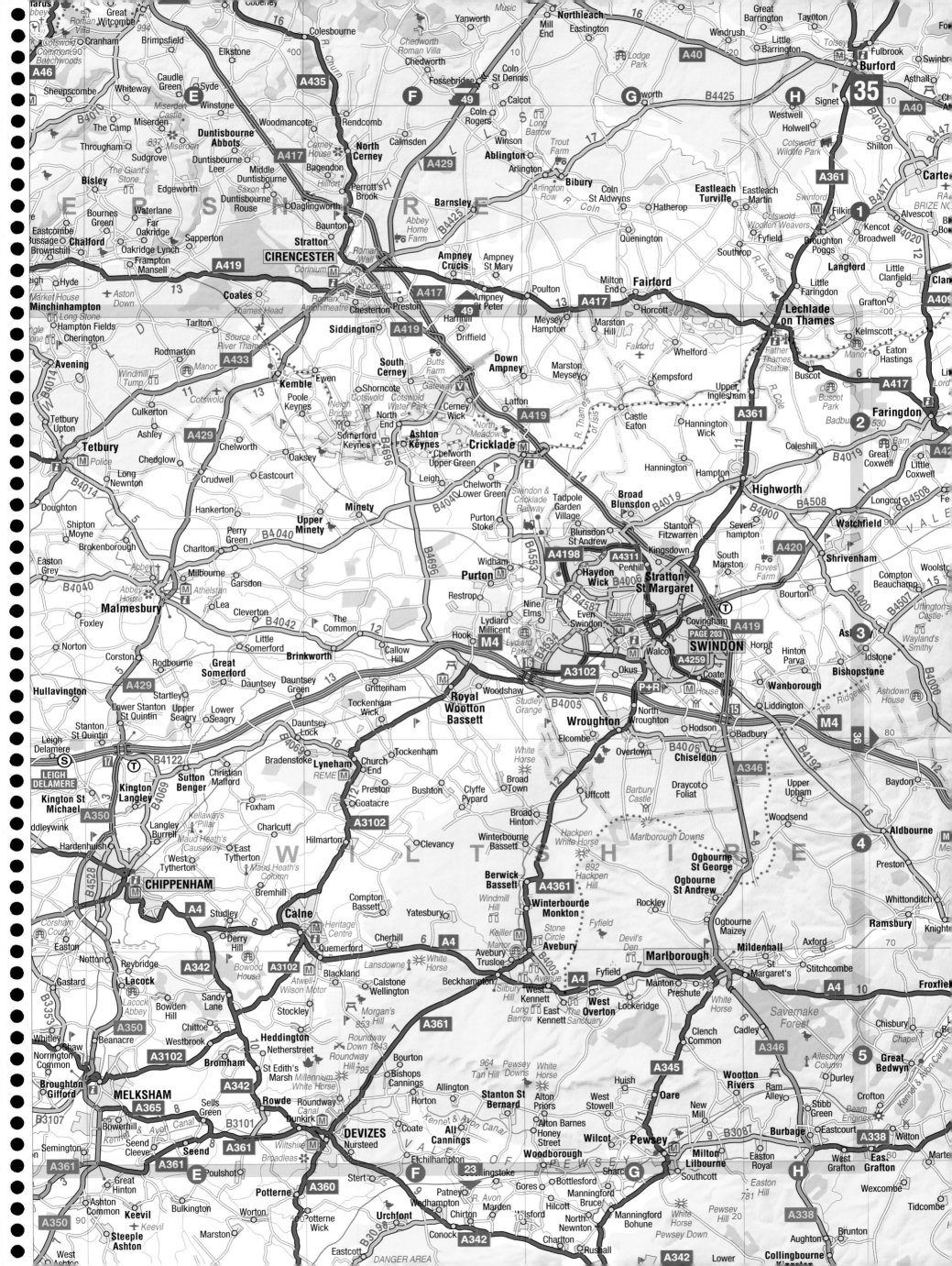

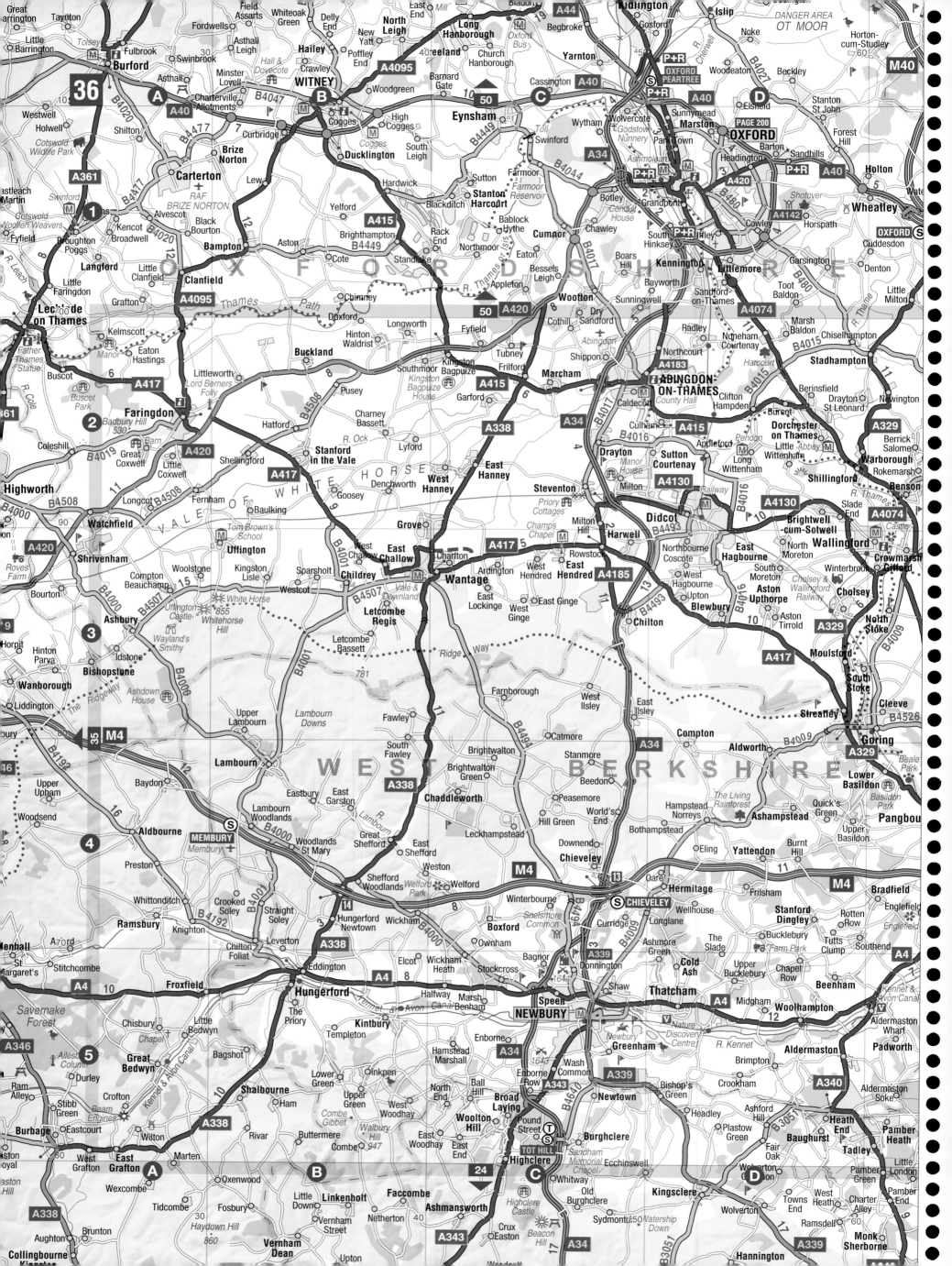

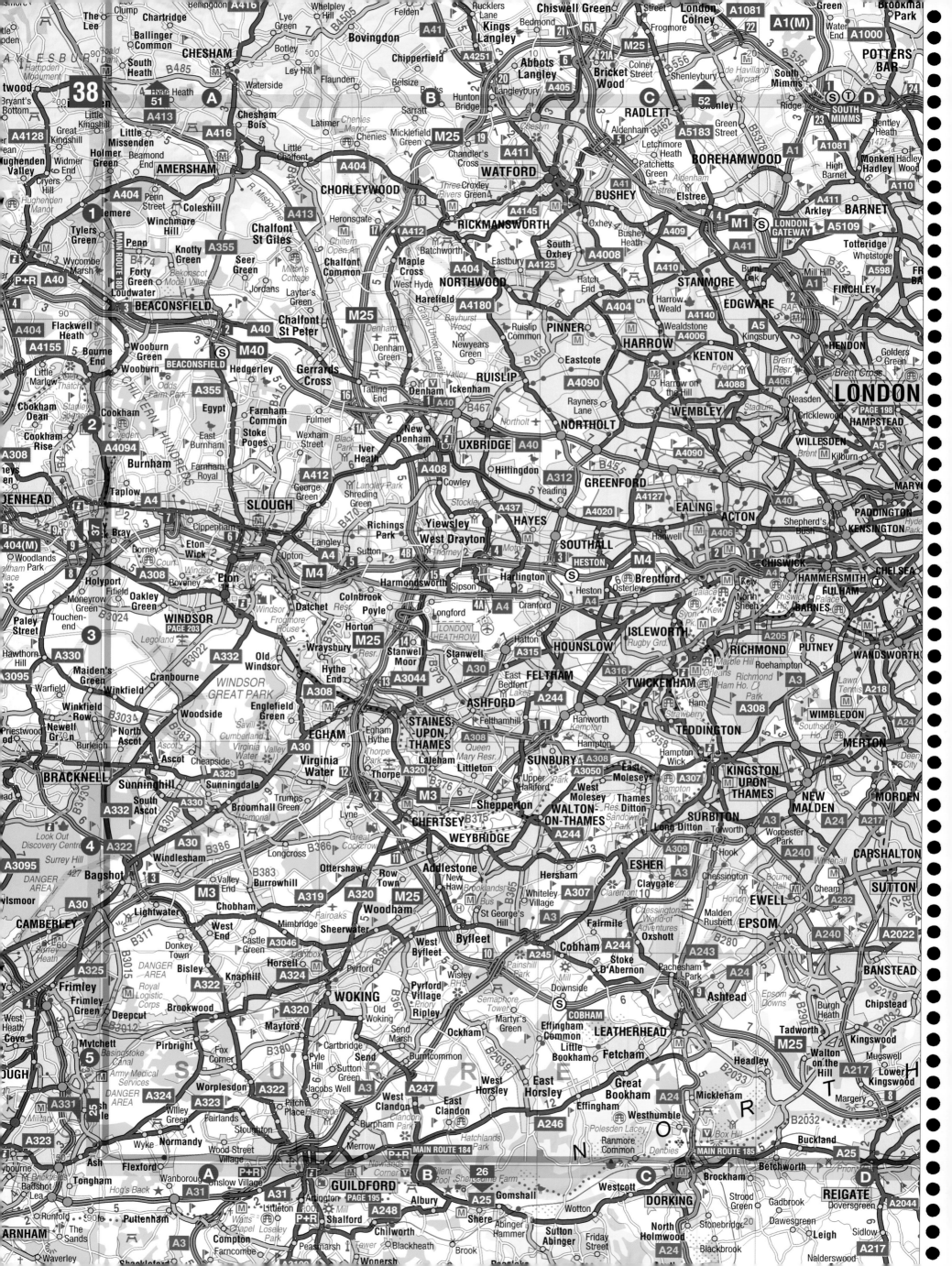

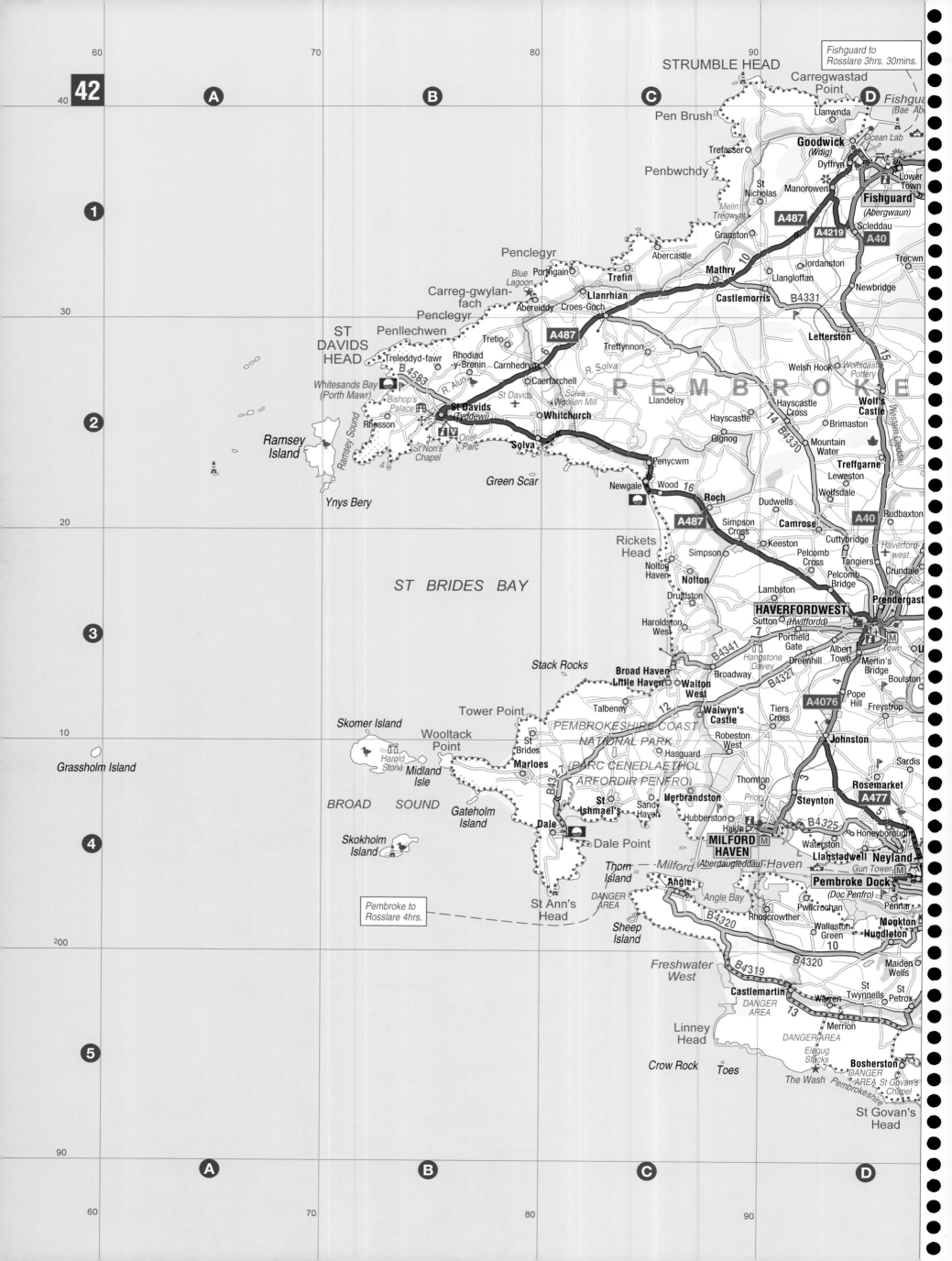

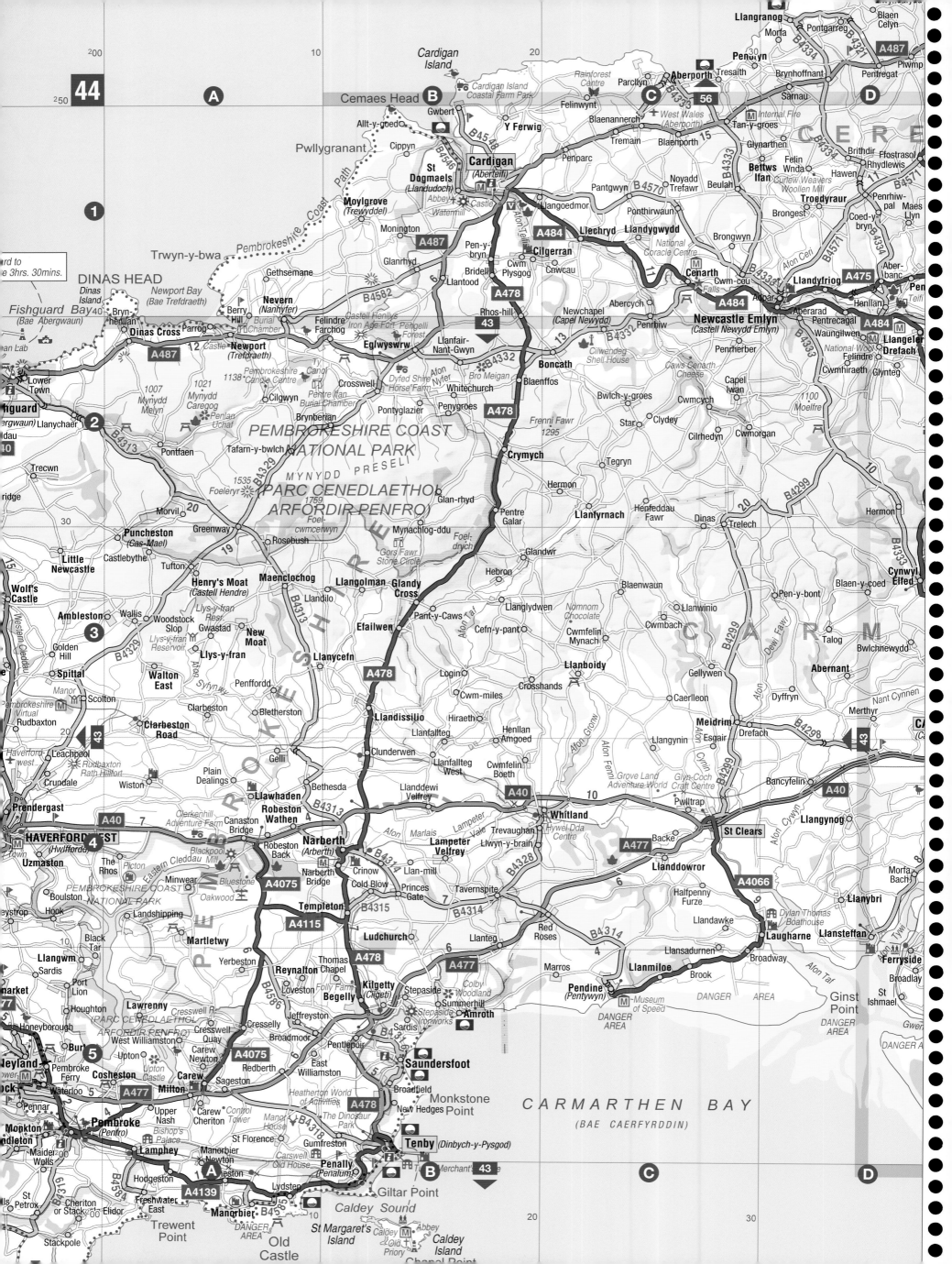

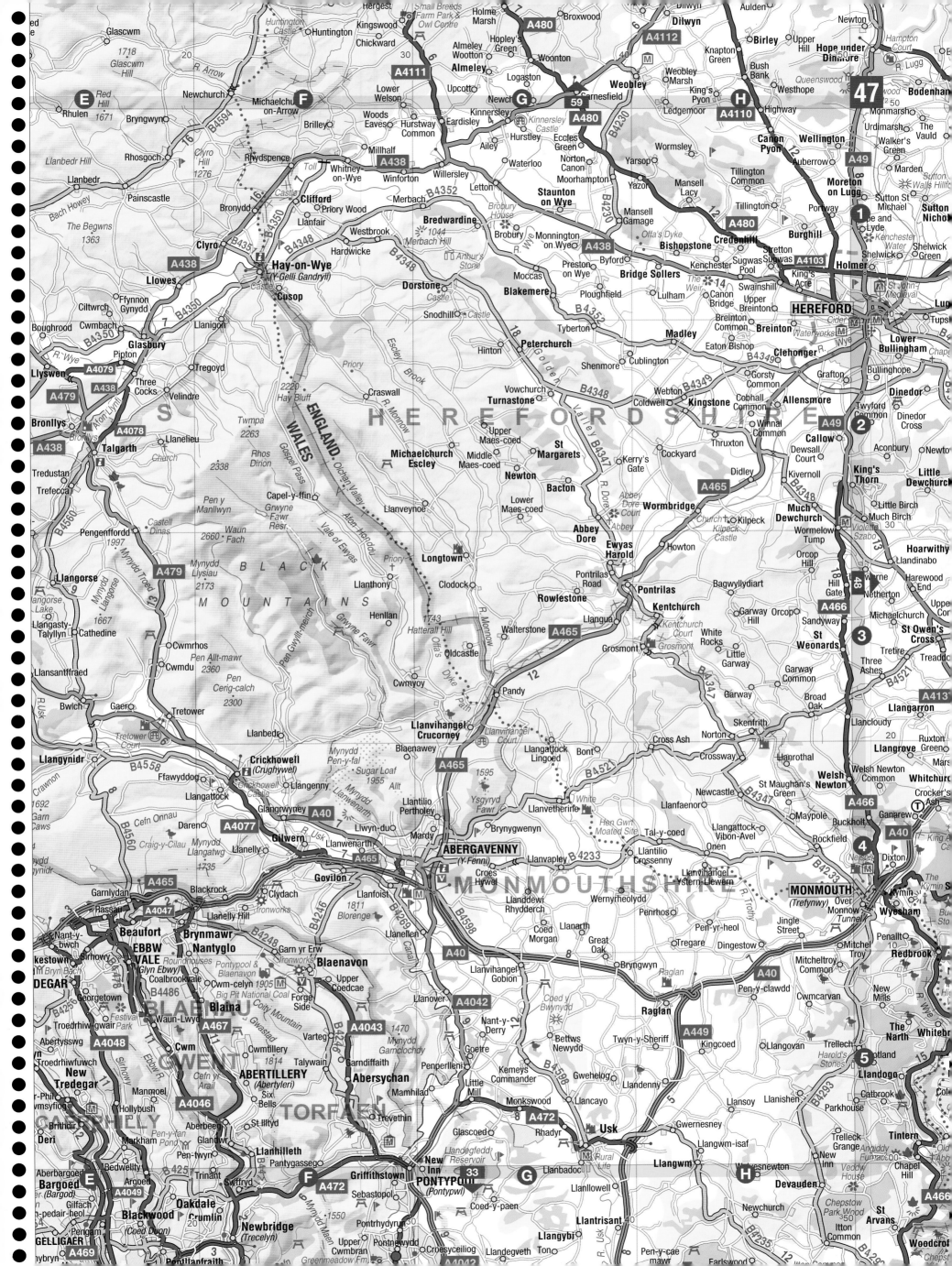

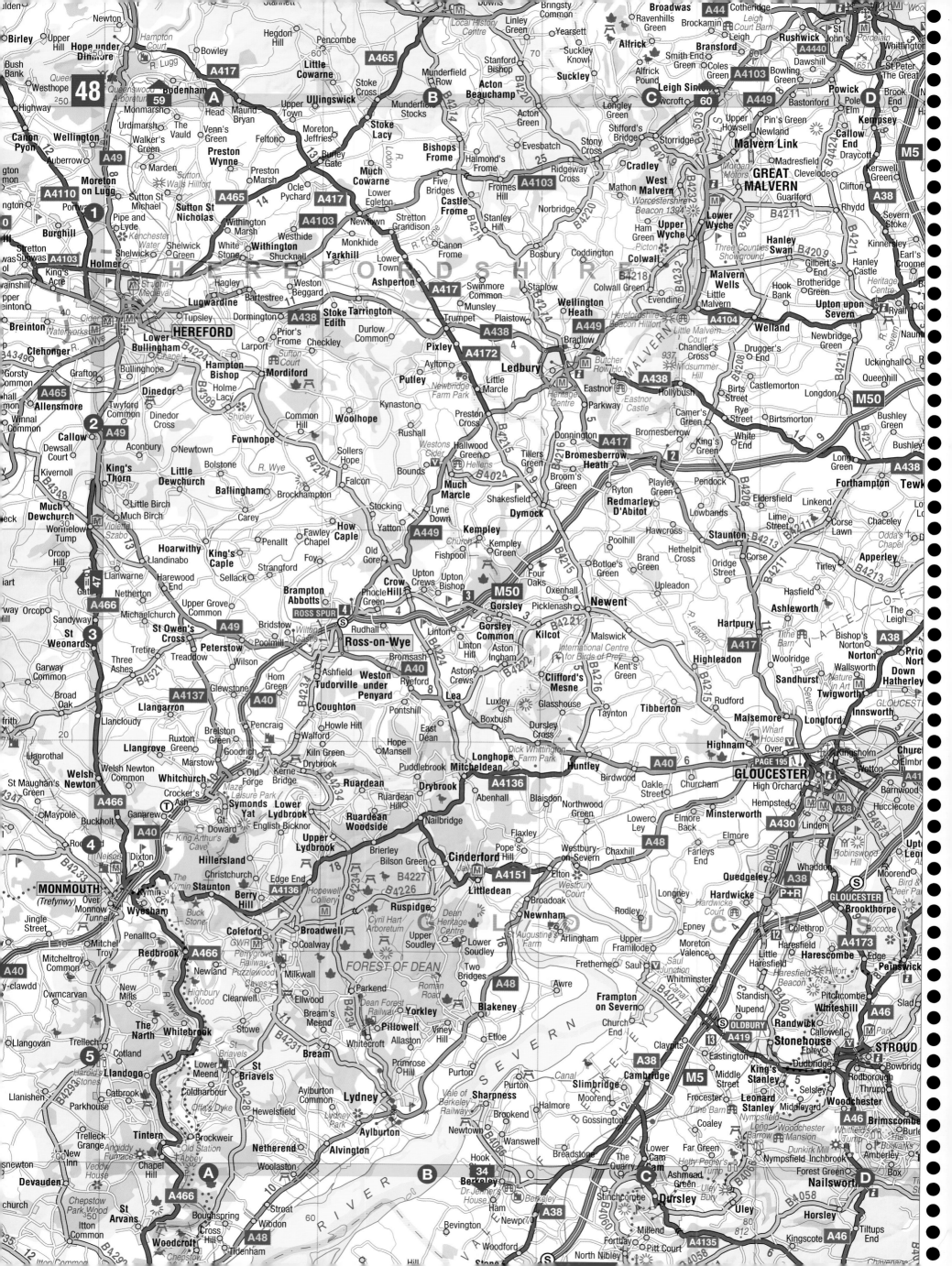

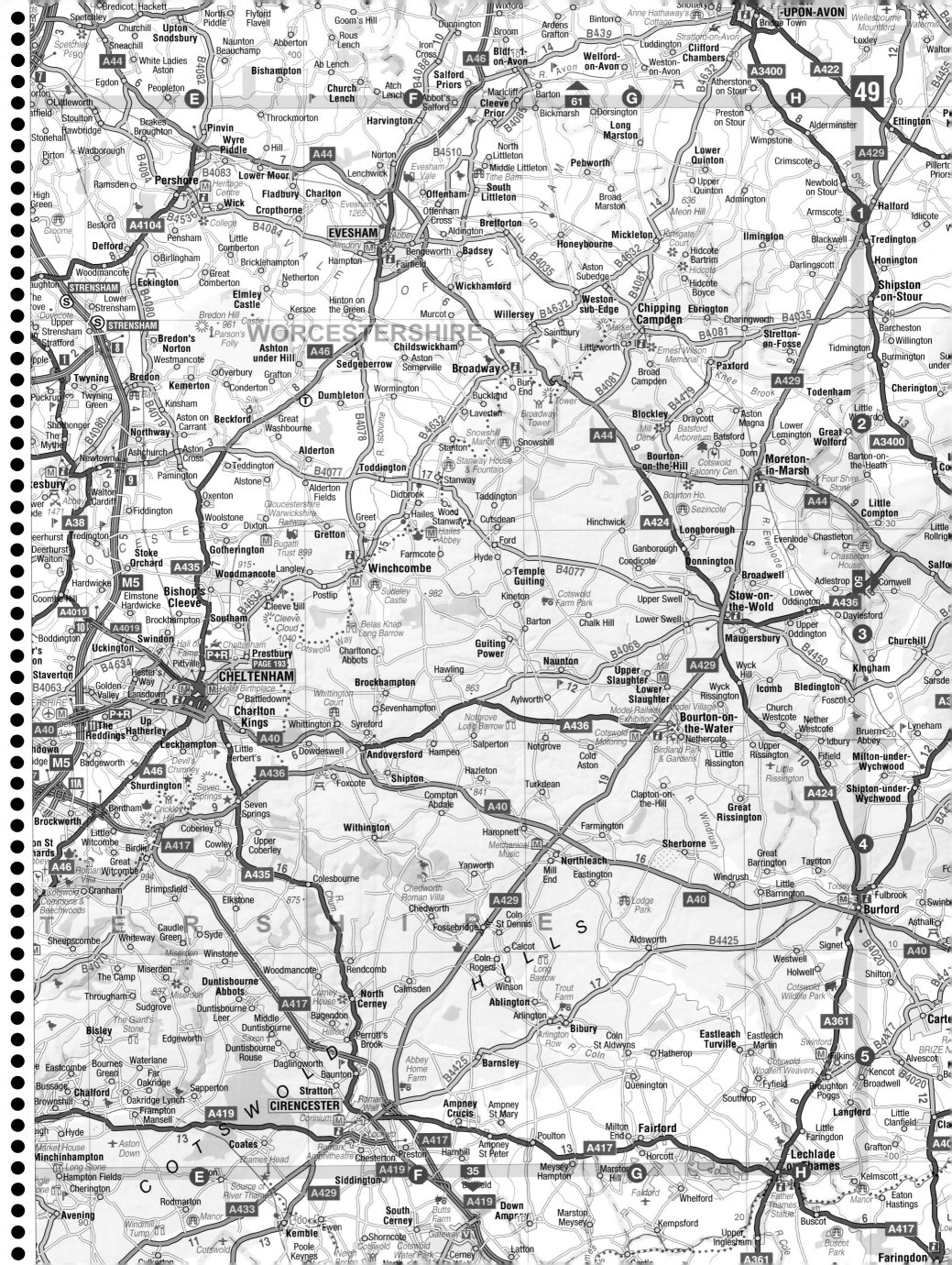

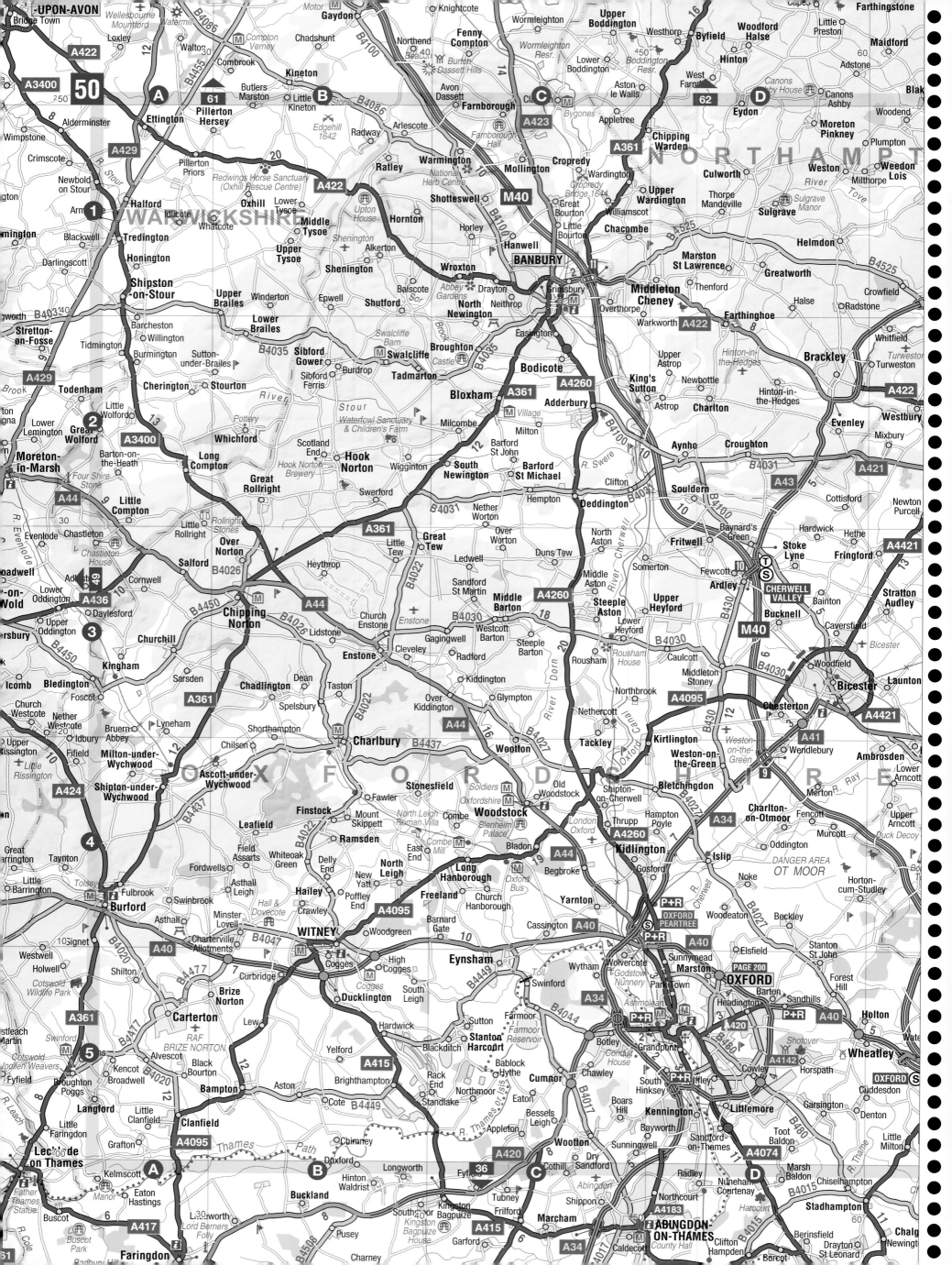

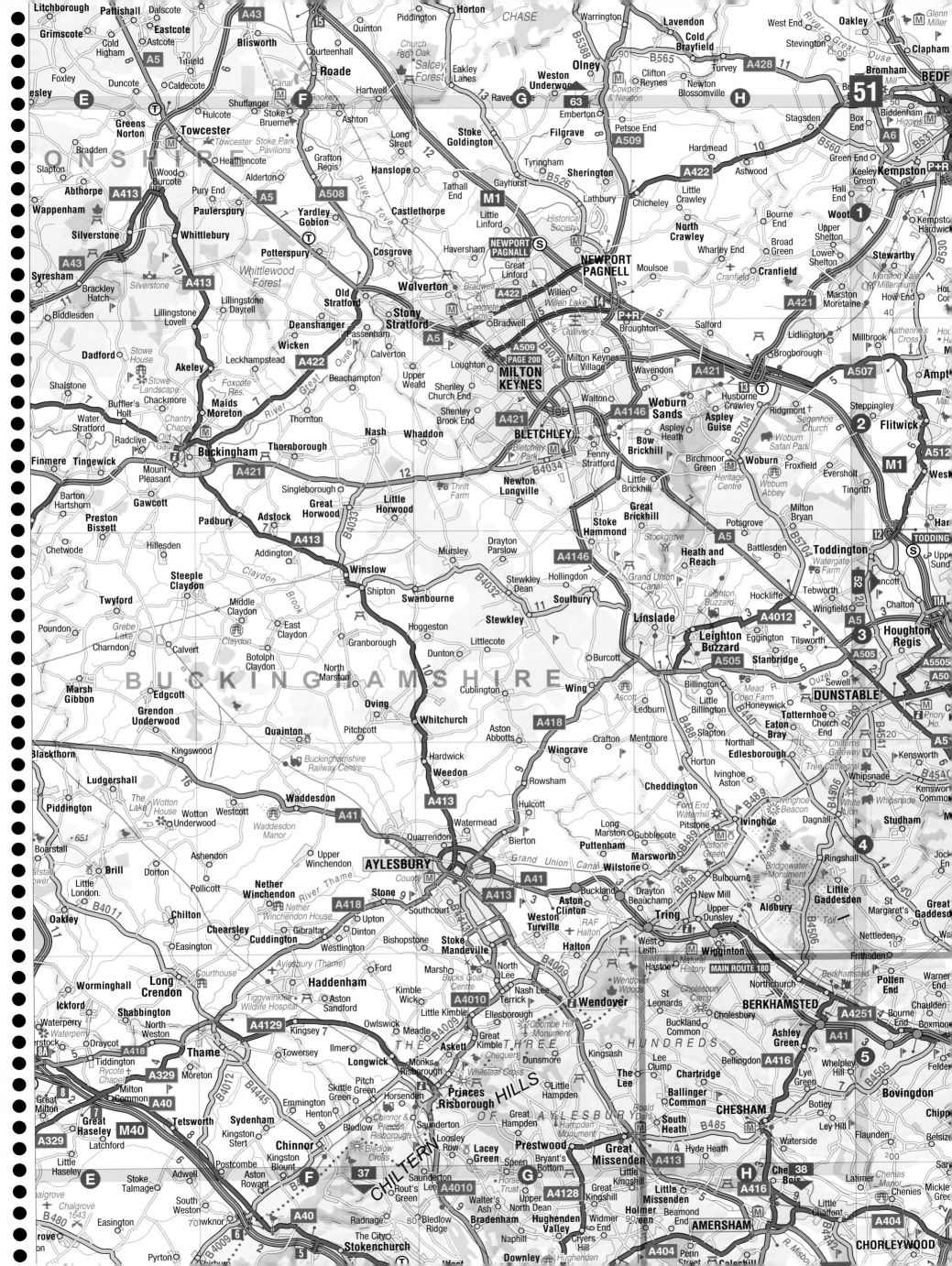

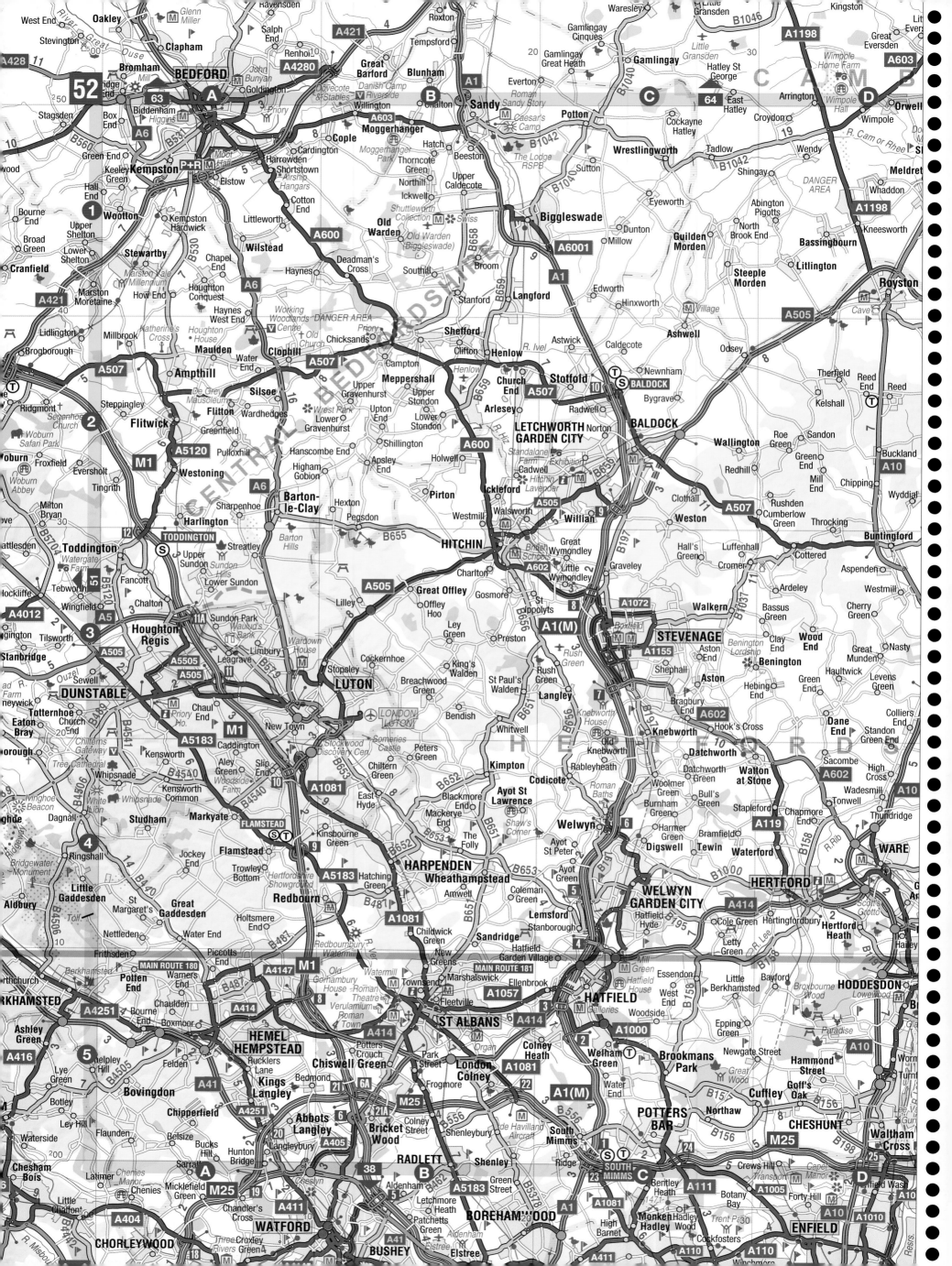

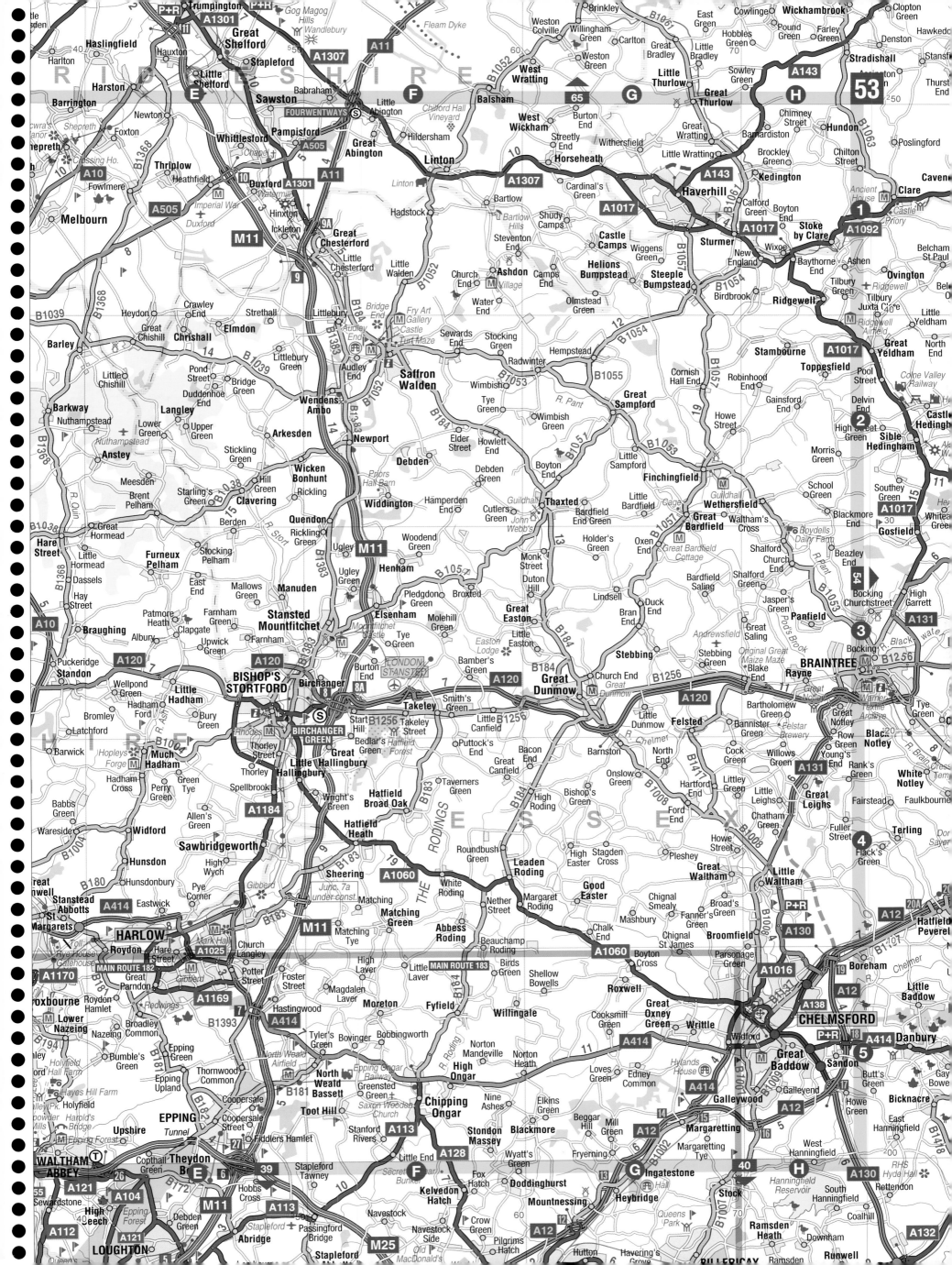

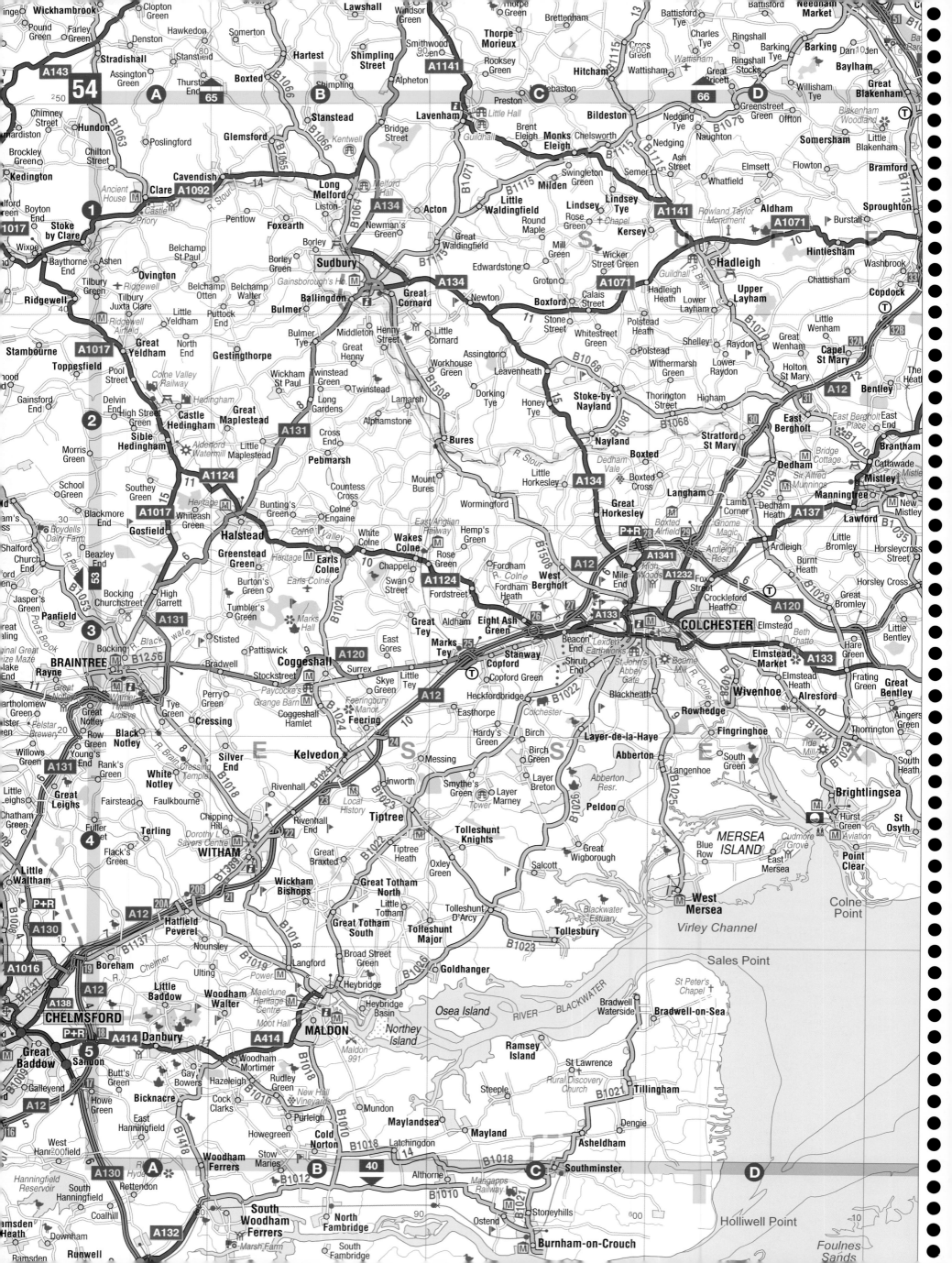

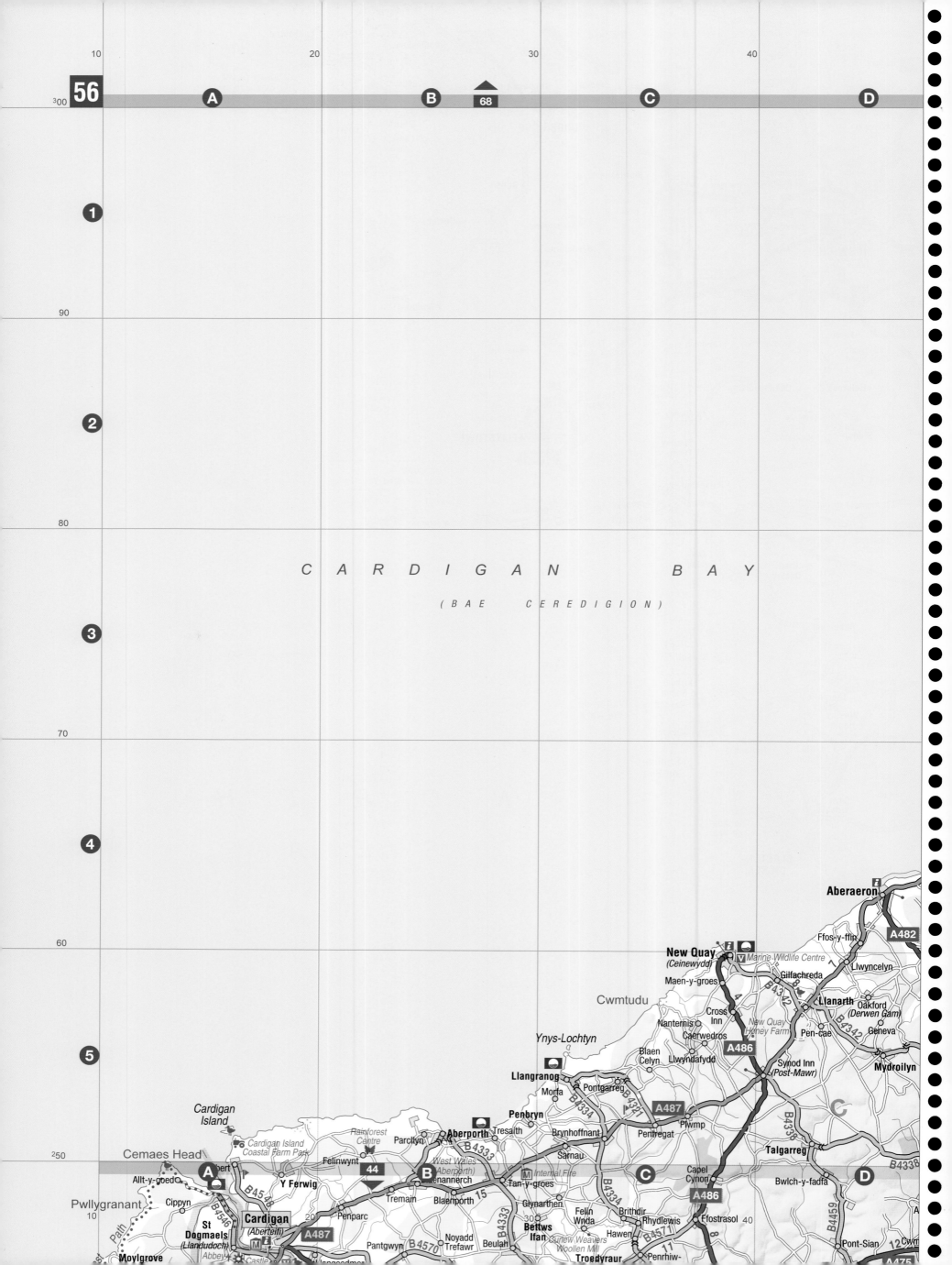

300

10   20   30   40

A   B   68   C   D

1

90

2

80

C A R D I G A N   B A Y

(B A E   C E R E D I G I O N)

3

70

4

Aberaeron

60

Ffos-y-ffin   A482

New Quay   Marine Wildlife Centre
(Ceinewydd)   Gilfachreda   Llwyncelyn

Maen-y-groes   Llanarth   Oakford
(Derwen Gam)

Cwmtudu   New Quay   Pen-cae   Geneva
Honey Farm

Nanternis   Caerwedros   Synod Inn   Mydroilyn
(Post-Mawr)

Ynys-Lochtyn   Blaen   Llwyndafydd
Celyn

5

Llangranog   Morfa   Pontgarreg   A486

Penbryn   A487   Plwmp

Cardigan   Tresaith   Brynhoffnant   Pentregat   Talgarreg
Island

Rainforest   Parcllyn   Aberporth   Sarnau
Centre

250   Cardigan Island
Coastal Farm Park   West Wales
(Aberporth)

Cemaes Head   B4333   Capel   Bwlch-y-fadfa
Cynon   D

A   Y Ferwig   Felinwynt   44   Henannerch   Tan-y-groes   Internal Fire   C   A486

Allt-y-goedo   Tremain   Blaenporth   15   Glynarthen   B4333
Pwllygranant

Cippyn   Penparc   20   Felin   Brithdir   Rhydlewis   Ffostrasol   40
Wnda

Cardigan   Noyadd   Hawen
(Aberteifi)   Trefawr   Bettws

St   A487   Pantgwyn   B4570   Beulah   Ifan   Surlew Weavers   B4571   Pont-Sian   12
Dogmaels   Woollen Mill

(Llandudoch)   Troedyraur   Penrhiw-

Moylgrove   Abbey   Castle   Llangoedmor

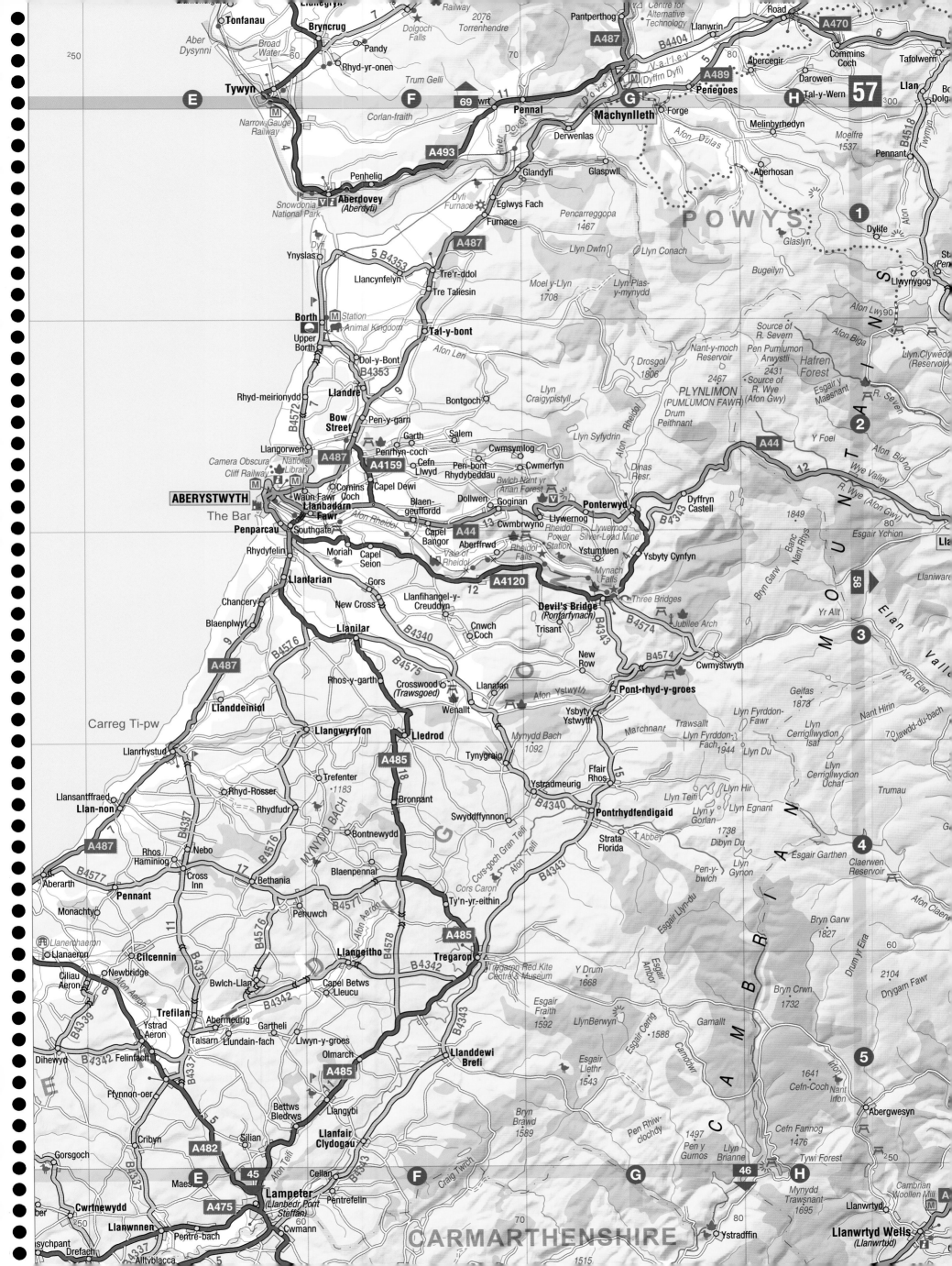

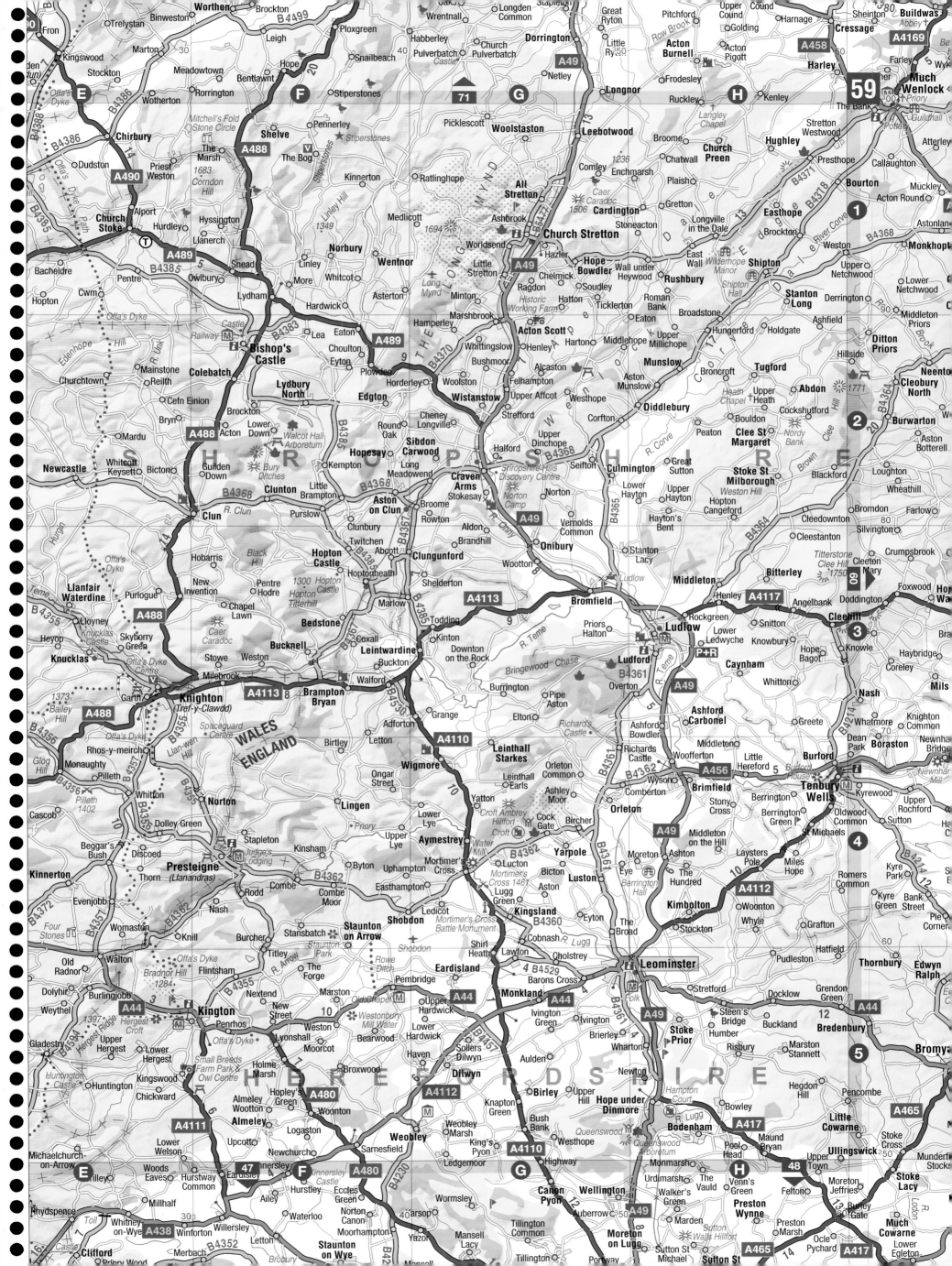

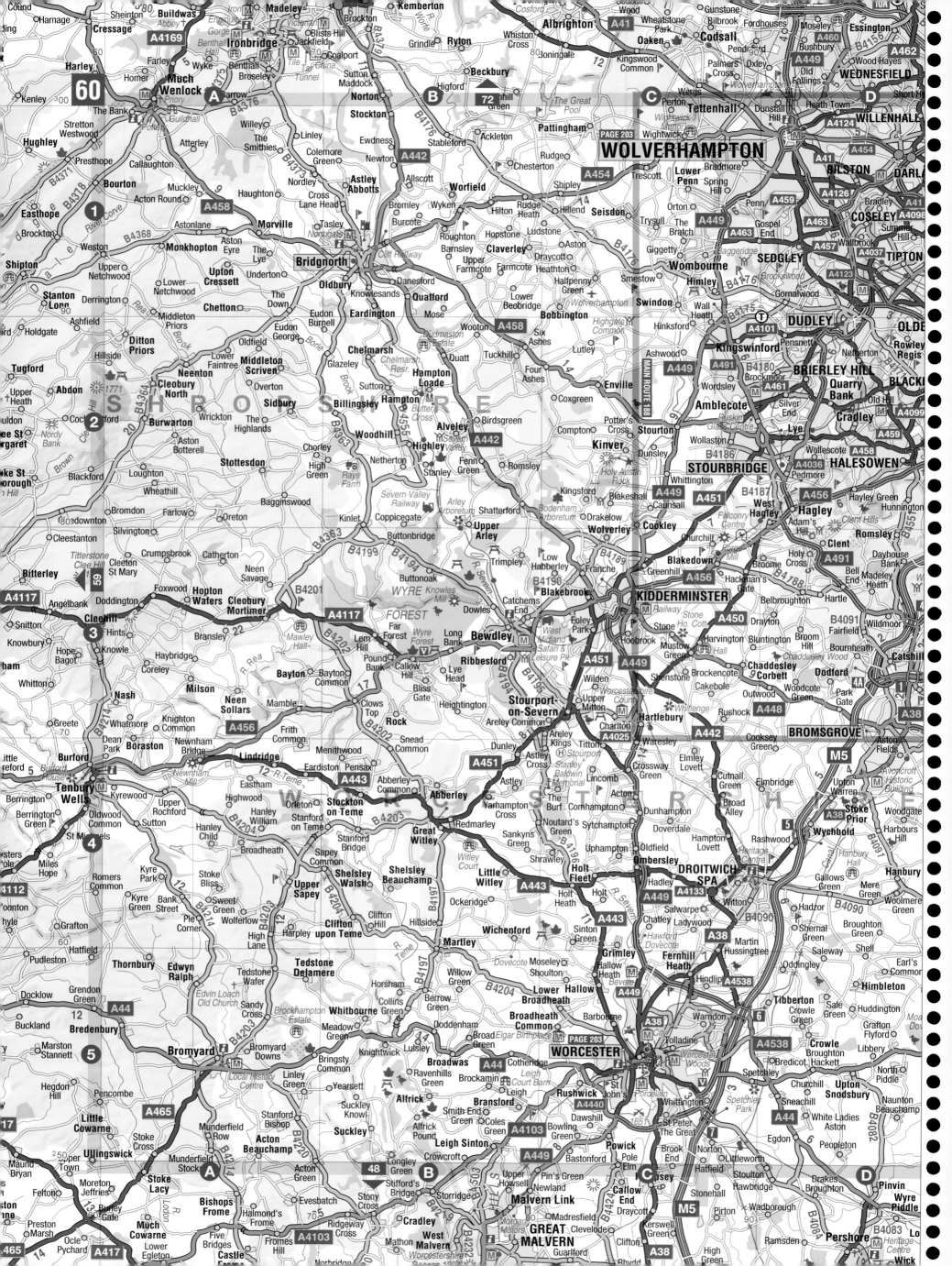

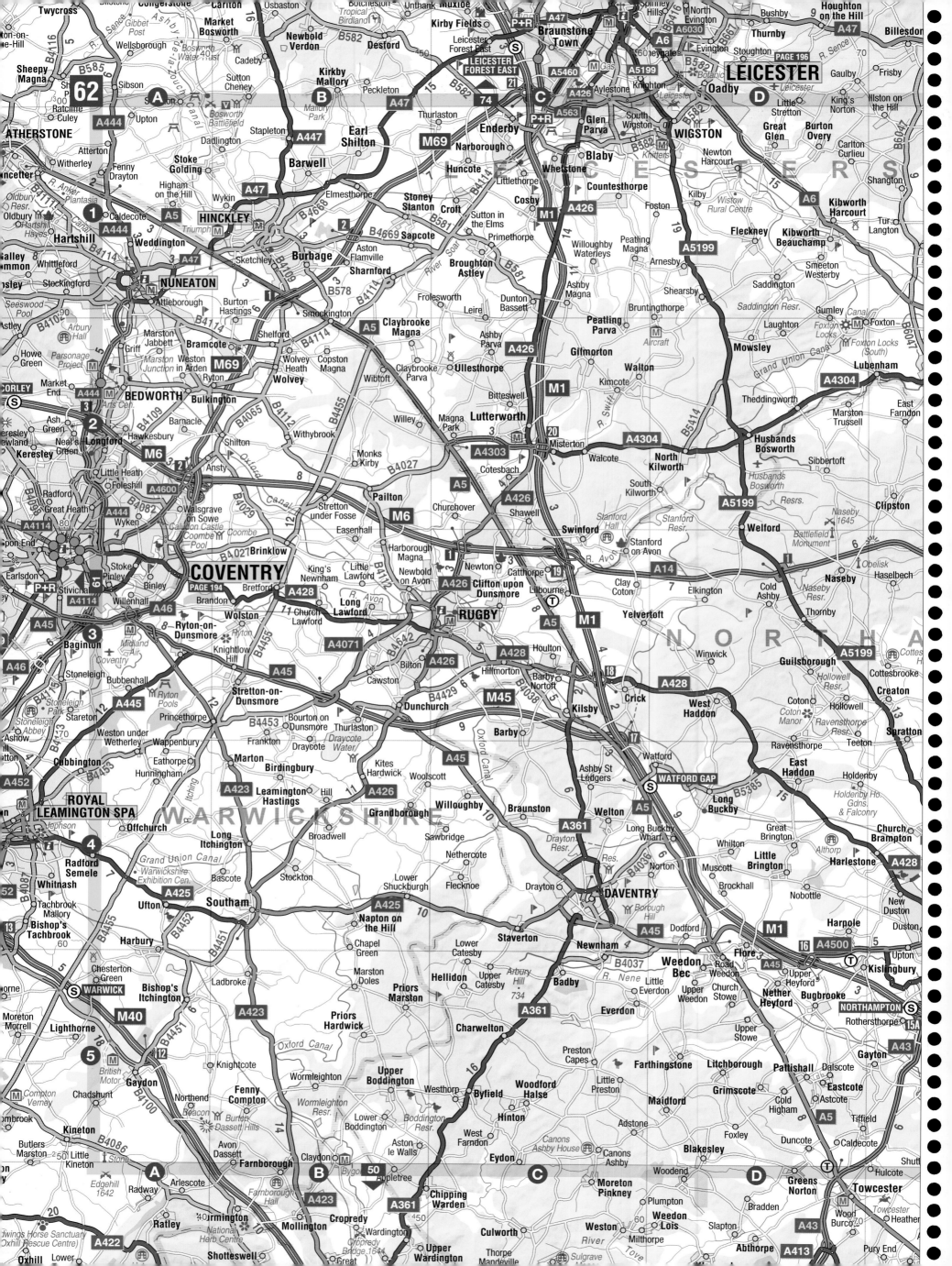

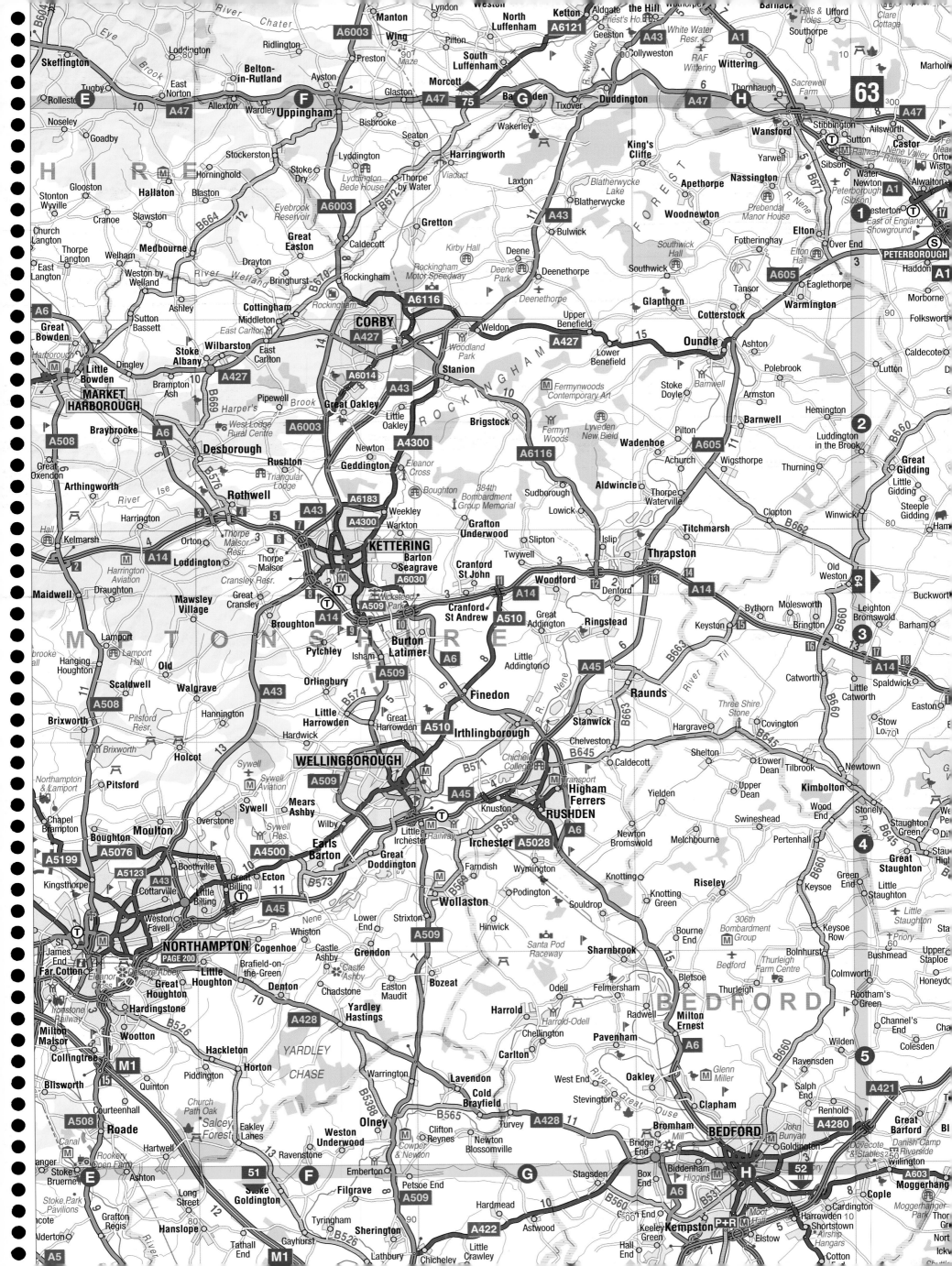

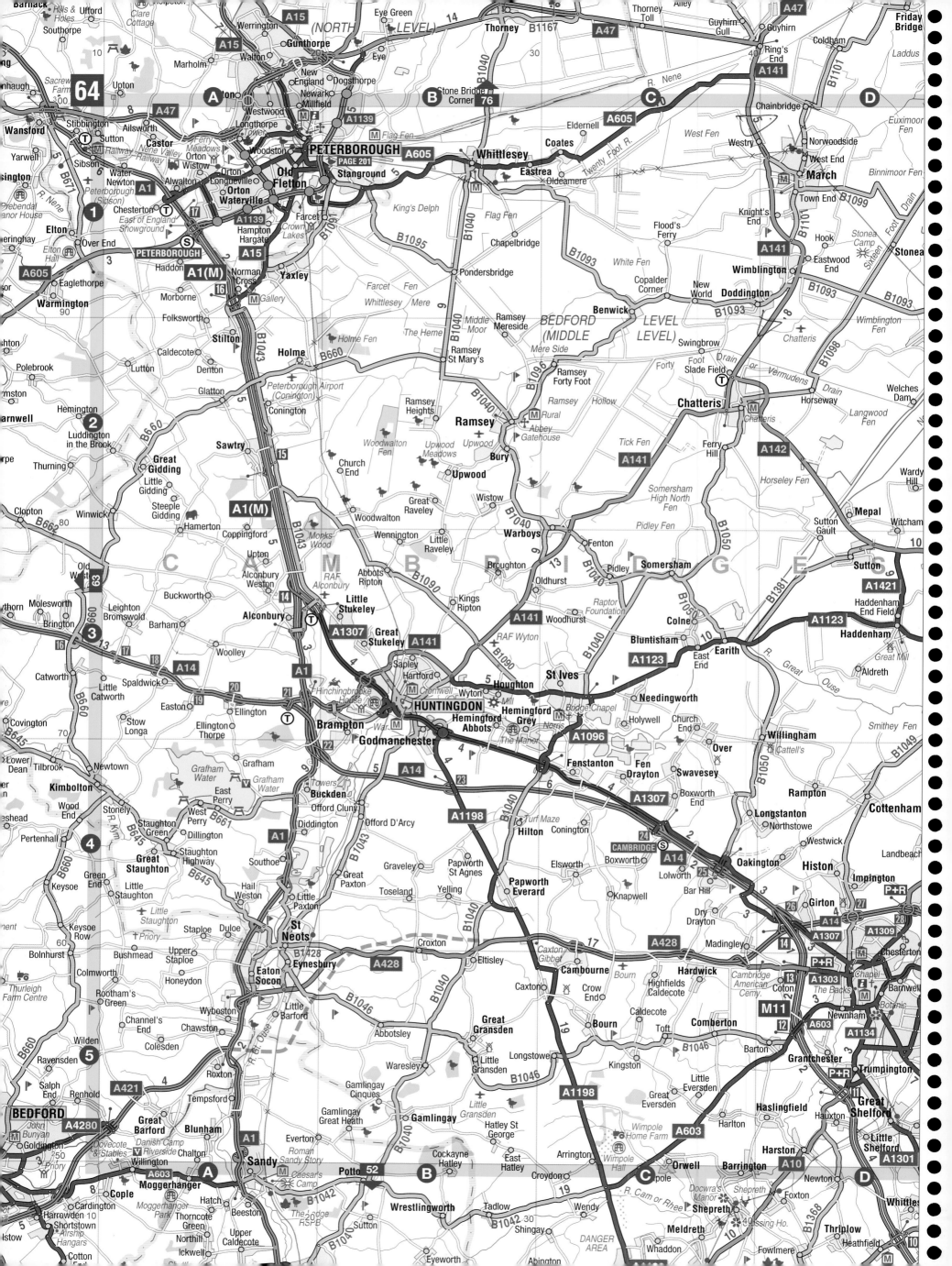

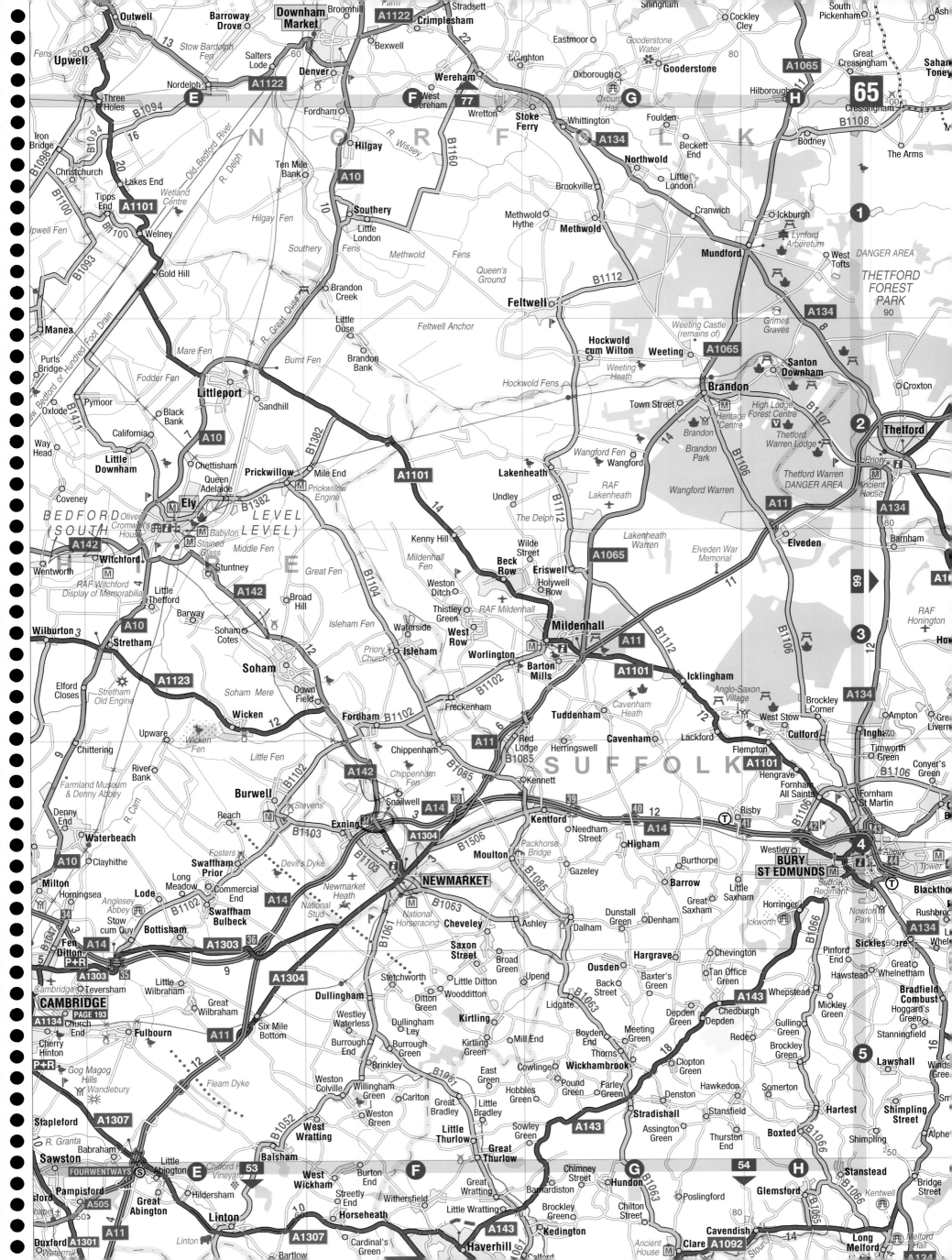

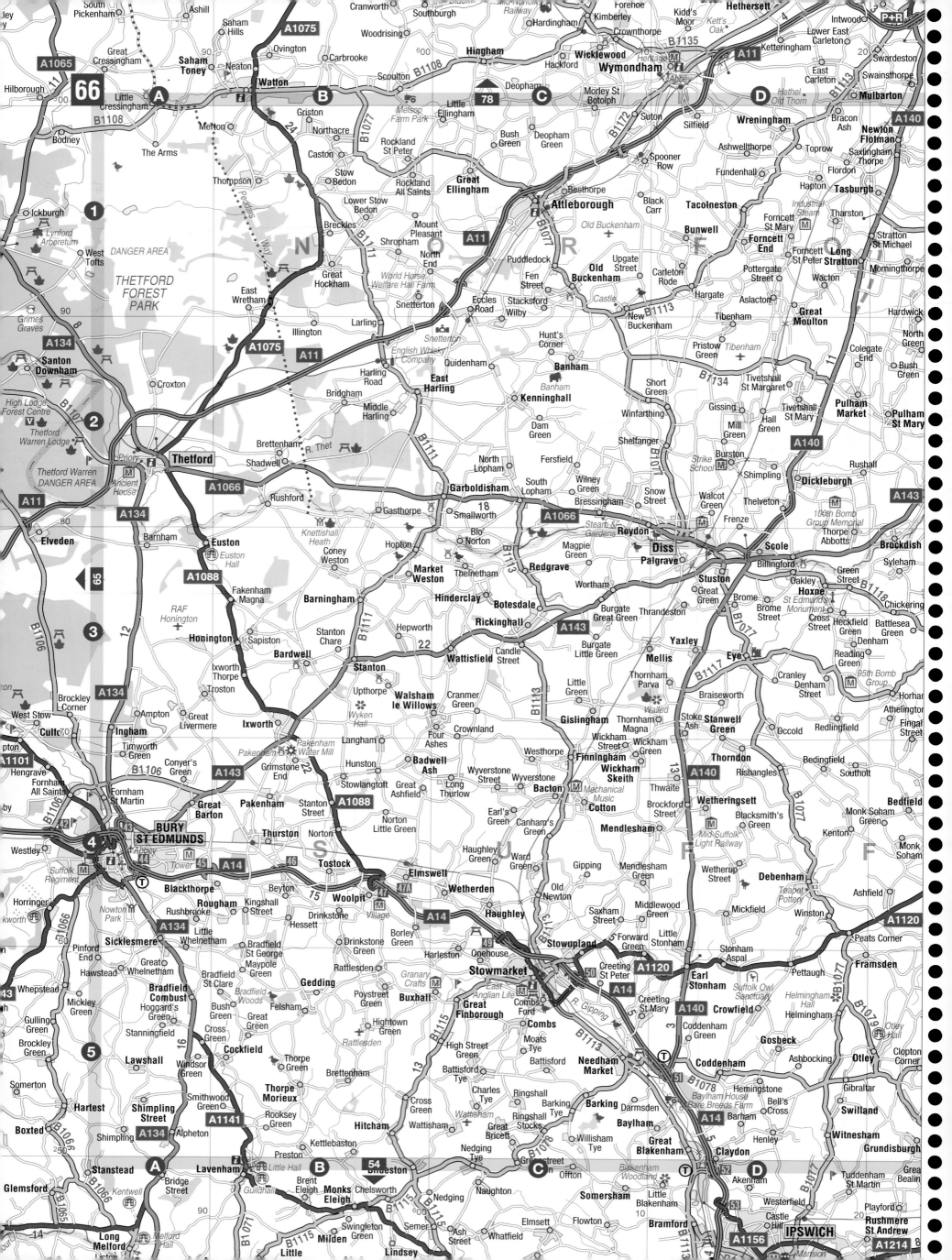

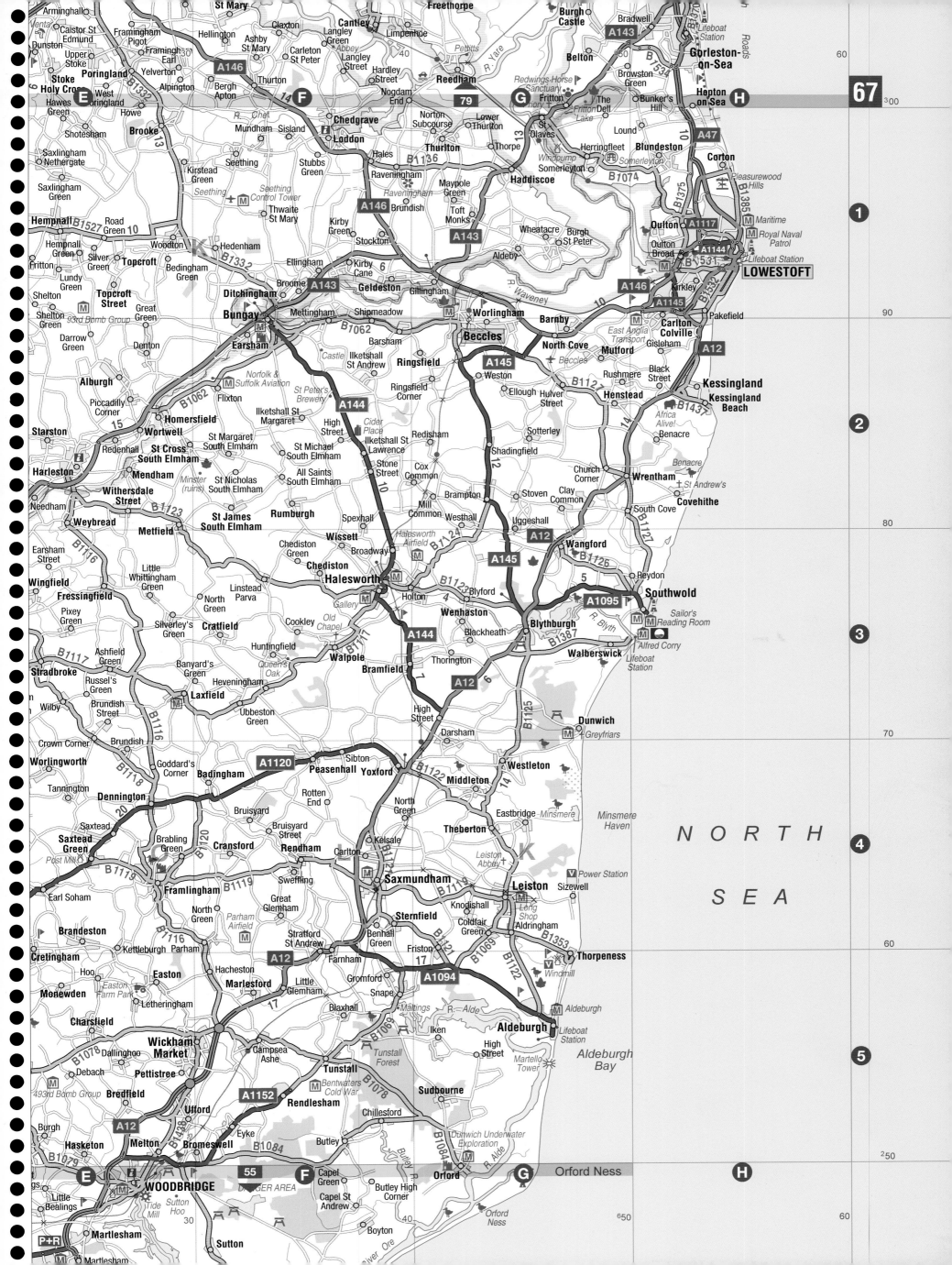

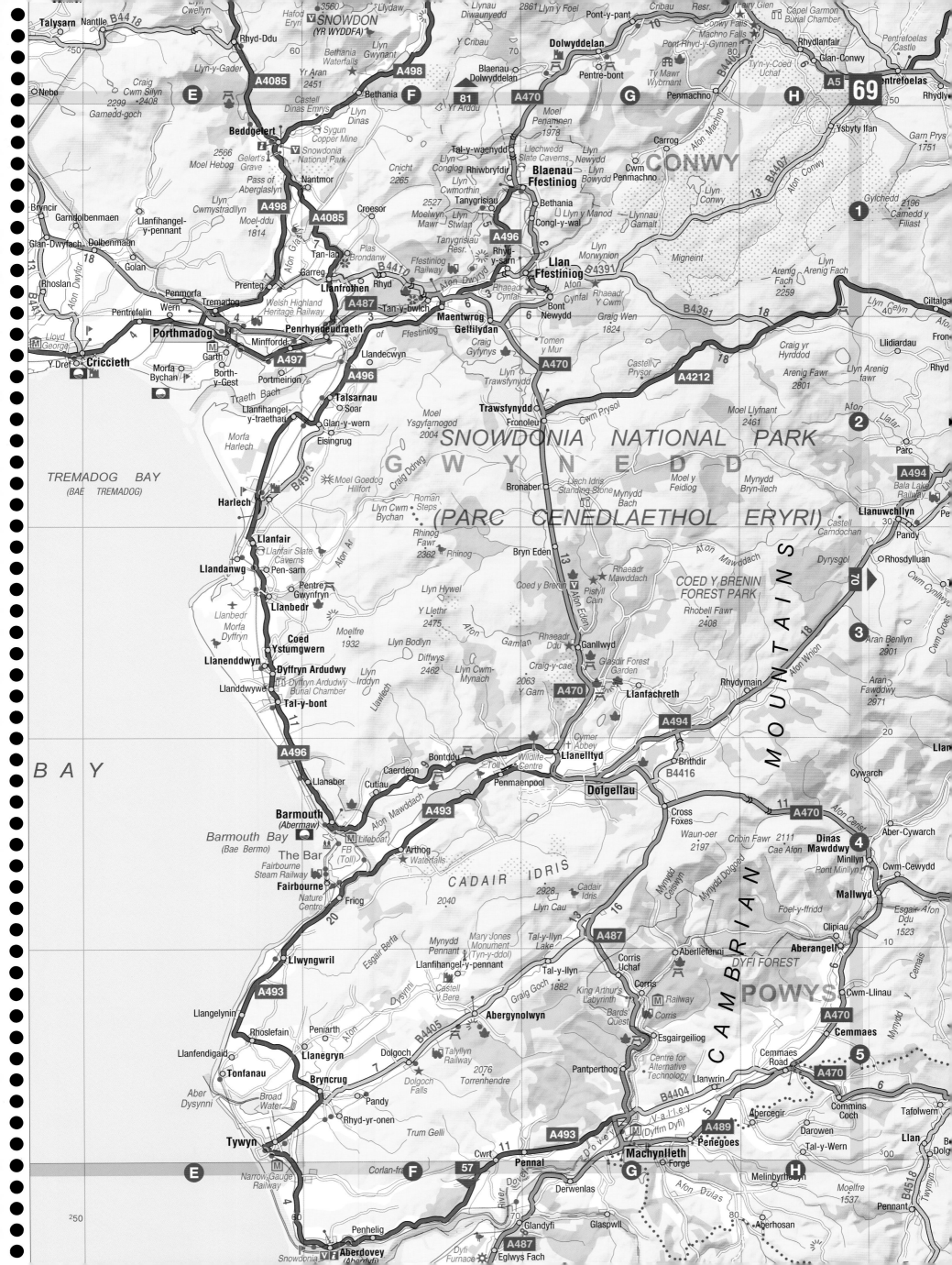

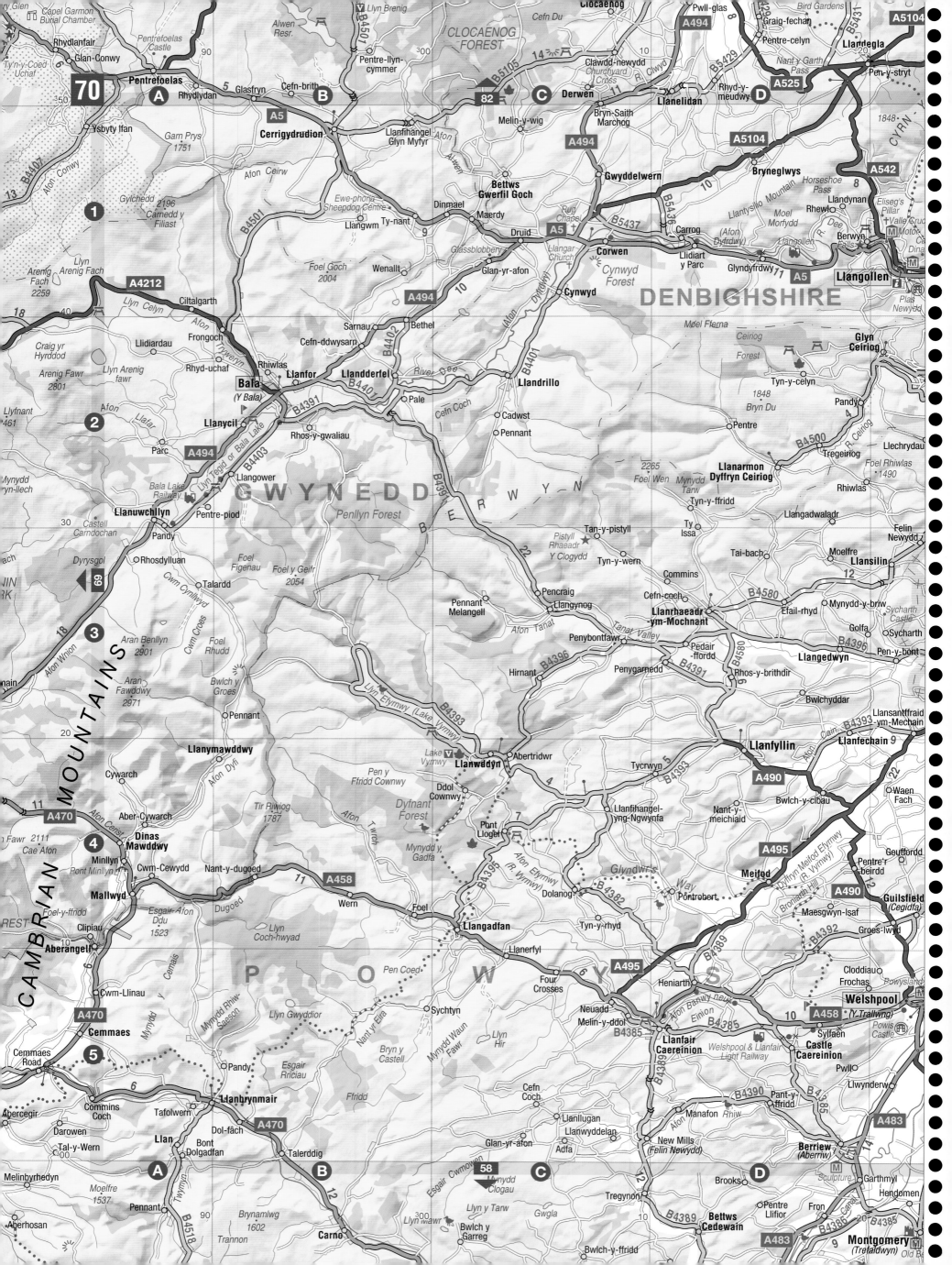

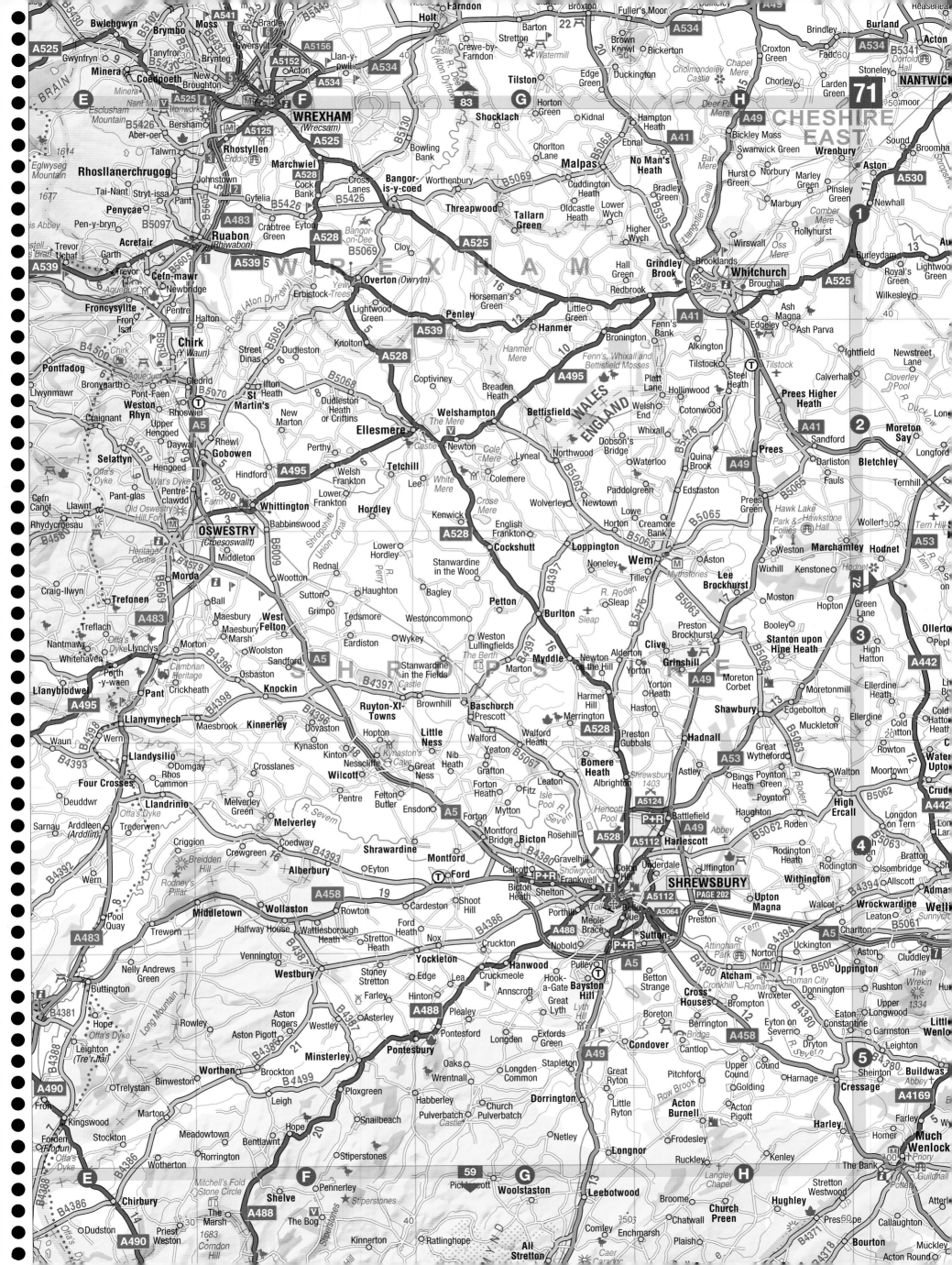

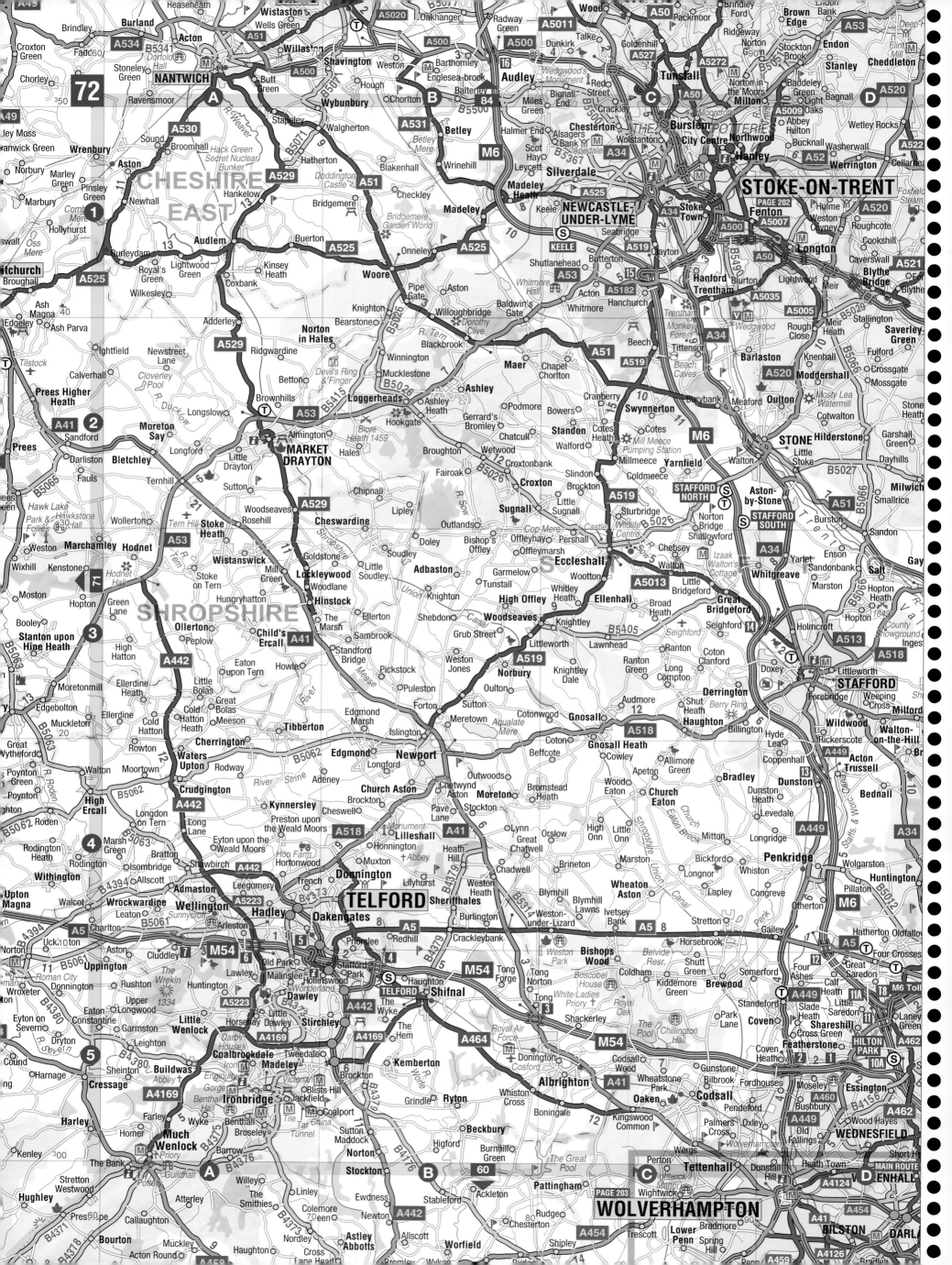

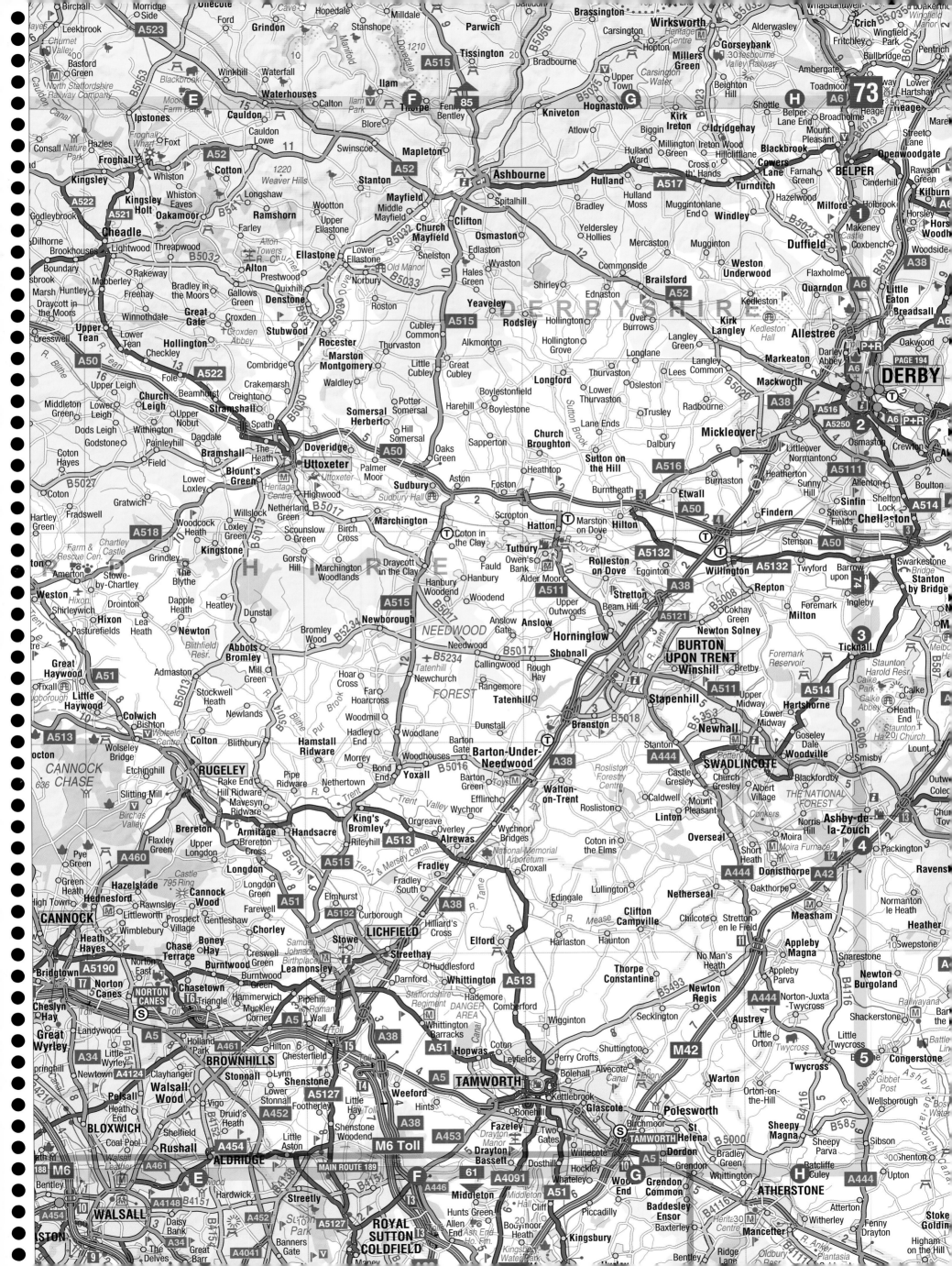

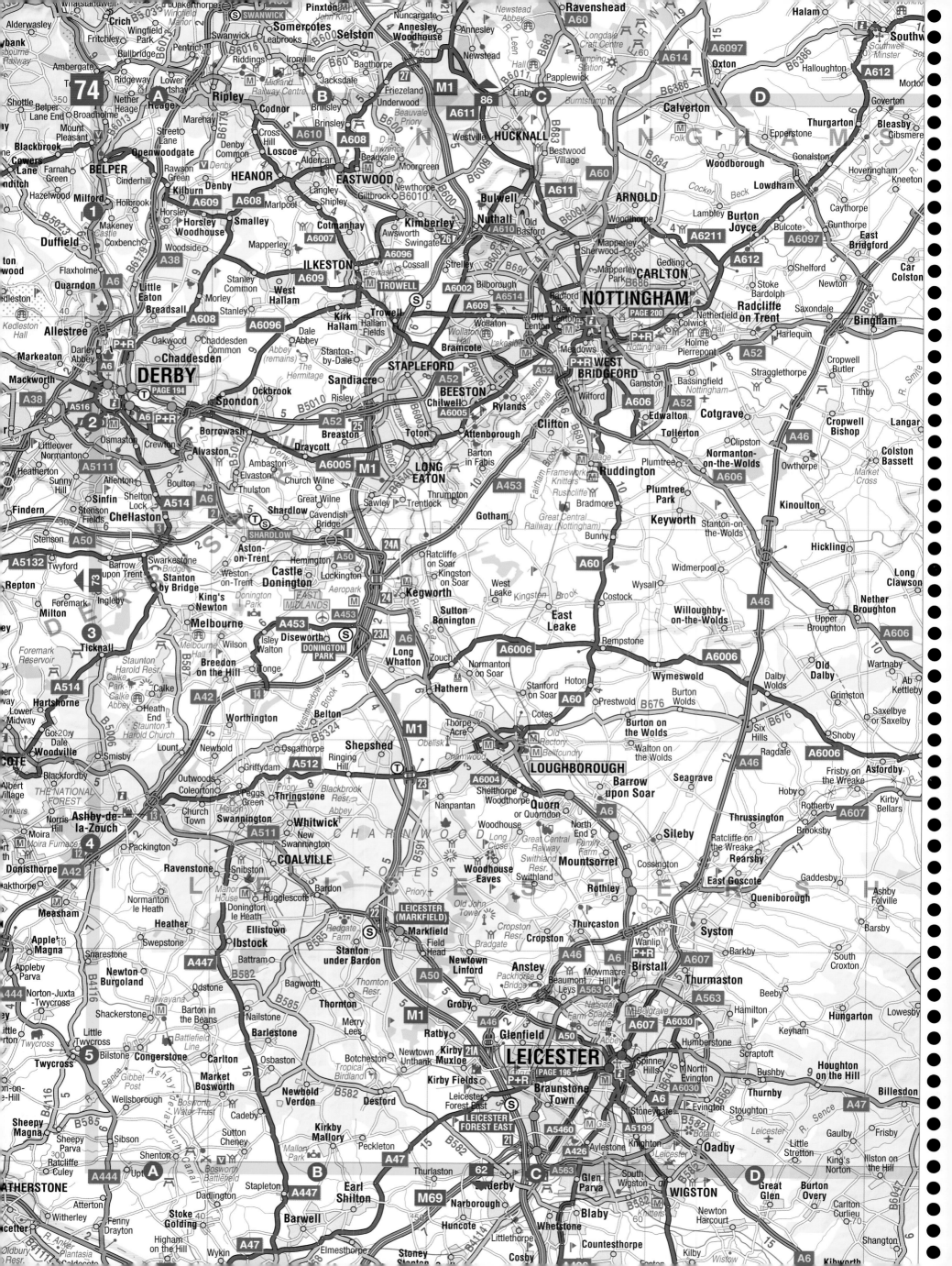

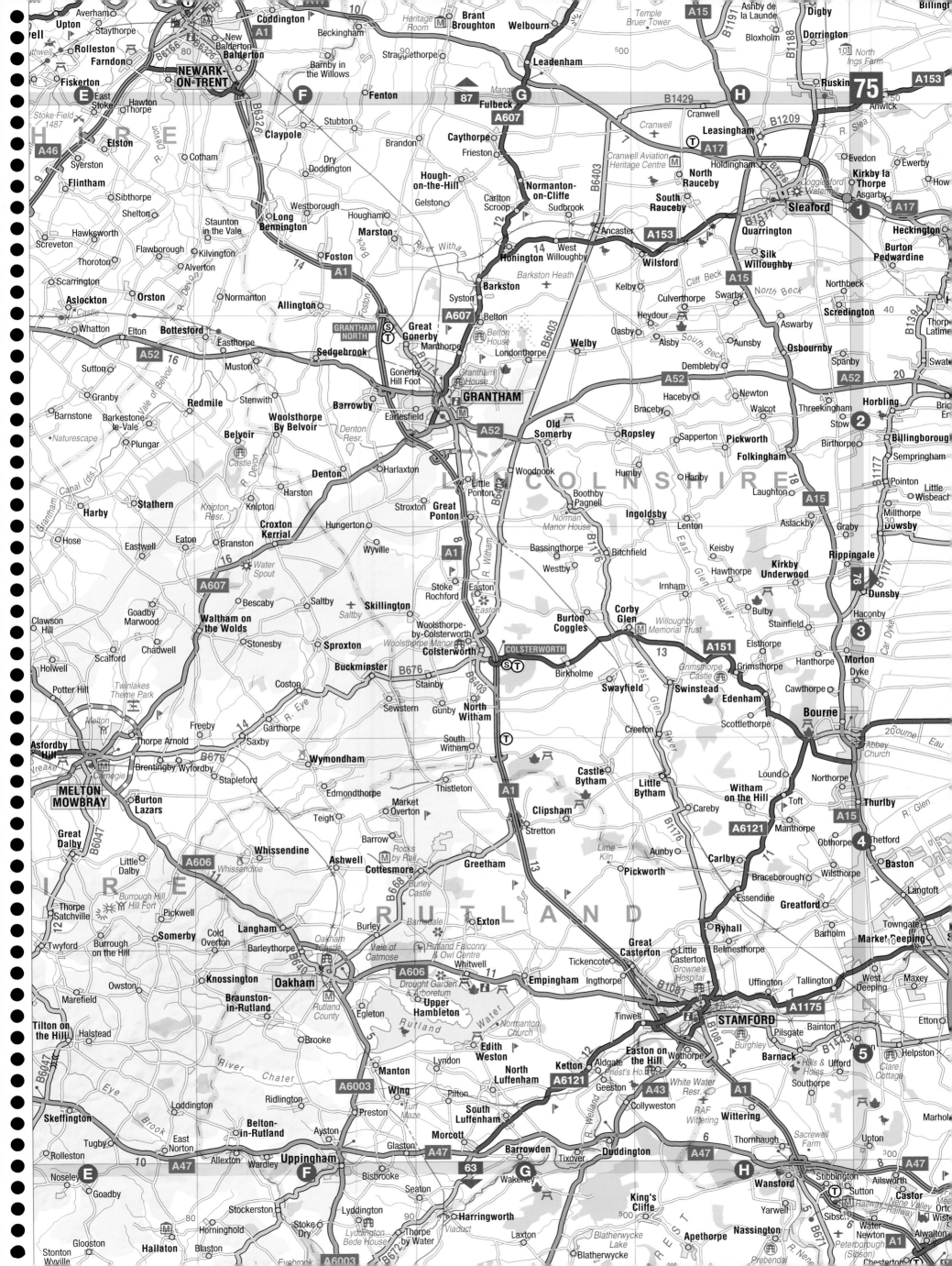

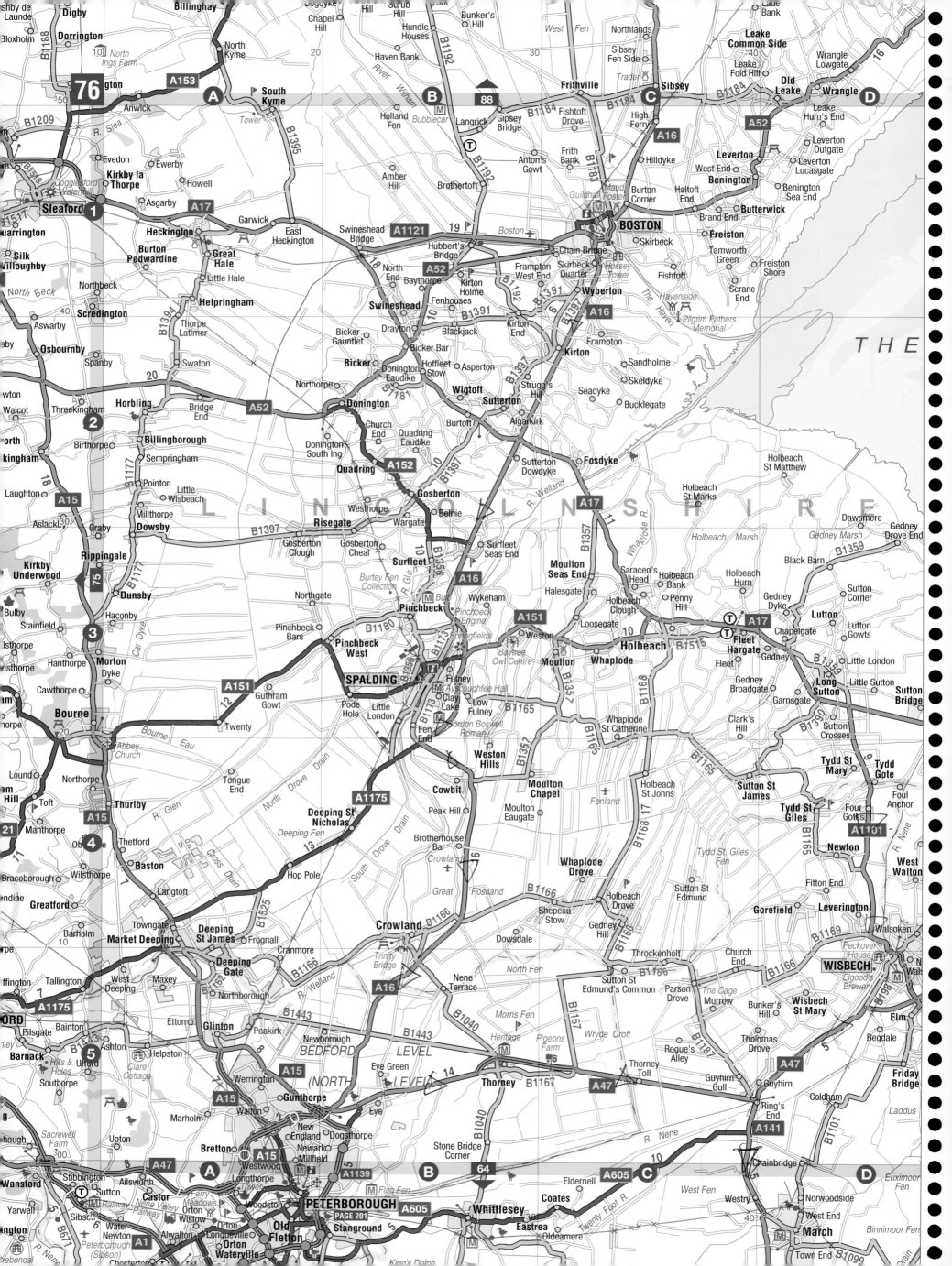

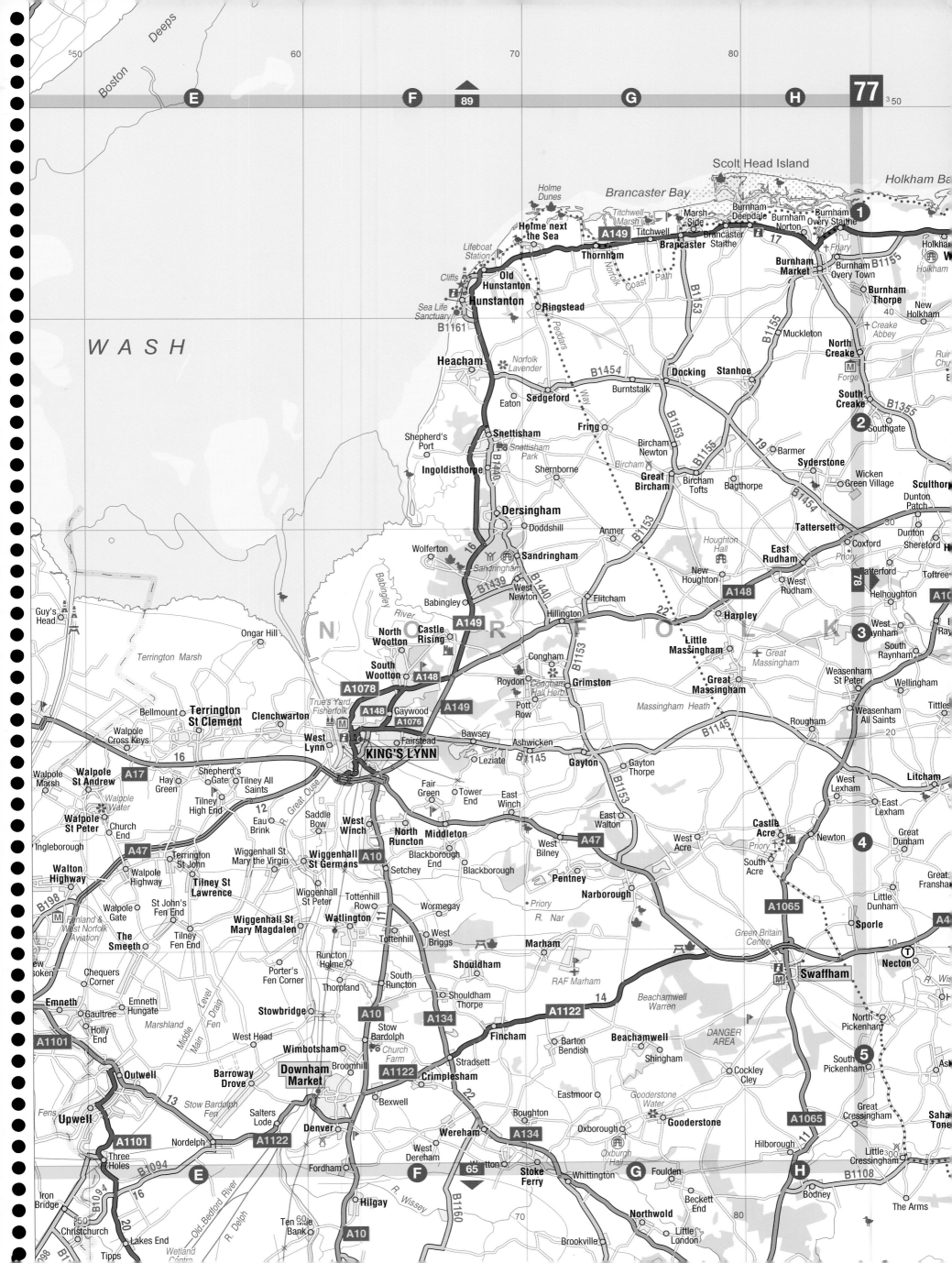

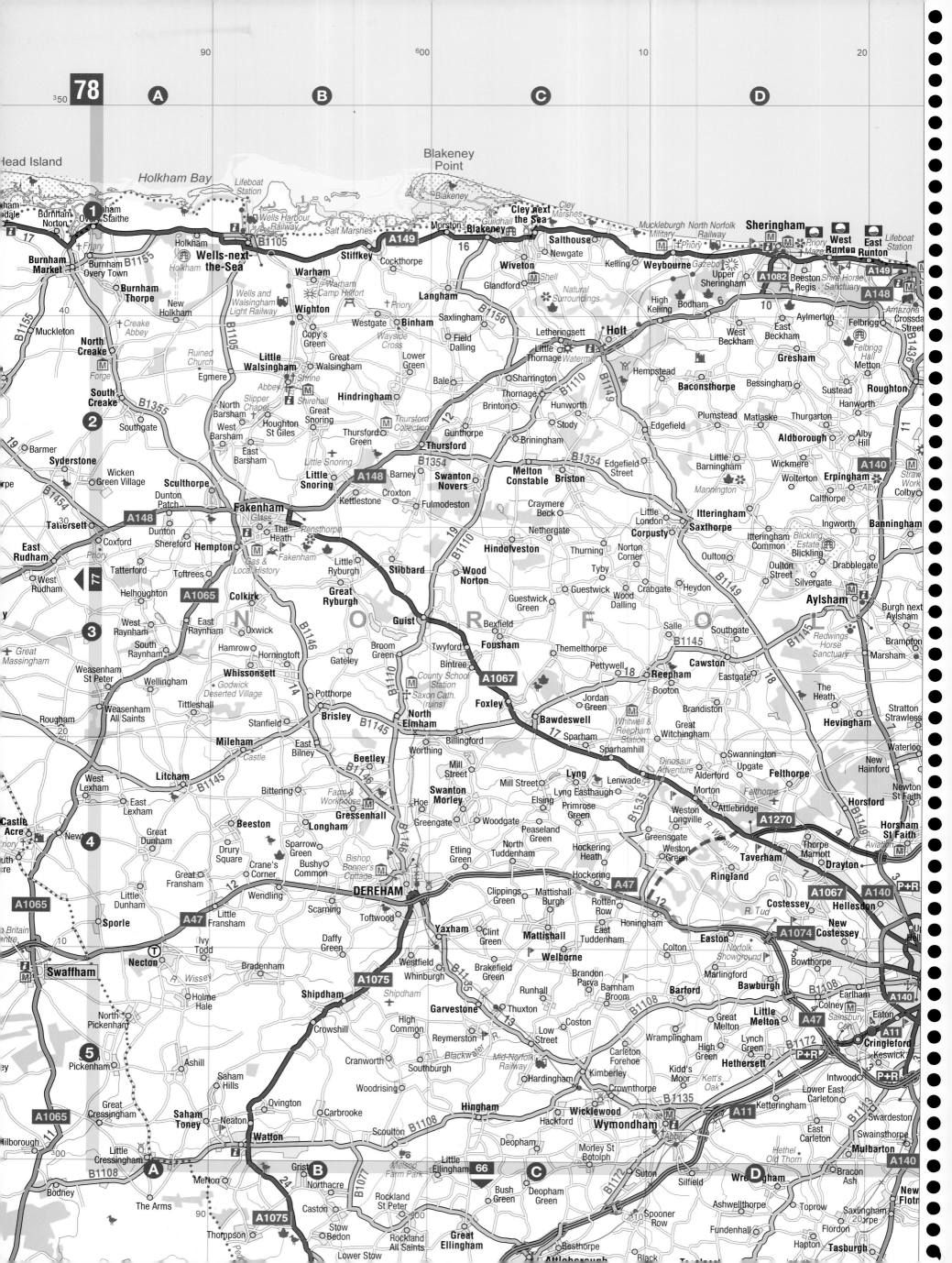

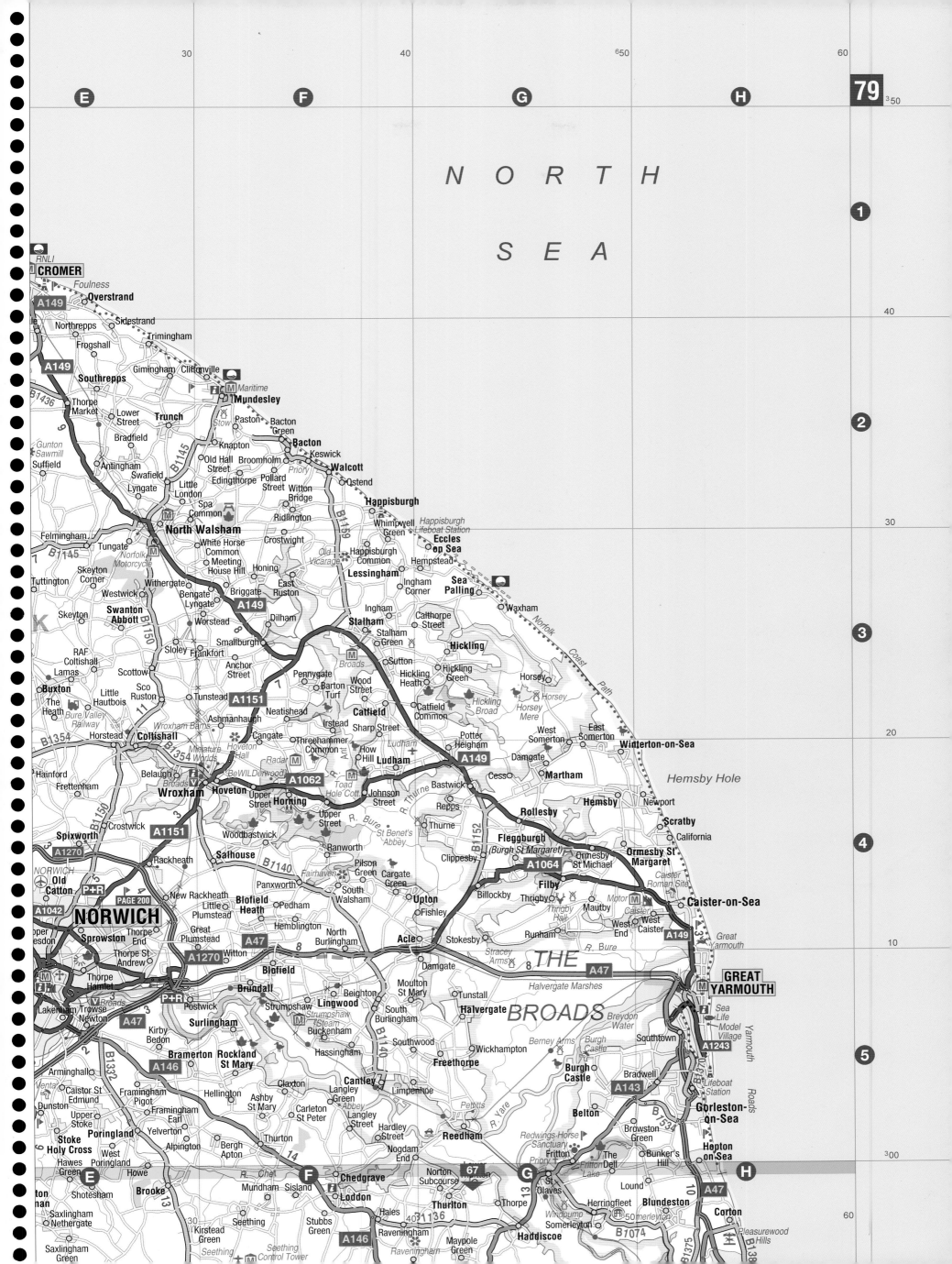

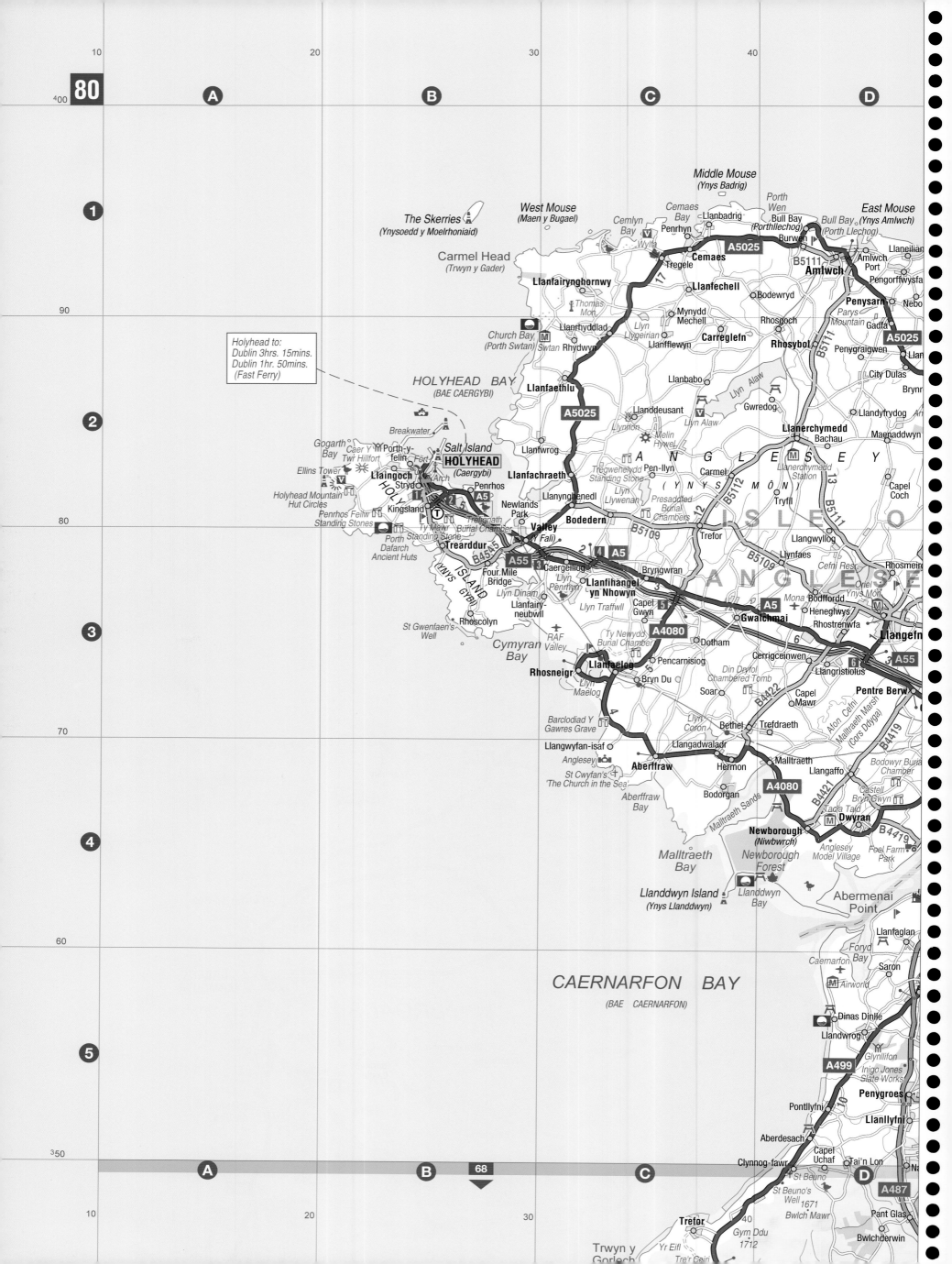

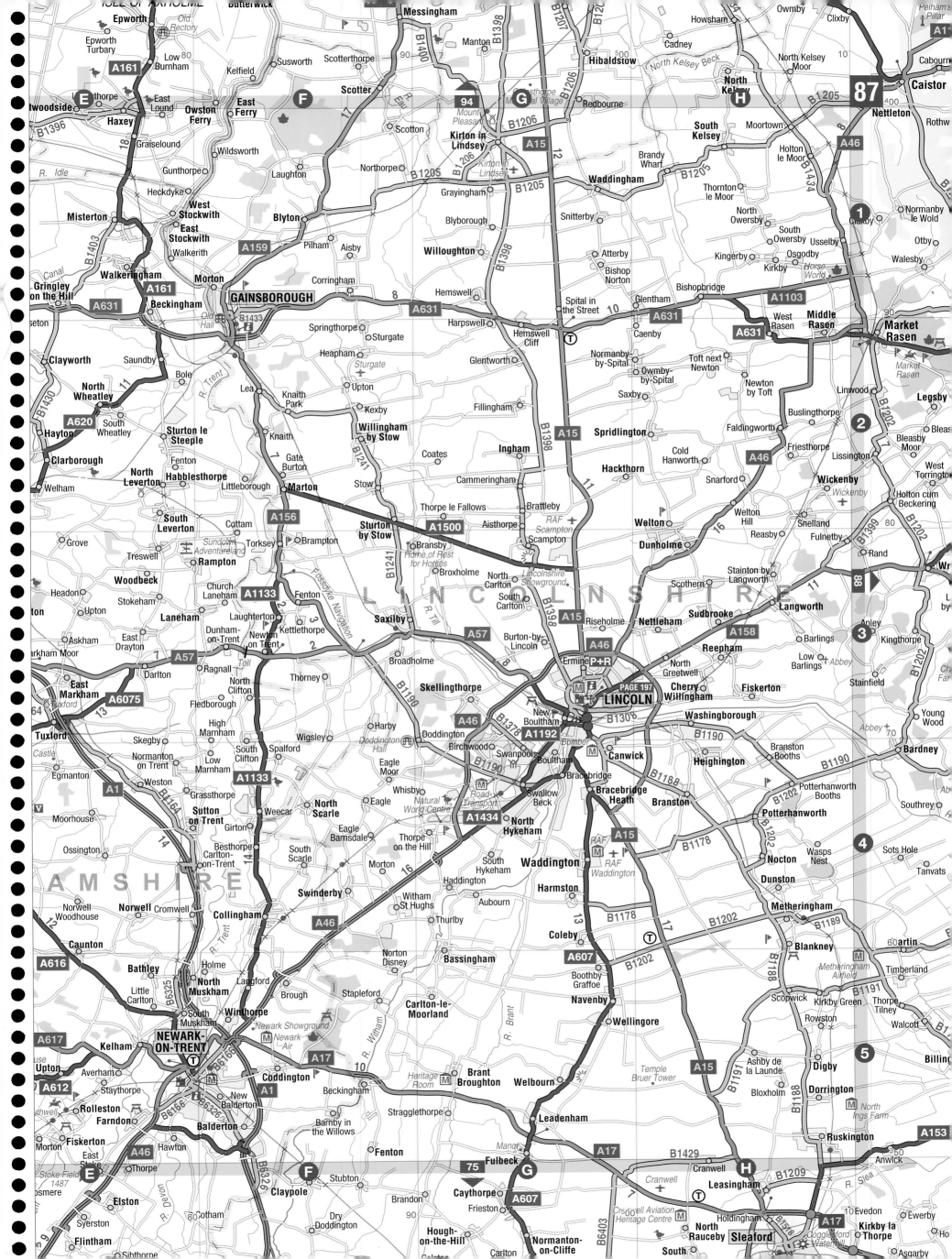

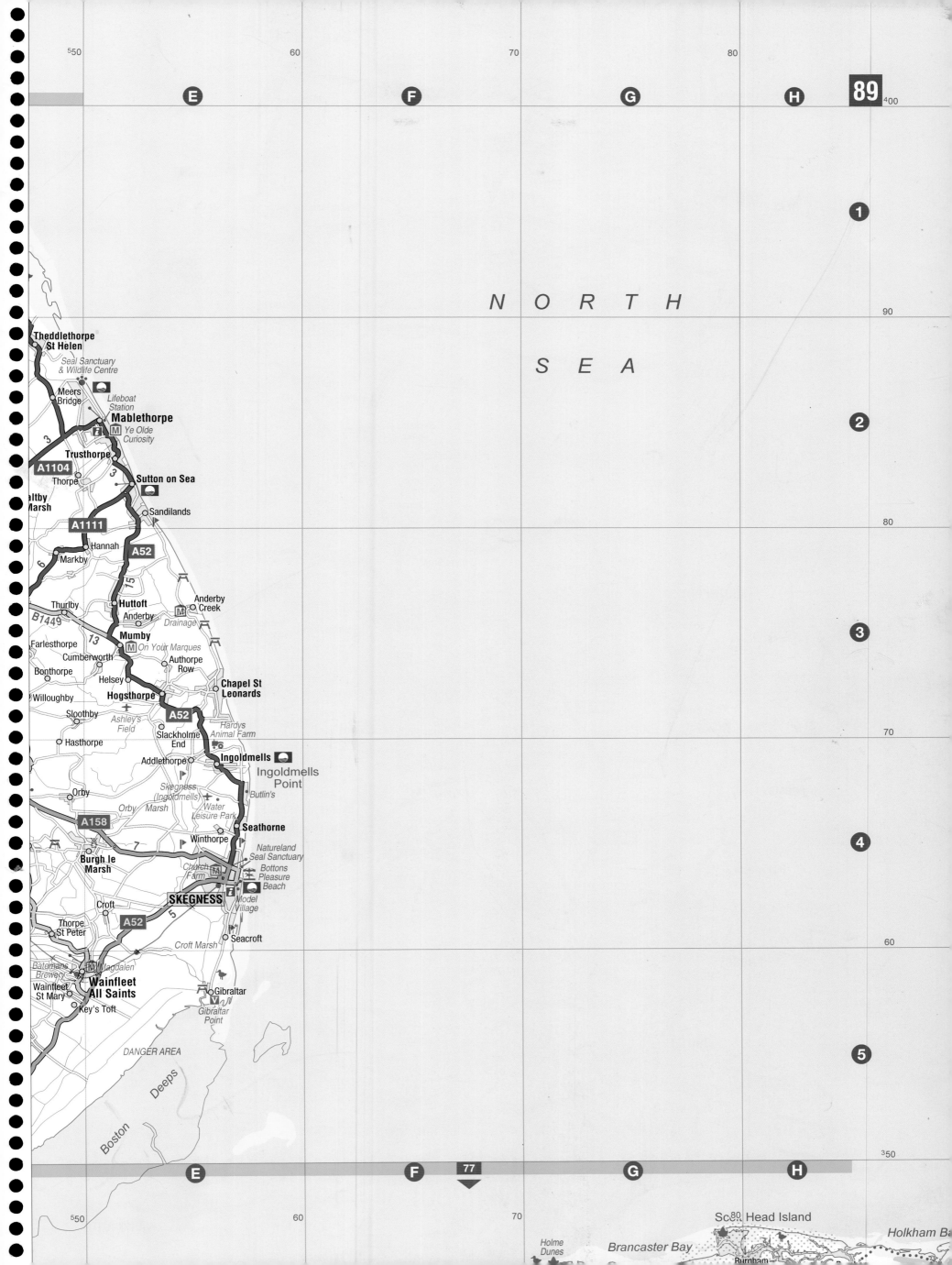

1

N O R T H

S E A

90

2

Theddlethorpe
St Helen

Seal Sanctuary
& Wildlife Centre

Meers
Bridge

Lifeboat
Station

Mablethorpe

Ye Olde
Curiosity

Trusthorpe

A1104

Thorpe

Sutton on Sea

altby
Marsh

Sandilands

80

A1111

Hannah

A52

Markby

6

15

Thurlby

Huttoft

Anderby
Creek

B1449

Anderby

Drainage

13

Mumby

On Your Marques

3

Farlesthorpe

Cumberworth

Authorpe
Row

Bonthorpe

Helsey

**Chapel St
Leonards**

Willoughby

Hogsthorpe

Sloothby

A52

Ashley's
Field

Hardys
Animal Farm

Hasthorpe

Slackholme
End

70

Addlethorpe

Ingoldmells

Ingoldmells
Point

Orby

Skegness
(Ingoldmells)

Butlin's

Orby Marsh

Water
Leisure Park

A158

Seathorne

Winthorpe

Natureland
Seal Sanctuary

4

**Burgh le
Marsh**

7

Church
Farm

Bottons
Pleasure
Beach

SKEGNESS

Model
Village

Croft

5

Thorpe
St Peter

A52

Seacroft

60

Croft Marsh

Batemans
Brewery

Magdalen

**Wainfleet
All Saints**

Wainfleet
St Mary

Gibraltar

Key's Toft

Gibraltar
Point

5

DANGER AREA

Deeps

Boston

350

Holme
Dunes

Brancaster Bay

Burnham

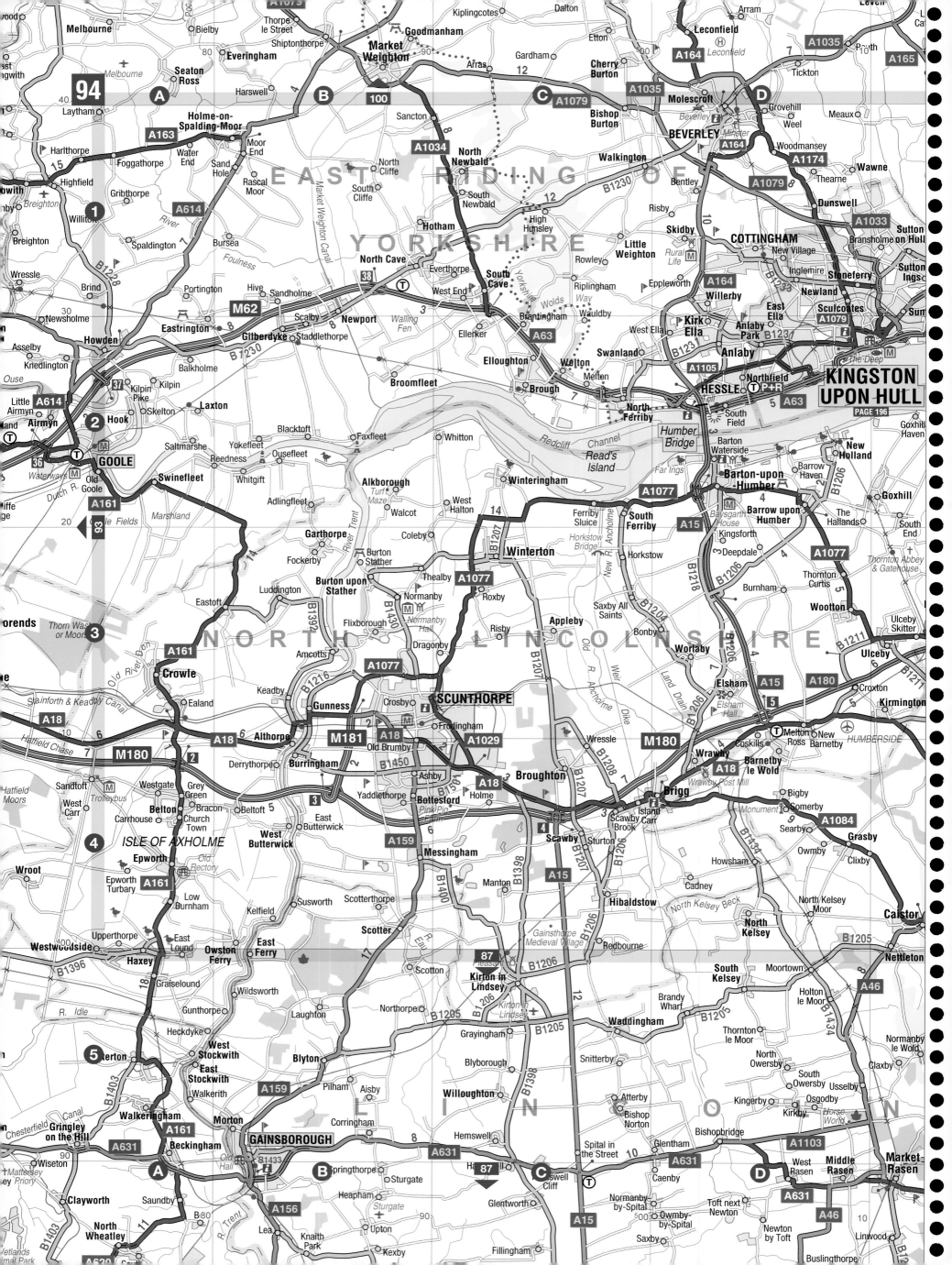

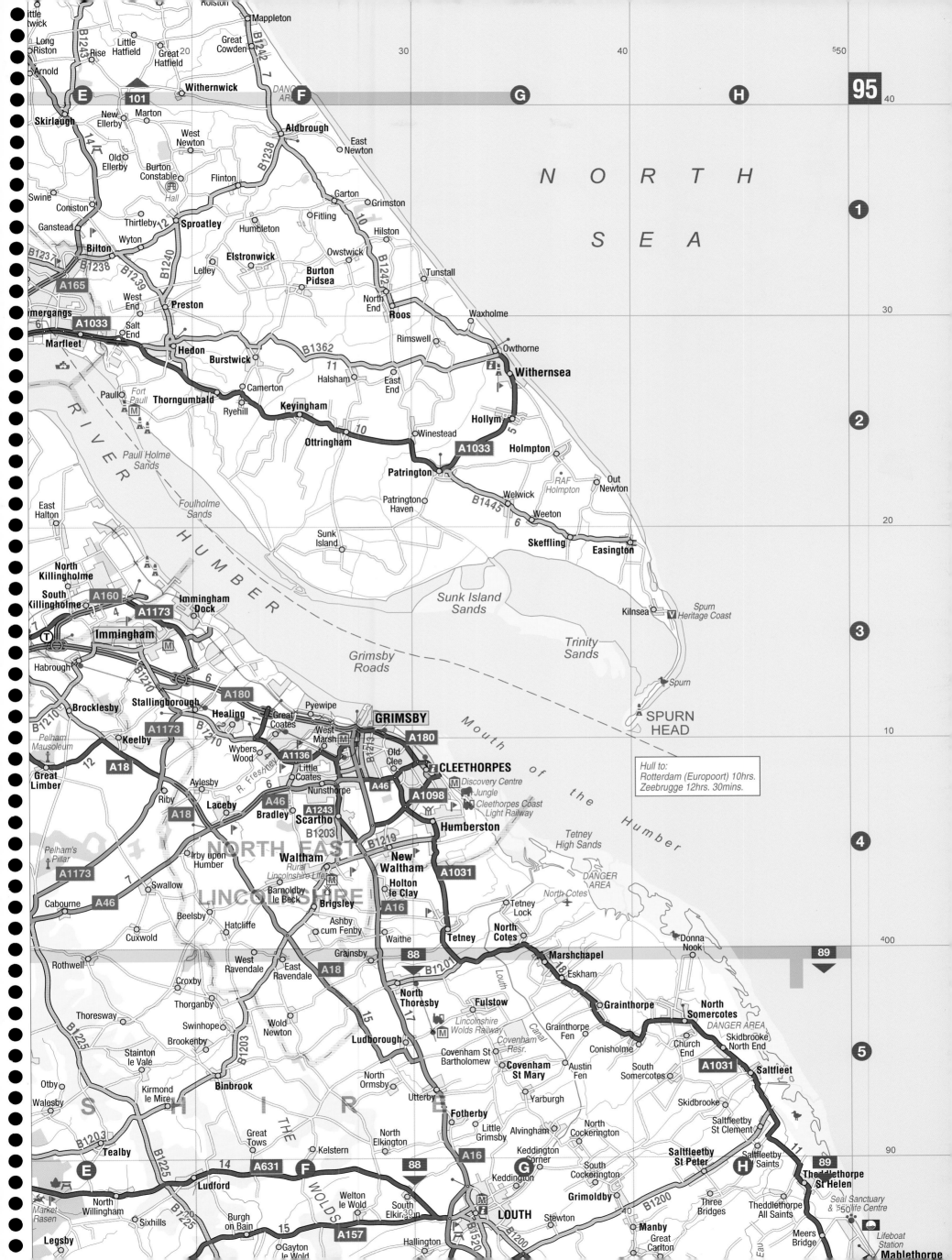

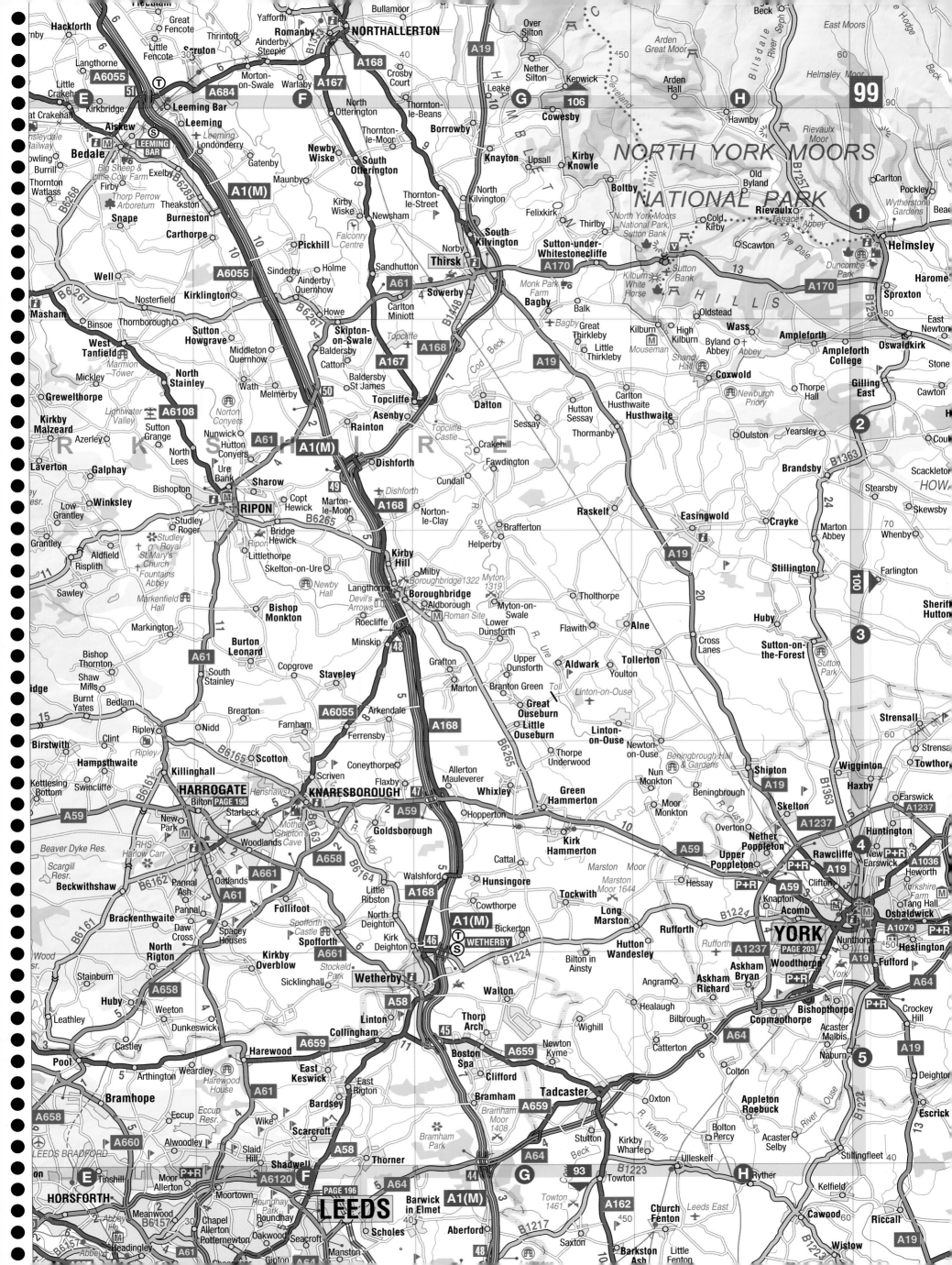

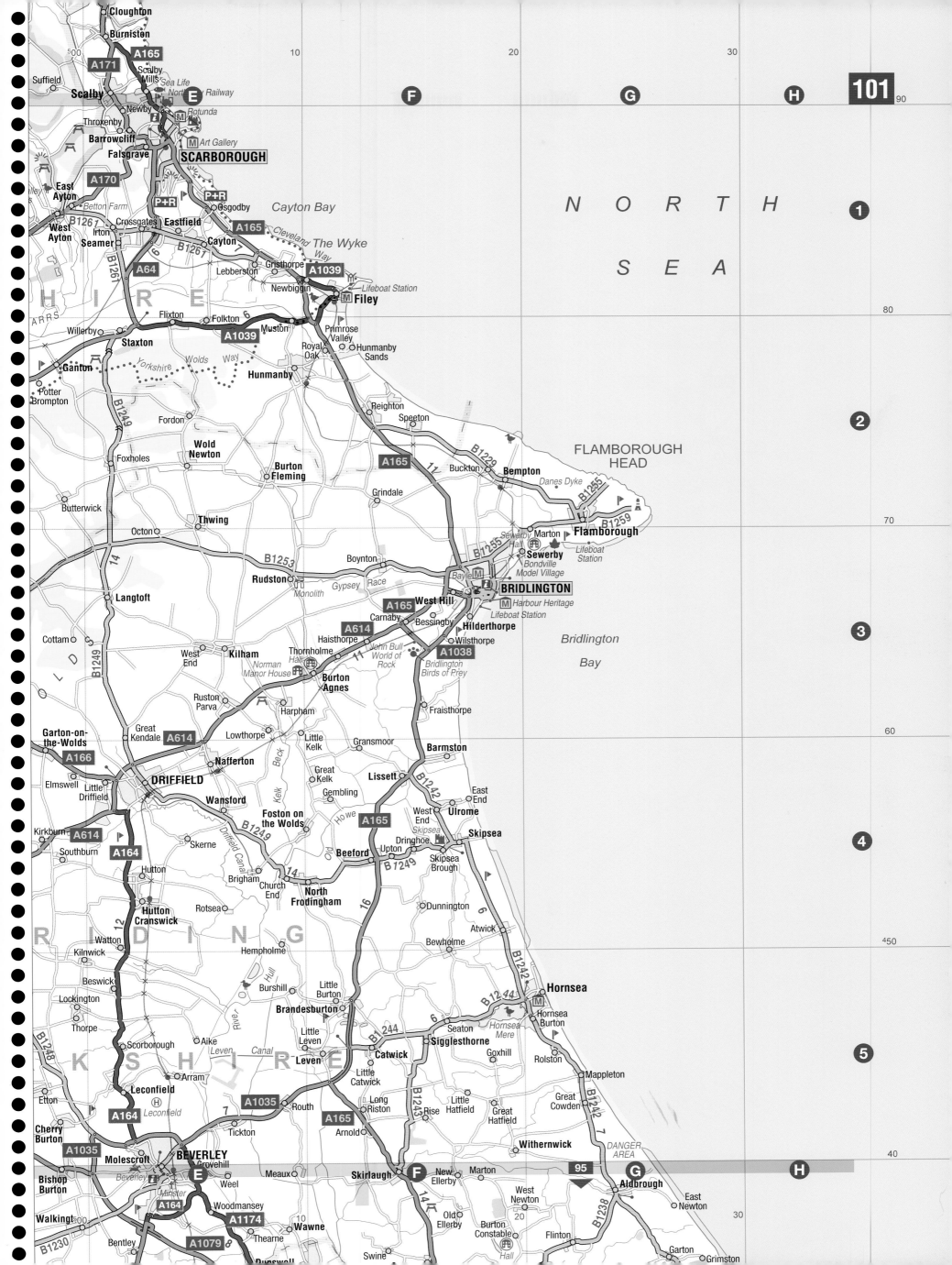

NORTH

SEA

FLAMBOROUGH
HEAD

Bridlington

Bay

Cayton Bay

The Wyke

Cloughton
Burniston
Suffield
Scalby
Scalby
Mills
Sea Life
North Bay Railway
Rotunda
Newby
Throxenby
Barrowcliff
Art Gallery
Falsgrave
SCARBOROUGH
East
Ayton
Betton Farm
West
Ayton
Crossgates
Eastfield
Osgodby
Irton
Seamer
Cayton
Lebberston
Gristhorpe
Newbiggin
Lifeboat Station
Filey
Flixton
Folkton
Muston
Willerby
Staxton
Primrose
Valley
Ganton
Yorkshire
Wolds
Way
Royal
Oak
Hunmanby
Sands
Potter
Brompton
Hunmanby
Butterwick
Foxholes
Wold
Newton
Burton
Fleming
Reighton
Speeton
Octon
Thwing
Grindale
Buckton
Bempton
Danes Dyke
Flamborough
Marton
Sewerby
Sewerby Hall
Bondville
Model Village
Rudston
Boynton
Monolith
Gypsy Race
Langtoft
West Hill
BRIDLINGTON
Bayle
Harbour Heritage
Lifeboat Station
Cottam
West
End
Kilham
Thornholme
Norman
Manor House
Carnaby
Bessingby
Hilderthorpe
Wilsthorpe
Haisthorpe
John Bull
World of Rock
Bridlington
Birds of Prey
Ruston
Parva
Burton
Agnes
Harpham
Fraisthorpe
Great
Kendale
Lowthorpe
Little
Kelk
Gransmoor
Barmston
Garton-on-
the-Wolds
Elmswell
Little
Driffield
Nafferton
Great
Kelk
Lissett
East
End
DRIFFIELD
Wansford
Gembling
West
End
Ulrome
Skipsea
Kirkburn
Foston on
the Wolds
Dringhoe
Skipsea
Brough
Southburn
Skerne
Beeford
Upton
Hutton
Brigham
Church
End
North
Frodingham
Watton
Rotsea
Dunnington
Kilnwick
Hemphome
Bewholme
Beswick
Atwick
Lockington
Burshill
Little
Burton
Thorpe
Brandesburton
Hornsea
Scorborough
Aike
Little
Leven
Seaton
Hornsea
Mere
Hornsea
Burton
Arram
Leven
Catwick
Sigglesthorne
Mappleton
Leconfield
Little
Catwick
Goxhill
Rolston
Leconfield
Routh
Long
Riston
Rise
Little
Hatfield
Great
Cowden
Cherry
Burton
Tickton
Arnold
Great
Hatfield
Withernwick
Etton
BEVERLEY
Grovehill
DANGER
AREA
Aldbrough
Bishop
Burton
Molescroft
Beverley
Minster
Weel
Meaux
Skirlaugh
New
Ellerby
Marton
95
Walking?
Woodmansey
West
Newton
East
Newton
Wawne
Old
Ellerby
Burton
Constable
Hall
Bentley
Thearne
Swine
Flinton
Garton
Dunswell
Grimston

A171
A165
500
A170
A64
B1261
B1261
B1261
6
7
A1039
A1039
B1249
A165
11
B1229
B1255
B1255
B1259
A165
A614
A1038
B1253
B1249
14
A614
A166
A614
A164
B1242
A165
Driffield Canal
12
14
16
B1249
6
B1242
B1244
B1244
B1243
6
B1248
A1035
A164
7
A165
B1238
A1035
A164
A1174
10
A1079
8
B1230

River Hull
Leven Canal
Kelk Beck
Howe Dike

RIDING

KSHIRE

HIRE

10
20
30
90
80
70
60
450
40
30

1
2
3
4
5

E
F
G
H
M
P+R
P+R
E
F
G
H

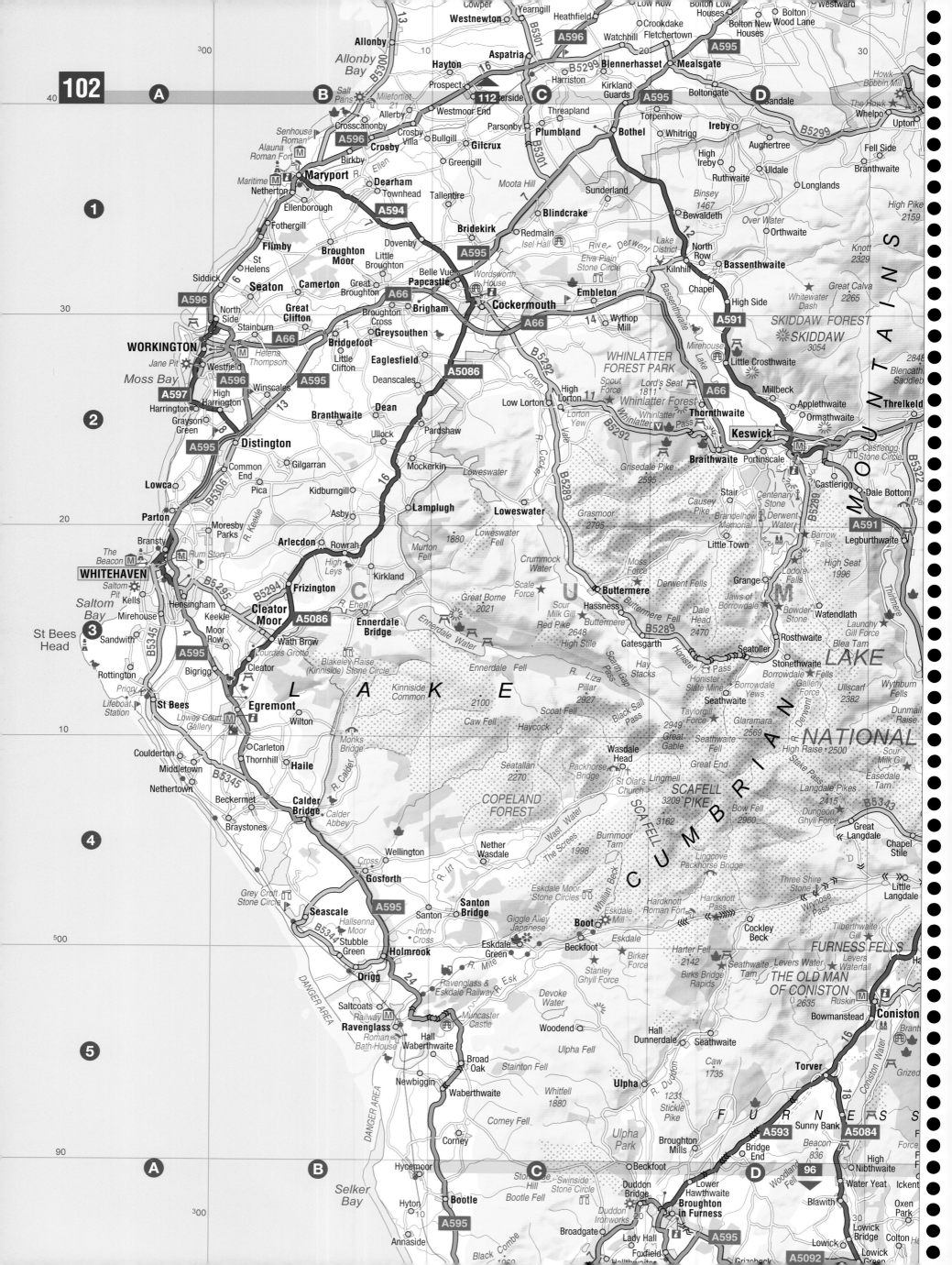

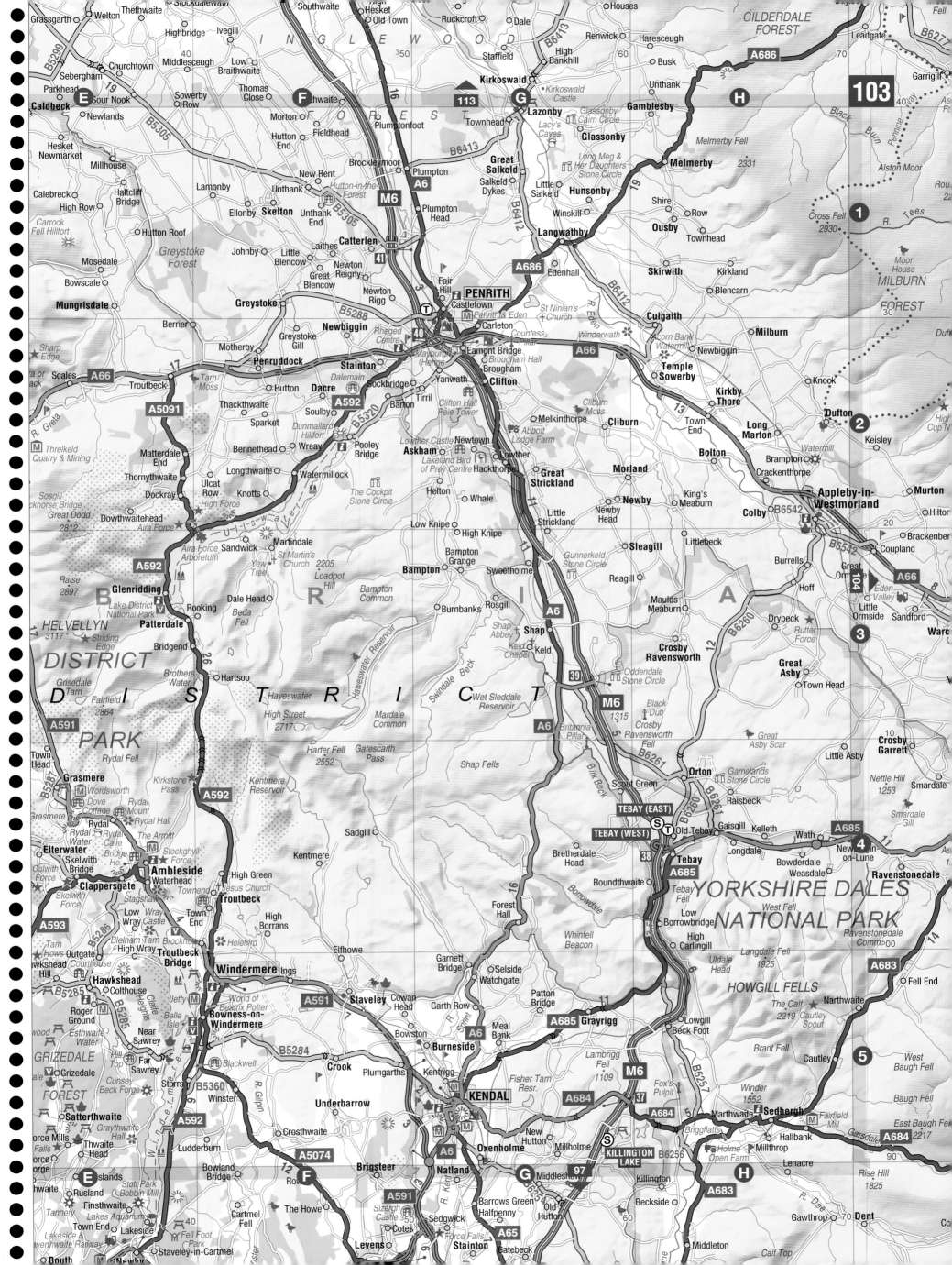

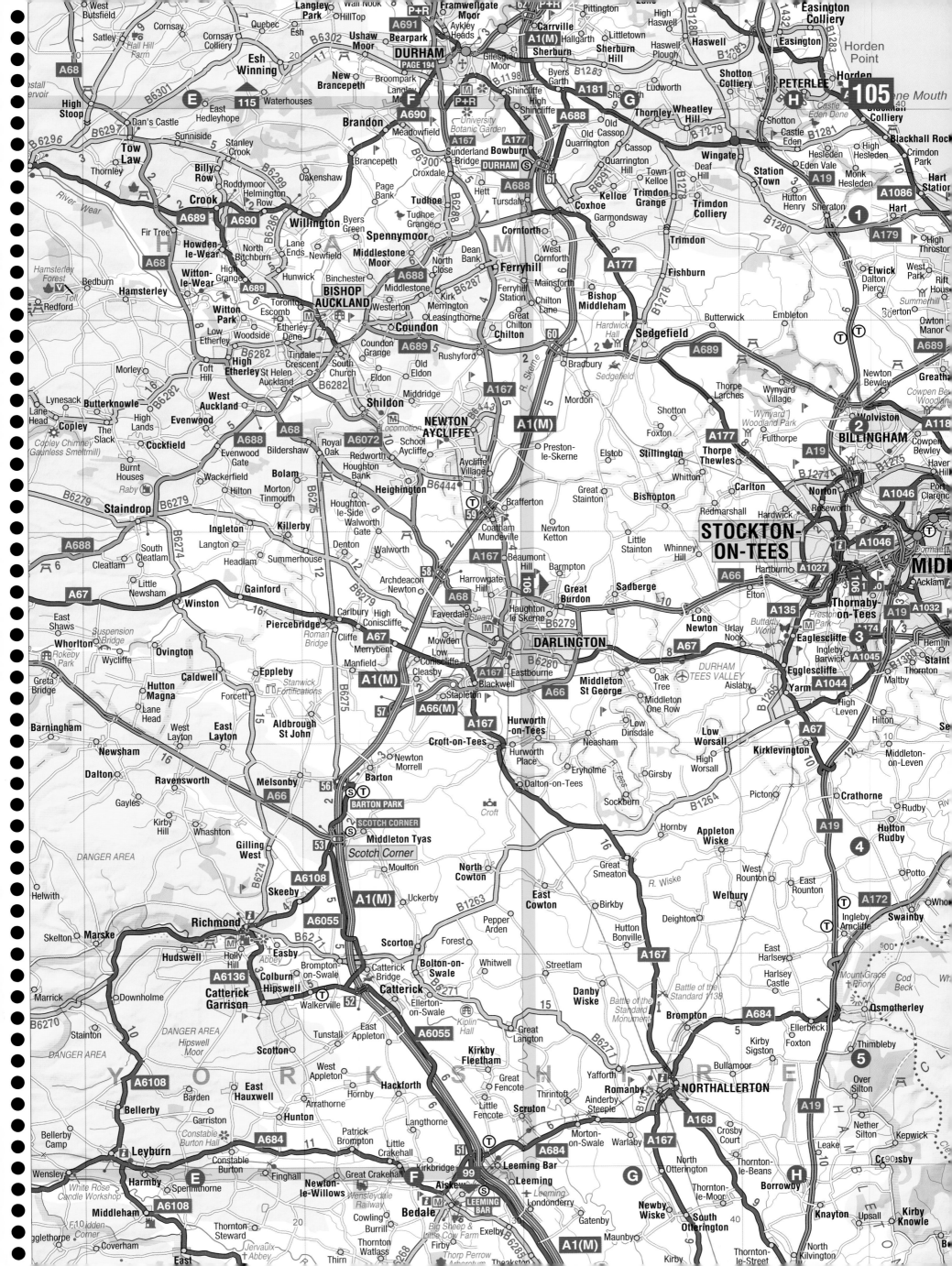

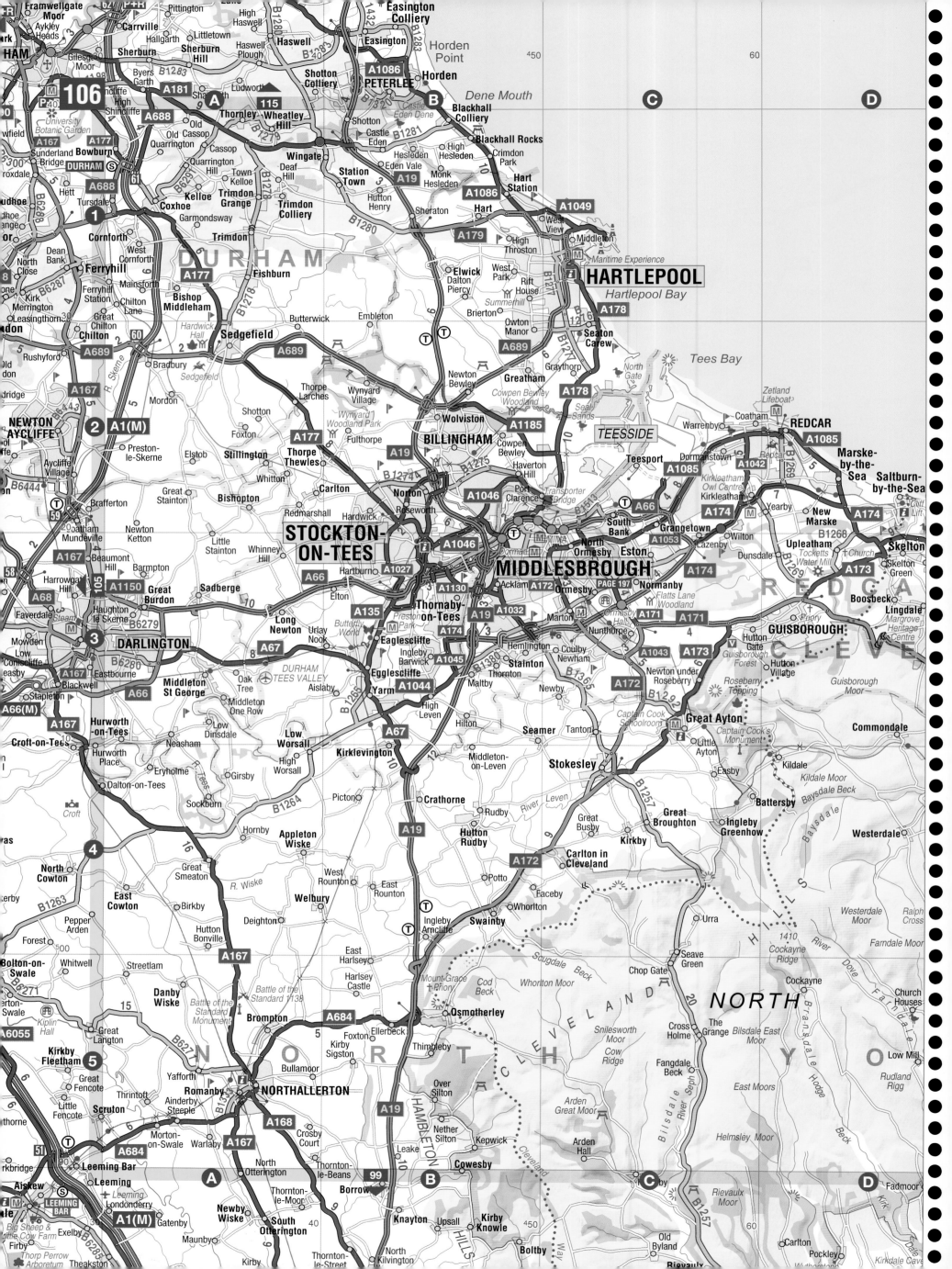

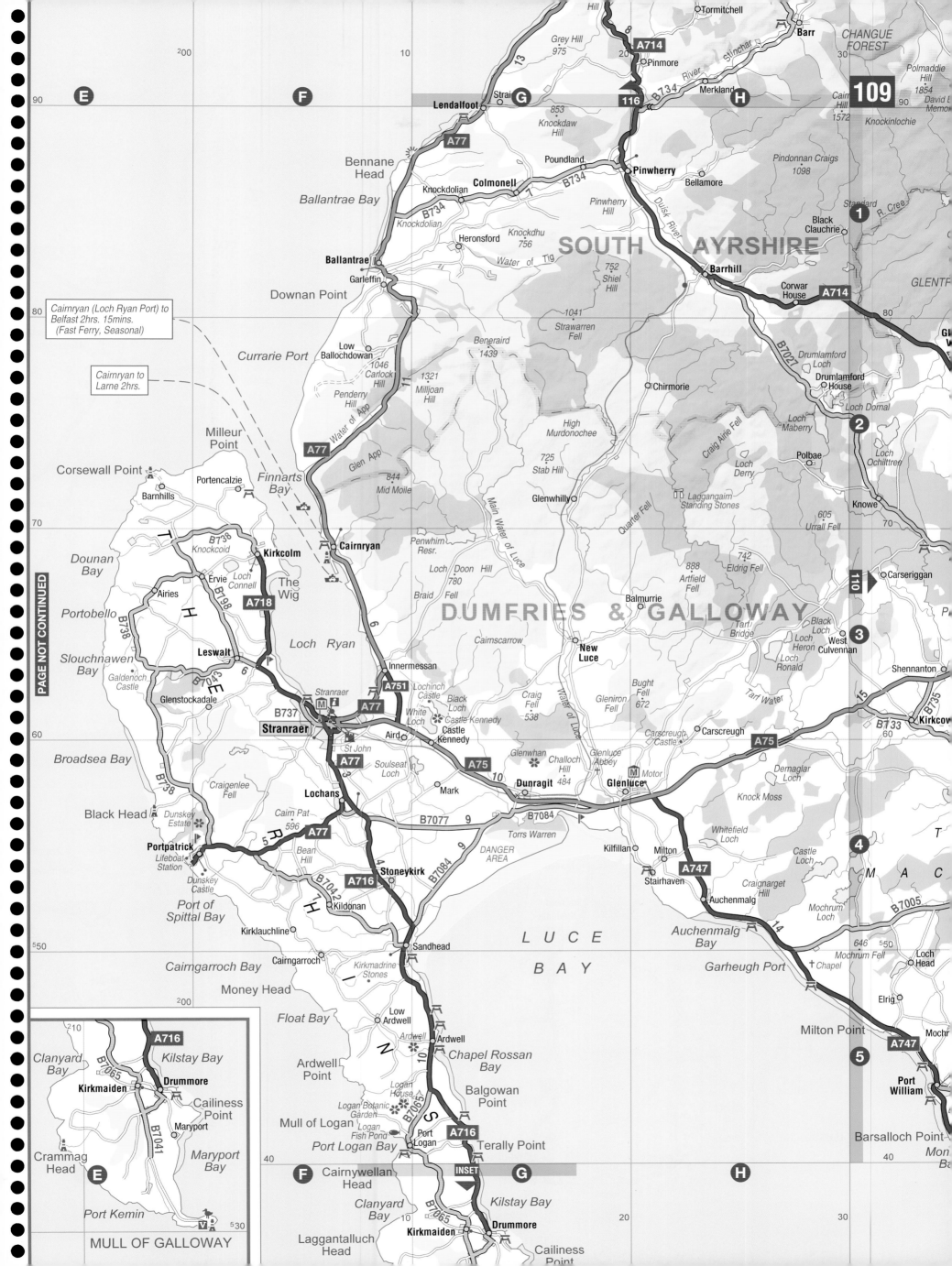

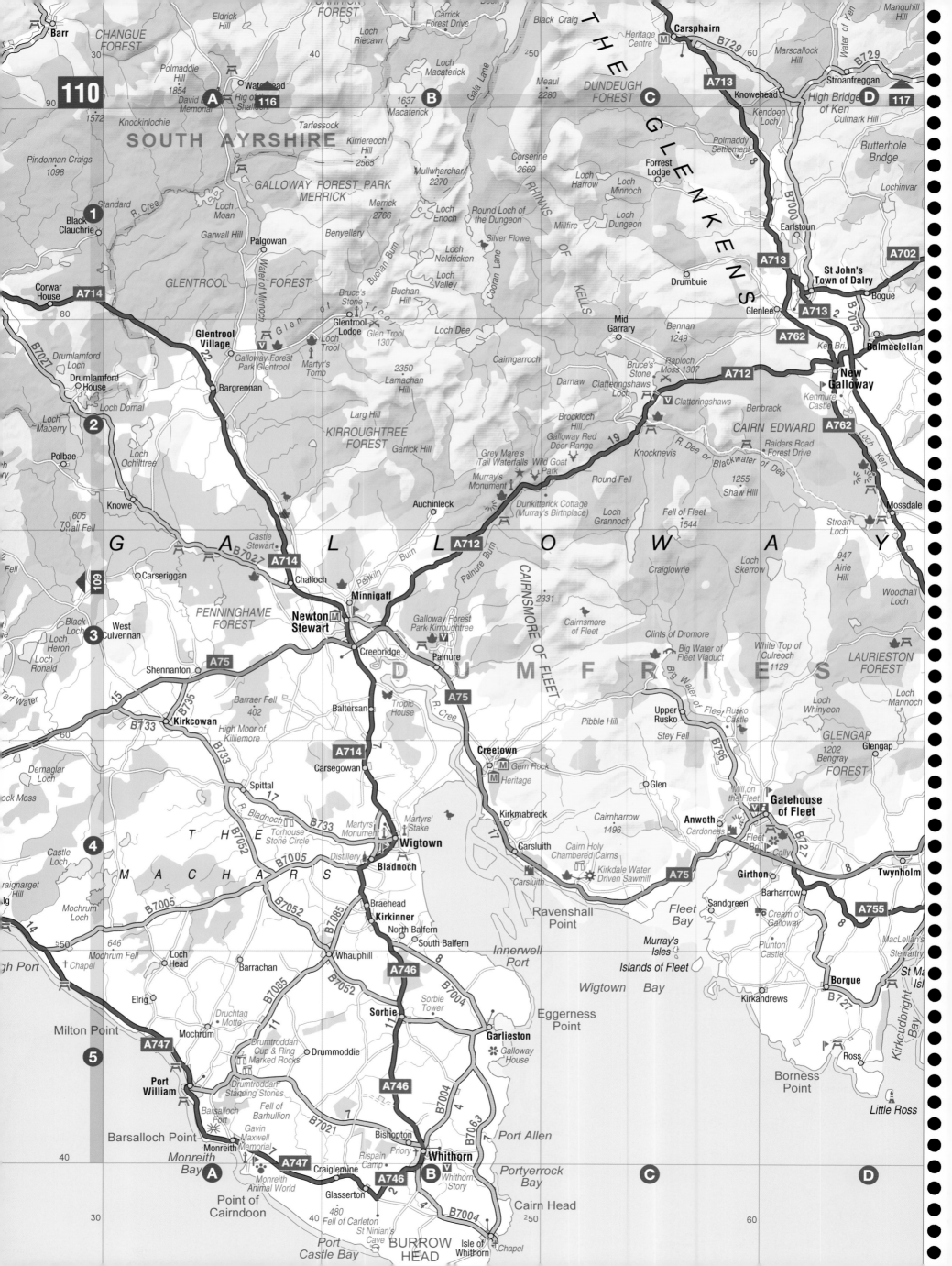

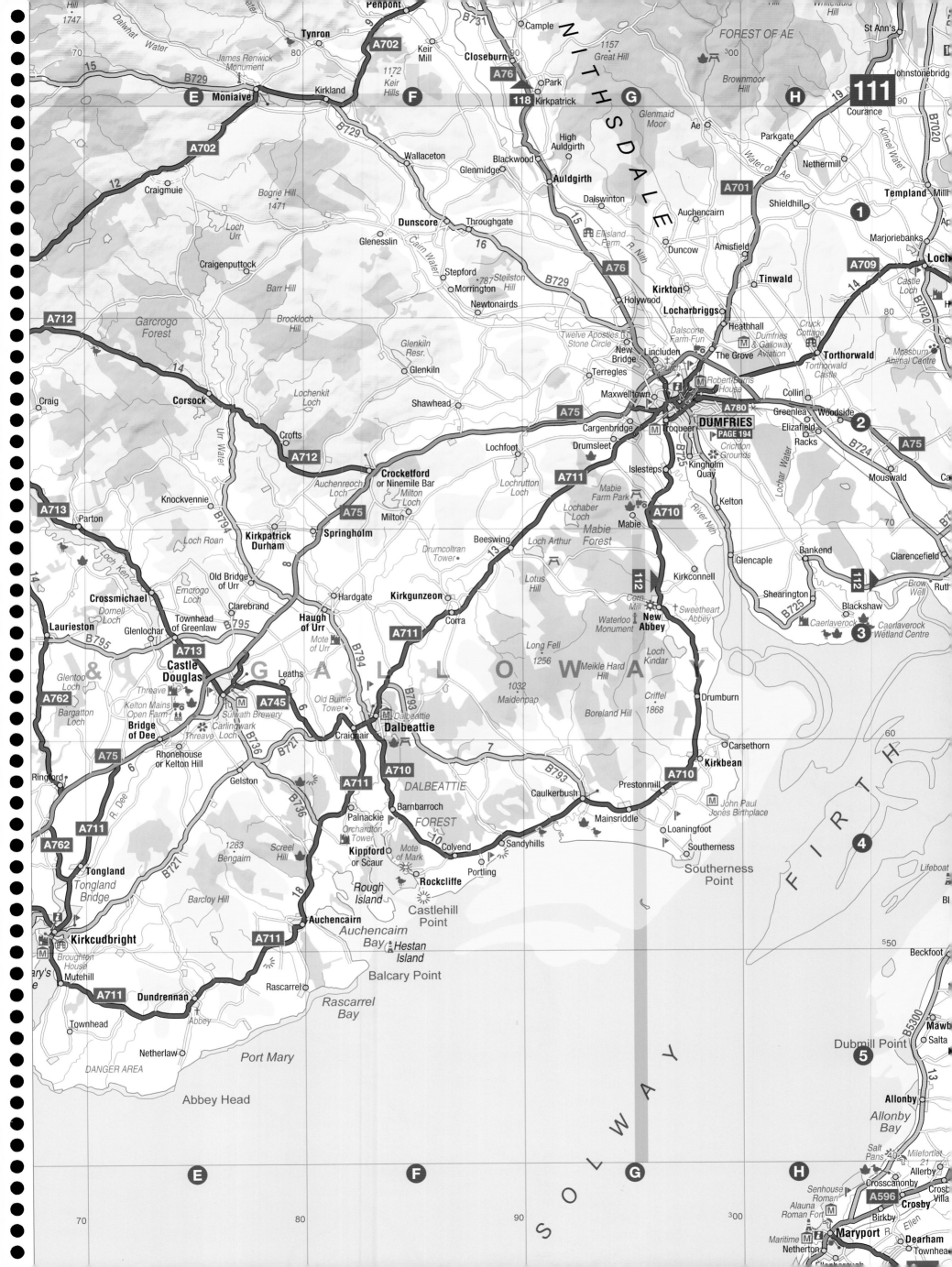

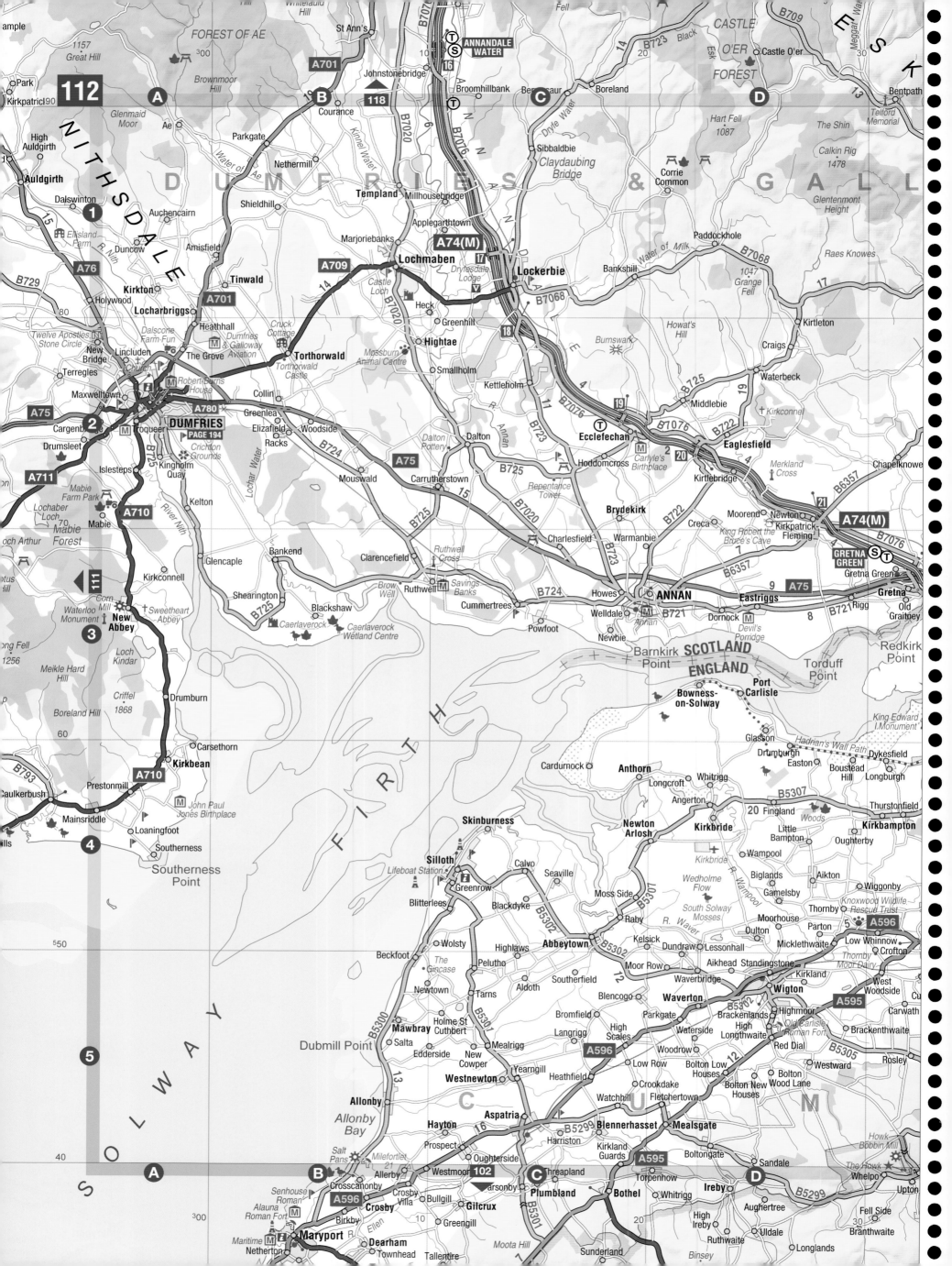

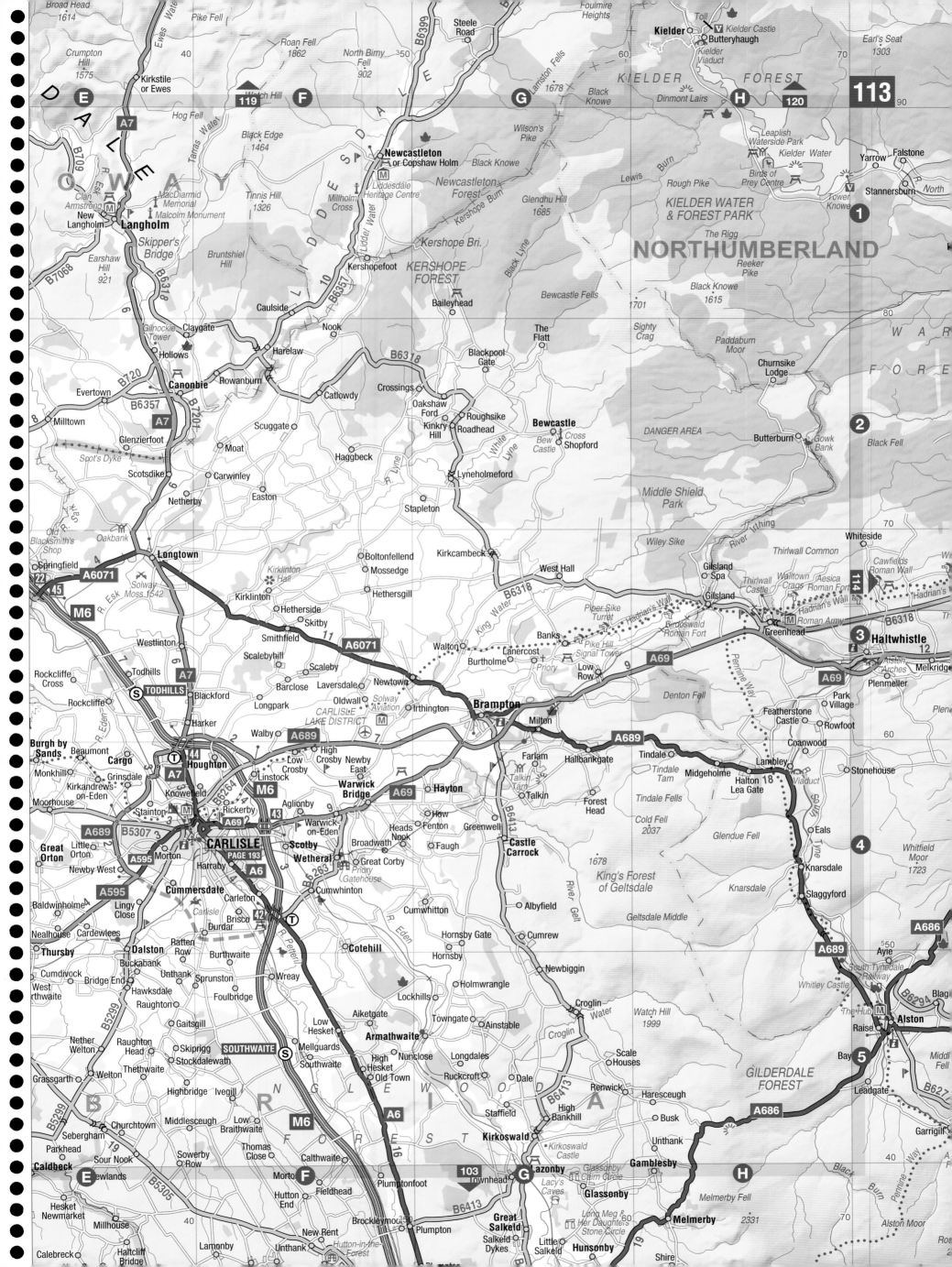

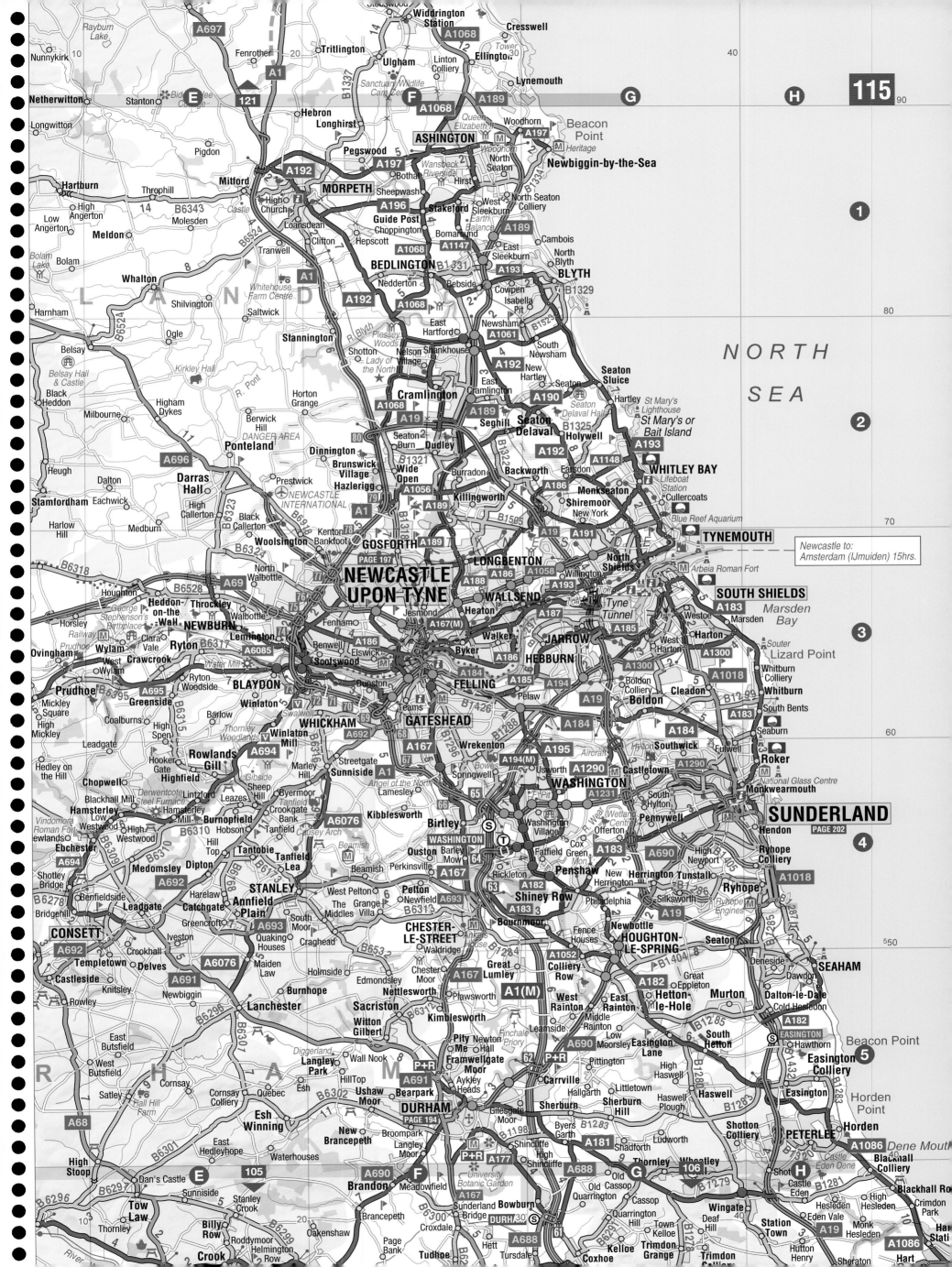

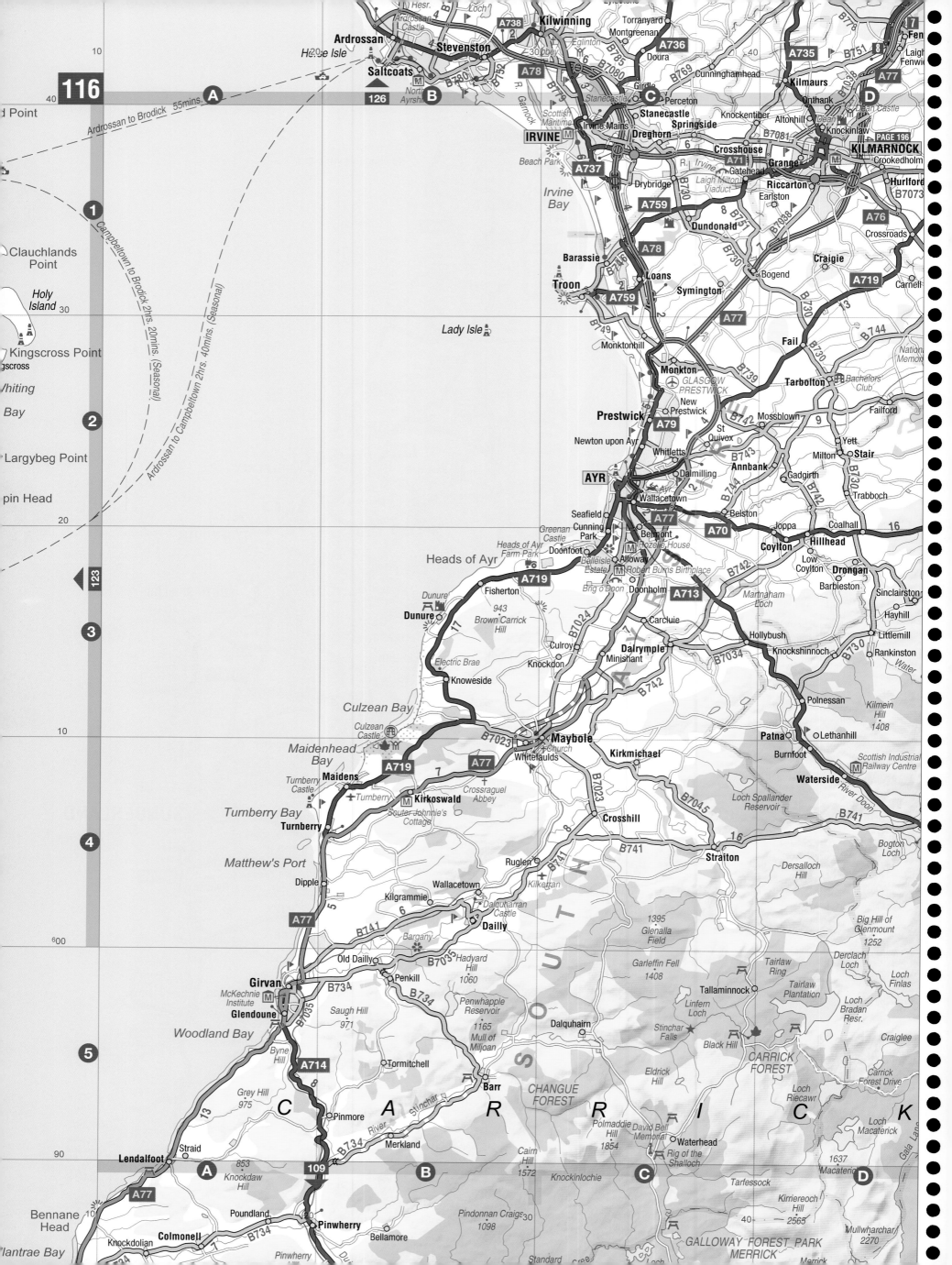

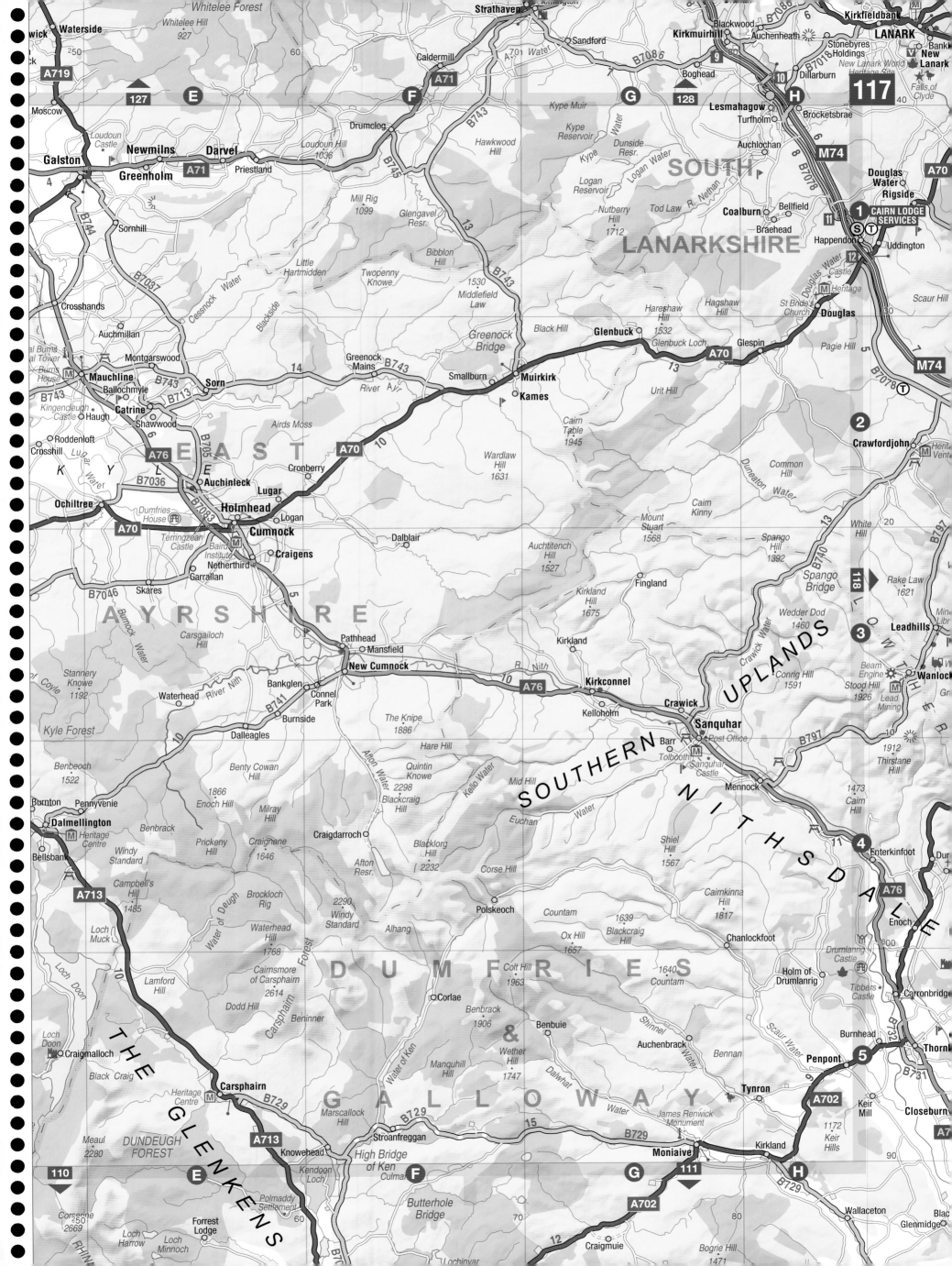

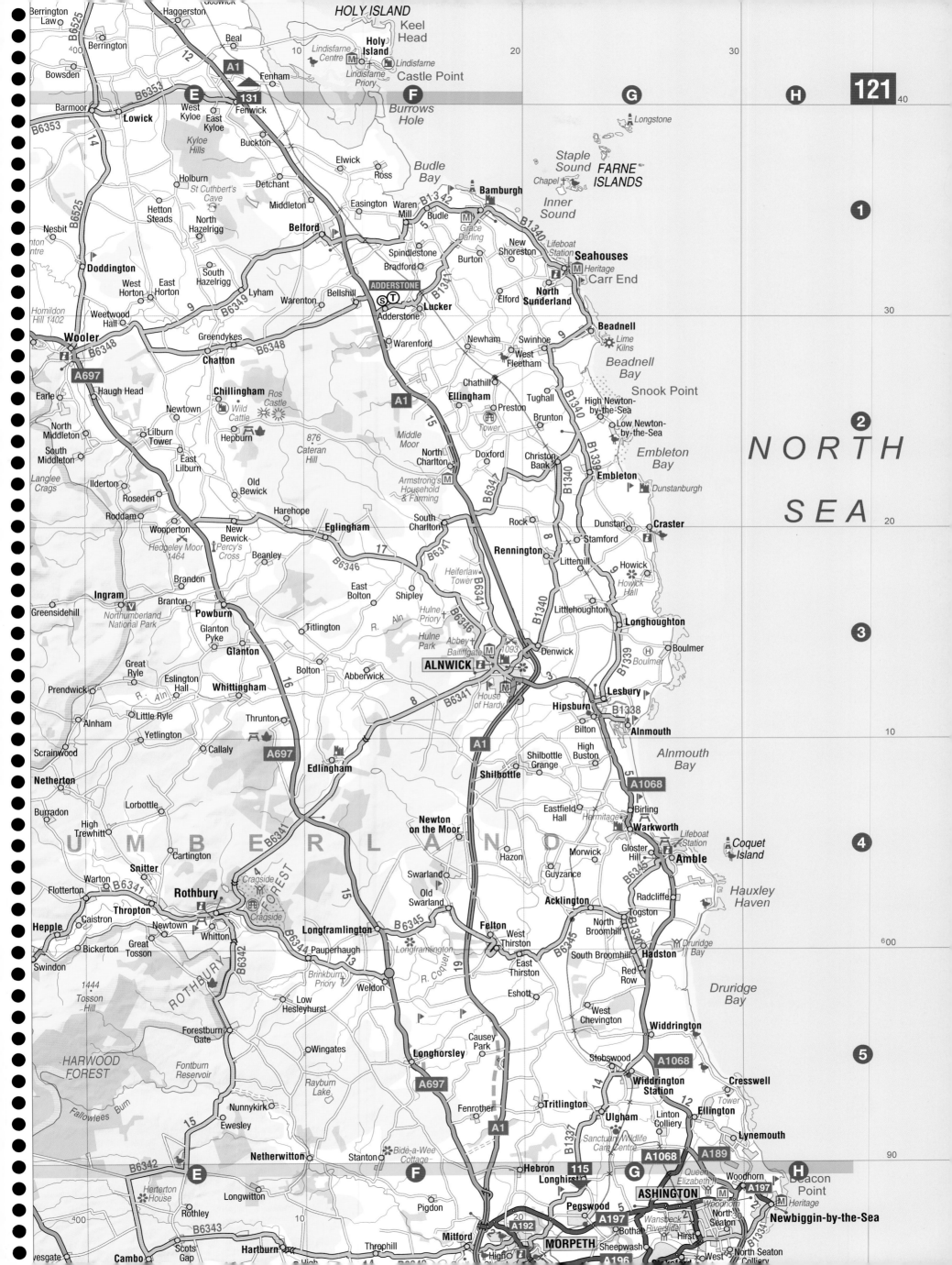

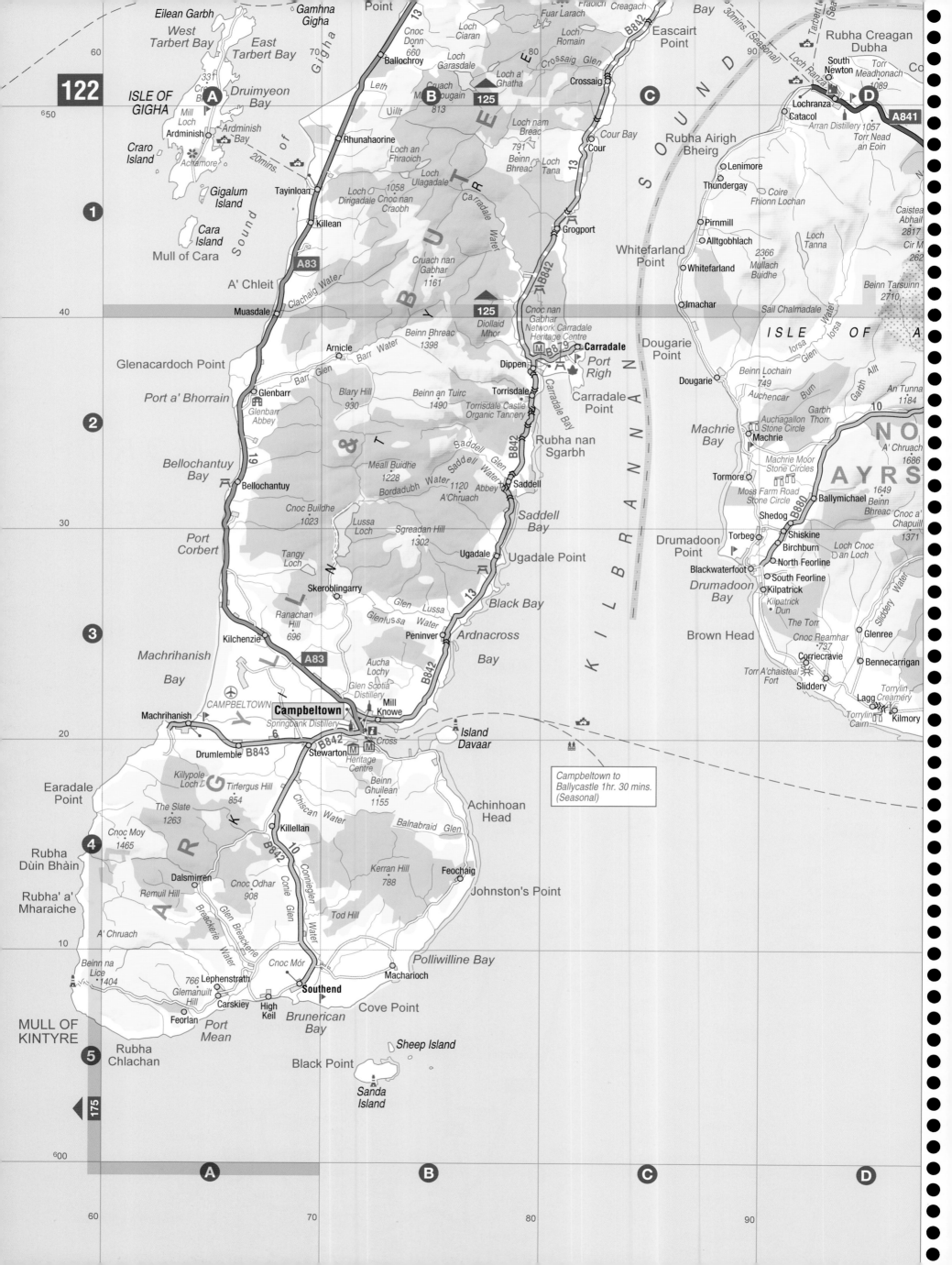

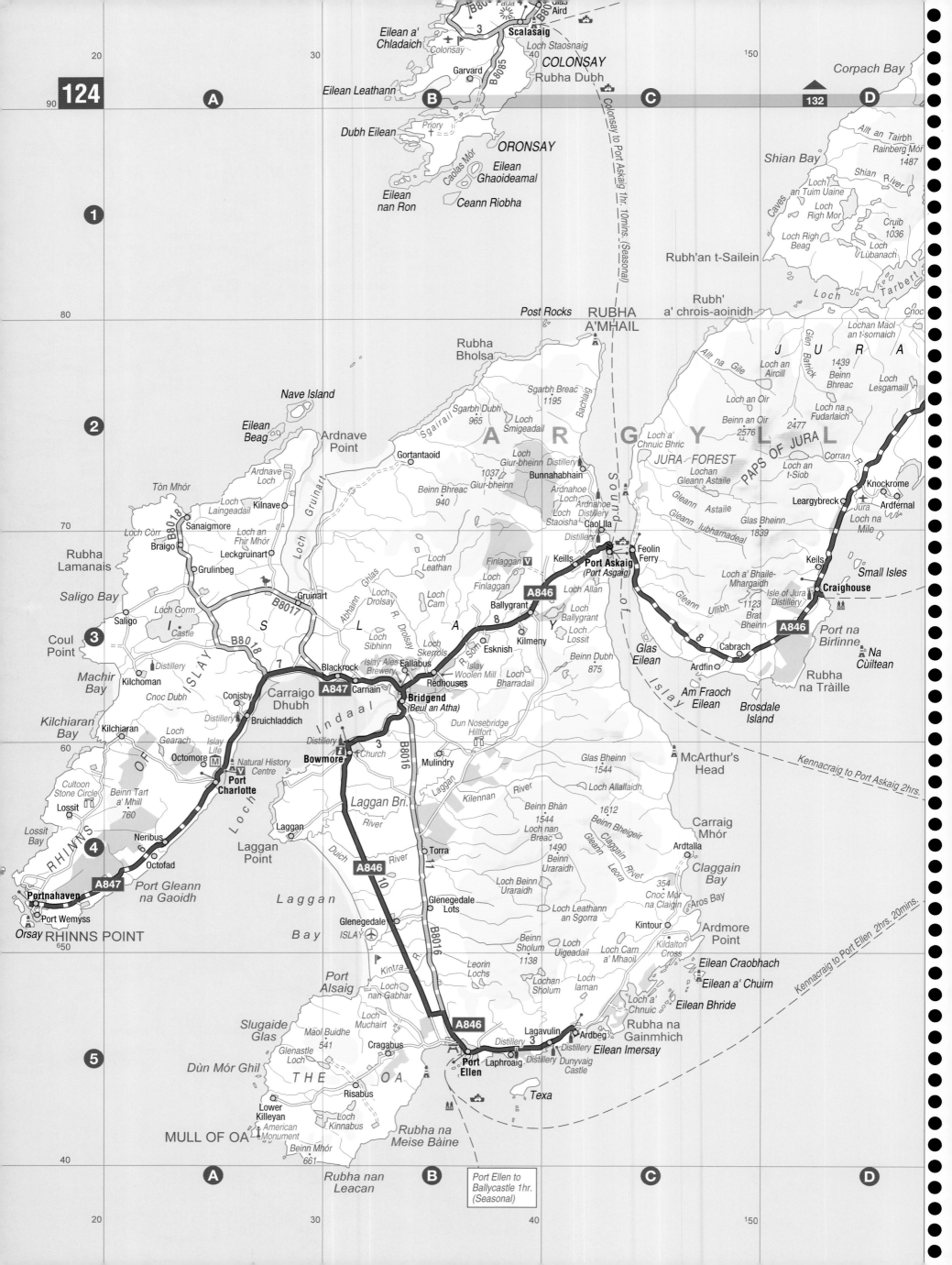

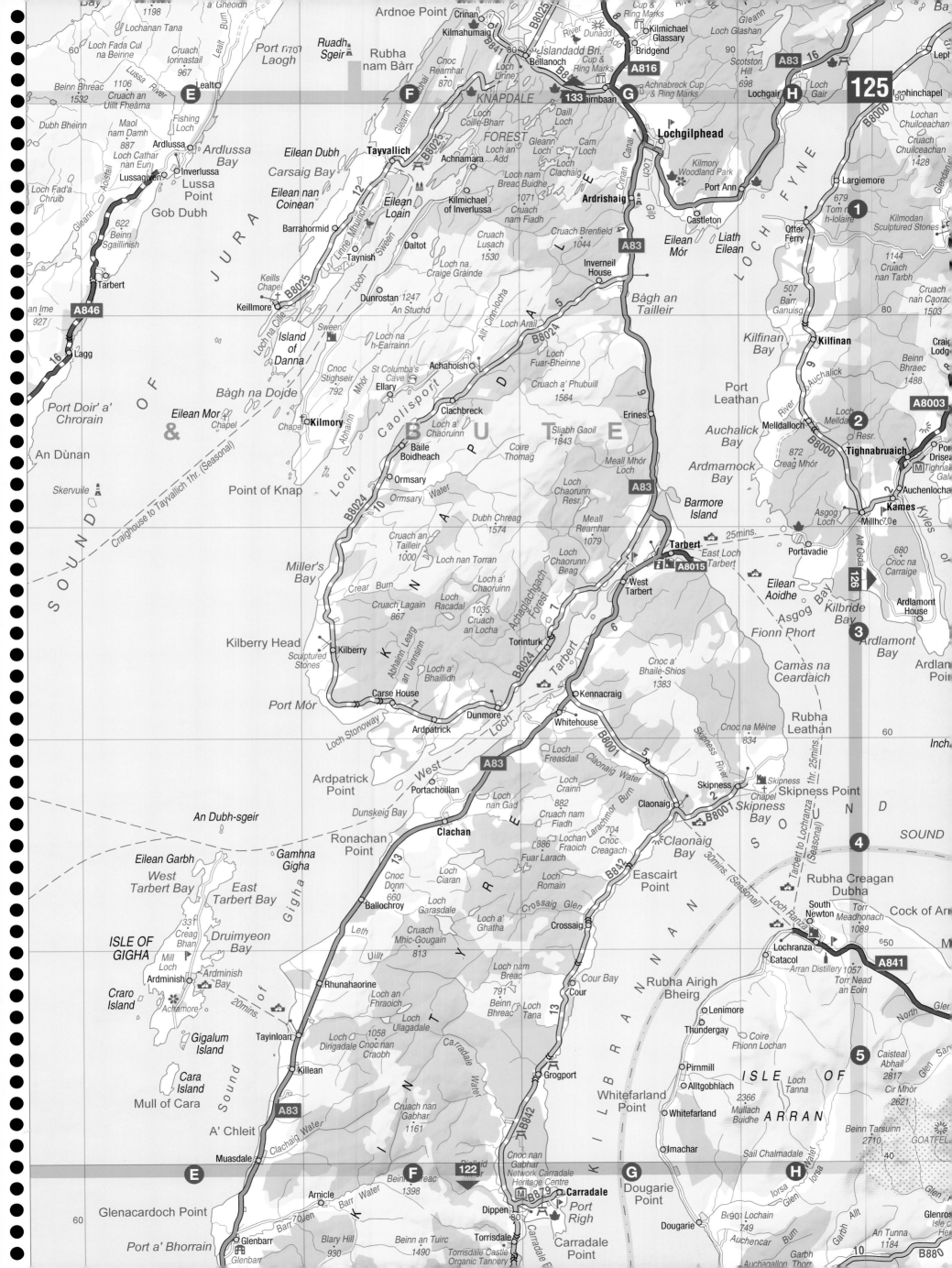

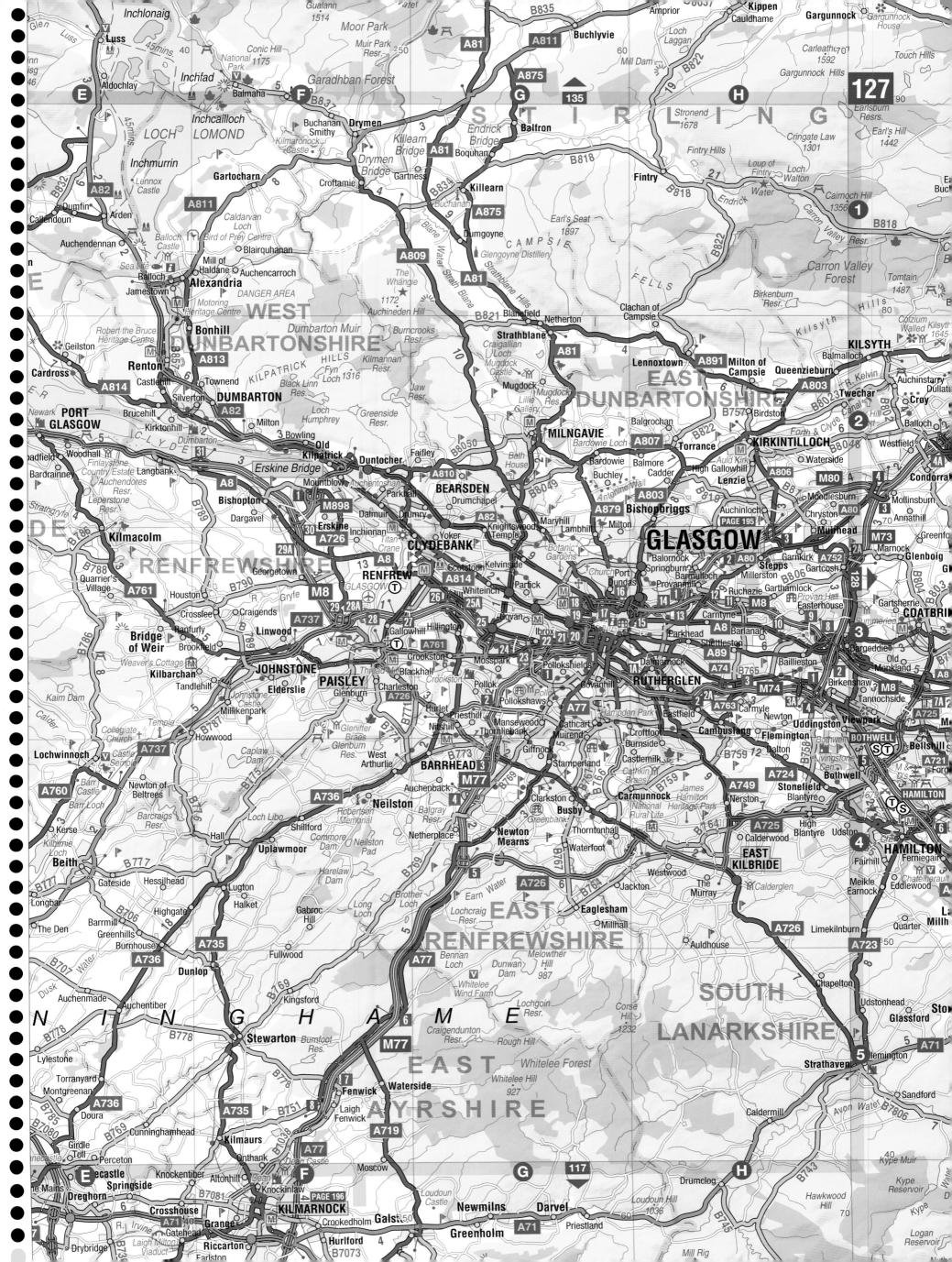

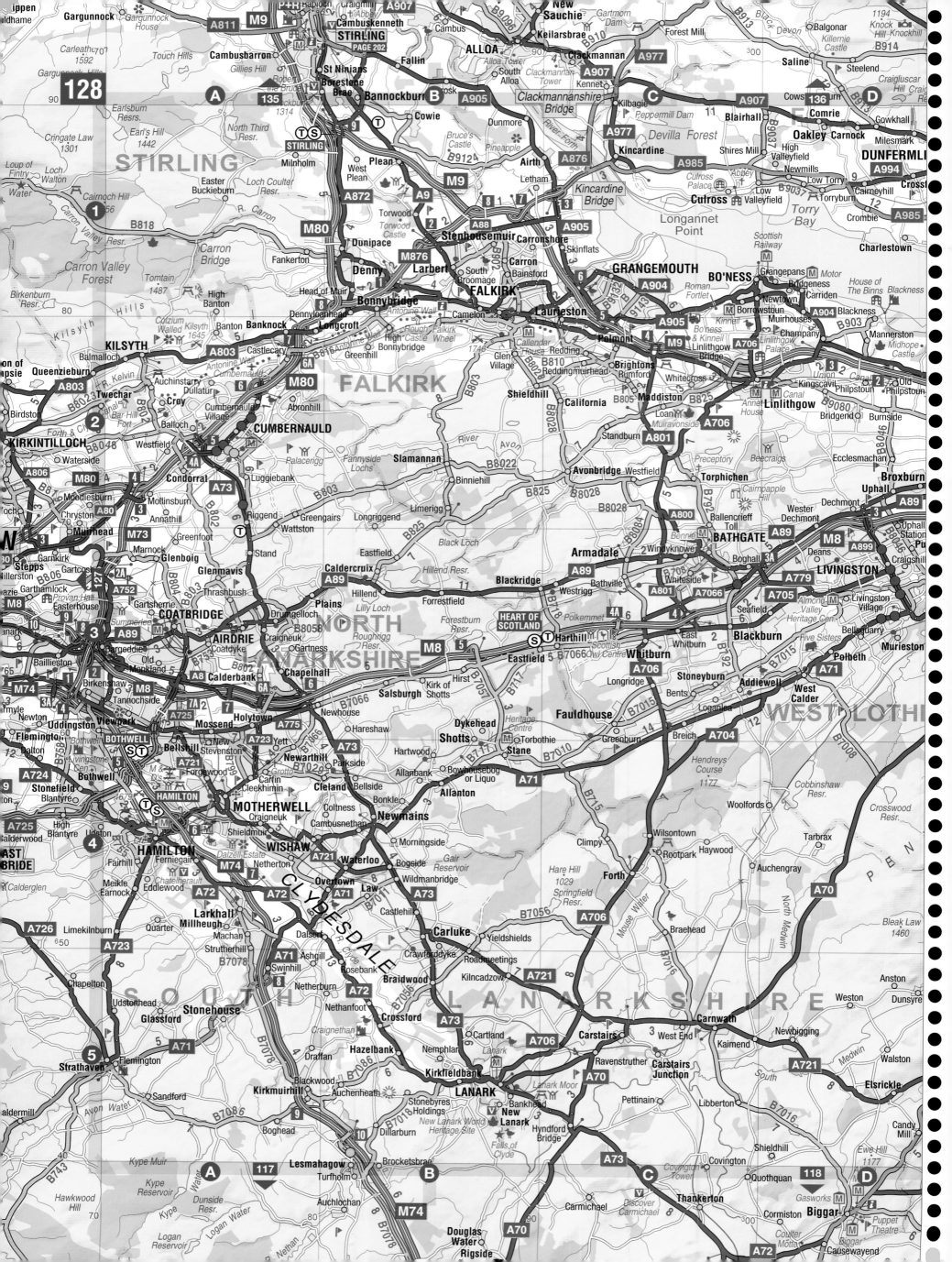

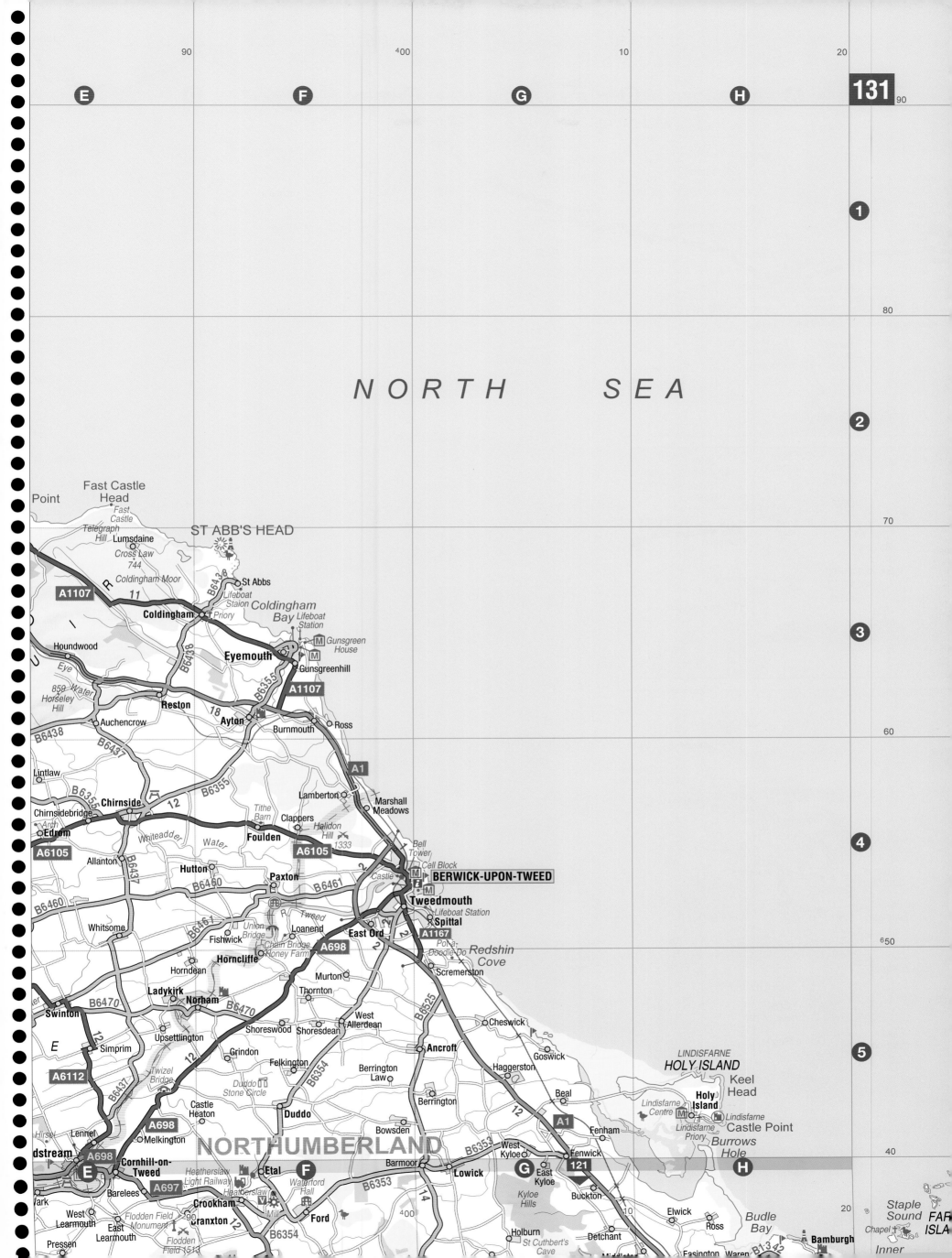

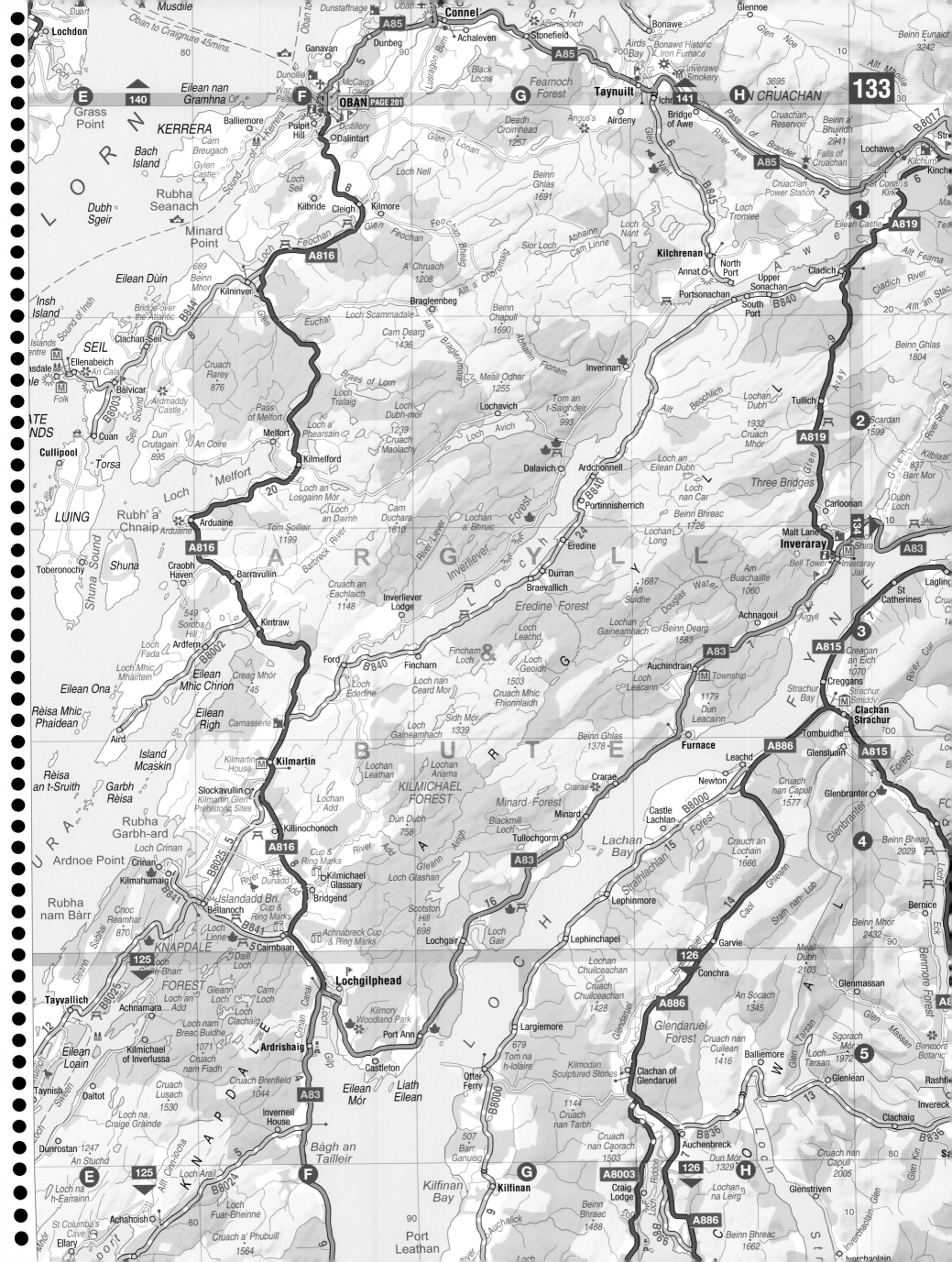

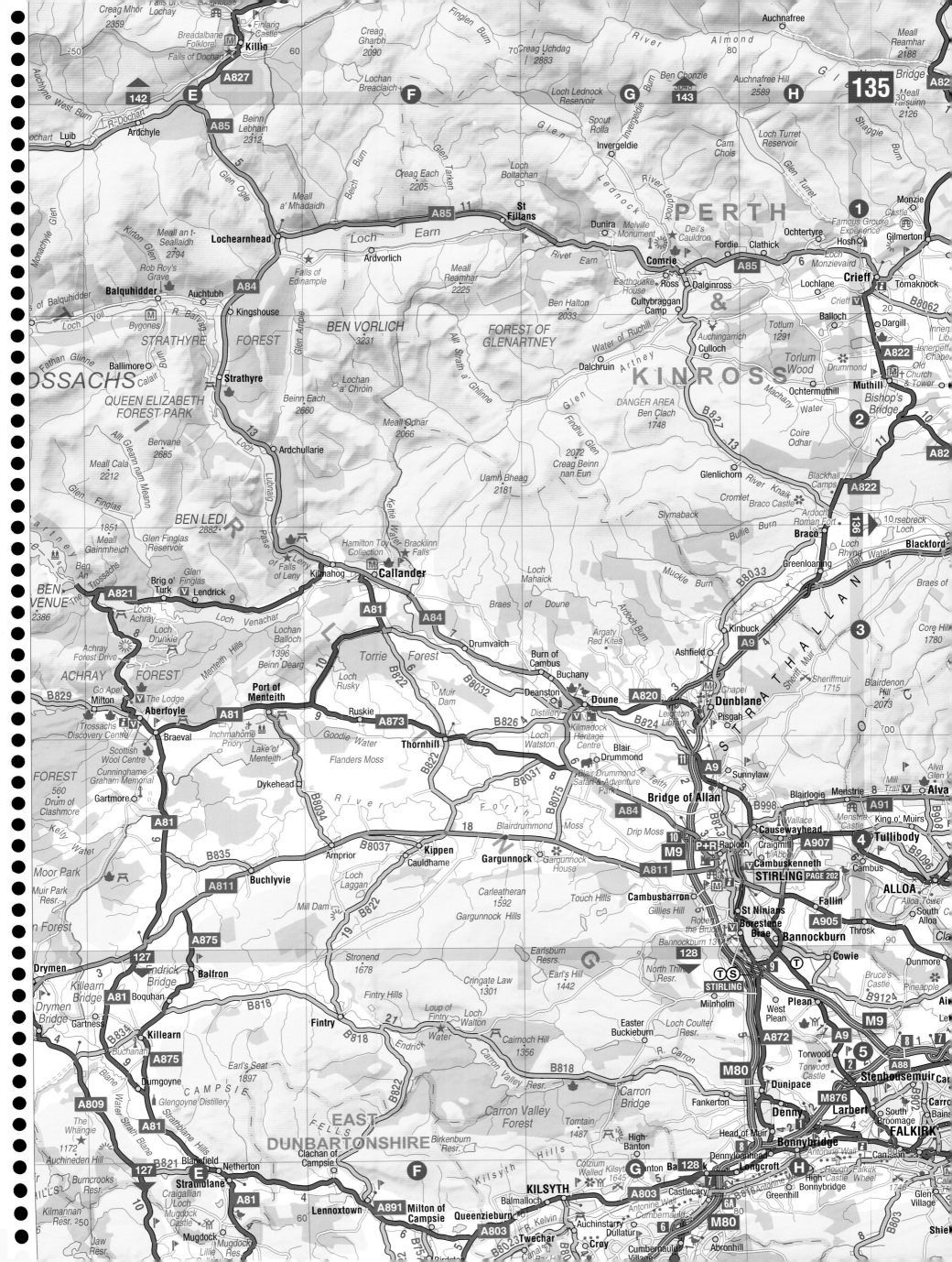

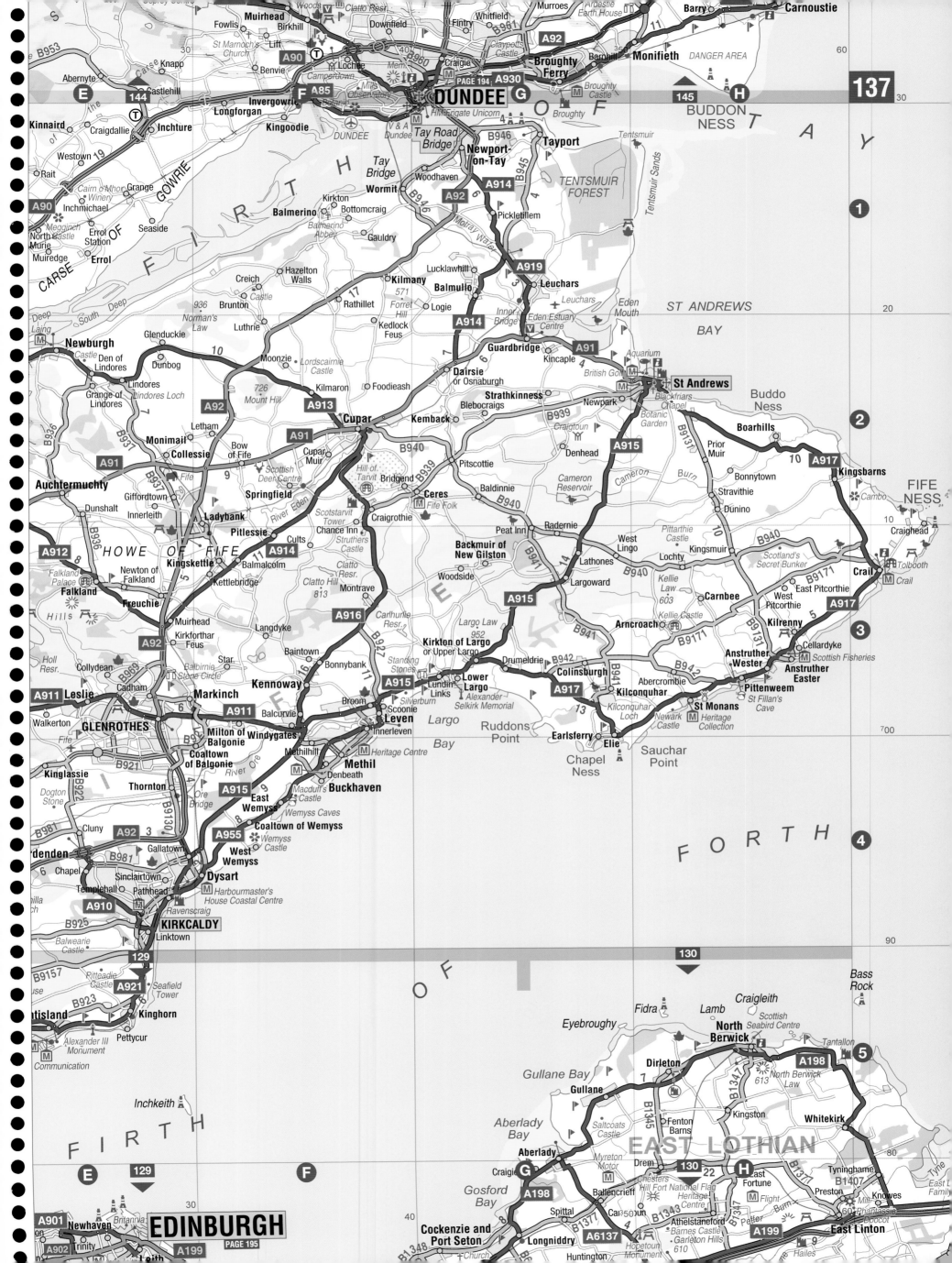

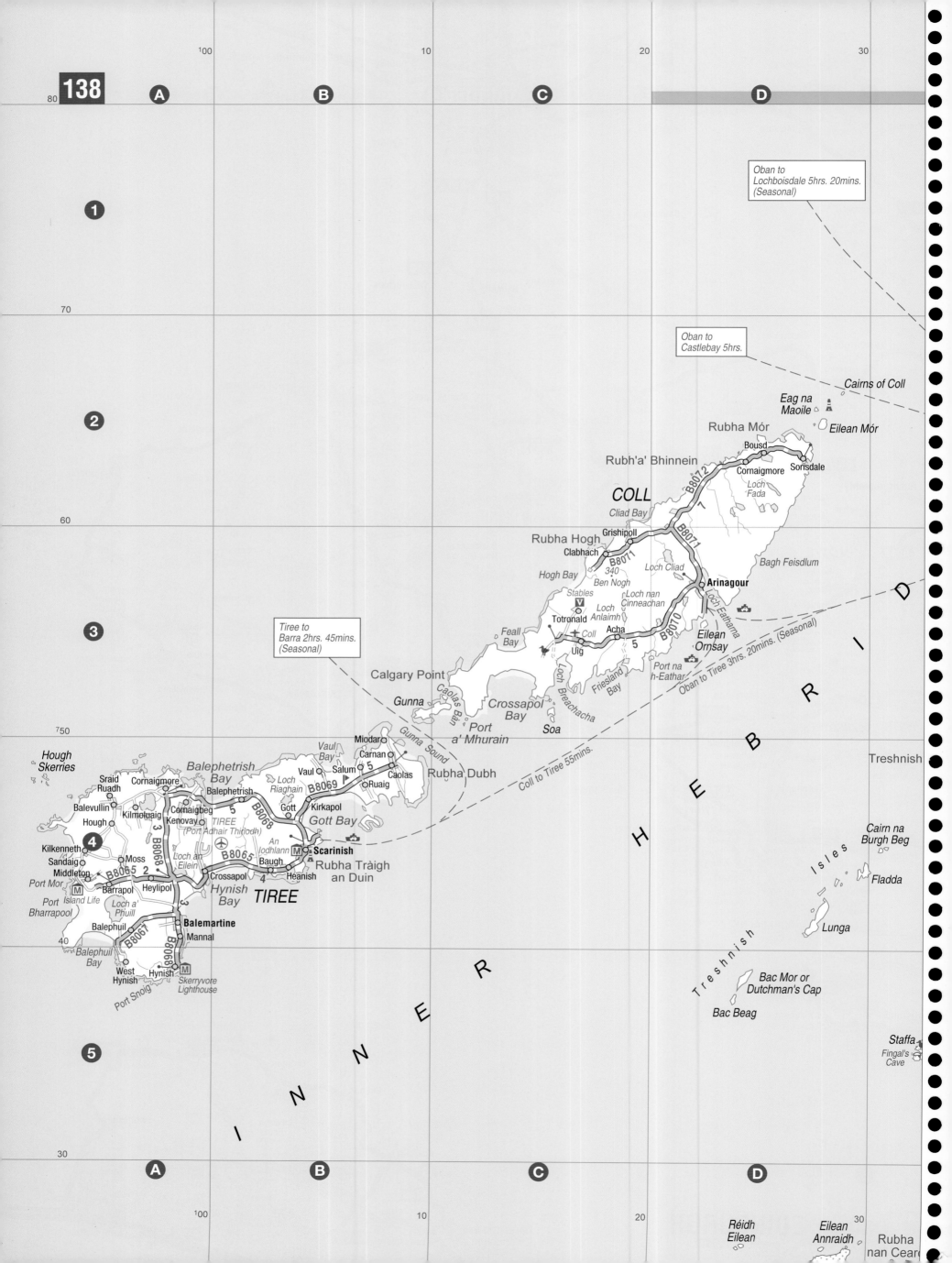

80   A   B   C   D

100   10   20   30

1

Oban to
Lochboisdale 5hrs. 20mins.
(Seasonal)

70

Oban to
Castlebay 5hrs.

Cairns of Coll

Eag na
Maoile

2   Rubha Mór   Eilean Mór

Rubh'a' Bhinnein   Bousd
                                                          Cornaigmore   Sorisdale

COLL

Cliad Bay   Loch
                                                          Fada

Rubha Hogh   Grishipoll
60   Clabhach   B8071   Bagh Feisdlum

Hogh Bay   340   Loch Cliad
                    Ben Nogh

Stables   Loch nan   Arinagour
Cinneachan

3   Feall   Totronald   Loch
Tiree to   Bay   Anlaimh   Coll   Acha
Barra 2hrs.   Uig   5   Eilean
45mins.   Ornsay
(Seasonal)   Calgary Point   Port na
                                                  h-Eathar
                    Gunna   Friesland
                    Caolas Bàn   Crossapol   Bay   Oban to Tiree 3hrs. 20mins. (Seasonal)
Hough   Balephetrish   Bay   Port   Soa
Skerries   Bay   Vaul   Miodaro   a' Mhurain   Treshnish
            Bay   Carnan   Gunna Sound
Sraid   Cornaigmore   Vaul   Salum   5   Rubha Dubh
Ruadh   Balephetrish   Loch   Ruaig   Caolas
Balevullin   Kilmoluaig   Cornaigbeg   Riaghain   Gott   B8069   Coll to Tiree 55mins.
Hough   Kenovay   Kirkapol   Cairn na
            TIREE   Gott Bay   Burgh Beg
4   Kilkenneth   (Port Adhair Thiriodh)   An   Scarinish   Isles
Sandaig   Moss   Iodhlann   Baugh   Fladda
Middleton   B8065   Loch an   Rubha Tràigh
Port Mor   Barrapol   Eilein   Héanish   an Duin   Lunga
Port   Island Life   Heylipol   Crossapol   TIREE
Bharrapool   Loch a'   Hynish
            Phuill   Bay   Bac Mor or
Balephuil   Balemartine   Dutchman's Cap
B8067   Mannal   Bac Beag
Balephuil   West   Hynish
Bay   Hynish   Skerryvore   Staffa
            Lighthouse   Fingal's
5   Port Snoig   Cave

I N N E R

30   A   B   C   D

100   10   20   30

Réidh   Eilean
Eilean   Annraidh   Rubha
                    nan Cear

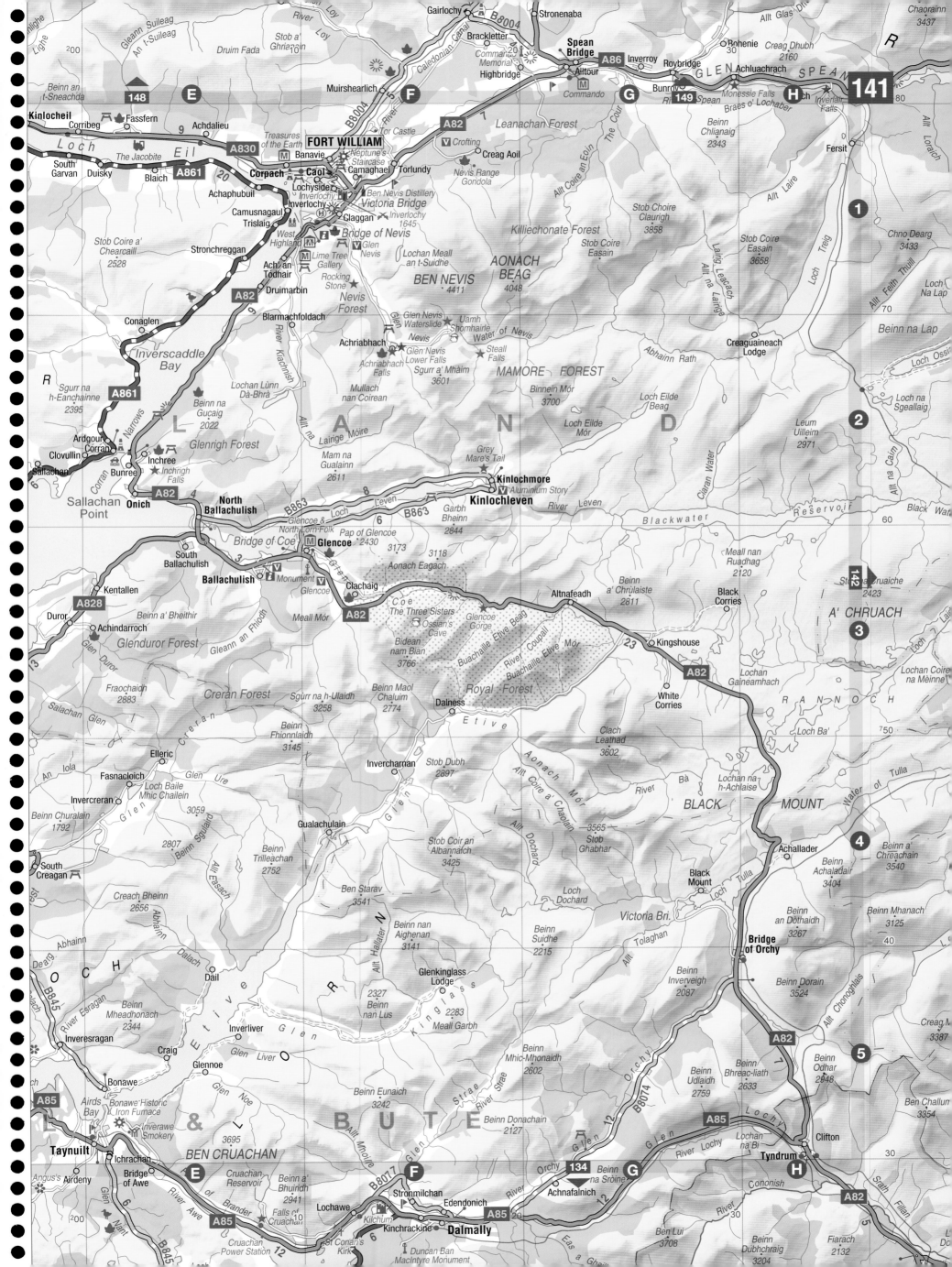

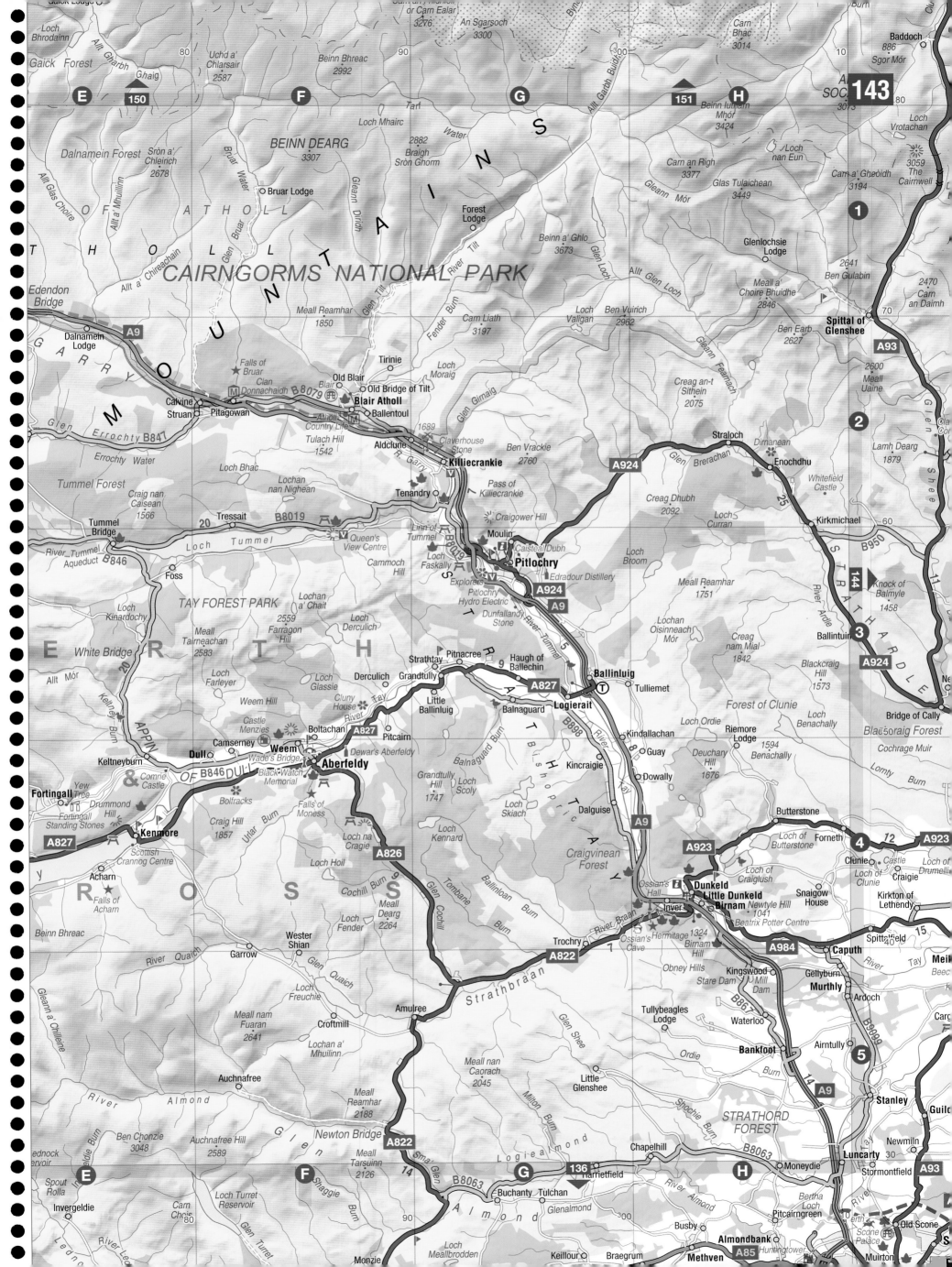

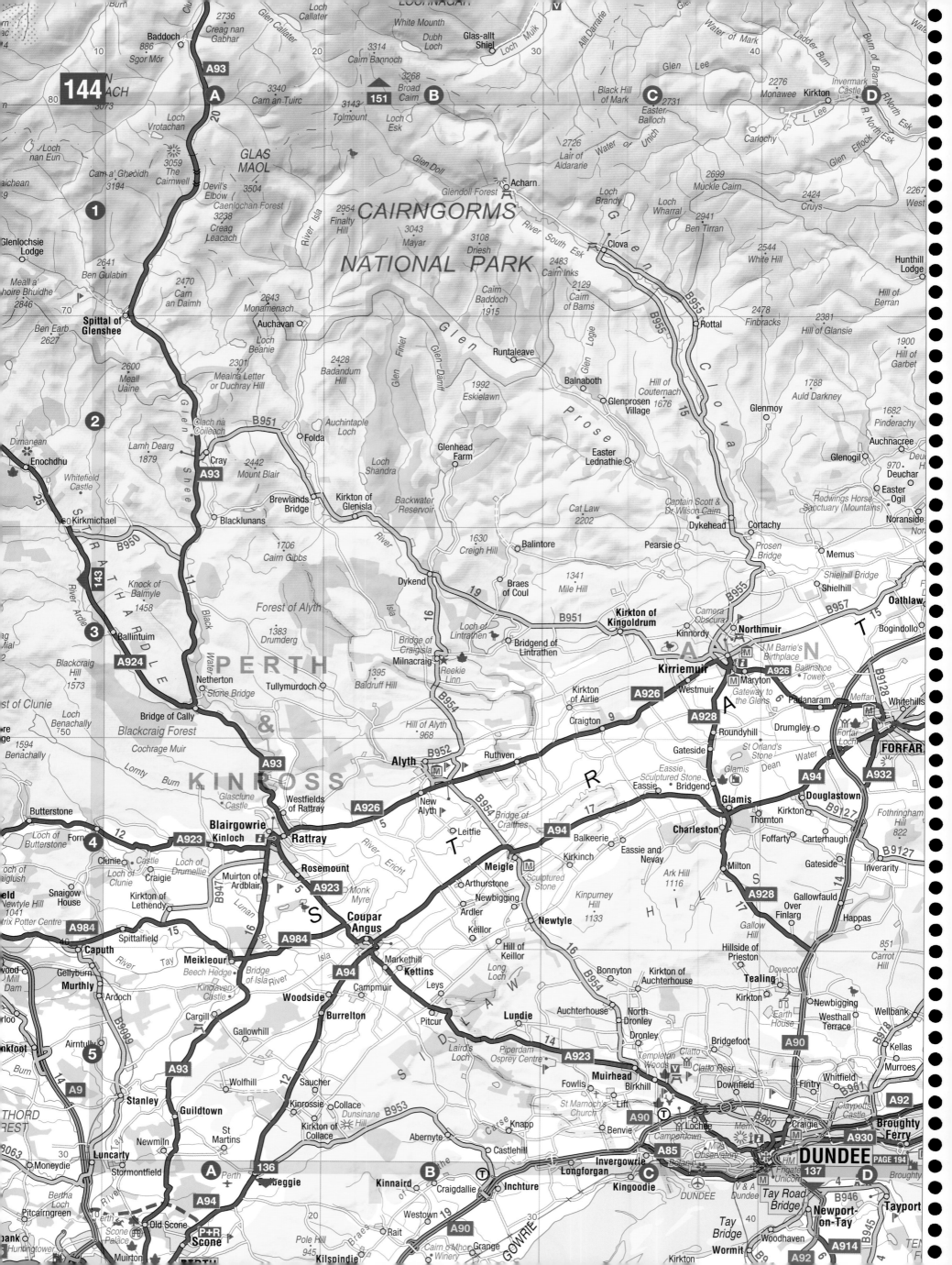

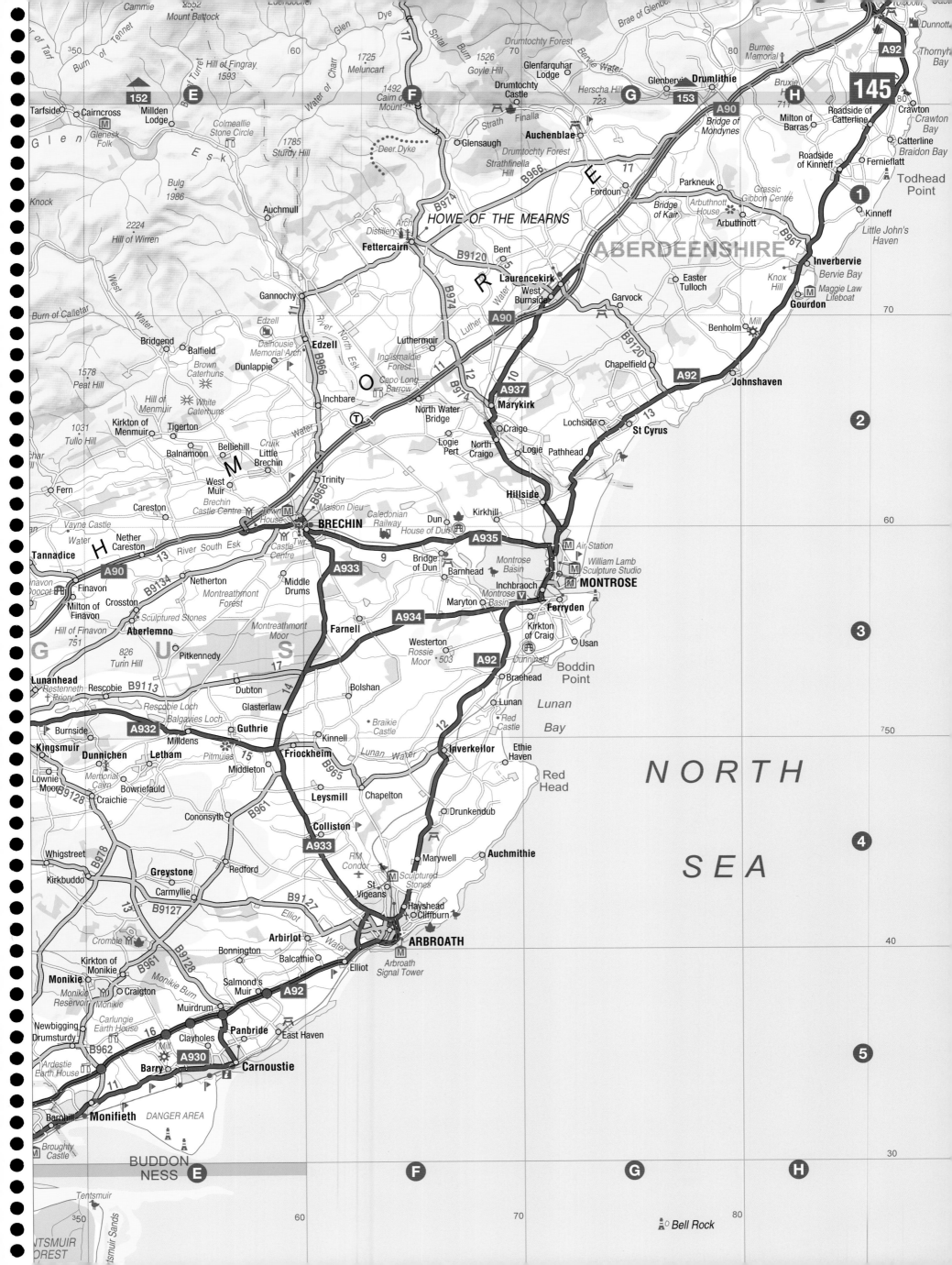

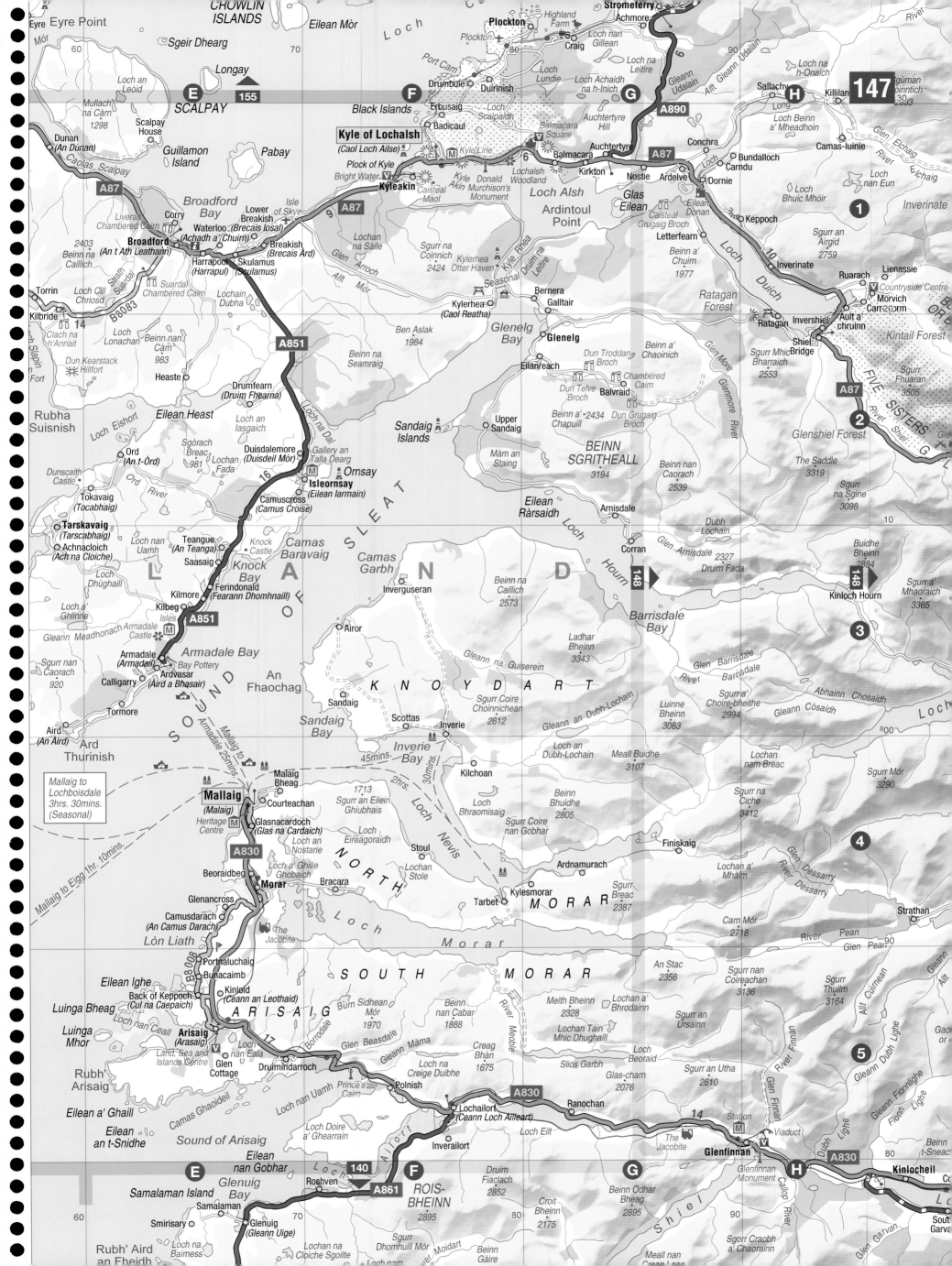

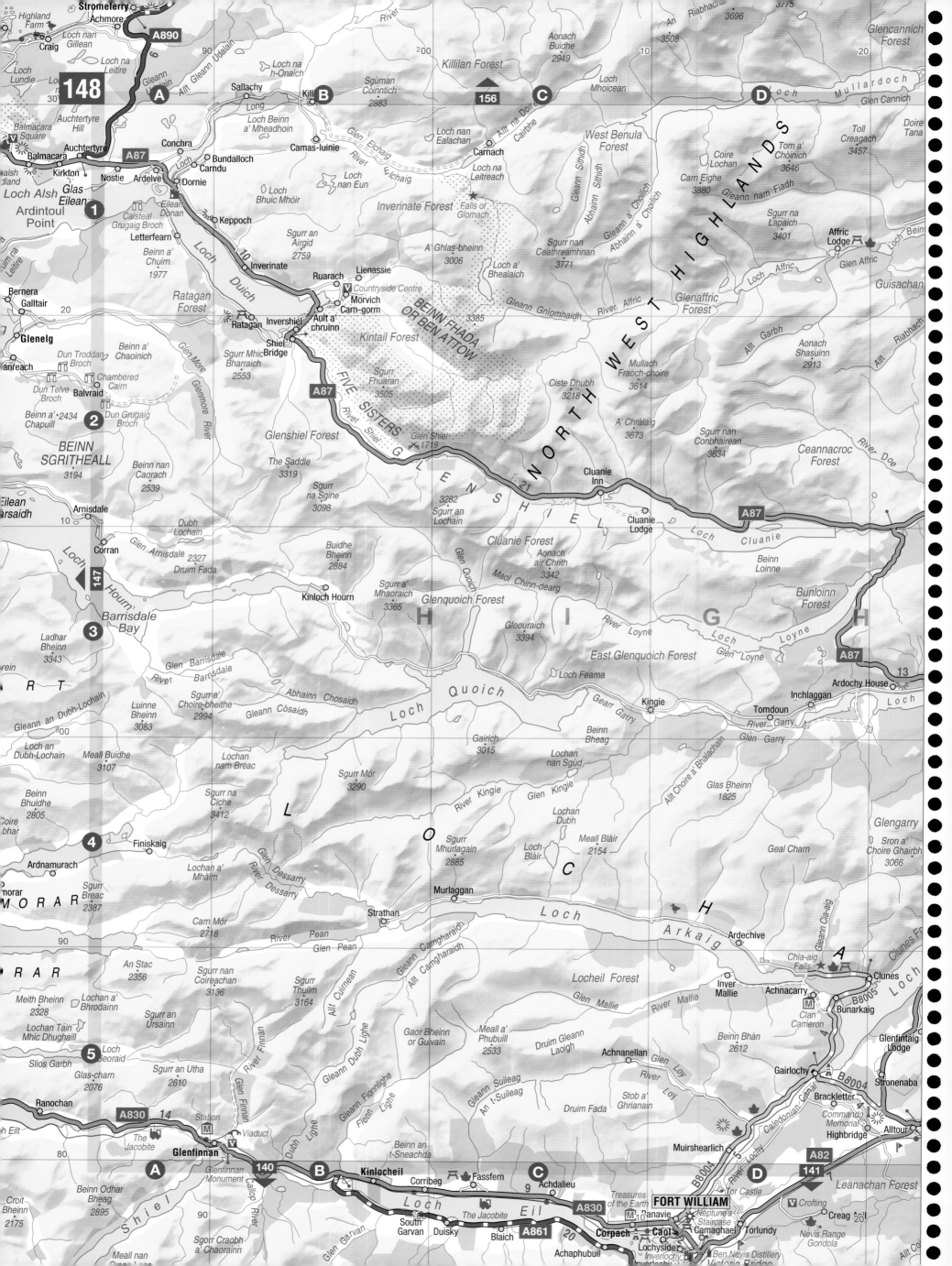

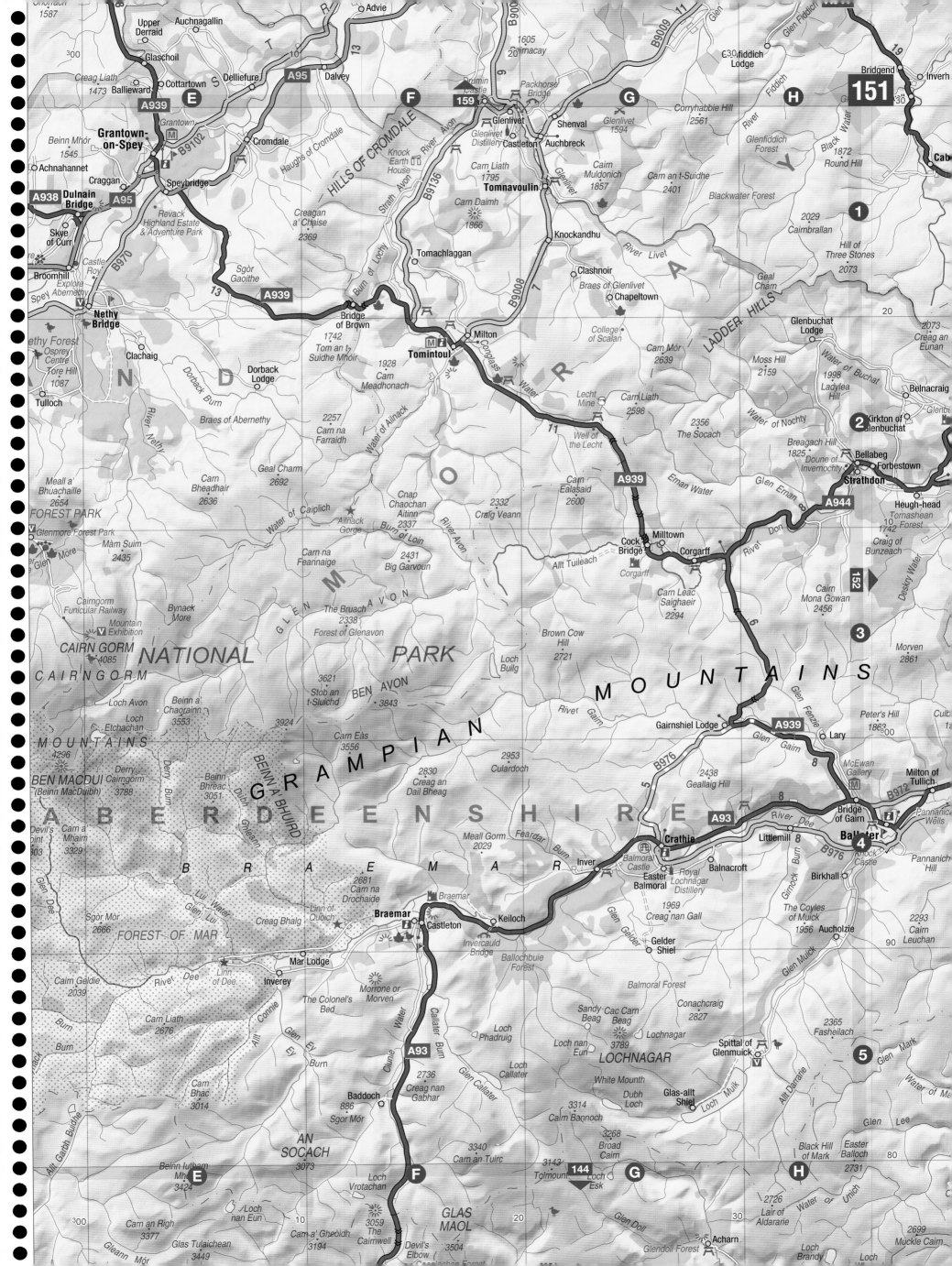

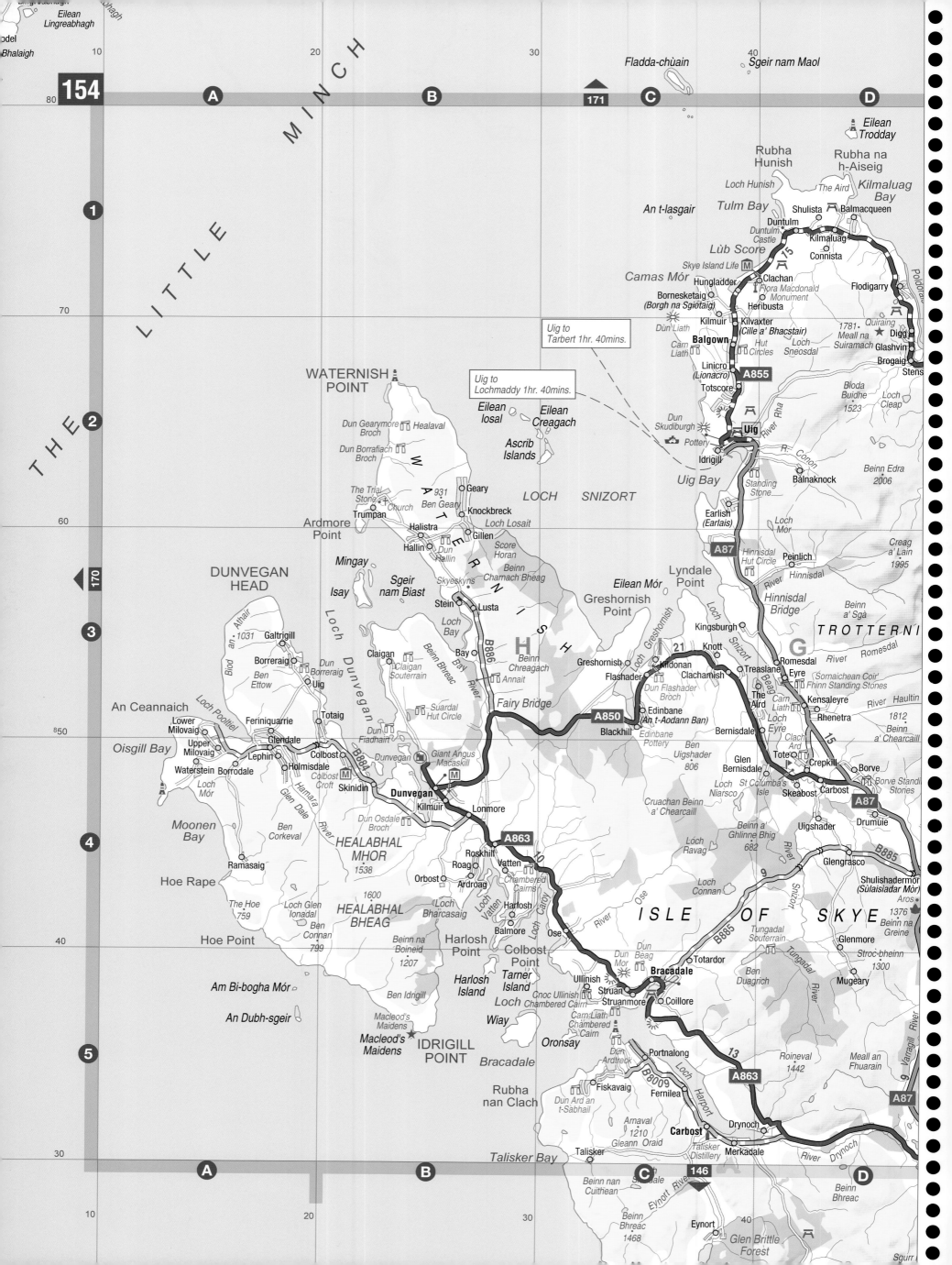

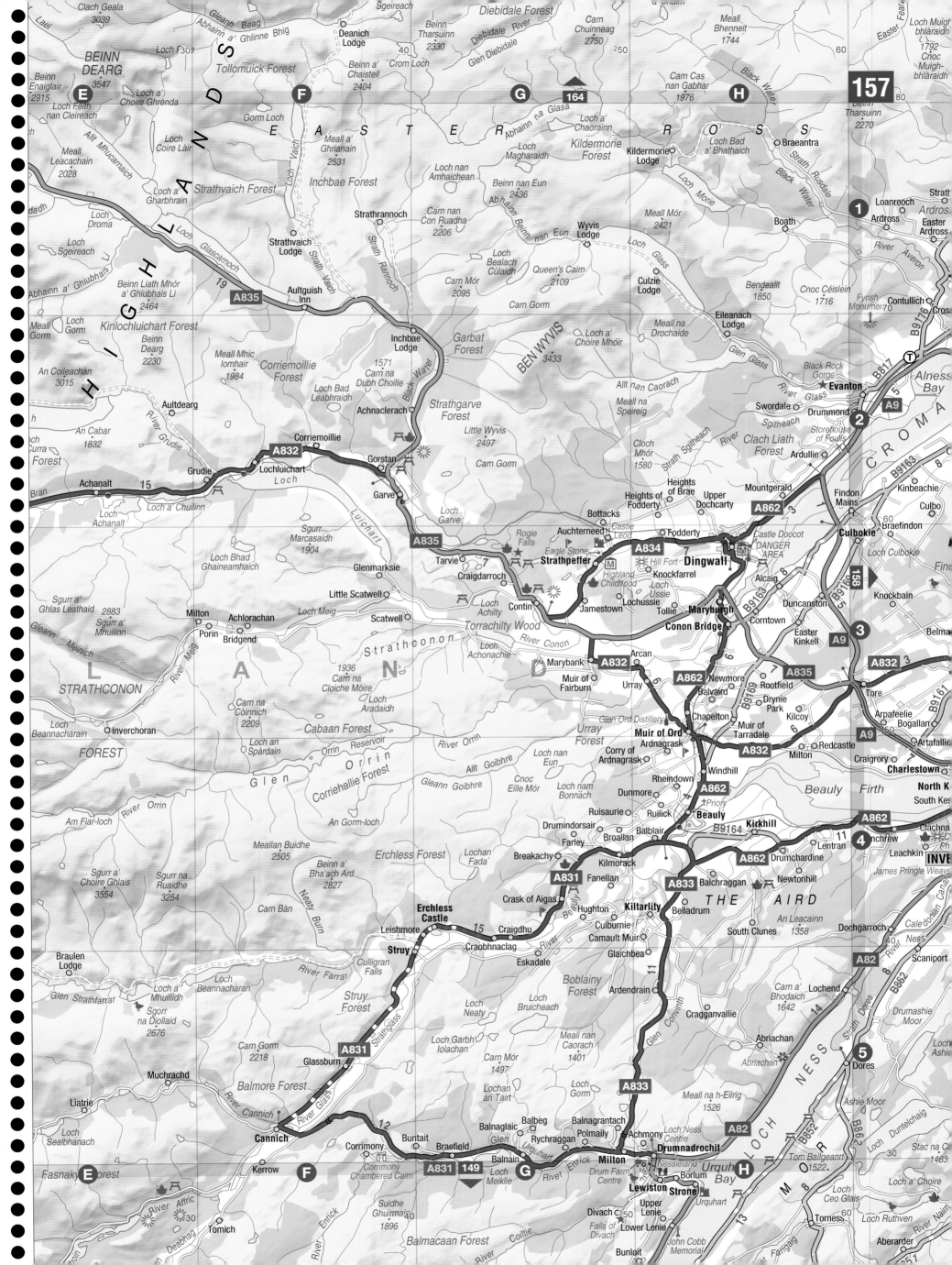

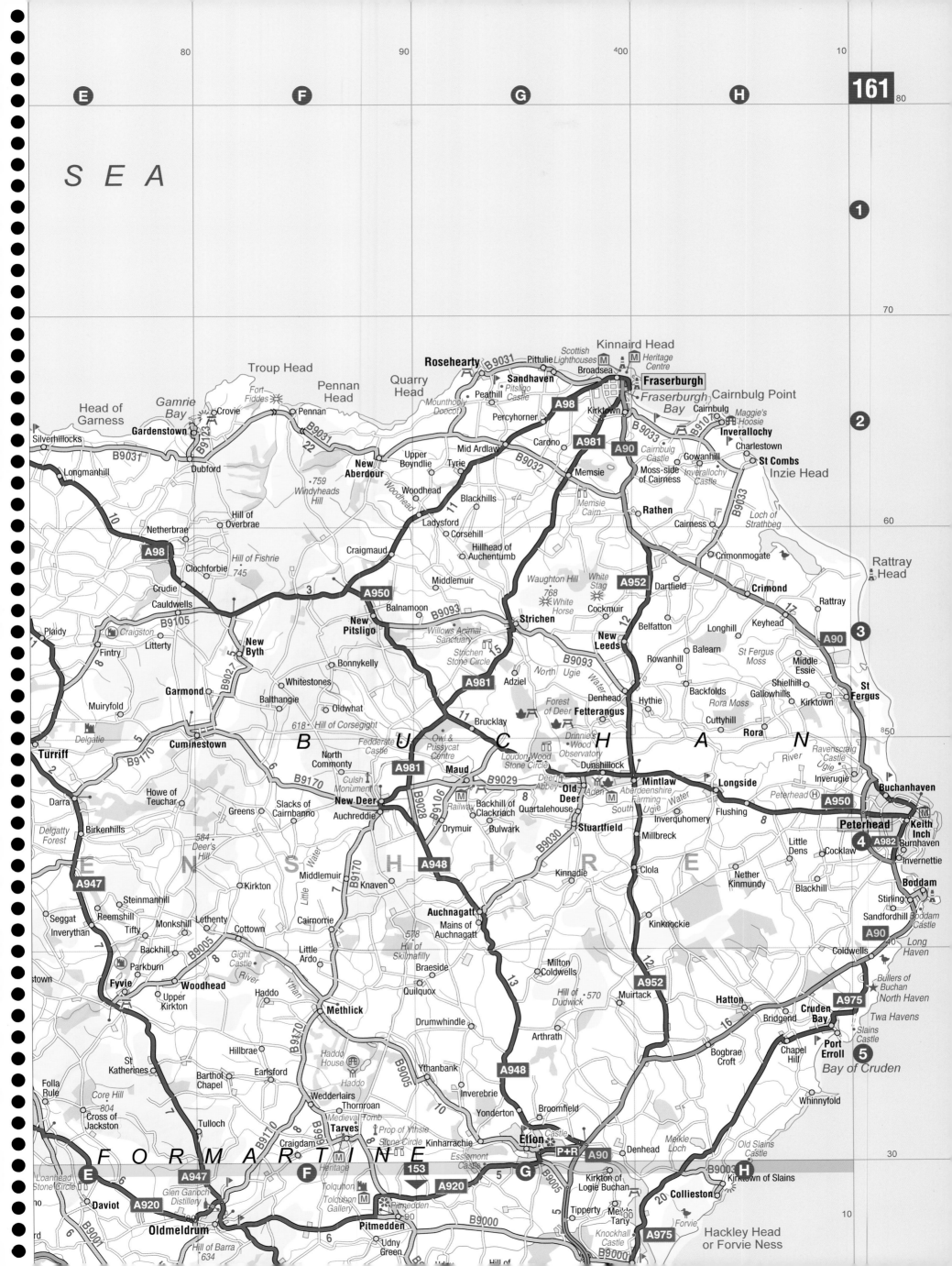

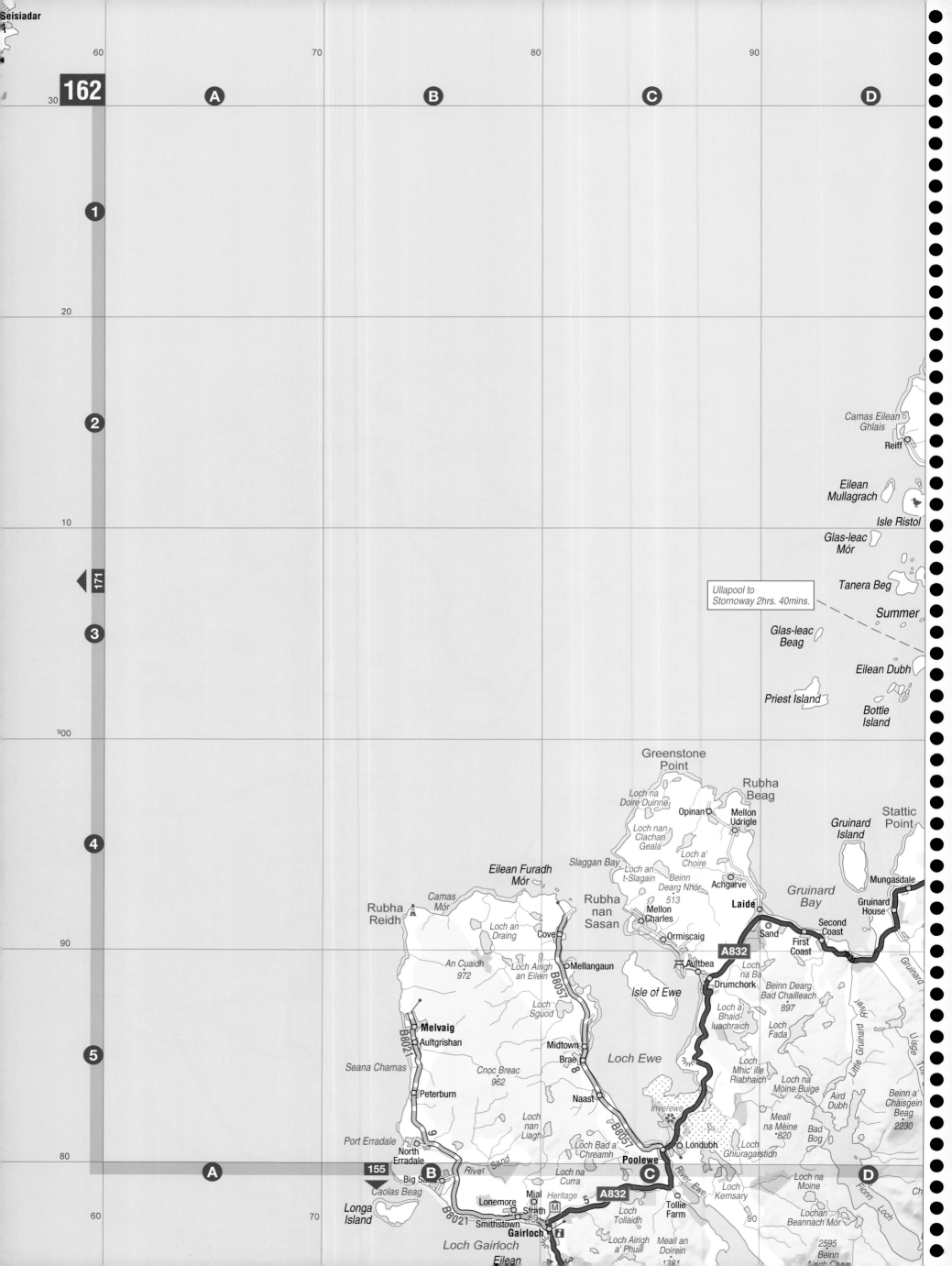

Seisiadar

162

A · B · C · D

171

Ullapool to
Stornoway 2hrs. 40mins.

Camas Eilean
Ghlais

Reiff

Eilean
Mullagrach

Isle Ristol

Glas-leac
Mór

Tanera Beg

Summer

Glas-leac
Beag

Eilean Dubh

Priest Island

Bottle
Island

Greenstone
Point

Rubha
Beag

Loch na
Doire Duinne

Opinan

Mellon
Udrigle

Loch nan
Clachan
Geala

Loch a'
Choire

Stattic
Point

Gruinard
Island

Mungasdale

Slaggan Bay

Loch an
t-Slagain

Beinn
Dearg Nhòr
513

Achgarve

Gruinard
Bay

Gruinard
House

Eilean Furadh
Mór

Rubha
nan
Sasan

Mellon
Charles

Laide

Rubha
Reidh

Camas
Mór

Loch an
Draing

Cove

Ormiscaig

Sand

Second
Coast

First
Coast

An Cuaidh
972

Loch Airigh
an Eilein

Mellangaun

Aultbea

A832

Loch
na Bà

Beinn Dearg
Bad Chailleach
897

Isle of Ewe

Drumchork

Aird
Dubh

Loch Sgùod

Loch a'
Bhaid-
luachraich

Loch
Fada

Melvaig

Aultgrishan

Midtown

Brae

Loch Ewe

Loch
Mhic' ille
Riabhaich

Loch na
Mòine Buige

Beinn a'
Chàisgein
Beag
2230

Seana Chamas

Cnoc Breac
962

Naast

Inverewe

Meall
na Mèine
·820

Bad
Bog

Peterburn

Loch
nan Liagh

Loch Bad a'
Chreamh

Londubh

Loch
Ghiuragarstidh

Port Erradale

North
Erradale

155

Poolewe

River Sand

Loch na
Curra

A832

Loch na
Moine

Big Sand

Caolas Beag

Lonemore

Mial

Heritage
M

Tollie
Farm

Loch
Kernsary

Lochan
Beannach Mór

Longa
Island

Strath

Smithstown

Gairloch

Loch
Tollaidh

River Ewe

2595
Beinn

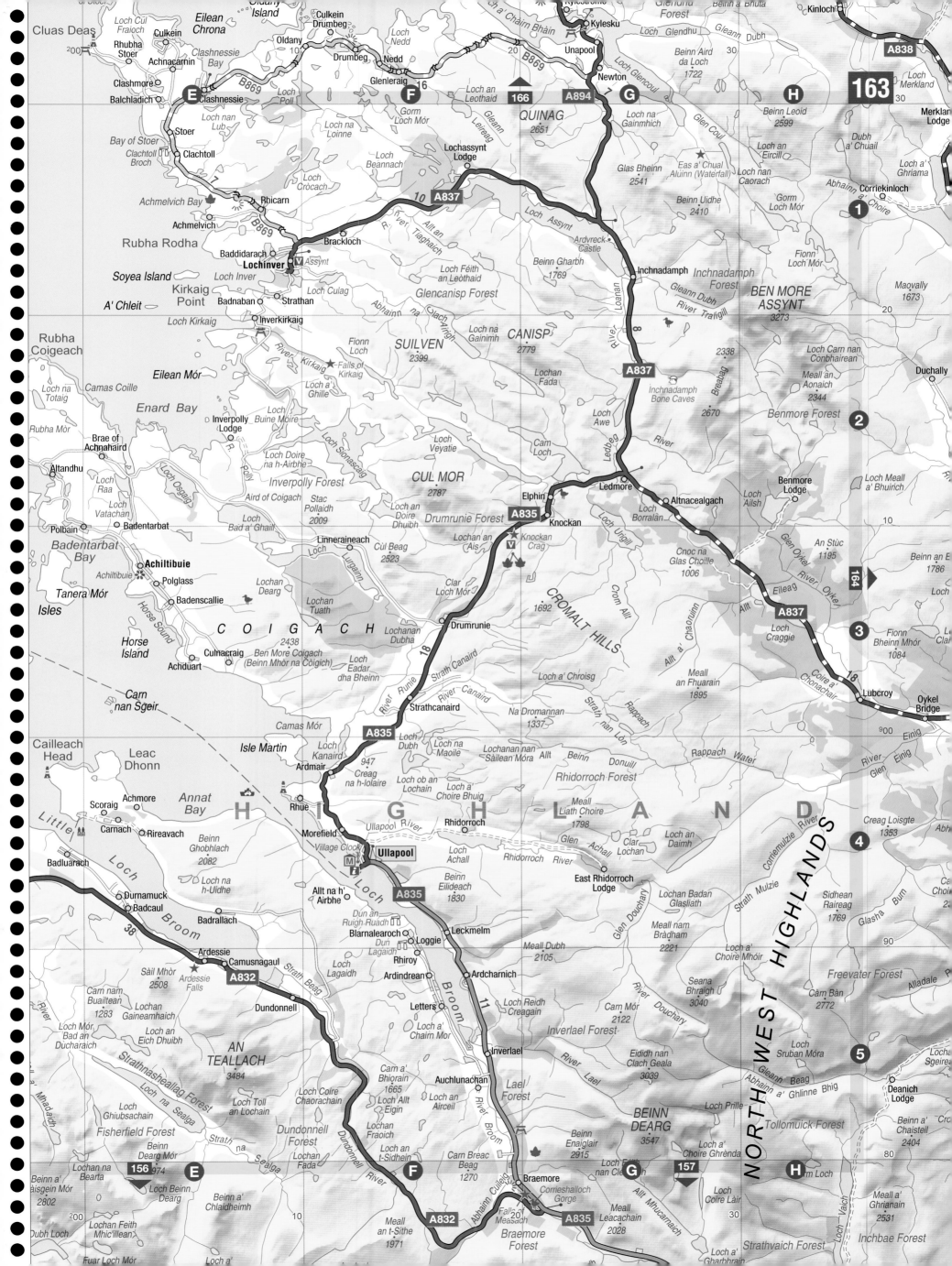

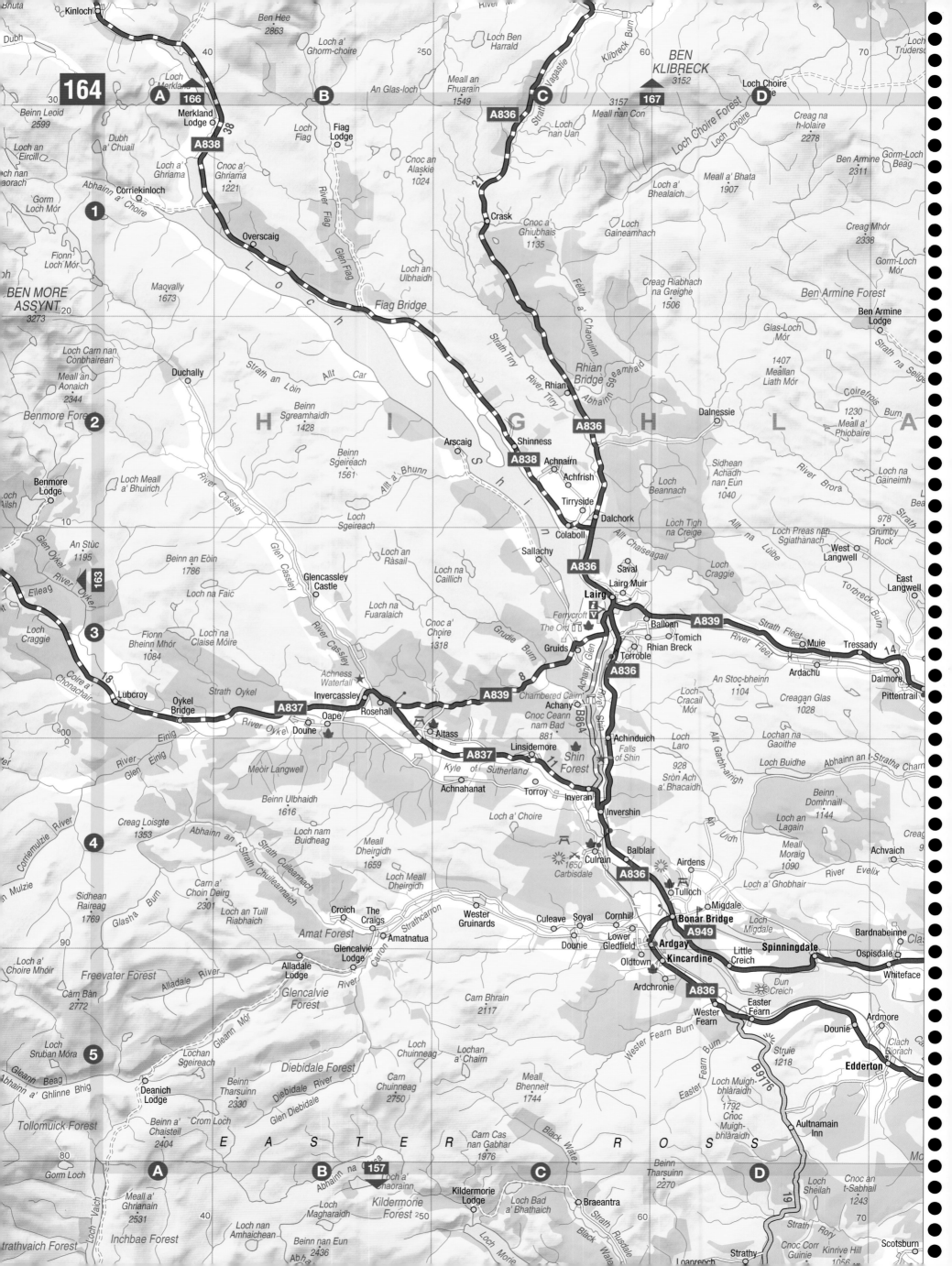

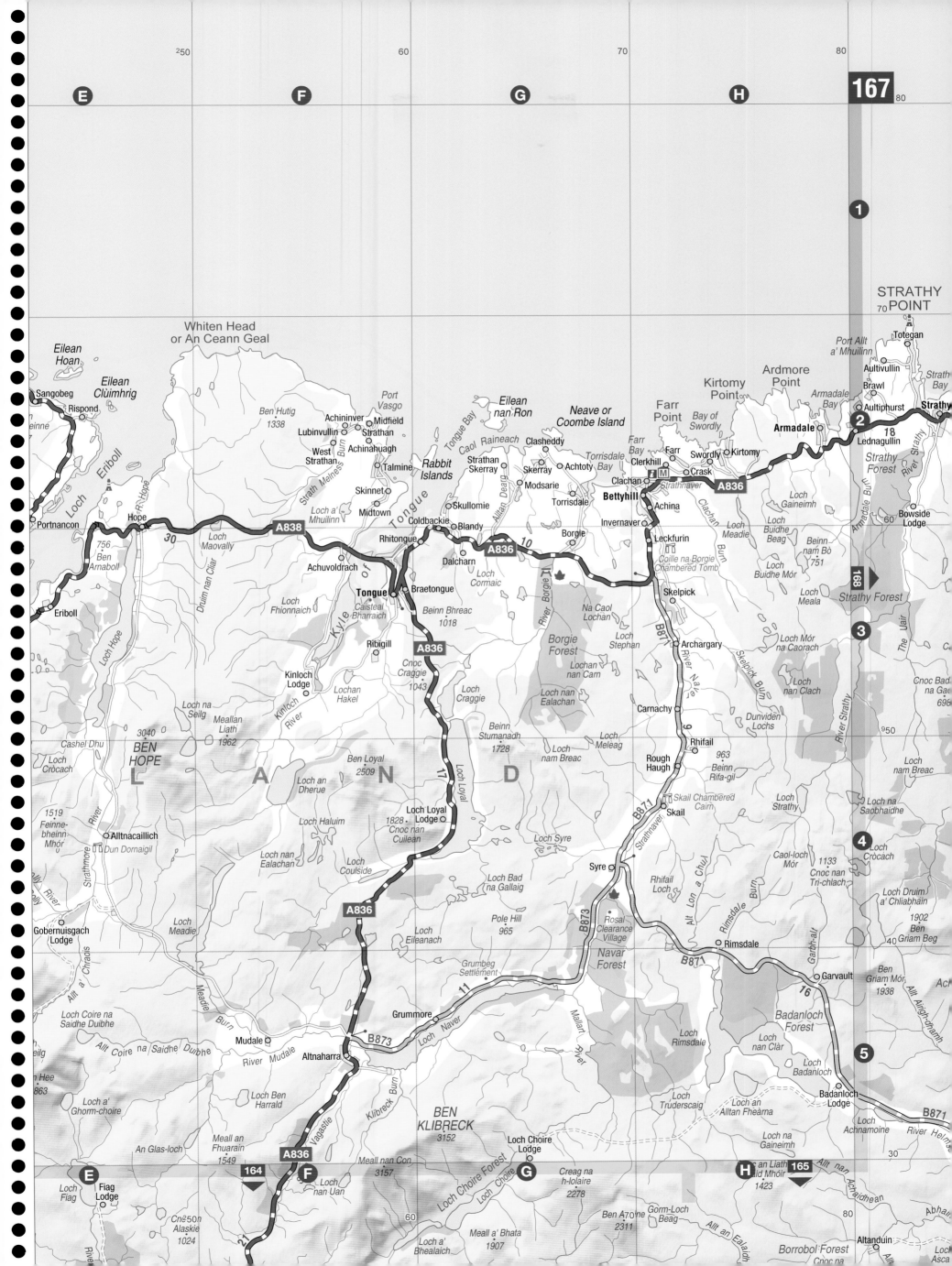

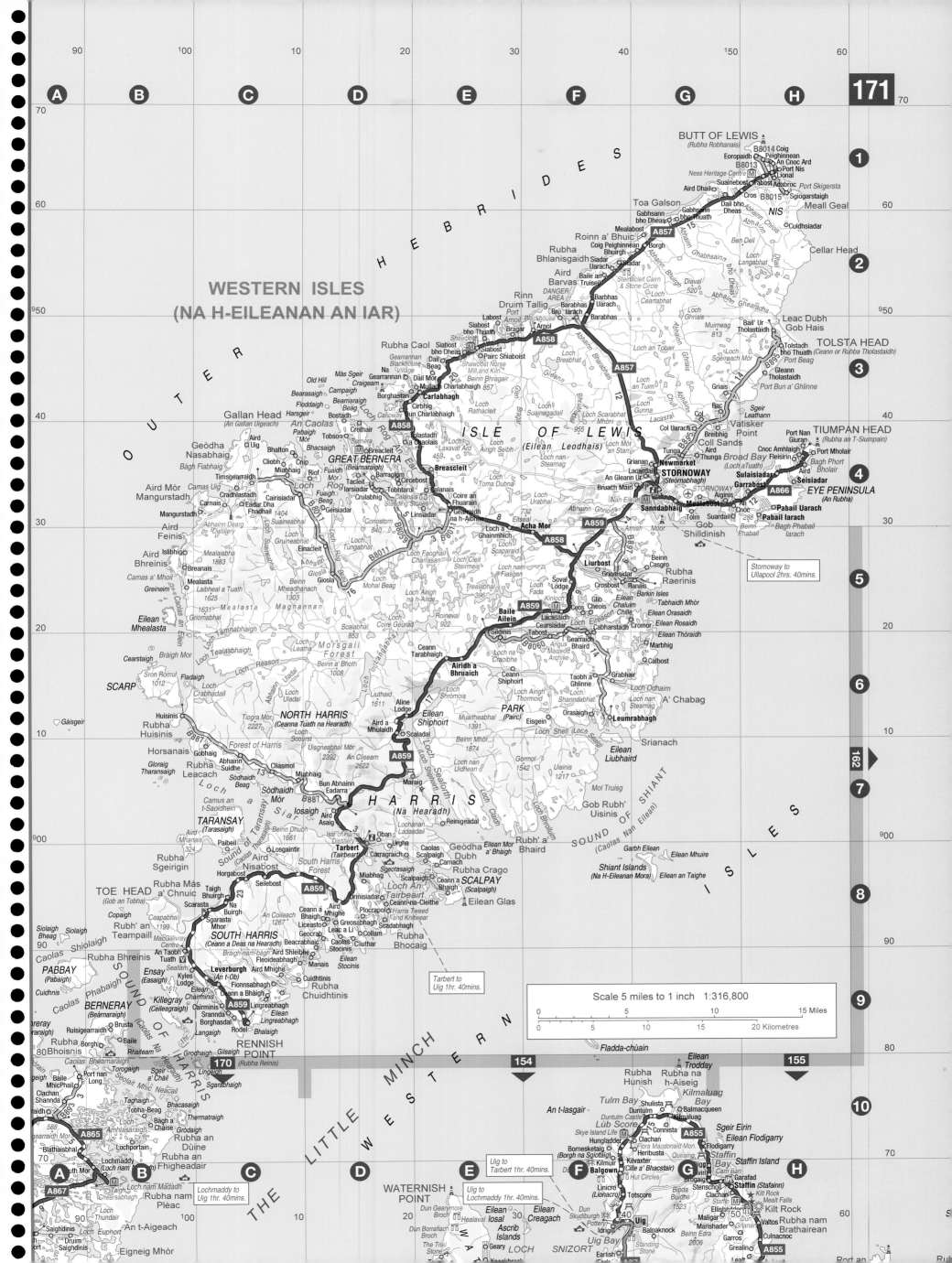

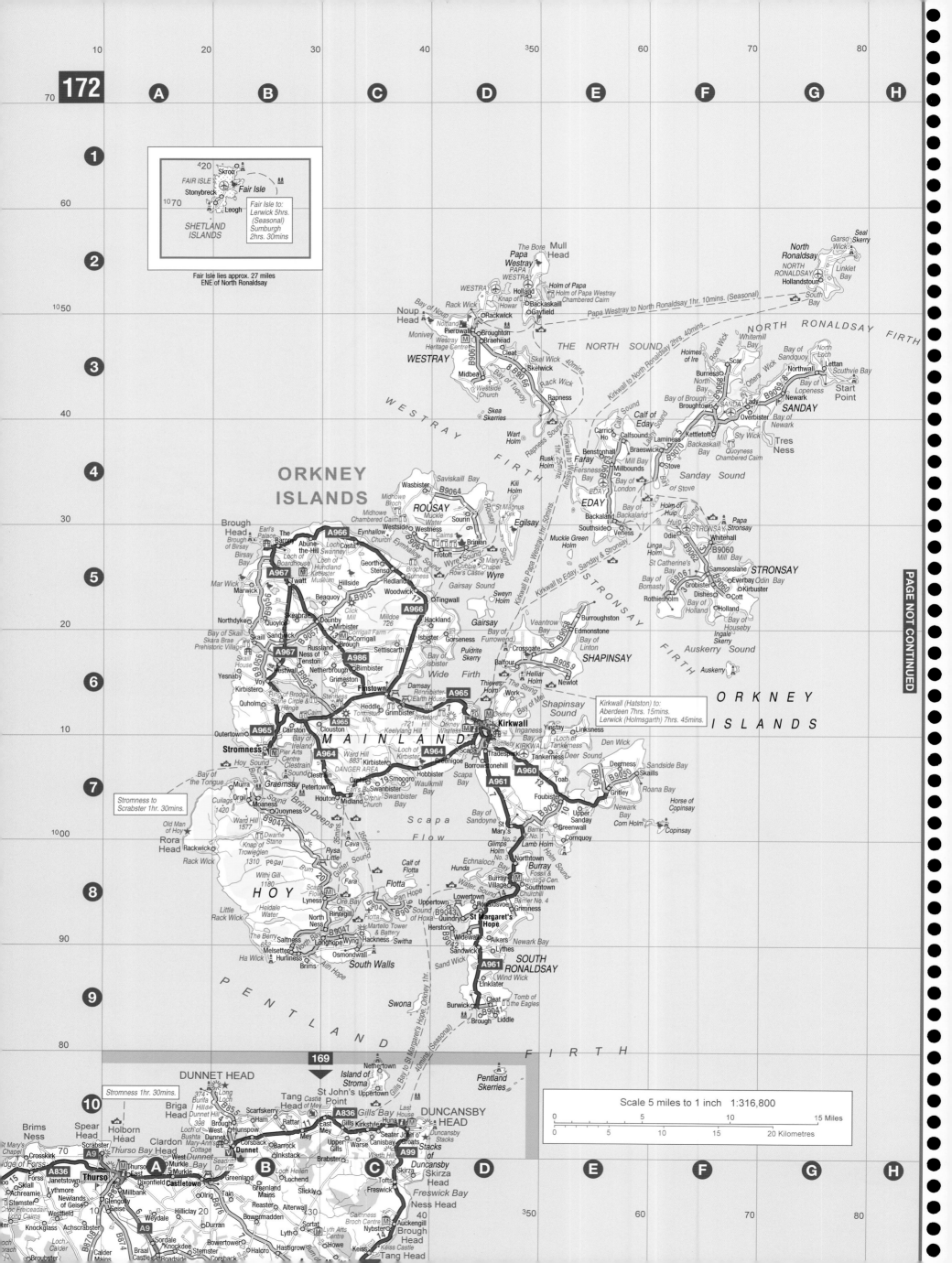

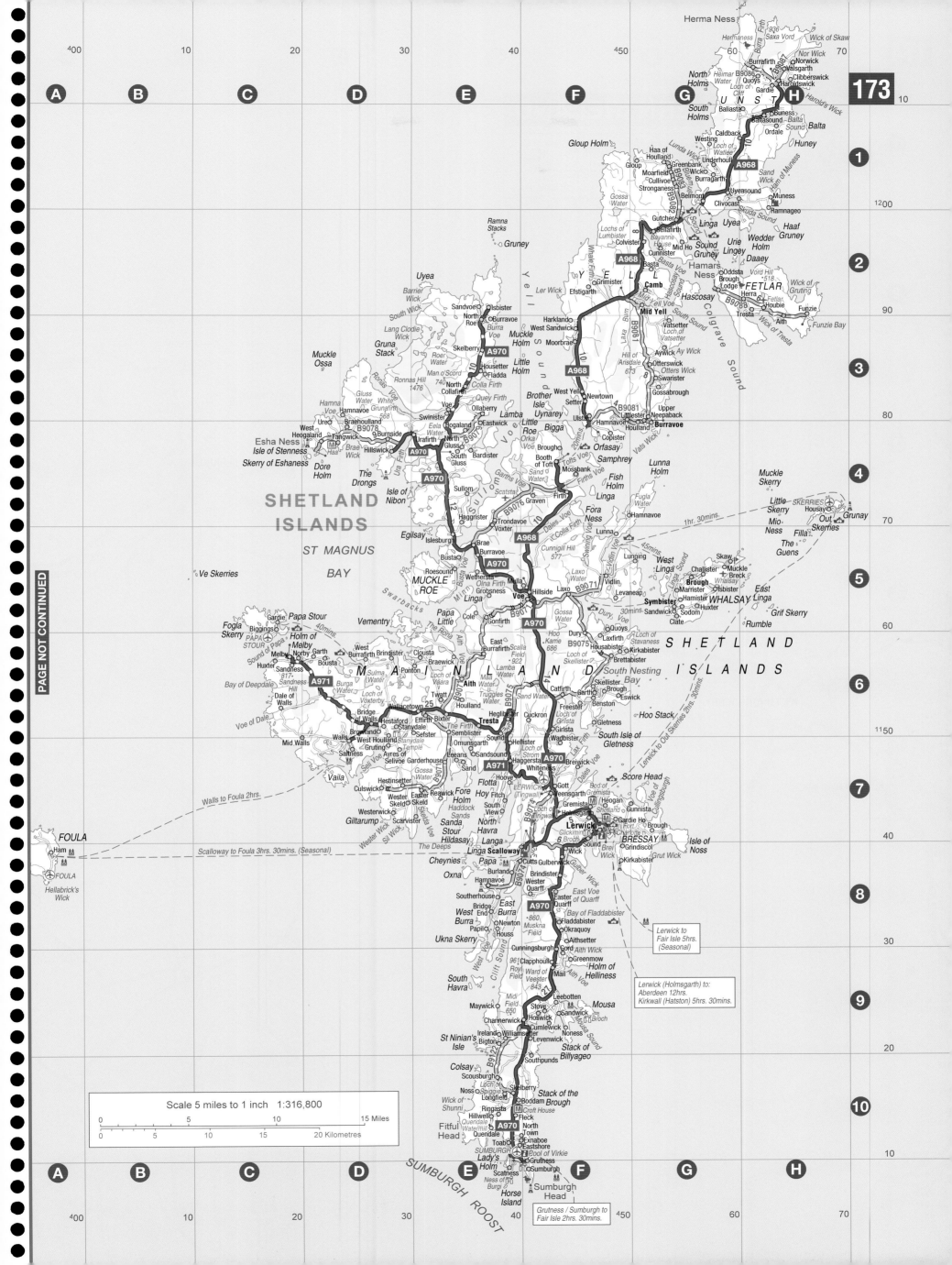

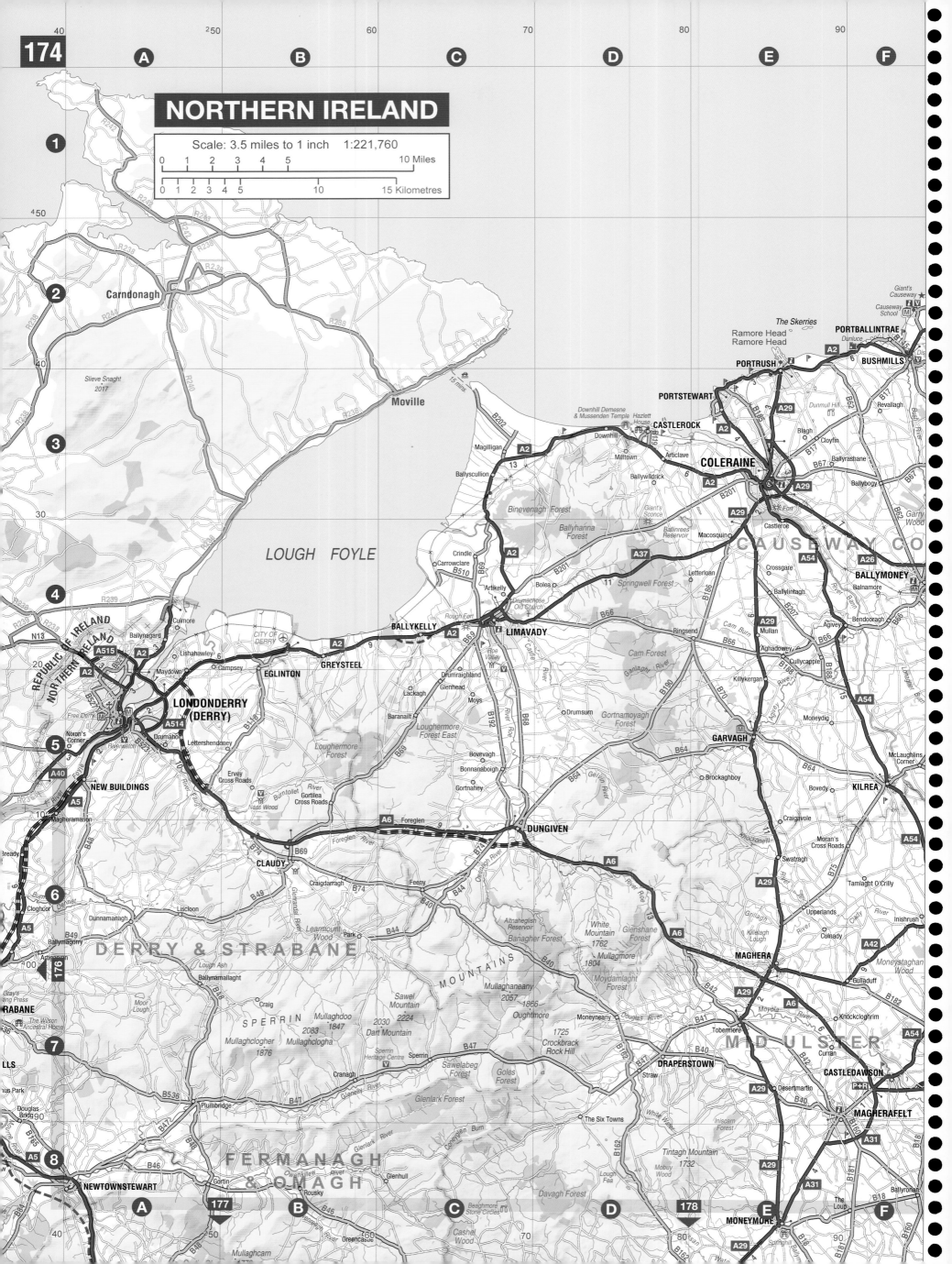

NORTHERN IRELAND

Scale: 3.5 miles to 1 inch   1:221,760

0 1 2 3 4 5   10 Miles

0 1 2 3 4 5   10   15 Kilometres

LOUGH FOYLE

Carndonagh

Slieve Snaght
2017

Moville

Giant's
Causeway
Causeway
School

The Skerries
Ramore Head
Ramore Head
PORTBALLINTRAE

PORTRUSH
Dunluce
BUSHMILLS

PORTSTEWART
Revallagh

Downhill Demesne
& Mussenden Temple
Hazlett
House
CASTLEROCK
Blagh
Cloyfin

Downhill
Milltown
Articlave
COLERAINE
Ballyrashane
Ballybogy

Magilligan
13
Ballywildrick
6
Castleroe
Garry
Wood

Ballyscullion
Binevenagh Forest
Giant's
Sconce
Ballinrees
Reservoir
Macosquin

Ballyhanna
Forest
CAUSEWAY CO
Crossgare
BALLYMONEY
Balnamore

Crindle
Carrowclare
Artikelly
Bolea
11
Springwell Forest
Letterloan
Ballylintagh
Agivey

Drumachose
Old Church
BALLYKELLY
Rough Fort
LIMAVADY
Ringsend
Cam Burn
Mullan
Aghadowey
Killykergan
Cullycapple

CITY OF
DERRY
Culmore
Ballynagard
Lishahawley
Campsey
GREYSTEEL
EGLINTON
Drumraighland
Glenhead
Cam Forest
Moneydig

Maydown
Lackagh
Moys
Drumsurn
Gortnamoyagh
Forest
GARVAGH

LONDONDERRY
(DERRY)
Baranailt
Loughermore
Forest East
River Roe
Bovevagh
Brockaghboy

Nixon's
Corner
Drumahoe
Lettershendoney
Loughermore
Forest
Bonnanaboigh
Gortnahey
Craigavole
McLaughlins
Corner

NEW BUILDINGS
Ervey
Cross Roads
Burntollet
Gortilea
Cross Roads
Dungiven
Knockoneill
Bovedy
KILREA

Magheramason
Ness Wood
A6
Foreglen
9
Moran's
Cross Roads

CLAUDY
B69
Craigdarragh
Foreglen River
Feeny
Swatragh
Tamlagh O'Crilly

Cloghcor
Dunnamanagh
Liscloon
B74
Learmount
Wood
Park
Altnaheglish
Reservoir
Banagher Forest
White
Mountain
1762
Glenshane
Forest
Upperlands
Culnady
Inishrush

Ballymagorry
Ballynamallaght
Lough Ash
Moydamlaght
Forest
Mullagmore
1804
MAGHERA
Gulladuff
Moneystaghan
Wood

DERRY & STRABANE
Craig
Moor
Lough
SPERRIN
Mullaghdoo
1847
2030
Dart Mountain
2224
Mullaghaneany
2057
1866
Oughtmore
Moneyneany
Douglas River
Tobermore
Moyola
A6
Knockcloghrim

STRABANE
The Wilson
Ancestral Home
Mullaghclogher
1876
Mullaghclogha
Sawel
Mountain
Sperrin
Heritage Centre
Sperrin
1725
Crockbrack
Rock Hill
Curran
MID ULSTER

NEWTOWNSTEWART
Gortin
Rousky
Cranagh
Sawelabeg
Forest
Goles
Forest
DRAPERSTOWN
Straw
Desertmartin
CASTLEDAWSON

Douglas
Bridge
Plumbridge
Glenlark Forest
The Six Towns
White Water
Iniscarn
Forest
MAGHERAFELT

FERMANAGH
& OMAGH
Glenhull
Lough Fea
Beaghmore
Stone Circles
Davagh Forest
Tintagh Mountain
1732
Mebuy
Wood

Mullaghcarn
Greencastle
Cashel
Wood
MONEYMORE
The Lou

177
176
178

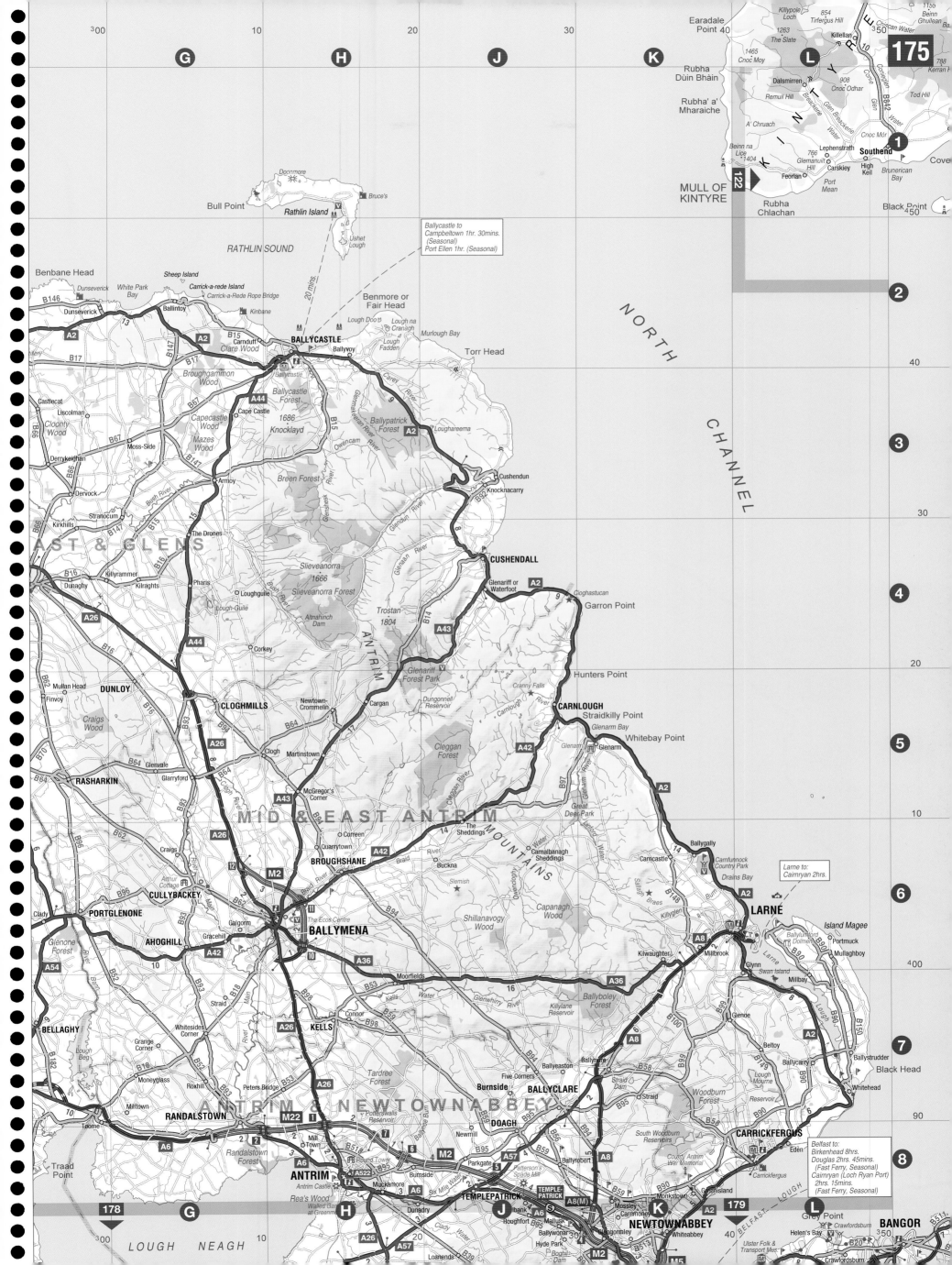

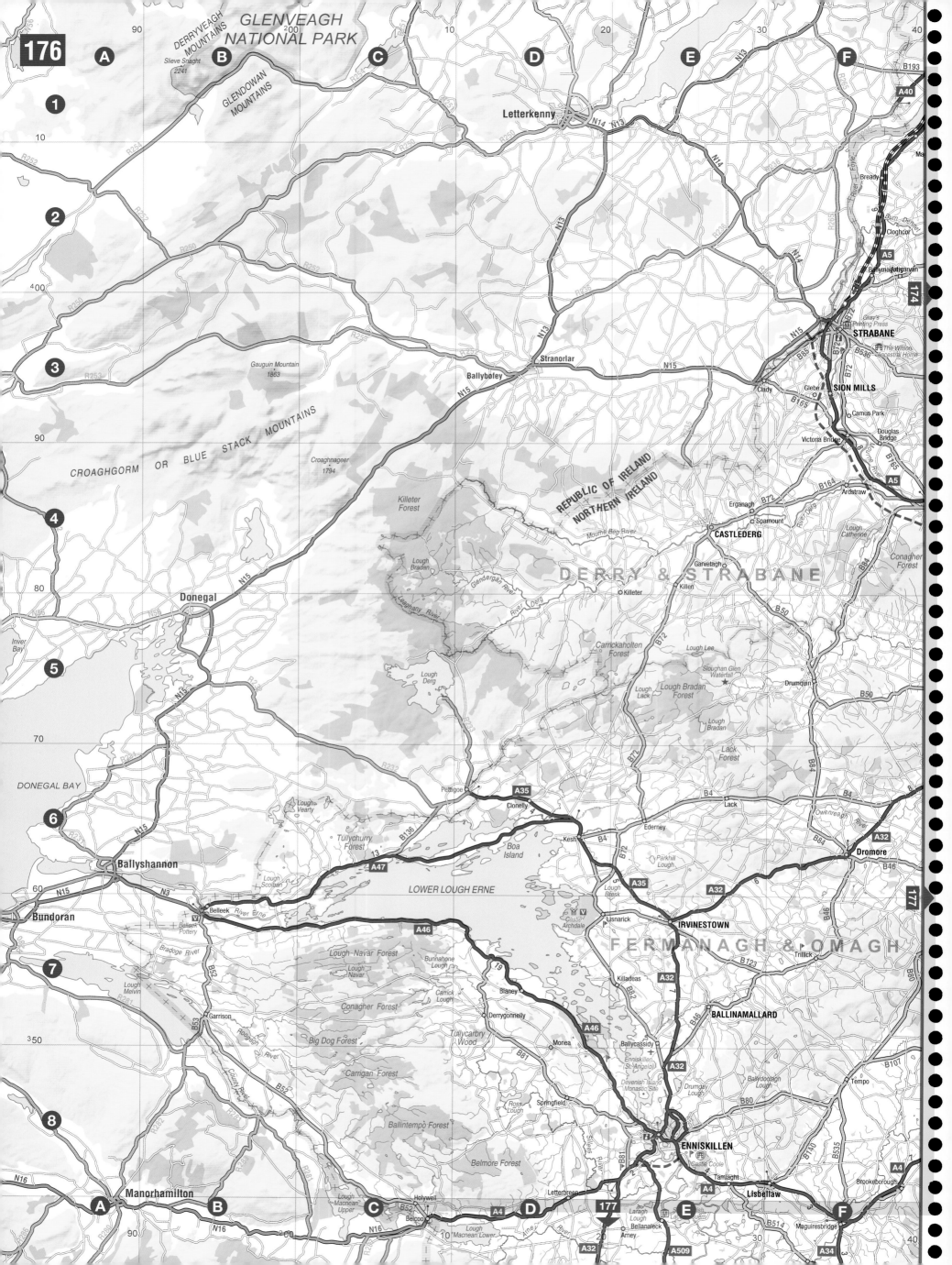

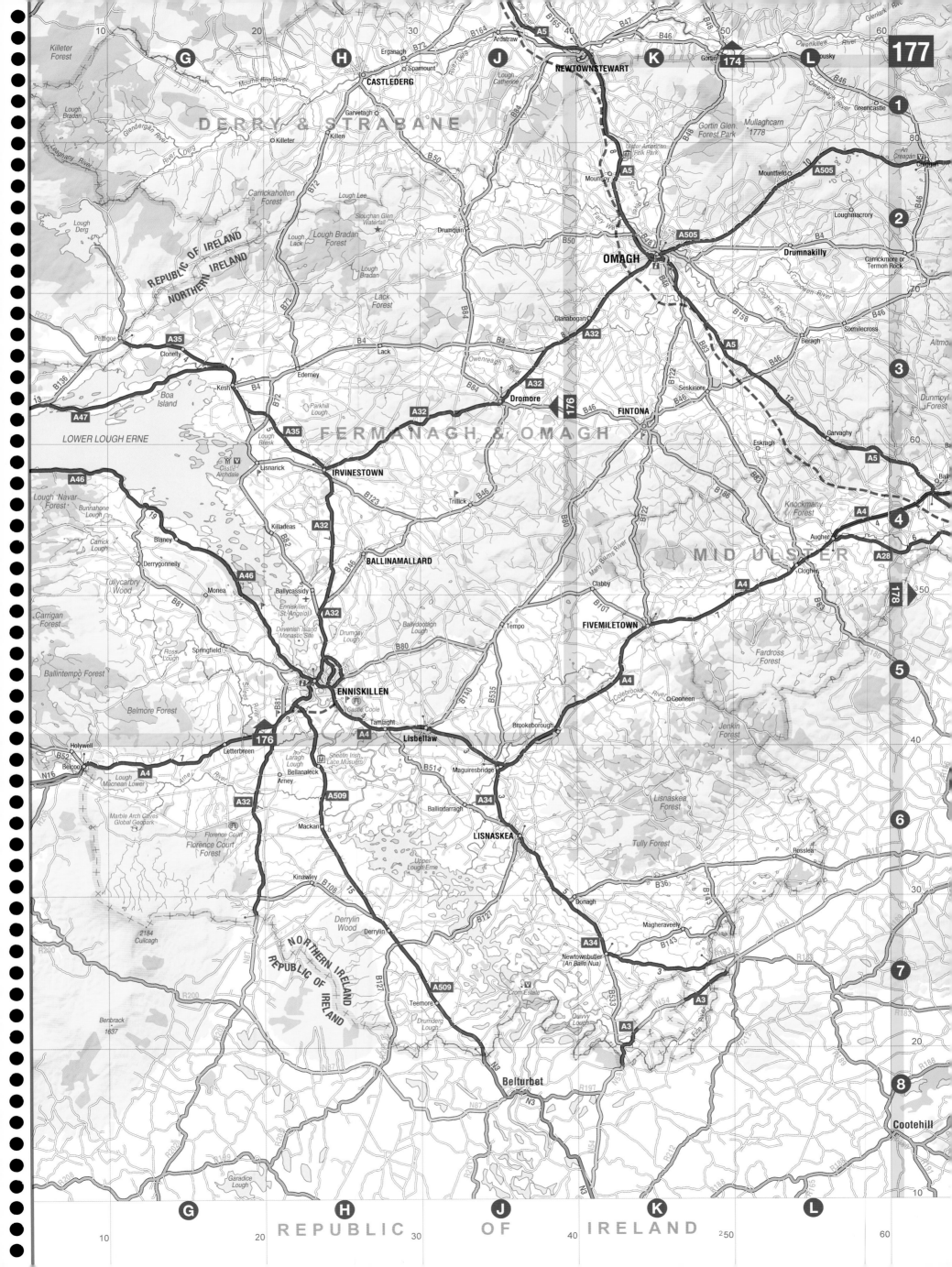

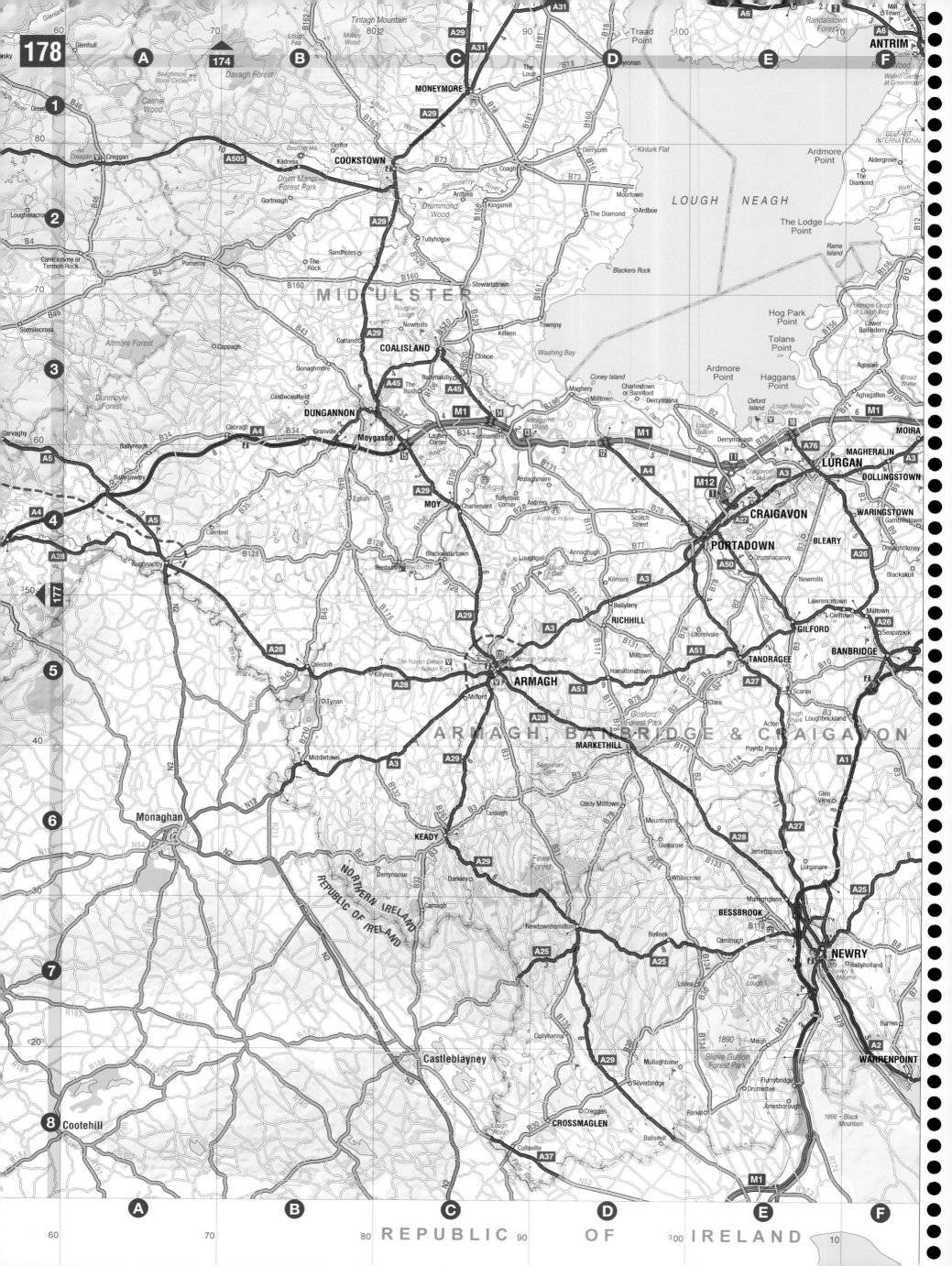

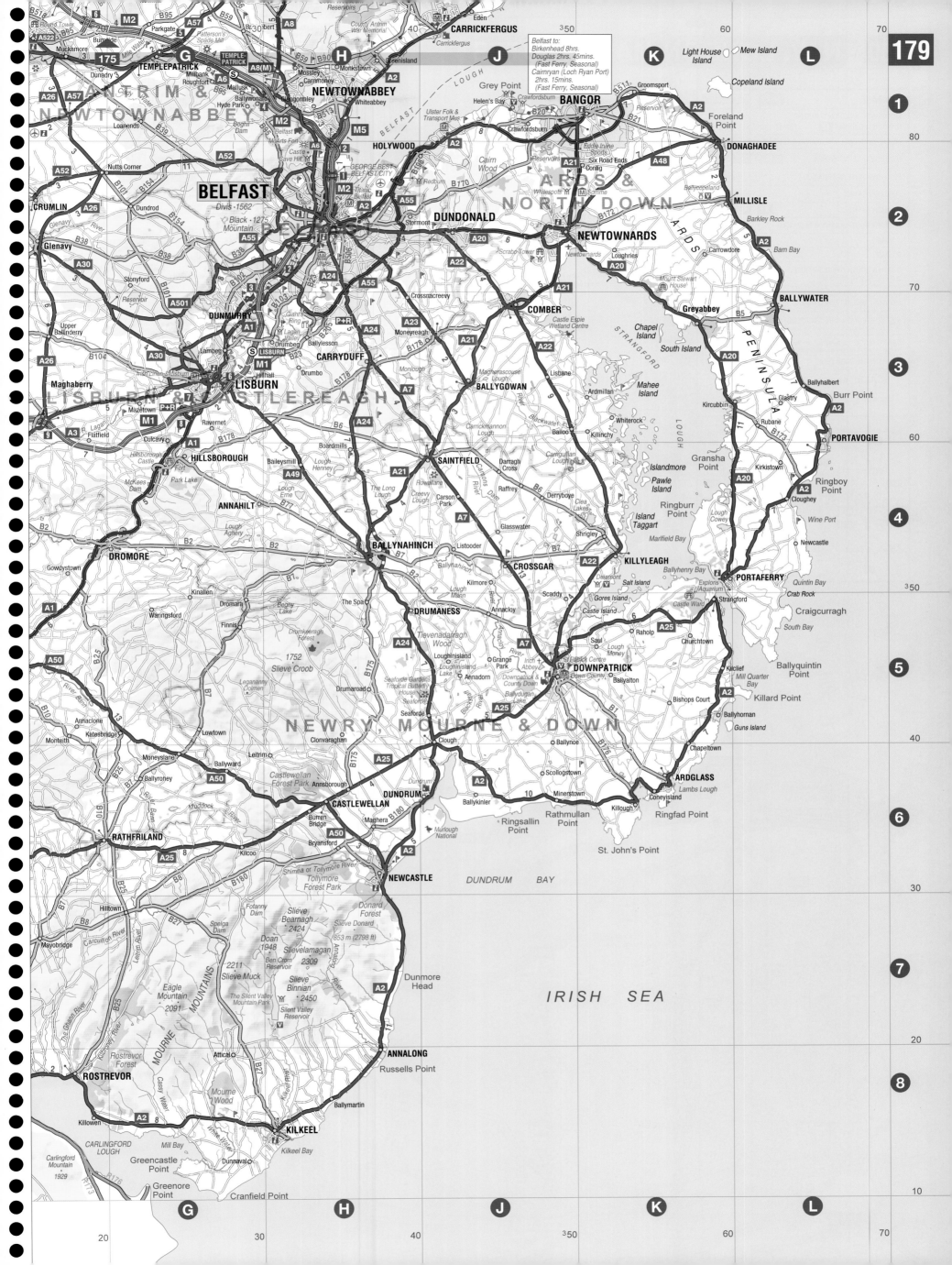

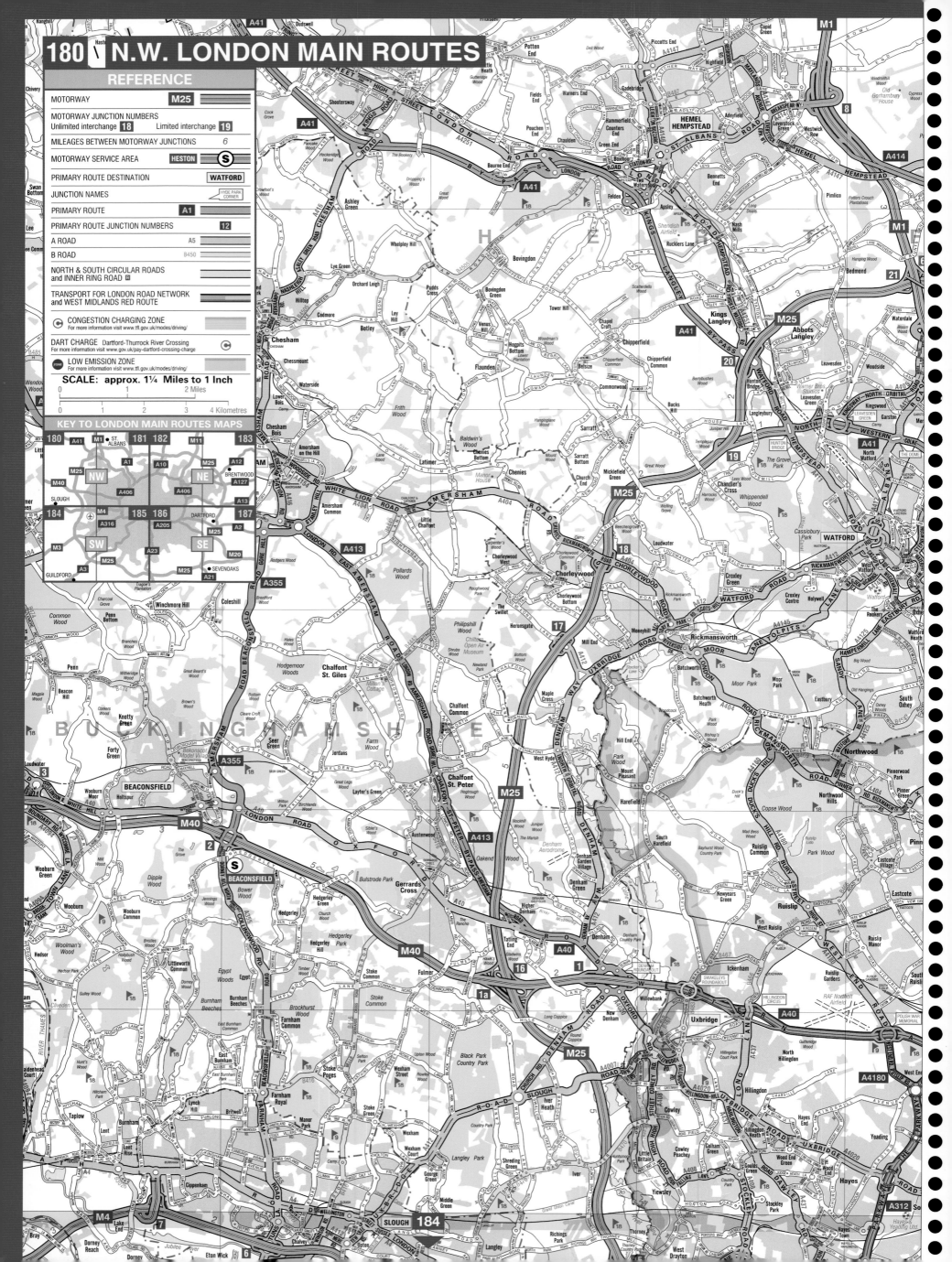

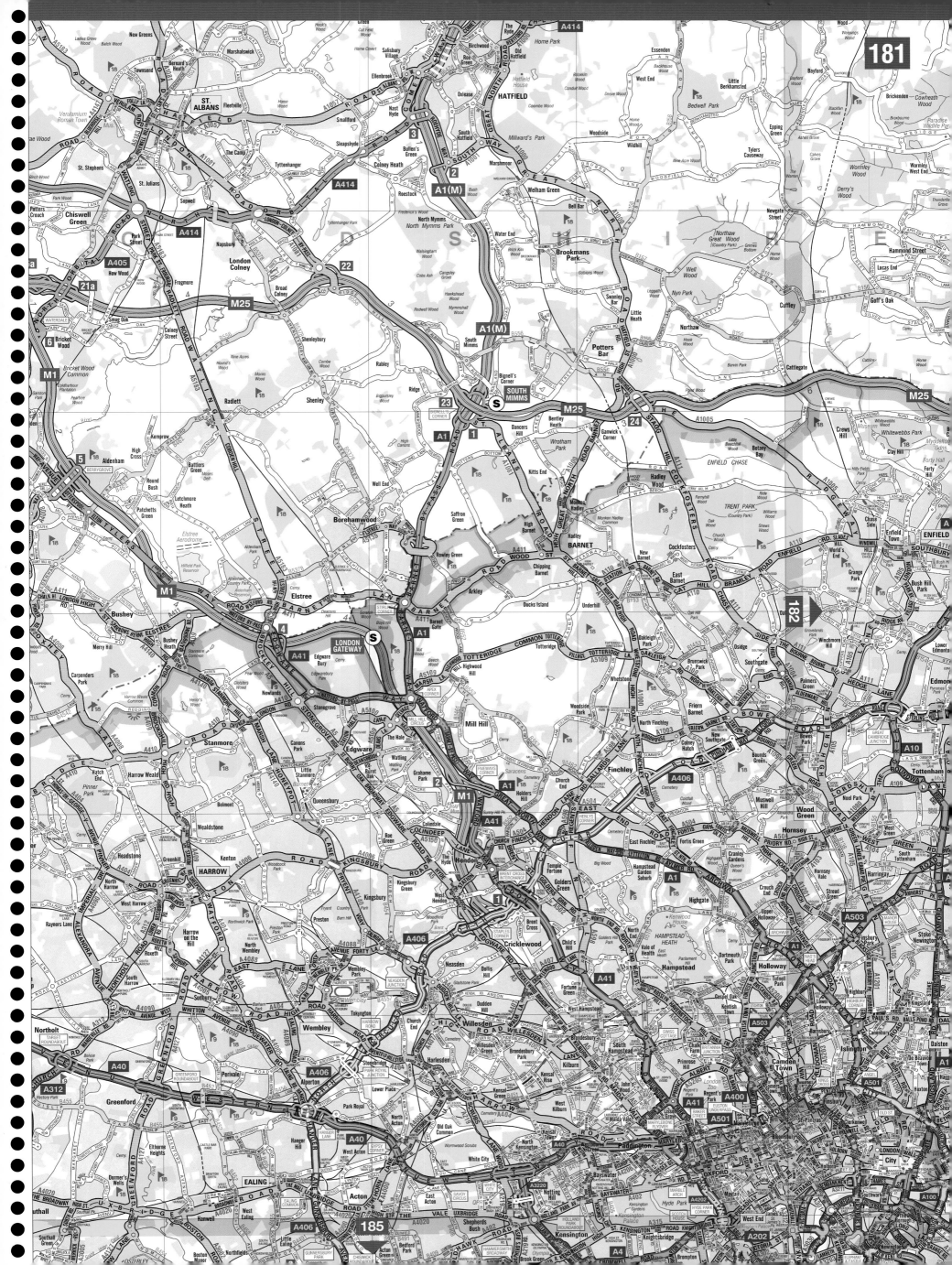

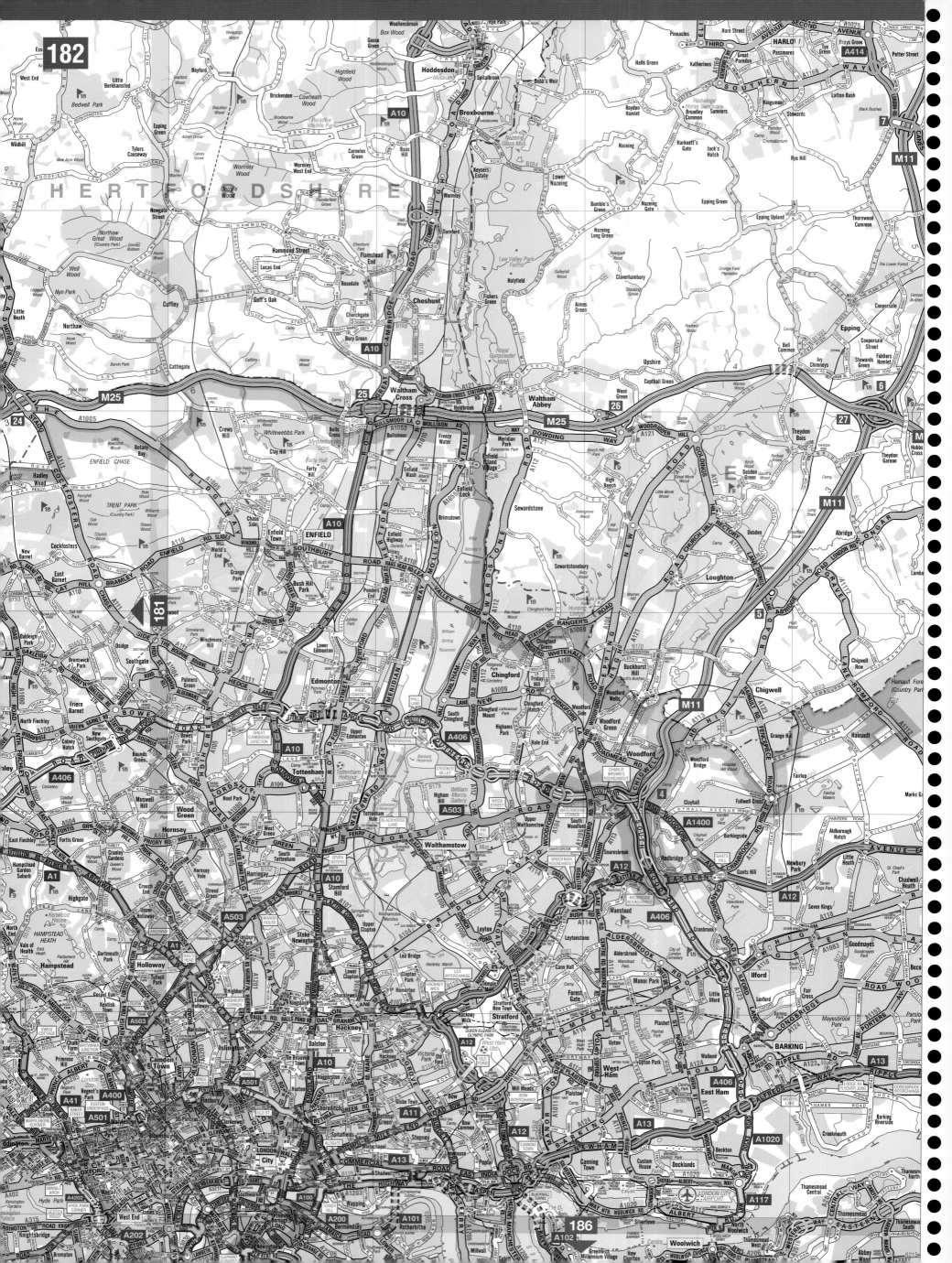

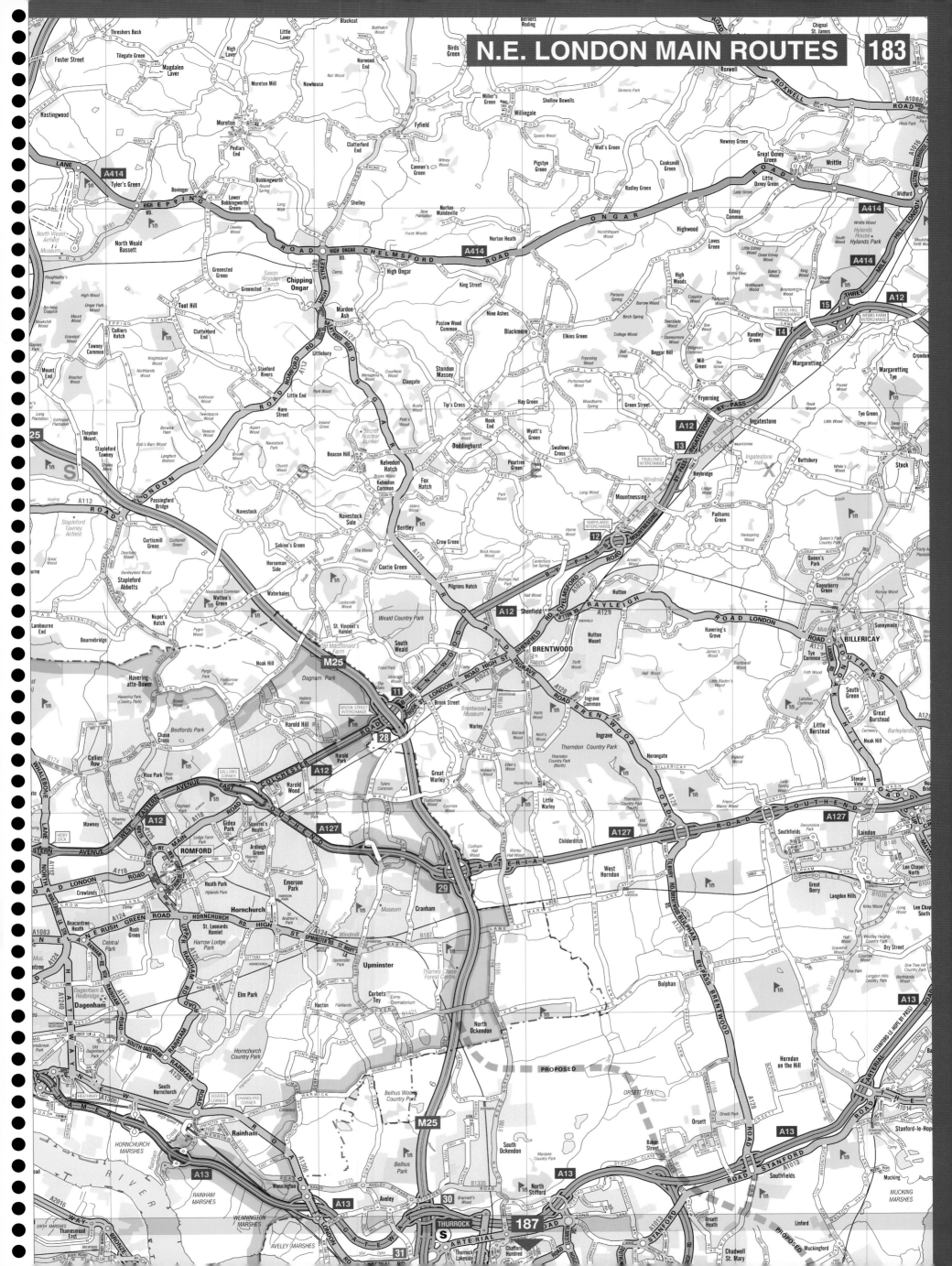

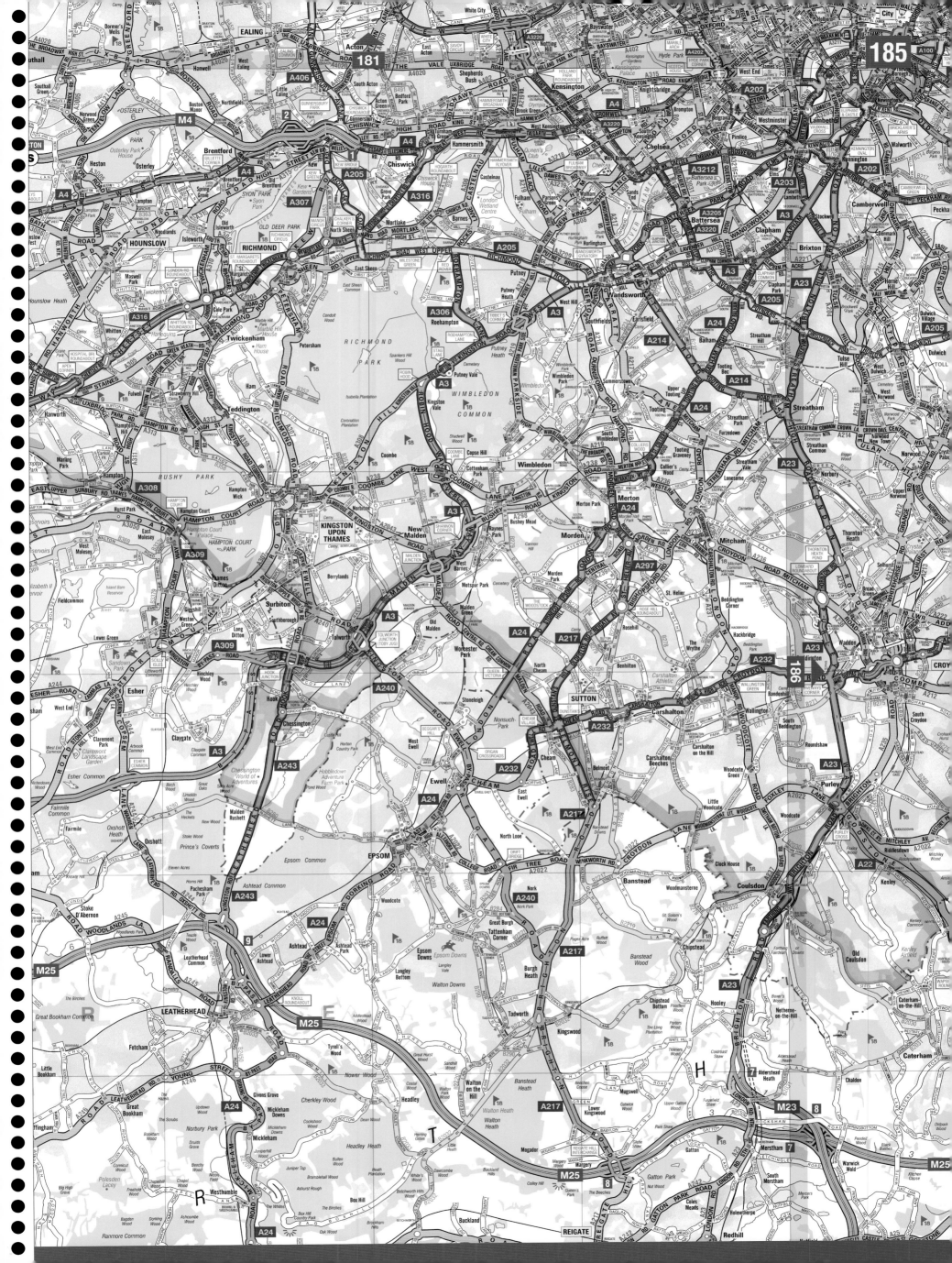

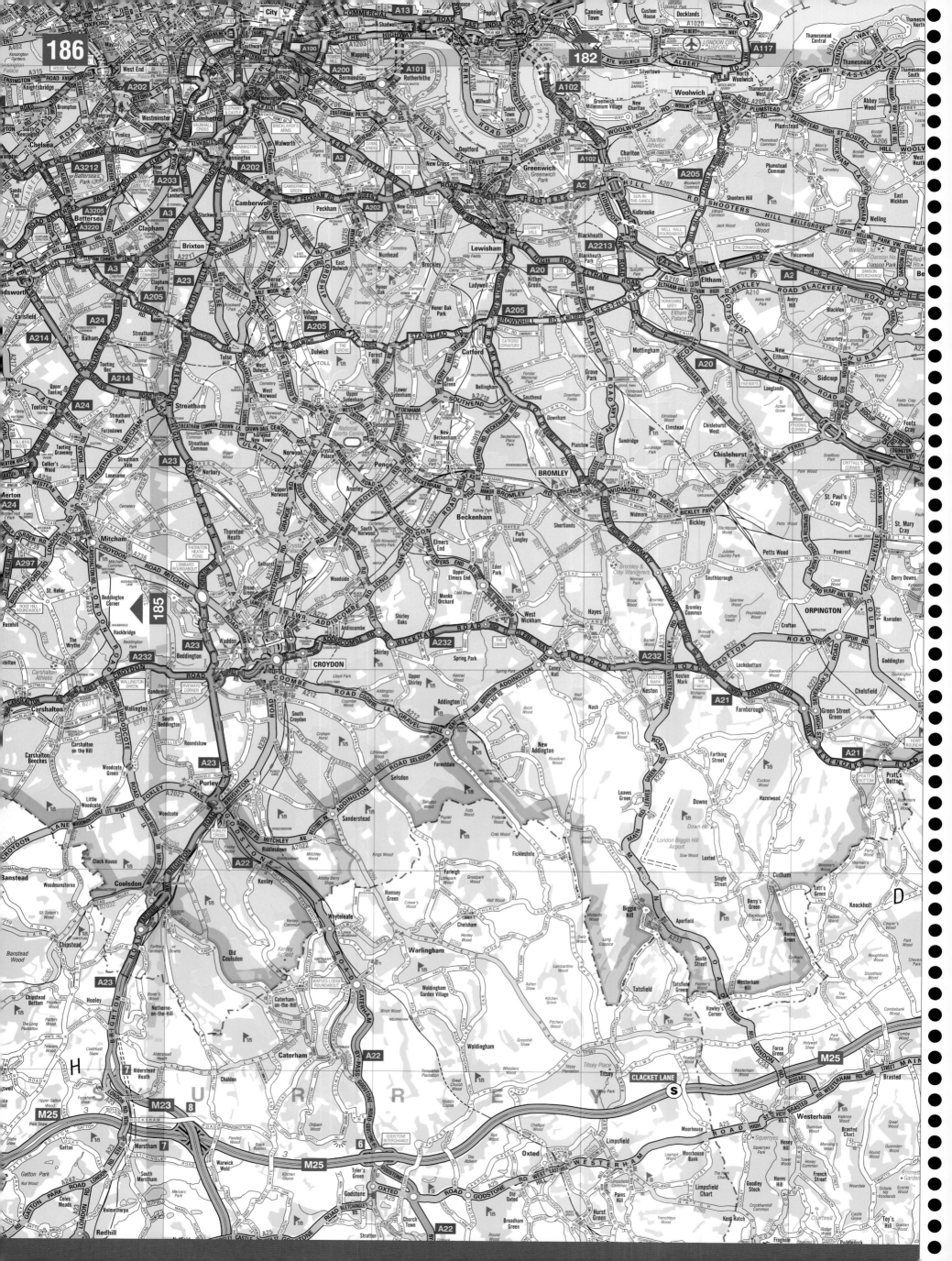

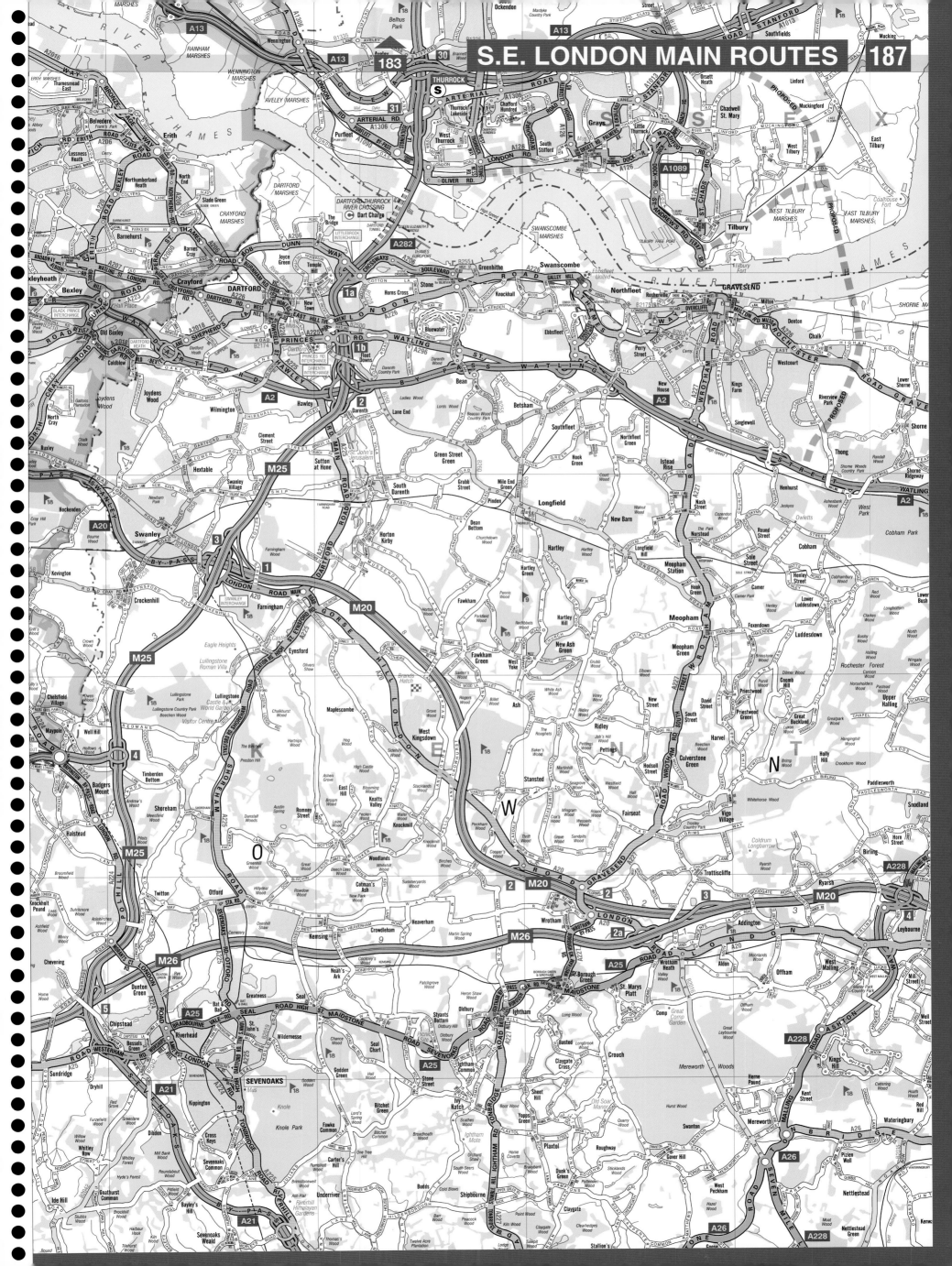

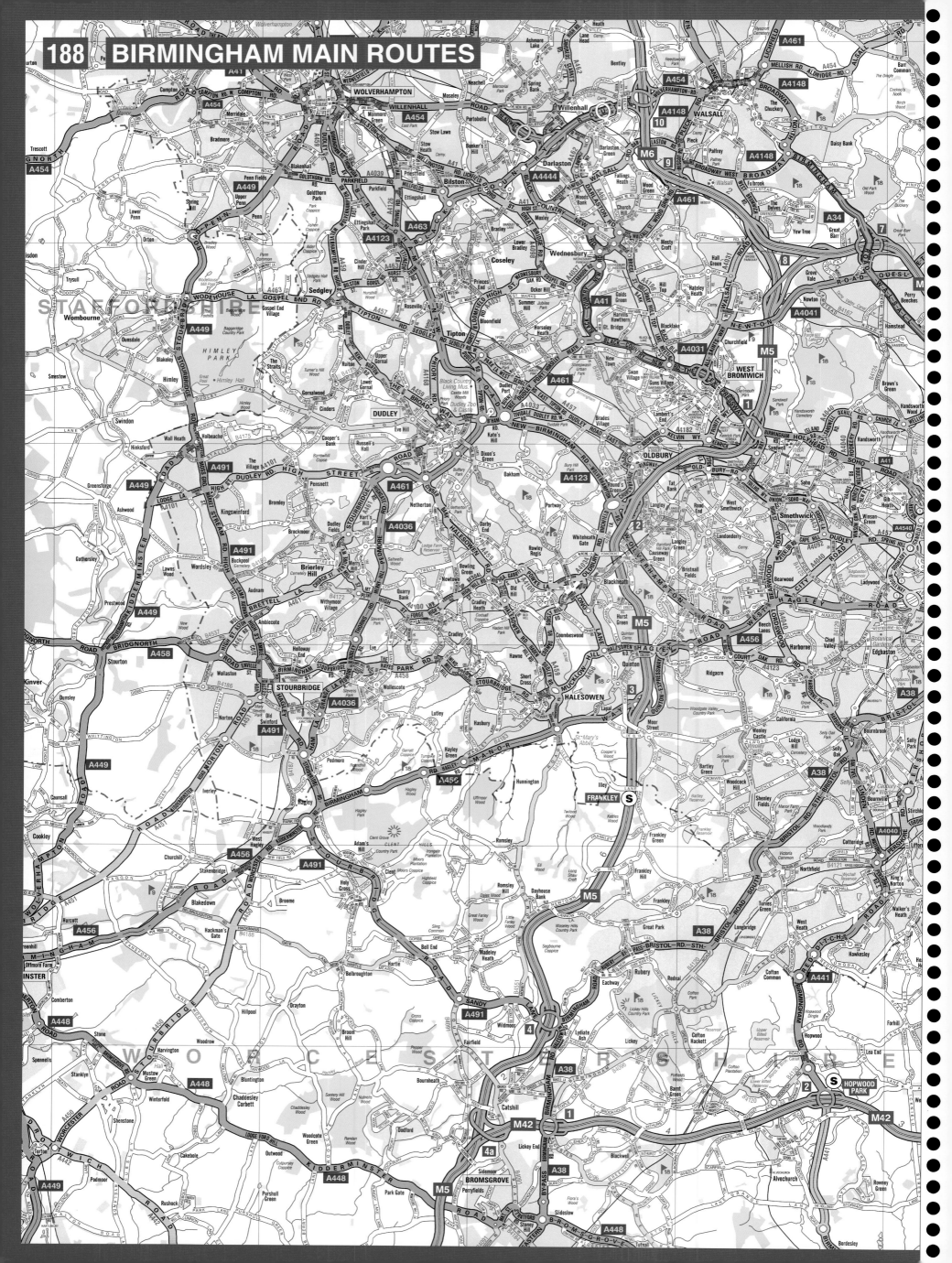

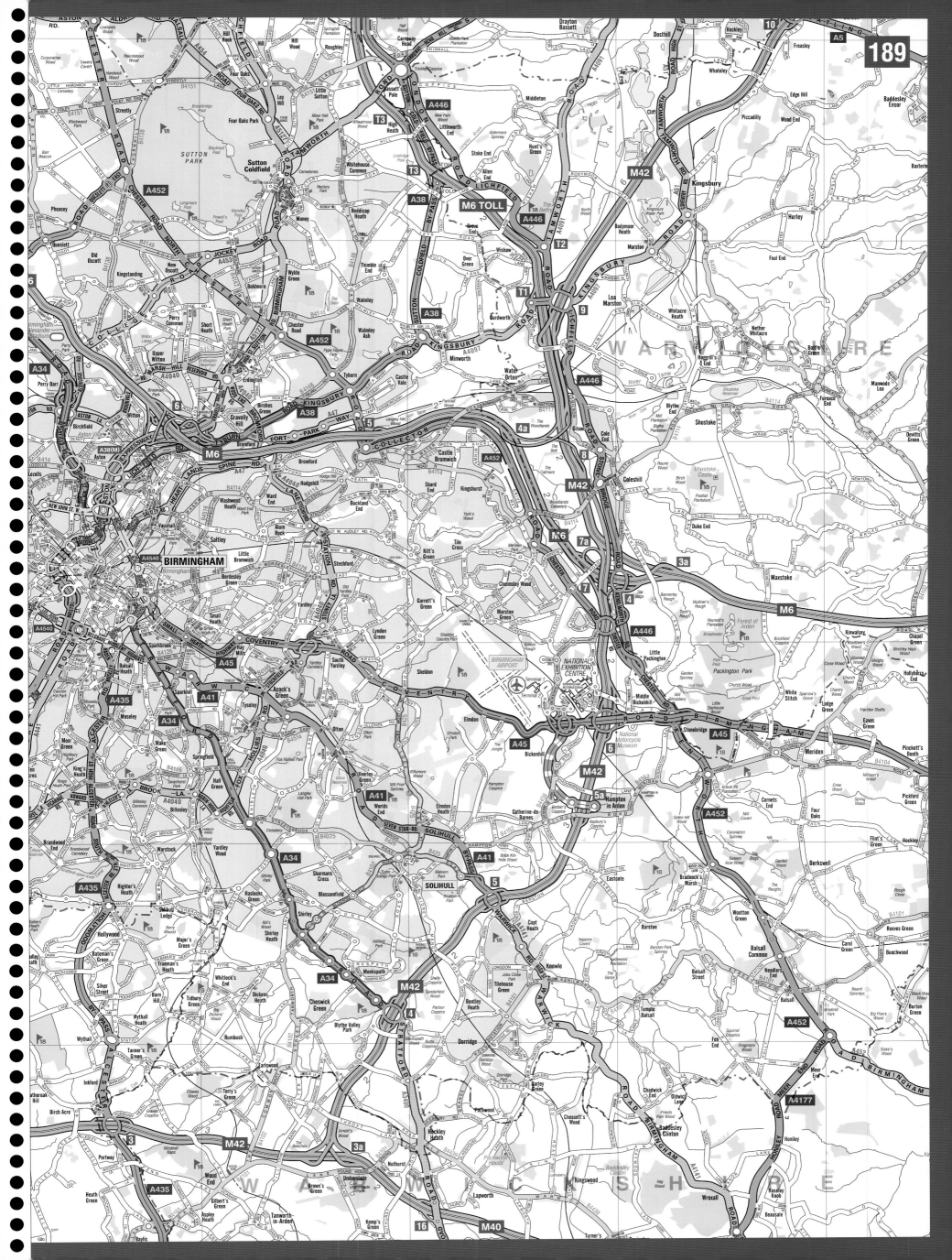

City & Town Centre Plans

Port Plans

Airport Plans

Reference to City & Town Plans   Légende   Zeichenerklärung

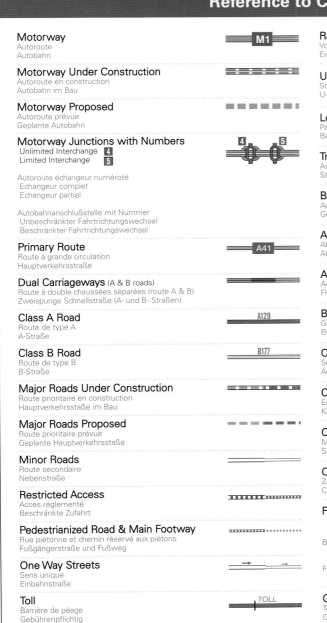

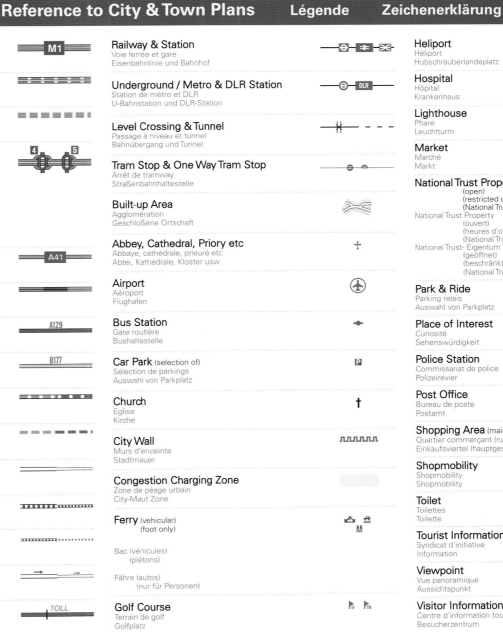

Motorway
Autoroute
Autobahn

Motorway Under Construction
Autoroute en construction
Autobahn im Bau

Motorway Proposed
Autoroute prévue
Geplante Autobahn

Motorway Junctions with Numbers
Unlimited Interchange **4**
Limited Interchange **5**

Autoroute échangeur numéroté
Echangeur complet
Echangeur partiel

Autobahnanschlußstelle mit Nummer
Unbeschränkter Fahrtrichtungswechsel
Beschränkter Fahrtrichtungswechsel

Primary Route
Route à grande circulation
Hauptverkehrsstraße

Dual Carriageways (A & B roads)
Route à double chaussées séparées (route A & B)
Zweispurige Schnellstraße (A- und B- Straßen)

Class A Road
Route de type A
A-Straße

Class B Road
Route de type B
B-Straße

Major Roads Under Construction
Route prioritaire en construction
Hauptverkehrsstraße im Bau

Major Roads Proposed
Route prioritaire prévue
Geplante Hauptverkehrsstraße

Minor Roads
Route secondaire
Nebenstraße

Restricted Access
Accès réglementé
Beschränkte Zufahrt

Pedestrianized Road & Main Footway
Rue piétonne et chemin réservé aux piétons
Fußgängerstraße und Fußweg

One Way Streets
Sens unique
Einbahnstraße

Toll
Barrière de péage
Gebührenpflichtig

Railway & Station
Voie ferrée et gare
Eisenbahnlinie und Bahnhof

Underground / Metro & DLR Station
Station de métro et DLR
U-Bahnstation und DLR-Station

Level Crossing & Tunnel
Passage à niveau et tunnel
Bahnübergang und Tunnel

Tram Stop & One Way Tram Stop
Arrêt de tramway
Straßenbahnhaltestelle

Built-up Area
Agglomération
Geschlossene Ortschaft

Abbey, Cathedral, Priory etc
Abbaye, cathédrale, prieuré etc
Abtei, Kathedrale, Kloster usw

Airport
Aéroport
Flughafen

Bus Station
Gare routière
Bushaltestelle

Car Park (selection of)
Sélection de parkings
Auswahl von Parkplatz

Church
Eglise
Kirche

City Wall
Murs d'enceinte
Stadtmauer

Congestion Charging Zone
Zone de péage urbain
City-Maut Zone

Ferry (vehicular)
(foot only)

Bac (véhicules)
(piétons)

Fähre (autos)
(nur für Personen)

Golf Course
Terrain de golf
Golfplatz

Heliport
Héliport
Hubschrauberlandeplatz

Hospital
Hôpital
Krankenhaus

Lighthouse
Phare
Leuchtturm

Market
Marché
Markt

National Trust Property
(open)   NT
(restricted opening)   NT
(National Trust for Scotland) NTS   NTS
National Trust Property
(ouvert)
(heures d'ouverture)
(National Trust for Scotland)
National Trust- Eigentum
(geöffnet)
(beschränkte Öffnungszeit)
(National Trust for Scotland)

Park & Ride
Parking relais
Auswahl von Parkplatz

Place of Interest
Curiosité
Sehenswürdigkeit

Police Station
Commissariat de police
Polizeirevier

Post Office
Bureau de poste
Postamt

Shopping Area (main street & precinct)
Quartier commerçant (rue et zone principales)
Einkaufsviertel (hauptgeschäftsstraße, fußgängerzone)

Shopmobility
Shopmobility
Shopmobility

Toilet
Toilettes
Toilette

Tourist Information Centre
Syndicat d'initiative
Information

Viewpoint
Vue panoramique
Aussichtspunkt

Visitor Information Centre
Centre d'information touristique
Besucherzentrum

ABERDEEN

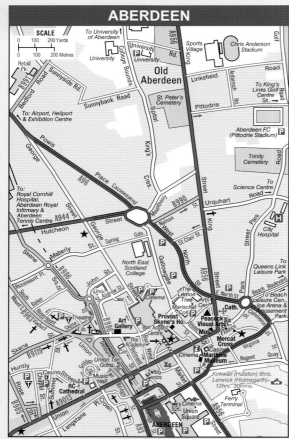

BATH

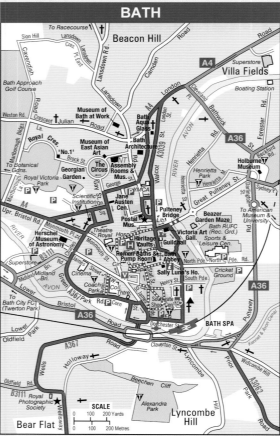

BLACKPOOL

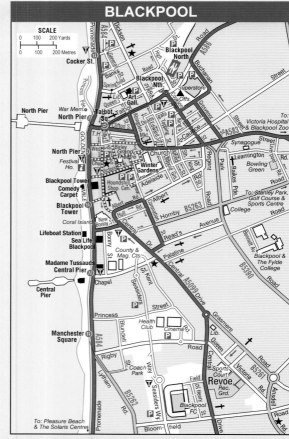

BIRMINGHAM (CITY CENTRE)

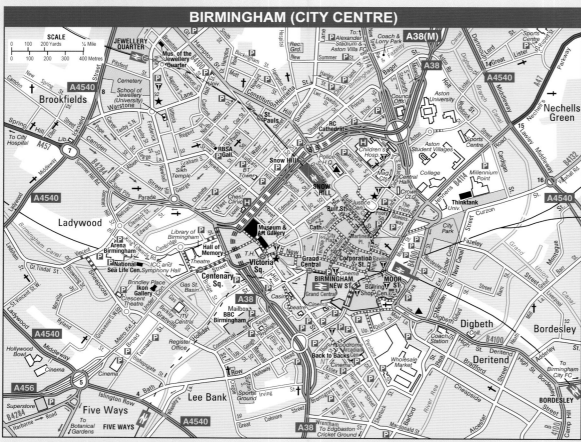

BOURNEMOUTH

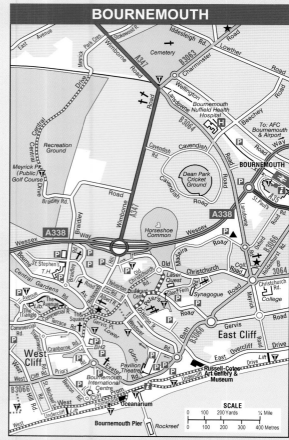

BRADFORD

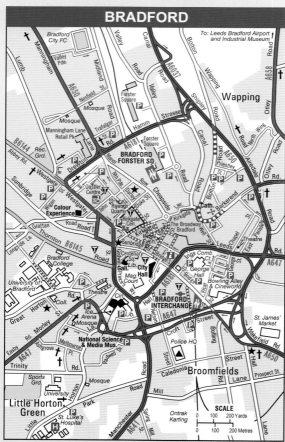

BRIGHTON and HOVE

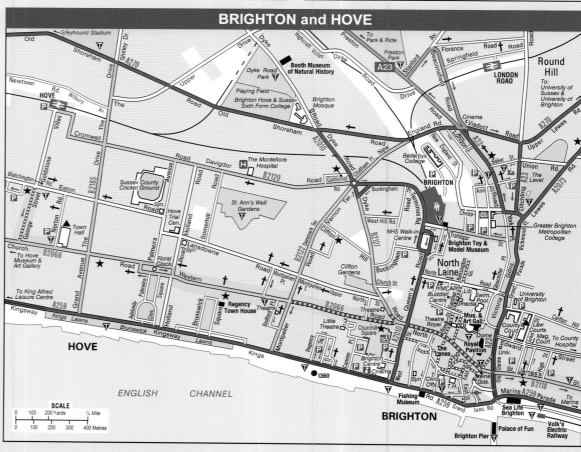

BRISTOL

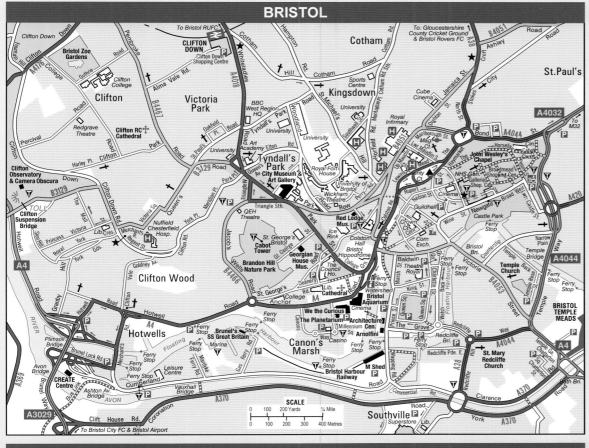

CANTERBURY

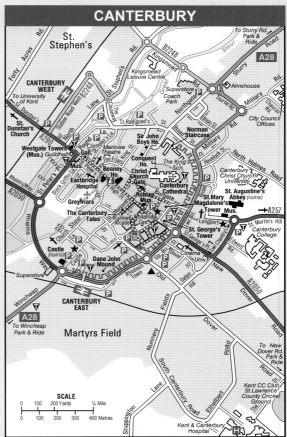

CAMBRIDGE

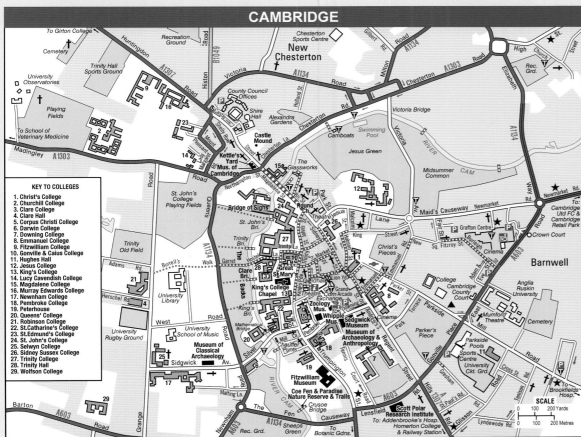

KEY TO COLLEGES
1. Christ's College
2. Churchill College
3. Clare College
4. Clare Hall
5. Corpus Christi College
6. Darwin College
7. Downing College
8. Emmanuel College
9. Fitzwilliam College
10. Gonville & Caius College
11. Hughes Hall
12. Jesus College
13. King's College
14. Lucy Cavendish College
15. Magdalene College
16. Murray Edwards College
17. Newnham College
18. Pembroke College
19. Peterhouse
20. Queens' College
21. Robinson College
22. St.Catharine's College
23. St.Edmund's College
24. St. John's College
25. Selwyn College
26. Sidney Sussex College
27. Trinity College
28. Trinity Hall
29. Wolfson College

CARLISLE

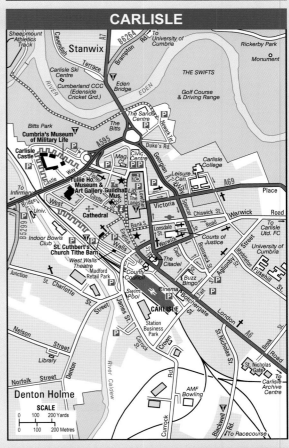

CARDIFF (CAERDYDD)

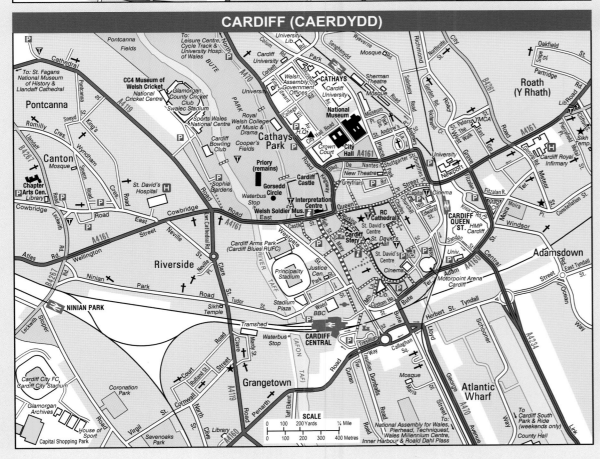

CHELTENHAM

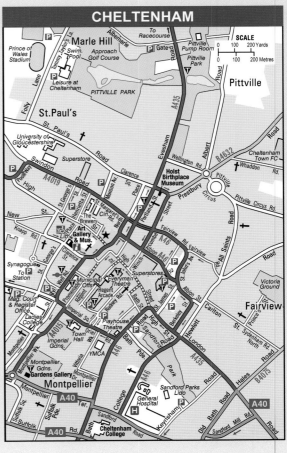

CHESTER

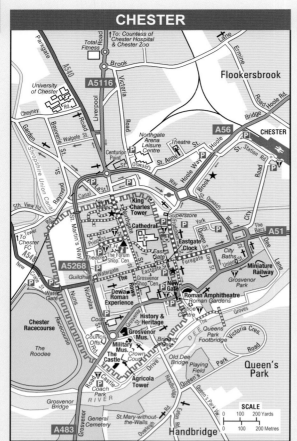

COVENTRY

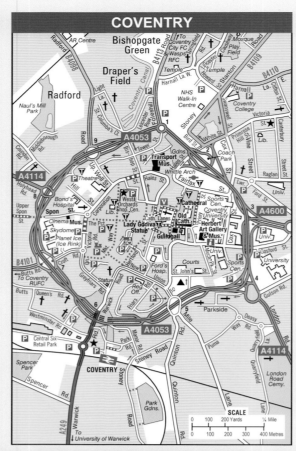

DERBY

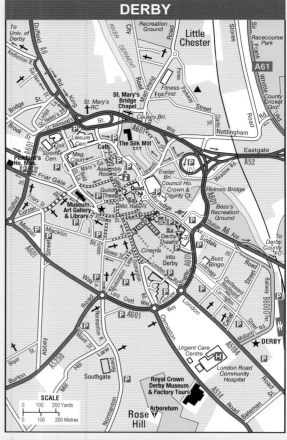

DOVER

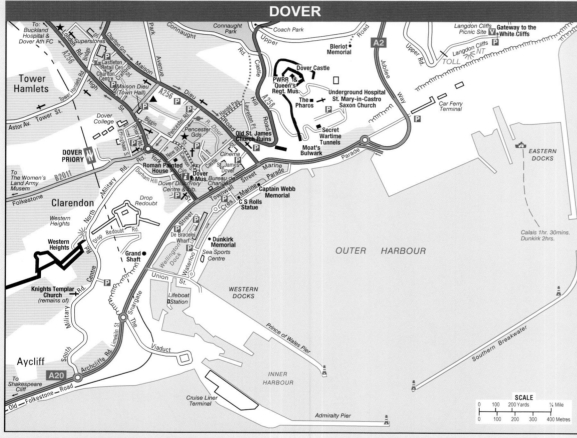

DUMFRIES

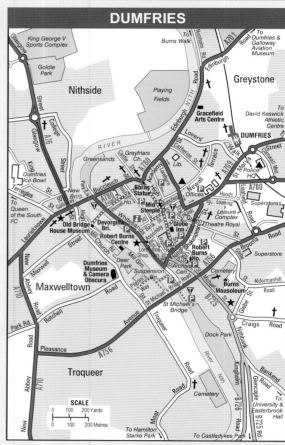

DUNDEE

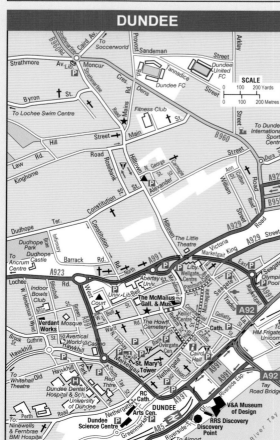

DURHAM

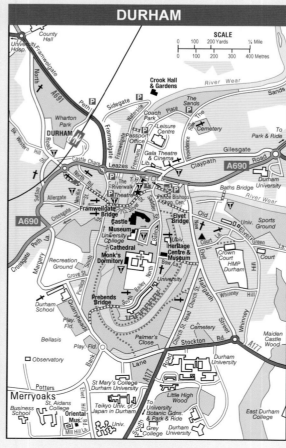

EASTBOURNE

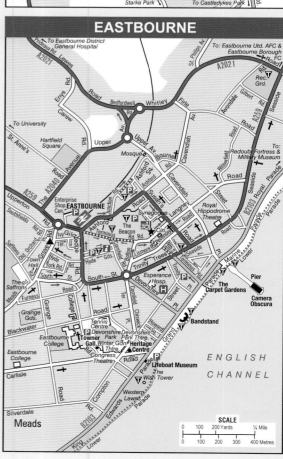

EDINBURGH

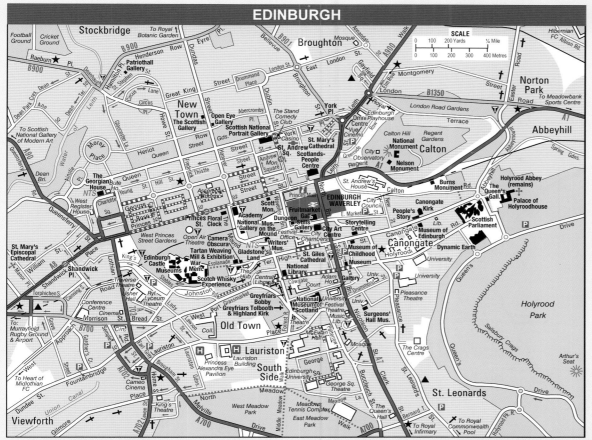

FOLKESTONE

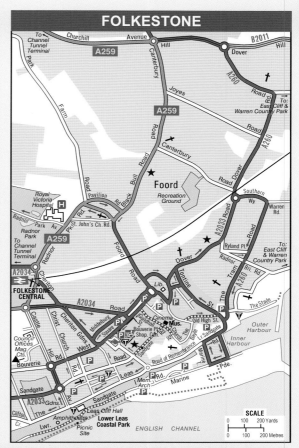

EXETER

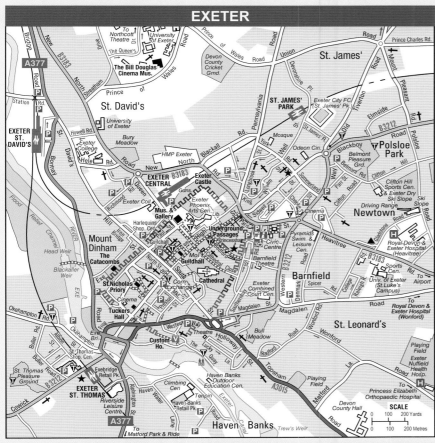

GUILDFORD

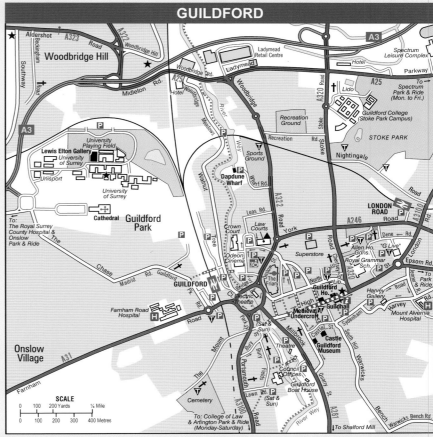

GLASGOW

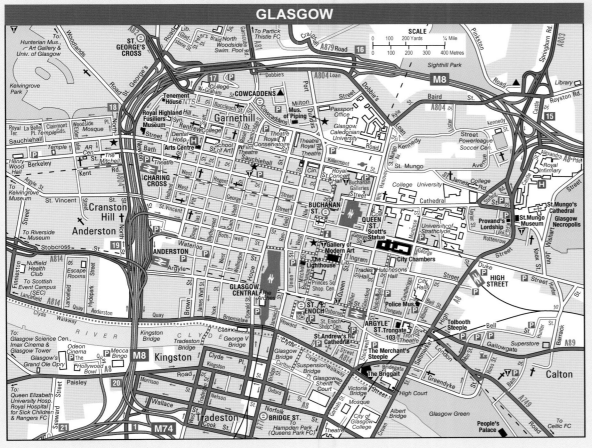

GLOUCESTER

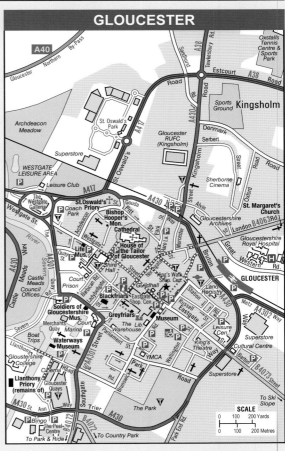

HARROGATE
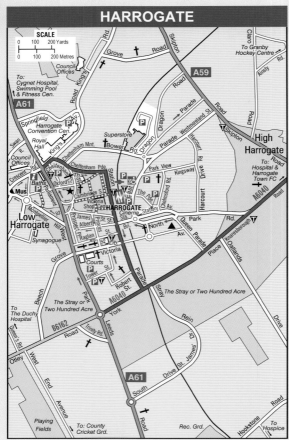

INVERNESS
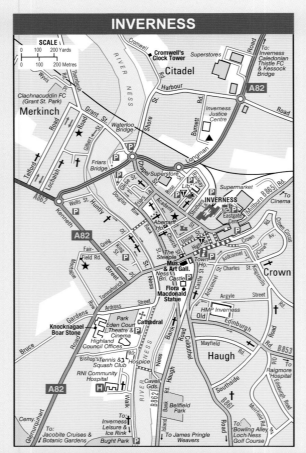

IPSWICH
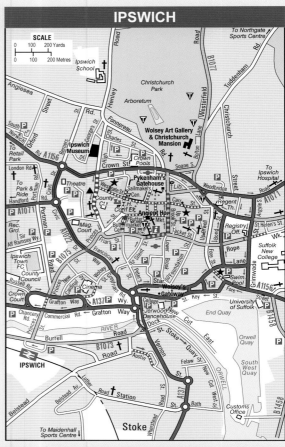

KILMARNOCK
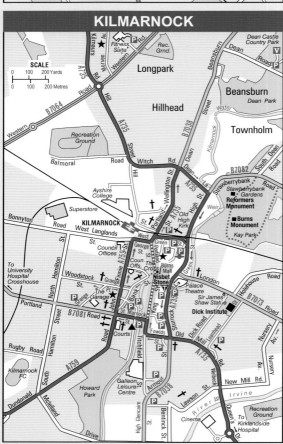

LEEDS
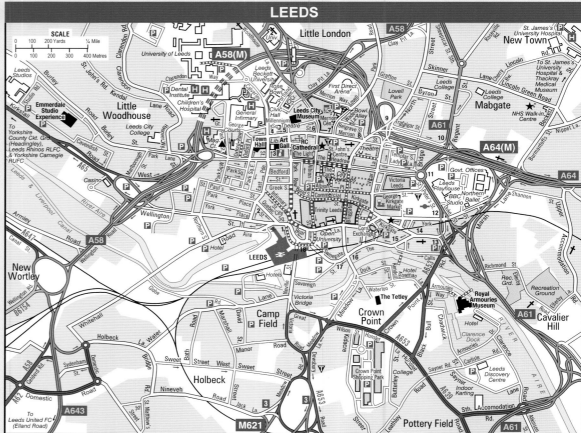

KINGSTON UPON HULL
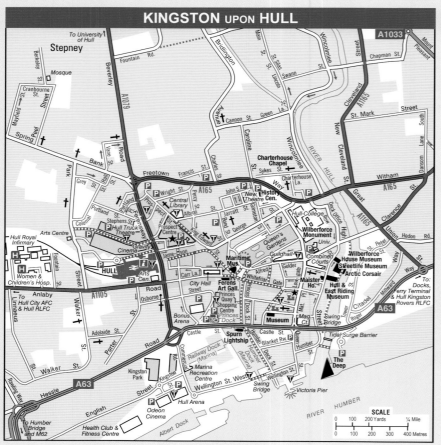

LEICESTER
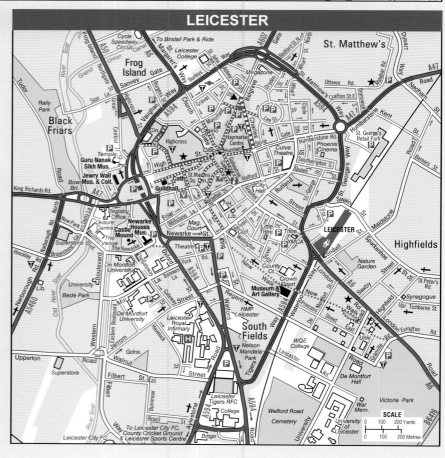

LINCOLN

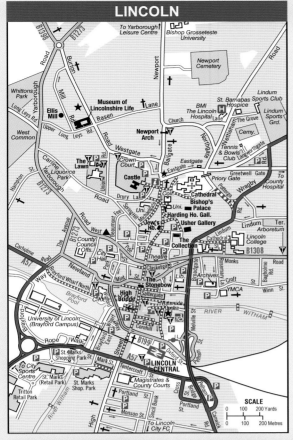

LIVERPOOL

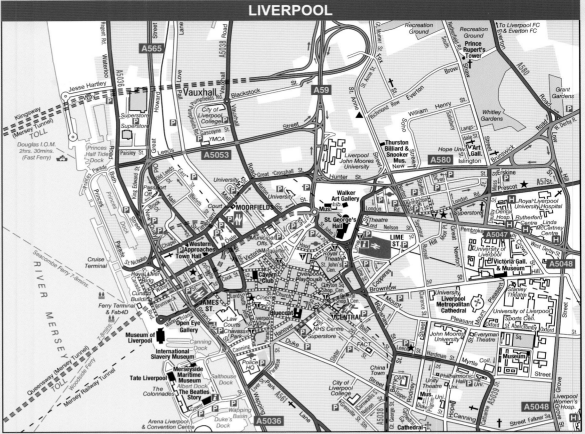

MANCHESTER (CITY CENTRE)

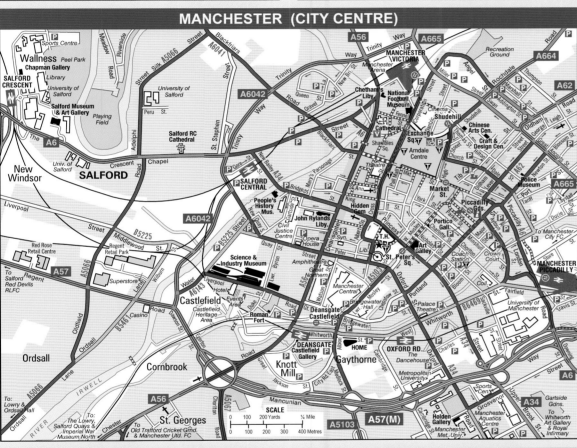

MIDDLESBROUGH

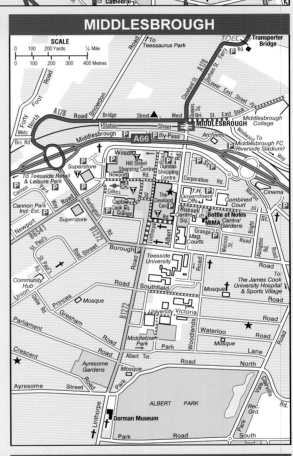

MEDWAY TOWNS

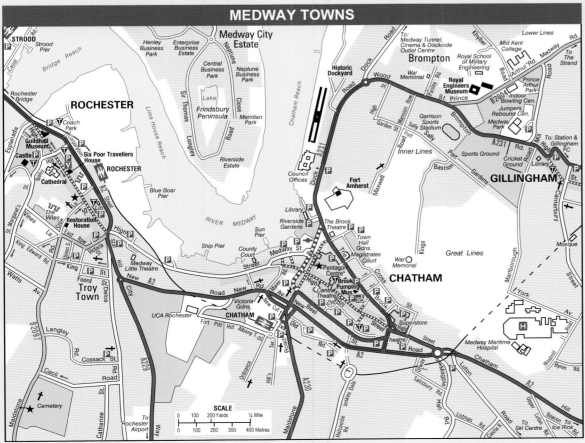

NEWCASTLE UPON TYNE

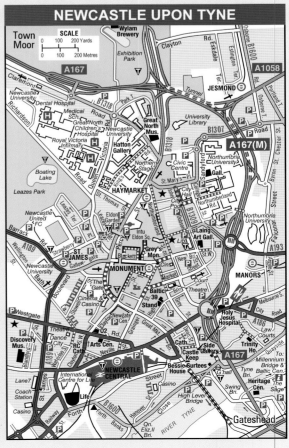

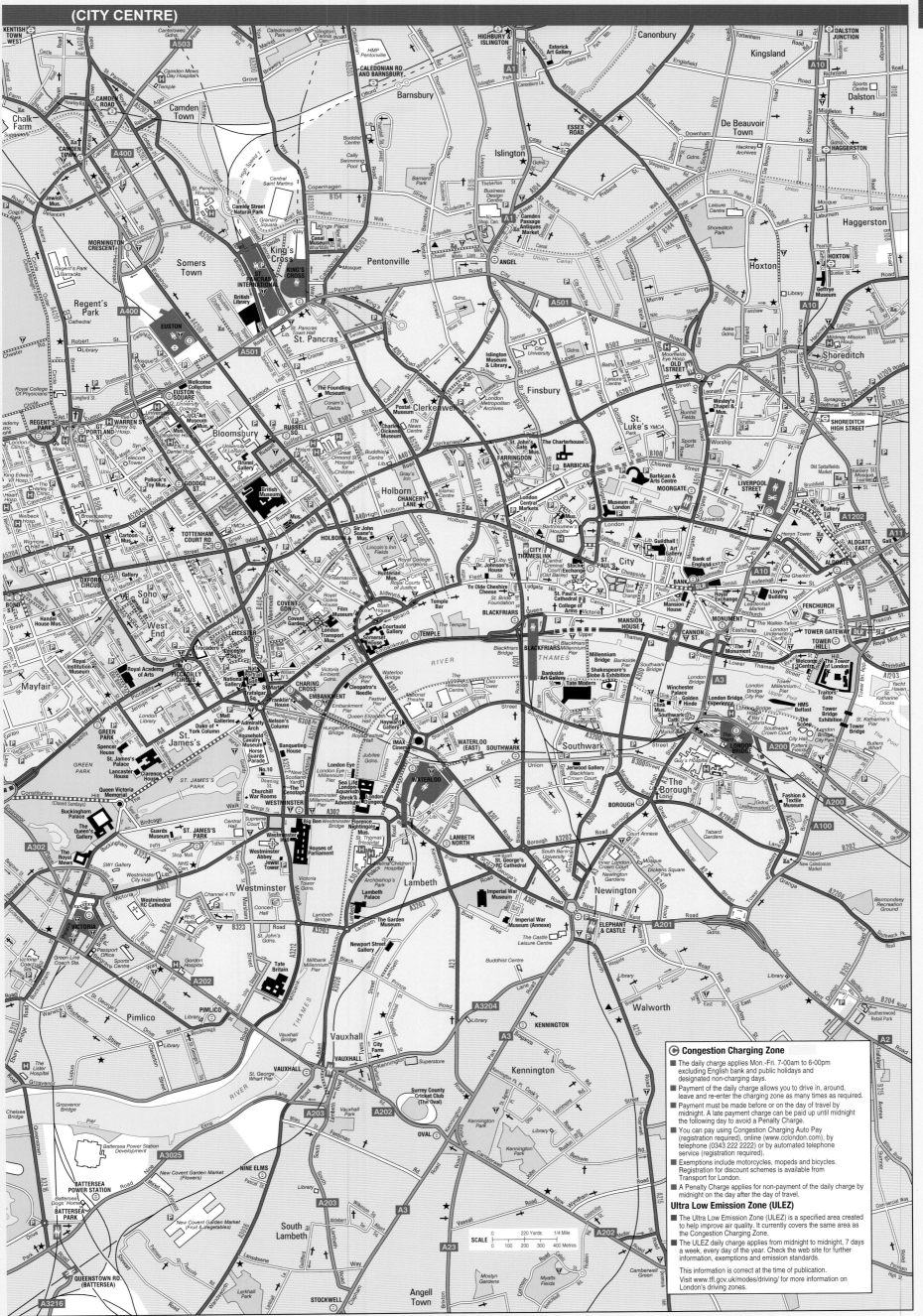

SCALE
0   220 Yards   1/4 Mile
0   100 200 300 400 Metres

MILTON KEYNES

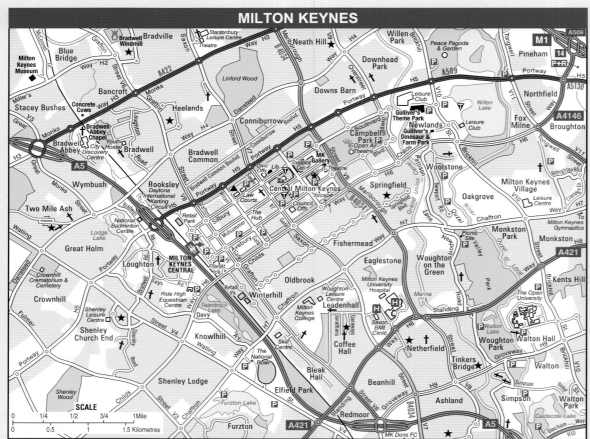

NEWPORT (CASNEWYDD)

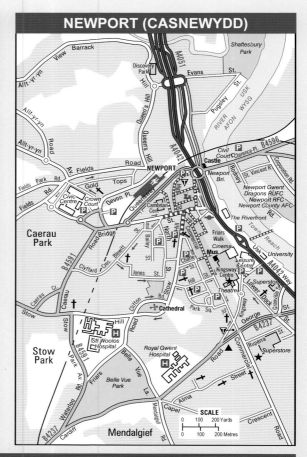

NORWICH

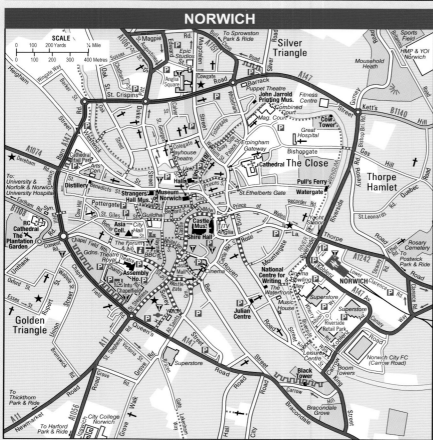

NOTTINGHAM

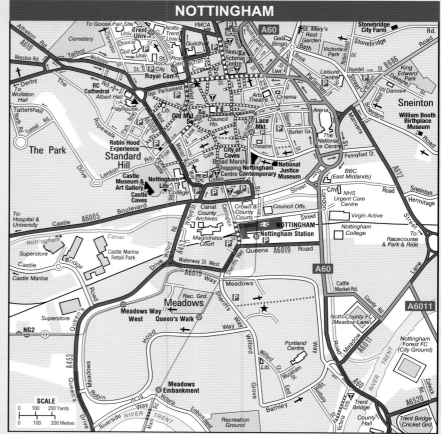

NORTHAMPTON

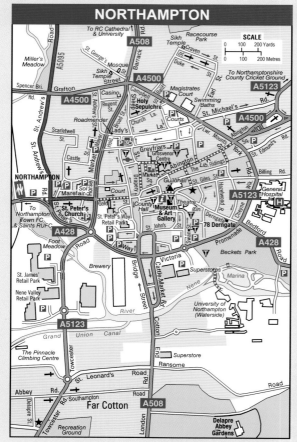

OXFORD

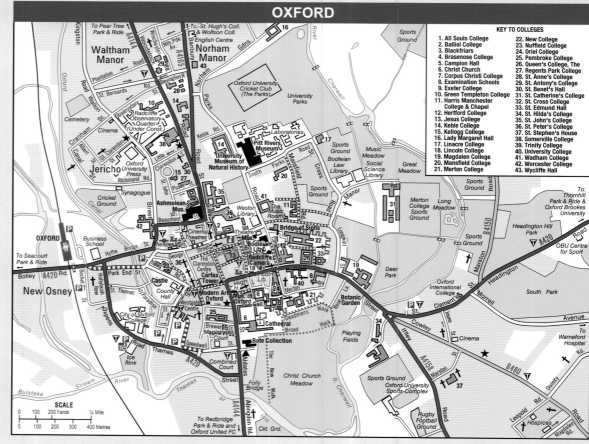

KEY TO COLLEGES

1. All Souls College
2. Balliol College
3. Blackfriars
4. Brasenose College
5. Campion Hall
6. Christ Church
7. Corpus Christi College
8. Examination Schools
9. Exeter College
10. Green Templeton College
11. Harris Manchester College & Chapel
12. Hertford College
13. Jesus College
14. Keble College
15. Kellogg College
16. Lady Margaret Hall
17. Linacre College
18. Lincoln College
19. Magdalen College
20. Mansfield College
21. Merton College
22. New College
23. Nuffield College
24. Oriel College
25. Pembroke College
26. Queen's College, The
27. Regents Park College
28. St. Anne's College
29. St. Antony's College
30. St. Benet's Hall
31. St. Catherine's College
32. St. Cross College
33. St. Edmund Hall
34. St. Hilda's College
35. St. John's College
36. St. Peter's College
37. St. Stephen's House
38. Somerville College
39. Trinity College
40. University College
41. Wadham College
42. Worcester College
43. Wycliffe Hall

OBAN
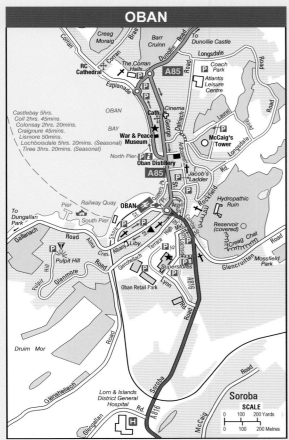

PERTH
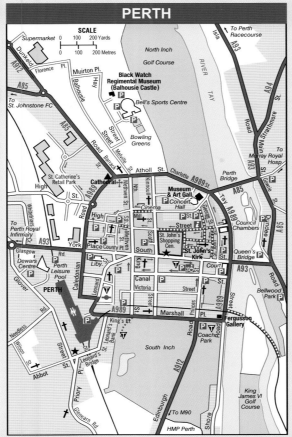

PETERBOROUGH
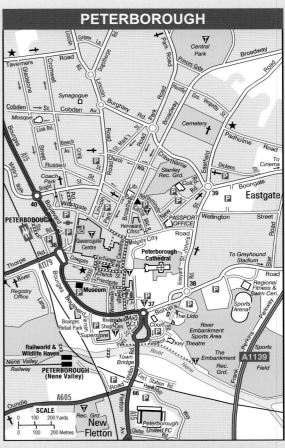

PLYMOUTH
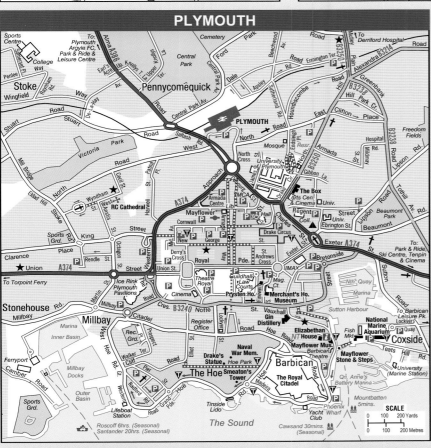

PORTSMOUTH
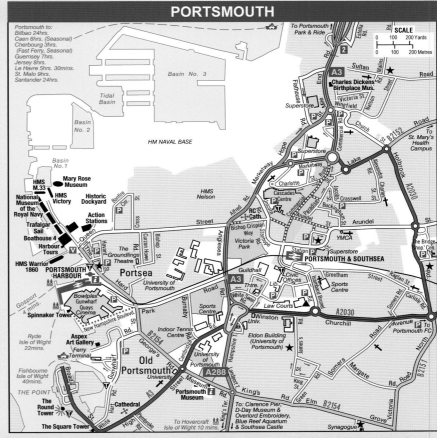

PRESTON
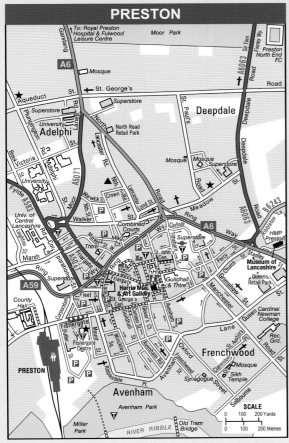

READING
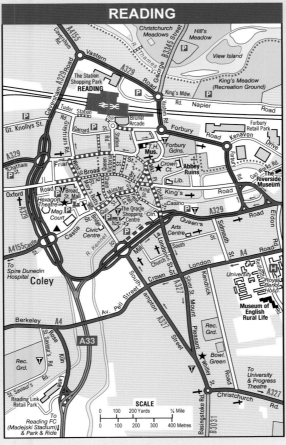

SALISBURY
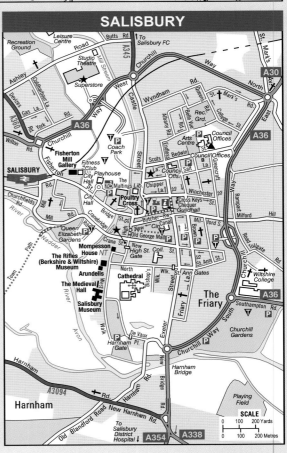

SHEFFIELD

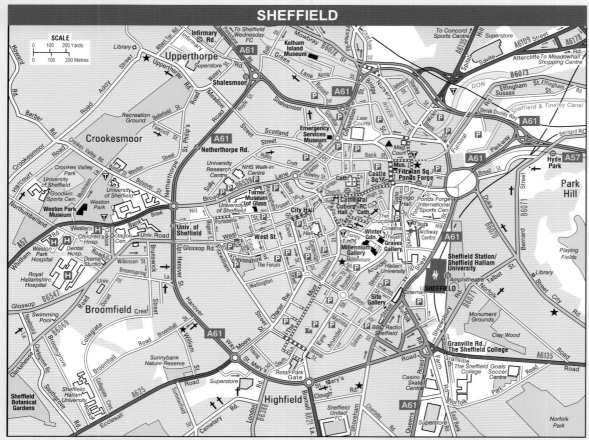

SHREWSBURY

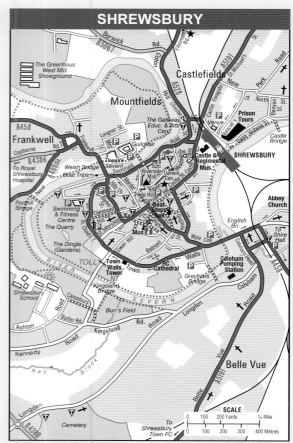

SOUTHAMPTON

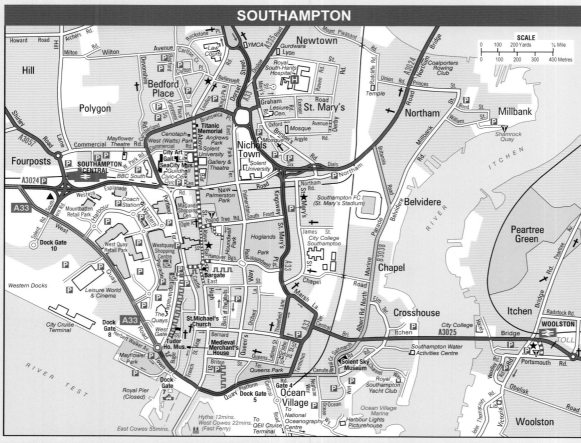

STIRLING

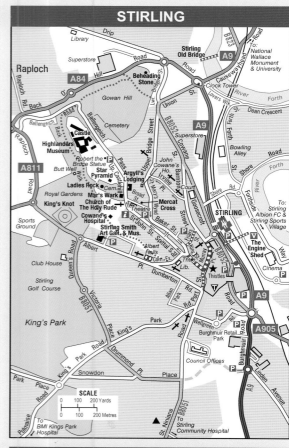

STOKE-ON-TRENT

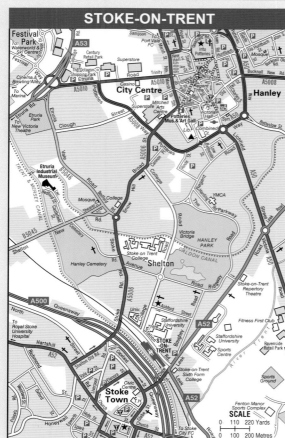

STRATFORD UPON AVON

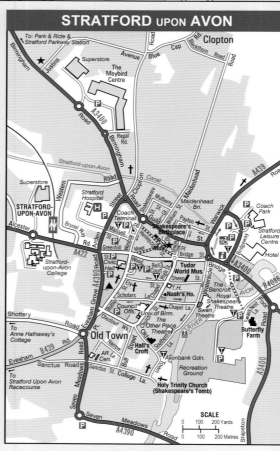

SUNDERLAND

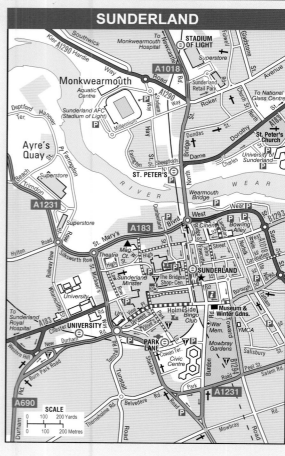

SWANSEA (ABERTAWE)
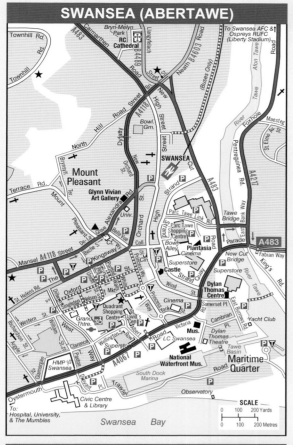

SWINDON
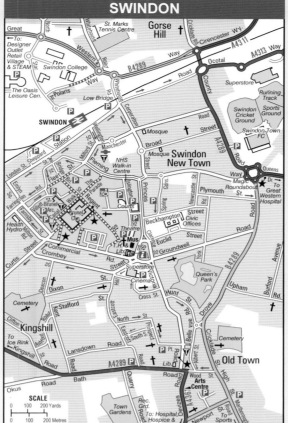

TAUNTON
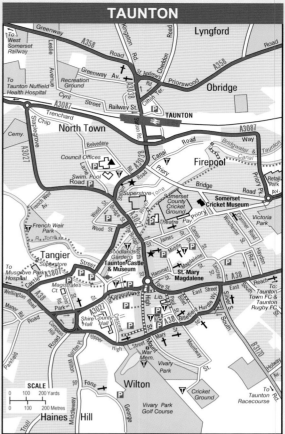

WINCHESTER
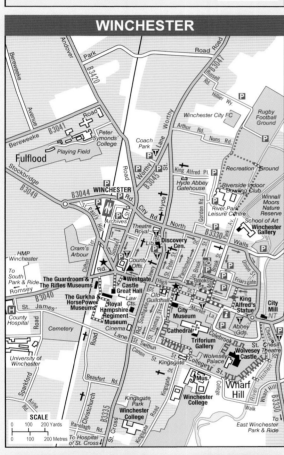

WINDSOR
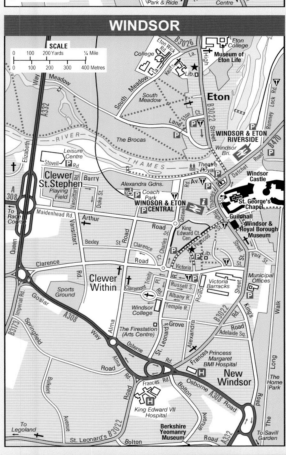

WOLVERHAMPTON
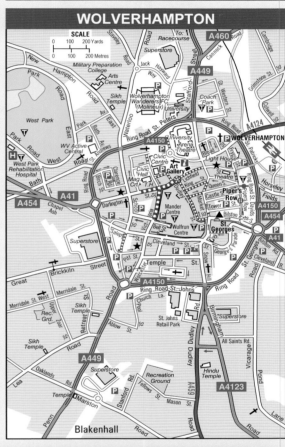

WORCESTER
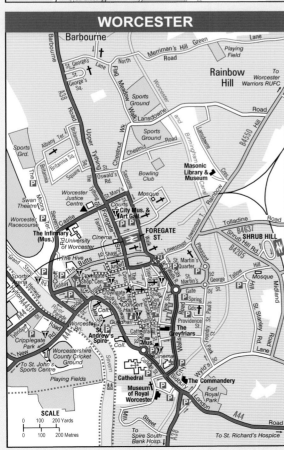

YORK
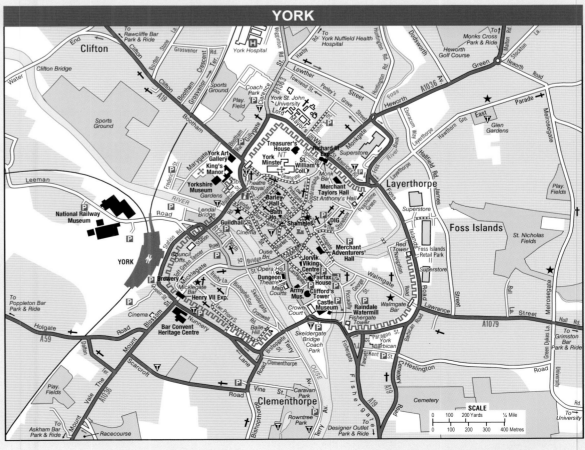

HARWICH

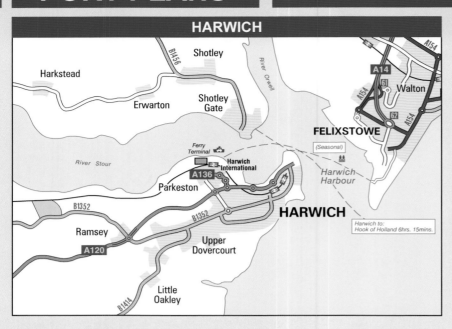

KINGSTON UPON HULL

NEWCASTLE UPON TYNE

NEWHAVEN

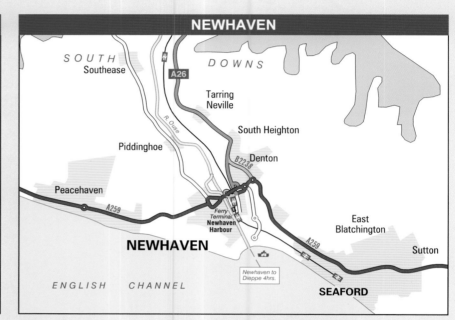

PEMBROKE DOCK (DOC PENFRO)

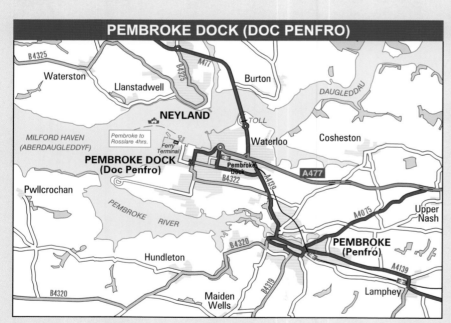

POOLE

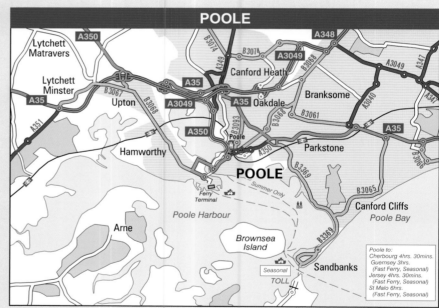

PORTSMOUTH

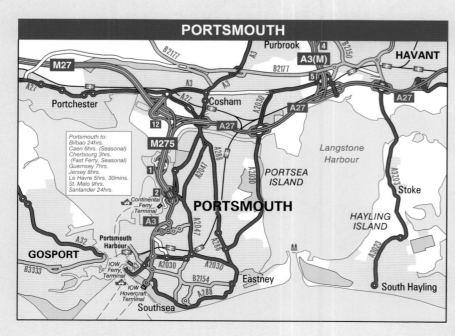

WEYMOUTH

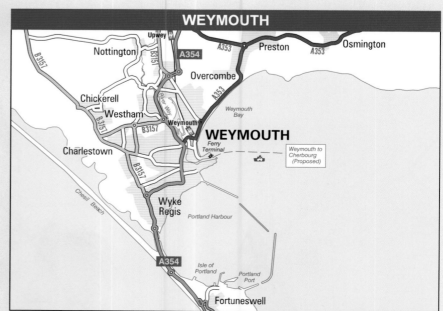

BIRMINGHAM

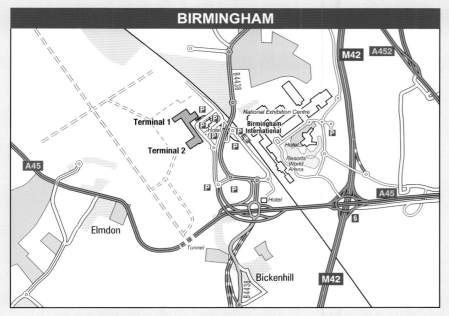

EAST MIDLANDS

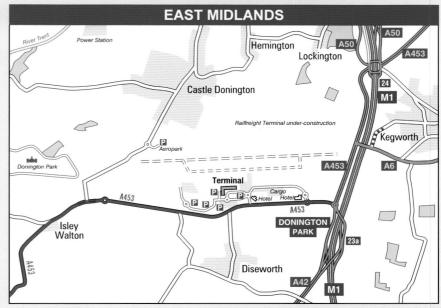

GLASGOW

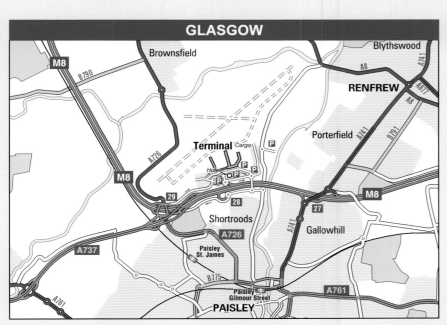

LONDON GATWICK

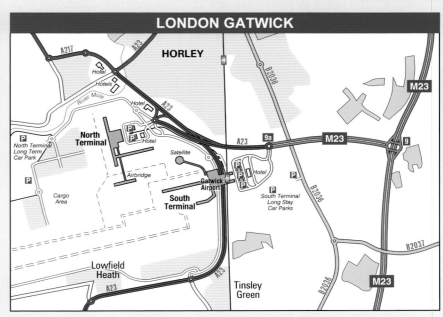

LONDON HEATHROW

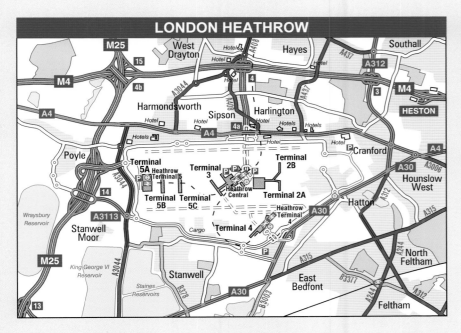

LONDON LUTON

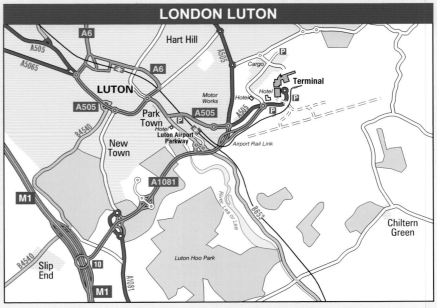

LONDON STANSTED

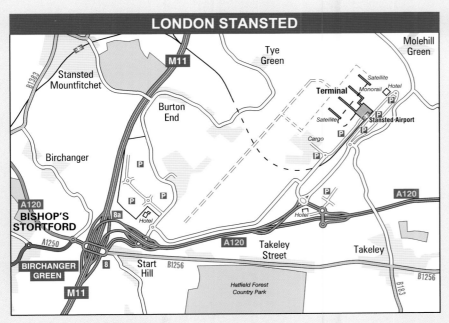

MANCHESTER

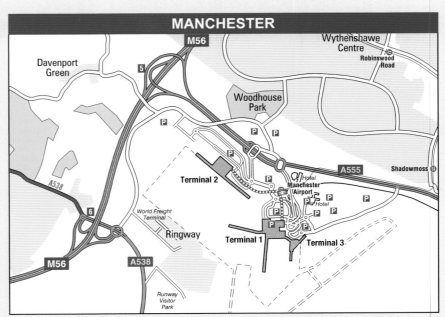

(1) A strict alphabetical order is used e.g. An Dùnan follows Andreas but precedes Andwell.

(2) The map reference given refers to the actual map square in which the town spot or built-up area is located and not to the place name.

(3) Major towns and destinations are shown in bold, i.e. **Aberdeen.** *Aber* 192 (3G 153)
Page references for Town Plan entries are shown first.

(4) Where two or more places of the same name occur in the same County or Unitary Authority, the nearest large town is also given;
e.g. Achiemore. *High* nr. Durness . . . .2D 166 indicates that Achiemore is located in square 2D on page 166 and is situated near Durness in the Unitary Authority of Highland.

(5) Only one reference is given although due to page overlaps the place may appear on more than one page.

COUNTIES and UNITARY AUTHORITIES with the abbreviations used in this index

Aberdeen : *Aber*
Aberdeenshire : *Abers*
Angus : *Ang*
Antrim & Newtownabbey : *Ant*
Ards & North Down : *Ards*
Argyll & Bute : *Arg*
Armagh, Banbridge & Craigavon : *Arm*
Bath & N E Somerset : *Bath*
Bedford : *Bed*
Belfast : *Bel*
Blackburn with Darwen : *Bkbn*
Blackpool : *Bkpl*
Blaenau Gwent : *Blae*
Bournemouth : *Bour*
Bracknell Forest : *Brac*
Bridgend : *B'end*
Brighton & Hove : *Brig*
Bristol : *Bris*
Buckinghamshire : *Buck*
Caerphilly : *Cphy*
Cambridgeshire : *Cambs*
Cardiff : *Card*

Carmarthenshire : *Carm*
Causeway Coast & Glens : *Caus*
Central Bedfordshire : *C Beds*
Ceredigion : *Cdgn*
Cheshire East : *Ches E*
Cheshire West & Chester : *Ches W*
Clackmannanshire : *Clac*
Conwy : *Cnwy*
Cornwall : *Corn*
Cumbria : *Cumb*
Darlington : *Darl*
Denbighshire : *Den*
Derby : *Derb*
Derbyshire : *Derbs*
Derry & Strabane : *Derr*
Devon : *Devn*
Dorset : *Dors*
Dumfries & Galloway : *Dum*
Dundee : *D'dee*
Durham : *Dur*
East Ayrshire : *E Ayr*
East Dunbartonshire : *E Dun*
East Lothian : *E Lot*

East Renfrewshire : *E Ren*
East Riding of Yorkshire : *E Yor*
East Sussex : *E Sus*
Edinburgh : *Edin*
Essex : *Essx*
Falkirk : *Falk*
Fermanagh & Omagh : *Ferm*
Fife : *Fife*
Flintshire : *Flin*
Glasgow : *Glas*
Gloucestershire : *Glos*
Greater London : *G Lon*
Greater Manchester : *G Man*
Gwynedd : *Gwyn*
Halton : *Hal*
Hampshire : *Hants*
Hartlepool : *Hart*
Herefordshire : *Here*
Hertfordshire : *Herts*
Highland : *High*
Inverclyde : *Inv*
Isle of Anglesey : *IOA*
Isle of Man : *IOM*

Isle of Wight : *IOW*
Isles of Scilly : *IOS*
Kent : *Kent*
Kingston upon Hull : *Hull*
Lancashire : *Lanc*
Leicester : *Leic*
Leicestershire : *Leics*
Lincolnshire : *Linc*
Lisburn & Castlereagh : *Lis*
Luton : *Lutn*
Medway : *Medw*
Merseyside : *Mers*
Merthyr Tydfil : *Mer T*
Mid & East Antrim : *ME Ant*
Middlesbrough : *Midd*
Midlothian : *Midl*
Mid Ulster : *M Ulst*
Milton Keynes : *Mil*
Monmouthshire : *Mon*
Moray : *Mor*
Neath Port Talbot : *Neat*
Newport : *Newp*
Newry, Mourne & Down : *New M*

Norfolk : *Norf*
Northamptonshire : *Nptn*
North Ayrshire : *N Ayr*
North East Lincolnshire : *NE Lin*
North Lanarkshire : *N Lan*
North Lincolnshire : *N Lin*
North Somerset : *N Som*
Northumberland : *Nmbd*
North Yorkshire : *N Yor*
Nottingham : *Nott*
Nottinghamshire : *Notts*
Orkney : *Orkn*
Oxfordshire : *Oxon*
Pembrokeshire : *Pemb*
Perth & Kinross : *Per*
Peterborough : *Pet*
Plymouth : *Plym*
Poole : *Pool*
Portsmouth : *Port*
Powys : *Powy*
Reading : *Read*
Redcar & Cleveland : *Red C*
Renfrewshire : *Ren*

Rhondda Cynon Taff : *Rhon*
Rutland : *Rut*
Scottish Borders : *Bord*
Shetland : *Shet*
Shropshire : *Shrp*
Slough : *Slo*
Somerset : *Som*
Southampton : *Sotn*
South Ayrshire : *S Ayr*
Southend-on-Sea : *S'end*
South Gloucestershire : *S Glo*
South Lanarkshire : *S Lan*
South Yorkshire : *S Yor*
Staffordshire : *Staf*
Stirling : *Stir*
Stockton-on-Tees : *Stoc T*
Stoke-on-Trent : *Stoke*
Suffolk : *Suff*
Surrey : *Surr*
Swansea : *Swan*
Swindon : *Swin*
Telford & Wrekin : *Telf*
Thurrock : *Thur*

Torbay : *Torb*
Torfaen : *Torf*
Tyne & Wear : *Tyne*
Vale of Glamorgan, The : *V Glam*
Warrington : *Warr*
Warwickshire : *Warw*
West Berkshire : *W Ber*
West Dunbartonshire : *W Dun*
Western Isles : *W Isl*
West Lothian : *W Lot*
West Midlands : *W Mid*
West Sussex : *W Sus*
West Yorkshire : *W Yor*
Wiltshire : *Wilts*
Windsor & Maidenhead : *Wind*
Wokingham : *Wok*
Worcestershire : *Worc*
Wrexham : *Wrex*
York : *York*

INDEX

Annscroft—Bampton

Annscroft. Shrp 5G 71
An Sailean. High 2A 140
Ansdell. Lanc 2B 90
Ansford. Som 3B 22
Ansley. Warw 1G 61
Anslow. Staf 3G 73
Anslow Gate. Staf 3F 73
Ansteadbrook. Surr 2A 26
Anstey. Herts 2E 53
Anstey. Leics 5C 74
Anston. S Lan 5D 128
Anstruther Easter. Fife 3H 137
Anstruther Wester. Fife 3H 137
Ansty. Warw 2A 62
Ansty. W Sus 3D 27
Ansty. Wilts 4E 23
An Taobh Tuath. W Isl 1E 170
An t-Aodann Ban. High 3C 154
An t Ath Leathann. High 1E 147
An Teanga. High 3E 147
Anthill Common. Hants 1E 17
Anthorn. Cumb 4C 112
Antingham. Norf 2E 79
An t-Ob. W Isl 9C 171
Anton's Gowt. Linc 1B 76
Antony. Corn 3A 8
An t-Ord. High 2E 147
Antrim. Ant 8H 175
Antrobus. Ches W 3A 84
Anvil Corner. Devn 2D 10
Anwick. Linc 5A 88
Anwoth. Dum 4C 110
Apethorpe. Nptn 1H 63
Apeton. Staf 4C 72
Apley. Linc 3A 88
Apperknowle. Derbs 3A 86
Apperley. Glos 3D 48
Apperley Dene. Nmbd 4D 114
Appersett. N Yor 5B 104
Appin. Arg 4D 140
Appleby. N Lin 3C 94
Appleby-in-Westmorland. Cumb 2H 103
Appleby Magna. Leics 5H 73
Appleby Parva. Leics 5H 73
Applecross. High 4G 155
Appledore. Devn
nr. Bideford 3E 19
nr. Tiverton 1D 12
Appledore. Kent 3D 28
Appledore Heath. Kent 2D 28
Appleford. Oxon 2D 36
Applegarthtown. Dum 1C 112
Applemore. Hants 2B 16
Appleshaw. Hants 2B 24
Applethwaite. Cumb 2D 102
Appleton. Hal 2H 83
Appleton. Oxon 5C 50
Appleton-le-Moors. N Yor 1B 100
Appleton-le-Street. N Yor 2B 100
Appleton Roebuck. N Yor 5H 99
Appleton Thorn. Warr 2A 84
Appleton Wiske. N Yor 4A 106
Appletree. Nptn 1C 50
Appletreehall. Bord 3H 119
Appletreewick. N Yor 3C 98
Appley. Som 4D 20
Appley Bridge. Lanc 3D 90
Apse Heath. IOW 4D 16
Apsley End. C Beds 2B 52
Apuldram. W Sus 2G 17
Arabella. High 1C 158
Arasaig. High 5E 147
Arbeadie. Abers 4D 152
Arberth. Pemb 3F 43
Arbirlot. Ang 4F 145
Arborfield. Wok 5F 37
Arborfield Cross. Wok 5F 37
Arborfield Garrison. Wok 5F 37
Arbourthorne. S Yor 2A 86
Arbroath. Ang 4F 145
Arbuthnott. Abers 1H 145
Arcan. High 3H 157
Archargary. High 3H 167
Archdeacon Newton. Darl 3F 105
Archiestown. Mor 4G 159
Arclid. Ches E 4B 84
Arclid Green. Ches E 4B 84
Ardachu. High 3D 164
Ardalanish. Arg 2A 132
Ardaneaskan. High 5H 155
Ardarroch. High 5H 155
Ardbeg. Arg
nr. Dunoon 1C 126
on Islay 5C 124
on Isle of Bute 3B 126
Ardboe. M Ulst 2D 178
Ardcharnich. High 5F 163
Ardchiavaig. Arg 2A 132
Ardchonnell. Arg 2G 133
Ardchrishnish. Arg 1B 132
Ardchronie. High 5D 164
Ardchullarie. Stir 2E 135
Ardchyle. Stir 1E 135
Ard-dhubh. High 4G 155
Arddleen. Powy 4E 71
Arddlîn. Powy 4E 71
Ardechive. High 4D 148
Ardeley. Herts 3D 52
Ardelve. High 1A 148
Arden. Arg 1E 127
Ardendrain. High 5H 157
Arden Hall. N Yor 5C 106
Ardens Grafton. Warw 5F 61
Ardentinny. Arg 1C 126
Ardeonaig. Stir 5D 142
Ardersier. High 3B 158
Ardery. High 2B 140
Ardessie. High 5E 163
Ardfern. Arg 3F 133
Ardfernal. Arg 2D 124
Ardfin. Arg 3C 124
Ardgartan. Arg 3B 134
Ardgay. High 4D 164
Ardglass. New M 6K 179
Ardgour. High 2E 141
Ardheslaig. High 3G 155
Ardindrean. High 5F 163
Ardingly. W Sus 3E 27
Ardington. Oxon 3C 36
Ardlamont House. Arg 3A 126
Ardleigh. Essx 3D 54
Ardler. Per 4B 144
Ardley. Oxon 3D 50
Ardlui. Arg 2C 134
Ardlussa. Arg 1E 125
Ardmair. High 4F 163
Ardmay. Arg 3B 134
Ardmillan. Ards 3K 179
Ardminish. Arg 5E 125
Ardmolich. High 1B 140
Ardmore. High
nr. Kinlochbervie 3C 166
nr. Tain 5E 164
Ardnacross. Arg 4G 139
Ardnadam. Arg 1C 126
Ardnagrask. High 4H 157
Ardnamurach. High 4G 147
Ardnarff. High 5A 156
Ardnastang. High 2C 140
Ardoch. Per 5H 143
Ardochy House. High 3E 148
Ardpatrick. Arg 3F 125
Ardrishaig. Arg 1G 125
Ardroag. High 4B 154
Ardross. High 1A 158
Ardrossan. N Ayr 5D 126
Ardshealach. High 2A 140
Ardsley. S Yor 4D 93
Ardslignish. High 2G 139
Ardstraw. Derr 4E 176
Ardtalla. Arg 4C 124
Ardtalnaig. Per 5E 142
Ardtoe. High 1A 140
Arduaine. Arg 2E 133
Ardullie. High 2H 157
Ardvasar. High 3E 147
Ardvorlich. Per 1F 135
Ardwell. Dum 5G 109
Ardwell. Mor 5A 160
Arean. High 1A 140
Areley Common. Worc 3C 60
Areley Kings. Worc 3C 60
Arford. Hants 3G 25
Argoed. Cphy 2E 33
Argoed Mill. Powy 4B 58
Aridhglas. Arg 2B 132
Arinacrinachd. High 3G 155
Arinagour. Arg 3D 138
Arisaig. High 5E 147
Ariundle. High 2C 140
Arivegaig. High 2A 140
Arkendale. N Yor 3F 99
Arkesden. Essx 2E 53
Arkholme. Lanc 2E 97
Arkle Town. N Yor 4D 104
Arkley. G Lon 1D 38
Arksey. S Yor 4F 93
Arkwright Town. Derbs 3B 86
Arlecdon. Cumb 3B 102
Arlescote. Warw 1B 50
Arlesey. C Beds 2B 52
Arleston. Telf 4A 72
Arley. Ches E 2A 84
Arlingham. Glos 4C 48
Arlington. Devn 2G 19
Arlington. E Sus 5G 27
Arlington. Glos 5G 49
Arlington Beccott. Devn 2G 19
Armadail. High 3E 147
Armadale. High
nr. Isleornsay 3E 147
nr. Strathy 2H 167
Armadale. W Lot 3C 128
Armagh. Arm 5C 178
Armathwaite. Cumb 5G 113
Arminghall. Norf 5E 79
Armitage. Staf 4E 73
Armitage Bridge. W Yor 3B 92
Armley. W Yor 1C 92
Armoy. Caus 3G 175
The Arms. Norf 1A 66
Armscote. Warw 1H 49
Armston. Nptn 2H 63
Armthorpe. S Yor 4G 93
Arncliffe. N Yor 2B 98
Arncliffe Cote. N Yor 2B 98
Arncroach. Fife 3H 137
Arne. Dors 4E 15
Arnesby. Leics 1D 62
Arnicle. Arg 2B 122
Arnisdale. High 2G 147
Arnish. High 4E 155
Arniston. Midl 3G 129
Arnol. W Isl 3F 171
Arnold. E Yor 5F 101
Arnold. Notts 1C 74
Arnprior. Stir 4F 135
Arnside. Cumb 2D 96
Aros Mains. Arg 4G 139
Arpafeelie. High 3A 158
Arrad Foot. Cumb 1C 96
Arram. E Yor 5E 101
Arras. E Yor 5D 100
Arrathorne. N Yor 5E 105
Arreton. IOW 4D 16
Arrington. Cambs 5C 64
Arrochar. Arg 3B 134
Arrow. Warw 5E 61
Arscaig. High 2C 164
Artafallie. High 4A 158
Arthington. W Yor 5E 99
Arthingworth. Nptn 2E 63
Arthog. Gwyn 4F 69
Arthrath. Abers 5G 161
Arthurstone. Per 4B 144
Articlave. Caus 3D 174
Artigarvan. Derr 2F 176
Artikelly. Caus 4C 174
Artington. Surr 1A 26
Arundel. W Sus 5B 26
Asby. Cumb 2B 102
Ascog. Arg 3C 126
Ascot. Wind 4A 38
Ascott-under-Wychwood. Oxon 4B 50
Asenby. N Yor 2F 99
Asfordby. Leics 4E 74
Asfordby Hill. Leics 4E 74
Asgarby. Linc
nr. Horncastle 4C 88
nr. Sleaford 1A 76
Ash. Devn 4E 9
Ash. Dors 1D 14
Ash. Kent
nr. Sandwich 5G 41
nr. Swanley 4H 39
Ash. Som 4H 21
Ash. Surr 1G 25
Ashampstead. W Ber 4D 36
Ashbocking. Suff 5D 66
Ashbourne. Derbs 1F 73
Ashbrittle. Som 4D 20
Ashbrook. Shrp 1G 59
Ashburton. Devn 2D 8
Ashbury. Devn 3F 11
Ashbury. Oxon 3A 36
Ashby. N Lin 4B 94
Ashby by Partney. Linc 4D 88
Ashby cum Fenby. NE Lin 4F 95
Ashby de la Launde. Linc 5H 87
Ashby-de-la-Zouch. Leics 4A 74
Ashby Folville. Leics 4E 74
Ashby Magna. Leics 1C 62
Ashby Parva. Leics 2C 62
Ashby Puerorum. Linc 3C 88
Ashby St Ledgars. Nptn 4C 62
Ashby St Mary. Norf 5F 79
Ashchurch. Glos 2E 49
Ashcombe. Devn 5C 12
Ashcott. Som 3H 21
Ashdon. Essx 1F 53
Ashe. Hants 2D 24
Asheldham. Essx 5C 54
Ashen. Essx 1H 53
Ashendon. Buck 4F 51
Ashey. IOW 4D 16
Ashfield. Hants 1B 16
Ashfield. Here 3A 48
Ashfield. Shrp 2H 59
Ashfield. Stir 3G 135
Ashfield. Suff 4E 66
Ashfield Green. Suff 3E 67
Ashfold Crossways. W Sus 3D 26
Ashford. Devn
nr. Barnstaple 3F 19
nr. Kingsbridge 4C 8
Ashford. Hants 1G 15
Ashford. Kent 1E 28
Ashford. Surr 3B 38
Ashford Bowdler. Shrp 3H 59
Ashford Carbonel. Shrp 3H 59
Ashford Hill. Hants 5D 36
Ashford in the Water. Derbs 4F 85
Ashgill. S Lan 5A 128
Ash Green. Warw 2H 61
Ashgrove. Mor 2G 159
Ashill. Devn 1D 12
Ashill. Norf 5A 78
Ashill. Som 1G 13
Ashingdon. Essx 1C 40
Ashington. Nmbd 1F 115
Ashington. W Sus 4C 26
Ashkirk. Bord 2G 119
Ashleworth. Glos 3D 48
Ashley. Cambs 4F 65
Ashley. Ches E 2B 84
Ashley. Dors 2G 15
Ashley. Glos 2E 35
Ashley. Hants
nr. New Milton 3A 16
nr. Winchester 3B 24
Ashley. Kent 1H 29
Ashley. Nptn 1E 63
Ashley. Staf 2B 72
Ashley. Wilts 5D 34
Ashley Green. Buck 5H 51
Ashley Heath. Dors 2G 15
Ashley Heath. Staf 2B 72
Ashley Moor. Here 4G 59
Ash Magna. Shrp 2H 71
Ashmanhaugh. Norf 3F 79
Ashmansworth. Hants 1C 24
Ashmansworthy. Devn 1D 10
Ashmead Green. Glos 2C 34
Ash Mill. Devn 4A 20
Ashmill. Devn 3D 11
Ashmore. Dors 1E 15
Ashmore Green. W Ber 5D 36
Ashorne. Warw 5H 61
Ashover. Derbs 4A 86
Ashow. Warw 3H 61
Ash Parva. Shrp 2H 71
Ashperton. Here 1B 48
Ashprington. Devn 3E 9
Ash Priors. Som 4E 21
Ashreigney. Devn 1G 11
Ash Street. Suff 1D 54
Ashtead. Surr 5C 38
Ash Thomas. Devn 1D 12
Ashton. Corn 4D 4
Ashton. Here 4H 59
Ashton. Inv 2D 126
Ashton. Nptn
nr. Oundle 2H 63
nr. Roade 1F 51
Ashton. Pet 5A 76
Ashton Common. Wilts 1D 23
Ashton Hayes. Ches W 4H 83
Ashton-in-Makerfield. G Man 1H 83
Ashton Keynes. Wilts 2F 35
Ashton under Hill. Worc 2E 49
Ashton-under-Lyne. G Man 1D 84
Ashton upon Mersey. G Man 1B 84
Ashurst. Hants 1B 16
Ashurst. Kent 2G 27
Ashurst. Lanc 4C 90
Ashurst. W Sus 4C 26
Ashurst Wood. W Sus 2F 27
Ash Vale. Surr 1G 25
Ashwater. Devn 3D 11
Ashwell. Herts 2C 52
Ashwell. Rut 4F 75
Ashwellthorpe. Norf 1D 66
Ashwick. Som 2B 22
Ashwicken. Norf 4G 77
Ashwood. Staf 2C 60
Askam in Furness. Cumb 2B 96
Askern. S Yor 3F 93
Askerswell. Dors 3A 14
Askett. Buck 5G 51
Askham. Cumb 2G 103
Askham. Notts 3E 87
Askham Bryan. York 5H 99
Askham Richard. York 5H 99
Askrigg. N Yor 5C 104
Askwith. N Yor 5D 98
Aslackby. Linc 2H 75
Aslacton. Norf 1D 66
Aslockton. Notts 1E 75
Aspatria. Cumb 5C 112
Aspenden. Herts 3D 52
Asperton. Linc 2B 76
Aspley Guise. C Beds 2H 51
Aspley Heath. C Beds 2H 51
Aspull. G Man 4E 90
Asselby. E Yor 2H 93
Assington. Suff 2C 54
Assington Green. Suff 5G 65
Astbury. Ches E 4C 84
Astcote. Nptn 5D 62
Asterby. Linc 3B 88
Asterley. Shrp 5F 71
Asterton. Shrp 1F 59
Asthall. Oxon 4A 50
Asthall Leigh. Oxon 4B 50
Astle. High 4E 165
Astley. G Man 4F 91
Astley. Shrp 4H 71
Astley. Warw 2H 61
Astley. Worc 4B 60
Astley Abbotts. Shrp 1B 60
Astley Bridge. G Man 3F 91
Astley Cross. Worc 4C 60
Aston. Ches E 1A 72
Aston. Ches W 3H 83
Aston. Derbs
nr. Hope 2F 85
nr. Sudbury 2F 73
Aston. Flin 4F 83
Aston. Here 4G 59
Aston. Herts 3C 52
Aston. Oxon 5B 50
Aston. Shrp
nr. Bridgnorth 1C 60
nr. Wem 3H 71
Aston. S Yor 2B 86
Aston. Staf 1B 72
Aston. Telf 5A 72
Aston. W Mid 1E 61
Aston. Wok 3F 37
Aston Abbotts. Buck 3G 51
Aston Botterell. Shrp 2A 60
Aston-by-Stone. Staf 2D 72
Aston Cantlow. Warw 5F 61
Aston Clinton. Buck 4G 51
Aston Crews. Here 3B 48
Aston Cross. Glos 2E 49
Aston End. Herts 3C 52
Aston Eyre. Shrp 1A 60
Aston Fields. Worc 4D 60
Aston Flamville. Leics 1B 62
Aston Ingham. Here 3B 48
Aston juxta Mondrum. Ches E 5A 84
Astonlane. Shrp 1A 60
Aston le Walls. Nptn 5B 62
Aston Magna. Glos 2G 49
Aston Munslow. Shrp 2H 59
Aston on Carrant. Glos 2E 49
Aston on Clun. Shrp 2F 59
Aston-on-Trent. Derbs 3B 74
Aston Pigott. Shrp 5F 71
Aston Rogers. Shrp 5F 71
Aston Rowant. Oxon 2F 37
Aston Sandford. Buck 5F 51
Aston Somerville. Worc 2F 49
Aston Subedge. Glos 1G 49
Aston Tirrold. Oxon 3D 36
Aston Upthorpe. Oxon 3D 36
Astrop. Nptn 2D 50
Astwick. C Beds 2C 52
Astwood. Mil 1H 51
Astwood Bank. Worc 4E 61
Aswarby. Linc 2H 75
Aswardby. Linc 3C 88
Atcham. Shrp 5H 71
Atch Lench. Worc 5E 61
Athelhampton. Dors 3C 14
Athelington. Suff 3E 66
Athelney. Som 4G 21
Athelstaneford. E Lot 2B 130
Atherfield Green. IOW 5C 16
Atherington. Devn 4F 19
Atherington. W Sus 5B 26
Athersley. S Yor 4D 92
Atherstone. Warw 1H 61
Atherstone on Stour. Warw 5G 61
Atherton. G Man 4E 91
Ath-Tharracail. High 2A 140
Atlow. Derbs 1G 73
Attadale. High 5B 156
Attenborough. Notts 2C 74
Atterby. Linc 1G 87
Atterley. Shrp 1A 60
Atterton. Leics 1A 62
Attical. New M 8G 179
Attleborough. Norf 1C 66
Attleborough. Warw 1A 62
Attlebridge. Norf 4D 78
Atwick. E Yor 4F 101
Atworth. Wilts 5D 34
Auberrow. Here 1H 47
Aubourn. Linc 4G 87
Aucharnie. Abers 4D 160
Auchattie. Abers 4D 152
Auchavan. Ang 2A 144
Auchbreck. Mor 1G 151
Auchenback. E Ren 4G 127
Auchenblae. Abers 1G 145
Auchenbrack. Dum 5G 117
Auchenbreck. Arg 1B 126
Auchencairn. Dum
nr. Dalbeattie 4E 111
nr. Dumfries 1A 112
Auchencarroch. W Dun 1F 127
Auchencrow. Bord 3E 131
Auchendennan. Arg 1E 127
Auchendinny. Midl 3F 129
Auchengray. S Lan 4C 128
Auchenhalrig. Mor 2A 160
Auchenheath. S Lan 5B 128
Auchenlochan. Arg 2A 126
Auchenmade. N Ayr 5E 127
Auchenmalg. Dum 4H 109
Auchentiber. N Ayr 5E 127
Auchenvennel. Arg 1D 126
Auchindrain. Arg 3H 133
Auchininna. Abers 4D 160
Auchinleck. Dum 2B 110
Auchinleck. E Ayr 2E 117
Auchinloch. N Lan 2H 127
Auchinstarry. N Lan 2A 128
Auchleven. Abers 1D 152
Auchlochan. S Lan 1H 117
Auchlunachan. High 5F 163
Auchmillan. E Ayr 2E 117
Auchmithie. Ang 4F 145
Auchmuirbridge. Fife 3E 136
Auchmull. Ang 1E 145
Auchnacree. Ang 2D 144
Auchnafree. Per 5F 143
Auchnagallin. High 5E 159
Auchnagatt. Abers 4G 161
Aucholzie. Abers 4H 151
Auchreddie. Abers 4F 161
Auchterarder. Per 2B 136
Auchteraw. High 3F 149
Auchterderran. Fife 4E 136
Auchterhouse. Ang 5C 144
Auchtermuchty. Fife 2E 137
Auchterneed. High 3G 157
Auchtertool. Fife 4E 136
Auchtertyre. High 1G 147
Auchtubh. Stir 1E 135
Auckengill. High 2F 169
Auckley. S Yor 4G 93
Audenshaw. G Man 1D 84
Audlem. Ches E 1A 72
Audley. Staf 5B 84
Audley End. Essx 2F 53
Audmore. Staf 3C 72
Auds. Abers 2D 160
Augher. M Ulst 4L 177
Aughertree. Cumb 1D 102
Aughnacloy. M Ulst 4A 178
Aughton. E Yor 1H 93
Aughton. Lanc
nr. Lancaster 3E 97
nr. Ormskirk 4B 90
Aughton. S Yor 2B 86
Aughton. Wilts 1H 23
Aughton Park. Lanc 4C 90
Auldearn. High 3D 158
Aulden. Here 5G 59
Auldgirth. Dum 1G 111
Auldhouse. S Lan 4H 127
Ault a' chruinn. High 1B 148
Aultbea. High 5C 162
Aultdearg. High 2E 157
Aultgrishan. High 5B 162
Aultguish Inn. High 1F 157
Ault Hucknall. Derbs 4B 86
Aultibea. High 1H 165
Aultiphurst. High 2A 168
Aultivullin. High 2A 168
Aultmore. Mor 3B 160
Aultnamain Inn. High 5D 164
Aunby. Linc 4H 75
Aunsby. Linc 2H 75
Aust. S Glo 3A 34
Austerfield. S Yor 1D 86
Austin Fen. Linc 1C 88
Austrey. Warw 5G 73
Austwick. N Yor 3G 97
Authorpe. Linc 2D 88
Authorpe Row. Linc 3E 89
Avebury. Wilts 5G 35
Avebury Trusloe. Wilts 5F 35
Aveley. Thur 2G 39
Avening. Glos 2D 35
Averham. Notts 5E 87
Aveton Gifford. Devn 4C 8
Avielochan. High 2D 150
Aviemore. High 2C 150
Avington. Hants 3D 24
Avoch. High 3B 158
Avon. Hants 3G 15
Avonbridge. Falk 2C 128
Avon Dassett. Warw 5B 62
Avonmouth. Bris 4A 34
Avonwick. Devn 3D 8
Awbridge. Hants 4B 24
Awliscombe. Devn 2E 13
Awre. Glos 5C 48
Awsworth. Notts 1B 74
Axbridge. Som 1H 21
Axford. Hants 2E 24
Axford. Wilts 5H 35
Axminster. Devn 3G 13
Axmouth. Devn 3F 13
Aycliffe Village. Dur 2F 105
Aydon. Nmbd 3D 114
Aykley Heads. Dur 5F 115
Aylburton. Glos 5B 48
Aylburton Common. Glos 5B 48
Ayle. Nmbd 5A 114
Aylesbeare. Devn 3D 12
Aylesbury. Buck 4G 51
Aylesby. NE Lin 4F 95
Aylescott. Devn 1G 11
Aylesford. Kent 5B 40
Aylesham. Kent 5G 41
Aylestone. Leic 5C 74
Aylmerton. Norf 2D 78
Aylsham. Norf 3D 78
Aylton. Here 2B 48
Aylworth. Glos 3G 49
Aymestrey. Here 4G 59
Aynho. Nptn 2D 50
Ayot Green. Herts 4C 52
Ayot St Lawrence. Herts 4B 52
Ayot St Peter. Herts 4C 52
Ayr. S Ayr 2C 116
Ayres of Selivoe. Shet 7D 173
Ayreville. Torb 2E 9
Aysgarth. N Yor 1C 98
Ayshford. Devn 1D 12
Ayside. Cumb 1C 96
Ayston. Rut 5F 75
Ayton. Bord 3F 131
Aywick. Shet 3G 173
Azerley. N Yor 2E 99

B

Babbacombe. Torb 2F 9
Babbinswood. Shrp 2F 71
Babbs Green. Herts 4D 53
Babcary. Som 4A 22
Babel. Carm 2B 46
Babell. Flin 3D 82
Babingley. Norf 3F 77
Bablock Hythe. Oxon 5C 50
Babraham. Cambs 5E 65
Babworth. Notts 2D 86
Bac. W Isl 3G 171
Bachau. IOA 2D 80
Bacheldre. Powy 1E 59
Bachymbyd Fawr. Den 4C 82
Backaland. Orkn 4E 172
Backaskaill. Orkn 2D 172
Backbarrow. Cumb 1C 96
Backe. Carm 3G 43
Backfolds. Abers 3H 161
Backford. Ches W 3G 83
Backhill. Abers 5E 161
Backhill of Clackriach. Abers 4G 161
Backies. High 3F 165
Backmuir of New Gilston. Fife 3G 137
Back of Keppoch. High 5E 147
Back Street. Suff 5G 65
Backwell. N Som 5H 33
Backworth. Tyne 2G 115
Bacon End. Essx 4G 53
Baconsthorpe. Norf 2D 78
Bacton. Here 2G 47
Bacton. Norf 2F 79
Bacton. Suff 4C 66
Bacton Green. Norf 2F 79
Bacup. Lanc 2G 91
Badachonacher. High 1A 158
Badachro. High 1G 155
Badanloch Lodge. High 5H 167
Badavanich. High 3D 156
Badbury. Swin 3G 35
Badby. Nptn 5C 62
Badcall. High 3C 166
Badcaul. High 4E 163
Baddeley Green. Stoke 5D 84
Baddesley Clinton. W Mid 3G 61
Baddesley Ensor. Warw 1G 61
Baddidarach. High 1E 163
Baddoch. Abers 5F 151
Badenscallie. High 3E 163
Badenscoth. Abers 5E 160
Badentarbat. High 2E 163
Badgall. Corn 4C 10
Badgers Mount. Kent 4F 39
Badgeworth. Glos 4E 49
Badgworth. Som 1G 21
Badicaul. High 1F 147
Badingham. Suff 4F 67
Badlesmere. Kent 5E 40
Badlipster. High 4E 169
Badluarach. High 4D 163
Badminton. S Glo 3D 34
Badnaban. High 1E 163
Badnabay. High 4C 166
Badnagie. High 5D 168
Badnellan. High 3F 165
Badninish. High 4E 165
Badrallach. High 4E 163
Badsey. Worc 1F 49
Badshot Lea. Surr 2G 25
Badsworth. W Yor 3E 93
Badwell Ash. Suff 4B 66
Bae Cinmel. Cnwy 2B 82
Bae Colwyn. Cnwy 3A 82
Bae Penrhyn. Cnwy 2H 81
Bagby. N Yor 1G 99
Bag Enderby. Linc 3C 88
Bagendon. Glos 5F 49
Bagginswood. Shrp 2A 60
Bàgh a Chàise. W Isl 1E 170
Bàgh a' Chaisteil. W Isl 9B 170
Bagham. Kent 5E 41
Baghasdal. W Isl 7C 170
Bagh Mor. W Isl 3D 170
Bagh Shiarabhagh. W Isl 8C 170
Bagillt. Flin 3E 82
Baginton. Warw 3H 61
Baglan. Neat 2A 32
Bagley. Shrp 3G 71
Bagley. Som 2H 21
Bagnall. Staf 5D 84
Bagnor. W Ber 5C 36
Bagshot. Surr 4A 38
Bagshot. Wilts 5B 36
Bagstone. S Glo 3B 34
Bagthorpe. Norf 2G 77
Bagthorpe. Notts 5B 86
Bagworth. Leics 5B 74
Bagwy Llydiart. Here 3H 47
Baildon. W Yor 1B 92
Baildon Green. W Yor 1B 92
Baile. W Isl 1E 170
Baile Ailein. W Isl 5E 171
Baile an Truiseil. W Isl 2F 171
Baile Boidheach. Arg 2F 125
Baile Glas. W Isl 3D 170
Bailemeonach. Arg 4A 140
Baile Mhartainn. W Isl 1C 170
Baile MhicPhail. W Isl 1D 170
Baile Mor. W Isl 2C 170
Baile Mór. Arg 2A 132
Baile nan Cailleach. W Isl 3C 170
Baile Raghaill. W Isl 2C 170
Bailey Green. Hants 4E 25
Baileyhead. Cumb 1G 113
Baileysmill. Lis 4H 179
Bailiesward. Abers 5B 160
Bail' Iochdrach. W Isl 3D 170
Baillieston. Glas 3H 127
Bailrigg. Lanc 4D 97
Bail Uachdraich. W Isl 2D 170
Bail' Ur Tholastaidh. W Isl 3H 171
Bainbridge. N Yor 5C 104
Bainsford. Falk 1B 128
Bainshole. Abers 5D 160
Bainton. E Yor 4D 100
Bainton. Oxon 3D 50
Bainton. Pet 5H 75
Baintown. Fife 3F 137
Baker Street. Thur 2H 39
Bakewell. Derbs 4G 85
Bala. Gwyn 2B 70
Y Bala. Gwyn 2B 70
Balachuirn. High 4E 155
Balbeg. High
nr. Cannich 5G 157
nr. Loch Ness 1G 149
Balbeggie. Per 1D 136
Balblair. High
nr. Bonar Bridge 4C 164
nr. Invergordon 2B 158
nr. Inverness 4H 157
Balby. S Yor 4F 93
Balcathie. Ang 5F 145
Balchladich. High 1E 163
Balchraggan. High 4H 157
Balchrick. High 3B 166
Balcombe. W Sus 2E 27
Balcombe Lane. W Sus 2E 27
Balcurvie. Fife 3F 137
Baldersby. N Yor 2F 99
Baldersby St James. N Yor 2F 99
Balderstone. Lanc 1E 91
Balderton. Ches W 4F 83
Balderton. Notts 5F 87
Baldinnie. Fife 2G 137
Baldock. Herts 2C 52
Baldrine. IOM 3D 108
Baldslow. E Sus 4C 28
Baldwin. IOM 3C 108
Baldwinholme. Cumb 4E 113
Baldwin's Gate. Staf 2B 72
Bale. Norf 2C 78
Balearn. Abers 3H 161
Balemartine. Arg 4A 138
Balephetrish. Arg 4B 138
Balephuil. Arg 4A 138
Balerno. Edin 3E 129
Balevullin. Arg 4A 138
Balfield. Ang 2E 145
Balfour. Orkn 6D 172
Balfron. Stir 1G 127
Balgaveny. Abers 4D 160
Balgonar. Fife 4C 136
Balgowan. High 4A 150
Balgown. High 2C 154
Balgrochan. E Dun 2H 127
Balgy. High 3H 155
Balhalgardy. Abers 1E 153
Baliasta. Shet 1H 173
Baligill. High 2A 168
Balintore. Ang 3B 144
Balintore. High 1C 158
Balintraid. High 1B 158
Balk. N Yor 1G 99
Balkeerie. Ang 4C 144
Balkholme. E Yor 2A 94
Ball. Shrp 3F 71
Ballabeg. IOM 4B 108
Ballacannell. IOM 3D 108
Ballacarnane Beg. IOM 3C 108
Ballachulish. High 3E 141
Ballagyr. IOM 3B 108
Ballajora. IOM 2D 108
Ballaleigh. IOM 3C 108
Ballamodha. IOM 4B 108
Ballantrae. S Ayr 1F 109
Ballards Gore. Essx 1D 40
Ballasalla. IOM
nr. Castletown 4B 108
nr. Kirk Michael 2C 108
Ballater. Abers 4A 152
Ballaugh. IOM 2C 108
Ballencrieff. E Lot 2A 130
Ballencrieff Toll. W Lot 2C 128
Ballentoul. Per 2F 143
Ball Hill. Hants 5C 36
Ballidon. Derbs 5G 85
Balliemore. Arg
nr. Dunoon 1B 126
nr. Oban 1F 133
Ballieward. High 5E 159
Ballig. IOM 3B 108
Ballimore. Stir 2E 135
Ballinamallard. Ferm 7E 176
Ballindarragh. Ferm 6J 177
Ballingdon. Suff 1B 54
Ballinger Common. Buck 5H 51
Ballingham. Here 2A 48
Ballingry. Fife 4D 136
Ballinluig. Per 3G 143
Ballintoy. Caus 2G 175
Ballintuim. Per 3A 144
Balliveolan. Arg 4C 140
Balloan. High 3C 164
Balloch. High 4B 158
Balloch. N Lan 2A 128
Balloch. Per 2H 135
Balloch. W Dun 1E 127
Ballochan. Abers 4C 152
Ballochgoy. Arg 3B 126
Ballochmyle. E Ayr 2E 117
Ballochroy. Arg 4F 125
Balloo. Ards 3J 179
Balls Cross. W Sus 3A 26
Ball's Green. E Sus 2F 27
Ballsmill. New M 8D 178
Ballyalton. New M 5K 179
Ballybogy. Caus 3F 174
Ballycarry. ME Ant 7L 175
Ballycassidy. Ferm 7E 176
Ballycastle. Caus 2H 175
Ballyclare. Ant 7J 175
Ballyeaston. Ant 7J 175
Ballygally. ME Ant 6K 175
Ballygawley. M Ulst 4A 178
Ballygowan. Ards 3J 179
Ballygown. Arg 4F 139
Ballygrant. Arg 3B 124
Ballyhalbert. Ards 3L 179
Ballyholland. New M 7F 178
Ballyhornan. New M 5K 179
Ballykelly. Caus 4C 174
Ballykinler. New M 6J 179
Ballylesson. Lis 3H 179
Ballymagorry. Derr 2F 176
Ballymartin. New M 8H 179
Ballymena. ME Ant 6H 175
Ballymichael. N Ayr 2D 122
Ballymoney. Caus 4F 174
Ballynagard. Derr 4A 174
Ballynahinch. New M 4H 179
Ballynakilly. M Ulst 3C 178
Ballynoe. New M 5J 179
Ballynure. Ant 7K 175
Ballyrashane. Caus 3E 174
Ballyrobert. Ant 8J 175
Ballyronan. M Ulst 8F 174
Ballyroney. Arm 6G 179
Ballyscullion. Caus 3C 174
Ballystrudder. ME Ant 7L 175
Ballyvoy. Caus 2H 175
Ballyward. New M 6G 179
Ballywalter. Ards 3L 179
Ballywonard. Ant 1G 179
Balmacara. High 1G 147
Balmaclellan. Dum 2D 110
Balmacqueen. High 1D 154
Balmaha. Stir 4D 134
Balmalcolm. Fife 3F 137
Balmalloch. N Lan 2A 128
Balmeanach. High 5E 155
Balmedie. Abers 2G 153
Balmerino. Fife 1F 137
Balmerlawn. Hants 2B 16
Balmore. E Dun 2H 127
Balmore. High 4B 154
Balmullo. Fife 1G 137
Balmurrie. Dum 3H 109
Balnaboth. Ang 2C 144
Balnabruaich. High 1B 158
Balnabruich. High 5D 168
Balnacoil. High 2F 165
Balnacra. High 4B 156
Balnacroft. Abers 4G 151
Balnageith. Mor 3E 159
Balnaglaic. High 5G 157
Balnagrantach. High 5G 157
Balnaguard. Per 3G 143
Balnahard. Arg 4B 132
Balnain. High 5G 157
Balnakeil. High 2D 166
Balnaknock. High 2D 154
Balnamoon. Abers 3G 161
Balnamoon. Ang 2E 145
Balnamore. Caus 4F 174
Balnapaling. High 2B 158
Balornock. Glas 3H 127
Balquhidder. Stir 1E 135
Balsall. W Mid 3G 61
Balsall Common. W Mid 3G 61
Balscote. Oxon 1B 50
Balsham. Cambs 5E 65
Baltasound. Shet 1H 173
Balterley. Staf 5B 84
Baltersan. Dum 3B 110
Balthangie. Abers 3F 161
Baltonsborough. Som 3A 22
Balvaird. High 3H 157
Balvaird. Per 2D 136
Balvenie. Mor 4H 159
Balvicar. Arg 2E 133
Balvraid. High 2G 147
Balvraid Lodge. High 5C 158
Bamber Bridge. Lanc 2D 90
Bamber's Green. Essx 3F 53
Bamburgh. Nmbd 1F 121
Bamford. Derbs 2G 85
Bamfurlong. G Man 4D 90
Bampton. Cumb 3G 103
Bampton. Devn 4C 20

Bampton—Bishampton

Bampton. Oxon 5B 50
Bampton Grange. Cumb 3G 103
Banavie. High 1F 141
Banbridge. Arm 5F 178
Banbury. Oxon 1C 50
Bancffosfelen. Carm 4E 45
Banchory. Abers 4D 152
Banchory-Devenick. Abers 3G 153
Bancycapel. Carm 4E 45
Bancyfelin. Carm 3H 43
Banc-y-ffordd. Carm 2E 45
Banff. Abers 2D 160
Bangor. Ards 1K 179
Bangor. Gwyn 3E 81
Bangor-is-y-coed. Wrex 1F 71
Bangors. Corn 3C 10
Bangor's Green. Lanc 4B 90
Banham. Norf 2C 66
Bank. Hants 2A 16
The Bank. Ches E 5C 84
The Bank. Shrp 1A 60
Bankend. Dum 3B 112
Bankfoot. Per 5H 143
Bankglen. E Ayr 3F 117
Bankhead. Aber 2F 153
Bankhead. Abers 3D 152
Bankhead. S Lan 5B 128
Bankland. Som 4G 21
Bank Newton. N Yor 4B 98
Banknock. Falk 2A 128
Banks. Cumb 3G 113
Banks. Lanc 2B 90
Bankshill. Dum 1C 112
Bank Street. Worc 4A 60
Bank Top. Lanc 4D 90
Banners Gate. W Mid 1E 61
Banningham. Norf 3E 78
Banniskirk. High 3D 168
Bannister Green. Essx 3G 53
Bannockburn. Stir 4H 135
Banstead. Surr 5D 38
Bantham. Devn 4C 8
Banton. N Lan 2A 128
Banwell. N Som 1G 21
Banyard's Green. Suff 3F 67
Bapchild. Kent 4D 40
Bapton. Wilts 3E 23
Barabhas. W Isl 2F 171
Barabhas Iarach. W Isl 3F 171
Baramore. High 1A 140
Barassie. S Ayr 1C 116
Baravullin. Arg 4D 140
Barbaraville. High 1B 158
Barber Booth. Derbs 2F 85
Barber Green. Cumb 1C 96
Barbhas Uarach. W Isl 2F 171
Barbieston. S Ayr 3D 116
Barbon. Cumb 1F 97
Barbourne. Worc 5C 60
Barbridge. Ches E 5A 84
Barbrook. Devn 2H 19
Barby. Nptn 3C 62
Barby Nortoft. Nptn 3C 62
Barcaldine. Arg 4D 140
Barcheston. Warw 2A 50
Barclose. Cumb 3F 113
Barcombe. E Sus 4F 27
Barcombe Cross. E Sus 4F 27
Barden. N Yor 5E 105
Barden Scale. N Yor 4C 98
Bardfield End Green. Essx 2G 53
Bardfield Saling. Essx 3G 53
Bardister. Shet 4E 173
Bardnabeinne. High 4E 164
Bardney. Linc 4A 88
Bardon. Leics 4B 74
Bardon Mill. Nmbd 3A 114
Bardowie. E Dun 2G 127
Bardrainney. Inv 2E 127
Bardsea. Cumb 2C 96
Bardsey. W Yor 5F 99
Bardsley. G Man 4H 91
Bardwell. Suff 3B 66
Bare. Lanc 3D 96
Barelees. Nmbd 1C 120
Barewood. Here 5F 59
Barford. Hants 3G 25
Barford. Norf 5D 78
Barford. Warw 4G 61
Barford St John. Oxon 2C 50
Barford St Martin. Wilts 3F 23
Barford St Michael. Oxon 2C 50
Barfrestone. Kent 5G 41
Bargeddie. N Lan 3H 127
Bargod. Cphy 2E 33
Bargoed. Cphy 2E 33
Bargrennan. Dum 2A 110
Barham. Cambs 3A 64
Barham. Kent 5G 41
Barham. Suff 5D 66
Barharrow. Dum 4D 110
Bar Hill. Cambs 4C 64
Barholm. Linc 4H 75
Barkby. Leics 5D 74
Barkestone-le-Vale. Leics 2E 75
Barkham. Wok 5F 37
Barking. G Lon 2F 39
Barking. Suff 5C 66
Barkingside. G Lon 2F 39
Barking Tye. Suff 5C 66
Barkisland. W Yor 3A 92
Barkston. Linc 1G 75
Barkston Ash. N Yor 1E 93
Barkway. Herts 2D 53
Barlanark. Glas 3H 127
Barlaston. Staf 2C 72
Barlavington. W Sus 4A 26
Barlborough. Derbs 3B 86
Barlby. N Yor 1G 93
Barlestone. Leics 5B 74
Barley. Herts 2D 53
Barley. Lanc 5H 97
Barley Mow. Tyne 4F 115
Barleythorpe. Rut 5F 75
Barling. Essx 2D 40
Barlings. Linc 3H 87
Barlow. Derbs 3H 85
Barlow. N Yor 2G 93
Barlow. Tyne 3E 115
Barmby Moor. E Yor 5B 100
Barmby on the Marsh. E Yor 2G 93
Barmer. Norf 2H 77
Barming. Kent 5B 40
Barming Heath. Kent 5B 40
Barmoor. Nmbd 1E 121
Barmouth. Gwyn 4F 69
Barmpton. Darl 3A 106
Barmston. E Yor 4F 101
Barmulloch. Glas 3H 127
Barnack. Pet 5H 75
Barnacle. Warw 2A 62
Barnard Castle. Dur 3D 104
Barnard Gate. Oxon 4C 50
Barnardiston. Suff 1H 53
Barnbarroch. Dum 4F 111
Barnburgh. S Yor 4E 93
Barnby. Suff 2G 67
Barnby Dun. S Yor 4G 93
Barnby in the Willows. Notts 5F 87
Barnby Moor. Notts 2D 86
Barnes. G Lon 3D 38
Barnes Street. Kent 1H 27
Barnet. G Lon 1D 38
Barnetby le Wold. N Lin 4D 94
Barney. Norf 2B 78
Barnham. Suff 3A 66
Barnham. W Sus 5A 26
Barnham Broom. Norf 5C 78
Barnhead. Ang 3F 145
Barnhill. D'dee 5D 145
Barnhill. Mor 3F 159
Barnhill. Per 1D 136
Barnhills. Dum 2E 109
Barningham. Dur 3D 105
Barningham. Suff 3B 66
Barnoldby le Beck. NE Lin 4F 95
Barnoldswick. Lanc 5A 98
Barns Green. W Sus 3C 26
Barnsley. Glos 5F 49
Barnsley. Shrp 1B 60
Barnsley. S Yor 4D 92
Barnstaple. Devn 3F 19
Barnston. Essx 4G 53
Barnston. Mers 2E 83
Barnstone. Notts 2E 75
Barnt Green. Worc 3E 61
Barnton. Ches W 3A 84
Barnwell. Cambs 5D 64
Barnwell. Nptn 2H 63
Barnwood. Glos 4D 48
Barons Cross. Here 5G 59
The Barony. Orkn 5B 172
Barr. Dum 4G 117
Barr. S Ayr 5B 116
Barra Airport. W Isl 8B 170
Barrachan. Dum 5A 110
Barraglom. W Isl 4D 171
Barrahormid. Arg 1F 125
Barrapol. Arg 4A 138
Barrasford. Nmbd 2C 114
Barravullin. Arg 3F 133
Barregarrow. IOM 3C 108
Barrhead. E Ren 4G 127
Barrhill. S Ayr 1H 109
Barri. V Glam 5E 32
Barrington. Cambs 1D 53
Barrington. Som 1G 13
Barripper. Corn 3D 4
Barrmill. N Ayr 4E 127
Barrock. High 1E 169
Barrow. Lanc 1F 91
Barrow. Rut 4F 75
Barrow. Shrp 5A 72
Barrow. Som 3C 22
Barrow. Suff 4G 65
Barroway Drove. Norf 5E 77
Barrow Bridge. G Man 3E 91
Barrowburn. Nmbd 3C 120
Barrowby. Linc 2F 75
Barrowcliff. N Yor 1E 101
Barrow Common. N Som 5A 34
Barrowden. Rut 5G 75
Barrowford. Lanc 1G 91
Barrow Gurney. N Som 5A 34
Barrow Haven. N Lin 2D 94
Barrow Hill. Derbs 3B 86
Barrow-in-Furness. Cumb 3B 96
Barrow Nook. Lanc 4C 90
Barrow's Green. Hal 2H 83
Barrows Green. Cumb 1E 97
Barrow Street. Wilts 3D 22
Barrow upon Humber. N Lin 2D 94
Barrow upon Soar. Leics 4C 74
Barrow upon Trent. Derbs 3A 74
Barry. Ang 5E 145
Barry. V Glam 5E 32
Barry Island. V Glam 5E 32
Barsby. Leics 4D 74
Barsham. Suff 2F 67
Barston. W Mid 3G 61
Bartestree. Here 1A 48
Barthol Chapel. Abers 5F 161
Bartholomew Green. Essx 3H 53
Barthomley. Ches E 5B 84
Bartley. Hants 1B 16
Bartley Green. W Mid 2E 61
Bartlow. Cambs 1F 53
Barton. Cambs 5D 64
Barton. Ches W 5G 83
Barton. Cumb 2F 103
Barton. Glos 3G 49
Barton. IOW 4D 16
Barton. Lanc
nr. Ormskirk 4B 90
nr. Preston 1D 90
Barton. N Som 1G 21
Barton. N Yor 4F 105
Barton. Oxon 5D 50
Barton. Torb 2F 9
Barton. Warw 5F 61
Barton Bendish. Norf 5G 77
Barton Gate. Staf 4F 73
Barton Green. Staf 4F 73
Barton Hartshorn. Buck 2E 51
Barton Hill. N Yor 3B 100
Barton in Fabis. Notts 2C 74
Barton in the Beans. Leics 5A 74
Barton-le-Clay. C Beds 2A 52
Barton-le-Street. N Yor 2B 100
Barton-le-Willows. N Yor 3B 100
Barton Mills. Suff 3G 65
Barton on Sea. Hants 3H 15
Barton-on-the-Heath. Warw 2A 50
Barton St David. Som 3A 22
Barton Seagrave. Nptn 3F 63
Barton Stacey. Hants 2C 24
Barton Town. Devn 2G 19
Barton Turf. Norf 3F 79
Barton-Under-Needwood. Staf 4F 73
Barton-upon-Humber. N Lin 2D 94
Barton Waterside. N Lin 2D 94
Barugh Green. S Yor 4D 92
Barway. Cambs 3E 65
Barwell. Leics 1B 62
Barwick. Herts 4D 53
Barwick. Som 1A 14
Barwick in Elmet. W Yor 1D 93
Baschurch. Shrp 3G 71
Bascote. Warw 4B 62
Basford Green. Staf 5D 85
Bashall Eaves. Lanc 5F 97
Bashall Town. Lanc 5G 97
Bashley. Hants 3H 15
Basildon. Essx 2B 40
Basingstoke. Hants 1E 25
Baslow. Derbs 3G 85
Bason Bridge. Som 2G 21
Bassaleg. Newp 3F 33
Bassendean. Bord 5C 130
Bassenthwaite. Cumb 1D 102
Bassett. Sotn 1C 16
Bassingbourn. Cambs 1D 52
Bassingfield. Notts 2D 74
Bassingham. Linc 4G 87
Bassingthorpe. Linc 3G 75
Bassus Green. Herts 3D 52
Basta. Shet 2G 173
Baston. Linc 4A 76
Bastonford. Worc 5C 60
Bastwick. Norf 4G 79
Batchley. Worc 4E 61
Batchworth. Herts 1B 38
Batcombe. Dors 2B 14
Batcombe. Som 3B 22
Bate Heath. Ches E 3A 84
Bath. Bath 192 (5C 34)
Bathampton. Bath 5C 34
Bathealton. Som 4D 20
Batheaston. Bath 5C 34
Bathford. Bath 5C 34
Bathgate. W Lot 3C 128
Bathley. Notts 5E 87
Bathpool. Corn 5C 10
Bathpool. Som 4F 21
Bathville. W Lot 3C 128
Bathway. Som 1A 22
Batley. W Yor 2C 92
Batsford. Glos 2G 49
Batson. Devn 5D 8
Battersby. N Yor 4C 106
Battersea. G Lon 3D 39
Battisborough Cross. Devn 4C 8
Battisford. Suff 5C 66
Battisford Tye. Suff 5C 66
Battle. E Sus 4B 28
Battle. Powy 2D 46
Battleborough. Som 1G 21
Battledown. Glos 3E 49
Battlefield. Shrp 4H 71
Battlesbridge. Essx 1B 40
Battlesden. C Beds 3H 51
Battlesea Green. Suff 3E 66
Battleton. Som 4C 20
Battram. Leics 5B 74
Battramsley. Hants 3B 16
Batt's Corner. Surr 2G 25
Bauds of Cullen. Mor 2B 160
Baugh. Arg 4B 138
Baughton. Worc 1D 49
Baughurst. Hants 5D 36
Baulking. Oxon 2B 36
Baumber. Linc 3B 88
Baunton. Glos 5F 49
Baverstock. Wilts 3F 23
Bawburgh. Norf 5D 78
Bawdeswell. Norf 3C 78
Bawdrip. Som 3G 21
Bawdsey. Suff 1G 55
Bawsey. Norf 4F 77
Bawtry. S Yor 1D 86
Baxenden. Lanc 2F 91
Baxterley. Warw 1G 61
Baxter's Green. Suff 5G 65
Bay. High 3B 154
Baybridge. Hants 4D 24
Baybridge. Nmbd 4C 114
Baycliff. Cumb 2B 96
Baydon. Wilts 4A 36
Bayford. Herts 5D 52
Bayford. Som 4C 22
Bayles. Cumb 5A 114
Baylham. Suff 5D 66
Baynard's Green. Oxon 3D 50
Bayston Hill. Shrp 5G 71
Baythorne End. Essx 1H 53
Baythorpe. Linc 1B 76
Bayton. Worc 3A 60
Bayton Common. Worc 3B 60
Bayworth. Oxon 5D 50
Beach. S Glo 4C 34
Beachampton. Buck 2F 51
Beachamwell. Norf 5G 77
Beachley. Glos 2A 34
Beacon. Devn 2E 13
Beacon End. Essx 3C 54
Beacon Hill. Surr 3G 25
Beacon's Bottom. Buck 2F 37
Beaconsfield. Buck 1A 38
Beacrabhaic. W Isl 8D 171
Beadlam. N Yor 1A 100
Beadnell. Nmbd 2G 121
Beaford. Devn 1F 11
Beal. Nmbd 5G 131
Beal. N Yor 2F 93
Bealsmill. Corn 5D 10
Beam Hill. Staf 3G 73
Beamhurst. Staf 2E 73
Beaminster. Dors 2H 13
Beamish. Dur 4F 115
Beamond End. Buck 1A 38
Beamsley. N Yor 4C 98
Bean. Kent 3G 39
Beanacre. Wilts 5E 35
Beanley. Nmbd 3E 121
Beaquoy. Orkn 5C 172
Beardwood. Bkbn 2E 91
Beare Green. Surr 1C 26
Bearley. Warw 4F 61
Bearpark. Dur 5F 115
Bearsbridge. Nmbd 4A 114
Bearsden. E Dun 2G 127
Bearsted. Kent 5B 40
Bearstone. Shrp 2B 72
Bearwood. Pool 3F 15
Bearwood. W Mid 2E 61
Beattock. Dum 4C 118
Beauchamp Roding. Essx 4F 53
Beauchief. S Yor 2H 85
Beaufort. Blae 4E 47
Beaulieu. Hants 2B 16
Beauly. High 4H 157
Beaumaris. IOA 3F 81
Beaumont. Cumb 4E 113
Beaumont. Essx 3E 55
Beaumont Hill. Darl 3F 105
Beaumont Leys. Leic 5C 74
Beausale. Warw 3G 61
Beauvale. Notts 1B 74
Beauworth. Hants 4D 24
Beaworthy. Devn 3E 11
Beazley End. Essx 3H 53
Bebington. Mers 2F 83
Bebside. Nmbd 1F 115
Beccles. Suff 2G 67
Becconsall. Lanc 2C 90
Beckbury. Shrp 5B 72
Beckenham. G Lon 4E 39
Beckermet. Cumb 4B 102
Beckett End. Norf 1G 65
Beck Foot. Cumb 5H 103
Beckfoot. Cumb
nr. Broughton in Furness 1A 96
nr. Seascale 4C 102
nr. Silloth 5B 112
Beckford. Worc 2E 49
Beckhampton. Wilts 5F 35
Beck Hole. N Yor 4F 107
Beckingham. Linc 5F 87
Beckingham. Notts 1E 87
Beckington. Som 1D 22
Beckley. E Sus 3C 28
Beckley. Hants 3H 15
Beckley. Oxon 4D 50
Beck Row. Suff 3F 65
Beck Side. Cumb
nr. Cartmel 1C 96
nr. Ulverston 1B 96
Beckside. Cumb 1F 97
Beckton. G Lon 2F 39
Beckwithshaw. N Yor 4E 99
Becontree. G Lon 2F 39
Bedale. N Yor 1E 99
Bedburn. Dur 1E 105
Bedchester. Dors 1D 14
Beddau. Rhon 3D 32
Beddgelert. Gwyn 1E 69
Beddingham. E Sus 5F 27
Beddington. G Lon 4E 39
Bedfield. Suff 4E 66
Bedford. Bed 1A 52
Bedford. G Man 1A 84
Bedham. W Sus 3B 26
Bedhampton. Hants 2F 17
Bedingfield. Suff 4D 66
Bedingham Green. Norf 1E 67
Bedlam. N Yor 3E 99
Bedlar's Green. Essx 3F 53
Bedlington. Nmbd 1F 115
Bedlinog. Mer T 5D 46
Bedminster. Bris 4A 34
Bedmond. Herts 5A 52
Bednall. Staf 4D 72
Bedrule. Bord 3A 120
Bedstone. Shrp 3F 59
Bedwas. Cphy 3E 33
Bedwellty. Cphy 5E 47
Bedworth. Warw 2A 62
Beeby. Leics 5D 74
Beech. Hants 3E 25
Beech. Staf 2C 72
Beechcliffe. W Yor 5C 98
Beech Hill. W Ber 5E 37
Beechingstoke. Wilts 1F 23
Beedon. W Ber 4C 36
Beeford. E Yor 4F 101
Beeley. Derbs 4G 85
Beelsby. NE Lin 4F 95
Beenham. W Ber 5D 36
Beeny. Corn 3B 10
Beer. Devn 4F 13
Beer. Som 3H 21
Beercrocombe. Som 4G 21
Beer Hackett. Dors 1B 14
Beesands. Devn 4E 9
Beesby. Linc 2D 88
Beeson. Devn 4E 9
Beeston. C Beds 1B 52
Beeston. Ches W 5H 83
Beeston. Norf 4B 78
Beeston. Notts 2C 74
Beeston. W Yor 1C 92
Beeston Regis. Norf 1D 78
Beeswing. Dum 3F 111
Beetham. Cumb 2D 97
Beetham. Som 1F 13
Beetley. Norf 4B 78
Beffcote. Staf 4C 72
Began. Card 3F 33
Begbroke. Oxon 4C 50
Begdale. Cambs 5D 76
Begelly. Pemb 4F 43
Beggar Hill. Essx 5G 53
Beggar's Bush. Powy 4E 59
Beggearn Huish. Som 3D 20
Beguildy. Powy 3D 58
Beighton. S Yor 2B 86
Beighton Hill. Derbs 5G 85
Beinn Casgro. W Isl 5G 171
Beith. N Ayr 4E 127
Bekesbourne. Kent 5F 41
Belaugh. Norf 4E 79
Belbroughton. Worc 3D 60
Belchalwell. Dors 2C 14
Belchalwell Street. Dors 2C 14
Belchamp Otten. Essx 1B 54
Belchamp St Paul. Essx 1A 54
Belchamp Walter. Essx 1B 54
Belchford. Linc 3B 88
Belcoo. Ferm 6F 177
Belfast. Bel 2H 179
Belfast City George Best Airport. Bel 4H 175
Belfast International Airport. Ant 1F 179
Belfatton. Abers 3H 161
Belford. Nmbd 1F 121
Belgrano. Cnwy 3B 82
Belhaven. E Lot 2C 130
Belhelvie. Abers 2G 153
Belhinnie. Abers 1B 152
Bellabeg. Abers 2A 152
Belladrum. High 4H 157
Bellaghy. M Ulst 7F 175
Bellamore. S Ayr 1H 109
Bellanaleck. Ferm 6H 177
Bellanoch. Arg 4F 133
Bell Busk. N Yor 4B 98
Belleau. Linc 3D 88
Belleek. Ferm 7B 176
Belleek. New M 7D 178
Belleheiglash. Mor 5F 159
Bell End. Worc 3D 60
Bellerby. N Yor 5E 105
Bellerby Camp. N Yor 5D 105
Bellever. Devn 5G 11
Belle Vue. Cumb 1C 102
Belle Vue. Shrp 4G 71
Bellfield. S Lan 1H 117
Belliehill. Ang 2E 145
Bellingdon. Buck 5H 51
Bellingham. Nmbd 1B 114
Belloch. Arg 2A 122
Bellochantuy. Arg 2A 122
Bellsbank. E Ayr 4D 117
Bell's Cross. Suff 5D 66
Bellshill. N Lan 4A 128
Bellshill. Nmbd 1F 121
Bellside. N Lan 4B 128
Bellspool. Bord 1D 118
Bellsquarry. W Lot 3D 128
Bells Yew Green. E Sus 2H 27
Belmaduthy. High 3A 158
Belmesthorpe. Rut 4H 75
Belmont. Bkbn 3E 91
Belmont. Shet 1G 173
Belmont. S Ayr 2C 116
Belnacraig. Abers 2A 152
Belnie. Linc 2B 76
Belowda. Corn 2D 6
Belper. Derbs 1A 74
Belper Lane End. Derbs 1H 73
Belph. Derbs 3C 86
Belsay. Nmbd 2E 115
Belsford. Devn 3D 8
Belsize. Herts 5A 52
Belstead. Suff 1E 55
Belston. S Ayr 2C 116
Belstone. Devn 3G 11
Belstone Corner. Devn 3G 11
Belthorn. Lanc 2F 91
Beltinge. Kent 4F 41
Beltoft. N Lin 4B 94
Belton. Leics 3B 74
Belton. Linc 2G 75
Belton. Norf 5G 79
Belton. N Lin 4A 94
Belton-in-Rutland. Rut 5F 75
Beltring. Kent 1A 28
Belts of Collonach. Abers 4D 152
Belvedere. G Lon 3F 39
Belvoir. Leics 2F 75
Bembridge. IOW 4E 17
Bemersyde. Bord 1H 119
Bemerton. Wilts 3G 23
Bempton. E Yor 2F 101
Benacre. Suff 2H 67
Ben Alder Lodge. High 1C 142
Ben Armine Lodge. High 2E 164
Benbecula Airport. W Isl 3C 170
Benbuie. Dum 5G 117
Benburb. M Ulst 4C 178
Benchill. G Man 2C 84
Benderloch. Arg 5D 140
Bendish. Herts 3B 52
Bendooragh. Caus 4F 174
Bendronaig Lodge. High 5C 156
Benenden. Kent 2C 28
Benfieldside. Dur 4D 115
Bengate. Norf 3F 79
Bengeworth. Worc 1F 49
Benhall Green. Suff 4F 67
Benholm. Abers 2H 145
Beningbrough. N Yor 4H 99
Benington. Herts 3C 52
Benington. Linc 1C 76
Benington Sea End. Linc 1D 76
Benllech. IOA 2E 81
Benmore Lodge. High 2H 163
Bennacott. Corn 3C 10
Bennah. Devn 4B 12
Bennecarrigan. N Ayr 3D 122
Bennethead. Cumb 2F 103
Benniworth. Linc 2B 88
Benover. Kent 1B 28
Benson. Oxon 2E 36
Benston. Shet 6F 173
Benstonhall. Orkn 4E 172
Bent. Abers 1F 145
Benthall. Shrp 5A 72
Bentham. Glos 4E 49
Bentlawnt. Shrp 5F 71
Bentley. E Yor 1D 94
Bentley. Hants 2F 25
Bentley. S Yor 4F 93
Bentley. Suff 2E 54
Bentley. Warw 1G 61
Bentley. W Mid 1D 61
Bentley Heath. Herts 1D 38
Bentley Heath. W Mid 3F 61
Bentpath. Dum 5F 119
Bents. W Lot 3C 128
Bentworth. Hants 2E 25
Benvie. D'dee 5C 144
Benville. Dors 2A 14
Benwell. Tyne 3F 115
Benwick. Cambs 1C 64
Beoley. Worc 4E 61
Beoraidbeg. High 4E 147
Bepton. W Sus 1G 17
Beragh. Ferm 3L 177
Berden. Essx 3E 53
Bere Alston. Devn 2A 8
Bere Ferrers. Devn 2A 8
Berepper. Corn 4D 4
Bere Regis. Dors 3D 14
Bergh Apton. Norf 5F 79
Berinsfield. Oxon 2D 36
Berkeley. Glos 2B 34
Berkhamsted. Herts 5H 51
Berkley. Som 2D 22
Berkswell. W Mid 3G 61
Bermondsey. G Lon 3E 39
Bernice. Arg 4A 134
Bernisdale. High 3D 154
Berrick Salome. Oxon 2E 36
Berriedale. High 1H 165
Berrier. Cumb 2E 103
Berriew. Powy 5D 70
Berrington. Nmbd 5G 131
Berrington. Shrp 5H 71
Berrington. Worc 4H 59
Berrington Green. Worc 4H 59
Berrington Law. Nmbd 5F 131
Berrow. Som 1G 21
Berrow Green. Worc 5B 60
Berry Cross. Devn 1E 11
Berry Down Cross. Devn 2F 19
Berry Hill. Glos 4A 48
Berry Hill. Pemb 1A 44
Berryhillock. Mor 2C 160
Berrynarbor. Devn 2F 19
Berry Pomeroy. Devn 2E 9
Berryscaur. Dum 5D 118
Berry's Green. G Lon 5F 39
Bersham. Wrex 1F 71
Berthengam. Flin 3D 82
Berwick. E Sus 5G 27
Berwick Bassett. Wilts 4G 35
Berwick Hill. Nmbd 2E 115
Berwick St James. Wilts 3F 23
Berwick St John. Wilts 4E 23
Berwick St Leonard. Wilts 3E 23
Berwick-upon-Tweed. Nmbd 4F 131
Berwyn. Den 1D 70
Bescaby. Leics 3F 75
Bescar. Lanc 3B 90
Besford. Worc 1E 49
Bessacarr. S Yor 4G 93
Bessbrook. New M 7E 178
Bessels Leigh. Oxon 5C 50
Bessingby. E Yor 3F 101
Bessingham. Norf 2D 78
Best Beech Hill. E Sus 2H 27
Besthorpe. Norf 1C 66
Besthorpe. Notts 4F 87
Bestwood Village. Notts 1C 74
Beswick. E Yor 5E 101
Betchworth. Surr 5D 38
Bethania. Cdgn 4E 57
Bethania. Gwyn
nr. Blaenau Ffestiniog 1G 69
nr. Caernarfon 5F 81
Bethel. Gwyn
nr. Bala 2B 70
nr. Caernarfon 4E 81
Bethel. IOA 3C 80
Bethersden. Kent 1D 28
Bethesda. Gwyn 4F 81
Bethesda. Pemb 3E 43
Bethlehem. Carm 3G 45
Bethnal Green. G Lon 2E 39
Betley. Staf 1B 72
Betsham. Kent 3H 39
Betteshanger. Kent 5H 41
Bettiscombe. Dors 3H 13
Bettisfield. Wrex 2G 71
Betton. Shrp 2A 72
Betton Strange. Shrp 5H 71
Bettws. B'end 3C 32
Bettws. Newp 2F 33
Bettws Bledrws. Cdgn 5E 57
Bettws Cedewain. Powy 1D 58
Bettws Gwerfil Goch. Den 1C 70
Bettws Ifan. Cdgn 1D 44
Bettws Newydd. Mon 5G 47
Bettyhill. High 2H 167
Betws. Carm 4G 45
Betws Garmon. Gwyn 5E 81
Betws-y-Coed. Cnwy 5G 81
Betws-yn-Rhos. Cnwy 3B 82
Beulah. Cdgn 1C 44
Beulah. Powy 5B 58
Beul an Atha. Arg 3B 124
Bevendean. Brig 5E 27
Bevercotes. Notts 3E 86
Beverley. E Yor 1D 94
Beverston. Glos 2D 34
Bevington. Glos 2B 34
Bewaldeth. Cumb 1D 102
Bewcastle. Cumb 2G 113
Bewdley. Worc 3B 60
Bewerley. N Yor 3D 98
Bewholme. E Yor 4F 101
Bexfield. Norf 3C 78
Bexhill. E Sus 5B 28
Bexley. G Lon 3F 39
Bexleyheath. G Lon 3F 39
Bexleyhill. W Sus 3A 26
Bexwell. Norf 5F 77
Beyton. Suff 4B 66
Bhalton. W Isl 4C 171
Bhatarsaigh. W Isl 9B 170
Bibbington. Derbs 3E 85
Bibury. Glos 5G 49
Bicester. Oxon 3D 50
Bickenhall. Som 1F 13
Bickenhill. W Mid 2F 61
Bicker. Linc 2B 76
Bicker Bar. Linc 2B 76
Bicker Gauntlet. Linc 2B 76
Bickershaw. G Man 4E 91
Bickerstaffe. Lanc 4C 90
Bickerton. Ches E 5H 83
Bickerton. Nmbd 4D 121
Bickerton. N Yor 4G 99
Bickford. Staf 4C 72
Bickington. Devn
nr. Barnstaple 3F 19
nr. Newton Abbot 5A 12
Bickleigh. Devn
nr. Plymouth 2B 8
nr. Tiverton 2C 12
Bickleton. Devn 3F 19
Bickley. N Yor 5G 107
Bickley Moss. Ches W 1H 71
Bickmarsh. Worc 1G 49
Bicknacre. Essx 5A 54
Bicknoller. Som 3E 20
Bicknor. Kent 5C 40
Bickton. Hants 1G 15
Bicton. Here 4G 59
Bicton. Shrp
nr. Bishop's Castle 2E 59
nr. Shrewsbury 4G 71
Bicton Heath. Shrp 4G 71
Bidborough. Kent 1G 27
Biddenden. Kent 2C 28
Biddenden Green. Kent 1C 28
Biddenham. Bed 5H 63
Biddestone. Wilts 4D 34
Biddisham. Som 1G 21
Biddlesden. Buck 1E 51
Biddlestone. Nmbd 4D 120
Biddulph. Staf 5C 84
Biddulph Moor. Staf 5D 84
Bideford. Devn 4E 19
Bidford-on-Avon. Warw 5E 61
Bidlake. Devn 4F 11
Bidston. Mers 2E 83
Bielby. E Yor 5B 100
Bieldside. Aber 3F 153
Bierley. IOW 5D 16
Bierley. W Yor 1B 92
Bierton. Buck 4G 51
Bigbury. Devn 4C 8
Bigbury-on-Sea. Devn 4C 8
Bigby. Linc 4D 94
Biggar. Cumb 3A 96
Biggar. S Lan 1C 118
Biggin. Derbs
nr. Hartington 5F 85
nr. Hulland 1G 73
Biggin. N Yor 1F 93
Biggings. Shet 5C 173
Biggin Hill. G Lon 5F 39
Biggleswade. C Beds 1B 52
Bighouse. High 2A 168
Bighton. Hants 3E 24
Biglands. Cumb 4D 112
Bignall End. Staf 5C 84
Bignor. W Sus 4A 26
Bigrigg. Cumb 3B 102
Big Sand. High 1G 155
Bigton. Shet 9E 173
Bilberry. Corn 3E 6
Bilborough. Nott 1C 74
Bilbrook. Som 2D 20
Bilbrook. Staf 5C 72
Bilbrough. N Yor 5H 99
Bilbster. High 3E 169
Bilby. Notts 2D 86
Bildershaw. Dur 2F 105
Bildeston. Suff 1C 54
Billericay. Essx 1A 40
Billesdon. Leics 5E 74
Billesley. Warw 5F 61
Billingborough. Linc 2A 76
Billinge. Mers 4D 90
Billingford. Norf
nr. Dereham 3C 78
nr. Diss 3D 66
Billingham. Stoc T 2B 106
Billinghay. Linc 5A 88
Billingley. S Yor 4E 93
Billingshurst. W Sus 3B 26
Billingsley. Shrp 2B 60
Billington. C Beds 3H 51
Billington. Lanc 1F 91
Billington. Staf 3C 72
Billockby. Norf 4G 79
Billy Row. Dur 1E 105
Bilsborrow. Lanc 5E 97
Bilsby. Linc 3D 88
Bilsham. W Sus 5A 26
Bilsington. Kent 2E 29
Bilson Green. Glos 4B 48
Bilsthorpe. Notts 4D 86
Bilston. Midl 3F 129
Bilston. W Mid 1D 60
Bilstone. Leics 5A 74
Bilting. Kent 1E 29
Bilton. E Yor 1E 95
Bilton. Nmbd 3G 121
Bilton. N Yor 4F 99
Bilton. Warw 3B 62
Bilton in Ainsty. N Yor 5G 99
Bimbister. Orkn 6C 172
Binbrook. Linc 1B 88
Binchester. Dur 1F 105
Bincombe. Dors 4B 14
Bindal. High 5G 165
Binegar. Som 2B 22
Bines Green. W Sus 4C 26
Binfield. Brac 4G 37
Binfield Heath. Oxon 4F 37
Bingfield. Nmbd 2C 114
Bingham. Notts 2E 74
Bingham's Melcombe. Dors 2C 14
Bingley. W Yor 1B 92
Bings Heath. Shrp 4H 71
Binham. Norf 2B 78
Binley. Hants 1C 24
Binley. W Mid 3A 62
Binnegar. Dors 4D 15
Binniehill. Falk 2B 128
Binsoe. N Yor 2E 99
Binstead. IOW 3D 16
Binsted. Hants 2F 25
Binsted. W Sus 5A 26
Binton. Warw 5F 61
Bintree. Norf 3C 78
Binweston. Shrp 5F 71
Birch. Essx 4C 54
Birch. G Man 4G 91
Birchall. Staf 5D 85
Bircham Newton. Norf 2G 77
Bircham Tofts. Norf 2G 77
Birchanger. Essx 3F 53
Birchburn. N Ayr 3D 122
Birch Cross. Staf 2F 73
Bircher. Here 4G 59
Birch Green. Essx 4C 54
Birchgrove. Card 3E 33
Birchgrove. Swan 3G 31
Birch Heath. Ches W 4H 83
Birch Hill. Ches W 3H 83
Birchill. Devn 2G 13
Birchington. Kent 4G 41
Birchley Heath. Warw 1G 61
Birchmoor. Warw 5G 73
Birchmoor Green. C Beds 2H 51
Birchover. Derbs 4G 85
Birch Vale. Derbs 2E 85
Birchview. Mor 5F 159
Birchwood. Linc 4G 87
Birchwood. Som 1F 13
Birchwood. Warr 1A 84
Bircotes. Notts 1D 86
Birdbrook. Essx 1H 53
Birdham. W Sus 2G 17
Birdholme. Derbs 4A 86
Birdingbury. Warw 4B 62
Birdlip. Glos 4E 49
Birdsall. N Yor 3C 100
Birds Edge. W Yor 4C 92
Birds Green. Essx 5F 53
Birdsgreen. Shrp 2B 60
Birdsmoorgate. Dors 2G 13
Birdston. E Dun 2H 127
Birdwell. S Yor 4D 92
Birdwood. Glos 4C 48
Birgham. Bord 1B 120
Birichen. High 4E 165
Birkby. Cumb 1B 102
Birkby. N Yor 4A 106
Birkdale. Mers 3B 90
Birkenhead. Mers 2F 83
Birkenhills. Abers 4E 161
Birkenshaw. N Lan 3H 127
Birkenshaw. W Yor 2C 92
Birkhall. Abers 4H 151
Birkhill. Ang 5C 144
Birkholme. Linc 3G 75
Birkin. N Yor 2F 93
Birley. Here 5G 59
Birling. Kent 4A 40
Birling. Nmbd 4G 121
Birling Gap. E Sus 5G 27
Birlingham. Worc 1E 49
Birmingham. W Mid 192 (2E 61)
Birmingham Airport. W Mid 205 (2F 61)
Birnam. Per 4H 143
Birse. Abers 4C 152
Birsemore. Abers 4C 152
Birstall. Leics 5C 74
Birstall. W Yor 2C 92
Birstall Smithies. W Yor 2C 92
Birstwith. N Yor 4E 99
Birthorpe. Linc 2A 76
Birtle. G Man 3G 91
Birtley. Here 4F 59
Birtley. Nmbd 2B 114
Birtley. Tyne 4F 115
Birtsmorton. Worc 2D 48
Birts Street. Worc 2C 48
Bisbrooke. Rut 1F 63
Bisham. Wind 3G 37
Bishampton. Worc 5D 61

Bish Mill—Bray

Bish Mill. Devn 4H 19
Bishop Auckland. Dur 2F 105
Bishopbridge. Linc 1H 87
Bishopbriggs. E Dun 2H 127
Bishop Burton. E Yor 1C 94
Bishopdown. Wilts 3G 23
Bishop Middleham. Dur 1A 106
Bishopmill. Mor 2G 159
Bishop Monkton. N Yor 3F 99
Bishop Norton. Linc 1G 87
Bishopsbourne. Kent 5F 41
Bishops Cannings. Wilts 5F 35
Bishop's Castle. Shrp 2F 59
Bishop's Caundle. Dors 1B 14
Bishop's Cleeve. Glos 3E 49
Bishops Court. New M 5K 179
Bishop's Down. Dors 1B 14
Bishop's Frome. Here 1B 48
Bishop's Green. Essx 4G 53
Bishop's Green. Hants 5D 36
Bishop's Hull. Som 4F 21
Bishop's Itchington. Warw 5A 62
Bishops Lydeard. Som 4E 21
Bishop's Norton. Glos 3D 48
Bishop's Nympton. Devn 4A 20
Bishop's Offley. Staf 3B 72
Bishop's Stortford. Herts 3E 53
Bishop's Sutton. Hants 3E 24
Bishop's Tachbrook.
Warw 4H 61
Bishop's Tawton. Devn 3F 19
Bishopsteignton. Devn 5C 12
Bishopstoke. Hants 1C 16
Bishopston. Swan 4E 31
Bishopstone. Buck 4G 51
Bishopstone. E Sus 5F 27
Bishopstone. Here 1H 47
Bishopstone. Swin 3H 35
Bishopstone. Wilts 4F 23
Bishopstrow. Wilts 2D 23
Bishop Sutton. Bath 1A 22
Bishop's Waltham. Hants 1D 16
Bishops Wood. Staf 5C 72
Bishopswood. Som 1F 13
Bishopsworth. Bris 5A 34
Bishop Thornton. N Yor 3E 99
Bishopthorpe. York 5H 99
Bishopton. Darl 2A 106
Bishopton. Dum 5B 110
Bishopton. N Yor 2E 99
Bishopton. Ren 2F 127
Bishopton. Warw 5F 61
Bishop Wilton. E Yor 4B 100
Bishton. Newp 3G 33
Bishton. Staf 3E 73
Bisley. Glos 5E 49
Bisley. Surr 5A 38
Bispham. Bkpl 5C 96
Bispham Green. Lanc 3C 90
Bissoe. Corn 4B 6
Bisterne. Hants 2G 15
Bisterne Close. Hants 2H 15
Bitchfield. Linc 3G 75
Bittadon. Devn 2F 19
Bittaford. Devn 3C 8
Bittering. Norf 4B 78
Bitterley. Shrp 3H 59
Bitterne. Sotn 1C 16
Bitteswell. Leics 2C 62
Bitton. S Glo 5B 34
Bix. Oxon 3F 37
Bixter. Shet 6E 173
Blaby. Leics 1C 62
Blackawton. Devn 3E 9
Black Bank. Cambs 2E 65
Black Barn. Linc 3D 76
Blackborough. Devn 2D 12
Blackborough. Norf 4F 77
Blackborough End. Norf 4F 77
Black Bourton. Oxon 5A 50
Blackboys. E Sus 3G 27
Blackbrook. Derbs 1H 73
Blackbrook. Mers 1H 83
Blackbrook. Staf 2B 72
Blackbrook. Surr 1C 26
Blackburn. Abers 2F 153
Blackburn. Bkbn 2E 91
Blackburn. W Lot 3C 128
Black Callerton. Tyne 3E 115
Black Carr. Norf 1C 66
Black Clauchrie. S Ayr 1H 109
Black Corries. High 3G 141
Black Crofts. Arg 5D 140
Black Cross. Corn 2D 6
Blackden Heath. Ches E 3B 84
Blackditch. Oxon 5C 50
Black Dog. Devn 2B 12
Blackdog. Abers 2G 153
Blackdown. Dors 2G 13
Blackdyke. Cumb 4C 112
Blacker Hill. S Yor 4D 92
Blackfen. G Lon 3F 39
Blackfield. Hants 2C 16
Blackford. Cumb 3E 113
Blackford. Per 3A 136
Blackford. Shrp 2H 59
Blackford. Som
nr. Burnham-on-Sea 2H 21
nr. Wincanton 4B 22
Blackfordby. Leics 4H 73
Blackgang. IOW 5C 16
Blackhall. Edin 2F 129
Blackhall. Ren 3F 127
Blackhall Colliery. Dur 1B 106
Blackhall Mill. Tyne 4E 115
Blackhall Rocks. Dur 1B 106
Blackham. E Sus 2F 27
Blackheath. Essx 3D 54
Blackheath. G Lon 3E 39
Blackheath. Suff 3G 67
Blackheath. Surr 1B 26
Blackheath. W Mid 2D 61
Black Heddon. Nmbd 2D 115
Black Hill. Warw 5G 61
Blackhill. Abers 4H 161
Blackhill. High 3C 154
Blackhills. Abers 2G 161
Blackhills. High 3D 158
Blackjack. Linc 2B 76
Blackland. Wilts 5F 35
Black Lane. G Man 4F 91
Blackleach. Lanc 1C 90
Blackley. G Man 4G 91
Blackley. W Yor 3B 92
Blacklunans. Per 2A 144
Blackmill. B'end 3C 32
Blackmoor. G Man 4E 91
Blackmoor. Hants 3F 25
Blackmoor Gate. Devn 2G 19
Blackmore. Essx 5G 53
Blackmore End. Essx 2H 53
Blackmore End. Herts 4B 52
Black Mount. Arg 4G 141
Blackness. Falk 2D 128
Blacknest. Hants 2F 25
Blackney. Dors 3H 13
Blacknoll. Dors 4D 14
Black Notley. Essx 3A 54
Blacko. Lanc 5A 98
Black Pill. Swan 3F 31
Blackpool. Bkpl 192 (1B 90)
Blackpool. Devn 4E 9
Blackpool Corner. Dors 3G 13
Blackpool Gate. Cumb 2G 113
Blackridge. W Lot 3B 128
Blackrock. Arg 3B 124
Blackrock. Mon 4F 47
Blackrod. G Man 3E 90
Blackshaw. Dum 3B 112
Blackshaw Head. W Yor 2H 91
Blackshaw Moor. Staf 5E 85
Blackskull. Arm 4F 178
Blacksmith's Green. Suff 4D 66
Blacksnape. Bkbn 2F 91
Blackstone. W Sus 4D 26
Black Street. Suff 2H 67
Black Tar. Pemb 4D 43
Blackthorn. Oxon 4E 50
Blackthorpe. Suff 4B 66
Blacktoft. E Yor 2B 94
Blacktop. Aber 3F 153
Black Torrington. Devn 2E 11
Blacktown. Newp 3F 33
Blackwall Tunnel. G Lon 2E 39
Blackwater. Corn 4B 6
Blackwater. Hants 1G 25
Blackwater. IOW 4D 16
Blackwater. Som 1F 13
Blackwaterfoot. N Ayr 3C 122
Blackwatertown. Arm 4C 178
Blackwell. Darl 3F 105
Blackwell. Derbs
nr. Alfreton 5B 86
nr. Buxton 3F 85
Blackwell. Som 4D 20
Blackwell. Warw 1H 49
Blackwell. Worc 3D 61
Blackwood. Cphy 2E 33
Blackwood. Dum 1G 111
Blackwood. S Lan 5A 128
Blackwood Hill. Staf 5D 84
Blacon. Ches W 4F 83
Bladnoch. Dum 4B 110
Bladon. Oxon 4C 50
Blaenannerch. Cdgn 1C 44
Blaenau Dolwyddelan.
Cnwy 5F 81
Blaenau Ffestiniog. Gwyn 1G 69
Blaenavon. Torf 5F 47
Blaenawey. Mon 4F 47
Blaen Celyn. Cdgn 5C 56
Blaen Clydach. Rhon 2C 32
Blaencwm. Rhon 2C 32
Blaendulais. Neat 5B 46
Blaenffos. Pemb 1F 43
Blaengarw. B'end 2C 32
Blaen-geuffordd. Cdgn 2F 57
Blaengwrach. Neat 5B 46
Blaengwynfi. Neat 2B 32
Blaenllechau. Rhon 2C 32
Blaenpennal. Cdgn 4F 57
Blaenplwyf. Cdgn 3E 57
Blaenporth. Cdgn 1C 44
Blaenrhondda. Rhon 5C 46
Blaenwaun. Carm 2G 43
Blaen-y-coed. Carm 2H 43
Blagdon. N Som 1A 22
Blagdon. Torb 2E 9
Blagdon Hill. Som 1F 13
Blagill. Cumb 5A 114
Blaguegate. Lanc 4C 90
Blaich. High 1E 141
Blain. High 2A 140
Blaina. Blae 5F 47
Blair Atholl. Per 2F 143
Blair Drummond. Stir 4G 135
Blairgowrie. Per 4A 144
Blairhall. Fife 1D 128
Blairingone. Per 4B 136
Blairlogie. Stir 4H 135
Blairmore. Abers 5B 160
Blairmore. Arg 1C 126
Blairmore. High 3B 166
Blairquhanan. W Dun 1F 127
Blaisdon. Glos 4C 48
Blakebrook. Worc 3C 60
Blakedown. Worc 3C 60
Blake End. Essx 3H 53
Blakemere. Here 1G 47
Blakeney. Glos 5B 48
Blakeney. Norf 1C 78
Blakenhall. Ches E 1B 72
Blakeshall. Worc 2C 60
Blakesley. Nptn 5D 62
Blanchland. Nmbd 4C 114
Blandford Camp. Dors 2E 15
Blandford Forum. Dors 2D 15
Blandford St Mary. Dors 2D 15
Bland Hill. N Yor 4E 98
Blandy. High 2G 167
Blanefield. Stir 2G 127
Blaney. Ferm 7D 176
Blankney. Linc 4H 87
Blantyre. S Lan 4H 127
Blarmachfoldach. High 2E 141
Blarnalearoch. High 4F 163
Blashford. Hants 2G 15
Blaston. Leics 1F 63
Blatchbridge. Som 2C 22
Blathaisbhal. W Isl 1D 170
Blatherwycke. Nptn 1G 63
Blawith. Cumb 1B 96
Blaxhall. Suff 5F 67
Blaxton. S Yor 4G 93
Blaydon. Tyne 3E 115
Bleadney. Som 2H 21
Bleadon. N Som 1G 21
Blean. Kent 4F 41
Bleary. Arm 4E 178
Bleasby. Linc 2A 88
Bleasby. Notts 1E 74
Bleasby Moor. Linc 2A 88
Blebocraigs. Fife 2G 137
Bleddfa. Powy 4E 58
Bledington. Glos 3H 49
Bledlow. Buck 5F 51
Bledlow Ridge. Buck 2F 37
Blencarn. Cumb 1H 103
Blencogo. Cumb 5C 112
Blendworth. Hants 1F 17
Blennerhasset. Cumb 5C 112
Bletchingdon. Oxon 4D 50
Bletchingley. Surr 5E 39
Bletchley. Mil 2G 51
Bletchley. Shrp 2A 72
Bletherston. Pemb 2E 43
Bletsoe. Bed 5H 63
Blewbury. Oxon 3D 36
Blickling. Norf 3D 78
Blidworth. Notts 5C 86
Blindburn. Nmbd 3C 120
Blindcrake. Cumb 1C 102
Blindley Heath. Surr 1E 27
Blindmoor. Som 1F 13
Blisland. Corn 5B 10
Blissford. Hants 1G 15
Bliss Gate. Worc 3B 60
Blists Hill. Telf 5A 72
Blisworth. Nptn 5E 63
Blithbury. Staf 3E 73
Blitterlees. Cumb 4C 112
Blockley. Glos 2G 49
Blofield. Norf 5F 79
Blofield Heath. Norf 4F 79
Blo' Norton. Norf 3C 66
Bloomfield. Bord 2H 119
Blore. Staf 1F 73
Blount's Green. Staf 2E 73
Bloxham. Oxon 2C 50
Bloxholm. Linc 5H 87
Bloxwich. W Mid 5D 73
Bloxworth. Dors 3D 15
Blubberhouses. N Yor 4D 98
Blue Anchor. Som 2D 20
Blue Anchor. Swan 3E 31
Blue Bell Hill. Kent 4B 40
Blue Row. Essx 4D 54
Bluetown. Kent 5D 40
Blundeston. Suff 1H 67
Blunham. C Beds 5A 64
Blunsdon St Andrew.
Swin 3G 35
Bluntington. Worc 3C 60
Bluntisham. Cambs 3C 64
Blunts. Corn 2H 7
Blurton. Stoke 1C 72
Blyborough. Linc 1G 87
Blyford. Suff 3G 67
Blymhill. Staf 4C 72
Blymhill Lawns. Staf 4C 72
Blyth. Nmbd 1G 115
Blyth. Notts 2D 86
Blyth. Bord 5E 129
Blyth Bank. Bord 5E 129
Blyth Bridge. Bord 5E 129
Blythburgh. Suff 3G 67
The Blythe. Staf 3E 73
Blythe Bridge. Staf 1D 72
Blythe Marsh. Staf 1D 72
Blyton. Linc 1F 87
Boardmills. Lis 4H 179
Boarhills. Fife 2H 137
Boarhunt. Hants 2E 16
Boar's Head. G Man 4D 90
Boarshead. E Sus 2G 27
Boars Hill. Oxon 5C 50
Boarstall. Buck 4E 51
Boasley Cross. Devn 3E 11
Boath. High 1H 157
Boat of Garten. High 2D 150
Bobbing. Kent 4C 40
Bobbington. Staf 1C 60
Bobbingworth. Essx 5F 53
Bocaddon. Corn 3F 7
Bocking. Essx 3A 54
Bocking Churchstreet.
Essx 3A 54
Boddam. Abers 4H 161
Boddam. Shet 10E 173
Boddington. Glos 3D 49
Bodedern. IOA 2C 80
Bodelwyddan. Den 3C 82
Bodenham. Here 5H 59
Bodenham. Wilts 4G 23
Bodewryd. IOA 1C 80
Bodfari. Den 3C 82
Bodffordd. IOA 3D 80
Bodham. Norf 1D 78
Bodiam. E Sus 3B 28
Bodicote. Oxon 2C 50
Bodieve. Corn 1D 6
Bodinnick. Corn 3F 7
Bodle Street Green. E Sus 4A 28
Bodmin. Corn 2E 7
Bodnant. Cnwy 3H 81
Bodney. Norf 1H 65
Bodorgan. IOA 4C 80
Bodrane. Corn 2G 7
Bodsham. Kent 1F 29
Boduan. Gwyn 2C 68
Bodymoor Heath. Warw 1F 61
The Bog. Shrp 1F 59
Bogallan. High 3A 158
Bogbrae Croft. Abers 5H 161
Bogend. S Ayr 1C 116
Boghall. Midl 3F 129
Boghall. W Lot 3C 128
Boghead. S Lan 5A 128
Bogindollo. Ang 3D 144
Bogmoor. Mor 2A 160
Bogniebrae. Abers 4C 160
Bognor Regis. W Sus 3H 17
Bograxie. Abers 2E 152
Bogside. N Lan 4B 128
Bogton. Abers 3D 160
Bogue. Dum 1D 110
Bohenie. High 5E 149
Bohortha. Corn 5C 6
Boirseam. W Isl 9C 171
Bokiddick. Corn 2E 7
Bolam. Dur 2E 105
Bolam. Nmbd 1D 115
Bolberry. Devn 5C 8
Bold Heath. Mers 2H 83
Boldon. Tyne 3G 115
Boldon Colliery. Tyne 3G 115
Boldre. Hants 3B 16
Boldron. Dur 3D 104
Bole. Notts 2E 87
Bolehall. Staf 5G 73
Bolehill. Derbs 5G 85
Bolenowe. Corn 5A 6
Boleside. Bord 1G 119
Bolham. Devn 1C 12
Bolham Water. Devn 1E 13
Bolingey. Corn 3B 6
Bollington. Ches E 3D 84
Bolney. W Sus 3D 26
Bolnhurst. Bed 5H 63
Bolshan. Ang 3F 145
Bolsover. Derbs 3B 86
Bolsterstone. S Yor 1G 85
Bolstone. Here 2A 48
Boltachan. Per 3F 143
Boltby. N Yor 1G 99
Bolton. Cumb 2H 103
Bolton. E Lot 2B 130
Bolton. E Yor 4B 100
Bolton. G Man 4F 91
Bolton. Nmbd 3F 121
Bolton Abbey. N Yor 4C 98
Bolton-by-Bowland. Lanc 5G 97
Boltonfellend. Cumb 3F 113
Boltongate. Cumb 5D 112
Bolton Green. Lanc 3D 90
Bolton-le-Sands. Lanc 3D 97
Bolton Low Houses.
Cumb 5D 112
Bolton New Houses.
Cumb 5D 112
Bolton-on-Swale. N Yor 5F 105
Bolton Percy. N Yor 5H 99
Bolton Town End. Lanc 3D 97
Bolton upon Dearne.
S Yor 4E 93
Bolton Wood Lane.
Cumb 5D 112
Bolventor. Corn 5B 10
Bomarsund. Nmbd 1F 115
Bomere Heath. Shrp 4G 71
Bonar Bridge. High 4D 164
Bonawe. Arg 5E 141
Bonby. N Lin 3D 94
Boncath. Pemb 1G 43
Bonchester Bridge. Bord 3H 119
Bonchurch. IOW 5D 16
Bond End. Staf 4F 73
Bondleigh. Devn 2G 11
Bonds. Lanc 5D 97
Bonehill. Devn 5H 11
Bonehill. Staf 5F 73
Bo'ness. Falk 1C 128
Boney Hay. Staf 4E 73
Bonham. Wilts 3C 22
Bonhill. W Dun 2E 127
Boningale. Shrp 5C 72
Bonjedward. Bord 2A 120
Bonkle. N Lan 4B 128
Bonnanaboigh. Caus 5C 174
Bonnington. Ang 5E 145
Bonnington. Edin 3E 129
Bonnington. Kent 2E 29
Bonnybank. Fife 3F 137
Bonnybridge. Falk 1B 128
Bonnykelly. Abers 3F 161
Bonnyrigg. Midl 3G 129
Bonnyton. Ang 5C 144
Bonnytown. Fife 2H 137
Bonsall. Derbs 5G 85
Bont. Mon 4G 47
Bontddu. Gwyn 4F 69
Bont Dolgadfan. Powy 5A 70
Y Bont-Faen. V Glam 4C 32
Bontgoch. Cdgn 2F 57
Bonthorpe. Linc 3D 89
Bont Newydd. Gwyn 1G 69
Bont-newydd. Cnwy 3C 82
Bontnewydd. Cdgn 4F 57
Bontnewydd. Gwyn 4D 81
Bontuchel. Den 5C 82
Bonvilston. V Glam 4D 32
Bon-y-maen. Swan 3F 31
Booker. Buck 2G 37
Booley. Shrp 3H 71
Boorley Green. Hants 1D 16
Boosbeck. Red C 3D 106
Boot. Cumb 4C 102
Booth. W Yor 2A 92
Boothby Graffoe. Linc 5G 87
Boothby Pagnell. Linc 2G 75
Booth Green. Ches E 2D 84
Booth of Toft. Shet 4F 173
Boothstown. G Man 4F 91
Boothville. Nptn 4E 63
Bootle. Cumb 1A 96
Bootle. Mers 1F 83
Booton. Norf 3D 78
Booze. N Yor 4D 104
Boquhan. Stir 1G 127
Boraston. Shrp 3A 60
Borden. Kent 4C 40
Borden. W Sus 4G 25
Bordlands. Bord 5E 129
Bordley. N Yor 3B 98
Bordon. Hants 3F 25
Boreham. Essx 5A 54
Boreham. Wilts 2D 23
Boreham Street. E Sus 4A 28
Borehamwood. Herts 1C 38
Boreland. Dum 5D 118
Boreston. Devn 3D 8
Borestone Brae. Stir 4G 135
Boreton. Shrp 5H 71
Borgh. W Isl
on Barra 8B 170
on Benbecula 3C 170
on Berneray 1E 170
on Isle of Lewis 2G 171
Borghasdal. W Isl 9C 171
Borghastan. W Isl 3D 171
Borgh na Sgiotaig. High 1C 154
Borgie. High 3G 167
Borgue. Dum 5D 110
Borgue. High 1H 165
Borley. Essx 1B 54
Borley Green. Essx 1B 54
Borley Green. Suff 4B 66
Borlum. High 1H 149
Bornais. W Isl 6C 170
Bornesketaig. High 1C 154
Borness. Dum 5D 110
Boroughbridge. N Yor 3F 99
Borough Green. Kent 5H 39
Borreraig. High 3A 154
Borrobol Lodge. High 1F 165
Borrodale. High 4A 154
Borrowash. Derbs 2B 74
Borrowby. N Yor
nr. Northallerton 1G 99
nr. Whitby 3E 107
Borrowston. High 4F 169
Borrowstonehill. Orkn 7D 172
Borrowstoun. Falk 1C 128
Borstal. Medw 4B 40
Borth. Cdgn 2F 57
Borthwick. Midl 4G 129
Borth-y-Gest. Gwyn 2E 69
Borve. High 4D 154
Borwick. Lanc 2E 97
Bosbury. Here 1B 48
Boscastle. Corn 3A 10
Boscombe. Bour 3G 15
Boscombe. Wilts 3H 23
Boscoppa. Corn 3E 7
Bosham. W Sus 2G 17
Bosherston. Pemb 5D 42
Bosley. Ches E 4D 84
Bossall. N Yor 3B 100
Bossiney. Corn 4A 10
Bossingham. Kent 1F 29
Bossington. Som 2B 20
Bostadh. W Isl 3D 171
Bostock Green. Ches W 4A 84
Boston. Linc 1C 76
Boston Spa. W Yor 5G 99
Boswarthen. Corn 3B 4
Boswinger. Corn 4D 6
Botallack. Corn 3A 4
Botany Bay. G Lon 1D 39
Botcheston. Leics 5B 74
Botesdale. Suff 3C 66
Bothal. Nmbd 1F 115
Bothampstead. W Ber 4D 36
Bothamsall. Notts 3D 86
Bothel. Cumb 1C 102
Bothenhampton. Dors 3H 13
Bothwell. S Lan 4A 128
Botley. Buck 5H 51
Botley. Hants 1D 16
Botley. Oxon 5C 50
Botloe's Green. Glos 3C 48
Botolph Claydon. Buck 3F 51
Botolphs. W Sus 5C 26
Bottacks. High 2G 157
Bottesford. Leics 2F 75
Bottesford. N Lin 4B 94
Bottisham. Cambs 4E 65
Bottlesford. Wilts 1G 23
Bottomcraig. Fife 1F 137
Bottom o' th' Moor. G Man 3E 91
Botton. N Yor 4D 107
Botton Head. Lanc 3F 97
Bottreaux Mill. Devn 4B 20
Botus Fleming. Corn 2A 8
Botwnnog. Gwyn 2B 68
Bough Beech. Kent 1F 27
Boughrood. Powy 2E 47
Boughspring. Glos 2A 34
Boughton. Norf 5F 77
Boughton. Nptn 4E 63
Boughton. Notts 4D 86
Boughton Aluph. Kent 1E 29
Boughton Green. Kent 5B 40
Boughton Lees. Kent 1E 28
Boughton Malherbe. Kent 1C 28
Boughton Monchelsea.
Kent 5B 40
Boughton under Blean.
Kent 5E 41
Boulby. Red C 3E 107
Bouldnor. IOW 4B 16
Bouldon. Shrp 2H 59
Boulmer. Nmbd 3G 121
Boulston. Pemb 3D 42
Boultham. Linc 4G 87
Boulton. Derb 2A 74
Boundary. Staf 1D 73
Bounds. Here 2B 48
Bourn. Cambs 5C 64
Bournbrook. W Mid 2E 61
Bourne. Linc 3H 75
The Bourne. Surr 2G 25
Bourne End. Bed 4H 63
Bourne End. Buck 3G 37
Bourne End. C Beds 1H 51
Bourne End. Herts 5A 52
Bournemouth.
Bour 192 (3F 15)
Bournemouth Airport.
Dors 3G 15
Bournes Green. Glos 5E 49
Bournes Green. S'end 2D 40
Bournheath. Worc 3D 60
Bournmoor. Dur 4G 115
Bournville. W Mid 2E 61
Bourton. Dors 3C 22
Bourton. N Som 5G 33
Bourton. Oxon 3H 35
Bourton. Shrp 1H 59
Bourton. Wilts 5F 35
Bourton on Dunsmore.
Warw 3B 62
Bourton-on-the-Hill. Glos 2G 49
Bourton-on-the-Water.
Glos 3G 49
Bousd. Arg 2D 138
Bousta. Shet 6D 173
Boustead Hill. Cumb 4D 112
Bouth. Cumb 1C 96
Bouthwaite. N Yor 2D 98
Boveney. Buck 3A 38
Boveridge. Dors 1F 15
Boverton. V Glam 5C 32
Bovey Tracey. Devn 5B 12
Bovingdon. Herts 5A 52
Bovingdon Green. Buck 3G 37
Bovinger. Essx 5F 53
Bovington Camp. Dors 4D 14
Bow. Devn 2H 11
Bowbank. Dur 2C 104
Bow Brickhill. Mil 2H 51
Bowbridge. Glos 5D 48
Bowburn. Dur 1A 106
Bowcombe. IOW 4C 16
Bowd. Devn 4E 12
Bowden. Devn 4E 9
Bowden. Bord 1H 119
Bowden Hill. Wilts 5E 35
Bowdens. Som 4H 21
Bowderdale. Cumb 4H 103
Bowdon. G Man 2B 84
Bower. Nmbd 1A 114
Bowerchalke. Wilts 4F 23
Bowerhill. Wilts 5E 35
Bower Hinton. Som 1H 13
Bowermadden. High 2E 169
Bowers. Staf 2C 72
Bowers Gifford. Essx 2B 40
Bowershall. Fife 4C 136
Bowertower. High 2E 169
Bowes. Dur 3C 104
Bowgreave. Lanc 5D 97
Bowhousebog. N Lan 4B 128
Bowithick. Corn 4B 10
Bowland Bridge. Cumb 1D 96
Bowlees. Dur 2C 104
Bowley. Here 5H 59
Bowlhead Green. Surr 2A 26
Bowling. W Dun 2F 127
Bowling. W Yor 1B 92
Bowling Bank. Wrex 1F 71
Bowling Green. Worc 5C 60
Bowlish. Som 2B 22
Bowmanstead. Cumb 5E 102
Bowmore. Arg 4B 124
Bowness-on-Solway.
Cumb 3D 112
Bowness-on-Windermere.
Cumb 5F 103
Bow of Fife. Fife 2F 137
Bowriefauld. Ang 4E 145
Bowscale. Cumb 1E 103
Bowsden. Nmbd 5F 131
Bowside Lodge. High 2A 168
Bowston. Cumb 5F 103
Bow Street. Cdgn 2F 57
Bowthorpe. Norf 5D 78
Box. Glos 5D 48
Box. Wilts 5D 34
Boxbush. Glos 3B 48
Box End. Bed 1A 52
Boxford. Suff 1C 54
Boxford. W Ber 4C 36
Boxgrove. W Sus 5A 26
Box Hill. Wilts 5D 34
Boxley. Kent 5B 40
Boxmoor. Herts 5A 52
Box's Shop. Corn 2C 10
Boxted. Essx 2C 54
Boxted. Suff 5H 65
Boxted Cross. Essx 2D 54
Boxworth. Cambs 4C 64
Boxworth End. Cambs 4C 64
Boyden End. Suff 5G 65
Boyden Gate. Kent 4G 41
Boylestone. Derbs 2F 73
Boylestonfield. Derbs 2F 73
Boyndie. Abers 2D 160
Boynton. E Yor 3F 101
Boys Hill. Dors 1B 14
Boythorpe. Derbs 4A 86
Boyton. Corn 3D 10
Boyton. Suff 1G 55
Boyton. Wilts 3E 23
Boyton Cross. Essx 5G 53
Boyton End. Essx 2G 53
Boyton End. Suff 1H 53
Bozeat. Nptn 5G 63
Braaid. IOM 4C 108
Braal Castle. High 3D 168
Brabling Green. Suff 4E 67
Brabourne. Kent 1F 29
Brabourne Lees. Kent 1E 29
Brabster. High 2F 169
Bracadale. High 5C 154
Bracara. High 4F 147
Braceborough. Linc 4H 75
Bracebridge. Linc 4G 87
Bracebridge Heath. Linc 4G 87
Braceby. Linc 2H 75
Bracewell. Lanc 5A 98
Brackenber. Cumb 3A 104
Brackenfield. Derbs 5A 86
Brackenlands. Cumb 5D 112
Brackenthwaite. Cumb 5D 112
Brackenthwaite. N Yor 4E 99
Brackla. B'end 4C 32
Brackla. High 3C 158
Bracklesham. W Sus 3G 17
Brackletter. High 5D 148
Brackley. Nptn 2D 50
Brackley Hatch. Nptn 1E 51
Brackloch. High 1F 163
Bracknell. Brac 5G 37
Braco. Per 3H 135
Bracobrae. Mor 3C 160
Bracon. N Lin 4A 94
Bracon Ash. Norf 1D 66
Bradbourne. Derbs 5G 85
Bradbury. Dur 2A 106
Bradda. IOM 4A 108
Bradden. Nptn 1E 51
Bradenham. Buck 2G 37
Bradenham. Norf 5B 78
Bradenstoke. Wilts 4F 35
Bradfield. Essx 2E 55
Bradfield. Norf 2E 79
Bradfield. W Ber 4E 36
Bradfield Combust. Suff 5A 66
Bradfield Green. Ches E 5A 84
Bradfield Heath. Essx 3E 55
Bradfield St Clare. Suff 5B 66
Bradfield St George. Suff 4B 66
Bradford. Derbs 4G 85
Bradford. Devn 2E 11
Bradford. Nmbd 1F 121
Bradford. W Yor 192 (1B 92)
Bradford Abbas. Dors 1A 14
Bradford Barton. Devn 1B 12
Bradford Leigh. Wilts 5D 34
Bradford-on-Avon. Wilts 5D 34
Bradford-on-Tone. Som 4E 21
Bradford Peverell. Dors 3B 14
Bradiford. Devn 3F 19
Brading. IOW 4E 16
Bradley. Ches W 3H 83
Bradley. Derbs 1G 73
Bradley. Glos 2C 34
Bradley. Hants 2E 25
Bradley. NE Lin 4F 95
Bradley. N Yor 1C 98
Bradley. Staf 4C 72
Bradley. W Mid 1D 60
Bradley. W Yor 2B 92
Bradley. Wrex 5F 83
Bradley Cross. Som 1H 21
Bradley Green. Ches W 1H 71
Bradley Green. Som 3F 21
Bradley Green. Warw 5G 73
Bradley Green. Worc 4D 61
Bradley in the Moors. Staf 1E 73
Bradley Mount. Ches E 3D 84
Bradley Stoke. S Glo 3B 34
Bradlow. Here 2C 48
Bradmore. Notts 2C 74
Bradmore. W Mid 1C 60
Bradninch. Devn 2D 12
Bradnop. Staf 5E 85
Bradpole. Dors 3H 13
Bradshaw. G Man 3F 91
Bradstone. Devn 4D 11
Bradwall Green. Ches E 4B 84
Bradway. S Yor 2H 85
Bradwell. Derbs 2F 85
Bradwell. Essx 3B 54
Bradwell. Mil 2G 51
Bradwell. Norf 5H 79
Bradwell-on-Sea. Essx 5D 54
Bradwell Waterside. Essx 5C 54
Bradworthy. Devn 1D 10
Brae. High 5C 162
Brae. Shet 5E 173
Braeantra. High 1H 157
Braefield. High 5G 157
Braefindon. High 3A 158
Braegrum. Per 1C 136
Braehead. Ang 3F 145
Braehead. Dum 4B 110
Braehead. Mor 4G 159
Braehead. Orkn 3D 172
Braehead. S Lan
nr. Coalburn 1H 117
nr. Forth 4C 128
Braehoulland. Shet 4D 173
Braemar. Abers 4F 151
Braemore. High
nr. Dunbeath 5C 168
nr. Ullapool 1D 156
Brae of Achnahaird. High 2E 163
Brae Roy Lodge. High 4F 149
Braeside. Abers 5G 161
Braeside. Inv 2D 126
Braes of Coul. Ang 3B 144
Braeswick. Orkn 4F 172
Braetongue. High 3F 167
Braeval. Stir 3E 135
Braevallich. Arg 3G 133
Braewick. Shet 6E 173
Brafferton. Darl 2F 105
Brafferton. N Yor 2G 99
Brafield-on-the-Green.
Nptn 5F 63
Bragar. W Isl 3E 171
Bragbury End. Herts 3C 52
Bragleenbeg. Arg 1G 133
Braichmelyn. Gwyn 4F 81
Braides. Lanc 4D 96
Braidwood. S Lan 5B 128
Braigo. Arg 3A 124
Brailsford. Derbs 1G 73
Braintree. Essx 3A 54
Braiseworth. Suff 3D 66
Braishfield. Hants 4B 24
Braithwaite. Cumb 2D 102
Braithwaite. S Yor 3G 93
Braithwaite. W Yor 5C 98
Braithwell. S Yor 1C 86
Brakefield Green. Norf 5C 78
Bramber. W Sus 4C 26
Brambridge. Hants 4C 24
Bramcote. Notts 2C 74
Bramcote. Warw 2B 62
Bramdean. Hants 4E 24
Bramerton. Norf 5E 79
Bramfield. Herts 4C 52
Bramfield. Suff 3F 67
Bramford. Suff 1E 54
Bramhall. G Man 2C 84
Bramham. W Yor 5G 99
Bramhope. W Yor 5E 99
Bramley. Hants 1E 25
Bramley. S Yor 1B 86
Bramley. Surr 1B 26
Bramley. W Yor 1C 92
Bramley Green. Hants 1E 25
Bramley Head. N Yor 4D 98
Bramley Vale. Derbs 4B 86
Bramling. Kent 5G 41
Brampford Speke. Devn 3C 12
Brampton. Cambs 3B 64
Brampton. Cumb
nr. Appleby-in-Westmorland
2H 103
nr. Carlisle 3G 113
Brampton. Linc 3F 87
Brampton. Norf 3E 78
Brampton. S Yor 4E 93
Brampton. Suff 2G 67
Brampton Abbotts. Here 3B 48
Brampton Ash. Nptn 2E 63
Brampton Bryan. Here 3F 59
Brampton en le Morthen.
S Yor 2B 86
Bramshall. Staf 2E 73
Bramshaw. Hants 1A 16
Bramshill. Hants 5F 37
Bramshott. Hants 3G 25
Branault. High 2G 139
Brancaster. Norf 1G 77
Brancaster Staithe. Norf 1G 77
Brancepeth. Dur 1F 105
Branch End. Nmbd 3D 114
Branchill. Mor 3E 159
Brand End. Linc 1C 76
Branderburgh. Mor 1G 159
Brandesburton. E Yor 5F 101
Brandeston. Suff 4E 67
Brand Green. Glos 3C 48
Brandhill. Shrp 3G 59
Brandis Corner. Devn 2E 11
Brandish Street. Som 2C 20
Brandiston. Norf 3D 78
Brandon. Dur 1F 105
Brandon. Linc 1G 75
Brandon. Nmbd 3E 121
Brandon. Suff 2G 65
Brandon. Warw 3B 62
Brandon Bank. Cambs 2F 65
Brandon Creek. Norf 1F 65
Brandon Parva. Norf 5C 78
Brandsby. N Yor 2H 99
Brandy Wharf. Linc 1H 87
Brane. Corn 4B 4
Bran End. Essx 3G 53
Branksome. Pool 3F 15
Bransbury. Hants 2C 24
Bransby. Linc 3F 87
Branscombe. Devn 4E 13
Bransford. Worc 5B 60
Bransgore. Hants 3G 15
Bransholme. Hull 1E 94
Bransley. Shrp 3A 60
Branston. Leics 3F 75
Branston. Linc 4H 87
Branston. Staf 3G 73
Branston Booths. Linc 4H 87
Branstone. IOW 4D 16
Bransty. Cumb 3A 102
Brant Broughton. Linc 5G 87
Brantham. Suff 2E 54
Branthwaite. Cumb
nr. Caldbeck 1D 102
nr. Workington 2B 102
Brantingham. E Yor 2C 94
Branton. Nmbd 3E 121
Branton. S Yor 4G 93
Branton Green. N Yor 3G 99
Branxholme. Bord 3G 119
Branxton. Nmbd 1C 120
Brassington. Derbs 5G 85
Brasted. Kent 5F 39
Brasted Chart. Kent 5F 39
The Bratch. Staf 1C 60
Brathens. Abers 4D 152
Bratoft. Linc 4D 88
Brattleby. Linc 2G 87
Bratton. Som 2C 20
Bratton. Telf 4A 72
Bratton. Wilts 1E 23
Bratton Clovelly. Devn 3E 11
Bratton Fleming. Devn 3G 19
Bratton Seymour. Som 4B 22
Braughing. Herts 3D 53
Braulen Lodge. High 5E 157
Braunston. Nptn 4C 62
Braunstone Town. Leics 5C 74
Braunston-in-Rutland. Rut 5F 75
Braunton. Devn 3E 19
Brawby. N Yor 2B 100
Brawl. High 2A 168
Brawlbin. High 3C 168
Bray. Wind 3A 38

Burton—Chapelknowe

Burton. Nmbd 1F 121
Burton. Pemb 4D 43
Burton. Som 2E 21
Burton. Wilts
  nr. Chippenham 4D 34
  nr. Warminster 3D 22
Burton. Wrex 5F 83
Burton Agnes. E Yor 3F 101
Burton Bradstock. Dors 4H 13
Burton-by-Lincoln. Linc 3G 87
Burton Coggles. Linc 3G 75
Burton Constable. E Yor 1E 95
Burton Corner. Linc 1C 76
Burton End. Cambs 1G 53
Burton End. Essx 3F 53
Burton Fleming. E Yor 2E 101
Burton Green. Warw 3G 61
Burton Green. Wrex 5F 83
Burton Hastings. Warw 2B 62
Burton-in-Kendal. Cumb 2E 97
Burton in Lonsdale. N Yor 2F 97
Burton Joyce. Notts 1D 74
Burton Latimer. Nptn 3G 63
Burton Lazars. Leics 4E 75
Burton Leonard. N Yor 3F 99
Burton on the Wolds. Leics 3C 74
Burton Overy. Leics 1D 62
Burton Pedwardine. Linc 1A 76
Burton Pidsea. E Yor 1F 95
Burton Salmon. N Yor 2E 93
Burton's Green. Essx 3B 54
Burton Stather. N Lin 3B 94
Burton upon Stather. N Lin 3B 94
Burton upon Trent. Staf 3G 73
Burton Wolds. Leics 3D 74
Burtonwood. Warr 1H 83
Burwardsley. Ches W 5H 83
Burwarton. Shrp 2A 60
Burwash. E Sus 3A 28
Burwash Common. E Sus 3H 27
Burwash Weald. E Sus 3A 28
Burwell. Cambs 4E 65
Burwell. Linc 3C 88
Burwen. IOA 1D 80
Burwick. Orkn 9D 172
Bury. Cambs 2B 64
Bury. G Man 3G 91
Bury. Som 4C 20
Bury. W Sus 4B 26
Burybank. Staf 2C 72
Bury End. Worc 2F 49
Bury Green. Herts 3E 53
Bury St Edmunds. Suff 4H 65
Burythorpe. N Yor 3B 100
Busbridge. Surr 1A 26
Busby. E Ren 4G 127
Busby. Per 1C 136
Buscot. Oxon 2H 35
Bush. Corn 2C 10
The Bush. M Ulst 3C 178
Bush Bank. Here 5G 59
Bushbury. W Mid 5D 72
Bushby. Leics 5D 74
Bushey. Dors 4E 15
Bushey. Herts 1C 38
Bushey Heath. Herts 1C 38
Bush Green. Norf
  nr. Attleborough 1C 66
  nr. Harleston 2E 66
Bush Green. Suff 5B 66
Bushley. Worc 2D 49
Bushley Green. Worc 2D 48
Bushmead. Bed 4A 64
Bushmills. Caus 2F 174
Bushmoor. Shrp 2G 59
Bushton. Wilts 4F 35
Bushy Common. Norf 4B 78
Busk. Cumb 5H 113
Buslingthorpe. Linc 2H 87
Bussage. Glos 5D 49
Bussex. Som 3G 21
Busta. Shet 5E 173
Butcher's Cross. E Sus 3G 27
Butcombe. N Som 5A 34
Bute Town. Cphy 5E 46
Butleigh. Som 3A 22
Butleigh Wootton. Som 3A 22
Butlers Marston. Warw 1B 50
Butley. Suff 5F 67
Butley High Corner. Suff 1G 55
Butlocks Heath. Hants 2C 16
Butterburn. Cumb 2H 113
Buttercrambe. N Yor 4B 100
Butterknowle. Dur 2E 105
Butterleigh. Devn 2C 12
Buttermere. Cumb 3C 102
Buttermere. Wilts 5B 36
Buttershaw. W Yor 2B 92
Butterstone. Per 4H 143
Butterton. Staf
  nr. Leek 5E 85
  nr. Stoke-on-Trent 1C 72
Butterwick. Dur 2A 106
Butterwick. Linc 1C 76
Butterwick. N Yor
  nr. Malton 2B 100
  nr. Weaverthorpe 2D 101
Butteryhaugh. Nmbd 5A 120
Butt Green. Ches E 5A 84
Buttington. Powy 5E 71
Buttonbridge. Shrp 3B 60
Buttonoak. Shrp 3B 60
Buttsash. Hants 2C 16
Butt's Green. Essx 5A 54
Butt Yeats. Lanc 3E 97
Buxhall. Suff 5C 66
Buxted. E Sus 3F 27
Buxton. Derbs 3E 85
Buxton. Norf 3E 79
Buxworth. Derbs 2E 85
Bwcle. Flin 4E 83
Bwlch. Powy 3E 47
Bwlchderwin. Gwyn 1D 68
Bwlchgwyn. Wrex 5E 83
Bwlch-Llan. Cdgn 5E 57
Bwlchnewydd. Carm 3D 44
Bwlchtocyn. Gwyn 3C 68
Bwlch-y-cibau. Powy 4D 70
Bwlchyddar. Powy 3D 70
Bwlch-y-fadfa. Cdgn 1E 45
Bwlch-y-ffridd. Powy 1C 58
Bwlch y Garreg. Powy 1C 58
Bwlch-y-groes. Pemb 1G 43
Bwlch-y-sarnau. Powy 3C 58
Bybrook. Kent 1E 28
Byermoor. Tyne 4E 115
Byers Garth. Dur 5G 115
Byers Green. Dur 1F 105
Byfield. Nptn 5C 62
Byfleet. Surr 4B 38
Byford. Here 1G 47
Bygrave. Herts 2C 52
Byker. Tyne 3F 115
Byland Abbey. N Yor 2H 99
Bylchau. Cnwy 4B 82
Byley. Ches W 4B 84
Bynea. Carm 3E 31
Byram. N Yor 2E 93
Byrness. Nmbd 4B 120
Bystock. Devn 4D 12
Bythorn. Cambs 3H 63
Byton. Here 4F 59
Bywell. Nmbd 3D 114
Byworth. W Sus 3A 26

C

Cabharstadh. W Isl 6F 171
Cabourne. Linc 4E 95
Cabrach. Arg 3C 124
Cabrach. Mor 1A 152
Cabragh. M Ulst 3B 178
Cabus. Lanc 5D 97
Cadbury. Devn 2C 12
Cadder. E Dun 2H 127
Caddington. C Beds 4A 52
Caddonfoot. Bord 1G 119
Cadeby. Leics 5B 74
Cadeby. S Yor 4F 93
Cadeleigh. Devn 2C 12
Cade Street. E Sus 3H 27
Cadgwith. Corn 5E 5
Cadham. Fife 3E 137
Cadishead. G Man 1B 84
Cadle. Swan 3F 31
Cadley. Lanc 1D 90
Cadley. Wilts
  nr. Ludgershall 1H 23
  nr. Marlborough 5H 35
Cadmore End. Buck 2F 37
Cadnam. Hants 1A 16
Cadney. N Lin 4D 94
Cadole. Flin 4E 82
Cadoxton-juxta-Neath. Neat 2A 32
Cadwell. Herts 2B 52
Cadwst. Den 2C 70
Caeathro. Gwyn 4E 81
Caehopkin. Powy 4B 46
Caenby. Linc 2H 87
Caerau. B'end 2B 32
Caerau. Card 4E 33
Cae'r-bont. Powy 4B 46
Cae'r-bryn. Carm 4F 45
Caerdeon. Gwyn 4F 69
Caerdydd. Card 193 (4E 33)
Caerfarchell. Pemb 2B 42
Caerffili. Cphy 3E 33
Caerfyrddin. Carm 4E 45
Caergeiliog. IOA 3C 80
Caergwrle. Flin 5F 83
Caergybi. IOA 2B 80
Caerlaverock. Per 2A 136
Caerleon. Newp 2G 33
Caerlleon. Carm 2G 43
Caerllion. Newp 2G 33
Caernarfon. Gwyn 4D 81
Caerphilly. Cphy 3E 33
Caersws. Powy 1C 58
Caerwedros. Cdgn 5C 56
Caerwent. Mon 2H 33
Caerwys. Flin 3D 82
Caim. IOA 2F 81
Caio. Carm 2G 45
Cairinis. W Isl 2D 170
Cairisiadar. W Isl 4C 171
Cairminis. W Isl 9C 171
Cairnbaan. Arg 4F 133
Cairnbulg. Abers 2H 161
Cairncross. Ang 1D 145
Cairndow. Arg 2A 134
Cairness. Abers 2H 161
Cairneyhill. Fife 1D 128
Cairngarroch. Dum 5F 109
Cairnhill. Abers 5D 160
Cairnie. Abers 4B 160
Cairnorrie. Abers 4F 161
Cairnryan. Dum 3F 109
Cairston. Orkn 6B 172
Caister-on-Sea. Norf 4H 79
Caistor. Linc 4E 94
Caistor St Edmund. Norf 5E 79
Caistron. Nmbd 4D 121
Cakebole. Worc 3C 60
Calais Street. Suff 1C 54
Calanais. W Isl 4E 171
Calbost. W Isl 6G 171
Calbourne. IOW 4C 16
Calceby. Linc 3C 88
Calcot. Glos 4F 49
Calcot Row. W Ber 4E 37
Calcott. Kent 4F 41
Calcott. Shrp 4G 71
Caldback. Shet 1H 173
Caldbeck. Cumb 5E 113
Caldbergh. N Yor 1C 98
Caldecote. Cambs
  nr. Cambridge 5C 64
  nr. Peterborough 2A 64
Caldecote. Herts 2C 52
Caldecote. Nptn 5D 62
Caldecote. Warw 1A 62
Caldecott. Nptn 4G 63
Caldecott. Oxon 2C 36
Caldecott. Rut 1F 63
Calderbank. N Lan 3A 128
Calder Bridge. Cumb 4B 102
Calderbrook. G Man 3H 91
Caldercruix. N Lan 3B 128
Calder Grove. W Yor 3D 92
Calder Mains. High 3C 168
Caldermill. S Lan 5H 127
Calder Vale. Lanc 5E 97
Calderwood. S Lan 4H 127
Caldicot. Mon 3H 33
Caldwell. Derbs 4G 73
Caldwell. N Yor 3E 105
Caldy. Mers 2E 83
Calebrack. Cumb 1E 103
Caledon. M Ulst 5B 178
Calf Heath. Staf 5D 72
Calford Green. Suff 1G 53
Calfsound. Orkn 4E 172
Calgary. Arg 3E 139
Califer. Mor 3E 159
California. Cambs 2E 65
California. Falk 2C 128
California. Norf 4H 79
California. Suff 1E 55
Calke. Derbs 3A 74
Callakille. High 3F 155
Callaly. Nmbd 4E 121
Callander. Stir 3F 135
Callaughton. Shrp 1A 60
Callendoun. Arg 1E 127
Callestick. Corn 3B 6
Calligarry. High 3E 147
Callington. Corn 2H 7
Callingwood. Staf 3F 73
Callow. Here 2H 47
Callow End. Worc 1D 48
Callow Hill. Wilts 3F 35
Callow Hill. Worc
  nr. Bewdley 3B 60
  nr. Redditch 4E 61
Calmore. Hants 1B 16
Calmsden. Glos 5F 49
Calne. Wilts 4E 35
Calow. Derbs 3B 86
Calshot. Hants 2C 16
Calstock. Corn 2A 8
Calstone Wellington. Wilts 5F 35
Calthorpe. Norf 2D 78
Calthorpe Street. Norf 3G 79
Calthwaite. Cumb 5F 113
Calton. N Yor 4B 98
Calton. Staf 5F 85
Calveley. Ches E 5H 83
Calver. Derbs 3G 85
Calverhall. Shrp 2A 72
Calverleigh. Devn 1C 12
Calverley. W Yor 1C 92
Calvert. Buck 3E 51
Calverton. Mil 2F 51
Calverton. Notts 1D 74
Calvine. Per 2F 143
Calvo. Cumb 4C 112
Cam. Glos 2C 34
Camaghael. High 1F 141
Camas-luinie. High 1B 148
Camasnacroise. High 3C 140
Camastianavaig. High 5E 155
Camasunary. High 2D 146
Camault Muir. High 4H 157
Camb. Shet 2G 173
Camber. E Sus 4D 28
Camberley. Surr 5G 37
Camberwell. G Lon 3E 39
Camblesforth. N Yor 2G 93
Cambo. Nmbd 1D 114
Cambois. Nmbd 1G 115
Camborne. Corn 5A 6
Cambourne. Cambs 5C 64
Cambridge. Cambs 193 (5D 64)
Cambridge. Glos 5C 48
Cambrose. Corn 4A 6
Cambus. Clac 4A 136
Cambusbarron. Stir 4G 135
Cambuskenneth. Stir 4H 135
Cambuslang. S Lan 3H 127
Cambusnethan. N Lan 4B 128
Cambus o' May. Abers 4B 152
Camden Town. G Lon 2D 39
Cameley. Bath 1B 22
Camelford. Corn 4B 10
Camelon. Falk 1B 128
Camelsdale. W Sus 3G 25
Camer's Green. Worc 2C 48
Camerton. Bath 1B 22
Camerton. Cumb 1B 102
Camerton. E Yor 2F 95
Camghouran. Per 3C 142
Camlough. New M 7E 178
Cammachmore. Abers 4G 153
Cammeringham. Linc 2G 87
Camore. High 4E 165
The Camp. Glos 5E 49
Campbelton. N Ayr 4C 126
Campbeltown. Arg 3B 122
Campbeltown Airport. Arg 3A 122
Cample. Dum 5A 118
Campmuir. Per 5B 144
Campsall. S Yor 3F 93
Campsea Ashe. Suff 5F 67
Camps End. Cambs 1G 53
Campsey. Derr 4A 174
Campton. C Beds 2B 52
Camptoun. E Lot 2B 130
Camptown. Bord 3A 120
Camrose. Pemb 2D 42
Camserney. Per 4F 143
Camster. High 4E 169
Camus Croise. High 2E 147
Camuscross. High 2E 147
Camusdarach. High 4E 147
Camusnagaul. High
  nr. Fort William 1E 141
  nr. Little Loch Broom 5E 163
Camus Park. Derr 3F 176
Camusteel. High 4G 155
Camusterrach. High 4G 155
Camusvrachan. Per 4D 142
Canada. Hants 1A 16
Canadia. E Sus 4B 28
Canaston Bridge. Pemb 3E 43
Candlesby. Linc 4D 88
Candle Street. Suff 3C 66
Candy Mill. S Lan 5D 128
Cane End. Oxon 4E 37
Canewdon. Essx 1D 40
Canford Cliffs. Pool 4F 15
Canford Heath. Pool 3F 15
Canford Magna. Pool 3F 15
Cangate. Norf 4F 79
Canham's Green. Suff 4C 66
Canholes. Derbs 3E 85
Canisbay. High 1F 169
Canley. W Mid 3H 61
Cann. Dors 4D 22
Cann Common. Dors 4D 23
Cannich. High 5F 157
Cannington. Som 3F 21
Cannock. Staf 4D 73
Cannock Wood. Staf 4E 73
Canonbie. Dum 2E 113
Canon Bridge. Here 1H 47
Canon Frome. Here 1B 48
Canon Pyon. Here 1H 47
Canons Ashby. Nptn 5C 62
Canonstown. Corn 3C 4
Canterbury. Kent 193 (5F 41)
Cantley. Norf 5F 79
Cantley. S Yor 4G 93
Cantlop. Shrp 5H 71
Canton. Card 4E 33
Cantray. High 4B 158
Cantraybruich. High 4B 158
Cantraywood. High 4B 158
Cantsdam. Fife 4D 136
Cantsfield. Lanc 2F 97
Canvey Island. Essx 2B 40
Canwick. Linc 4G 87
Canworthy Water. Corn 3C 10
Caol. High 1F 141
Caolas. Arg 4B 138
Caolas. W Isl 9B 170
Caolas Liubharsaigh. W Isl 4D 170
Caolas Scalpaigh. W Isl 8E 171
Caolas Stocinis. W Isl 8D 171
Caol Ila. Arg 2C 124
Caol Loch Ailse. High 1F 147
Caol Reatha. High 1F 147
Capel. Kent 1H 27
Capel. Surr 1C 26
Capel Bangor. Cdgn 2F 57
Capel Betws Lleucu. Cdgn 5F 57
Capel Coch. IOA 2D 80
Capel Curig. Cnwy 5G 81
Capel Cynon. Cdgn 1D 45
Capel Dewi. Carm 3E 45
Capel Dewi. Cdgn
  nr. Aberystwyth 2F 57
  nr. Llandysul 1E 45
Capel Garmon. Cnwy 5H 81
Capel Green. Suff 1G 55
Capel Gwyn. IOA 3C 80
Capel Gwynfe. Carm 3H 45
Capel Hendre. Carm 4F 45
Capel Isaac. Carm 3F 45
Capel Iwan. Carm 1G 43
Capel-le-Ferne. Kent 2G 29
Capel Llanilltern. Card 4D 32
Capel Mawr. IOA 3D 80
Capel Newydd. Pemb 1G 43
Capel St Andrew. Suff 1G 55
Capel St Mary. Suff 2D 54
Capel Seion. Carm 4F 45
Capel Seion. Cdgn 3F 57
Capel Uchaf. Gwyn 1D 68
Capel-y-ffin. Powy 2F 47
Capenhurst. Ches W 3F 83
Capernwray. Lanc 2E 97
Capheaton. Nmbd 1D 114
Cappagh. M Ulst 3A 178
Cappercleuch. Bord 2E 119
Capplegill. Dum 4D 118
Capton. Devn 3E 9
Capton. Som 3D 20
Caputh. Per 5H 143
Caradon Town. Corn 5C 10
Carbis Bay. Corn 3C 4
Carbost. High
  nr. Loch Harport 5C 154
  nr. Portree 4D 154
Carbrook. S Yor 2A 86
Carbrooke. Norf 5B 78
Carburton. Notts 3D 86
Carcluie. S Ayr 3C 116
Car Colston. Notts 1E 74
Carcroft. S Yor 4F 93
Cardenden. Fife 4E 136
Cardeston. Shrp 4F 71
Cardewlees. Cumb 4E 113
Cardiff. Card 193 (4E 33)
Cardiff Airport. V Glam 5D 32
Cardigan. Cdgn 1B 44
Cardinal's Green. Cambs 1G 53
Cardington. Bed 1A 52
Cardington. Shrp 1H 59
Cardinham. Corn 2F 7
Cardno. Abers 2G 161
Cardow. Mor 4F 159
Cardross. Arg 2E 127
Cardurnock. Cumb 4C 112
Careby. Linc 4H 75
Careston. Ang 2E 145
Carew. Pemb 4E 43
Carew Cheriton. Pemb 4E 43
Carew Newton. Pemb 4E 43
Carey. Here 2A 48
Carfin. N Lan 4A 128
Carfrae. Bord 4B 130
Cargan. ME Ant 5H 175
Cargate Green. Norf 4F 79
Cargenbridge. Dum 2G 111
Cargill. Per 5A 144
Cargo. Cumb 4E 113
Cargreen. Corn 2A 8
Carham. Nmbd 1C 120
Carhampton. Som 2D 20
Carharrack. Corn 4B 6
Carie. Per
  nr. Loch Rannah 3D 142
  nr. Loch Tay 5D 142
Carisbrooke. IOW 4C 16
Cark. Cumb 2C 96
Carkeel. Corn 2A 8
Carlabhagh. W Isl 3E 171
Carland Cross. Corn 3C 6
Carlbury. Darl 3F 105
Carlby. Linc 4H 75
Carlecotes. S Yor 4B 92
Carleen. Corn 4D 4
Carlesmoor. N Yor 2D 98
Carleton. Cumb
  nr. Carlisle 4F 113
  nr. Egremont 4B 102
  nr. Penrith 2G 103
Carleton. Lanc 5C 96
Carleton. N Yor 5B 98
Carleton. W Yor 2E 93
Carleton Forehoe. Norf 5C 78
Carleton Rode. Norf 1D 66
Carleton St Peter. Norf 5F 79
Carlidnack. Corn 4E 5
Carlingcott. Bath 1B 22
Carlin How. Red C 3E 107
Carlisle. Cumb 193 (4F 113)
Carloonan. Arg 2H 133
Carlops. Bord 4E 129
Carlton. Bed 5G 63
Carlton. Cambs 5F 65
Carlton. Leics 5A 74
Carlton. N Yor
  nr. Helmsley 1A 100
  nr. Middleham 1C 98
  nr. Selby 2G 93
Carlton. Notts 1D 74
Carlton. S Yor 3D 92
Carlton. Stoc T 2A 106
Carlton. Suff 4F 67
Carlton. W Yor 2D 92
Carlton Colville. Suff 1H 67
Carlton Curlieu. Leics 1D 62
Carlton Husthwaite. N Yor 2G 99
Carlton in Cleveland. N Yor 4C 106
Carlton in Lindrick. Notts 2C 86
Carlton-le-Moorland. Linc 5G 87
Carlton Miniott. N Yor 1F 99
Carlton-on-Trent. Notts 4F 87
Carlton Scroop. Linc 1G 75
Carluke. S Lan 4B 128
Carlyon Bay. Corn 3E 7
Carmarthen. Carm 4E 45
Carmel. Carm 4F 45
Carmel. Flin 3D 82
Carmel. Gwyn 5D 81
Carmel. IOA 2C 80
Carmichael. S Lan 1B 118
Carmunnock. Glas 4H 127
Carmyle. Glas 3H 127
Carmyllie. Ang 4E 145
Carnaby. E Yor 3F 101
Carnach. High
  nr. Lochcarron 1C 148
  nr. Ullapool 4E 163
Carnach. Mor 4E 159
Carnach. W Isl 8E 171
Carnachy. High 3H 167
Carnain. Arg 3B 124
Carnais. W Isl 4C 171
Carnan. Arg 4B 138
Carnan. W Isl 4C 170
Carnbee. Fife 3H 137
Carnbo. Per 3C 136
Carn Brea Village. Corn 4A 6
Carndu. High 1A 148
Carnduff. Caus 2G 175
Carne. Corn 5D 6
Carnforth. Lanc 2E 97
Carn-gorm. High 1B 148
Carnhedryn. Pemb 2C 42
Carnhell Green. Corn 3D 4
Carnie. Abers 3F 153
Carnkie. Corn
  nr. Falmouth 5B 6
  nr. Redruth 5A 6
Carnkief. Corn 3B 6
Carnlough. ME Ant 5J 175
Carnmoney. Ant 1H 179
Carno. Powy 1B 58
Carnock. Fife 1D 128
Carnon Downs. Corn 4B 6
Carnoustie. Ang 5E 145
Carnteel. M Ulst 4A 178
Carntyne. Glas 3H 127
Carnwath. S Lan 5C 128
Carnyorth. Corn 3A 4
Carol Green. W Mid 3G 61
Carpalla. Corn 3D 6
Carperby. N Yor 1C 98
Carradale. Arg 2C 122
Carragraich. W Isl 8D 171
Carrbridge. High 1D 150
Carr Cross. Lanc 3B 90
Carreglefn. IOA 2C 80
Carrhouse. N Lin 4A 94
Carrick Castle. Arg 4A 134
Carrickfergus. ME Ant 8L 175
Carrickmore. Ferm 2A 178
Carriden. Falk 1D 128
Carrington. G Man 1B 84
Carrington. Linc 5C 88
Carrington. Midl 3G 129
Carrog. Cnwy 1G 69
Carrog. Den 1D 70
Carron. Falk 1B 128
Carron. Mor 4G 159
Carronbridge. Dum 5A 118
Carronshore. Falk 1B 128
Carrowclare. Caus 4C 174
Carrowdore. Ards 2K 179
Carrow Hill. Mon 2H 33
Carr Shield. Nmbd 5B 114
Carrutherstown. Dum 2C 112
Carr Vale. Derbs 4B 86
Carrville. Dur 5G 115
Carryduff. Lis 3H 179
Carsaig. Arg 1C 132
Carscreugh. Dum 3H 109
Carsegowan. Dum 4B 110
Carse House. Arg 3F 125
Carseriggan. Dum 3A 110
Carsethorn. Dum 4A 112
Carshalton. G Lon 4D 39
Carsington. Derbs 5G 85
Carskiey. Arg 5A 122
Carsluith. Dum 4B 110
Carsphairn. Dum 5E 117
Carstairs. S Lan 5C 128
Carstairs Junction. S Lan 5C 128
Cartbridge. Surr 5B 38
Carterhaugh. Ang 4D 144
Carter's Clay. Hants 4B 24
Carterton. Oxon 5A 50
Carterway Heads. Nmbd 4D 114
Carthew. Corn 3E 6
Carthorpe. N Yor 1F 99
Cartington. Nmbd 4E 121
Cartland. S Lan 5B 128
Cartmel. Cumb 2C 96
Cartmel Fell. Cumb 1D 96
Cartworth. W Yor 4B 92
Carwath. Cumb 5E 112
Carway. Carm 5E 45
Carwinley. Cumb 2F 113
Cascob. Powy 4E 59
Cas-gwent. Mon 2A 34
Cash Feus. Fife 3E 136
Cashlie. Per 4B 142
Cashmoor. Dors 1E 15
Cas-Mael. Pemb 2E 43
Casnewydd. Newp 200 (3G 33)
Cassington. Oxon 4C 50
Cassop. Dur 1A 106
Castell. Cnwy 4G 81
Castell. Den 4D 82
Castell Hendre. Pemb 2E 43
Castell-Nedd. Neat 2A 32
Castell Newydd Emlyn. Carm 1D 44
Castell-y-bwch. Torf 2F 33
Casterton. Cumb 2F 97
Castle. Som 2A 22
Castle Acre. Norf 4H 77
Castle Ashby. Nptn 5F 63
Castlebay. W Isl 9B 170
Castle Bolton. N Yor 5D 104
Castle Bromwich. W Mid 2F 61
Castle Bytham. Linc 4G 75
Castlebythe. Pemb 2E 43
Castle Caereinion. Powy 5D 70
Castle Camps. Cambs 1G 53
Castle Carrock. Cumb 4G 113
Castle Cary. Som 3B 22
Castlecary. N Lan 2A 128
Castlecaulfield. M Ulst 3B 178
Castle Combe. Wilts 4D 34
Castlecraig. High 2C 158
Castledawson. M Ulst 7F 174
Castlederg. Derr 4E 176
Castle Donington. Leics 3B 74
Castle Douglas. Dum 3E 111
Castle Eaton. Swin 2G 35
Castle Eden. Dur 1B 106
Castleford. W Yor 2E 93
Castle Frome. Here 1B 48
Castle Green. Surr 4A 38
Castle Green. Warw 3G 61
Castle Gresley. Derbs 4G 73
Castle Heaton. Nmbd 5F 131
Castle Hedingham. Essx 2A 54
Castle Hill. Kent 1A 28
Castle Hill. Suff 1E 55
Castlehill. Per 5B 144
Castlehill. S Lan 4B 128
Castlehill. W Dun 2E 127
Castle Kennedy. Dum 4G 109
Castle Lachlan. Arg 4H 133
Castlemartin. Pemb 5D 42
Castlemilk. Glas 4H 127
Castlemorris. Pemb 1D 42
Castlemorton. Worc 2C 48
Castle O'er. Dum 5E 119
Castle Park. N Yor 3F 107
Castlerigg. Cumb 2D 102
Castle Rising. Norf 3F 77
Castlerock. Caus 3D 174
Castleroe. Caus 4E 174
Castleside. Dur 5D 115
Castlethorpe. Mil 1F 51
Castleton. Abers 4F 151
Castleton. Arg 1G 125
Castleton. Derbs 2F 85
Castleton. G Man 3G 91
Castleton. Mor 1F 151
Castleton. Newp 3F 33
Castleton. N Yor 4D 107
Castleton. Per 2B 136
Castletown. Cumb 1G 103
Castletown. Dors 5B 14
Castletown. High 2D 169
Castletown. IOM 5B 108
Castletown. Tyne 4G 115
Castlewellan. New M 6H 179
Castley. N Yor 5E 99
Caston. Norf 1B 66
Castor. Pet 1A 64
Caswell. Swan 4E 31
Catacol. N Ayr 5H 125
Catbrook. Mon 5A 48
Catchems End. Worc 3B 60
Catchgate. Dur 4E 115
Catcleugh. Nmbd 4B 120
Catcliffe. S Yor 2B 86
Catcott. Som 3G 21
Caterham. Surr 5E 39
Catfield. Norf 3F 79
Catfield Common. Norf 3F 79
Catfirth. Shet 6F 173
Catford. G Lon 3E 39
Catforth. Lanc 1C 90
Cathcart. Glas 3G 127
Cathedine. Powy 3E 47
Catherine-de-Barnes. W Mid 2F 61
Catherington. Hants 1E 17
Catherston Leweston. Dors 3G 13
Catherton. Shrp 3A 60
Catisfield. Hants 2D 16
Catlodge. High 4A 150
Catlowdy. Cumb 2F 113
Catmore. W Ber 3C 36
Caton. Devn 5A 12
Caton. Lanc 3E 97
Catrine. E Ayr 2E 117
Cat's Ash. Newp 2G 33
Catsfield. E Sus 4B 28
Catsgore. Som 4A 22
Catshill. Worc 3D 60
Cattal. N Yor 4G 99
Cattawade. Suff 2E 54
Catterall. Lanc 5E 97
Catterick. N Yor 5F 105
Catterick Bridge. N Yor 5F 105
Catterick Garrison. N Yor 5E 105
Catterlen. Cumb 1F 103
Catterline. Abers 1H 145
Catterton. N Yor 5H 99
Catteshall. Surr 1A 26
Catthorpe. Leics 3C 62
Cattistock. Dors 3A 14
Catton. Nmbd 4B 114
Catton. N Yor 2F 99
Catwick. E Yor 5F 101
Catworth. Cambs 3H 63
Caudle Green. Glos 4E 49
Caulcott. Oxon 3D 50
Cauldhame. Stir 4F 135
Cauldmill. Bord 3H 119
Cauldon. Staf 1E 73
Cauldon Lowe. Staf 1E 73
Cauldwells. Abers 3E 161
Caulkerbush. Dum 4G 111
Caulside. Dum 1F 113
Caunsall. Worc 2C 60
Caunton. Notts 4E 87
Causewayend. S Lan 1C 118
Causewayhead. Stir 4H 135
Causey Park. Nmbd 5F 121
Caute. Devn 1E 11
Cautley. Cumb 5H 103
Cavendish. Suff 1B 54
Cavendish Bridge. Leics 3B 74
Cavenham. Suff 3G 65
Caversfield. Oxon 3D 50
Caversham. Read 4F 37
Caversham Heights. Read 4F 37
Caverswall. Staf 1D 72
Cawdor. High 3C 158
Cawkwell. Linc 2B 88
Cawood. N Yor 1F 93
Cawsand. Corn 3A 8
Cawston. Norf 3D 78
Cawston. Warw 3B 62
Cawthorne. N Yor 1B 100
Cawthorne. S Yor 4C 92
Cawthorpe. Linc 3H 75
Cawton. N Yor 2A 100
Caxton. Cambs 5C 64
Caynham. Shrp 3H 59
Caythorpe. Linc 1G 75
Caythorpe. Notts 1D 74
Cayton. N Yor 1E 101
Ceallan. W Isl 3D 170
Ceann a Bhaigh. W Isl
  on North Uist 2C 170
  on Scalpay 8E 171
  on South Harris 8D 171
Ceann a Bhàigh. W Isl 9C 171
Ceannacroc Lodge. High 2E 149
Ceann a Deas Loch Baghasdail. W Isl 7C 170
Ceann an Leothaid. High 5E 147
Ceann a Tuath Loch Baghasdail. W Isl 6C 170
Ceann Loch Ailleart. High 5F 147
Ceann Loch Muideirt. High 1B 140
Ceann-na-Cleithe. W Isl 8D 171
Ceann Shiphoirt. W Isl 6E 171
Ceann Tarabhaigh. W Isl 6E 171
Cearsiadar. W Isl 5F 171
Ceathramh Meadhanach. W Isl 1D 170
Cefn Berain. Cnwy 4B 82
Cefn-brith. Cnwy 5B 82
Cefn-bryn-brain. Carm 4H 45
Cefn Bychan. Cphy 2F 33
Cefn-bychan. Flin 4D 82
Cefncaeau. Carm 3E 31
Cefn Canol. Powy 2E 71
Cefn Coch. Powy 5C 70
Cefn-coch. Powy 3D 70
Cefn-coed-y-cymmer. Mer T 5D 46
Cefn Cribwr. B'end 3B 32
Cefn-ddwysarn. Gwyn 2B 70
Cefn Einion. Shrp 2E 59
Cefneithin. Carm 4F 45
Cefn Glas. B'end 3B 32
Cefngorwydd. Powy 1C 46
Cefn Llwyd. Cdgn 2F 57
Cefn-mawr. Wrex 1E 71
Cefn-y-bedd. Flin 5F 83
Cefn-y-coed. Powy 1D 58
Cefn-y-pant. Carm 2F 43
Cegidfa. Powy 4E 70
Ceinewydd. Cdgn 5C 56
Cellan. Cdgn 1G 45
Cellardyke. Fife 3H 137
Cellarhead. Staf 1D 72
Cemaes. IOA 1C 80
Cemmaes. Powy 5H 69
Cemmaes Road. Powy 5H 69
Cenarth. Cdgn 1C 44
Cenin. Gwyn 1D 68
Ceos. W Isl 5F 171
Ceres. Fife 2G 137
Ceri. Powy 2D 58
Cerist. Powy 2B 58
Cerne Abbas. Dors 2B 14
Cerney Wick. Glos 2F 35
Cerrigceinwen. IOA 3D 80
Cerrigydrudion. Cnwy 1B 70
Cess. Norf 4G 79
Cessford. Bord 2B 120
Ceunant. Gwyn 4E 81
Chaceley. Glos 2D 48
Chacewater. Corn 4B 6
Chackmore. Buck 2E 51
Chacombe. Nptn 1C 50
Chadderton. G Man 4H 91
Chaddesden. Derb 2A 74
Chaddesden Common. Derb 2A 74
Chaddesley Corbett. Worc 3C 60
Chaddlehanger. Devn 5E 11
Chaddleworth. W Ber 4C 36
Chadlington. Oxon 3B 50
Chadshunt. Warw 5H 61
Chadstone. Nptn 5F 63
Chad Valley. W Mid 2E 61
Chadwell. Leics 3E 75
Chadwell. Shrp 4B 72
Chadwell Heath. G Lon 2F 39
Chadwell St Mary. Thur 3H 39
Chadwick End. W Mid 3G 61
Chadwick Green. Mers 1H 83
Chaffcombe. Som 1G 13
Chafford Hundred. Thur 3H 39
Chagford. Devn 4H 11
Chailey. E Sus 4E 27
Chain Bridge. Linc 1C 76
Chainbridge. Cambs 5D 76
Chainhurst. Kent 1B 28
Chalbury. Dors 2F 15
Chalbury Common. Dors 2F 15
Chaldon. Surr 5E 39
Chaldon Herring. Dors 4C 14
Chale. IOW 5C 16
Chale Green. IOW 5C 16
Chalfont Common. Buck 1B 38
Chalfont St Giles. Buck 1A 38
Chalfont St Peter. Buck 2B 38
Chalford. Glos 5D 49
Chalgrove. Oxon 2E 37
Chalk. Kent 3A 40
Chalk End. Essx 4G 53
Chalk Hill. Glos 3G 49
Challaborough. Devn 4C 8
Challacombe. Devn 2G 19
Challister. Shet 5G 173
Challoch. Dum 3A 110
Challock. Kent 5E 40
Chalton. C Beds
  nr. Bedford 5A 64
  nr. Luton 3A 52
Chalton. Hants 1F 17
Chalvington. E Sus 5G 27
Champany. Falk 2D 128
Chance Inn. Fife 2F 137
Chancery. Cdgn 3E 57
Chandler's Cross. Herts 1B 38
Chandler's Cross. Worc 2C 48
Chandler's Ford. Hants 4C 24
Chanlockfoot. Dum 4G 117
Channel's End. Bed 5A 64
Channel Tunnel. Kent 2F 29
Channerwick. Shet 9F 173
Chantry. Som 2C 22
Chantry. Suff 1E 55
Chapel. Cumb 1D 102
Chapel. Fife 4E 137
Chapel Allerton. Som 1H 21
Chapel Allerton. W Yor 1C 92
Chapel Amble. Corn 1D 6
Chapel Brampton. Nptn 4E 63
Chapelbridge. Cambs 1B 64
Chapel Chorlton. Staf 2C 72
Chapel Cleeve. Som 2D 20
Chapel End. C Beds 1A 52
Chapel-en-le-Frith. Derbs 2E 85
Chapelfield. Abers 2G 145
Chapelgate. Linc 3D 76
Chapel Green. Warw
  nr. Coventry 2G 61
  nr. Southam 4B 62
Chapel Haddlesey. N Yor 2F 93
Chapelhall. N Lan 3A 128
Chapel Hill. Abers 5H 161
Chapel Hill. Linc 5B 88
Chapel Hill. Mon 5A 48
Chapelhill. Per
  nr. Glencarse 1E 136
  nr. Harrietfield 5H 143
Chapelknowe. Dum 2E 112

Chapel Lawn—Coggeshall

Chapel Lawn. Shrp 3F 59
Chapel le Dale. N Yor 2G 97
Chapel Milton. Derbs 2E 85
Chapel of Garioch. Abers 1E 152
Chapel Row. W Ber 5D 36
Chapels. Cumb 1B 96
Chapel St Leonards. Linc 3E 89
Chapel Stile. Cumb 4E 102
Chapelthorpe. W Yor 3D 92
Chapelton. Ang 4F 145
Chapelton. Devn 4F 19
Chapelton. High
nr. Grantown-on-Spey 2D 150
nr. Inverness 3H 157
Chapelton. S Lan 5H 127
Chapel Town. Corn 3C 6
Chapeltown. Bkbn 3F 91
Chapeltown. Mor 1G 151
Chapeltown. New M 6K 179
Chapeltown. S Yor 1A 86
Chapmanslade. Wilts 2D 22
Chapmans Well. Devn 3D 10
Chapmore End. Herts 4D 52
Chappel. Essx 3B 54
Chard. Som 2G 13
Chard Junction. Dors 2G 13
Chardstock. Devn 2G 13
Charfield. S Glo 2C 34
Charing. Kent 1D 28
Charing Heath. Kent 1D 28
Charing Hill. Kent 5D 40
Charingworth. Glos 2H 49
Charlbury. Oxon 4B 50
Charlcombe. Bath 5C 34
Charlcutt. Wilts 4E 35
Charlecote. Warw 5G 61
Charlemont. Arm 4C 178
Charles. Devn 3G 19
Charlesfield. Dum 3C 112
Charleshill. Surr 2G 25
Charleston. Ang 4C 144
Charleston. Ren 3F 127
Charlestown. Aber 3G 153
Charlestown. Abers 2H 161
Charlestown. Corn 3E 7
Charlestown. Dors 5B 14
Charlestown. Fife 1D 128
Charlestown. G Man 4G 91
Charlestown. High
nr. Gairloch 1H 155
nr. Inverness 4A 158
Charlestown. W Yor 2H 91
Charlestown of Aberlour. Mor 4G 159
Charles Tye. Suff 5C 66
Charlesworth. Derbs 1E 85
Charlton. G Lon 3F 39
Charlton. Hants 2B 24
Charlton. Herts 3B 52
Charlton. Nptn 2D 50
Charlton. Nmbd 1B 114
Charlton. Oxon 3C 36
Charlton. Som
nr. Radstock 1B 22
nr. Shepton Mallet 2B 22
nr. Taunton 4F 21
Charlton. Telf 4H 71
Charlton. W Sus 1G 17
Charlton. Wilts
nr. Malmesbury 3E 35
nr. Pewsey 1G 23
nr. Shaftesbury 4E 23
Charlton. Worc
nr. Evesham 1F 49
nr. Stourport-on-Severn 3C 60
Charlton Abbots. Glos 3F 49
Charlton Adam. Som 4A 22
Charlton All Saints. Wilts 4G 23
Charlton Down. Dors 3B 14
Charlton Horethorne. Som 4B 22
Charlton Kings. Glos 3E 49
Charlton Mackrell. Som 4A 22
Charlton Marshall. Dors 2E 15
Charlton Musgrove. Som 4C 22
Charlton-on-Otmoor. Oxon 4D 50
Charlton on the Hill. Dors 2D 15
Charlwood. Hants 3E 25
Charlwood. Surr 1D 26
Charlynch. Som 3F 21
Charminster. Dors 3B 14
Charmouth. Dors 3G 13
Charndon. Buck 3E 51
Charney Bassett. Oxon 2B 36
Charnock Green. Lanc 3D 90
Charnock Richard. Lanc 3D 90
Charsfield. Suff 5E 67
The Chart. Kent 5F 39
Chart Corner. Kent 5B 40
Charter Alley. Hants 1D 24
Charterhouse. Som 1H 21
Charterville Allotments. Oxon 4B 50
Chartham. Kent 5F 41
Chartham Hatch. Kent 5F 41
Chartridge. Buck 5H 51
Chart Sutton. Kent 5B 40
Charvil. Wok 4F 37
Charwelton. Nptn 5C 62
Chase Terrace. Staf 5E 73
Chasetown. Staf 5E 73
Chastleton. Oxon 3H 49
Chasty. Devn 2D 10
Chatburn. Lanc 5G 97
Chatcull. Staf 2B 72
Chatham. Medw ... **Medway Towns 197** (4B 40)
Chatham Green. Essx 4H 53
Chathill. Nmbd 2F 121
Chatley. Worc 4C 60
Chattenden. Medw 3B 40
Chatteris. Cambs 2C 64
Chattisham. Suff 1D 54
Chatton. Nmbd 2E 121
Chatwall. Shrp 1H 59
Chaulden. Herts 5A 52
Chaul End. C Beds 3A 52
Chawleigh. Devn 1H 11
Chawley. Oxon 5C 50
Chawston. Bed 5A 64
Chawton. Hants 3F 25
Chaxhill. Glos 4C 48
Cheadle. G Man 2C 84
Cheadle. Staf 1E 73
Cheadle Hulme. G Man 2C 84
Cheam. G Lon 4D 38
Cheapside. Wind 4A 38
Chearsley. Buck 4F 51
Chebsey. Staf 3C 72
Checkendon. Oxon 3E 37
Checkley. Ches E 1B 72
Checkley. Here 2A 48
Checkley. Staf 2E 73
Chedburgh. Suff 5G 65
Cheddar. Som 1H 21
Cheddington. Buck 4H 51
Cheddleton. Staf 5D 84
Cheddon Fitzpaine. Som 4F 21
Chedglow. Wilts 2E 35
Chedgrave. Norf 1F 67
Chedington. Dors 2H 13
Chediston. Suff 3F 67
Chediston Green. Suff 3F 67
Chedworth. Glos 4F 49
Chedzoy. Som 3G 21
Cheeseman's Green. Kent 2E 29
Cheetham Hill. G Man 4G 91
Cheglinch. Devn 2F 19
Cheldon. Devn 1H 11
Chelford. Ches E 3C 84
Chellaston. Derb 2A 74
Chellington. Bed 5G 63
Chelmarsh. Shrp 2B 60
Chelmick. Shrp 1G 59
Chelmondiston. Suff 2F 55
Chelmorton. Derbs 4F 85
Chelmsford. Essx 5H 53
Chelsea. G Lon 3D 38
Chelsfield. G Lon 4F 39
Chelsham. Surr 5E 39
Chelston. Som 4E 21
Chelsworth. Suff 1C 54
Cheltenham. Glos **193** (3E 49)
Chelveston. Nptn 4G 63
Chelvey. N Som 5H 33
Chelwood. Bath 5B 34
Chelwood Common. E Sus 3F 27
Chelwood Gate. E Sus 3F 27
Chelworth. Wilts 2E 35
Chelworth Lower Green. Wilts 2F 35
Chelworth Upper Green. Wilts 2F 35
Chelynch. Som 2B 22
Cheney Longville. Shrp 2G 59
Chenies. Buck 1B 38
Chepstow. Mon 2A 34
Chequerfield. W Yor 2E 93
Chequers Corner. Norf 5D 77
Cherhill. Wilts 4F 35
Cherington. Glos 2E 35
Cherington. Warw 2A 50
Cheriton. Devn 2H 19
Cheriton. Hants 4D 24
Cheriton. Kent 2G 29
Cheriton. Pemb 5D 43
Cheriton. Swan 3D 30
Cheriton Bishop. Devn 3A 12
Cheriton Cross. Devn 3A 12
Cheriton Fitzpaine. Devn 2B 12
Cherrington. Telf 3A 72
Cherrybank. Per 1D 136
Cherry Burton. E Yor 5D 101
Cherry Green. Herts 3D 52
Cherry Hinton. Cambs 5D 65
Cherry Willingham. Linc 3H 87
Chertsey. Surr 4B 38
Cheselbourne. Dors 3C 14
Chesham. Buck 5H 51
Chesham. G Man 3G 91
Chesham Bois. Buck 1A 38
Cheshunt. Herts 5D 52
Cheslyn Hay. Staf 5D 73
Chessetts Wood. Warw 3F 61
Chessington. G Lon 4C 38
Chester. Ches W **194** (4G 83)
Chesterblade. Som 2B 22
Chesterfield. Derbs 3A 86
Chesterfield. Staf 5F 73
Chesterhope. Nmbd 1C 114
Chester-le-Street. Dur 4F 115
Chester Moor. Dur 5F 115
Chesters. Bord 3A 120
Chesterton. Cambs
nr. Cambridge 4D 64
nr. Peterborough 1A 64
Chesterton. Glos 5F 49
Chesterton. Oxon 3D 50
Chesterton. Shrp 1B 60
Chesterton. Staf 1C 72
Chesterton Green. Warw 5H 61
Chesterwood. Nmbd 3B 114
Chestfield. Kent 4F 41
Cheston. Devn 3C 8
Cheswardine. Shrp 2B 72
Cheswell. Telf 4B 72
Cheswick. Nmbd 5G 131
Cheswick Green. W Mid 3F 61
Chetnole. Dors 2B 14
Chettiscombe. Devn 1C 12
Chettisham. Cambs 2E 65
Chettle. Dors 1E 15
Chetton. Shrp 1A 60
Chetwode. Buck 3E 51
Chetwynd Aston. Telf 4B 72
Cheveley. Cambs 4F 65
Chevening. Kent 5F 39
Chevington. Suff 5G 65
Chevithorne. Devn 1C 12
Chew Magna. Bath 5A 34
Chew Moor. G Man 4E 91
Chew Stoke. Bath 5A 34
Chewton Keynsham. Bath 5B 34
Chewton Mendip. Som 1A 22
Chichacott. Devn 3G 11
Chicheley. Mil 1H 51
Chichester. W Sus 2G 17
Chickerell. Dors 4B 14
Chickering. Suff 3E 66
Chicklade. Wilts 3E 23
Chicksands. C Beds 2B 52
Chickward. Here 5E 59
Chidden. Hants 1E 17
Chiddingfold. Surr 2A 26
Chiddingly. E Sus 4G 27
Chiddingstone. Kent 1G 27
Chiddingstone Causeway. Kent 1G 27
Chiddingstone Hoath. Kent 1F 27
Chideock. Dors 3H 13
Chidgley. Som 3D 20
Chidham. W Sus 2F 17
Chieveley. W Ber 4C 36
Chignal St James. Essx 5G 53
Chignal Smealy. Essx 4G 53
Chigwell. Essx 1F 39
Chigwell Row. Essx 1F 39
Chilbolton. Hants 2B 24
Chilcomb. Hants 4D 24
Chilcombe. Dors 3A 14
Chilcompton. Som 1B 22
Chilcote. Leics 4G 73
Childer Thornton. Ches W 3F 83
Child Okeford. Dors 1D 14
Childrey. Oxon 3B 36
Child's Ercall. Shrp 3A 72
Childswickham. Worc 2F 49
Childwall. Mers 2G 83
Childwick Green. Herts 4B 52
Chilfrome. Dors 3A 14
Chilgrove. W Sus 1G 17
Chilham. Kent 5E 41
Chilhampton. Wilts 3F 23
Chilla. Devn 2E 11
Chilland. Hants 3D 24
Chillaton. Devn 4E 11
Chillenden. Kent 5G 41
Chillerton. IOW 4C 16
Chillesford. Suff 5F 67
Chillingham. Nmbd 2E 121
Chillington. Devn 4D 9
Chillington. Som 1G 13
Chilmark. Wilts 3E 23
Chilmington Green. Kent 1D 28
Chilson. Oxon 4B 50
Chilsworthy. Corn 5E 11
Chilsworthy. Devn 2D 10
Chiltern Green. C Beds 4B 52
Chilthorne Domer. Som 1A 14
Chilton. Buck 4E 51
Chilton. Devn 2B 12
Chilton. Dur 2F 105
Chilton. Oxon 3C 36
Chilton Candover. Hants 2D 24
Chilton Cantelo. Som 4A 22
Chilton Foliat. Wilts 4B 36
Chilton Lane. Dur 1A 106
Chilton Polden. Som 3G 21
Chilton Street. Suff 1A 54
Chilton Trinity. Som 3F 21
Chilwell. Notts 2C 74
Chilworth. Hants 1C 16
Chilworth. Surr 1B 26
Chimney. Oxon 5B 50
Chimney Street. Suff 1H 53
Chineham. Hants 1E 25
Chingford. G Lon 1E 39
Chinley. Derbs 2E 85
Chinnor. Oxon 5F 51
Chipley. Som 4E 20
Chipnall. Shrp 2B 72
Chippenham. Cambs 4F 65
Chippenham. Wilts 4E 35
Chipperfield. Herts 5A 52
Chipping. Herts 2D 52
Chipping. Lanc 5F 97
Chipping Campden. Glos 2G 49
Chipping Hill. Essx 4B 54
Chipping Norton. Oxon 3B 50
Chipping Ongar. Essx 5F 53
Chipping Sodbury. S Glo 3C 34
Chipping Warden. Nptn 1C 50
Chipstable. Som 4D 20
Chipstead. Kent 5G 39
Chipstead. Surr 5D 38
Chirbury. Shrp 1E 59
Chirk. Wrex 2E 71
Chirmorie. S Ayr 2H 109
Chirnside. Bord 4E 131
Chirnsidebridge. Bord 4E 131
Chirton. Wilts 1F 23
Chisbridge Cross. Buck 3G 37
Chisbury. Wilts 5A 36
Chiselborough. Som 1H 13
Chiseldon. Swin 4G 35
Chiselhampton. Oxon 2D 36
Chiserley. W Yor 2A 92
Chislehurst. G Lon 3F 39
Chislet. Kent 4G 41
Chiswell. Dors 5B 14
Chiswell Green. Herts 5B 52
Chiswick. G Lon 3D 38
Chisworth. Derbs 1D 85
Chitcombe. E Sus 3C 28
Chithurst. W Sus 4G 25
Chittering. Cambs 4D 65
Chitterley. Devn 2C 12
Chitterne. Wilts 2E 23
Chittlehamholt. Devn 4G 19
Chittlehampton. Devn 4G 19
Chittoe. Wilts 5E 35
Chivelstone. Devn 5D 9
Chivenor. Devn 3F 19
Chobham. Surr 4A 38
Cholderton. Wilts 2H 23
Cholesbury. Buck 5H 51
Chollerford. Nmbd 2C 114
Chollerton. Nmbd 2C 114
Cholsey. Oxon 3D 36
Cholstrey. Here 5G 59
Chop Gate. N Yor 5C 106
Choppington. Nmbd 1F 115
Chopwell. Tyne 4E 115
Chorley. Ches E 5H 83
Chorley. Lanc 3D 90
Chorley. Shrp 2A 60
Chorley. Staf 4E 73
Chorleywood. Herts 1B 38
Chorlton. Ches E 5B 84
Chorlton-cum-Hardy. G Man 1C 84
Chorlton Lane. Ches W 1G 71
Choulton. Shrp 2F 59
Chrishall. Essx 2E 53
Christchurch. Cambs 1D 65
Christchurch. Dors 3G 15
Christchurch. Glos 4A 48
Christian Malford. Wilts 4E 35
Christleton. Ches W 4G 83
Christmas Common. Oxon 2F 37
Christon. N Som 1G 21
Christon Bank. Nmbd 2G 121
Christow. Devn 4B 12
Chryston. N Lan 2H 127
Chuck Hatch. E Sus 2F 27
Chudleigh. Devn 5B 12
Chudleigh Knighton. Devn 5B 12
Chulmleigh. Devn 1G 11
Chunal. Derbs 1E 85
Church. Lanc 2F 91
Churcham. Glos 4C 48
Church Aston. Telf 4B 72
Church Brampton. Nptn 4E 62
Church Brough. Cumb 3A 104
Church Broughton. Derbs 2G 73
Church Corner. Suff 2G 67
Church Crookham. Hants 1G 25
Churchdown. Glos 3D 49
Church Eaton. Staf 4C 72
Church End. Cambs
nr. Cambridge 5D 65
nr. Over 3C 64
nr. Sawtry 2A 64
nr. Wisbech 5C 76
Church End. C Beds
nr. Stotfold 2B 52
nr. Totternhoe 3H 51
Church End. E Yor 4E 101
Church End. Essx
nr. Braintree 3H 53
nr. Great Dunmow 3G 53
nr. Saffron Walden 1F 53
Church End. Glos 5C 48
Church End. Hants 1E 25
Church End. Linc
nr. Donington 2B 76
nr. North Somercotes 1D 88
Church End. Norf 4E 77
Church End. Warw
nr. Coleshill 1G 61
nr. Nuneaton 1G 61
Church End. Wilts 4F 35
Churchend. Essx 1E 40
Church Enstone. Oxon 3B 50
Church Fenton. N Yor 1F 93
Church Green. Devn 3E 13
Church Gresley. Derbs 4G 73
Church Hanborough. Oxon 4C 50
Church Hill. Ches W 4A 84
Church Hill. Worc 4E 61
Church Hougham. Kent 1G 29
Church Houses. N Yor 5D 106
Churchill. Devn
nr. Axminster 2G 13
nr. Barnstaple 2F 19
Churchill. N Som 1H 21
Churchill. Oxon 3A 50
Churchill. Worc
nr. Kidderminster 3C 60
nr. Worcester 5D 60
Churchinford. Som 1F 13
Church Knowle. Dors 4E 15
Church Laneham. Notts 3F 87
Church Langley. Essx 5E 53
Church Langton. Leics 1E 62
Church Lawford. Warw 3B 62
Church Lawton. Ches E 5C 84
Church Leigh. Staf 2E 73
Church Lench. Worc 5E 61
Church Mayfield. Staf 1F 73
Church Minshull. Ches E 4A 84
Church Norton. W Sus 3G 17
Churchover. Warw 2C 62
Church Preen. Shrp 1H 59
Church Pulverbatch. Shrp 5G 71
Churchstanton. Som 1E 13
Church Stoke. Powy 1E 59
Churchstow. Devn 4D 8
Church Stowe. Nptn 5D 62
Church Street. Kent 3B 40
Church Stretton. Shrp 1G 59
Church Town. Leics 4A 74
Church Town. N Lin 4A 94
Churchtown. Cumb 5E 113
Churchtown. Derbs 4G 85
Churchtown. Devn 2G 19
Churchtown. IOM 2D 108
Churchtown. Lanc 5D 97
Churchtown. Mers 3B 90
Churchtown. New M 5K 179
Churchtown. Shrp 2E 59
Church Village. Rhon 3D 32
Church Warsop. Notts 4C 86
Church Westcote. Glos 3H 49
Church Wilne. Derbs 2B 74
Churnsike Lodge. Nmbd 2H 113
Churston Ferrers. Torb 3F 9
Churt. Surr 3G 25
Churton. Ches W 5G 83
Churwell. W Yor 2C 92
Chute Standen. Wilts 1B 24
Chwilog. Gwyn 2D 68
Chwitffordd. Flin 3D 82
Chyandour. Corn 3B 4
Cilan Uchaf. Gwyn 3B 68
Cilcain. Flin 4D 82
Cilcennin. Cdgn 4E 57
Cilfrew. Neat 5A 46
Cilfynydd. Rhon 2D 32
Cilgerran. Pemb 1B 44
Cilgeti. Pemb 4F 43
Cilgwyn. Carm 3H 45
Cilgwyn. Pemb 1E 43
Ciliau Aeron. Cdgn 5D 57
Cill Amhlaidh. W Isl 4C 170
Cill Donnain. W Isl 6C 170
Cille a' Bhacstair. High 2C 154
Cille Bhrighde. W Isl 7C 170
Cille Pheadair. W Isl 7C 170
Cilmaengwyn. Neat 5H 45
Cilmeri. Powy 5C 58
Cilmery. Powy 5C 58
Cilrhedyn. Pemb 1G 43
Cilsan. Carm 3F 45
Ciltalgarth. Gwyn 1A 70
Cilybebyll. Neat 5H 45
Cilycwm. Carm 2A 46
Cimla. Neat 2A 32
Cinderford. Glos 4B 48
Cinderhill. Derbs 1A 74
Cippenham. Slo 2A 38
Cippyn. Pemb 1B 44
Cirbhig. W Isl 3D 171
Circebost. W Isl 4D 171
Cirencester. Glos 5F 49
City. Powy 1E 58
City. V Glam 4C 32
The City. Buck 2F 37
City Airport. G Lon 2F 39
City Centre. Stoke ... **Stoke 202** (1C 72)
City Dulas. IOA 2D 80
City of Derry Airport. Derr 4B 174
City of London. G Lon ... **London 199** (2E 39)
Civiltown. Arm 5F 178
Clabby. Ferm 4K 177
Clabhach. Arg 3C 138
Clachaig. Arg 1C 126
Clachaig. High
nr. Kinlochleven 3F 141
nr. Nethy Bridge 2E 151
Clachamish. High 3C 154
Clachan. Arg
on Kintyre 4F 125
on Lismore 4C 140
Clachan. High
nr. Bettyhill 2H 167
nr. Staffin 2D 155
nr. Uig 1D 154
on Raasay 5E 155
Clachan Farm. Arg 2A 134
Clachan na Luib. W Isl 2D 170
Clachan of Campsie. E Dun 2H 127
Clachan of Glendaruel. Arg 1A 126
Clachan-Seil. Arg 2E 133
Clachan Shannda. W Isl 1D 170
Clachan Strachur. Arg 3H 133
Clachbreck. Arg 2F 125
Clachnaharry. High 4A 158
Clachtoll. High 1E 163
Clackmannan. Clac 4B 136
Clackmannanshire Bridge. Clac 1C 128
Clackmarras. Mor 3G 159
Clacton-on-Sea. Essx 4E 55
Cladach a Chaolais. W Isl 2C 170
Cladach Chairinis. W Isl 3D 170
Cladach Chirceboist. W Isl 2C 170
Cladach Iolaraigh. W Isl 2C 170
Cladich. Arg 1H 133
Cladswell. Worc 5E 61
Clady. Derr 3E 176
Clady. M Ulst 6F 175
Claggan. High
nr. Fort William 1F 141
nr. Lochaline 3B 140
Claigan. High 3B 154
Clandown. Bath 1B 22
Clanfield. Hants 1E 17
Clanfield. Oxon 5A 50
Clanville. Hants 2B 24
Clanville. Som 3B 22
Claonaig. Arg 4G 125
Clapgate. Dors 2F 15
Clapgate. Herts 3E 53
Clapham. Bed 5H 63
Clapham. Devn 4B 12
Clapham. G Lon 3D 39
Clapham. N Yor 3G 97
Clapham. W Sus 5B 26
Clap Hill. Kent 2E 29
Clappers. Bord 4F 131
Clappersgate. Cumb 4E 103
Clapphoull. Shet 9F 173
Clapton. Som
nr. Crewkerne 2H 13
nr. Radstock 1B 22
Clapton in Gordano. N Som 4H 33
Clapton-on-the-Hill. Glos 4G 49
Clapworthy. Devn 4G 19
Clara Vale. Tyne 3E 115
Clarbeston. Pemb 2E 43
Clarbeston Road. Pemb 2E 43
Clarborough. Notts 2E 87
Clare. Arm 5E 178
Clare. Suff 1A 54
Clarebrand. Dum 3E 111
Clarencefield. Dum 3B 112
Clarilaw. Bord 3H 119
Clark's Green. Surr 2C 26
Clark's Hill. Linc 3C 76
Clarkston. E Ren 4G 127
Clasheddy. High 2G 167
Clashindarroch. Abers 5B 160
Clashmore. High
nr. Dornoch 5E 165
nr. Stoer 1E 163
Clashnessie. High 5A 166
Clashnoir. Mor 1G 151
Clate. Shet 5G 173
Clathick. Per 1H 135
Clathy. Per 2B 136
Clatt. Abers 1C 152
Clatter. Powy 1B 58
Clatterford. IOW 4C 16
Clatworthy. Som 3D 20
Claudy. Derr 6B 174
Claughton. Lanc
nr. Caton 3E 97
nr. Garstang 5E 97
Claughton. Mers 2E 83
Claverdon. Warw 4F 61
Claverham. N Som 5H 33
Clavering. Essx 2E 53
Claverley. Shrp 1B 60
Claverton. Bath 5C 34
Clawdd-coch. V Glam 4D 32
Clawdd-newydd. Den 5C 82
Clawson Hill. Leics 3E 75
Clawton. Devn 3D 10
Claxby. Linc
nr. Alford 3D 88
nr. Market Rasen 1A 88
Claxton. Norf 5F 79
Claxton. N Yor 3A 100
Claybrooke Magna. Leics 2B 62
Claybrooke Parva. Leics 2B 62
Clay Common. Suff 2G 67
Clay Coton. Nptn 3C 62
Clay Cross. Derbs 4A 86
Claydon. Oxon 5B 62
Claydon. Suff 5D 66
Clay End. Herts 3D 52
Claygate. Dum 2E 113
Claygate. Kent 1B 28
Claygate. Surr 4C 38
Claygate Cross. Kent 5H 39
Clayhall. Hants 3E 16
Clayhanger. Devn 4D 20
Clayhanger. W Mid 5E 73
Clayhidon. Devn 1E 13
Clay Hill. Bris 4B 34
Clayhill. E Sus 3C 28
Clayhill. Hants 2B 16
Clayhithe. Cambs 4E 65
Clayholes. Ang 5E 145
Clay Lake. Linc 3B 76
Claylock. High 3D 168
Claypits. Glos 5C 48
Claypole. Linc 1F 75
Claythorpe. Linc 3D 88
Clayton. G Man 1C 84
Clayton. S Yor 4E 93
Clayton. Staf 1C 72
Clayton. W Sus 4E 27
Clayton. W Yor 1B 92
Clayton Green. Lanc 2D 90
Clayton-le-Moors. Lanc 1F 91
Clayton-le-Woods. Lanc 2D 90
Clayton West. W Yor 3C 92
Clayworth. Notts 2E 87
Cleadale. High 5C 146
Cleadon. Tyne 3G 115
Clearbrook. Devn 2B 8
Clearwell. Glos 5A 48
Cleasby. N Yor 3F 105
Cleat. Orkn
nr. Braehead 3D 172
nr. St Margaret's Hope 9D 172
Cleatlam. Dur 3E 105
Cleator. Cumb 3B 102
Cleator Moor. Cumb 3B 102
Cleckheaton. W Yor 2B 92
Cleedownton. Shrp 2H 59
Cleehill. Shrp 3H 59
Cleekhimin. N Lan 4A 128
Clee St Margaret. Shrp 2H 59
Cleestanton. Shrp 3H 59
Cleethorpes. NE Lin 4G 95
Cleeton St Mary. Shrp 3A 60
Cleeve. N Som 5H 33
Cleeve. Oxon 3E 36
Cleeve Hill. Glos 3E 49
Cleeve Prior. Worc 1F 49
Clehonger. Here 2H 47
Cleigh. Arg 1F 133
Cleish. Per 4C 136
Cleland. N Lan 4B 128
Clench Common. Wilts 5G 35
Clenchwarton. Norf 3E 77
Clennell. Nmbd 4D 120
Clent. Worc 3D 60
Cleobury Mortimer. Shrp 3A 60
Cleobury North. Shrp 2A 60
Clephanton. High 3C 158
Clerkhill. High 2H 167
Clestrain. Orkn 7C 172
Clevancy. Wilts 4F 35
Clevedon. N Som 4H 33
Cleveley. Oxon 3B 50
Cleveleys. Lanc 5C 96
Clevelode. Worc 1D 48
Cleverton. Wilts 3E 35
Clewer. Som 1H 21
Cley next the Sea. Norf 1C 78
Cliaid. W Isl 8B 170
Cliasmol. W Isl 7C 171
Cliburn. Cumb 2G 103
Cliddesden. Hants 2E 25
Clieves Hills. Lanc 4B 90
Cliff. Warw 1G 61
Cliffburn. Ang 4F 145
Cliffe. Medw 3B 40
Cliffe. N Yor
nr. Darlington 3F 105
nr. Selby 1G 93
Cliff End. E Sus 4C 28
Cliffe Woods. Medw 3B 40
Clifford. Here 1F 47
Clifford. W Yor 5G 99
Clifford Chambers. Warw 5F 61
Clifford's Mesne. Glos 3C 48
Cliffsend. Kent 4H 41
Clifton. Bris 4A 34
Clifton. C Beds 2B 52
Clifton. Cumb 2G 103
Clifton. Derbs 1F 73
Clifton. Devn 2G 19
Clifton. G Man 4F 91
Clifton. Lanc 1C 90
Clifton. Nmbd 1F 115
Clifton. N Yor 5D 98
Clifton. Nott 2C 74
Clifton. Oxon 2C 50
Clifton. S Yor 1C 86
Clifton. Stir 5H 141
Clifton. W Yor 2B 92
Clifton. Worc 1D 48
Clifton. York 4H 99
Clifton Campville. Staf 4G 73
Clifton Hampden. Oxon 2D 36
Clifton Hill. Worc 4B 60
Clifton Reynes. Mil 5G 63
Clifton upon Dunsmore. Warw 3C 62
Clifton upon Teme. Worc 4B 60
Cliftonville. Kent 3H 41
Cliftonville. Norf 2F 79
Climping. W Sus 5A 26
Climpy. S Lan 4C 128
Clink. Som 2C 22
Clint. N Yor 4E 99
Clint Green. Norf 4C 78
Clintmains. Bord 1A 120
Cliobh. W Isl 4C 171
Clipiau. Gwyn 4H 69
Clippesby. Norf 4G 79
Clippings Green. Norf 4C 78
Clipsham. Rut 4G 75
Clipston. Nptn 2E 62
Clipston. Notts 2D 74
Clipstone. Notts 4C 86
Clitheroe. Lanc 5G 97
Cliuthar. W Isl 8D 171
Clive. Shrp 3H 71
Clivocast. Shet 1G 173
Clixby. Linc 4D 94
Clocaenog. Den 5C 82
Clochan. Mor 2B 160
Clochforbie. Abers 3F 161
Clock Face. Mers 1H 83
Cloddiau. Powy 5E 70
Cloddymoss. Mor 2D 159
Clodock. Here 3G 47
Cloford. Som 2C 22
Clogh. ME Ant 5G 175
Clogher. M Ulst 4L 177
Cloghmills. Caus 5G 175
Clola. Abers 4H 161
Clonoe. M Ulst 3C 178
Clonvaraghan. New M 5H 179
Clophill. C Beds 2A 52
Clopton. Nptn 2H 63
Clopton Corner. Suff 5E 66
Clopton Green. Suff 5G 65
Closeburn. Dum 5A 118
Close Clark. IOM 4B 108
Closworth. Som 1A 14
Clothall. Herts 2C 52
Clotton. Ches W 4H 83
Clough. G Man 3H 91
Clough. New M 5J 179
Clough. W Yor 3A 92
Cloughey. Ards 4L 179
Clough Foot. W Yor 2H 91
Cloughton. N Yor 5H 107
Cloughton Newlands. N Yor 5H 107
Clousta. Shet 6E 173
Clouston. Orkn 6B 172
Clova. Abers 1B 152
Clova. Ang 1C 144
Clovelly. Devn 4D 18
Clovenfords. Bord 1G 119
Clovenstone. Abers 2E 153
Clovullin. High 2E 141
Clowne. Derbs 3B 86
Clows Top. Worc 3B 60
Cloy. Wrex 1F 71
Cloyfin. Caus 3E 174
Cluanie Inn. High 2C 148
Cluanie Lodge. High 2C 148
Cluddley. Telf 4A 72
Clun. Shrp 2F 59
Y Clun. Neat 5B 46
Clunas. High 4C 158
Clunbury. Shrp 2F 59
Clunderwen. Pemb 3F 43
Clune. High 1B 150
Clunes. High 5E 148
Clungunford. Shrp 3F 59
Clunie. Per 4A 144
Clunton. Shrp 2F 59
Cluny. Fife 4E 137
Clutton. Bath 1B 22
Clutton. Ches W 5G 83
Clwt-y-bont. Gwyn 4E 81
Clwydfagwyr. Mer T 5D 46
Clydach. Mon 4F 47
Clydach. Swan 5G 45
Clydebank. W Dun 3G 127
Clydach Vale. Rhon 2C 32
Clydey. Pemb 1G 43
Clyffe Pypard. Wilts 4F 35
Clynder. Arg 1D 126
Clyne. Neat 5B 46
Clynelish. High 3F 165
Clynnog-fawr. Gwyn 1D 68
Clyro. Powy 1F 47
Clyst Honiton. Devn 3C 12
Clyst Hydon. Devn 2D 12
Clyst St George. Devn 4C 12
Clyst St Lawrence. Devn 2D 12
Clyst St Mary. Devn 3C 12
Clyth. High 5E 169
Cnip. W Isl 4C 171
Cnoc Amhlaigh. W Isl 4H 171
Cnwcau. Pemb 1C 44
Cnwch Coch. Cdgn 3F 57
Coad's Green. Corn 5C 10
Coagh. M Ulst 2C 178
Coal Aston. Derbs 3A 86
Coalbrookdale. Telf 5A 72
Coalbrookvale. Blae 5E 47
Coalburn. S Lan 1H 117
Coalburns. Tyne 3E 115
Coalcleugh. Nmbd 5B 114
Coaley. Glos 5C 48
Coalford. Abers 4F 153
Coalhall. E Ayr 3D 116
Coalhill. Essx 1B 40
Coalisland. M Ulst 3C 178
Coalpit Heath. S Glo 3B 34
Coal Pool. W Mid 5E 73
Coalport. Telf 5B 72
Coalsnaughton. Clac 4B 136
Coaltown of Balgonie. Fife 4F 137
Coaltown of Wemyss. Fife 4F 137
Coalville. Leics 4B 74
Coalway. Glos 4A 48
Coanwood. Nmbd 4H 113
Coat. Som 4H 21
Coatbridge. N Lan 3A 128
Coatdyke. N Lan 3A 128
Coate. Swin 3G 35
Coate. Wilts 5F 35
Coates. Cambs 1C 64
Coates. Glos 5E 49
Coates. Linc 2G 87
Coates. W Sus 4A 26
Coatham. Red C 2C 106
Coatham Mundeville. Darl 2F 105
Cobbaton. Devn 4G 19
Coberley. Glos 4E 49
Cobhall Common. Here 2H 47
Cobham. Kent 4A 40
Cobham. Surr 5C 38
Cobnash. Here 4G 59
Coburg. Devn 5B 12
Cockayne. N Yor 5D 106
Cockayne Hatley. C Beds 1C 52
Cock Bank. Wrex 1F 71
Cock Bridge. Abers 3G 151
Cockburnspath. Bord 2D 130
Cock Clarks. Essx 5B 54
Cockenzie and Port Seton. E Lot 2H 129
Cockerham. Lanc 4D 96
Cockermouth. Cumb 1C 102
Cockernhoe. Herts 3B 52
Cockfield. Dur 2E 105
Cockfield. Suff 5B 66
Cockfosters. G Lon 1D 39
Cock Gate. Here 4G 59
Cock Green. Essx 4G 53
Cocking. W Sus 1G 17
Cocking Causeway. W Sus 1G 17
Cockington. Torb 2E 9
Cocklake. Som 2H 21
Cocklaw. Abers 4H 161
Cocklaw. Nmbd 2C 114
Cockley Beck. Cumb 4D 102
Cockley Cley. Norf 5G 77
Cockmuir. Abers 3G 161
Cockpole Green. Wok 3F 37
Cockshutford. Shrp 2H 59
Cockshutt. Shrp 3G 71
Cockthorpe. Norf 1B 78
Cockwood. Devn 4C 12
Cockyard. Derbs 3E 85
Cockyard. Here 2H 47
Codda. Corn 5B 10
Coddenham. Suff 5D 66
Coddenham Green. Suff 5D 66
Coddington. Ches W 5G 83
Coddington. Here 1C 48
Coddington. Notts 5F 87
Codford. Wilts 3E 23
Codicote. Herts 4C 52
Codmore Hill. W Sus 3B 26
Codnor. Derbs 1B 74
Codrington. S Glo 4C 34
Codsall. Staf 5C 72
Codsall Wood. Staf 5C 72
Coed Duon. Cphy 2E 33
Coedely. Rhon 3D 32
Coedglasson. Powy 4C 58
Coedkernew. Newp 3F 33
Coed Morgan. Mon 4G 47
Coedpoeth. Wrex 5E 83
Coedway. Powy 4F 71
Coed-y-bryn. Cdgn 1D 44
Coed-y-paen. Mon 2G 33
Coed Ystumgwern. Gwyn 3E 69
Coelbren. Powy 4B 46
Coffinswell. Devn 2E 9
Cofton Hackett. Worc 3E 61
Cogan. V Glam 4E 33
Cogenhoe. Nptn 4F 63
Cogges. Oxon 5B 50
Coggeshall. Essx 3B 54

212 A-Z Great Britain Road Atlas

Crosby Ravensworth—Dorsington

Crosby Ravensworth.
Cumb 3H 103
Crosby Villa. *Cumb* 1B 102
Croscombe. *Som* 2A 22
Crosland Moor. *W Yor* 3B 92
Cross. *Som* 1H 21
Crossaig. *Arg* 4G 125
Crossapol. *Arg* 4A 138
Cross Ash. *Mon* 4H 47
Cross-at-Hand. *Kent* 1B 28
Crossbush. *W Sus* 5B 26
Crosscanonby. *Cumb* 1B 102
Crossdale Street. *Norf* 2E 79
Cross End. *Essx* 2B 54
Crossens. *Mers* 2B 90
Crossford. *Fife* 1D 128
Crossford. *S Lan* 5B 128
Cross Foxes. *Gwyn* 4G 69
Crossgar. *New M* 4J 179
Crossgate. *Orkn* 6D 172
Crossgate. *Staf* 2D 72
Crossgatehall. *E Lot* 3G 129
Cross Gates. *W Yor* 1D 92
Crossgates. *Fife* 1E 129
Crossgates. *N Yor* 1E 101
Crossgates. *Powy* 4C 58
Crossgill. *Lanc* 3E 97
Cross Green. *Devn* 4D 11
Cross Green. *Staf* 5D 72
Cross Green. *Suff*
nr. Cockfield 5A 66
nr. Hitcham 5B 66
Cross Hands. *Carm* 4F 45
Crosshands. *Carm* 2F 43
Crosshands. *E Ayr* 1D 117
Cross Hill. *Derbs* 1B 74
Cross Hill. *Glos* 2A 34
Crosshill. *E Ayr* 2D 117
Crosshill. *Fife* 4D 136
Crosshill. *S Ayr* 4C 116
Cross Hills. *N Yor* 5C 98
Crosshills. *High* 1A 158
Cross Holme. *N Yor* 5C 106
Crosshouse. *E Ayr* 1C 116
Cross Houses. *Shrp* 5H 71
Crossings. *Cumb* 2G 113
Cross in Hand. *E Sus* 3G 27
Cross Inn. *Cdgn*
nr. Aberaeron 4E 57
nr. New Quay 5C 56
Cross Inn. *Rhon* 3D 32
Crosskeys. *Cphy* 2F 33
Crosskirk. *High* 2C 168
Crosslands. *Cumb* 1C 96
Cross Lane Head. *Shrp* 1B 60
Cross Lanes. *Corn* 4D 5
Cross Lanes. *Dur* 3D 104
Cross Lanes. *N Yor* 3H 99
Cross Lanes. *Wrex* 1F 71
Crosslanes. *Shrp* 4F 71
Crosslee. *Ren* 3F 127
Crossmaglen. *New M* 8D 178
Crossmichael. *Dum* 3E 111
Crossmoor. *Lanc* 1C 90
Crossnacreevy. *Lis* 3H 179
Cross Oak. *Powy* 3E 46
Cross of Jackston. *Abers* 5E 161
Cross o' th' Hands. *Derbs* 1G 73
Crossroads. *Abers*
nr. Aberdeen 3G 153
nr. Banchory 4E 153
Crossroads. *E Ayr* 1D 116
Cross Side. *Devn* 4B 20
Cross Street. *Suff* 3D 66
Crosston. *Ang* 3E 145
Cross Town. *Ches E* 3B 84
Crossway. *Mon* 4H 47
Crossway. *Powy* 5C 58
Crossway Green. *Mon* 2A 34
Crossway Green. *Worc* 4C 60
Crossways. *Dors* 4C 14
Crosswell. *Pemb* 1F 43
Crosswood. *Cdgn* 3F 57
Crosthwaite. *Cumb* 5F 103
Croston. *Lanc* 3C 90
Crostwick. *Norf* 4E 79
Crostwight. *Norf* 3F 79
Crothair. *W Isl* 4D 171
Crouch. *Kent* 5H 39
Croucheston. *Wilts* 4F 23
Crouch Hill. *Dors* 1C 14
Croughton. *Nptn* 2D 50
Crovie. *Abers* 2F 161
Crow. *Hants* 2G 15
Crowan. *Corn* 3D 4
Crowborough. *E Sus* 2G 27
Crowcombe. *Som* 3E 21
Crowcroft. *Worc* 5B 60
Crowdecote. *Derbs* 4F 85
Crowden. *Derbs* 1E 85
Crowden. *Devn* 3E 11
Crowdhill. *Hants* 1C 16
Crowdon. *N Yor* 5G 107
Crow Edge. *S Yor* 4B 92
Crow End. *Cambs* 5C 64
Crowfield. *Nptn* 1E 50
Crowfield. *Suff* 5D 66
Crow Green. *Essx* 1G 39
Crow Hill. *Here* 3B 48
Crowhurst. *E Sus* 4B 28
Crowhurst. *Surr* 1E 27
Crowhurst Lane End. *Surr* 1E 27
Crowland. *Linc* 4B 76
Crowland. *Suff* 3C 66
Crowlas. *Corn* 3C 4
Crowle. *N Lin* 3A 94
Crowle. *Worc* 5D 60
Crowle Green. *Worc* 5D 60
Crowmarsh Gifford. *Oxon* 3E 36
Crown Corner. *Suff* 3E 67
Crownthorpe. *Norf* 5C 78
Crowntown. *Corn* 3D 4
Crows-an-wra. *Corn* 4A 4
Crowshill. *Norf* 5B 78
Crowthorne. *Brac* 5G 37
Crowton. *Ches W* 3H 83
Croxall. *Staf* 4F 73
Croxby. *Linc* 1A 88
Croxdale. *Dur* 1F 105
Croxden. *Staf* 2E 73
Croxley Green. *Herts* 1B 38
Croxton. *Cambs* 4B 64
Croxton. *Norf*
nr. Fakenham 2B 78
nr. Thetford 2A 66
Croxton. *N Lin* 3D 94
Croxton. *Staf* 2B 72
Croxtonbank. *Staf* 2B 72
Croxton Green. *Ches E* 5H 83
Croxton Kerrial. *Leics* 3F 75
Croy. *High* 4B 158
Croy. *N Lan* 2A 128
Croyde. *Devn* 3E 19
Croydon. *Cambs* 1D 52
Croydon. *G Lon* 4E 39
Crubenbeg. *High* 4A 150
Crubenmore Lodge. *High* 4A 150
Cruckmeole. *Shrp* 5G 71
Cruckton. *Shrp* 4G 71
Cruden Bay. *Abers* 5H 161
Crudgington. *Telf* 4A 72
Crudie. *Abers* 3E 161
Crudwell. *Wilts* 2E 35
Cruft. *Devn* 3F 11
Crug. *Powy* 3D 58
Crughywel. *Powy* 4F 47
Crugmeer. *Corn* 1D 6
Crugybar. *Carm* 2G 45
Crug-y-byddar. *Powy* 2D 58
Crulabhig. *W Isl* 4D 171
Crumlin. *Ant* 2F 179
Crumlin. *Cphy* 2F 33
Crumpsall. *G Man* 4G 91
Crumpsbrook. *Shrp* 3A 60
Crundale. *Kent* 1E 29
Crundale. *Pemb* 3D 42
Cruwys Morchard. *Devn* 1B 12
Crux Easton. *Hants* 1C 24
Cruxton. *Dors* 3B 14
Crwbin. *Carm* 4E 45
Cryers Hill. *Buck* 2G 37
Crymych. *Pemb* 1F 43
Crynant. *Neat* 5A 46
Crystal Palace. *G Lon* 3E 39
Cuaich. *High* 5A 150
Cuaig. *High* 3G 155
Cuan. *Arg* 2E 133
Cubbington. *Warw* 4H 61
Cubert. *Corn* 3B 6
Cubley. *S Yor* 4C 92
Cubley Common. *Derbs* 2F 73
Cublington. *Buck* 3G 51
Cublington. *Here* 2G 47
Cuckfield. *W Sus* 3E 27
Cucklington. *Som* 4C 22
Cuckney. *Notts* 3C 86
Cuckron. *Shet* 6F 173
Cuddesdon. *Oxon* 5E 50
Cuddington. *Buck* 4F 51
Cuddington. *Ches W* 3A 84
Cuddington Heath.
Ches W 1G 71
Cuddy Hill. *Lanc* 1C 90
Cudham. *G Lon* 5F 39
Cudlipptown. *Devn* 5F 11
Cudworth. *Som* 1G 13
Cudworth. *S Yor* 4D 93
Cudworth. *Surr* 1D 26
Cuerdley Cross. *Warr* 2H 83
Cuffley. *Herts* 5D 52
Cuidhir. *W Isl* 8B 170
Cuidhsiadar. *W Isl* 2H 171
Cuidhtinis. *W Isl* 9C 171
Culbo. *High* 2A 158
Culbokie. *High* 3A 158
Culburnie. *High* 4G 157
Culcabock. *High* 4A 158
Culcavy. *Lis* 3G 179
Culcharry. *High* 3C 158
Culcheth. *Warr* 1A 84
Culduie. *High* 4G 155
Culeave. *High* 4C 164
Culford. *Suff* 3H 65
Culgaith. *Cumb* 2H 103
Culham. *Oxon* 2D 36
Culkein. *High* 1E 163
Culkein Drumbeg. *High* 5B 166
Culkerton. *Glos* 2E 35
Cullaville. *New M* 8C 178
Cullen. *Mor* 2C 160
Cullercoats. *Tyne* 2G 115
Cullicudden. *High* 2A 158
Cullingworth. *W Yor* 1A 92
Cullipool. *Arg* 2E 133
Cullivoe. *Shet* 1G 173
Culloch. *Per* 2G 135
Culloden. *High* 4B 158
Cullompton. *Devn* 2D 12
Cullybackey. *ME Ant* 6G 175
Cullycapple. *Caus* 4E 174
Cullyhanna. *New M* 7D 178
Culm Davy. *Devn* 1E 13
Culmington. *Shrp* 2G 59
Culmore. *Derr* 4A 174
Culmstock. *Devn* 1E 12
Cul na Caepaich. *High* 5E 147
Culnacnoc. *High* 2E 155
Culnacraig. *High* 3E 163
Culnady. *M Ulst* 6E 174
Culrain. *High* 4C 164
Culross. *Fife* 1C 128
Culroy. *S Ayr* 3C 116
Culswick. *Shet* 7D 173
Cults. *Aber* 3F 153
Cults. *Abers* 5C 160
Cults. *Fife* 3F 137
Cultybraggan Camp. *Per* 1G 135
Culver. *Devn* 3B 12
Culverlane. *Devn* 2D 8
Culverstone Green. *Kent* 4H 39
Culverthorpe. *Linc* 1H 75
Culworth. *Nptn* 1D 50
Culzie Lodge. *High* 1H 157
Cumberlow Green. *Herts* 2D 52
Cumbernauld. *N Lan* 2A 128
Cumbernauld Village.
N Lan 2A 128
Cumberworth. *Linc* 3E 89
Cumdivock. *Cumb* 5E 113
Cuminestown. *Abers* 3F 161
Cumledge Mill. *Bord* 4D 130
Cumlewick. *Shet* 9F 173
Cummersdale. *Cumb* 4E 113
Cummertrees. *Dum* 3C 112
Cummingstown. *Mor* 2F 159
Cumnock. *E Ayr* 2E 117
Cumnor. *Oxon* 5C 50
Cumrew. *Cumb* 4G 113
Cumwhinton. *Cumb* 4F 113
Cumwhitton. *Cumb* 4G 113
Cundall. *N Yor* 2G 99
Cunninghamhead. *N Ayr* 5E 127
Cunning Park. *S Ayr* 3C 116
Cunningsburgh. *Shet* 9F 173
Cunnister. *Shet* 2G 173
Cupar. *Fife* 2F 137
Cupar Muir. *Fife* 2F 137
Cupernham. *Hants* 4B 24
Curbar. *Derbs* 3G 85
Curborough. *Staf* 4F 73
Curbridge. *Hants* 1D 16
Curbridge. *Oxon* 5B 50
Curdridge. *Hants* 1D 16
Curdworth. *Warw* 1F 61
Curland. *Som* 1F 13
Curland Common. *Som* 1F 13
Curran. *M Ulst* 7E 174
Curridge. *W Ber* 4C 36
Currie. *Edin* 3E 129
Curry Mallet. *Som* 4G 21
Curry Rivel. *Som* 4G 21
Curtisden Green. *Kent* 1B 28
Curtisknowle. *Devn* 3D 8
Cury. *Corn* 4D 5
Cusgarne. *Corn* 4B 6
Cushendall. *Caus* 4J 175
Cushendun. *Caus* 3J 175
Cusop. *Here* 1F 47
Cusworth. *S Yor* 4F 93
Cutcombe. *Som* 3C 20
Cuthill. *E Lot* 2G 129
Cutiau. *Gwyn* 4F 69
Cutlers Green. *Essx* 2F 53
Cutmadoc. *Corn* 2E 7
Cutnall Green. *Worc* 4C 60
Cutsdean. *Glos* 2F 49
Cutthorpe. *Derbs* 3H 85
Cuttiford's Door. *Som* 1G 13
Cuttivett. *Corn* 2H 7
Cutts. *Shet* 8E 173
Cuttybridge. *Pemb* 3D 42
Cuttyhill. *Abers* 3H 161
Cuxham. *Oxon* 2E 37
Cuxton. *Medw* 4B 40
Cuxwold. *Linc* 4E 95
Cwm. *Blae* 5E 47
Cwm. *Den* 3C 82
Cwm. *Powy* 1E 59
Cwmafan. *Neat* 2A 32
Cwmaman. *Rhon* 2C 32
Cwmann. *Carm* 1F 45
Cwmbach. *Carm* 2G 43
Cwmbach. *Powy* 2E 47
Cwmbach. *Rhon* 5D 46
Cwmbach Llechrhyd.
Powy 5C 58
Cwmbelan. *Powy* 2B 58
Cwmbran. *Torf* 2F 33
Cwmbrwyno. *Cdgn* 2G 57
Cwm Capel. *Carm* 5E 45
Cwmcarn. *Cphy* 2F 33
Cwmcarvan. *Mon* 5H 47
Cwm-celyn. *Blae* 5F 47
Cwmcerdinen. *Swan* 5G 45
Cwm-Cewydd. *Gwyn* 4A 70
Cwm-cou. *Cdgn* 1C 44
Cwmcych. *Pemb* 1G 43
Cwmdare. *Rhon* 5C 46
Cwmdu. *Carm* 2G 45
Cwmdu. *Powy* 3E 47
Cwmduad. *Carm* 2D 45
Cwm Dulais. *Swan* 5G 45
Cwmerfyn. *Cdgn* 2F 57
Cwmfelin. *B'end* 3B 32
Cwmfelin Boeth. *Carm* 3F 43
Cwmfelinfach. *Cphy* 2E 33
Cwmfelin Mynach. *Carm* 2G 43
Cwmffrwd. *Carm* 4E 45
Cwmgiedd. *Powy* 4A 46
Cwmgors. *Neat* 4H 45
Cwmgwili. *Carm* 4F 45
Cwmgwrach. *Neat* 5B 46
Cwmhiraeth. *Carm* 1H 43
Cwmifor. *Carm* 3G 45
Cwmisfael. *Carm* 4E 45
Cwm-Llinau. *Powy* 5H 69
Cwmllynfell. *Neat* 4H 45
Cwm-mawr. *Carm* 4F 45
Cwm-miles. *Carm* 2F 43
Cwmorgan. *Carm* 1G 43
Cwmparc. *Rhon* 2C 32
Cwm Penmachno. *Cnwy* 1G 69
Cwmpennar. *Rhon* 5D 46
Cwm Plysgog. *Pemb* 1B 44
Cwmrhos. *Powy* 3E 47
Cwmsychpant. *Cdgn* 1E 45
Cwmsyfiog. *Cphy* 5E 47
Cwmsymlog. *Cdgn* 2F 57
Cwmtillery. *Blae* 5F 47
Cwm-twrch Isaf. *Powy* 5A 46
Cwm-twrch Uchaf. *Powy* 4A 46
Cwmwysg. *Powy* 3B 46
Cwm-y-glo. *Gwyn* 4E 81
Cwmyoy. *Mon* 3G 47
Cwmystwyth. *Cdgn* 3G 57
Cwrt. *Gwyn* 5F 69
Cwrtnewydd. *Cdgn* 1E 45
Cwrt-y-Cadno. *Carm* 1G 45
Cydweli. *Carm* 5E 45
Cyffylliog. *Den* 5C 82
Cymau. *Flin* 5E 83
Cymer. *Neat* 2B 32
Cymmer. *Neat* 2B 32
Cymmer. *Rhon* 2D 32
Cyncoed. *Card* 3E 33
Cynghordy. *Carm* 2B 46
Cynheidre. *Carm* 5E 45
Cynonville. *Neat* 2B 32
Cynwyd. *Den* 1C 70
Cynwyl Elfed. *Carm* 3D 44
Cywarch. *Gwyn* 4A 70

D

Dacre. *Cumb* 2F 103
Dacre. *N Yor* 3D 98
Dacre Banks. *N Yor* 3D 98
Daddry Shield. *Dur* 1B 104
Dadford. *Buck* 2E 51
Dadlington. *Leics* 1B 62
Dafen. *Carm* 5F 45
Daffy Green. *Norf* 5B 78
Dagdale. *Staf* 2E 73
Dagenham. *G Lon* 2F 39
Daggons. *Dors* 1G 15
Daglingworth. *Glos* 5E 49
Dagnall. *Buck* 4H 51
Dagtail End. *Worc* 4E 61
Dail. *Arg* 5E 141
Dail Beag. *W Isl* 3E 171
Dail bho Dheas. *W Isl* 1G 171
Dailly. *S Ayr* 4B 116
Dail Mor. *W Isl* 3E 171
Dairsie. *Fife* 2G 137
Daisy Bank. *W Mid* 1E 61
Daisy Hill. *G Man* 4E 91
Daisy Hill. *W Yor* 1B 92
Dalabrog. *W Isl* 6C 170
Dalavich. *Arg* 2G 133
Dalbeattie. *Dum* 3F 111
Dalblair. *E Ayr* 3F 117
Dalbury. *Derbs* 2G 73
Dalby. *IOM* 4B 108
Dalby Wolds. *Leics* 3D 74
Dalchalm. *High* 3G 165
Dalcharn. *High* 3G 167
Dalchork. *High* 2C 164
Dalchreichart. *High* 2E 149
Dalchruin. *Per* 2G 135
Dalcross. *High* 4B 158
Dalderby. *Linc* 4B 88
Dale. *Cumb* 5G 113
Dale. *Pemb* 4C 42
Dale Abbey. *Derbs* 2B 74
Dalebank. *Derbs* 4A 86
Dale Bottom. *Cumb* 2D 102
Dale Head. *Cumb* 3F 103
Dalehouse. *N Yor* 3E 107
Dalelia. *High* 2B 140
Dale of Walls. *Shet* 6C 173
Dalgarven. *N Ayr* 5D 126
Dalgety Bay. *Fife* 1E 129
Dalginross. *Per* 1G 135
Dalguise. *Per* 4G 143
Dalhalvaig. *High* 3A 168
Dalham. *Suff* 4G 65
Dalintart. *Arg* 1F 133
Dalkeith. *Midl* 3G 129
Dallas. *Mor* 3F 159
Dalleagles. *E Ayr* 3E 117
Dall House. *Per* 3C 142
Dallinghoo. *Suff* 5E 67
Dallington. *E Sus* 4A 28
Dallow. *N Yor* 2D 98
Dalmally. *Arg* 1A 134
Dalmarnock. *Glas* 3H 127
Dalmellington. *E Ayr* 4D 117
Dalmeny. *Edin* 2E 129
Dalmigavie. *High* 2B 150
Dalmilling. *S Ayr* 2C 116
Dalmore. *High*
nr. Alness 2A 158
nr. Rogart 3E 164
Dalmuir. *W Dun* 2F 127
Dalmunach. *Mor* 4G 159
Dalnabreck. *High* 2B 140
Dalnacardoch Lodge. *Per* 1E 142
Dalnamein Lodge. *Per* 2E 143
Dalnaspidal Lodge. *Per* 1D 142
Dalnatrat. *High* 3D 140
Dalnavie. *High* 1A 158
Dalnawillan Lodge. *High* 4C 168
Dalness. *High* 3F 141
Dalnessie. *High* 2D 164
Dalqueich. *Per* 3C 136
Dalquhairn. *S Ayr* 5C 116
Dalreavoch. *High* 3E 165
Dalreoch. *Per* 2C 136
Dalry. *Edin* 2F 129
Dalry. *N Ayr* 5D 126
Dalrymple. *E Ayr* 3C 116
Dalscote. *Nptn* 5D 62
Dalserf. *S Lan* 4B 128
Dalsmirren. *Arg* 4A 122
Dalston. *Cumb* 4E 113
Dalswinton. *Dum* 1G 111
Dalton. *Dum* 2C 112
Dalton. *Lanc* 4C 90
Dalton. *Nmbd*
nr. Hexham 4C 114
nr. Ponteland 2E 115
Dalton. *N Yor*
nr. Richmond 4E 105
nr. Thirsk 2G 99
Dalton. *S Lan* 4H 127
Dalton. *S Yor* 1B 86
Dalton-in-Furness. *Cumb* 2B 96
Dalton-le-Dale. *Dur* 5H 115
Dalton Magna. *S Yor* 1B 86
Dalton-on-Tees. *N Yor* 4F 105
Dalton Piercy. *Hart* 1B 106
Daltot. *Arg* 1F 125
Dalvey. *High* 5F 159
Dalwhinnie. *High* 5A 150
Dalwood. *Devn* 2F 13
Damerham. *Hants* 1G 15
Damgate. *Norf*
nr. Acle 5G 79
nr. Martham 4G 79
Dam Green. *Norf* 2C 66
Damhead. *Mor* 3E 159
Danaway. *Kent* 4C 40
Danbury. *Essx* 5A 54
Danby. *N Yor* 4E 107
Danby Botton. *N Yor* 4D 107
Danby Wiske. *N Yor* 5A 106
Danderhall. *Midl* 3G 129
Danebank. *Ches E* 2D 85
Danebridge. *Ches E* 4D 84
Dane End. *Herts* 3D 52
Danehill. *E Sus* 3F 27
Danesford. *Shrp* 1B 60
Daneshill. *Hants* 1E 25
Danesmoor. *Derbs* 4B 86
Danestone. *Aber* 2G 153
Dangerous Corner. *Lanc* 3D 90
Daniel's Water. *Kent* 1D 28
Dan's Castle. *Dur* 1E 105
Danzey Green. *Warw* 4F 61
Dapple Heath. *Staf* 3E 73
Daren. *Powy* 4F 47
Darenth. *Kent* 3G 39
Daresbury. *Hal* 2H 83
Darfield. *S Yor* 4E 93
Dargate. *Kent* 4E 41
Dargill. *Per* 2A 136
Darite. *Corn* 2G 7
Darlaston. *W Mid* 1D 61
Darley. *N Yor* 4E 98
Darley Abbey. *Derb* 2H 73
Darley Bridge. *Derbs* 4G 85
Darley Dale. *Derbs* 4G 85
Darley Head. *N Yor* 4D 98
Darlingscott. *Warw* 1H 49
Darlington. *Darl* 3F 105
Darliston. *Shrp* 2H 71
Darlton. *Notts* 3E 87
Darmsden. *Suff* 5C 66
Darnall. *S Yor* 2A 86
Darnford. *Abers* 4E 153
Darnford. *Staf* 5F 73
Darnhall. *Ches W* 4A 84
Darnick. *Bord* 1H 119
Darowen. *Powy* 5H 69
Darra. *Abers* 4E 161
Darracott. *Devn* 3E 19
Darragh Cross. *New M* 4J 179
Darras Hall. *Nmbd* 2E 115
Darrington. *W Yor* 2E 93
Darrow Green. *Norf* 2E 67
Darsham. *Suff* 4G 67
Dartfield. *Abers* 3H 161
Dartford. *Kent* 3G 39
Dartford-Thurrock River Crossing.
Kent 3G 39
Dartington. *Devn* 2D 9
Dartmeet. *Devn* 5G 11
Dartmouth. *Devn* 3E 9
Darton. *S Yor* 3D 92
Darvel. *E Ayr* 1E 117
Darwen. *Bkbn* 2E 91
Dassels. *Herts* 3D 53
Datchet. *Wind* 3A 38
Datchworth. *Herts* 4C 52
Datchworth Green. *Herts* 4C 52
Daubhill. *G Man* 4F 91
Dauntsey. *Wilts* 3E 35
Dauntsey Green. *Wilts* 3E 35
Dauntsey Lock. *Wilts* 3E 35
Dava. *Mor* 5E 159
Davenham. *Ches W* 3A 84
Daventry. *Nptn* 4C 62
Davidson's Mains. *Edin* 2F 129
Davidston. *High* 2B 158
Davidstow. *Corn* 4B 10
David's Well. *Powy* 3C 58
Davington. *Dum* 4E 119
Daviot. *Abers* 1E 153
Daviot. *High* 5B 158
Davyhulme. *G Man* 1B 84
Daw Cross. *N Yor* 4E 99
Dawdon. *Dur* 5H 115
Dawesgreen. *Surr* 1D 26
Dawley. *Telf* 5A 72
Dawlish. *Devn* 5C 12
Dawlish Warren. *Devn* 5C 12
Dawn. *Cnwy* 3A 82
Daws Heath. *Essx* 2C 40
Dawshill. *Worc* 5C 60
Daw's House. *Corn* 4D 10
Dawsmere. *Linc* 2D 76
Dayhills. *Staf* 2D 72
Dayhouse Bank. *Worc* 3D 60
Daylesford. *Glos* 3H 49
Daywall. *Shrp* 2E 71
Ddol. *Flin* 3D 82
Ddol Cownwy. *Powy* 4C 70
Deadman's Cross. *C Beds* 1B 52
Deadwater. *Nmbd* 5A 120
Deaf Hill. *Dur* 1A 106
Deal. *Kent* 5H 41
Dean. *Cumb* 2B 102
Dean. *Devn*
nr. Combe Martin 2G 19
nr. Lynton 2H 19
Dean. *Dors* 1E 15
Dean. *Hants*
nr. Bishop's Waltham 1D 16
nr. Winchester 3C 24
Dean. *Oxon* 3B 50
Dean. *Som* 2B 22
Dean Bank. *Dur* 1F 105
Deanburnhaugh. *Bord* 3F 119
Dean Cross. *Devn* 2F 19
Deane. *Hants* 1D 24
Deanich Lodge. *High* 5A 164
Deanland. *Dors* 1E 15
Deanlane End. *W Sus* 1F 17
Dean Park. *Shrp* 4A 60
Dean Prior. *Devn* 2D 8
Dean Row. *Ches E* 2C 84
Deans. *W Lot* 3D 128
Deanscales. *Cumb* 2B 102
Deanshanger. *Nptn* 1F 51
Deanston. *Stir* 3G 135
Dearham. *Cumb* 1B 102
Dearne Valley. *S Yor* 4D 93
Debach. *Suff* 5E 67
Debden. *Essx* 2F 53
Debden Green. *Essx*
nr. Loughton 1F 39
nr. Saffron Walden 2F 53
Debenham. *Suff* 4D 66
Dechmont. *W Lot* 2D 128
Deddington. *Oxon* 2C 50
Dedham. *Essx* 2D 54
Dedham Heath. *Essx* 2D 54
Deebank. *Abers* 4D 152
Deene. *Nptn* 1G 63
Deenethorpe. *Nptn* 1G 63
Deepcar. *S Yor* 1G 85
Deepcut. *Surr* 5A 38
Deepdale. *Cumb* 1G 97
Deepdale. *N Lin* 3D 94
Deepdale. *N Yor* 2A 98
Deeping Gate. *Pet* 5A 76
Deeping St James. *Linc* 5A 76
Deeping St Nicholas. *Linc* 4B 76
Deerhill. *Mor* 3B 160
Deerhurst. *Glos* 3D 48
Deerhurst Walton. *Glos* 3D 49
Deerness. *Orkn* 7E 172
Defford. *Worc* 1E 49
Defynnog. *Powy* 3C 46
Deganwy. *Cnwy* 3G 81
Deighton. *N Yor* 4A 106
Deighton. *W Yor* 3B 92
Deighton. *York* 5A 100
Deiniolen. *Gwyn* 4E 81
Delabole. *Corn* 4A 10
Delamere. *Ches W* 4H 83
Delfour. *High* 3C 150
The Dell. *Suff* 1G 67
Delliefure. *High* 5E 159
Delly End. *Oxon* 4B 50
Delny. *High* 1B 158
Delph. *G Man* 4H 91
Delves. *Dur* 5E 115
The Delves. *W Mid* 1E 61
Delvin End. *Essx* 2A 54
Dembleby. *Linc* 2H 75
Demelza. *Corn* 2D 6
The Den. *N Ayr* 4E 127
Denaby Main. *S Yor* 1B 86
Denbeath. *Fife* 4F 137
Denbigh. *Den* 4C 82
Denbury. *Devn* 2E 9
Denby. *Derbs* 1A 74
Denby Common. *Derbs* 1B 74
Denby Dale. *W Yor* 4C 92
Denchworth. *Oxon* 2B 36
Dendron. *Cumb* 2B 96
Deneside. *Dur* 5H 115
Denford. *Nptn* 3G 63
Dengie. *Essx* 5C 54
Denham. *Buck* 2B 38
Denham. *Suff*
nr. Bury St Edmunds 4G 65
nr. Eye 3D 66
Denham Green. *Buck* 2B 38
Denham Street. *Suff* 3D 66
Denhead. *Abers*
nr. Ellon 5G 161
nr. Strichen 3G 161
Denhead. *Fife* 2G 137
Denholm. *Bord* 3H 119
Denholme. *W Yor* 1A 92
Denholme Clough. *W Yor* 1A 92
Denholme Gate. *W Yor* 1A 92
Denio. *Gwyn* 2C 68
Denmead. *Hants* 1E 17
Dennington. *Suff* 4E 67
Denny. *Falk* 1B 128
Denny End. *Cambs* 4D 65
Dennyloanhead. *Falk* 1B 128
Den of Lindores. *Fife* 2E 137
Denshaw. *G Man* 3H 91
Denside. *Abers* 4F 153
Densole. *Kent* 1G 29
Denston. *Suff* 5G 65
Denstone. *Staf* 1F 73
Denstroude. *Kent* 4F 41
Dent. *Cumb* 1G 97
Denton. *Cambs* 2A 64
Denton. *Darl* 3F 105
Denton. *E Sus* 5F 27
Denton. *G Man* 1D 84
Denton. *Kent* 1G 29
Denton. *Linc* 2F 75
Denton. *Norf* 2E 67
Denton. *Nptn* 5F 63
Denton. *N Yor* 5D 98
Denton. *Oxon* 5D 50
Denver. *Norf* 5F 77
Denwick. *Nmbd* 3G 121
Deopham. *Norf* 5C 78
Deopham Green. *Norf* 1C 66
Depden. *Suff* 5G 65
Depden Green. *Suff* 5G 65
Deptford. *G Lon* 3E 39
Deptford. *Wilts* 3F 23
Derby. *Derb* 194 (2A 74)
Derbyhaven. *IOM* 5B 108
Derculich. *Per* 3F 143
Dereham. *Norf* 4B 78
Deri. *Cphy* 5E 47
Derril. *Devn* 2D 10
Derringstone. *Kent* 1G 29
Derrington. *Shrp* 1A 60
Derrington. *Staf* 3C 72
Derriton. *Devn* 2D 10
Derry. *Derr* 5A 174
Derryboye. *New M* 4J 179
Derrycrin. *M Ulst* 2D 178
Derrygonnelly. *Ferm* 7D 176
Derryguaig. *Arg* 5F 139
Derry Hill. *Wilts* 4E 35
Derrykeighan. *Caus* 3F 175
Derrylin. *Ferm* 7H 177
Derrymacash. *Arm* 4E 178
Derrythorpe. *N Lin* 4B 94
Derrytrasna. *Arm* 3D 178
Dersingham. *Norf* 2F 77
Dervaig. *Arg* 3F 139
Dervock. *Caus* 3F 175
Derwen. *Den* 5C 82
Derwen Gam. *Cdgn* 5D 56
Derwenlas. *Powy* 1G 57
Desborough. *Nptn* 2F 63
Desertmartin. *M Ulst* 7E 174
Desford. *Leics* 5B 74
Detchant. *Nmbd* 1E 121
Dethick. *Derbs* 5H 85
Detling. *Kent* 5B 40
Deuchar. *Ang* 2D 144
Deuddwr. *Powy* 4E 71
Devauden. *Mon* 2H 33
Devil's Bridge. *Cdgn* 3G 57
Devitts Green. *Warw* 1G 61
Devizes. *Wilts* 5F 35
Devonport. *Plym* 3A 8
Devonside. *Clac* 4B 136
Devoran. *Corn* 5B 6
Dewartown. *Midl* 3G 129
Dewlish. *Dors* 3C 14
Dewsall Court. *Here* 2H 47
Dewsbury. *W Yor* 2C 92
Dexbeer. *Devn* 2C 10
Dhoon. *IOM* 3D 108
Dhoor. *IOM* 2D 108
Dhowin. *IOM* 1D 108
Dial Green. *W Sus* 3A 26
Dial Post. *W Sus* 4C 26
The Diamond. *M Ulst* 2D 178
Dibberford. *Dors* 2H 13
Dibden. *Hants* 2C 16
Dibden Purlieu. *Hants* 2C 16
Dickleburgh. *Norf* 2D 66
Didbrook. *Glos* 2F 49
Didcot. *Oxon* 2D 36
Diddington. *Cambs* 4A 64
Diddlebury. *Shrp* 2H 59
Didley. *Here* 2H 47
Didling. *W Sus* 1G 17
Didmarton. *Glos* 3D 34
Didsbury. *G Man* 1C 84
Didworthy. *Devn* 2C 8
Digby. *Linc* 5H 87
Digg. *High* 2D 154
Diggle. *G Man* 4A 92
Digmoor. *Lanc* 4C 90
Digswell. *Herts* 4C 52
Dihewyd. *Cdgn* 5D 57
Dilham. *Norf* 3F 79
Dilhorne. *Staf* 1D 72
Dillarburn. *S Lan* 5B 128
Dillington. *Cambs* 4A 64
Dilston. *Nmbd* 3C 114
Dilton Marsh. *Wilts* 2D 22
Dilwyn. *Here* 5G 59
Dimmer. *Som* 3B 22
Dimple. *G Man* 3F 91
Dinas. *Carm* 1G 43
Dinas. *Gwyn*
nr. Caernarfon 5D 81
nr. Tudweiliog 2B 68
Dinas Cross. *Pemb* 1E 43
Dinas Dinlle. *Gwyn* 5D 80
Dinas Mawddwy. *Gwyn* 4A 70
Dinas Powys. *V Glam* 4E 33
Dinbych. *Den* 4C 82
Dinbych-y-Pysgod. *Pemb* 4F 43
Dinckley. *Lanc* 1E 91
Dinder. *Som* 2A 22
Dinedor. *Here* 2A 48
Dinedor Cross. *Here* 2A 48
Dingestow. *Mon* 4H 47
Dingle. *Mers* 2F 83
Dingleden. *Kent* 2C 28
Dingleton. *Bord* 1H 119
Dingley. *Nptn* 2E 63
Dingwall. *High* 3H 157
Dinmael. *Cnwy* 1C 70
Dinnet. *Abers* 4B 152
Dinnington. *Som* 1H 13
Dinnington. *S Yor* 2C 86
Dinnington. *Tyne* 2F 115
Dinorwig. *Gwyn* 4E 81
Dinton. *Buck* 4F 51
Dinton. *Wilts* 3F 23
Dinworthy. *Devn* 1D 10
Dipley. *Hants* 1F 25
Dippen. *Arg* 2B 122
Dippenhall. *Surr* 2G 25
Dippertown. *Devn* 4E 11
Dippin. *N Ayr* 3E 123
Dipple. *S Ayr* 4B 116
Diptford. *Devn* 3D 8
Dipton. *Dur* 4E 115
Dirleton. *E Lot* 1B 130
Dirt Pot. *Nmbd* 5B 114
Discoed. *Powy* 4E 59
Diseworth. *Leics* 3B 74
Dishes. *Orkn* 5F 172
Dishforth. *N Yor* 2F 99
Disley. *Ches E* 2D 85
Diss. *Norf* 3D 66
Disserth. *Powy* 5C 58
Distington. *Cumb* 2B 102
Ditchampton. *Wilts* 3F 23
Ditcheat. *Som* 3B 22
Ditchingham. *Norf* 1F 67
Ditchling. *E Sus* 4E 27
Ditteridge. *Wilts* 5D 34
Dittisham. *Devn* 3E 9
Ditton. *Hal* 2G 83
Ditton. *Kent* 5B 40
Ditton Green. *Cambs* 5F 65
Ditton Priors. *Shrp* 2A 60
Divach. *High* 1G 149
Dixonfield. *High* 2D 168
Dixton. *Glos* 2E 49
Dixton. *Mon* 4A 48
Dizzard. *Corn* 3B 10
Doagh. *Ant* 8J 175
Dobcross. *G Man* 4H 91
Dobs Hill. *Flin* 4F 83
Dobson's Bridge. *Shrp* 2G 71
Dobwalls. *Corn* 2G 7
Doccombe. *Devn* 4A 12
Dochgarroch. *High* 4A 158
Docking. *Norf* 2G 77
Docklow. *Here* 5H 59
Dockray. *Cumb* 2E 103
Doc Penfro. *Pemb* 204 (4D 42)
Dodbrooke. *Devn* 4D 8
Doddenham. *Worc* 5B 60
Doddinghurst. *Essx* 1G 39
Doddington. *Cambs* 1C 64
Doddington. *Kent* 5D 40
Doddington. *Linc* 3G 87
Doddington. *Nmbd* 1D 121
Doddington. *Shrp* 3A 60
Doddiscombsleigh. *Devn* 4B 12
Doddshill. *Norf* 2G 77
Dodford. *Nptn* 4D 62
Dodford. *Worc* 3D 60
Dodington. *Som* 2E 21
Dodington. *S Glo* 3C 34
Dodleston. *Ches W* 4F 83
Dods Leigh. *Staf* 2E 73
Dodworth. *S Yor* 4D 92
Doe Lea. *Derbs* 4B 86
Dogdyke. *Linc* 5B 88
Dogmersfield. *Hants* 1F 25
Dogsthorpe. *Pet* 5B 76
Dog Village. *Devn* 3C 12
Dolanog. *Powy* 4C 70
Dolau. *Powy* 4D 58
Dolau. *Rhon* 3D 32
Dolbenmaen. *Gwyn* 1E 69
Doley. *Staf* 3B 72
Dol-fâch. *Powy* 5B 70
Dolfach. *Powy* 3B 58
Dolfor. *Powy* 2D 58
Dolgarrog. *Cnwy* 4G 81
Dolgellau. *Gwyn* 4G 69
Dolgoch. *Gwyn* 5F 69
Dol-gran. *Carm* 2E 45
Dolhelfa. *Powy* 3B 58
Doll. *High* 3F 165
Dollar. *Clac* 4B 136
Dolley Green. *Powy* 4E 59
Dollingstown. *Arm* 4F 178
Dollwen. *Cdgn* 2F 57
Dolphin. *Flin* 3D 82
Dolphinholme. *Lanc* 4E 97
Dolphinton. *S Lan* 5E 129
Dolton. *Devn* 1F 11
Dolwen. *Cnwy* 3A 82
Dolwyddelan. *Cnwy* 5G 81
Dol-y-Bont. *Cdgn* 2F 57
Dolyhir. *Powy* 5E 59
Domgay. *Powy* 4E 71
Donagh. *Ferm* 7J 177
Donaghadee. *Ards* 2K 179
Donaghcloney. *Arm* 4F 178
Donaghmore. *M Ulst* 3B 178
Doncaster. *S Yor* 4F 93
Doncaster Sheffield Airport.
S Yor 1D 86
Donhead St Andrew. *Wilts* 4E 23
Donhead St Mary. *Wilts* 4E 23
Doniford. *Som* 2D 20
Donington. *Linc* 2B 76
Donington. *Shrp* 5C 72
Donington Eaudike. *Linc* 2B 76
Donington le Heath. *Leics* 4B 74
Donington on Bain. *Linc* 2B 88
Donington South Ing.
Linc 2B 76
Donisthorpe. *Leics* 4H 73
Donkey Street. *Kent* 2F 29
Donkey Town. *Surr* 4A 38
Donna Nook. *Linc* 1D 88
Donnington. *Glos* 3G 49
Donnington. *Here* 2C 48
Donnington. *Shrp* 5H 71
Donnington. *Telf* 4B 72
Donnington. *W Ber* 5C 36
Donnington. *W Sus* 2G 17
Donyatt. *Som* 1G 13
Doomsday Green. *W Sus* 3C 26
Doonfoot. *S Ayr* 3C 116
Doonholm. *S Ayr* 3C 116
Dorback Lodge. *High* 2E 151
Dorchester. *Dors* 3B 14
Dorchester on Thames.
Oxon 2D 36
Dordon. *Warw* 5G 73
Dore. *S Yor* 2H 85
Dores. *High* 5H 157
Dorking. *Surr* 1C 26
Dorking Tye. *Suff* 2C 54
Dormansland. *Surr* 1F 27
Dormans Park. *Surr* 1E 27
Dormanstown. *Red C* 2C 106
Dormington. *Here* 1A 48
Dormston. *Worc* 5D 61
Dorn. *Glos* 2H 49
Dorney. *Buck* 3A 38
Dornie. *High* 1A 148
Dornoch. *High* 5E 165
Dornock. *Dum* 3D 112
Dorrery. *High* 3C 168
Dorridge. *W Mid* 3F 61
Dorrington. *Linc* 5H 87
Dorrington. *Shrp* 5G 71
Dorsington. *Warw* 1G 49

Dorstone—Eccleshall

Dorstone. Here 1G 47
Dorton. Buck 4E 51
Dosthill. Staf 5G 73
Dotham. IOA 3C 80
Dottery. Dors 3H 13
Doublebois. Corn 2F 7
Dougarie. N Ayr 2C 122
Doughton. Glos 2D 35
Douglas. IOM 2C 108
Douglas. S Lan 1H 117
Douglas Bridge. Derr 3F 176
Douglastown. Ang 4D 144
Douglas Water. S Lan 1A 118
Doulting. Som 2B 22
Dounby. Orkn 5B 172
Doune. High
nr. Kingussie 2C 150
nr. Lairg 3B 164
Doune. Stir 3G 135
Dounie. High
nr. Bonar Bridge 4C 164
nr. Tain 5D 164
Dounreay, Upper & Lower.
High 2B 168
Doura. N Ayr 5E 127
Dousland. Devn 2B 8
Dovaston. Shrp 3F 71
Dove Holes. Derbs 3E 85
Dovenby. Cumb 1B 102
Dover. Kent 194 (1H 29)
Dovercourt. Essx 2F 55
Doverdale. Worc 4C 60
Doveridge. Derbs 2F 73
Doversgreen. Surr 1D 26
Dowally. Per 4H 143
Dowbridge. Lanc 1C 90
Dowdeswell. Glos 4F 49
Dowlais. Mer T 5D 46
Dowland. Devn 1F 11
Dowlands. Devn 3F 13
Dowles. Worc 3B 60
Dowlesgreen. Wok 5G 37
Dowlish Wake. Som 1G 13
The Down. Shrp 1A 60
Downall Green. Mers 4D 90
Down Ampney. Glos 2G 35
Downderry. Corn
nr. Looe 3H 7
nr. St Austell 3D 6
Downe. G Lon 4F 39
Downend. IOW 4D 16
Downend. S Glo 4B 34
Downend. W Ber 4C 36
Down Field. Cambs 3F 65
Downfield. D'dee 5C 144
Downgate. Corn
nr. Kelly Bray 5D 10
nr. Upton Cross 5C 10
Downham. Essx 1B 40
Downham. Lanc 5G 97
Downham. Nmbd 1C 120
Downham Market. Norf 5F 77
Down Hatherley. Glos 3D 48
Downhead. Som
nr. Frome 2B 22
nr. Yeovil 4A 22
Downhill. Caus 3D 174
Downholland Cross. Lanc 4B 90
Downholme. N Yor 5E 105
Downies. Abers 4G 153
Downley. Buck 2G 37
Downpatrick. New M 5J 179
Down St Mary. Devn 2H 11
Downside. Som
nr. Chilcompton 1B 22
nr. Shepton Mallet 2B 22
Downside. Surr 5C 38
Down Thomas. Devn 3B 8
Downton. Hants 3A 16
Downton. Wilts 4G 23
Downton on the Rock.
Here 3G 59
Dowsby. Linc 3A 76
Dowsdale. Linc 4B 76
Dowthwaitehead. Cumb 2E 103
Doxey. Staf 3D 72
Doxford. Nmbd 2F 121
Doynton. S Glo 4C 34
Drabblegate. Norf 3E 78
Draethen. Cphy 3F 33
Draffan. S Lan 5A 128
Dragonby. N Lin 3C 94
Dragon's Green. W Sus 3C 26
Drakelow. Worc 2C 60
Drakemyre. N Ayr 4D 126
Drakes Broughton. Worc 1E 49
Drakes Cross. Worc 3E 61
Drakewalls. Corn 5E 11
Draperstown. M Ulst 7D 174
Draughton. Nptn 3E 63
Draughton. N Yor 4C 98
Drax. N Yor 2G 93
Draycot. Oxon 5E 51
Draycote. Warw 3B 62
Draycot Foliat. Swin 4G 35
Draycott. Derbs 2B 74
Draycott. Glos 2G 49
Draycott. Shrp 1C 60
Draycott. Som
nr. Cheddar 1H 21
nr. Yeovil 4A 22
Draycott. Worc 1D 48
Draycott in the Clay. Staf 3F 73
Draycott in the Moors.
Staf 1D 73
Drayford. Devn 1A 12
Drayton. Leics 1F 63
Drayton. Linc 2B 76
Drayton. Norf 4D 78
Drayton. Nptn 4C 62
Drayton. Oxon
nr. Abingdon 2C 36
nr. Banbury 1C 50
Drayton. Port 2E 17
Drayton. Som 4H 21
Drayton. Warw 5F 61
Drayton. Worc 3D 60
Drayton Bassett. Staf 5F 73
Drayton Beauchamp.
Buck 4H 51
Drayton Parslow. Buck 3G 51
Drayton St Leonard. Oxon 2D 36
Drebley. N Yor 4C 98
Dreenhill. Pemb 3D 42
Y Dref. Gwyn 2D 69
Drefach. Carm
nr. Meidrim 4F 45
nr. Newcastle Emlyn 2D 44
nr. Tumble 2G 43
Drefach. Cdgn 1E 45
Dreghorn. N Ayr 1C 116
Drellingore. Kent 1G 29
Drem. E Lot 2B 130
Y Drenewydd. Powy 1D 58
Dreumasdal. W Isl 5C 170
Drewsteignton. Devn 3H 11
Driby. Linc 3C 88
Driffield. E Yor 4E 101
Driffield. Glos 2F 35
Drift. Corn 4B 4
Drigg. Cumb 5B 102
Drighlington. W Yor 2C 92
Drimnin. High 3G 139
Drimpton. Dors 2H 13
Dringhoe. E Yor 4F 101
Drinisiadar. W Isl 8D 171
Drinkstone. Suff 4B 66
Drinkstone Green. Suff 4B 66
Drointon. Staf 3E 73
Droitwich Spa. Worc 4C 60
Droman. High 3B 166
Dromara. Lis 5G 179
Dromore. Arm 4G 179
Dromore. Ferm 6F 176
Dron. Per 2D 136
Dronfield. Derbs 3A 86
Dronfield Woodhouse.
Derbs 3H 85
Drongan. E Ayr 3D 116
Dronley. Ang 5C 144
Droop. Dors 2C 14
Drope. V Glam 4E 32
Droxford. Hants 1E 16
Droylsden. G Man 1C 84
Druggers End. Worc 2C 48
Druid. Den 1C 70
Druid's Heath. W Mid 5E 73
Druidston. Pemb 3C 42
Druim. High 3D 158
Druimarbin. High 1E 141
Druim Fhearna. High 2E 147
Druimindarroch. High 5E 147
Druim Saighdinis. W Isl 2D 170
Drum. Per 3C 136
Drumaness. New M 5H 179
Drumaroad. New M 5H 179
Drumbeg. High 5B 166
Drumblade. Abers 4C 160
Drumbo. Lis 3H 179
Drumbuie. Dum 1C 110
Drumbuie. High 5G 155
Drumburgh. Cumb 4D 112
Drumburn. Dum 3A 112
Drumchapel. Glas 2G 127
Drumchardine. High 4H 157
Drumchork. High 5C 162
Drumclog. S Lan 1F 117
Drumeldrie. Fife 3G 137
Drumelzier. Bord 1D 118
Drumfearn. High 2E 147
Drumgask. High 4A 150
Drumgelloch. N Lan 3A 128
Drumgley. Ang 3D 144
Drumguish. High 4B 150
Drumin. Mor 5F 159
Drumindorsair. High 4G 157
Drumintee. New M 8E 178
Drumlamford House.
S Ayr 2H 109
Drumlasie. Abers 3D 152
Drumlemble. Arg 4A 122
Drumlithie. Abers 5E 153
Drummoddie. Dum 5A 110
Drummond. High 2A 158
Drummore. Dum 5E 109
Drummuir. Mor 4A 160
Drumnacanvy. Arm 4E 178
Drumnadrochit. High 5H 157
Drumnagorrach. Mor 3C 160
Drumnakilly. Ferm 2L 177
Drumoak. Abers 4E 153
Drumquin. Ferm 5F 176
Drumraighland. Caus 4C 174
Drumrunie. High 3F 163
Drumry. W Dun 2G 127
Drums. Abers 1G 153
Drumsleet. Dum 2G 111
Drumsmittal. High 4A 158
Drums of Park. Abers 3C 160
Drumsturdy. Ang 5D 145
Drumsurn. Caus 5D 174
Drumtochty Castle.
Abers 5D 152
Drumuie. High 4D 154
Drumuillie. High 1D 150
Drumvaich. Stir 3F 135
Drumwhindle. Abers 5G 161
Drunkendub. Ang 4F 145
Drury. Flin 4E 83
Drury Square. Norf 4B 78
Drybeck. Cumb 3H 103
Drybridge. Mor 2B 160
Drybridge. N Ayr 1C 116
Drybrook. Glos 4B 48
Drybrook. Here 4A 48
Dryburgh. Bord 1H 119
Dry Doddington. Linc 1F 75
Dry Drayton. Cambs 4C 64
Drym. Corn 3D 4
Drymen. Stir 1F 127
Drymuir. Abers 4G 161
Drynachan Lodge. High 5C 158
Drynie Park. High 3H 157
Drynoch. High 5D 154
Dry Sandford. Oxon 5C 50
Dryslwyn. Carm 3F 45
Dry Street. Essx 2A 40
Dryton. Shrp 5H 71
Dubford. Abers 2E 161
Dubiton. Abers 3D 160
Dubton. Ang 3E 145
Duchally. High 2A 164
Duck End. Essx 3G 53
Duckington. Ches W 5G 83
Ducklington. Oxon 5B 50
Duckmanton. Derbs 3B 86
Duck Street. Hants 2B 24
Dudbridge. Glos 5D 48
Duddenhoe End. Essx 2E 53
Duddingston. Edin 2F 129
Duddington. Nptn 5G 75
Duddleswell. E Sus 3F 27
Duddo. Nmbd 5F 131
Duddon. Ches W 4H 83
Duddon Bridge. Cumb 1A 96
Dudleston. Shrp 2F 71
Dudleston Heath. Shrp 2F 71
Dudley. Tyne 2F 115
Dudley. W Mid 2D 60
Dudston. Shrp 1E 59
Dudwells. Pemb 2D 42
Duffield. Derbs 1H 73
Duffryn. Neat 2B 32
Dufftown. Mor 4H 159
Duffus. Mor 2F 159
Dufton. Cumb 2H 103
Duggleby. N Yor 3C 100
Duirinish. High 5G 155
Duisdalemore. High 2E 147
Duisdeil Mòr. High 2E 147
Duisky. High 1E 141
Dukesfield. Nmbd 4C 114
Dukestown. Blae 5E 47
Dukinfield. G Man 1D 84
Dulas. IOA 2D 81
Dulcote. Som 2A 22
Dulford. Devn 2D 12
Dull. Per 4F 143
Dullatur. N Lan 2A 128
Dullingham. Cambs 5F 65
Dullingham Ley. Cambs 5F 65
Dulnain Bridge. High 1D 151
Duloe. Bed 4A 64
Duloe. Corn 3G 7
Dulverton. Som 4C 20
Dulwich. G Lon 3E 39
Dumbarton. W Dun 2F 127
Dumbleton. Glos 2F 49
Dumfin. Arg 1E 127
Dumfries. Dum 194 (2A 112)
Dumgoyne. Stir 1G 127
Dummer. Hants 2D 24
Dumpford. W Sus 4G 25
Dun. Ang 2F 145
Dunadry. Ant 1F 179
Dunaghy. Caus 4F 175
Dunagoil. Arg 4B 126
Dunalastair. Per 3E 142
Dunan. High 1D 147
Dunball. Som 2G 21
Dunbar. E Lot 2C 130
Dunbeath. High 5D 168
Dunbeg. Arg 5C 140
Dunblane. Stir 3G 135
Dunbog. Fife 2E 137
Dunbridge. Hants 4B 24
Duncanston. Abers 1C 152
Duncanston. High 3H 157
Dun Charlabhaigh. W Isl 3D 171
Dunchideock. Devn 4B 12
Dunchurch. Warw 3B 62
Duncote. Nptn 5D 62
Duncow. Dum 1A 112
Duncrievie. Per 3D 136
Duncton. W Sus 4A 26
Dundee. D'dee 194 (5D 144)
Dundee Airport. D'dee 1F 137
Dundon. Som 3H 21
Dundonald. Lis 2J 179
Dundonald. S Ayr 1C 116
Dundonnell. High 5E 163
Dundraw. Cumb 5D 112
Dundreggan. High 2F 149
Dundrennan. Dum 5E 111
Dundridge. Hants 1D 16
Dundrod. Lis 2G 179
Dundrum. New M 6J 179
Dundry. N Som 5A 34
Dunecht. Abers 3E 153
Dunfermline. Fife 1D 129
Dunford Bridge. S Yor 4B 92
Dungannon. M Ulst 3B 178
Dungate. Kent 5D 40
Dunge. Wilts 1D 23
Dungeness. Kent 4E 29
Dungiven. Caus 6C 174
Dungworth. S Yor 2G 85
Dunham-on-the-Hill.
Ches W 3G 83
Dunham-on-Trent. Notts 3F 87
Dunhampton. Worc 4C 60
Dunham Town. G Man 2B 84
Dunham Woodhouses.
G Man 2B 84
Dunholme. Linc 3H 87
Dunino. Fife 2H 137
Dunipace. Falk 1B 128
Dunira. Per 1G 135
Dunkeld. Per 4H 143
Dunkerton. Bath 1C 22
Dunkeswell. Devn 2E 13
Dunkeswick. N Yor 5F 99
Dunkirk. Kent 5E 41
Dunkirk. S Glo 3C 34
Dunkirk. Staf 5C 84
Dunkirk. Wilts 5E 35
Dunk's Green. Kent 5H 39
Dunlappie. Ang 2E 145
Dunley. Hants 1C 24
Dunley. Worc 4B 60
Dunlichity Lodge. High 5A 158
Dunlop. E Ayr 5F 127
Dunloy. Caus 5G 175
Dunmaglass Lodge.
High 1H 149
Dunmore. Arg 3F 125
Dunmore. Falk 1B 128
Dunmore. High 4H 157
Dunmurry. Bel 3G 179
Dunnamanagh. Derr 6A 174
Dunnaval. New M 8G 179
Dunnet. High 1E 169
Dunnichen. Ang 4E 145
Dunning. Per 2C 136
Dunnington. E Yor 4F 101
Dunnington. Warw 5E 61
Dunnington. York 4A 100
Dunningwell. Cumb 1A 96
Dunnockshaw. Lanc 2G 91
Dunoon. Arg 2C 126
Dunphail. Mor 4E 159
Dunragit. Dum 4G 109
Dunrostan. Arg 1F 125
Duns. Bord 4D 130
Dunsby. Linc 3A 76
Dunscar. G Man 3F 91
Dunscore. Dum 1F 111
Dunscroft. S Yor 4G 93
Dunsdale. Red C 3D 106
Dunsden Green. Oxon 4F 37
Dunsfold. Surr 2B 26
Dunsford. Devn 4B 12
Dunshalt. Fife 2E 137
Dunshillock. Abers 4G 161
Dunsley. N Yor 3F 107
Dunsley. Staf 2C 60
Dunsmore. Buck 5G 51
Dunsop Bridge. Lanc 4F 97
Dunstable. C Beds 3A 52
Dunstal. Staf 3E 73
Dunstall. Staf 3F 73
Dunstall Green. Suff 4G 65
Dunstall Hill. W Mid 5D 72
Dunstan. Nmbd 3G 121
Dunster. Som 2C 20
Duns Tew. Oxon 3C 50
Dunston. Linc 4H 87
Dunston. Norf 5E 79
Dunston. Staf 4D 72
Dunston. Tyne 3F 115
Dunstone. Devn 3B 8
Dunston Heath. Staf 4D 72
Dunsville. S Yor 4G 93
Dunswell. E Yor 1D 94
Dunsyre. S Lan 5D 128
Dunterton. Devn 5D 11
Duntisbourne Abbots.
Glos 5E 49
Duntisbourne Leer. Glos 5E 49
Duntisbourne Rouse. Glos 5E 49
Duntish. Dors 2B 14
Duntocher. W Dun 2F 127
Dunton. Buck 3G 51
Dunton. C Beds 1C 52
Dunton. Norf 2A 78
Dunton Bassett. Leics 1C 62
Dunton Green. Kent 5G 39
Dunton Patch. Norf 2A 78
Duntulm. High 1D 154
Dunure. S Ayr 3B 116
Dunvant. Swan 3E 31
Dunvegan. High 4B 154
Dunwich. Suff 3G 67
Dunwood. Staf 5D 84
Durdar. Cumb 4F 113
Durgates. E Sus 2H 27
Durham. Dur 194 (5F 115)
Durham Tees Valley Airport.
Darl 3A 106
Durisdeer. Dum 4A 118
Durisdeermill. Dum 4A 118
Durkar. W Yor 3D 92
Durleigh. Som 3F 21
Durley. Hants 1D 16
Durley. Wilts 5H 35
Durley Street. Hants 1D 16
Durlow Common. Here 2B 48
Durnamuck. High 4E 163
Durness. High 2E 166
Durno. Abers 1E 152
Durns Town. Hants 3A 16
Duror. High 3D 141
Durran. Arg 3G 133
Durran. High 2D 169
Durrant Green. Kent 2C 28
Durrants. Hants 1F 17
Durrington. W Sus 5C 26
Durrington. Wilts 2G 23
Dursley. Glos 2C 34
Dursley Cross. Glos 4B 48
Durston. Som 4F 21
Durweston. Dors 2D 14
Dury. Shet 6F 173
Duston. Nptn 4E 63
Duthil. High 1D 150
Dutlas. Powy 3E 58
Duton Hill. Essx 3G 53
Dutson. Corn 4D 10
Dutton. Ches W 3H 83
Duxford. Cambs 1E 53
Duxford. Oxon 2B 36
Dwygyfylchi. Cnwy 3G 81
Dwyran. IOA 4D 80
Dyce. Aber 2F 153
Dyffryn. B'end 2B 32
Dyffryn. Carm 2H 43
Dyffryn. Pemb 1D 42
Dyffryn. V Glam 4D 32
Dyffryn Ardudwy. Gwyn 3E 69
Dyffryn Castell. Cdgn 2G 57
Dyffryn Ceidrych. Carm 3H 45
Dyffryn Cellwen. Neat 5B 46
Dyke. Linc 3A 76
Dyke. Mor 3D 159
Dykehead. Ang 2C 144
Dykehead. N Lan 3B 128
Dykehead. Stir 4E 135
Dykend. Ang 3B 144
Dykesfield. Cumb 4E 112
Dylife. Powy 1A 58
Dymchurch. Kent 3F 29
Dymock. Glos 2C 48
Dyrham. S Glo 4C 34
Dysart. Fife 4F 137
Dyserth. Den 3C 82

E

Eachwick. Nmbd 2E 115
Eadar Dha Fhadhail.
W Isl 4C 171
Eagland Hill. Lanc 5D 96
Eagle. Linc 4F 87
Eagle Barnsdale. Linc 4F 87
Eagle Moor. Linc 4F 87
Eaglescliffe. Stoc T 3B 106
Eaglesfield. Cumb 2B 102
Eaglesfield. Dum 2D 112
Eaglesham. E Ren 4G 127
Eaglethorpe. Nptn 1H 63
Eagley. G Man 3F 91
Eairy. IOM 4B 108
Eakley Lanes. Mil 5F 63
Eakring. Notts 4D 86
Ealand. N Lin 3A 94
Ealing. G Lon 2C 38
Eallabus. Arg 3B 124
Eals. Nmbd 4H 113
Eamont Bridge. Cumb 2G 103
Earby. Lanc 5B 98
Earcroft. Bkbn 2E 91
Eardington. Shrp 1B 60
Eardisland. Here 5G 59
Eardisley. Here 1G 47
Eardiston. Shrp 3F 71
Eardiston. Worc 4A 60
Earith. Cambs 3C 64
Earlais. High 2C 154
Earle. Nmbd 2D 121
Earlesfield. Linc 2G 75
Earlestown. Mers 1H 83
Earley. Wok 4F 37
Earlham. Norf 5D 78
Earlish. High 2C 154
Earls Barton. Nptn 4F 63
Earls Colne. Essx 3B 54
Earls Common. Worc 5D 60
Earl's Croome. Worc 1D 48
Earlsdon. W Mid 3H 61
Earlsferry. Fife 3G 137
Earlsford. Abers 5F 161
Earl's Green. Suff 4C 66
Earlsheaton. W Yor 2C 92
Earl Shilton. Leics 1B 62
Earl Soham. Suff 4E 67
Earl Sterndale. Derbs 4E 85
Earlston. E Ayr 1D 116
Earlston. Bord 1H 119
Earl Stonham. Suff 5D 66
Earlstoun. Dum 1D 110
Earlswood. Mon 2H 33
Earlswood. Warw 3F 61
Earlyvale. Bord 4F 129
Earnley. W Sus 3G 17
Earsairidh. W Isl 9C 170
Earsdon. Tyne 2G 115
Earsham. Norf 2F 67
Earsham Street. Suff 3E 67
Earswick. York 4A 100
Eartham. W Sus 5A 26
Earthcott Green. S Glo 3B 34
Easby. N Yor
nr. Great Ayton 4C 106
nr. Richmond 4E 105
Easdale. Arg 2E 133
Easebourne. W Sus 4G 25
Easenhall. Warw 3B 62
Eashing. Surr 1A 26
Easington. Buck 4E 51
Easington. Dur 5H 115
Easington. E Yor 3G 95
Easington. Nmbd 1F 121
Easington. Oxon
nr. Banbury 2C 50
nr. Watlington 2E 37
Easington. Red C 3E 107
Easington Colliery. Dur 5H 115
Easington Lane. Tyne 5G 115
Easingwold. N Yor 2H 99
Eassie. Ang 4C 144
Eassie and Nevay. Ang 4C 144
East Aberthaw. V Glam 5D 32
Eastacombe. Devn 4F 19
Eastacott. Devn 4G 19
East Allington. Devn 4D 8
East Anstey. Devn 4B 20
East Anton. Hants 2B 24
East Appleton. N Yor 5F 105
East Ardsley. W Yor 2D 92
East Ashley. Devn 1G 11
East Ashling. W Sus 2G 17
East Aston. Hants 2C 24
East Ayton. N Yor 1D 101
East Barkwith. Linc 2A 88
East Barnby. N Yor 3F 107
East Barnet. G Lon 1D 39
East Barns. E Lot 2D 130
East Barsham. Norf 2B 78
East Beach. W Sus 3G 17
East Beckham. Norf 2D 78
East Bedfont. G Lon 3B 38
East Bennan. N Ayr 3D 123
East Bergholt. Suff 2D 54
East Bierley. W Yor 2B 92
East Bilney. Norf 4B 78
East Blatchington. E Sus 5F 27
East Bloxworth. Dors 3D 15
East Boldre. Hants 2B 16
East Bolton. Nmbd 3F 121
Eastbourne. Darl 3F 105
Eastbourne. E Sus 194 (5H 27)
East Brent. Som 1G 21
East Bridge. Suff 4G 67
East Bridgford. Notts 1D 74
East Briscoe. Dur 3C 104
East Buckland. Devn
nr. Barnstaple 3G 19
nr. Thurlestone 4C 8
East Budleigh. Devn 4D 12
Eastburn. W Yor 5C 98
East Burnham. Buck 2A 38
East Burrafirth. Shet 6E 173
East Burton. Dors 4D 14
Eastbury. Herts 1B 38
Eastbury. W Ber 4B 36
East Butsfield. Dur 5E 115
East Butterleigh. Devn 2C 12
East Butterwick. N Lin 4B 94
Eastby. N Yor 4C 98
East Calder. W Lot 3D 129
East Carleton. Norf 5D 78
East Carlton. Nptn 2F 63
East Carlton. W Yor 5E 98
East Chaldon. Dors 4C 14
East Challow. Oxon 3B 36
East Charleton. Devn 4D 8
East Chelborough. Dors 2A 14
East Chiltington. E Sus 4E 27
East Chinnock. Som 1H 13
East Chisenbury. Wilts 1G 23
Eastchurch. Kent 3D 40
East Clandon. Surr 5B 38
East Claydon. Buck 3F 51
East Clevedon. N Som 4H 33
East Clyne. High 3F 165
East Clyth. High 5E 169
East Coker. Som 1A 14
East Combe. Som 3E 21
Eastcombe. Glos 5D 49
East Common. N Yor 1G 93
East Compton. Som 2B 22
East Cornworthy. Devn 3E 9
Eastcote. G Lon 2C 38
Eastcote. Nptn 5D 62
Eastcote. W Mid 3F 61
Eastcott. Corn 1C 10
Eastcott. Wilts 1F 23
East Cottingwith. E Yor 5B 100
Eastcourt. Wilts
nr. Pewsey 5H 35
nr. Tetbury 2E 35
East Cowes. IOW 3D 16
East Cowick. E Yor 2G 93
East Cowton. N Yor 4A 106
East Cramlington. Nmbd 2F 115
East Cranmore. Som 2B 22
East Creech. Dors 4E 15
East Croachy. High 1A 150
East Dean. E Sus 5G 27
East Dean. Glos 3B 48
East Dean. Hants 4A 24
East Dean. W Sus 4A 26
East Down. Devn 2G 19
East Drayton. Notts 3E 87
East Dundry. N Som 5A 34
East Ella. Hull 2D 94
East End. Cambs 3C 64
East End. Dors 3E 15
East End. E Yor
nr. Ulrome 4F 101
nr. Withernsea 2F 95
East End. Hants
nr. Lymington 3B 16
nr. Newbury 5C 36
East End. Herts 3E 53
East End. Kent
nr. Minster 3D 40
nr. Tenterden 2C 28
East End. N Som 4H 33
East End. Oxon 4B 50
East End. Som 1A 22
East End. Suff 2E 54
Easter Ardross. High 1A 158
Easter Balgedie. Per 3D 136
Easter Balmoral. Abers 4G 151
Easter Brae. High 2A 158
Easter Buckieburn. Stir 1A 128
Easter Compton. S Glo 3A 34
Easter Fearn. High 5D 164
Easter Galcantray. High 4C 158
Eastergate. W Sus 5A 26
Easterhouse. Glas 3H 127
Easter Howgate. Midl 3F 129
Easter Kinkell. High 3H 157
Easter Lednathie. Ang 2C 144
Easter Ogil. Ang 2D 144
Easter Ord. Abers 3F 153
Easter Quarff. Shet 8F 173
Easter Rhynd. Per 2D 136
Easter Skeld. Shet 7E 173
Easter Suddie. High 3A 158
Easterton. Wilts 1F 23
Eastertown. Som 1G 21
Easter Tulloch. Abers 1G 145
East Everleigh. Wilts 1H 23
East Farleigh. Kent 5B 40
East Farndon. Nptn 2E 62
East Ferry. Linc 1F 87
Eastfield. N Lan
nr. Caldercruix 3B 128
nr. Harthill 3B 128
Eastfield. N Yor 1E 101
Eastfield. S Lan 3H 127
Eastfield Hall. Nmbd 4G 121
East Fortune. E Lot 2B 130
East Garforth. W Yor 1E 93
East Garston. W Ber 4B 36
Eastgate. Dur 1C 104
Eastgate. Norf 3D 78
East Ginge. Oxon 3C 36
East Gores. Essx 3B 54
East Goscote. Leics 4D 74
East Grafton. Wilts 5A 36
East Green. Suff 5F 65
East Grimstead. Wilts 4H 23
East Grinstead. W Sus 2E 27
East Guldeford. E Sus 3D 28
East Haddon. Nptn 4D 62
East Hagbourne. Oxon 3D 36
East Halton. N Lin 2E 95
East Ham. G Lon 2F 39
Eastham. Mers 2F 83
Eastham. Worc 4A 60
Eastham Ferry. Mers 2F 83
Easthampstead. Brac 5G 37
Easthampton. Here 4G 59
East Hanney. Oxon 2C 36
East Hanningfield. Essx 5A 54
East Hardwick. W Yor 3E 93
East Harling. Norf 2B 66
East Harlsey. N Yor 5B 106
East Harptree. Bath 1A 22
East Hartford. Nmbd 2F 115
East Harting. W Sus 1G 17
East Hatch. Wilts 4E 23
East Hatley. Cambs 5B 64
Easthaugh. Norf 4C 78
East Hauxwell. N Yor 5E 105
East Haven. Ang 5E 145
Eastheath. Wok 5G 37
East Heckington. Linc 1A 76
East Hedleyhope. Dur 5E 115
East Helmsdale. High 2H 165
East Hendred. Oxon 3C 36
East Heslerton. N Yor 2D 100
East Hoathly. E Sus 4G 27
East Holme. Dors 4D 15
Easthope. Shrp 1H 59
Easthorpe. Essx 3C 54
Easthorpe. Leics 2F 75
East Horrington. Som 2A 22
East Horsley. Surr 5B 38
East Horton. Nmbd 1E 121
Easthouses. Midl 3G 129
East Howe. Bour 3F 15
East Huntspill. Som 2G 21
East Hyde. C Beds 4B 52
East Ilsley. W Ber 3C 36
Eastington. Devn 2H 11
Eastington. Glos
nr. Northleach 4G 49
nr. Stonehouse 5C 48
East Keal. Linc 4C 88
East Kennett. Wilts 5G 35
East Keswick. W Yor 5F 99
East Kilbride. S Lan 4H 127
East Kirkby. Linc 4C 88
East Knapton. N Yor 2C 100
East Knighton. Dors 4D 14
East Knowstone. Devn 4B 20
East Knoyle. Wilts 3D 23
East Kyloe. Nmbd 1E 121
East Lambrook. Som 1H 13
East Langdon. Kent 1H 29
East Langton. Leics 1E 63
East Langwell. High 3E 164
East Lavant. W Sus 2G 17
East Lavington. W Sus 4A 26
East Layton. N Yor 4E 105
Eastleach Martin. Glos 5H 49
Eastleach Turville. Glos 5G 49
East Leake. Notts 3C 74
East Learmouth. Nmbd 1C 120
East Leigh. Devn
nr. Crediton 2G 11
nr. Modbury 3C 8
Eastleigh. Devn 4E 19
Eastleigh. Hants 1C 16
East Lexham. Norf 4A 78
East Lilburn. Nmbd 2E 121
Eastling. Kent 5D 40
East Linton. E Lot 2B 130
East Liss. Hants 4F 25
East Lockinge. Oxon 3C 36
East Looe. Corn 3G 7
East Lound. N Lin 1E 87
East Lulworth. Dors 4D 14
East Lutton. N Yor 3D 100
East Lydford. Som 3A 22
East Lyng. Som 4G 21
East Mains. Abers 4D 152
East Malling. Kent 5B 40
East Marden. W Sus 1G 17
East Markham. Notts 3E 87
East Marton. N Yor 4B 98
East Meon. Hants 4E 25
East Mersea. Essx 4D 54
East Mey. High 1F 169
East Midlands Airport.
Leics 205 (3B 74)
East Molesey. Surr 4C 38
Eastmoor. Norf 5G 77
East Morden. Dors 3E 15
East Morton. W Yor 5D 98
East Ness. N Yor 2A 100
East Newton. E Yor 1F 95
East Newton. N Yor 2A 100
Eastney. Port 3E 17
Eastnor. Here 2C 48
East Norton. Leics 5E 75
East Nynehead. Som 4E 21
East Oakley. Hants 1D 24
Eastoft. N Lin 3B 94
East Ogwell. Devn 5B 12
Easton. Cambs 3A 64
Easton. Cumb
nr. Burgh by Sands 4D 112
nr. Longtown 2F 113
Easton. Devn 4H 11
Easton. Dors 5B 14
Easton. Hants 3D 24
Easton. Linc 3G 75
Easton. Norf 4D 78
Easton. Som 2A 22
Easton. Suff 5E 67
Easton. Wilts 4D 35
Easton Grey. Wilts 3D 35
Easton-in-Gordano.
N Som 4A 34
Easton Maudit. Nptn 5F 63
Easton on the Hill. Nptn 5H 75
Easton Royal. Wilts 5H 35
East Orchard. Dors 1D 14
East Ord. Nmbd 4F 131
East Panson. Devn 3D 10
East Peckham. Kent 1A 28
East Pennard. Som 3A 22
East Perry. Cambs 4A 64
East Pitcorthie. Fife 3H 137
East Portlemouth. Devn 5D 8
East Prawle. Devn 5D 9
East Preston. W Sus 5B 26
East Putford. Devn 1D 10
East Quantoxhead. Som 2E 21
East Rainton. Tyne 5G 115
East Ravendale. NE Lin 1B 88
East Raynham. Norf 3A 78
Eastrea. Cambs 1B 64
East Rhidorroch Lodge.
High 4G 163
Eastriggs. Dum 3D 112
East Rigton. W Yor 5F 99
Eastrington. E Yor 2A 94
East Rounton. N Yor 4B 106
East Row. N Yor 3F 107
East Rudham. Norf 3H 77
East Runton. Norf 1D 78
East Ruston. Norf 3F 79
Eastry. Kent 5H 41
East Saltoun. E Lot 3A 130
East Shaws. Dur 3D 105
East Shefford. W Ber 4B 36
Eastshore. Shet 10E 173
East Sleekburn. Nmbd 1F 115
East Somerton. Norf 4G 79
East Stockwith. Linc 1E 87
East Stoke. Dors 4D 14
East Stoke. Notts 1E 75
East Stoke. Som 1H 13
East Stour. Dors 4D 22
East Stourmouth. Kent 4G 41
East Stowford. Devn 4G 19
East Stratton. Hants 2D 24
East Studdal. Kent 1H 29
East Taphouse. Corn 2F 7
East-the-Water. Devn 4E 19
East Thirston. Nmbd 5F 121
East Tilbury. Thur 3A 40
East Tisted. Hants 3F 25
East Torrington. Linc 2A 88
East Tuddenham. Norf 4C 78
East Tytherley. Hants 4A 24
East Tytherton. Wilts 4E 35
East Village. Devn 2B 12
Eastville. Linc 5D 88
East Wall. Shrp 1H 59
East Walton. Norf 4G 77
East Week. Devn 3G 11
Eastwell. Leics 3E 75
East Wellow. Hants 4B 24
East Wemyss. Fife 4F 137
East Whitburn. W Lot 3C 128
Eastwick. Herts 4E 53
Eastwick. Shet 4E 173
East Williamston. Pemb 4E 43
East Winch. Norf 4F 77
East Winterslow. Wilts 3H 23
East Wittering. W Sus 3F 17
East Witton. N Yor 1D 98
Eastwood. Notts 1B 74
Eastwood. S'end 2C 40
Eastwood End. Cambs 1D 64
East Woodburn. Nmbd 1C 114
East Woodhay. Hants 5C 36
East Woodlands. Som 2C 22
East Worldham. Hants 3F 25
East Worlington. Devn 1A 12
East Wretham. Norf 1B 66
East Youlstone. Devn 1C 10
Eathorpe. Warw 4A 62
Eaton. Ches E 4C 84
Eaton. Ches W 4H 83
Eaton. Leics 3E 75
Eaton. Norf
nr. Heacham 2F 77
nr. Norwich 5E 78
Eaton. Notts 3E 86
Eaton. Oxon 5C 50
Eaton. Shrp
nr. Bishop's Castle 2F 59
nr. Church Stretton 2H 59
Eaton Bishop. Here 2H 47
Eaton Bray. C Beds 3H 51
Eaton Constantine. Shrp 5H 71
Eaton Hastings. Oxon 2A 36
Eaton Socon. Cambs 5A 64
Eaton upon Tern. Shrp 3A 72
Eau Brink. Norf 4E 77
Eaves Green. W Mid 2G 61
Ebberley Hill. Devn 1F 11
Ebberston. N Yor 1C 100
Ebbesbourne Wake. Wilts 4E 23
Ebblake. Dors 2G 15
Ebbsfleet. Kent 3H 39
Ebbw Vale. Blae 5E 47
Ebchester. Dur 4E 115
Ebernoe. W Sus 3A 26
Ebford. Devn 4C 12
Ebley. Glos 5D 48
Ebnal. Ches W 1G 71
Ebrington. Glos 1G 49
Ecchinswell. Hants 1D 24
Ecclefechan. Dum 2C 112
Eccles. G Man 1B 84
Eccles. Kent 4B 40
Eccles. Bord 5D 130
Ecclesall. S Yor 2H 85
Ecclesfield. S Yor 1A 86
Eccles Green. Here 1G 47
Eccleshall. Staf 3C 72

Eccleshill—Fiskerton

Eccleshill. W Yor 1B 92
Ecclesmachan. W Lot 2D 128
Eccles on Sea. Norf 3G 79
Eccles Road. Norf 1C 66
Eccleston. Ches W 4G 83
Eccleston. Lanc 3D 90
Eccleston. Mers 1G 83
Eccup. W Yor 5E 99
Echt. Abers 3E 153
Eckford. Bord 2B 120
Eckington. Derbs 3B 86
Eckington. Worc 1E 49
Ecton. Nptn 4F 63
Edale. Derbs 2F 85
Eday Airport. Orkn 4E 172
Edburton. W Sus 4D 26
Edderside. Cumb 5C 112
Edderton. High 5E 164
Eddington. Kent 4F 41
Eddington. W Ber 5B 36
Eddleston. Bord 5F 129
Eddlewood. S Lan 4A 128
Eden. ME Ant 8L 175
Edenbridge. Kent 1F 27
Edendonich. Arg 1A 134
Edenfield. Lanc 3F 91
Edenhall. Cumb 1G 103
Edenham. Linc 3H 75
Edensor. Derbs 3G 85
Edentaggart. Arg 4C 134
Edenthorpe. S Yor 4G 93
Eden Vale. Dur 1B 106
Edern. Gwyn 2B 68
Ederney. Ferm 6E 176
Edgarley. Som 3A 22
Edgbaston. W Mid 2E 61
Edgcott. Buck 3E 51
Edgcott. Som 3B 20
Edge. Glos 5D 48
Edge. Shrp 5F 71
Edgebolton. Shrp 3H 71
Edge End. Glos 4A 48
Edgefield. Norf 2C 78
Edgefield Street. Norf 2C 78
Edge Green. Ches W 5G 83
Edgehead. Midl 3G 129
Edgeley. Shrp 1H 71
Edgeside. Lanc 2G 91
Edgeworth. Glos 5E 49
Edgiock. Worc 4E 61
Edgmond. Telf 4B 72
Edgmond Marsh. Telf 3B 72
Edgton. Shrp 2F 59
Edgware. G Lon 1C 38
Edgworth. Bkbn 3F 91
Edinbane. High 3C 154
Edinburgh. Edin 195 (2F 129)
Edinburgh Airport. Edin 2E 129
Edingale. Staf 4G 73
Edingley. Notts 5D 86
Edingthorpe. Norf 2F 79
Edington. Som 3G 21
Edington. Wilts 1E 23
Edingworth. Som 1G 21
Edistone. Devn 4C 18
Edithmead. Som 2G 21
Edith Weston. Rut 5G 75
Edlaston. Derbs 1F 73
Edlesborough. Buck 4H 51
Edlingham. Nmbd 4F 121
Edlington. Linc 3B 88
Edmondsham. Dors 1F 15
Edmondsley. Dur 5F 115
Edmondthorpe. Leics 4F 75
Edmonstone. Orkn 5E 172
Edmonton. Corn 1D 6
Edmonton. G Lon 1E 39
Edmundbyers. Dur 4D 114
Ednam. Bord 1B 120
Ednaston. Derbs 1G 73
Edney Common. Essx 5G 53
Edrom. Bord 4E 131
Edstaston. Shrp 2H 71
Edstone. Warw 4F 61
Edwalton. Notts 2C 74
Edwardstone. Suff 1C 54
Edwardsville. Mer T 2D 32
Edwinsford. Carm 2G 45
Edwinstowe. Notts 4D 86
Edworth. C Beds 1C 52
Edwyn Ralph. Here 5A 60
Edzell. Ang 2F 145
Efail-fach. Neat 2A 32
Efail Isaf. Rhon 3D 32
Efailnewydd. Gwyn 2C 68
Efail-rhyd. Powy 3D 70
Efailwen. Carm 2F 43
Efenechtyd. Den 5D 82
Effingham. Surr 5C 38
Effingham Common. Surr 5C 38
Effirth. Shet 6E 173
Efflinch. Staf 4F 73
Efford. Devn 2B 12
Efstigarth. Shet 2F 173
Egbury. Hants 1C 24
Egdon. Worc 5D 60
Egerton. G Man 3F 91
Egerton. Kent 1D 28
Egerton Forstal. Kent 1C 28
Eggborough. N Yor 2F 93
Eggbuckland. Plym 3A 8
Eggesford. Devn 1G 11
Eggington. C Beds 3H 51
Egginton. Derbs 3G 73
Egglescliffe. Stoc T 3B 106
Eggleston. Dur 2C 104
Egham. Surr 3B 38
Egham Hythe. Surr 3B 38
Egleton. Rut 5F 75
Eglingham. Nmbd 3F 121
Eglinton. Derr 4B 174
Eglish. M Ulst 4B 178
Egloshayle. Corn 5A 10
Egloskerry. Corn 4C 10
Eglwysbach. Cnwy 3H 81
Eglwys-Brewis. V Glam 5D 32
Eglwys Fach. Cdgn 1F 57
Eglwyswrw. Pemb 1F 43
Egmanton. Notts 4E 87
Egmere. Norf 2B 78
Egremont. Cumb 3B 102
Egremont. Mers 1F 83
Egton. N Yor 4F 107
Egton Bridge. N Yor 4F 107
Egypt. Buck 2A 38
Egypt. Hants 2C 24
Eight Ash Green. Essx 3C 54
Eight Mile Burn. Midl 4E 129
Eignaig. High 4B 140
Eilanreach. High 2G 147
Eildon. Bord 1H 119
Eileanach Lodge. High 2H 157
Eilean Fhlodaigh. W Isl 3D 170
Eilean Iarmain. High 2F 147
Einacleit. W Isl 5D 171
Eisgein. W Isl 6F 171
Eisingrug. Gwyn 2F 69
Elan Village. Powy 4B 58
Elberton. S Glo 3B 34
Elbridge. W Sus 5A 26
Elburton. Plym 3B 8
Elcho. Per 1D 136
Elcombe. Swin 3G 35
Elcot. W Ber 5B 36
Eldernell. Cambs 1C 64
Eldersfield. Worc 2D 48
Elderslie. Ren 3F 127
Elder Street. Essx 2F 53
Eldon. Dur 2F 105
Eldroth. N Yor 3G 97
Eldwick. W Yor 5D 98
Elfhowe. Cumb 5F 103
Elford. Nmbd 1F 121
Elford. Staf 4F 73
Elford Closes. Cambs 3D 65
Elgin. Mor 2G 159
Elgol. High 2D 146
Elham. Kent 1F 29
Elie. Fife 3G 137
Eling. Hants 1B 16
Eling. W Ber 4D 36
Elishaw. Nmbd 5C 120
Elizafield. Dum 2B 112
Elkesley. Notts 3D 86
Elkington. Nptn 3D 62
Elkins Green. Essx 5G 53
Elkstone. Glos 4E 49
Ellan. High 1C 150
Elland. W Yor 2B 92
Ellary. Arg 2F 125
Ellastone. Staf 1F 73
Ellbridge. Corn 2A 8
Ellel. Lanc 4D 97
Ellemford. Bord 3D 130
Ellenabeich. Arg 2E 133
Ellenborough. Cumb 1B 102
Ellenbrook. Herts 5C 52
Ellenhall. Staf 3C 72
Ellen's Green. Surr 2B 26
Ellerbeck. N Yor 5B 106
Ellerburn. N Yor 1C 100
Ellerby. N Yor 3E 107
Ellerdine. Telf 3A 72
Ellerdine Heath. Telf 3A 72
Ellerhayes. Devn 2C 12
Elleric. Arg 4E 141
Ellerker. E Yor 2C 94
Ellerton. E Yor 1H 93
Ellerton. Shrp 3B 72
Ellerton-on-Swale. N Yor 5F 105
Ellesborough. Buck 5G 51
Ellesmere. Shrp 2G 71
Ellesmere Port. Ches W 3G 83
Ellingham. Hants 2G 15
Ellingham. Norf 1F 67
Ellingham. Nmbd 2F 121
Ellingstring. N Yor 1D 98
Ellington. Cambs 3A 64
Ellington. Nmbd 5G 121
Ellington Thorpe. Cambs 3A 64
Elliot. Ang 5F 145
Ellisfield. Hants 2E 25
Ellishadder. High 2E 155
Ellistown. Leics 4B 74
Ellon. Abers 5G 161
Ellonby. Cumb 1F 103
Ellough. Suff 2G 67
Elloughton. E Yor 2C 94
Ellwood. Glos 5A 48
Elm. Cambs 5D 76
Elmbridge. Glos 4D 48
Elmbridge. Worc 4D 60
Elmdon. Essx 2E 53
Elmdon. W Mid 2F 61
Elmdon Heath. W Mid 2F 61
Elmesthorpe. Leics 1B 62
Elmfield. IOW 3E 16
Elm Hill. Dors 4D 22
Elmhurst. Staf 4F 73
Elmley Castle. Worc 1E 49
Elmley Lovett. Worc 4C 60
Elmore. Glos 4C 48
Elmore Back. Glos 4C 48
Elm Park. G Lon 2G 39
Elmscott. Devn 4C 18
Elmsett. Suff 1D 54
Elmstead. Essx 3D 54
Elmstead Heath. Essx 3D 54
Elmstead Market. Essx 3D 54
Elmsted. Kent 1F 29
Elmstone. Kent 4G 41
Elmstone Hardwicke. Glos 3E 49
Elmswell. E Yor 4D 101
Elmswell. Suff 4B 66
Elmton. Derbs 3C 86
Elphin. High 2G 163
Elphinstone. E Lot 2G 129
Elrick. Abers 3F 153
Elrick. Mor 1B 152
Elrig. Dum 5A 110
Elsdon. Nmbd 5D 120
Elsecar. S Yor 1A 86
Elsenham. Essx 3F 53
Elsfield. Oxon 4D 50
Elsham. N Lin 3D 94
Elsing. Norf 4C 78
Elslack. N Yor 5B 98
Elsrickle. S Lan 5D 128
Elstead. Surr 1A 26
Elsted. W Sus 1G 17
Elsted Marsh. W Sus 4G 25
Elsthorpe. Linc 3H 75
Elstob. Dur 2A 106
Elston. Devn 2A 12
Elston. Lanc 1E 90
Elston. Notts 1E 75
Elston. Wilts 2F 23
Elstone. Devn 1G 11
Elstow. Bed 1A 52
Elstree. Herts 1C 38
Elstronwick. E Yor 1F 95
Elswick. Lanc 1C 90
Elswick. Tyne 3F 115
Elsworth. Cambs 4C 64
Elterwater. Cumb 4E 103
Eltham. G Lon 3F 39
Eltisley. Cambs 5B 64
Elton. Cambs 1H 63
Elton. Ches W 3G 83
Elton. Derbs 4G 85
Elton. Glos 4C 48
Elton. G Man 3F 91
Elton. Here 3G 59
Elton. Notts 2E 75
Elton. Stoc T 3B 106
Elton Green. Ches W 3G 83
Eltringham. Nmbd 3D 115
Elvanfoot. S Lan 3B 118
Elvaston. Derbs 2B 74
Elveden. Suff 3H 65
Elvetham Heath. Hants 1F 25
Elvingston. E Lot 2A 130
Elvington. Kent 5G 41
Elvington. York 5B 100
Elwick. Hart 1B 106
Elwick. Nmbd 1F 121
Elworth. Ches E 4B 84
Elworth. Dors 4A 14
Elworthy. Som 3D 20
Ely. Cambs 2E 65
Ely. Card 4E 33
Emberton. Mil 1G 51
Embleton. Cumb 1C 102
Embleton. Hart 2B 106
Embleton. Nmbd 2G 121
Embo. High 4F 165
Emborough. Som 1B 22
Embo Street. High 4F 165
Embsay. N Yor 4C 98
Emery Down. Hants 2A 16
Emley. W Yor 3C 92
Emmbrook. Wok 5F 37
Emmer Green. Read 4F 37
Emmington. Oxon 5F 51
Emneth. Norf 5D 77
Emneth Hungate. Norf 5E 77
Empingham. Rut 5G 75
Empshott. Hants 3F 25
Emsworth. Hants 2F 17
Enborne. W Ber 5C 36
Enborne Row. W Ber 5C 36
Enchmarsh. Shrp 1H 59
Enderby. Leics 1C 62
Endmoor. Cumb 1E 97
Endon. Staf 5D 84
Endon Bank. Staf 5D 84
Enfield. G Lon 1E 39
Enfield Wash. G Lon 1E 39
Enford. Wilts 1G 23
Engine Common. S Glo 3B 34
Englefield. W Ber 4E 37
Englefield Green. Surr 3A 38
Englesea-brook. Ches E 5B 84
English Bicknor. Glos 4A 48
Englishcombe. Bath 5C 34
English Frankton. Shrp 3G 71
Enham Alamein. Hants 2B 24
Enmore. Som 3F 21
Ennerdale Bridge. Cumb 3B 102
Enniscaven. Corn 3D 6
Enniskillen. Ferm 8E 176
Enoch. Dum 4A 118
Enochdhu. Per 2H 143
Ensay. Arg 4E 139
Ensbury. Bour 3F 15
Ensdon. Shrp 4G 71
Ensis. Devn 4F 19
Enson. Staf 3D 72
Enstone. Oxon 3B 50
Enterkinfoot. Dum 4A 118
Enville. Staf 2C 60
Eolaigearraidh. W Isl 8C 170
Eorabus. Arg 1A 132
Eoropaidh. W Isl 1H 171
Epney. Glos 4C 48
Epperstone. Notts 1D 74
Epping. Essx 5E 53
Epping Green. Essx 5E 53
Epping Green. Herts 5C 52
Epping Upland. Essx 5E 53
Eppleby. N Yor 3E 105
Eppleworth. E Yor 1D 94
Epsom. Surr 4D 38
Epwell. Oxon 1B 50
Epworth. N Lin 4A 94
Epworth Turbary. N Lin 4A 94
Erbistock. Wrex 1F 71
Erbusaig. High 1F 147
Erchless Castle. High 4G 157
Erdington. W Mid 1F 61
Eredine. Arg 3G 133
Eriganagh. Derr 4F 176
Eriboll. High 3E 167
Ericstane. Dum 3C 118
Eridge Green. E Sus 2G 27
Erines. Arg 2G 125
Eriswell. Suff 3G 65
Erith. G Lon 3G 39
Erlestoke. Wilts 1E 23
Ermine. Linc 3G 87
Ermington. Devn 3C 8
Ernesettle. Plym 3A 8
Erpingham. Norf 2D 78
Erriott Wood. Kent 5D 40
Errogie. High 1H 149
Errol. Per 1E 137
Errol Station. Per 1E 137
Erskine. Ren 2F 127
Erskine Bridge. Ren 2F 127
Ervie. Dum 3F 109
Erwarton. Suff 2F 55
Erwood. Powy 1D 46
Eryholme. N Yor 4A 106
Eryrys. Den 5E 82
Escalls. Corn 4A 4
Escomb. Dur 1E 105
Escrick. N Yor 5A 100
Esgair. Carm
nr. Carmarthen 3D 45
nr. St Clears 3G 43
Esgairgeiliog. Powy 5G 69
Esh. Dur 5E 115
Esher. Surr 4C 38
Esholt. W Yor 5D 98
Eshott. Nmbd 5G 121
Eshton. N Yor 4B 98
Esh Winning. Dur 5E 115
Eskadale. High 5G 157
Eskbank. Midl 3G 129
Eskdale Green. Cumb 4C 102
Eskdalemuir. Dum 5E 119
Eskham. Linc 1C 88
Esknish. Arg 3B 124
Esk Valley. N Yor 4F 107
Eslington Hall. Nmbd 3E 121
Esprick. Lanc 1C 90
Essendine. Rut 4H 75
Essendon. Herts 5C 52
Essich. High 5A 158
Essington. Staf 5D 72
Eston. Red C 3C 106
Estover. Plym 3B 8
Eswick. Shet 6F 173
Etal. Nmbd 1D 120
Etchilhampton. Wilts 5F 35
Etchingham. E Sus 3B 28
Etchinghill. Kent 2F 29
Etchinghill. Staf 4E 73
Etherley Dene. Dur 2E 105
Ethie Haven. Ang 4F 145
Etling Green. Norf 4C 78
Etloe. Glos 5B 48
Eton. Wind 3A 38
Eton Wick. Wind 3A 38
Etteridge. High 4A 150
Ettersgill. Dur 2B 104
Ettiley Heath. Ches E 4B 84
Ettington. Warw 1A 50
Etton. E Yor 5D 101
Etton. Pet 5A 76
Ettrick. Bord 3E 119
Ettrickbridge. Bord 2F 119
Etwall. Derbs 2G 73
Eudon Burnell. Shrp 2B 60
Eudon George. Shrp 2A 60
Euston. Suff 3A 66
Euxton. Lanc 3D 90
Evanstown. B'end 3C 32
Evanton. High 2A 158
Evedon. Linc 1H 75
Evelix. High 4E 165
Evendine. Here 1C 48
Evenjobb. Powy 4E 59
Evenley. Nptn 2D 50
Evenlode. Glos 3H 49
Even Swindon. Swin 3G 35
Evenwood. Dur 2E 105
Evenwood Gate. Dur 2E 105
Everbay. Orkn 5F 172
Evercreech. Som 3B 22
Everdon. Nptn 5C 62
Everingham. E Yor 5C 100
Everleigh. Wilts 1H 23
Everley. N Yor 1D 100
Eversholt. C Beds 2H 51
Evershot. Dors 2A 14
Eversley. Hants 5F 37
Eversley Centre. Hants 5F 37
Eversley Cross. Hants 5F 37
Everthorpe. E Yor 1C 94
Everton. C Beds 5B 64
Everton. Hants 3A 16
Everton. Mers 1F 83
Everton. Notts 1D 86
Evertown. Dum 2E 113
Evesbatch. Here 1B 48
Evesham. Worc 1F 49
Evington. Leic 5D 74
Ewden Village. S Yor 1G 85
Ewdness. Shrp 1B 60
Ewell. Surr 4D 38
Ewell Minnis. Kent 1G 29
Ewelme. Oxon 2E 37
Ewen. Glos 2F 35
Ewenny. V Glam 4C 32
Ewerby. Linc 1A 76
Ewes. Dum 5F 119
Ewesley. Nmbd 5E 121
Ewhurst. Surr 1B 26
Ewhurst Green. E Sus 3B 28
Ewhurst Green. Surr 2B 26
Ewlo. Flin 4E 83
Ewloe. Flin 4E 83
Ewood Bridge. Lanc 2F 91
Eworthy. Devn 3E 11
Ewshot. Hants 1G 25
Ewyas Harold. Here 3G 47
Exbourne. Devn 2G 11
Exbury. Hants 2C 16
Exceat. E Sus 5G 27
Exebridge. Som 4C 20
Exelby. N Yor 1E 99
Exeter. Devn 195 (3C 12)
Exeter Airport. Devn 3D 12
Exford. Som 3B 20
Exfords Green. Shrp 5G 71
Exhall. Warw 5F 61
Exlade Street. Oxon 3E 37
Exminster. Devn 4C 12
Exmouth. Devn 4D 12
Exnaboe. Shet 10E 173
Exning. Suff 4F 65
Exton. Devn 4C 12
Exton. Hants 4E 24
Exton. Rut 4G 75
Exton. Som 3C 20
Exwick. Devn 3C 12
Eyam. Derbs 3G 85
Eydon. Nptn 5C 62
Eye. Here 4G 59
Eye. Pet 5B 76
Eye. Suff 3D 66
Eye Green. Pet 5B 76
Eyemouth. Bord 3F 131
Eyeworth. C Beds 1C 52
Eyhorne Street. Kent 5C 40
Eyke. Suff 5F 67
Eynesbury. Cambs 5A 64
Eynort. High 1B 146
Eynsford. Kent 4G 39
Eynsham. Oxon 5C 50
Eyre. High
on Isle of Skye 3D 154
on Raasay 5E 155
Eythorne. Kent 1G 29
Eyton. Here 4G 59
Eyton. Shrp
nr. Bishop's Castle 2F 59
nr. Shrewsbury 4F 71
Eyton. Wrex 1F 71
Eyton on Severn. Shrp 5H 71
Eyton upon the Weald Moors. Telf 4A 72

F

Faccombe. Hants 1B 24
Faceby. N Yor 4B 106
Faddiley. Ches E 5H 83
Fadmoor. N Yor 1A 100
Fagwyr. Swan 5G 45
Faichem. High 3E 149
Faifley. W Dun 2G 127
Fail. S Ayr 2D 116
Failand. N Som 4A 34
Failford. S Ayr 2D 116
Failsworth. G Man 4H 91
Fairbourne. Gwyn 4F 69
Fairbourne Heath. Kent 5C 40
Fairburn. N Yor 2E 93
Fairfield. Derbs 3E 85
Fairfield. Kent 3D 28
Fairfield. Worc
nr. Bromsgrove 3D 60
nr. Evesham 1F 49
Fairford. Glos 5G 49
Fair Green. Norf 4F 77
Fair Hill. Cumb 1G 103
Fairhill. S Lan 4A 128
Fair Isle Airport. Shet 1B 172
Fairlands. Surr 5A 38
Fairlie. N Ayr 4D 126
Fairlight. E Sus 4C 28
Fairlight Cove. E Sus 4C 28
Fairmile. Devn 3D 12
Fairmile. Surr 4C 38
Fairmilehead. Edin 3F 129
Fair Oak. Devn 1D 12
Fair Oak. Hants
nr. Eastleigh 1C 16
nr. Kingsclere 5D 36
Fairoak. Staf 2B 72
Fair Oak Green. Hants 5E 37
Fairseat. Kent 4H 39
Fairstead. Essx 4A 54
Fairstead. Norf 4F 77
Fairwarp. E Sus 3F 27
Fairwater. Card 4E 33
Fairy Cross. Devn 4E 19
Fakenham. Norf 2B 78
Fakenham Magna. Suff 3B 66
Fala. Midl 3H 129
Fala Dam. Midl 3H 129
Falcon. Here 2B 48
Faldingworth. Linc 2H 87
Falfield. S Glo 2B 34
Y Fali. IOA 3B 80
Falkenham. Suff 2F 55
Falkirk. Falk 1B 128
Falkland. Fife 3E 137
Fallin. Stir 4H 135
Fallowfield. G Man 1C 84
Falmer. E Sus 5E 27
Falmouth. Corn 5C 6
Falsgrave. N Yor 1E 101
Falstone. Nmbd 1A 114
Fanagmore. High 4B 166
Fancott. C Beds 3A 52
Fanellan. High 4G 157
Fangdale Beck. N Yor 5C 106
Fangfoss. E Yor 4B 100
Fankerton. Falk 1A 128
Fanmore. Arg 4F 139
Fanner's Green. Essx 4G 53
Fannich Lodge. High 2E 156
Fans. Bord 5C 130
Farcet. Cambs 1B 64
Far Cotton. Nptn 5E 63
Fareham. Hants 2D 16
Farewell. Staf 4E 73
Far Forest. Worc 3B 60
Farforth. Linc 3C 88
Far Green. Glos 5C 48
Far Hoarcross. Staf 3F 73
Faringdon. Oxon 2A 36
Farington. Lanc 2D 90
Farlam. Cumb 4G 113
Farleigh. N Som 5H 33
Farleigh. Surr 4E 39
Farleigh Hungerford. Som 1D 22
Farleigh Wallop. Hants 2E 24
Farleigh Wick. Wilts 5D 34
Farlesthorpe. Linc 3D 88
Farleton. Cumb 1E 97
Farleton. Lanc 3E 97
Farley. High 4G 157
Farley. Shrp
nr. Shrewsbury 5F 71
nr. Telford 5A 72
Farley. Staf 1E 73
Farley. Wilts 4H 23
Farley Green. Suff 5G 65
Farley Green. Surr 1B 26
Farley Hill. Wok 5F 37
Farley's End. Glos 4C 48
Farlington. N Yor 3A 100
Farlington. Port 2E 17
Farlow. Shrp 2A 60
Farmborough. Bath 5B 34
Farmcote. Glos 3F 49
Farmcote. Shrp 1B 60
Farmington. Glos 4G 49
Far Moor. G Man 4D 90
Farmoor. Oxon 5C 50
Farmtown. Mor 3C 160
Farnah Green. Derbs 1H 73
Farnborough. G Lon 4F 39
Farnborough. Hants 1G 25
Farnborough. Warw 1C 50
Farnborough. W Ber 3C 36
Farncombe. Surr 1A 26
Farndish. Bed 4G 63
Farndon. Ches W 5G 83
Farndon. Notts 5E 87
Farnell. Ang 3F 145
Farnham. Dors 1E 15
Farnham. Essx 3E 53
Farnham. N Yor 3F 99
Farnham. Suff 4F 67
Farnham. Surr 2G 25
Farnham Common. Buck 2A 38
Farnham Green. Essx 3E 53
Farnham Royal. Buck 2A 38
Farnhill. N Yor 5C 98
Farningham. Kent 4G 39
Farnley. N Yor 5E 98
Farnley Tyas. W Yor 3B 92
Farnsfield. Notts 5D 86
Farnworth. G Man 4F 91
Farnworth. Hal 2H 83
Far Oakridge. Glos 5E 49
Farr. High
nr. Bettyhill 2H 167
nr. Inverness 5A 158
nr. Kingussie 3C 150
Farraline. High 1H 149
Farringdon. Devn 3D 12
Farrington. Dors 1D 14
Farrington Gurney. Bath 1B 22
Far Sawrey. Cumb 5E 103
Farsley. W Yor 1C 92
Farthinghoe. Nptn 2D 50
Farthingstone. Nptn 5D 62
Farthorpe. Linc 3B 88
Fartown. W Yor 3B 92
Farway. Devn 3E 13
Fasag. High 3A 156
Fascadale. High 1G 139
Fasnacloich. Arg 4E 141
Fassfern. High 1E 141
Fatfield. Tyne 4G 115
Faugh. Cumb 4G 113
Fauld. Staf 3F 73
Fauldhouse. W Lot 3C 128
Faulkbourne. Essx 4A 54
Faulkland. Som 1C 22
Fauls. Shrp 2H 71
Faverdale. Darl 3F 105
Faversham. Kent 4E 40
Fawdington. N Yor 2G 99
Fawfieldhead. Staf 4E 85
Fawkham Green. Kent 4G 39
Fawler. Oxon 4B 50
Fawley. Buck 3F 37
Fawley. Hants 2C 16
Fawley. W Ber 3B 36
Fawley Chapel. Here 3A 48
Fawton. Corn 2F 7
Faxfleet. E Yor 2B 94
Faygate. W Sus 2D 26
Fazakerley. Mers 1F 83
Fazeley. Staf 5F 73
Feagour. High 4H 149
Fearann Dhomhnaill. High 3E 147
Fearby. N Yor 1D 98
Fearn. High 1C 158
Fearnan. Per 4E 142
Fearnbeg. High 3G 155
Fearnhead. Warr 1A 84
Fearnmore. High 2G 155
Featherstone. Staf 5D 72
Featherstone. W Yor 2E 93
Featherstone Castle. Nmbd 3H 113
Feckenham. Worc 4E 61
Feeny. Caus 6C 174
Feering. Essx 3B 54
Feetham. N Yor 5C 104
Feizor. N Yor 3G 97
Felbridge. Surr 2E 27
Felbrigg. Norf 2E 78
Felcourt. Surr 1E 27
Felden. Herts 5A 52
Felhampton. Shrp 2G 59
Felindre. Carm
nr. Llandeilo 3F 45
nr. Llandovery 2G 45
nr. Newcastle Emlyn 2D 44
Felindre. Powy 2D 58
Felindre. Swan 5G 45
Felindre Farchog. Pemb 1F 43
Felinfach. Cdgn 5E 57
Felinfach. Powy 2D 46
Felinfoel. Carm 5F 45
Felingwmisaf. Carm 3F 45
Felingwmuchaf. Carm 3F 45
Y Felinheli. Gwyn 4E 81
Felin Newydd. Powy
nr. Newtown 5C 70
nr. Oswestry 3E 70
Felin Wnda. Cdgn 1D 44
Felinwynt. Cdgn 5B 56
Felixkirk. N Yor 1G 99
Felixstowe. Suff 2F 55
Felixstowe Ferry. Suff 2G 55
Felkington. Nmbd 5F 131
Fell End. Cumb 5A 104
Felling. Tyne 3F 115
Fell Side. Cumb 1E 102
Felmersham. Bed 5G 63
Felmingham. Norf 3E 79
Felpham. W Sus 3H 17
Felsham. Suff 5B 66
Felsted. Essx 3G 53
Feltham. G Lon 3C 38
Felthamhill. Surr 3B 38
Felthorpe. Norf 4D 78
Felton. Here 1A 48
Felton. N Som 5A 34
Felton. Nmbd 4F 121
Felton Butler. Shrp 4F 71
Feltwell. Norf 1G 65
Fenay Bridge. W Yor 3B 92
Fence. Lanc 1G 91
Fence Houses. Tyne 4G 115
Fencott. Oxon 4D 50
Fen Ditton. Cambs 4D 65
Fen Drayton. Cambs 4C 64
Fen End. Linc 3B 76
Fen End. W Mid 3G 61
Fenham. Nmbd 5G 131
Fenham. Tyne 3F 115
Fenhouses. Linc 1B 76
Feniscowles. Bkbn 2E 91
Feniton. Devn 3D 12
Fenn Green. Shrp 2B 60
Y Fenni. Mon 4G 47
Fenn's Bank. Wrex 2H 71
Fenn Street. Medw 3B 40
Fenny Bentley. Derbs 5F 85
Fenny Bridges. Devn 3E 12
Fenny Compton. Warw 5B 62
Fenny Drayton. Leics 1H 61
Fenny Stratford. Mil 2G 51
Fenrother. Nmbd 5F 121
Fenstanton. Cambs 4C 64
Fen Street. Norf 1C 66
Fenton. Cambs 3C 64
Fenton. Cumb 4G 113
Fenton. Linc
nr. Caythorpe 5F 87
nr. Saxilby 3F 87
Fenton. Nmbd 1D 120
Fenton. Notts 2E 87
Fenton. Stoke 1C 72
Fentonadle. Corn 5A 10
Fenton Barns. E Lot 1B 130
Fenwick. E Ayr 5F 127
Fenwick. Nmbd
nr. Berwick-upon-Tweed 5G 131
nr. Hexham 2D 114
Fenwick. S Yor 3F 93
Feochaig. Arg 4B 122
Feock. Corn 5C 6
Feolin Ferry. Arg 3C 124
Feorlan. Arg 5A 122
Ferindonald. High 3E 147
Feriniquarrie. High 3A 154
Fern. Ang 2D 145
Ferndale. Rhon 2C 32
Ferndown. Dors 2F 15
Ferness. High 4D 158
Fernham. Oxon 2A 36
Fernhill. W Sus 1E 27
Fernhill Heath. Worc 5C 60
Fernhurst. W Sus 4G 25
Fernieflatt. Abers 1H 145
Ferniegair. S Lan 4A 128
Fernilea. High 5C 154
Fernilee. Derbs 3E 85
Ferrensby. N Yor 3F 99
Ferriby Sluice. N Lin 2C 94
Ferring. W Sus 5B 26
Ferrybridge. W Yor 2E 93
Ferryden. Ang 3G 145
Ferry Hill. Cambs 2C 64
Ferryhill. Dur 1F 105
Ferryhill Station. Dur 1A 106
Ferryside. Carm 4D 44
Ferryton. High 2A 158
Fersfield. Norf 2C 66
Fersit. High 1A 142
Y Ferwig. Cdgn 1B 44
Feshiebridge. High 3C 150
Fetcham. Surr 5C 38
Fetterangus. Abers 3G 161
Fettercairn. Abers 1F 145
Fewcott. Oxon 3D 50
Fewston. N Yor 4D 98
Ffairfach. Carm 3G 45
Ffair Rhos. Cdgn 4G 57
Ffaldybrenin. Carm 1G 45
Ffarmers. Carm 1G 45
Ffawyddog. Powy 4F 47
Y Fflint. Flin 3E 83
Ffodun. Powy 5E 71
Ffont-y-gari. V Glam 5D 32
Y Ffor. Gwyn 2C 68
Fforest. Carm 5F 45
Fforest-fach. Swan 3F 31
Fforest Goch. Neat 5H 45
Ffostrasol. Cdgn 1D 44
Ffos-y-ffin. Cdgn 4D 56
Ffrith. Flin 5E 83
Ffwl-y-mwn. V Glam 5D 32
Ffynnon-ddrain. Carm 3E 45
Ffynnongroyw. Flin 2D 82
Ffynnon Gynydd. Powy 1E 47
Ffynnon-oer. Cdgn 5E 57
Fiag Lodge. High 1B 164
Fidden. Arg 2B 132
Fiddington. Glos 2E 49
Fiddington. Som 2F 21
Fiddleford. Dors 1D 14
Fiddlers Hamlet. Essx 5E 53
Field. Staf 2E 73
Field Assarts. Oxon 4B 50
Field Broughton. Cumb 1C 96
Field Dalling. Norf 2C 78
Field Head. Leics 5B 74
Fieldhead. Cumb 1F 103
Fifehead Magdalen. Dors 4C 22
Fifehead Neville. Dors 1C 14
Fifehead St Quintin. Dors 1C 14
Fife Keith. Mor 3B 160
Fifield. Oxon 4H 49
Fifield. Wilts 1G 23
Fifield. Wind 3A 38
Fifield Bavant. Wilts 4F 23
Figheldean. Wilts 2G 23
Filby. Norf 4G 79
Filey. N Yor 1F 101
Filford. Dors 3H 13
Filgrave. Mil 1G 51
Filkins. Oxon 5H 49
Filleigh. Devn
nr. Crediton 1H 11
nr. South Molton 4G 19
Fillingham. Linc 2G 87
Fillongley. Warw 2G 61
Filton. S Glo 4B 34
Fimber. E Yor 3C 100
Finavon. Ang 3D 145
Fincham. Norf 5F 77
Finchampstead. Wok 5F 37
Fincharn. Arg 3G 133
Finchdean. Hants 1F 17
Finchingfield. Essx 2G 53
Finchley. G Lon 1D 38
Findern. Derbs 2H 73
Findhorn. Mor 2E 159
Findhorn Bridge. High 1C 150
Findochty. Mor 2B 160
Findo Gask. Per 1C 136
Findon. Abers 4G 153
Findon. W Sus 5C 26
Findon Mains. High 2A 158
Findon Valley. W Sus 5C 26
Finedon. Nptn 3G 63
Fingal Street. Suff 3E 66
Fingest. Buck 2F 37
Finghall. N Yor 1D 98
Fingland. Cumb 4D 112
Fingland. Dum 3G 117
Finglesham. Kent 5H 41
Fingringhoe. Essx 3D 54
Finiskaig. High 4A 148
Finmere. Oxon 2E 51
Finnart. Per 3C 142
Finningham. Suff 4C 66
Finningley. S Yor 1D 86
Finnygaud. Abers 3D 160
Finsbury. G Lon 2E 39
Finstall. Worc 4D 61
Finsthwaite. Cumb 1C 96
Finstock. Oxon 4B 50
Finstown. Orkn 6C 172
Fintona. Ferm 3K 177
Fintry. Abers 3E 161
Fintry. D'dee 5D 144
Fintry. Stir 1H 127
Finvoy. Caus 5F 175
Finwood. Warw 4F 61
Finzean. Abers 4D 152
Fionnphort. Arg 2B 132
Fionnsabhagh. W Isl 9C 171
Firbeck. S Yor 2C 86
Firby. N Yor
nr. Bedale 1E 99
nr. Malton 3B 100
Firgrove. G Man 3H 91
Firle. E Sus 5F 27
Firsby. Linc 4D 88
Firsdown. Wilts 3H 23
First Coast. High 4D 162
Firth. Shet 4F 173
Fir Tree. Dur 1E 105
Fishbourne. IOW 3D 16
Fishbourne. W Sus 2G 17
Fishburn. Dur 1A 106
Fishcross. Clac 4A 136
Fisherford. Abers 5D 160
Fisherrow. E Lot 2G 129
Fisher's Pond. Hants 4C 24
Fisher's Row. Lanc 5D 96
Fisherstreet. W Sus 2A 26
Fisherton. High 3B 158
Fisherton. S Ayr 3B 116
Fisherton de la Mere. Wilts 3E 23
Fishguard. Pemb 1D 42
Fishlake. S Yor 3G 93
Fishley. Norf 4G 79
Fishnish. Arg 4A 140
Fishpond Bottom. Dors 3G 13
Fishponds. Bris 4B 34
Fishpool. Glos 3B 48
Fishpool. G Man 3G 91
Fishpools. Powy 4D 58
Fishtoft. Linc 1C 76
Fishtoft Drove. Linc 1C 76
Fishwick. Bord 4F 131
Fiskavaig. High 5C 154
Fiskerton. Linc 3H 87

Fiskerton—Glenancross

Fiskerton. Notts 5E 87
Fitch. Shet 7E 173
Fitling. E Yor 1F 95
Fittleton. Wilts 2G 23
Fittleworth. W Sus 4B 26
Fitton End. Cambs 4D 76
Fitz. Shrp 4G 71
Fitzhead. Som 4E 20
Fitzwilliam. W Yor 3E 93
Fiunary. High 4A 140
Five Ash Down. E Sus 3F 27
Five Ashes. E Sus 3G 27
Five Bells. Som 2D 20
Five Bridges. Here 1B 48
Fivehead. Som 4G 21
Fivelanes. Corn 4C 10
Fivemiletown. M Ulst 5K 177
Five Oak Green. Kent 1H 27
Five Oaks. W Sus 3B 26
Five Roads. Carm 5E 45
Five Ways. Warw 3G 61
Flack's Green. Essx 4A 54
Flackwell Heath. Buck 3G 37
Fladbury. Worc 1E 49
Fladda. Shet 3E 173
Fladdabister. Shet 8F 173
Flagg. Derbs 4F 85
Flamborough. E Yor 2G 101
Flamstead. Herts 4A 52
Flansham. W Sus 5A 26
Flasby. N Yor 4B 98
Flash. Staf 4E 85
Flashader. High 3C 154
The Flatt. Cumb 2G 113
Flaunden. Herts 5A 52
Flawborough. Notts 1E 75
Flawith. N Yor 3G 99
Flax Bourton. N Som 5A 34
Flaxby. N Yor 4F 99
Flaxholme. Derbs 1H 73
Flaxley. Glos 4B 48
Flaxley Green. Staf 4E 73
Flaxpool. Som 3E 21
Flaxton. N Yor 3A 100
Fleck. Shet 10E 173
Fleckney. Leics 1D 62
Flecknoe. Warw 4C 62
Fledborough. Notts 3F 87
Fleet. Dors 4B 14
Fleet. Hants
nr. Farnborough 1G 25
Fleet. Hants
nr. South Hayling 2F 17
Fleet. Linc 3C 76
Fleet Hargate. Linc 3C 76
Fleetville. Herts 5B 52
Fleetwood. Lanc 5C 96
Fleggburgh. Norf 4G 79
Fleisirin. W Isl 4H 171
Flemingston. V Glam 5D 32
Flemington. S Lan
nr. Glasgow 3H 127
nr. Strathaven 5A 128
Flempton. Suff 4H 65
Fleoideabhagh. W Isl 9C 171
Fletcher's Green. Kent 1G 27
Fletchertown. Cumb 5D 112
Fletching. E Sus 3F 27
Fleuchary. High 4E 165
Flexbury. Corn 2C 10
Flexford. Surr 1A 26
Flimby. Cumb 1B 102
Flimwell. E Sus 2B 28
Flint. Flin 3E 83
Flintham. Notts 1E 75
Flint Mountain. Flin 3E 83
Flinton. E Yor 1F 95
Flintsham. Here 5F 59
Flishinghurst. Kent 2B 28
Flitcham. Norf 3G 77
Flitton. C Beds 2A 52
Flitwick. C Beds 2A 52
Flixborough. N Lin 3B 94
Flixton. G Man 1B 84
Flixton. N Yor 2E 101
Flixton. Suff 2F 67
Flockton. W Yor 3C 92
Flodden. Nmbd 1D 120
Flodigarry. High 1D 154
Flood's Ferry. Cambs 1C 64
Flookburgh. Cumb 2C 96
Flordon. Norf 1D 66
Flore. Nptn 4D 62
Flotterton. Nmbd 4D 121
Flowton. Suff 1D 54
Flushing. Abers 4H 161
Flushing. Corn 5C 6
Fluxton. Devn 3D 12
Flyford Flavell. Worc 5D 61
Fobbing. Thur 2B 40
Fochabers. Mor 3H 159
Fochriw. Cphy 5E 46
Fockerby. N Lin 3B 94
Fodderty. High 3H 157
Foddington. Som 4A 22
Foel. Powy 4B 70
Foffarty. Ang 4D 144
Foggathorpe. E Yor 1A 94
Fogo. Bord 5D 130
Fogorig. Bord 5D 130
Foindle. High 4B 166
Folda. Ang 2A 144
Fole. Staf 2E 73
Foleshill. W Mid 2A 62
Foley Park. Worc 3C 60
Folke. Dors 1B 14
Folkestone. Kent 195 (2G 29)
Folkingham. Linc 2H 75
Folkington. E Sus 5G 27
Folksworth. Cambs 2A 64
Folkton. N Yor 2E 101
Folla Rule. Abers 5E 161
Follifoot. N Yor 4F 99
The Folly. Herts 4B 52
Folly Cross. Devn 2E 11
Folly Gate. Devn 3F 11
Fonmon. V Glam 5D 32
Fonthill Bishop. Wilts 3E 23
Fonthill Gifford. Wilts 3E 23
Fontmell Magna. Dors 1D 14
Fontwell. W Sus 5A 26
Font-y-gary. V Glam 5D 32
Foodieash. Fife 2F 137
Foolow. Derbs 3F 85
Footdee. Aber 3G 153
Footherley. Staf 5F 73
Foots Cray. G Lon 3F 39
Forbestown. Abers 2A 152
Force Forge. Cumb 5E 103
Force Mills. Cumb 5E 103
Forcett. N Yor 3E 105
Ford. Arg 3F 133
Ford. Buck 5F 51
Ford. Derbs 2B 86
Ford. Devn
nr. Bideford 4E 19
nr. Holbeton 3C 8
nr. Salcombe 4D 9
Ford. Glos 3F 49
Ford. Nmbd 1D 120
Ford. Plym 3A 8
Ford. Shrp 4G 71
Ford. Som
nr. Wells 1A 22
nr. Wiveliscombe 4D 20
Ford. Staf 5E 85
Ford. W Sus 5B 26
Ford. Wilts
nr. Chippenham 4D 34
nr. Salisbury 3G 23
Forda. Devn 3E 19
Ford Barton. Devn 1C 12
Fordcombe. Kent 1G 27
Fordell. Fife 1E 129
Forden. Powy 5E 71
Ford End. Essx 4G 53
Forder Green. Devn 2D 9
Ford Green. Lanc 5D 97
Fordham. Cambs 3F 65
Fordham. Essx 3C 54
Fordham. Norf 1F 65
Fordham Heath. Essx 3C 54
Ford Heath. Shrp 4G 71
Fordhouses. W Mid 5D 72
Fordie. Per 1G 135
Fordingbridge. Hants 1G 15
Fordington. Linc 3D 88
Fordon. E Yor 2E 101
Fordoun. Abers 1G 145
Ford Street. Essx 3C 54
Ford Street. Som 1E 13
Fordton. Devn 3B 12
Fordwells. Oxon 4B 50
Fordwich. Kent 5F 41
Fordyce. Abers 2C 160
Forebridge. Staf 3D 72
Foreglen. Caus 6C 174
Foremark. Derbs 3H 73
Forest. N Yor 4F 105
Forestburn Gate. Nmbd 5E 121
Foresterseat. Mor 3F 159
Forest Green. Glos 2D 34
Forest Green. Surr 1C 26
Forest Hall. Cumb 4G 103
Forest Head. Cumb 4G 113
Forest Hill. Oxon 5E 50
Forest-in-Teesdale. Dur 2B 104
Forest Lodge. Per 1G 143
Forest Mill. Clac 4B 136
Forest Row. E Sus 2F 27
Forestside. W Sus 1F 17
Forest Town. Notts 4C 86
Forfar. Ang 3D 144
Forgandenny. Per 2C 136
Forge. Powy 1G 57
The Forge. Here 5F 59
Forge Side. Torf 5F 47
Forgewood. N Lan 4A 128
Forgie. Mor 3A 160
Forgue. Abers 4D 160
Forkill. New M 8E 178
Formby. Mers 4B 90
Forncett End. Norf 1D 66
Forncett St Mary. Norf 1D 66
Forncett St Peter. Norf 1D 66
Forneth. Per 4H 143
Fornham All Saints. Suff 4H 65
Fornham St Martin. Suff 4A 66
Forres. Mor 3E 159
Forrestfield. N Lan 3B 128
Forrest Lodge. Dum 1C 110
Forsbrook. Staf 1D 72
Forse. High 5E 169
Forsinard. High 4A 168
Forss. High 2C 168
The Forstal. Kent 2E 29
Forston. Dors 3B 14
Fort Augustus. High 3F 149
Forteviot. Per 2C 136
Fort George. High 3B 158
Forth. S Lan 4C 128
Forthampton. Glos 2D 48
Forthay. Glos 2C 34
Fortingall. Per 4E 143
Fort Matilda. Inv 2D 126
Forton. Hants 2C 24
Forton. Lanc 4D 97
Forton. Shrp 4G 71
Forton. Som 2G 13
Forton. Staf 3B 72
Forton Heath. Shrp 4G 71
Fortrie. Abers 4D 160
Fortrose. High 3B 158
Fortuneswell. Dors 5B 14
Fort William. High 1F 141
Forty Green. Buck 1A 38
Forty Hill. G Lon 1E 39
Forward Green. Suff 5C 66
Fosbury. Wilts 1B 24
Foscot. Oxon 3H 49
Fosdyke. Linc 2C 76
Foss. Per 3E 143
Fossebridge. Glos 4F 49
Foster Street. Essx 5E 53
Foston. Derbs 2F 73
Foston. Leics 1D 62
Foston. Linc 1F 75
Foston. N Yor 3A 100
Foston on the Wolds.
E Yor 4F 101
Fotherby. Linc 1C 88
Fothergill. Cumb 1B 102
Fotheringhay. Nptn 1H 63
Foubister. Orkn 7E 172
Foula Airport. Shet 8A 173
Foul Anchor. Cambs 4D 76
Foulbridge. Cumb 5F 113
Foulden. Norf 1G 65
Foulden. Bord 4F 131
Foul Mile. E Sus 4H 27
Foulridge. Lanc 5A 98
Foulsham. Norf 3C 78
Fountainhall. Bord 5H 129
The Four Alls. Shrp 2A 72
Four Ashes. Staf
nr. Cannock 5D 72
nr. Kinver 2C 60
Four Ashes. Suff 3C 66
Four Crosses. Powy
nr. Llanerfyl 5C 70
nr. Llanymynech 4E 71
Four Crosses. Staf 5D 72
Four Elms. Kent 1F 27
Four Forks. Som 3F 21
Four Gotes. Cambs 4D 76
Four Lane End. S Yor 4C 92
Four Lane Ends. Lanc 4E 97
Four Lanes. Corn 5A 6
Fourlanes End. Ches E 5C 84
Four Marks. Hants 3E 25
Four Mile Bridge. IOA 3B 80
Four Oaks. E Sus 3C 28
Four Oaks. Glos 3B 48
Four Oaks. W Mid 2G 61
Four Roads. Carm 5E 45
Four Roads. IOM 5B 108
Fourstones. Nmbd 3B 114
Four Throws. Kent 3B 28
Fovant. Wilts 4F 23
Foveran. Abers 1G 153
Fowey. Corn 3F 7
Fowlershill. Aber 2G 153
Fowley Common. Warr 1A 84
Fowlis. Ang 5C 144
Fowlis Wester. Per 1B 136
Fowlmere. Cambs 1E 53
Fownhope. Here 2A 48
Fox Corner. Surr 5A 38
Foxcote. Glos 4F 49
Foxcote. Som 1C 22
Foxdale. IOM 4B 108
Foxearth. Essx 1B 54
Foxfield. Cumb 1B 96
Foxham. Wilts 4E 35
Fox Hatch. Essx 1G 39
Foxhole. Corn 3D 6
Foxholes. N Yor 2E 101
Foxhunt Green. E Sus 4G 27
Fox Lane. Hants 1G 25
Foxley. Norf 3C 78
Foxley. Nptn 5D 62
Foxley. Wilts 3D 35
Foxlydiate. Worc 4E 61
Fox Street. Essx 3D 54
Foxt. Staf 1E 73
Foxton. Cambs 1E 53
Foxton. Dur 2A 106
Foxton. Leics 2D 62
Foxton. N Yor 5B 106
Foxup. N Yor 2A 98
Foxwist Green. Ches W 4A 84
Foxwood. Shrp 3A 60
Foy. Here 3A 48
Foyers. High 1G 149
Foynesfield. High 3C 158
Fraddam. Corn 3C 4
Fraddon. Corn 3D 6
Fradley. Staf 4F 73
Fradley South. Staf 4F 73
Fradswell. Staf 2D 73
Fraisthorpe. E Yor 3F 101
Framfield. E Sus 3F 27
Framingham Earl. Norf 5E 79
Framingham Pigot. Norf 5E 79
Framlingham. Suff 4E 67
Frampton. Dors 3B 14
Frampton. Linc 2C 76
Frampton Cotterell. S Glo 3B 34
Frampton Mansell. Glos 5E 49
Frampton on Severn. Glos 5C 48
Frampton West End. Linc 1B 76
Framsden. Suff 5D 66
Framwellgate Moor. Dur 5F 115
Franche. Worc 3C 60
Frandley. Ches W 3A 84
Frankby. Mers 2E 83
Frankfort. Norf 3F 79
Frankley. Worc 2D 61
Frank's Bridge. Powy 5D 58
Frankton. Warw 3B 62
Frankwell. Shrp 4G 71
Frant. E Sus 2G 27
Fraserburgh. Abers 2G 161
Frating Green. Essx 3D 54
Fratton. Port 2E 17
Freathy. Corn 3A 8
Freckenham. Suff 3F 65
Freckleton. Lanc 2C 90
Freeby. Leics 3F 75
Freefolk Priors. Hants 2C 24
Freehay. Staf 1E 73
Freeland. Oxon 4C 50
Freester. Shet 6F 173
Freethorpe. Norf 5G 79
Freiston. Linc 1C 76
Freiston Shore. Linc 1C 76
Fremington. Devn 3F 19
Fremington. N Yor 5D 104
Frenchay. S Glo 4B 34
Frenchbeer. Devn 4G 11
Frenich. Stir 3D 134
Frensham. Surr 2G 25
Frenze. Norf 2D 66
Fresgoe. High 2B 168
Freshfield. Mers 4A 90
Freshford. Bath 5C 34
Freshwater. IOW 4B 16
Freshwater Bay. IOW 4B 16
Freshwater East. Pemb 5E 43
Fressingfield. Suff 3E 67
Freston. Suff 2E 55
Freswick. High 2F 169
Fretherne. Glos 5C 48
Frettenham. Norf 4E 79
Freuchie. Fife 3E 137
Freystrop. Pemb 3D 42
Friar's Gate. E Sus 2F 27
Friar Waddon. Dors 4B 14
Friday Bridge. Cambs 5D 76
Friday Street. E Sus 5H 27
Friday Street. Surr 1C 26
Fridaythorpe. E Yor 4C 100
Friden. Derbs 4F 85
Friern Barnet. G Lon 1D 39
Friesthorpe. Linc 2H 87
Frieston. Linc 1G 75
Frieth. Buck 2F 37
Friezeland. Notts 5B 86
Frilford. Oxon 2C 36
Frilsham. W Ber 4D 36
Frimley. Surr 1G 25
Frimley Green. Surr 1G 25
Frindsbury. Medw 4B 40
Fring. Norf 2G 77
Fringford. Oxon 3E 50
Frinsted. Kent 5C 40
Frinton-on-Sea. Essx 4F 55
Friockheim. Ang 4E 145
Friog. Gwyn 4F 69
Frisby. Leics 5E 74
Frisby on the Wreake.
Leics 4D 74
Friskney. Linc 5D 88
Friskney Eaudyke. Linc 5D 88
Friston. E Sus 5G 27
Friston. Suff 4G 67
Fritchley. Derbs 5A 86
Fritham. Hants 1H 15
Frith Bank. Linc 1C 76
Frith Common. Worc 4A 60
Frithelstock. Devn 1E 11
Frithelstock Stone. Devn 1E 11
Frithsden. Herts 5A 52
Frithville. Linc 5C 88
Frittenden. Kent 1C 28
Frittiscombe. Devn 4E 9
Fritton. Norf
nr. Great Yarmouth 5G 79
nr. Long Stratton 1E 67
Fritwell. Oxon 3D 50
Frizinghall. W Yor 1B 92
Frizington. Cumb 3B 102
Frobost. W Isl 6C 170
Frocester. Glos 5C 48
Frochas. Powy 5D 70
Frodesley. Shrp 5H 71
Frodingham. N Lin 3C 94
Frodsham. Ches W 3H 83
Froggatt. Derbs 3G 85
Froghall. Staf 1E 73
Frogham. Hants 1G 15
Frogham. Kent 5G 41
Frogmore. Devn 4D 8
Frogmore. Hants 5G 37
Frogmore. Herts 5B 52
Frognall. Linc 4A 76
Frogshall. Norf 2E 79
Frogwell. Corn 2H 7
Frolesworth. Leics 1C 62
Frome. Som 2C 22
Fromefield. Som 2C 22
Frome St Quintin. Dors 2A 14
Fromes Hill. Here 1B 48
Fron. Gwyn 2C 68
Fron. Powy
nr. Llandrindod Wells 4C 58
nr. Newtown 1D 58
nr. Welshpool 5E 71
Y Fron. Gwyn 5E 81
Froncysyllte. Wrex 1E 71
Frongoch. Gwyn 2B 70
Fron Isaf. Wrex 1E 71
Fronoleu. Gwyn 2G 69
Frosterley. Dur 1D 104
Frotoft. Orkn 5D 172
Froxfield. C Beds 2H 51
Froxfield. Wilts 5A 36
Froxfield Green. Hants 4F 25
Fryern Hill. Hants 4C 24
Fryerning. Essx 5G 53
Fryton. N Yor 2A 100
Fugglestone St Peter.
Wilts 3G 23
Fulbeck. Linc 5G 87
Fulbourn. Cambs 5E 65
Fulbrook. Oxon 4A 50
Fulflood. Hants 3C 24
Fulford. Som 4F 21
Fulford. Staf 2D 72
Fulford. York 5A 100
Fulham. G Lon 3D 38
Fulking. W Sus 4D 26
Fuller's Moor. Ches W 5G 83
Fuller Street. Essx 4H 53
Fullerton. Hants 3B 24
Fulletby. Linc 3B 88
Full Sutton. E Yor 4B 100
Fullwood. E Ayr 4F 127
Fulmer. Buck 2A 38
Fulmodestone. Norf 2B 78
Fulnetby. Linc 3H 87
Fulney. Linc 3B 76
Fulstow. Linc 1C 88
Fulthorpe. Stoc T 2B 106
Fulwell. Tyne 4G 115
Fulwood. Lanc 1D 90
Fulwood. Notts 5B 86
Fulwood. Som 1F 13
Fulwood. S Yor 2G 85
Fundenhall. Norf 1D 66
Funtington. W Sus 2G 17
Funtley. Hants 2D 16
Funzie. Shet 2H 173
Furley. Devn 2F 13
Furnace. Arg 3H 133
Furnace. Carm 5F 45
Furnace. Cdgn 1F 57
Furner's Green. E Sus 3F 27
Furness Vale. Derbs 2E 85
Furneux Pelham. Herts 3E 53
Furzebrook. Dors 4E 15
Furzehill. Devn 2H 19
Furzehill. Dors 2F 15
Furzeley Corner. Hants 1E 17
Furzey Lodge. Hants 2B 16
Furzley. Hants 1A 16
Fyfield. Essx 5F 53
Fyfield. Glos 5H 49
Fyfield. Hants 2A 24
Fyfield. Oxon 2C 36
Fyfield. Wilts 5G 35
The Fylde. Lanc 1B 90
Fylingthorpe. N Yor 4G 107
Fyning. W Sus 4G 25
Fyvie. Abers 5E 161

G

Gabhsann bho Dheas.
W Isl 2G 171
Gabhsann bho Thuath.
W Isl 2G 171
Gabroc Hill. E Ayr 4F 127
Gadbrook. Surr 1D 26
Gaddesby. Leics 4D 74
Gadfa. IOA 2D 80
Gadgirth. S Ayr 2D 116
Gaer. Powy 3E 47
Gaerwen. IOA 3D 81
Gagingwell. Oxon 3C 50
Gaick Lodge. High 5B 150
Gailey. Staf 4D 72
Gainford. Dur 3E 105
Gainsborough. Linc 1F 87
Gainsborough. Suff 1E 55
Gainsford End. Essx 2H 53
Gairletter. Arg 1C 126
Gairloch. Abers 3E 153
Gairloch. High 1H 155
Gairlochy. High 5D 148
Gairney Bank. Per 4D 136
Gairnshiel Lodge. Abers 3G 151
Gaitsgill. Cumb 5E 113
Galashiels. Bord 1G 119
Galgate. Lanc 4D 97
Galgorm. ME Ant 6G 175
Galhampton. Som 4B 22
Gallatown. Fife 4E 137
Galley Common. Warw 1H 61
Galleyend. Essx 5H 53
Galleywood. Essx 5H 53
Gallin. Per 4C 142
Gallowfauld. Ang 4D 144
Gallowhill. Per 5A 144
Gallowhill. Ren 3F 127
Gallowhills. Abers 3H 161
Gallows Green. Staf 1E 73
Gallows Green. Worc 4D 60
Gallowstree Common.
Oxon 3E 37
Galltair. High 1G 147
Gallt Melyd. Den 2C 82
Galmington. Som 4F 21
Galmisdale. High 5C 146
Galmpton. Devn 4C 8
Galmpton. Torb 3E 9
Galmpton Warborough.
Torb 3E 9
Galphay. N Yor 2E 99
Galston. E Ayr 1D 117
Galton. Dors 4C 14
Galtrigill. High 3A 154
Gamblesby. Cumb 1H 103
Gamblestown. Arm 4F 178
Gamelsby. Cumb 4D 112
Gamesley. Derbs 1E 85
Gamlingay. Cambs 5B 64
Gamlingay Cinques.
Cambs 5B 64
Gamlingay Great Heath.
Cambs 5B 64
Gammaton. Devn 4E 19
Gammersgill. N Yor 1C 98
Gamston. Notts
nr. Nottingham 2D 74
nr. Retford 3E 86
Ganarew. Here 4A 48
Ganavan. Arg 5C 140
Ganborough. Glos 3G 49
Gang. Corn 2H 7
Ganllwyd. Gwyn 3G 69
Gannochy. Ang 1E 145
Gannochy. Per 1D 136
Gansclet. High 4F 169
Ganstead. E Yor 1E 95
Ganthorpe. N Yor 2A 100
Ganton. N Yor 2D 101
Gants Hill. G Lon 2F 39
Gappah. Devn 5B 12
Garafad. High 2D 155
Garboldisham. Norf 2C 66
Garden City. Flin 4F 83
Gardeners Green. Wok 5G 37
Gardenstown. Abers 2F 161
Garden Village. S Yor 1G 85
Garden Village. Swan 3E 31
Garderhouse. Shet 7E 173
Gardham. E Yor 5D 100
Gardie. Shet
on Papa Stour 5C 173
on Unst 1H 173
Gardie Ho. Shet 7F 173
Gare Hill. Wilts 2C 22
Garelochhead. Arg 4B 134
Garford. Oxon 2C 36
Garforth. W Yor 1E 93
Gargrave. N Yor 4B 98
Gargunnock. Stir 4G 135
Garleffin. S Ayr 1F 109
Garlieston. Dum 5B 110
Garlinge Green. Kent 5F 41
Garlogie. Abers 3E 153
Garmelow. Staf 3B 72
Garmond. Abers 3F 161
Garmondsway. Dur 1A 106
Garmony. Arg 4A 140
Garmouth. Mor 2H 159
Garmston. Shrp 5A 72
Garnant. Carm 4G 45
Garndiffaith. Torf 5F 47
Garndolbenmaen. Gwyn 1D 69
Garnett Bridge. Cumb 5G 103
Garnfadryn. Gwyn 2B 68
Garnkirk. N Lan 3H 127
Garnlydan. Blae 4E 47
Garnsgate. Linc 3D 76
Garnswllt. Swan 5G 45
Garn yr Erw. Torf 4F 47
Garrabost. W Isl 4H 171
Garrallan. E Ayr 3E 117
Garras. Corn 4E 5
Garreg. Gwyn 1F 69
Garrigill. Cumb 5A 114
Garriston. Ferm 7B 176
Garriston. N Yor 5E 105
Garrogie Lodge. High 2H 149
Garros. High 2D 155
Garrow. Per 4F 143
Garsdale. Cumb 1G 97
Garsdale Head. Cumb 5A 104
Garsdon. Wilts 3E 35
Garshall Green. Staf 2D 72
Garsington. Oxon 5D 50
Garstang. Lanc 5D 97
Garston. Mers 2G 83
Garswood. Mers 1H 83
Gartcosh. N Lan 3H 127
Garth. B'end 2B 32
Garth. Cdgn 2F 57
Garth. Gwyn 2E 69
Garth. IOM 4C 108
Garth. Powy
nr. Builth Wells 1C 46
nr. Knighton 3E 59
Garth. Shet
nr. Sandness 6D 173
nr. Skellister 6F 173
Garth. Wrex 1E 71
Garthamlock. Glas 3H 127
Garthbrengy. Powy 2D 46
Gartheli. Cdgn 5E 57
Garthmyl. Powy 1D 58
Garthorpe. Leics 3F 75
Garthorpe. N Lin 3B 94
Garth Owen. Powy 1D 58
Garth Place. Cphy 3E 33
Garth Row. Cumb 5G 103
Gartly. Abers 5C 160
Gartmore. Stir 4E 135
Gartness. N Lan 3A 128
Gartness. Stir 1G 127
Gartocharn. W Dun 1F 127
Garton. E Yor 1F 95
Garton-on-the-Wolds.
E Yor 4D 101
Gartsherrie. N Lan 3A 128
Gartymore. High 2H 165
Garvagh. Caus 5E 174
Garvaghy. Ferm 3L 177
Garvald. E Lot 2B 130
Garvamore. High 4H 149
Garvard. Arg 4A 132
Garvault. High 5H 167
Garve. High 2F 157
Garvestone. Norf 5C 78
Garvetagh. Derr 4E 176
Garvie. Arg 4H 133
Garvock. Abers 1G 145
Garvock. Inv 2D 126
Garway. Here 3H 47
Garway Common. Here 3H 47
Garway Hill. Here 3H 47
Garwick. Linc 1A 76
Gaskan. High 1C 140
Gasper. Wilts 3C 22
Gastard. Wilts 5D 35
Gasthorpe. Norf 2B 66
Gatcombe. IOW 4C 16
Gateacre. Mers 2G 83
Gatebeck. Cumb 1E 97
Gate Burton. Linc 2F 87
Gateforth. N Yor 2F 93
Gatehead. E Ayr 1C 116
Gate Helmsley. N Yor 4A 100
Gatehouse. Nmbd 1A 114
Gatehouse of Fleet. Dum 4D 110
Gatelawbridge. Dum 5B 118
Gateley. Norf 3B 78
Gatenby. N Yor 1F 99
Gatesgarth. Cumb 3C 102
Gateshead. Tyne 3F 115
Gatesheath. Ches W 4G 83
Gateside. Ang
nr. Forfar 4D 144
nr. Kirriemuir 4C 144
Gateside. Fife 3D 136
Gateside. N Ayr 4E 127
Gathurst. G Man 4D 90
Gatley. G Man 2C 84
Gatton. Surr 5D 39
Gattonside. Bord 1H 119
Gatwick Airport.
W Sus 205 (1D 26)
Gaufron. Powy 4B 58
Gaulby. Leics 5D 74
Gauldry. Fife 1F 137
Gaultree. Norf 5D 77
Gaunt's Common. Dors 2F 15
Gaunt's Earthcott. S Glo 3B 34
Gautby. Linc 3A 88
Gavinton. Bord 4D 130
Gawber. S Yor 4D 92
Gawcott. Buck 2E 51
Gawsworth. Ches E 4C 84
Gawthorpe. W Yor 2C 92
Gawthrop. Cumb 1F 97
Gawthwaite. Cumb 1B 96
Gay Bowers. Essx 5A 54
Gaydon. Warw 5A 62
Gayfield. Orkn 2D 172
Gayhurst. Mil 1G 51
Gayle. N Yor 1A 98
Gayles. N Yor 4E 105
Gay Street. W Sus 3B 26
Gayton. Mers 2E 83
Gayton. Norf 4G 77
Gayton. Nptn 5E 62
Gayton. Staf 3D 73
Gayton le Marsh. Linc 2D 88
Gayton le Wold. Linc 2B 88
Gayton Thorpe. Norf 4G 77
Gaywood. Norf 3F 77
Gazeley. Suff 4G 65
Geanies. High 1C 158
Gearraidh Bhailteas.
W Isl 6C 170
Gearraidh Bhaird. W Isl 6F 171
Gearraidh ma Monadh.
W Isl 7C 170
Gearraidh na h-Aibhne.
W Isl 4E 171
Geary. High 2B 154
Geddes. High 3C 158
Gedding. Suff 5B 66
Geddington. Nptn 2F 63
Gedintailor. High 5E 155
Gedling. Notts 1D 74
Gedney. Linc 3D 76
Gedney Broadgate. Linc 3D 76
Gedney Drove End. Linc 3D 76
Gedney Dyke. Linc 3D 76
Gedney Hill. Linc 4C 76
Gee Cross. G Man 1D 84
Geeston. Rut 5G 75
Geilston. Arg 2E 127
Geirinis. W Isl 4C 170
Geise. High 2D 168
Geisiadar. W Isl 4D 171
Gelder Shiel. Abers 5G 151
Geldeston. Norf 1F 67
Gell. Cnwy 4A 82
Gelli. Pemb 3E 43
Gelli. Rhon 2C 32
Gellifor. Den 4D 82
Gelligaer. Cphy 2E 33
Y Gelli Gandryll. Powy 1F 47
Gellilydan. Gwyn 2F 69
Gellinudd. Neat 5H 45
Gellyburn. Per 5H 143
Gellywen. Carm 2G 43
Gelston. Dum 4E 111
Gelston. Linc 1G 75
Gembling. E Yor 4F 101
Geneva. Cdgn 5D 56
Gentleshaw. Staf 4E 73
Geocrab. W Isl 8D 171
George Best Belfast City Airport.
Bel 2H 179
George Green. Buck 2A 38
Georgeham. Devn 3E 19
George Nympton. Devn 4H 19
Georgetown. Blae 5E 47
Georgetown. Ren 3F 127
Georth. Orkn 5C 172
Gerlan. Gwyn 4F 81
Germansweek. Devn 3E 11
Germoe. Corn 4C 4
Gerrans. Corn 5C 6
Gerrard's Bromley. Staf 2B 72
Gerrards Cross. Buck 2A 38
Gerston. High 3D 168
Gestingthorpe. Essx 2B 54
Gethsemane. Pemb 1A 44
Geuffordd. Powy 4E 70
Gibraltar. Buck 4F 51
Gibraltar. Linc 5E 89
Gibraltar. Suff 5D 66
Gibsmere. Notts 1E 74
Giddeahall. Wilts 4D 34
Gidea Park. G Lon 2G 39
Gidleigh. Devn 4G 11
Giffnock. E Ren 4G 127
Gifford. E Lot 3B 130
Giffordtown. Fife 2E 137
Giggetty. Staf 1C 60
Giggleswick. N Yor 3H 97
Gignog. Pemb 2C 42
Gilberdyke. E Yor 2B 94
Gilbert's End. Worc 1D 48
Gilbert's Green. Warw 3F 61
Gilchriston. E Lot 3A 130
Gilcrux. Cumb 1C 102
Gildersome. W Yor 2C 92
Gildingwells. S Yor 2C 86
Gilesgate Moor. Dur 5F 115
Gileston. V Glam 5D 32
Gilfach. Cphy 2E 33
Gilfach Goch. Rhon 3C 32
Gilfachreda. Cdgn 5D 56
Gilford. Arm 5E 178
Gilgarran. Cumb 2B 102
Gillamoor. N Yor 5D 107
Gillan. Corn 4E 5
Gillar's Green. Mers 1G 83
Gillen. High 3B 154
Gilling East. N Yor 2A 100
Gillingham. Dors 4D 22
Gillingham. Medw
Medway Towns 197 (4B 40)
Gillingham. Norf 1G 67
Gilling West. N Yor 4E 105
Gillock. High 3E 169
Gillow Heath. Staf 5C 84
Gills. High 1F 169
Gill's Green. Kent 2B 28
Gilmanscleuch. Bord 2F 119
Gilmerton. Edin 3F 129
Gilmerton. Per 1A 136
Gilmonby. Dur 3C 104
Gilmorton. Leics 2C 62
Gilsland. Nmbd 3H 113
Gilsland Spa. Cumb 3H 113
Gilston. Bord 4H 129
Giltbrook. Notts 1B 74
Gilwern. Mon 4F 47
Gimingham. Norf 2E 79
Giosla. W Isl 5D 171
Gipping. Suff 4C 66
Gipsey Bridge. Linc 1B 76
Gipton. W Yor 1D 92
Girdle Toll. N Ayr 5E 127
Girlsta. Shet 6F 173
Girsby. N Yor 4A 106
Girthon. Dum 4D 110
Girton. Cambs 4D 64
Girton. Notts 4F 87
Girvan. S Ayr 5A 116
Gisburn. Lanc 5H 97
Gisleham. Suff 2H 67
Gislingham. Suff 3C 66
Gissing. Norf 2D 66
Gittisham. Devn 3E 13
Gladestry. Powy 5E 59
Gladsmuir. E Lot 2A 130
Glaichbea. High 5H 157
Glais. Swan 5H 45
Glaisdale. N Yor 4E 107
Glame. High 4E 155
Glamis. Ang 4C 144
Glanaman. Carm 4G 45
Glan-Conwy. Cnwy 5H 81
Glandford. Norf 1C 78
Glan Duar. Carm 1F 45
Glandwr. Blae 5F 47
Glandwr. Pemb 2F 43
Glan-Dwyfach. Gwyn 1D 69
Glandy Cross. Carm 2F 43
Glandyfi. Cdgn 1F 57
Glangrwyney. Powy 4F 47
Glanmule. Powy 1D 58
Glan-rhyd. Pemb 1F 43
Glan-rhyd. Powy 5A 46
Glanrhyd. Gwyn 2B 68
Glanrhyd. Pemb 1B 44
Glanton. Nmbd 3E 121
Glanton Pyke. Nmbd 3E 121
Glanvilles Wootton. Dors 2B 14
Glan-y-don. Flin 3D 82
Glan-y-nant. Powy 2B 58
Glan-yr-afon. Gwyn 1C 70
Glan-yr-afon. IOA 2F 81
Glan-yr-afon. Powy 5C 70
Glan-y-wern. Gwyn 2F 69
Glapthorn. Nptn 1H 63
Glapwell. Derbs 4B 86
Glarryford. ME Ant 5G 175
Glas Aird. Arg 4A 132
Glas-allt Shiel. Abers 5G 151
Glasbury. Powy 2E 47
Glaschoil. High 5E 159
Glascoed. Den 3B 82
Glascoed. Mon 5G 47
Glascote. Staf 5G 73
Glascwm. Powy 5D 58
Glasfryn. Cnwy 5B 82
Glasgow. Glas 195 (3G 127)
Glasgow Airport.
Ren 205 (3F 127)
Glasgow Prestwick Airport.
S Ayr 2C 116
Glashvin. High 2D 154
Glasinfryn. Gwyn 4E 81
Glas na Cardaich. High 4E 147
Glasnacardoch. High 4E 147
Glasnakille. High 2D 146
Glaspwll. Cdgn 1G 57
Glassburn. High 5F 157
Glassenbury. Kent 2B 28
Glasserton. Dum 5B 110
Glassford. S Lan 5A 128
Glassgreen. Mor 2G 159
Glasshouse. Glos 3C 48
Glasshouses. N Yor 3D 98
Glasson. Cumb 3D 112
Glasson. Lanc 4D 96
Glassonby. Cumb 1G 103
Glasswater. New M 4J 179
Glasterlaw. Ang 3E 145
Glaston. Rut 5F 75
Glastonbury. Som 3H 21
Glatton. Cambs 2A 64
Glazebrook. Warr 1A 84
Glazebury. Warr 1A 84
Glazeley. Shrp 2B 60
Gleadless. S Yor 2A 86
Gleadsmoss. Ches E 4C 84
Gleann Dail bho Dheas.
W Isl 7C 170
Gleann Tholastaidh.
W Isl 3H 171
Gleann Uige. High 1A 140
Gleaston. Cumb 2B 96
Glebe. Derr 3F 176
Glecknabae. Arg 3B 126
Gledrid. Shrp 2E 71
Gleiniant. Powy 1B 58
Glemsford. Suff 1B 54
Glen. Dum 4C 110
Glenancross. High 4E 147

Glenanne—Hackman's Gate

Glenanne. Arm 6D 178
Glenariff. Caus 4J 175
Glenarm. ME Ant 5K 175
Glen Auldyn. IOM 2D 108
Glenavy. Lis 2F 179
Glenbarr. Arg 2A 122
Glenbeg. High 2G 139
Glen Bernisdale. High 4D 154
Glenbervie. Abers 5E 153
Glenboig. N Lan 3A 128
Glenborrodale. High 2A 140
Glenbranter. Arg 4A 134
Glenbreck. Bord 2C 118
Glenbrein Lodge. High 2G 149
Glenbrittle. High 1C 146
Glenbuchat Lodge.
Abers 2H 151
Glenbuck. E Ayr 2G 117
Glenburn. Ren 3F 127
Glencalvie Lodge. High 5B 164
Glencaple. Dum 3A 112
Glencarron Lodge. High 3C 156
Glencarse. Per 1D 136
Glencassley Castle. High 3B 164
Glencat. Abers 4C 152
Glencoe. High 3F 141
Glen Cottage. High 5E 147
Glencraig. Fife 4D 136
Glendale. High 4A 154
Glendevon. Per 3B 136
Glendoebeg. High 3G 149
Glendoick. Per 1E 136
Glendoune. S Ayr 5A 116
Glenduckie. Fife 2E 137
Gleneagles. Per 3B 136
Glenegedale. Arg 4B 124
Glenegedale Lots. Arg 4B 124
Glenelg. High 2G 147
Glenernie. Mor 4E 159
Glenesslin. Dum 1F 111
Glenfarg. Per 2D 136
Glenfarquhar Lodge.
Abers 5E 152
Glenferness Mains. High 4D 158
Glenfeshie Lodge. High 4C 150
Glenfiddich Lodge. Mor 5H 159
Glenfield. Leics 5C 74
Glenfinnan. High 5B 148
Glenfintaig Lodge. High 5E 148
Glenfoot. Per 2D 136
Glenfyne Lodge. Arg 2B 134
Glengap. Dum 4D 110
Glengarnock. N Ayr 4E 126
Glengolly. High 2D 168
Glengorm Castle. Arg 3F 139
Glengormley. Ant 1H 179
Glengrasco. High 4D 154
Glenhead Farm. Ang 2B 144
Glenholm. Bord 1D 118
Glen House. Bord 1E 119
Glenhurich. High 2C 140
Glenkerry. Bord 3E 119
Glenkiln. Dum 2F 111
Glenkindie. Abers 2B 152
Glenkinglass Lodge. Arg 5F 141
Glenkirk. Bord 2C 118
Glenlean. Arg 1B 126
Glenlee. Dum 1D 110
Glenleraig. High 5B 166
Glenlichorn. Per 2G 135
Glenlivet. Mor 1F 151
Glenlochar. Dum 3E 111
Glenlochsie Lodge. Per 1H 143
Glenluce. Dum 4G 109
Glenmarksie. High 3F 157
Glenmassan. Arg 1C 126
Glenmavis. N Lan 3A 128
Glen Maye. IOM 4B 108
Glenmazeran Lodge.
High 1B 150
Glenmidge. Dum 1F 111
Glen Mona. IOM 3D 108
Glenmore. High
nr. Glenborrodale 2G 139
nr. Kingussie 3D 151
on Isle of Skye 4D 154
Glenmoy. Ang 2D 144
Glennoe. Arg 5E 141
Glen of Coachford.
Abers 4B 160
Glenogil. Ang 2D 144
Glen Parva. Leics 1C 62
Glenprosen Village. Ang 2C 144
Glenree. N Ayr 3D 122
Glenridding. Cumb 3E 103
Glenrosa. N Ayr 2E 123
Glenrothes. Fife 3E 137
Glensanda. High 4C 140
Glensaugh. Abers 1F 145
Glenshero Lodge. High 4H 149
Glensluain. Arg 4H 133
Glenstockadale. Dum 3F 109
Glenstriven. Arg 2B 126
Glen Tanar House. Abers 4B 152
Glentham. Linc 1H 87
Glenton. Abers 1D 152
Glentress. Bord 1E 119
Glentromie Lodge. High 4B 150
Glentrool Lodge. Dum 1B 110
Glentrool Village. Dum 2A 110
Glentruim House. High 4A 150
Glentworth. Linc 2G 87
Glenuig. High 1A 140
Glen View. New M 6E 178
Glen Village. Falk 2B 128
Glen Vine. IOM 4C 108
Glenwhilly. Dum 2G 109
Glenzierfoot. Dum 2E 113
Glespin. S Lan 2H 117
Gletness. Shet 6F 173
Glewstone. Here 3A 48
Glib Cheois. W Isl 5F 171
Glinton. Pet 5A 76
Glooston. Leics 1E 63
Glossop. Derbs 1E 85
Gloster Hill. Nmbd 4G 121
Gloucester. Glos 195 (4D 48)
Gloucestershire Airport.
Glos 3D 49
Gloup. Shet 1G 173
Glusburn. N Yor 5C 98
Glutt Lodge. High 5B 168
Glutton Bridge. Derbs 4E 85
Gluvian. Corn 2D 6
Glympton. Oxon 3C 50
Glyn. Cnwy 3A 82
Glynarthen. Cdgn 1D 44
Glynbrochan. Powy 2B 58
Glyn Ceiriog. Wrex 2E 70
Glyncoch. Rhon 2D 32
Glyncorrwg. Neat 2B 32
Glynde. E Sus 5F 27
Glyndebourne. E Sus 4F 27
Glyndyfrdwy. Den 1D 70
Glyn Ebwy. Blae 5E 47
Glynllan. B'end 3C 32
Glynn. ME Ant 7L 175
Glyn-neath. Neat 5B 46
Glynogwr. B'end 3C 32
Glyntaff. Rhon 3D 32
Glyntawe. Powy 4B 46
Glynteg. Carm 2D 44
Gnosall. Staf 3C 72
Gnosall Heath. Staf 3C 72
Goadby. Leics 1E 63
Goadby Marwood. Leics 3E 75
Goatacre. Wilts 4F 35
Goathill. Dors 1B 14
Goathland. N Yor 4F 107
Goathurst. Som 3F 21
Goathurst Common. Kent 5F 39
Goat Lees. Kent 1E 28
Gobernuisgach Lodge.
High 4E 167
Gobernuisgeach. High 5B 168
Gobhaig. W Isl 7C 171
Gobowen. Shrp 2F 71
Godalming. Surr 1A 26
Goddard's Corner. Suff 4E 67
Goddard's Green. Kent
nr. Benenden 2C 28
nr. Cranbrook 2B 28
Goddards' Green. W Sus 3D 27
Godford Cross. Devn 2E 13
Godleybrook. Staf 1D 73
Godmanchester. Cambs 3B 64
Godmanstone. Dors 3B 14
Godmersham. Kent 5E 41
Godolphin Cross. Corn 3D 4
Godre'r-graig. Neat 5A 46
Godshill. Hants 1G 15
Godshill. IOW 4D 16
Godstone. Staf 2E 73
Godstone. Surr 5E 39
Goetre. Mon 5G 47
Goff's Oak. Herts 5D 52
Gogar. Edin 2E 129
Goginan. Cdgn 2F 57
Golan. Gwyn 1E 69
Golant. Corn 3F 7
Golberdon. Corn 5D 10
Golborne. G Man 1A 84
Golcar. W Yor 3A 92
Goldcliff. Newp 3G 33
Golden Cross. E Sus 4G 27
Golden Green. Kent 1H 27
Golden Grove. Carm 4F 45
Golden Grove. N Yor 4F 107
Golden Hill. Pemb 2D 43
Goldenhill. Stoke 5C 84
Golden Pot. Hants 2F 25
Golden Valley. Glos 3E 49
Golders Green. G Lon 2D 38
Goldhanger. Essx 5C 54
Gold Hill. Norf 1E 65
Golding. Shrp 5H 71
Goldington. Bed 5H 63
Goldsborough. N Yor
nr. Harrogate 4F 99
nr. Whitby 3F 107
Goldsithney. Corn 3C 4
Goldstone. Kent 4G 41
Goldstone. Shrp 3B 72
Goldthorpe. S Yor 4E 93
Goldworthy. Devn 4D 19
Golfa. Powy 3D 70
Gollanfield. High 3C 158
Gollinglith Foot. N Yor 1D 98
Golsoncott. Som 3D 20
Golspie. High 4F 165
Gomeldon. Wilts 3G 23
Gomersal. W Yor 2C 92
Gometra House. Arg 4E 139
Gomshall. Surr 1B 26
Gonalston. Notts 1D 74
Gonerby Hill Foot. Linc 2G 75
Gonfirth. Shet 5E 173
Good Easter. Essx 4G 53
Gooderstone. Norf 5G 77
Goodleigh. Devn 3G 19
Goodmanham. E Yor 5C 100
Goodmayes. G Lon 2F 39
Goodnestone. Kent
nr. Aylesham 5G 41
nr. Faversham 4E 41
Goodrich. Here 4A 48
Goodrington. Torb 3E 9
Goodshaw. Lanc 2G 91
Goodshaw Fold. Lanc 2G 91
Goodstone. Devn 5A 12
Goodwick. Pemb 1D 42
Goodworth Clatford.
Hants 2B 24
Goole. E Yor 2H 93
Goom's Hill. Worc 5E 61
Goonabarn. Corn 3D 6
Goonbell. Corn 4B 6
Goonhavern. Corn 3B 6
Goonlaze. Corn 5B 6
Goonvrea. Corn 4B 6
Goose Green. Cumb 1E 97
Goose Green. S Glo 3C 34
Gooseham. Corn 1C 10
Goosewell. Plym 3B 8
Goosey. Oxon 2B 36
Goosnargh. Lanc 1D 90
Goostrey. Ches E 3B 84
Gorcott Hill. Warw 4E 61
Gord. Shet 9F 173
Gordon. Bord 5C 130
Gordonbush. High 3F 165
Gordonstown. Abers
nr. Cornhill 3C 160
nr. Fyvie 5E 160
Gorebridge. Midl 3G 129
Gorefield. Cambs 4D 76
Gores. Wilts 1G 23
Gorgie. Edin 2F 129
Goring. Oxon 3E 36
Goring-by-Sea. W Sus 5C 26
Goring Heath. Oxon 4E 37
Gorleston-on-Sea. Norf 5H 79
Gornalwood. W Mid 1D 60
Gorran Churchtown. Corn 4D 6
Gorran Haven. Corn 4E 6
Gorran High Lanes. Corn 4D 6
Gors. Cdgn 3F 57
Gorsedd. Flin 3D 82
Gorseinon. Swan 3E 31
Gorseness. Orkn 6D 172
Gorseybank. Derbs 5G 85
Gorsgoch. Cdgn 5D 57
Gorslas. Carm 4F 45
Gorsley. Glos 3B 48
Gorsley Common. Here 3B 48
Gorstan. High 2F 157
Gorstella. Ches W 4F 83
Gorsty Common. Here 2H 47
Gorsty Hill. Staf 3F 73
Gortantaoid. Arg 2B 124
Gorteneorn. High 2A 140
Gortenfern. High 2A 140
Gortin. Ferm 8A 174
Gortnahey. Caus 5C 174
Gorton. G Man 1C 84
Gosbeck. Suff 5D 66
Gosberton. Linc 2B 76
Gosberton Cheal. Linc 3B 76
Gosberton Clough. Linc 3A 76
Goseley Dale. Derbs 3H 73
Gosfield. Essx 3A 54
Gosford. Oxon 4C 50
Gosforth. Cumb 4B 102
Gosforth. Tyne 3F 115
Gosmore. Herts 3B 52
Gospel End. Staf 1C 60
Gosport. Hants 3E 16
Gossabrough. Shet 3G 173
Gossington. Glos 5C 48
Gossops Green. W Sus 2D 26
Goswick. Nmbd 5G 131
Gotham. Notts 2C 74
Gotherington. Glos 3E 49
Gott. Arg 4B 138
Gott. Shet 7F 173
Goudhurst. Kent 2B 28
Goulceby. Linc 3B 88
Gourdon. Abers 1H 145
Gourock. Inv 2D 126
Govan. Glas 3G 127
Govanhill. Glas 3G 127
Goverton. Notts 1E 74
Goveton. Devn 4D 8
Govilon. Mon 4F 47
Gowanhill. Abers 2H 161
Gowdall. E Yor 2G 93
Gowdystown. Arm 4F 179
Gowerton. Swan 3E 31
Gowkhall. Fife 1D 128
Gowthorpe. E Yor 4B 100
Goxhill. E Yor 5F 101
Goxhill. N Lin 2E 94
Goxhill Haven. N Lin 2E 94
Goytre. Neat 3A 32
Grabhair. W Isl 6F 171
Graby. Linc 3H 75
Gracehill. ME Ant 6G 175
Graffham. W Sus 4A 26
Grafham. Cambs 4A 64
Grafham. Surr 1B 26
Grafton. Here 2H 47
Grafton. N Yor 3G 99
Grafton. Oxon 5A 50
Grafton. Shrp 4G 71
Grafton. Worc
nr. Evesham 2E 49
nr. Leominster 4H 59
Grafton Flyford. Worc 5D 60
Grafton Regis. Nptn 1F 51
Grafton Underwood. Nptn 2G 63
Grafty Green. Kent 1C 28
Graianrhyd. Den 5E 82
Graig. Carm 5E 45
Graig. Cnwy 3H 81
Graig. Den 3C 82
Graig-fechan. Den 5D 82
Graig Penllyn. V Glam 4C 32
Grain. Medw 3C 40
Grainsby. Linc 1B 88
Grainthorpe. Linc 1C 88
Grainthorpe Fen. Linc 1C 88
Graiselound. N Lin 1E 87
Gramasdail. W Isl 3D 170
Grampound. Corn 4D 6
Grampound Road. Corn 3D 6
Granborough. Buck 3F 51
Granby. Notts 2E 75
Grandborough. Warw 4B 62
Grandpont. Oxon 5D 50
Grandtully. Per 3G 143
Grange. Cumb 3D 102
Grange. E Ayr 1D 116
Grange. Here 3G 59
Grange. Mers 2E 82
Grange. Per 1E 137
The Grange. N Yor 5C 106
Grange Corner. ME Ant 7G 175
Grange Crossroads. Mor 3B 160
Grange Hill. Essx 1F 39
Grangemill. Derbs 5G 85
Grange Moor. W Yor 3C 92
Grangemouth. Falk 1C 128
Grange of Lindores. Fife 2E 137
Grange-over-Sands.
Cumb 2D 96
Grangepans. Falk 1D 128
Grange Park. New M 5J 179
Grangetown. Card 4E 33
Grangetown. Red C 2C 106
Grange Villa. Dur 4F 115
Granish. High 2C 150
Gransmoor. E Yor 4F 101
Granston. Pemb 1C 42
Grantchester. Cambs 5D 64
Grantham. Linc 2G 75
Grantley. N Yor 3E 99
Grantlodge. Abers 2E 152
Granton. Edin 2F 129
Grantown-on-Spey. High 1E 151
Grantshouse. Bord 3E 130
Grappenhall. Warr 2A 84
Grasby. Linc 4D 94
Grasmere. Cumb 4E 103
Grasscroft. G Man 4H 91
Grassendale. Mers 2F 83
Grassgarth. Cumb 5E 113
Grassholme. Dur 2C 104
Grassington. N Yor 3C 98
Grassmoor. Derbs 4B 86
Grassthorpe. Notts 4E 87
Grateley. Hants 2A 24
Gratton. Devn 1D 11
Gratton. Staf 5D 84
Gratwich. Staf 2E 73
Graveley. Cambs 4B 64
Graveley. Herts 3C 52
Gravelhill. Shrp 4G 71
Gravel Hole. G Man 4H 91
Gravelly Hill. W Mid 1F 61
Graven. Shet 4F 173
Graveney. Kent 4E 41
Gravesend. Kent 3H 39
Grayingham. Linc 1G 87
Grayrigg. Cumb 5G 103
Grays. Thur 3H 39
Grayshott. Hants 3G 25
Grayson Green. Cumb 2A 102
Grayswood. Surr 2A 26
Graythorp. Hart 2C 106
Grazeley. Wok 5E 37
Grealin. High 2E 155
Greasbrough. S Yor 1B 86
Greasby. Mers 2E 83
Great Abington. Cambs 1F 53
Great Addington. Nptn 3G 63
Great Alne. Warw 5F 61
Great Altcar. Lanc 4B 90
Great Amwell. Herts 4D 52
Great Asby. Cumb 3H 103
Great Ashfield. Suff 4B 66
Great Ayton. N Yor 3C 106
Great Baddow. Essx 5H 53
Great Bardfield. Essx 2G 53
Great Barford. Bed 5A 64
Great Barr. W Mid 1E 61
Great Barrington. Glos 4H 49
Great Barrow. Ches W 4G 83
Great Barton. Suff 4A 66
Great Barugh. N Yor 2B 100
Great Bavington. Nmbd 1C 114
Great Bealings. Suff 1F 55
Great Bedwyn. Wilts 5A 36
Great Bentley. Essx 3E 54
Great Billing. Nptn 4F 63
Great Bircham. Norf 2G 77
Great Blakenham. Suff 5D 66
Great Blencow. Cumb 1F 103
Great Bolas. Telf 3A 72
Great Bookham. Surr 5C 38
Great Bosullow. Corn 3B 4
Great Bourton. Oxon 1C 50
Great Bowden. Leics 2E 63
Great Bradley. Suff 5F 65
Great Braxted. Essx 4B 54
Great Bricett. Suff 5C 66
Great Brickhill. Buck 2H 51
Great Bridgeford. Staf 3C 72
Great Brington. Nptn 4D 62
Great Bromley. Essx 3D 54
Great Broughton. Cumb 1B 102
Great Broughton. N Yor 4C 106
Great Budworth. Ches W 3A 84
Great Burdon. Darl 3A 106
Great Burstead. Essx 1A 40
Great Busby. N Yor 4C 106
Great Canfield. Essx 4F 53
Great Carlton. Linc 2D 88
Great Casterton. Rut 5G 75
Great Chalfield. Wilts 5D 34
Great Chart. Kent 1D 28
Great Chatwell. Staf 4B 72
Great Chesterford. Essx 1F 53
Great Cheverell. Wilts 1E 23
Great Chilton. Dur 1F 105
Great Chishill. Cambs 2E 53
Great Clacton. Essx 4E 55
Great Cliff. W Yor 3D 92
Great Clifton. Cumb 2B 102
Great Coates. NE Lin 3F 95
Great Comberton. Worc 1E 49
Great Corby. Cumb 4F 113
Great Cornard. Suff 1B 54
Great Cowden. E Yor 5G 101
Great Coxwell. Oxon 2A 36
Great Crakehall. N Yor 5F 105
Great Cransley. Nptn 3F 63
Great Cressingham. Norf 5A 78
Great Crosby. Mers 4B 90
Great Cubley. Derbs 2F 73
Great Dalby. Leics 4E 75
Great Doddington. Nptn 4F 63
Great Doward. Here 4A 48
Great Dunham. Norf 4A 78
Great Dunmow. Essx 3G 53
Great Durnford. Wilts 3G 23
Great Easton. Essx 3G 53
Great Easton. Leics 1F 63
Great Eccleston. Lanc 5D 96
Great Edstone. N Yor 1B 100
Great Ellingham. Norf 1C 66
Great Elm. Som 2C 22
Great Eppleton. Tyne 5G 115
Great Eversden. Cambs 5C 64
Great Fencote. N Yor 5F 105
Great Finborough. Suff 5C 66
Greatford. Linc 4H 75
Great Fransham. Norf 4A 78
Great Gaddesden. Herts 4A 52
Great Gate. Staf 1E 73
Great Gidding. Cambs 2A 64
Great Givendale. E Yor 4C 100
Great Glemham. Suff 4F 67
Great Glen. Leics 1D 62
Great Gonerby. Linc 2F 75
Great Gransden. Cambs 5B 64
Great Green. Norf 2E 67
Great Green. Suff
nr. Lavenham 5B 66
nr. Palgrave 3D 66
Great Habton. N Yor 2B 100
Great Hale. Linc 1A 76
Great Hallingbury. Essx 4F 53
Greatham. Hants 3F 25
Greatham. Hart 2B 106
Greatham. W Sus 4B 26
Great Hampden. Buck 5G 51
Great Harrowden. Nptn 3F 63
Great Harwood. Lanc 1F 91
Great Haseley. Oxon 5E 51
Great Hatfield. E Yor 5F 101
Great Haywood. Staf 3D 73
Great Heath. W Mid 2H 61
Great Heck. N Yor 2F 93
Great Henny. Essx 2B 54
Great Hinton. Wilts 1E 23
Great Hockham. Norf 1B 66
Great Holland. Essx 4F 55
Great Horkesley. Essx 2C 54
Great Hormead. Herts 2E 53
Great Horton. W Yor 1B 92
Great Horwood. Buck 2F 51
Great Houghton. Nptn 5E 63
Great Houghton. S Yor 4E 93
Great Hucklow. Derbs 3F 85
Great Kelk. E Yor 4F 101
Great Kendale. E Yor 3E 101
Great Kimble. Buck 5G 51
Great Kingshill. Buck 2G 37
Great Langdale. Cumb 4D 102
Great Langton. N Yor 5F 105
Great Leighs. Essx 4H 53
Great Limber. Linc 4E 95
Great Linford. Mil 1G 51
Great Livermere. Suff 3A 66
Great Longstone. Derbs 3G 85
Great Lumley. Dur 5F 115
Great Lyth. Shrp 5G 71
Great Malvern. Worc 1C 48
Great Maplestead. Essx 2B 54
Great Marton. Bkpl 1B 90
Great Massingham. Norf 3G 77
Great Melton. Norf 5D 78
Great Milton. Oxon 5E 51
Great Missenden. Buck 5G 51
Great Mitton. Lanc 1F 91
Great Mongeham. Kent 5H 41
Great Moulton. Norf 1D 66
Great Munden. Herts 3D 52
Great Musgrave. Cumb 3A 104
Great Ness. Shrp 4F 71
Great Notley. Essx 3H 53
Great Oak. Mon 5G 47
Great Oakley. Essx 3E 55
Great Oakley. Nptn 2F 63
Great Offley. Herts 3B 52
Great Ormside. Cumb 3A 104
Great Orton. Cumb 4E 113
Great Ouseburn. N Yor 3G 99
Great Oxendon. Nptn 2E 63
Great Oxney Green. Essx 5G 53
Great Parndon. Essx 5E 53
Great Paxton. Cambs 4B 64
Great Plumpton. Lanc 1B 90
Great Plumstead. Norf 4F 79
Great Ponton. Linc 2G 75
Great Potheridge. Devn 1F 11
Great Preston. W Yor 2E 93
Great Raveley. Cambs 2B 64
Great Rissington. Glos 4G 49
Great Rollright. Oxon 2B 50
Great Ryburgh. Norf 3B 78
Great Ryle. Nmbd 3E 121
Great Ryton. Shrp 5G 71
Great Saling. Essx 3H 53
Great Salkeld. Cumb 1G 103
Great Sampford. Essx 2G 53
Great Sankey. Warr 2H 83
Great Saredon. Staf 5D 72
Great Saxham. Suff 4G 65
Great Shefford. W Ber 4B 36
Great Shelford. Cambs 5D 64
Great Shoddesden. Hants 2A 24
Great Smeaton. N Yor 4A 106
Great Snoring. Norf 2B 78
Great Somerford. Wilts 3E 35
Great Stainton. Darl 2A 106
Great Stambridge. Essx 1C 40
Great Staughton. Cambs 4A 64
Great Steeping. Linc 4D 88
Great Stonar. Kent 5H 41
Greatstone-on-Sea. Kent 3E 29
Great Strickland. Cumb 2G 103
Great Stukeley. Cambs 3B 64
Great Sturton. Linc 3B 88
Great Sutton. Ches W 3F 83
Great Sutton. Shrp 2H 59
Great Swinburne. Nmbd 2C 114
Great Tew. Oxon 3B 50
Great Tey. Essx 3B 54
Great Thirkleby. N Yor 2G 99
Great Thorness. IOW 3C 16
Great Thurlow. Suff 5F 65
Great Torr. Devn 4C 8
Great Torrington. Devn 1E 11
Great Tosson. Nmbd 4E 121
Great Totham North. Essx 4B 54
Great Totham South. Essx 4B 54
Great Tows. Linc 1B 88
Great Urswick. Cumb 2B 96
Great Wakering. Essx 2D 40
Great Waldingfield. Suff 1C 54
Great Walsingham. Norf 2B 78
Great Waltham. Essx 4G 53
Great Warley. Essx 1G 39
Great Washbourne. Glos 2E 49
Great Wenham. Suff 2D 54
Great Whelnetham. Suff 5A 66
Great Whittington.
Nmbd 2D 114
Great Wigborough. Essx 4C 54
Great Wilbraham. Cambs 5E 65
Great Wilne. Derbs 2B 74
Great Wishford. Wilts 3F 23
Great Witchingham. Norf 3D 78
Great Witcombe. Glos 4E 49
Great Witley. Worc 4B 60
Great Wolford. Warw 2H 49
Greatworth. Nptn 1D 50
Great Wratting. Suff 1G 53
Great Wymondley. Herts 3C 52
Great Wyrley. Staf 5D 73
Great Wytheford. Shrp 4H 71
Great Yarmouth. Norf 5H 79
Great Yeldham. Essx 2A 54
Grebby. Linc 4D 88
Greeba Castle. IOM 3C 108
The Green. Cumb 1A 96
The Green. Wilts 3D 22
Greenbank. Shet 1G 173
Greenbottom. Corn 4B 6
Greenburn. W Lot 3C 128
Greencastle. Ferm 1L 177
Greencroft. Dur 4E 115
Greendown. Som 1A 22
Greendykes. Nmbd 2E 121
Green End. Bed
nr. Bedford 1A 52
nr. Little Staughton 4A 64
Green End. Herts
nr. Buntingford 2D 52
nr. Stevenage 3D 52
Green End. N Yor 4F 107
Green End. Warw 2G 61
Greenfield. Arg 4B 134
Greenfield. C Beds 2A 52
Greenfield. Flin 3D 82
Greenfield. G Man 4H 91
Greenfield. Oxon 2F 37
Greenfoot. N Lan 3A 128
Greenford. G Lon 2C 38
Greengairs. N Lan 2A 128
Greengate. Norf 4C 78
Greengill. Cumb 1C 102
Greenhalgh. Lanc 1C 90
Greenham. Dors 2H 13
Greenham. Som 4D 20
Greenham. W Ber 5C 36
Green Hammerton. N Yor 4G 99
Greenhaugh. Nmbd 1A 114
Greenhead. Nmbd 3H 113
Green Heath. Staf 4D 73
Greenhill. Dum 2C 112
Greenhill. Falk 2B 128
Greenhill. Kent 4F 41
Greenhill. S Yor 2H 85
Greenhill. Worc 3C 60
Greenhills. N Ayr 4E 127
Greenhithe. Kent 3G 39
Greenholm. E Ayr 1E 117
Greenhow Hill. N Yor 3D 98
Greenigoe. Orkn 7D 172
Greenisland. ME Ant 8K 175
Greenland. High 2E 169
Greenland Mains. High 2E 169
Greenlands. Worc 4E 61
Green Lane. Shrp 3A 72
Green Lane. Worc 4E 61
Greenlaw. Bord 5D 130
Greenlea. Dum 2B 112
Greenloaning. Per 3H 135
Greenmount. G Man 3F 91
Greenmow. Shet 9F 173
Greenock. Inv 2D 126
Greenock Mains. E Ayr 2F 117
Greenodd. Cumb 1C 96
Green Ore. Som 1A 22
Greenrow. Cumb 4C 112
Greens. Abers 4F 161
Greensgate. Norf 4D 78
Greenside. Tyne 3E 115
Greensidehill. Nmbd 3D 121
Greens Norton. Nptn 1E 51
Greenstead Green. Essx 3B 54
Greensted Green. Essx 5F 53
Green Street. Herts 1C 38
Green Street. Suff 3D 66
Green Street Green. G Lon 4F 39
Green Street Green. Kent 3G 39
Greenstreet Green. Suff 1D 54
Green Tye. Herts 4E 53
Greenwall. Orkn 7E 172
Greenway. Pemb 1E 43
Greenway. V Glam 4D 32
Greenwell. Cumb 4G 113
Greenwich. G Lon 3E 39
Greet. Glos 2F 49
Greete. Shrp 3H 59
Greetham. Linc 3C 88
Greetham. Rut 4G 75
Greetland. W Yor 2A 92
Gregson Lane. Lanc 2D 90
Grein. W Isl 8B 170
Greinetobht. W Isl 1D 170
Greinton. Som 3H 21
Gremista. Shet 7F 173
Grenaby. IOM 4B 108
Grendon. Nptn 4F 63
Grendon. Warw 1G 61
Grendon Common. Warw 1G 61
Grendon Green. Here 5H 59
Grendon Underwood.
Buck 3E 51
Grenofen. Devn 5E 11
Grenoside. S Yor 1H 85
Greosabhagh. W Isl 8D 171
Gresford. Wrex 5F 83
Gresham. Norf 2D 78
Greshornish. High 3C 154
Gressenhall. Norf 4B 78
Gressingham. Lanc 3E 97
Greta Bridge. Dur 3D 105
Gretna. Dum 3E 112
Gretna Green. Dum 3E 112
Gretton. Glos 2F 49
Gretton. Nptn 1G 63
Gretton. Shrp 1H 59
Grewelthorpe. N Yor 2E 99
Greyabbey. Ards 3K 179
Greygarth. N Yor 2D 98
Grey Green. N Lin 4A 94
Greylake. Som 3G 21
Greysouthen. Cumb 2B 102
Greysteel. Caus 4B 174
Greystoke. Cumb 1F 103
Greystoke Gill. Cumb 2F 103
Greystone. Ang 4E 145
Greystones. S Yor 2H 85
Greywell. Hants 1F 25
Griais. W Isl 3G 171
Grianan. W Isl 4G 171
Gribthorpe. E Yor 1A 94
Gribun. Arg 5F 139
Griff. Warw 2A 62
Griffithstown. Torf 2F 33
Griffydam. Leics 4B 74
Griggs Green. Hants 3G 25
Grimbister. Orkn 6C 172
Grimeford Village. Lanc 3E 90
Grimeston. Orkn 6C 172
Grimethorpe. S Yor 4E 93
Griminis. W Isl
on Benbecula 3C 170
on North Uist 1C 170
Grimister. Shet 2F 173
Grimley. Worc 4C 60
Grimness. Orkn 8D 172
Grimoldby. Linc 2C 88
Grimpo. Shrp 3F 71
Grimsargh. Lanc 1D 90
Grimsbury. Oxon 1C 50
Grimsby. NE Lin 4F 95
Grimscote. Nptn 5D 62
Grimscott. Corn 2C 10
Grimshaw. Bkbn 2F 91
Grimshaw Green. Lanc 3C 90
Grimsthorpe. Linc 3H 75
Grimston. E Yor 1F 95
Grimston. Leics 3D 74
Grimston. Norf 3G 77
Grimston. York 4A 100
Grimstone. Dors 3B 14
Grimstone End. Suff 4B 66
Grinacombe Moor. Devn 3E 11
Grindale. E Yor 2F 101
Grindhill. Devn 3E 11
Grindiscol. Shet 8F 173
Grindle. Shrp 5B 72
Grindleford. Derbs 3G 85
Grindleton. Lanc 5G 97
Grindley. Staf 3E 73
Grindley Brook. Shrp 1H 71
Grindlow. Derbs 3F 85
Grindon. Nmbd 5F 131
Grindon. Staf 5E 85
Gringley on the Hill. Notts 1E 87
Grinsdale. Cumb 4E 113
Grinshill. Shrp 3H 71
Grinton. N Yor 5D 104
Griomsidar. W Isl 5G 171
Grishipoll. Arg 3C 138
Grisling Common. E Sus 3F 27
Gristhorpe. N Yor 1E 101
Griston. Norf 1B 66
Gritley. Orkn 7E 172
Grittenham. Wilts 3F 35
Grittleton. Wilts 3D 34
Grizebeck. Cumb 1B 96
Grizedale. Cumb 5E 103
Grobister. Orkn 5F 172
Grobsness. Shet 5E 173
Groby. Leics 5C 74
Groes. Cnwy 4C 82
Groes. Neat 3A 32
Groes-faen. Rhon 3D 32
Groesffordd. Gwyn 2B 68
Groesffordd. Powy 3D 46
Groeslon. Gwyn 5D 81
Groes-lwyd. Powy 4E 70
Groes-wen. Cphy 3E 33
Grogport. Arg 5G 125
Groigearraidh. W Isl 4C 170
Gromford. Suff 5F 67
Gronant. Flin 2C 82
Groombridge. E Sus 2G 27
Groomsport. Ards 1K 179
Grosmont. Mon 3H 47
Grosmont. N Yor 4F 107
Groton. Suff 1C 54
Grove. Dors 5B 14
Grove. Kent 4G 41
Grove. Notts 3E 87
Grove. Oxon 2B 36
The Grove. Dum 2A 112
The Grove. Worc 1D 48
Grovehill. E Yor 1D 94
Grove Park. G Lon 3F 39
Grovesend. Swan 5F 45
Grub Street. Staf 3B 72
Grudie. High 2F 157
Gruids. High 3C 164
Gruinard House. High 4D 162
Gruinart. Arg 3A 124
Grulinbeg. Arg 3A 124
Gruline. Arg 4G 139
Grummore. High 5G 167
Grundisburgh. Suff 5E 66
Gruting. Shet 7D 173
Grutness. Shet 10F 173
Gualachulain. High 4F 141
Gualin House. High 3D 166
Guardbridge. Fife 2G 137
Guarlford. Worc 1D 48
Guay. Per 4H 143
Gubblecote. Herts 4H 51
Guestling Green. E Sus 4C 28
Guestling Thorn. E Sus 4C 28
Guestwick. Norf 3C 78
Guestwick Green. Norf 3C 78
Guide. Bkbn 2F 91
Guide Post. Nmbd 1F 115
Guilden Down. Shrp 2F 59
Guilden Morden. Cambs 1C 52
Guilden Sutton. Ches W 4G 83
Guildford. Surr 195 (1A 26)
Guildtown. Per 5A 144
Guilsborough. Nptn 3D 62
Guilsfield. Powy 4E 70
Guineaford. Devn 3F 19
Guisborough. Red C 3D 106
Guiseley. W Yor 5D 98
Guist. Norf 3B 78
Guiting Power. Glos 3F 49
Gulberwick. Shet 8F 173
Gulladuff. M Ulst 7F 174
Gullane. E Lot 1A 130
Gulling Green. Suff 5H 65
Gulval. Corn 3B 4
Gulworthy. Devn 5E 11
Gumfreston. Pemb 4F 43
Gumley. Leics 1D 62
Gunby. E Yor 1H 93
Gunby. Linc 3G 75
Gundleton. Hants 3E 24
Gun Green. Kent 2B 28
Gun Hill. E Sus 4G 27
Gunn. Devn 3G 19
Gunnerside. N Yor 5C 104
Gunnerton. Nmbd 2C 114
Gunness. N Lin 3B 94
Gunnislake. Corn 5E 11
Gunnista. Shet 7F 173
Gunsgreenhill. Bord 3F 131
Gunstone. Staf 5C 72
Gunthorpe. Norf 2C 78
Gunthorpe. N Lin 1F 87
Gunthorpe. Notts 1D 74
Gunthorpe. Pet 5A 76
Gunville. IOW 4C 16
Gupworthy. Som 3C 20
Gurnard. IOW 3C 16
Gurney Slade. Som 2B 22
Gurnos. Powy 5A 46
Gussage All Saints. Dors 1F 15
Gussage St Andrew. Dors 1E 15
Gussage St Michael. Dors 1E 15
Guston. Kent 1H 29
Gutcher. Shet 2G 173
Guthram Gowt. Linc 3A 76
Guthrie. Ang 3E 145
Guyhirn. Cambs 5D 76
Guyhirn Gull. Cambs 5C 76
Guy's Head. Linc 3D 77
Guy's Marsh. Dors 4D 22
Guyzance. Nmbd 4G 121
Gwaelod-y-garth. Card 3E 32
Gwaenynog Bach. Den 4C 82
Gwaenysgor. Flin 2C 82
Gwalchmai. IOA 3C 80
Gwastad. Pemb 2E 43
Gwaun-Cae-Gurwen. Neat 4H 45
Gwbert. Cdgn 1B 44
Gweek. Corn 4E 5
Gwehelog. Mon 5G 47
Gwenddwr. Powy 1D 46
Gwennap. Corn 4B 6
Gwenter. Corn 5E 5
Gwernaffield. Flin 4E 82
Gwernesney. Mon 5H 47
Gwernogle. Carm 2F 45
Gwern-y-go. Powy 1E 58
Gwernymynydd. Flin 4E 82
Gwersyllt. Wrex 5F 83
Gwespyr. Flin 2D 82
Gwinear. Corn 3C 4
Gwithian. Corn 2C 4
Gwredog. IOA 2D 80
Gwyddelwern. Den 1C 70
Gwyddgrug. Carm 2E 45
Gwynfryn. Wrex 5E 83
Gwystre. Powy 4C 58
Gwytherin. Cnwy 4A 82
Gyfelia. Wrex 1F 71
Gyffin. Cnwy 3G 81

H

Haa of Houlland. Shet 1G 173
Habberley. Shrp 5G 71
Habblesthorpe. Notts 2E 87
Habergham. Lanc 1G 91
Habin. W Sus 4G 25
Habrough. NE Lin 3E 95
Haceby. Linc 2H 75
Hacheston. Suff 5F 67
Hackenthorpe. S Yor 2B 86
Hackford. Norf 5C 78
Hackforth. N Yor 5F 105
Hackland. Orkn 5C 172
Hackleton. Nptn 5F 63
Hackman's Gate. Worc 3C 60

Hackness—Heol-y-Cyw

Hackness. N Yor 5G 107
Hackness. Orkn 8C 172
Hackney. G Lon 2E 39
Hackthorn. Linc 2G 87
Hackthorpe. Cumb 2G 103
Haclait. W Isl 4D 170
Haconby. Linc 3A 76
Hadden. Bord 1B 120
Haddenham. Buck 5F 51
Haddenham. Cambs 3D 64
Haddenham End Field. Cambs 3D 64
Haddington. E Lot 2B 130
Haddington. Linc 4G 87
Haddiscoe. Norf 1G 67
Haddo. Abers 5F 161
Haddon. Cambs 1A 64
Hademore. Staf 5F 73
Hadfield. Derbs 1E 85
Hadham Cross. Herts 4E 53
Hadham Ford. Herts 3E 53
Hadleigh. Essx 2C 40
Hadleigh. Suff 1D 54
Hadleigh Heath. Suff 1C 54
Hadley. Telf 4A 72
Hadley. Worc 4C 60
Hadley End. Staf 3F 73
Hadley Wood. G Lon 1D 38
Hadlow. Kent 1H 27
Hadlow Down. E Sus 3G 27
Hadnall. Shrp 3H 71
Hadstock. Essx 1F 53
Hadston. Nmbd 4G 121
Hady. Derbs 3A 86
Hadzor. Worc 4D 60
Haffenden Quarter. Kent 1C 28
Haggate. Lanc 1G 91
Haggbeck. Cumb 2F 113
Haggersta. Shet 7E 173
Haggerston. Nmbd 5G 131
Haggrister. Shet 4E 173
Hagley. Here 1A 48
Hagley. Worc 2D 60
Hagnaby. Linc 4C 88
Hagworthingham. Linc 4C 88
Haigh. G Man 4E 90
Haigh Moor. W Yor 2C 92
Haighton Green. Lanc 1D 90
Haile. Cumb 4B 102
Hailes. Glos 2F 49
Hailey. Herts 4D 52
Hailey. Oxon 4B 50
Hailsham. E Sus 5G 27
Hail Weston. Cambs 4A 64
Hainault. G Lon 1F 39
Hainford. Norf 4E 78
Hainton. Linc 2A 88
Hainworth. W Yor 1A 92
Haisthorpe. E Yor 3F 101
Hakin. Pemb 4C 42
Halam. Notts 5D 86
Halbeath. Fife 1E 129
Halberton. Devn 1D 12
Halcro. High 2E 169
Hale. Cumb 2E 97
Hale. G Man 2B 84
Hale. Hal 2G 83
Hale. Hants 1G 15
Hale. Surr 2G 25
Hale Bank. Hal 2G 83
Halebarns. G Man 2B 84
Hales. Norf 1F 67
Hales. Staf 2B 72
Halesgate. Linc 3C 76
Hales Green. Derbs 1F 73
Halesowen. W Mid 2D 60
Hale Street. Kent 1A 28
Halesworth. Suff 3F 67
Halewood. Mers 2G 83
Halford. Shrp 2G 59
Halford. Warw 1A 50
Halfpenny. Cumb 1E 97
Halfpenny Furze. Carm 3G 43
Halfpenny Green. Staf 1C 60
Halfway. Carm
nr. Llandeilo 2G 45
nr. Llandovery 2B 46
Halfway. S Yor 2B 86
Halfway. W Ber 5C 36
Halfway House. Shrp 4F 71
Halfway Houses. Kent 3D 40
Halgabron. Corn 4A 10
Halifax. W Yor 2A 92
Halistra. High 3B 154
Halket. E Ayr 4F 127
Halkirk. High 3D 168
Halkyn. Flin 3E 82
Hall. E Ren 4F 127
Hallam Fields. Derbs 1B 74
Halland. E Sus 4G 27
The Hallands. N Lin 2D 94
Hallaton. Leics 1E 63
Hallatrow. Bath 1B 22
Hallbank. Cumb 5H 103
Hallbankgate. Cumb 4G 113
Hall Dunnerdale. Cumb 5D 102
Hallen. S Glo 3A 34
Hall End. Bed 1A 52
Hallgarth. Dur 5G 115
Hall Green. Ches E 5C 84
Hall Green. Norf 2D 66
Hall Green. W Mid 2F 61
Hall Green. W Yor 3D 92
Hall Green. Wrex 1G 71
Halliburton. Bord 5C 130
Hallin. High 3B 154
Halling. Medw 4B 40
Hallington. Linc 2C 88
Hallington. Nmbd 2C 114
Halloughton. Notts 5D 86
Hallow. Worc 5C 60
Hallow Heath. Worc 5C 60
Hallowsgate. Ches W 4H 83
Hallsands. Devn 5E 9
Hall's Green. Herts 3C 52
Hallspill. Devn 4E 19
Hallthwaites. Cumb 1A 96
Hall Waberthwaite. Cumb 5C 102
Hallwood Green. Glos 2B 48
Hallworthy. Corn 4B 10
Hallyne. Bord 5E 129
Halmer End. Staf 1C 72
Halmond's Frome. Here 1B 48
Halmore. Glos 5B 48
Halnaker. W Sus 5A 26
Halsall. Lanc 3B 90
Halse. Nptn 1D 50
Halse. Som 4E 21
Halsetown. Corn 3C 4
Halsham. E Yor 2F 95
Halsinger. Devn 3F 19
Halstead. Essx 2B 54
Halstead. Kent 4F 39
Halstead. Leics 5E 75
Halstock. Dors 2A 14
Halsway. Som 3E 21
Haltcliff Bridge. Cumb 1E 103
Haltham. Linc 4B 88
Haltoft End. Linc 1C 76
Halton. Buck 5G 51
Halton. Hal 2H 83
Halton. Lanc 3E 97
Halton. Nmbd 3C 114
Halton. W Yor 1D 92
Halton. Wrex 2F 71
Halton East. N Yor 4C 98
Halton Fenside. Linc 4D 88
Halton Gill. N Yor 2A 98
Halton Holegate. Linc 4D 88
Halton Lea Gate. Nmbd 4H 113
Halton Moor. W Yor 1D 92
Halton Shields. Nmbd 3D 114
Halton West. N Yor 4H 97
Haltwhistle. Nmbd 3A 114
Halvergate. Norf 5G 79
Halwell. Devn 3D 9
Halwill. Devn 3E 11
Halwill Junction. Devn 3E 11
Ham. Devn 2F 13
Ham. Glos 2B 34
Ham. G Lon 3C 38
Ham. High 1E 169
Ham. Kent 5H 41
Ham. Plym 3A 8
Ham. Shet 8A 173
Ham. Som
nr. Ilminster 1F 13
nr. Taunton 4F 21
nr. Wellington 1E 13
Ham. Wilts 5B 36
Hambleden. Buck 3F 37
Hambledon. Hants 1E 17
Hambledon. Surr 2A 26
Hamble-le-Rice. Hants 2C 16
Hambleton. Lanc 5C 96
Hambleton. N Yor 1F 93
Hambridge. Som 4G 21
Hambrook. S Glo 4B 34
Hambrook. W Sus 2F 17
Ham Common. Dors 4D 22
Hameringham. Linc 4C 88
Hamerton. Cambs 3A 64
Ham Green. Here 1C 48
Ham Green. Kent 4C 40
Ham Green. N Som 4A 34
Ham Green. Worc 4E 61
Ham Hill. Kent 4A 40
Hamilton. Leic 5D 74
Hamilton. S Lan 4A 128
Hamiltonsbawn. Arm 5D 178
Hamister. Shet 5G 173
Hammer. W Sus 3G 25
Hammersmith. G Lon 3D 38
Hammerwich. Staf 5E 73
Hammerwood. E Sus 2F 27
Hammill. Kent 5G 41
Hammond Street. Herts 5D 52
Hammoon. Dors 1D 14
Hamnavoe. Shet
nr. Braehoulland 3D 173
nr. Burland 8E 173
nr. Lunna 4F 173
on Yell 3F 173
Hamp. Som 3G 21
Hampden Park. E Sus 5G 27
Hampen. Glos 4F 49
Hamperden End. Essx 2F 53
Hamperley. Shrp 2G 59
Hampnett. Glos 4F 49
Hampole. S Yor 3F 93
Hampreston. Dors 3F 15
Hampstead. G Lon 2D 38
Hampstead Norreys. W Ber 4D 36
Hampsthwaite. N Yor 4E 99
Hampton. Devn 3F 13
Hampton. G Lon 3C 38
Hampton. Kent 4F 41
Hampton. Shrp 2B 60
Hampton. Swin 2G 35
Hampton. Worc 1F 49
Hampton Bishop. Here 2A 48
Hampton Fields. Glos 2D 35
Hampton Hargate. Pet 1A 64
Hampton Heath. Ches W 1H 71
Hampton in Arden. W Mid 2G 61
Hampton Loade. Shrp 2B 60
Hampton Lovett. Worc 4C 60
Hampton Lucy. Warw 5G 61
Hampton Magna. Warw 4G 61
Hampton on the Hill. Warw 4G 61
Hampton Poyle. Oxon 4D 50
Hampton Wick. G Lon 4C 38
Hamptworth. Wilts 1H 15
Hamrow. Norf 3B 78
Hamsey. E Sus 4F 27
Hamsey Green. Surr 5E 39
Hamstall Ridware. Staf 4F 73
Hamstead. IOW 3C 16
Hamstead. W Mid 1E 61
Hamstead Marshall. W Ber 5C 36
Hamsterley. Dur
nr. Consett 4E 115
nr. Wolsingham 1E 105
Hamsterley Mill. Dur 4E 115
Ham Street. Som 3A 22
Hamstreet. Kent 2E 28
Hamworthy. Pool 3E 15
Hanbury. Staf 3F 73
Hanbury. Worc 4D 60
Hanbury Woodend. Staf 3F 73
Hanby. Linc 2H 75
Hanchurch. Staf 1C 72
Hand and Pen. Devn 3D 12
Handbridge. Ches W 4G 83
Handcross. W Sus 2D 26
Handforth. Ches E 2C 84
Handley. Ches W 5G 83
Handley. Derbs 4A 86
Handsacre. Staf 4E 73
Handsworth. S Yor 2B 86
Handsworth. W Mid 1E 61
Handy Cross. Buck 2G 37
Hanford. Dors 1D 14
Hanford. Stoke 1C 72
Hangersley. Hants 2G 15
Hanging Houghton. Nptn 3E 63
Hanging Langford. Wilts 3F 23
Hangleton. Brig 5D 26
Hangleton. W Sus 5B 26
Hanham. S Glo 4B 34
Hanham Green. S Glo 4B 34
Hankelow. Ches E 1A 72
Hankerton. Wilts 2E 35
Hankham. E Sus 5H 27
Hanley. Stoke **Stoke 202** (1C 72)
Hanley Castle. Worc 1D 48
Hanley Childe. Worc 4A 60
Hanley Swan. Worc 1D 48
Hanley William. Worc 4A 60
Hanlith. N Yor 3B 98
Hanmer. Wrex 2G 71
Hannaborough. Devn 2F 11
Hannaford. Devn 4G 19
Hannah. Linc 3E 89
Hannington. Hants 1D 24
Hannington. Nptn 3F 63
Hannington. Swin 2G 35
Hannington Wick. Swin 2G 35
Hanscombe End. C Beds 2B 52
Hanslope. Mil 1G 51
Hanthorpe. Linc 3H 75
Hanwell. G Lon 2C 38
Hanwell. Oxon 1C 50
Hanwood. Shrp 5G 71
Hanworth. G Lon 3C 38
Hanworth. Norf 2D 78
Happas. Ang 4D 144
Happendon. S Lan 1A 118
Happisburgh. Norf 2F 79
Happisburgh Common. Norf 3F 79
Hapsford. Ches W 3G 83
Hapton. Lanc 1F 91
Hapton. Norf 1D 66
Harberton. Devn 3D 9
Harbertonford. Devn 3D 9
Harbledown. Kent 5F 41
Harborne. W Mid 2E 61
Harborough Magna. Warw 3B 62
Harbottle. Nmbd 4D 120
Harbourneford. Devn 2D 8
Harbours Hill. Worc 4D 60
Harbridge. Hants 1G 15
Harbury. Warw 4A 62
Harby. Leics 2E 75
Harby. Notts 3F 87
Harcombe. Devn 3E 13
Harcombe Bottom. Devn 3G 13
Harcourt. Corn 5C 6
Harden. W Yor 1A 92
Hardenhuish. Wilts 4E 35
Hardgate. Abers 3E 153
Hardgate. Dum 3F 111
Hardham. W Sus 4B 26
Hardingham. Norf 5C 78
Hardingstone. Nptn 5E 63
Hardings Wood. Staf 5C 84
Hardington. Som 1C 22
Hardington Mandeville. Som 1A 14
Hardington Marsh. Som 2A 14
Hardington Moor. Som 1A 14
Hardley. Hants 2C 16
Hardley Street. Norf 5F 79
Hardmead. Mil 1H 51
Hardraw. N Yor 5B 104
Hardstoft. Derbs 4B 86
Hardway. Hants 2E 16
Hardway. Som 3C 22
Hardwick. Buck 4G 51
Hardwick. Cambs 5C 64
Hardwick. Norf 2E 66
Hardwick. Nptn 4F 63
Hardwick. Oxon
nr. Bicester 3D 50
nr. Witney 5B 50
Hardwick. Shrp 1F 59
Hardwick. S Yor 2B 86
Hardwick. Stoc T 2B 106
Hardwick. W Mid 1E 61
Hardwicke. Glos
nr. Cheltenham 3E 49
nr. Gloucester 4C 48
Hardwicke. Here 1F 47
Hardwick Village. Notts 3D 86
Hardy's Green. Essx 3C 54
Hare. Som 1F 13
Hareby. Linc 4C 88
Hareden. Lanc 4F 97
Harefield. G Lon 1B 38
Hare Green. Essx 3D 54
Hare Hatch. Wok 4G 37
Harehill. Derbs 2F 73
Harehills. W Yor 1D 92
Harehope. Nmbd 2E 121
Harelaw. Dum 2F 113
Harelaw. Dur 4E 115
Hareplain. Kent 2C 28
Harescough. Cumb 5H 113
Harescombe. Glos 4D 48
Haresfield. Glos 4D 48
Haresfinch. Mers 1H 83
Hareshaw. N Lan 3B 128
Hare Street. Essx 5E 53
Hare Street. Herts 3D 53
Harewood. W Yor 5F 99
Harewood End. Here 3A 48
Harford. Devn 3C 8
Hargate. Norf 1D 66
Hargatewall. Derbs 3F 85
Hargrave. Ches W 4G 83
Hargrave. Nptn 3H 63
Hargrave. Suff 5G 65
Harker. Cumb 3E 113
Harkland. Shet 3F 173
Harkstead. Suff 2E 55
Harlaston. Staf 4G 73
Harlaxton. Linc 2F 75
Harlech. Gwyn 2E 69
Harlequin. Notts 2D 74
Harlescott. Shrp 4H 71
Harleston. Devn 4D 9
Harleston. Norf 2E 67
Harleston. Suff 4C 66
Harlestone. Nptn 4E 62
Harley. Shrp 5H 71
Harley. S Yor 1A 86
Harling Road. Norf 2B 66
Harlington. C Beds 2A 52
Harlington. G Lon 3B 38
Harlington. S Yor 4E 93
Harlosh. High 4B 154
Harlow. Essx 4E 53
Harlow Hill. Nmbd 3D 115
Harlsey Castle. N Yor 5B 106
Harlthorpe. E Yor 1H 93
Harlton. Cambs 5C 64
Harlyn Bay. Corn 1C 6
Harman's Cross. Dors 4E 15
Harmby. N Yor 1D 98
Harmer Green. Herts 4C 52
Harmer Hill. Shrp 3G 71
Harmondsworth. G Lon 3B 38
Harmston. Linc 4G 87
Harnage. Shrp 5H 71
Harnham. Nmbd 1D 115
Harnham. Wilts 4G 23
Harnhill. Glos 5F 49
Harold Hill. G Lon 1G 39
Haroldston West. Pemb 3C 42
Haroldswick. Shet 1H 173
Harold Wood. G Lon 1G 39
Harome. N Yor 1A 100
Harpenden. Herts 4B 52
Harpford. Devn 3D 12
Harpham. E Yor 3E 101
Harpley. Norf 3G 77
Harpley. Worc 4A 60
Harpole. Nptn 4D 62
Harpsdale. High 3D 168
Harpsden. Oxon 3F 37
Harpswell. Linc 2G 87
Harpurhey. G Man 4G 91
Harpur Hill. Derbs 3E 85
Harraby. Cumb 4F 113
Harracott. Devn 4F 19
Harrapool. High 1E 147
Harrapul. High 1E 147
Harrietfield. Per 1B 136
Harrietsham. Kent 5C 40
Harrington. Cumb 2A 102
Harrington. Linc 3C 88
Harrington. Nptn 2E 63
Harringworth. Nptn 1G 63
Harriseahead. Staf 5C 84
Harriston. Cumb 5C 112
Harrogate. N Yor **196** (4F 99)
Harrold. Bed 5G 63
Harrop Dale. G Man 4A 92
Harrow. G Lon 2C 38
Harrowbarrow. Corn 2H 7
Harrowden. Bed 1A 52
Harrowgate Hill. Darl 3F 105
Harrow on the Hill. G Lon 2C 38
Harrow Weald. G Lon 1C 38
Harry Stoke. S Glo 4B 34
Harston. Cambs 5D 64
Harston. Leics 2F 75
Harswell. E Yor 5C 100
Hart. Hart 1B 106
Hartburn. Nmbd 1D 115
Hartburn. Stoc T 3B 106
Hartest. Suff 5H 65
Hartfield. E Sus 2F 27
Hartford. Cambs 3B 64
Hartford. Ches W 3A 84
Hartford. Som 4C 20
Hartford Bridge. Hants 1F 25
Hartford End. Essx 4G 53
Harthill. Ches W 5H 83
Harthill. N Lan 3C 128
Harthill. S Yor 2B 86
Hartington. Derbs 4F 85
Hartland. Devn 4C 18
Hartland Quay. Devn 4C 18
Hartle. Worc 3D 60
Hartlebury. Worc 3C 60
Hartlepool. Hart 1C 106
Hartley. Cumb 4A 104
Hartley. Kent
nr. Cranbrook 2B 28
nr. Dartford 4H 39
Hartley. Nmbd 2G 115
Hartley Green. Staf 3D 73
Hartley Mauditt. Hants 3F 25
Hartley Wespall. Hants 1E 25
Hartley Wintney. Hants 1F 25
Hartlip. Kent 4C 40
Hartmoor Holdings. High 1B 158
Hartoft End. N Yor 5E 107
Harton. N Yor 3B 100
Harton. Shrp 2G 59
Harton. Tyne 3G 115
Hartpury. Glos 3D 48
Hartshead. W Yor 2B 92
Hartshill. Warw 1H 61
Hartshorne. Derbs 3H 73
Hartsop. Cumb 3F 103
Hart Station. Hart 1B 106
Hartswell. Som 4D 20
Hartwell. Nptn 5E 63
Hartwood. Lanc 3D 90
Hartwood. N Lan 4B 128
Harvel. Kent 4A 40
Harvington. Worc
nr. Evesham 1F 49
nr. Kidderminster 3C 60
Harwell. Oxon 3C 36
Harwich. Essx **204** (2F 55)
Harwood. Dur 1B 104
Harwood. G Man 3F 91
Harwood Dale. N Yor 5G 107
Harworth. Notts 1D 86
Hascombe. Surr 2A 26
Haselbech. Nptn 3E 62
Haselbury Plucknett. Som 1H 13
Haseley. Warw 4G 61
Hasfield. Glos 3D 48
Hasguard. Pemb 4C 42
Haskayne. Lanc 4B 90
Hasketon. Suff 5E 67
Hasland. Derbs 4A 86
Haslemere. Surr 2A 26
Haslingden. Lanc 2F 91
Haslingfield. Cambs 5D 64
Haslington. Ches E 5B 84
Hassall. Ches E 5B 84
Hassall Green. Ches E 5B 84
Hassell Street. Kent 1E 29
Hassendean. Bord 2H 119
Hassingham. Norf 5F 79
Hassness. Cumb 3C 102
Hassocks. W Sus 4E 27
Hassop. Derbs 3G 85
Haster. High 3F 169
Hasthorpe. Linc 4D 89
Hastigrow. High 2E 169
Hastingleigh. Kent 1E 29
Hastings. E Sus 5C 28
Hastingwood. Essx 5E 53
Hastoe. Herts 5H 51
Haston. Shrp 3H 71
Haswell. Dur 5G 115
Haswell Plough. Dur 5G 115
Hatch. C Beds 1B 52
Hatch Beauchamp. Som 4G 21
Hatch End. G Lon 1C 38
Hatch Green. Som 1G 13
Hatching Green. Herts 4B 52
Hatchmere. Ches W 3H 83
Hatch Warren. Hants 2E 24
Hatcliffe. NE Lin 4F 95
Hatfield. Here 5H 59
Hatfield. Herts 5C 52
Hatfield. S Yor 4G 93
Hatfield. Worc 5C 60
Hatfield Broad Oak. Essx 4F 53
Hatfield Garden Village. Herts 5C 52
Hatfield Heath. Essx 4F 53
Hatfield Hyde. Herts 4C 52
Hatfield Peverel. Essx 4A 54
Hatfield Woodhouse. S Yor 4G 93
Hatford. Oxon 2B 36
Hatherden. Hants 1B 24
Hatherleigh. Devn 2F 11
Hathern. Leics 3B 74
Hatherop. Glos 5G 49
Hathersage. Derbs 2G 85
Hathersage Booths. Derbs 2G 85
Hatherton. Ches E 1A 72
Hatherton. Staf 4D 72
Hatley St George. Cambs 5B 64
Hatt. Corn 2H 7
Hattersley. G Man 1D 85
Hattingley. Hants 3E 25
Hatton. Abers 5H 161
Hatton. Derbs 2G 73
Hatton. G Lon 3B 38
Hatton. Linc 3A 88
Hatton. Shrp 1G 59
Hatton. Warr 2A 84
Hatton. Warw 4G 61
Hattoncrook. Abers 1F 153
Hatton Heath. Ches W 4G 83
Hatton of Fintray. Abers 2F 153
Haugh. E Ayr 2D 117
Haugh. Linc 3D 88
Haugham. Linc 2C 88
Haugh Head. Nmbd 2E 121
Haughley. Suff 4C 66
Haughley Green. Suff 4C 66
Haugh of Ballechin. Per 3G 143
Haugh of Glass. Mor 5B 160
Haugh of Urr. Dum 3F 111
Haughton. Ches E 5H 83
Haughton. Notts 3D 86
Haughton. Shrp
nr. Bridgnorth 1A 60
nr. Oswestry 3F 71
nr. Shifnal 5B 72
nr. Shrewsbury 4H 71
Haughton. Staf 3C 72
Haughton Green. G Man 1D 84
Haughton le Skerne. Darl 3A 106
Haultwick. Herts 3D 52
Haunn. Arg 4E 139
Haunn. W Isl 7C 170
Haunton. Staf 4G 73
Hauxton. Cambs 5D 64
Havannah. Ches E 4C 84
Havant. Hants 2F 17
Haven. Here 5G 59
The Haven. W Sus 2B 26
Haven Bank. Linc 5B 88
Havenstreet. IOW 3D 16
Havercroft. W Yor 3D 93
Haverfordwest. Pemb 3D 42
Haverhill. Suff 1G 53
Haverigg. Cumb 2A 96
Havering-Atte-Bower. G Lon 1G 39
Haversham. Mil 1G 51
Haverthwaite. Cumb 1C 96
Haverton Hill. Stoc T 2B 106
Havyatt. Som 3A 22
Hawarden. Flin 4F 83
Hawbridge. Worc 1E 49
Hawcoat. Cumb 2B 96
Hawcross. Glos 2C 48
Hawen. Cdgn 1D 44
Hawes. N Yor 1A 98
Hawes Green. Norf 1E 67
Hawick. Bord 3H 119
Hawkchurch. Devn 2G 13
Hawkedon. Suff 5G 65
Hawkenbury. Kent 1C 28
Hawkeridge. Wilts 1D 22
Hawkerland. Devn 4D 12
Hawkesbury. S Glo 3C 34
Hawkesbury. Warw 2A 62
Hawkesbury Upton. S Glo 3C 34
Hawkes End. W Mid 2G 61
Hawk Green. G Man 2D 84
Hawkhurst. Kent 2B 28
Hawkhurst Common. E Sus 4G 27
Hawkinge. Kent 1G 29
Hawkley. Hants 4F 25
Hawkridge. Som 3B 20
Hawksdale. Cumb 5E 113
Hawkshaw. G Man 3F 91
Hawkshead. Cumb 5E 103
Hawkshead Hill. Cumb 5E 103
Hawkswick. N Yor 2B 98
Hawksworth. Notts 1E 75
Hawksworth. W Yor 5D 98
Hawkwell. Essx 1C 40
Hawley. Hants 1G 25
Hawley. Kent 3G 39
Hawling. Glos 3F 49
Hawnby. N Yor 1H 99
Haworth. W Yor 1A 92
Hawstead. Suff 5A 66
Hawthorn. Dur 5H 115
Hawthorn Hill. Brac 4G 37
Hawthorn Hill. Linc 5B 88
Hawthorpe. Linc 3H 75
Hawton. Notts 5E 87
Haxby. York 4A 100
Haxey. N Lin 1E 87
Haybridge. Shrp 3A 60
Haybridge. Som 2A 22
Haydock. Mers 1H 83
Haydon. Bath 1B 22
Haydon. Dors 1B 14
Haydon. Som 4F 21
Haydon Bridge. Nmbd 3B 114
Haydon Wick. Swin 3G 35
Haye. Corn 2H 7
Hayes. G Lon
nr. Bromley 4F 39
Hayes. G Lon
nr. Uxbridge 2B 38
Hayfield. Derbs 2E 85
Hay Green. Norf 4E 77
Hayhill. E Ayr 3D 116
Haylands. IOW 3D 16
Hayle. Corn 3C 4
Hayley Green. W Mid 2D 60
Hayling Island. Hants 3F 17
Hayne. Devn 2B 12
Haynes. C Beds 1A 52
Haynes West End. C Beds 1A 52
Hay-on-Wye. Powy 1F 47
Hayscastle. Pemb 2C 42
Hayscastle Cross. Pemb 2D 42
Hayshead. Ang 4F 145
Hay Street. Herts 3D 53
Hayton. Aber 3G 153
Hayton. Cumb
nr. Aspatria 5C 112
nr. Brampton 4G 113
Hayton. E Yor 5C 100
Hayton. Notts 2E 87
Hayton's Bent. Shrp 2H 59
Haytor Vale. Devn 5A 12
Haytown. Devn 1D 11
Haywards Heath. W Sus 3E 27
Haywood. S Lan 4C 128
Hazelbank. S Lan 5B 128
Hazelbury Bryan. Dors 2C 14
Hazeleigh. Essx 5B 54
Hazeley. Hants 1F 25
Hazel Grove. G Man 2D 84
Hazelhead. S Yor 4B 92
Hazelslade. Staf 4E 73
Hazel Street. Kent 2A 28
Hazelton Walls. Fife 1F 137
Hazelwood. Derbs 1H 73
Hazlemere. Buck 2G 37
Hazler. Shrp 1G 59
Hazlerigg. Tyne 2F 115
Hazles. Staf 1E 73
Hazleton. Glos 4F 49
Hazon. Nmbd 4F 121
Heacham. Norf 2F 77
Headbourne Worthy. Hants 3C 24
Headcorn. Kent 1C 28
Headingley. W Yor 1C 92
Headington. Oxon 5D 50
Headlam. Dur 3E 105
Headless Cross. Worc 4E 61
Headley. Hants
nr. Haslemere 3G 25
nr. Kingsclere 5D 36
Headley. Surr 5D 38
Headley Down. Hants 3G 25
Headley Heath. Worc 3E 61
Headley Park. Bris 5A 34
Head of Muir. Falk 1B 128
Headon. Notts 3E 87
Heads Nook. Cumb 4F 113
Heage. Derbs 5A 86
Healaugh. N Yor
nr. Grinton 5D 104
nr. York 5H 99
Heald Green. G Man 2C 84
Heale. Devn 2G 19
Healey. G Man 3G 91
Healey. Nmbd 4D 114
Healey. N Yor 1D 98
Healeyfield. Dur 5D 114
Healing. NE Lin 3F 95
Heamoor. Corn 3B 4
Heanish. Arg 4B 138
Heanor. Derbs 1B 74
Heanton Punchardon. Devn 3F 19
Heapham. Linc 2F 87
Heartsease. Powy 4D 58
Heasley Mill. Devn 3H 19
Heaste. High 2E 147
Heath. Derbs 4B 86
The Heath. Norf
nr. Buxton 3E 79
nr. Fakenham 3B 78
nr. Hevingham 3D 78
The Heath. Staf 2E 73
The Heath. Suff 2E 55
Heath and Reach. C Beds 3H 51
Heath Common. W Sus 4C 26
Heathcote. Derbs 4F 85
Heath Cross. Devn 3H 11
Heathencote. Nptn 1F 51
Heath End. Hants 5D 36
Heath End. Leics 3A 74
Heath End. W Mid 5E 73
Heather. Leics 4A 74
Heatherfield. High 4D 155
Heatherton. Derb 2H 73
Heathfield. Cambs 1E 53
Heathfield. Cumb 5C 112
Heathfield. Devn 5B 12
Heathfield. E Sus 3G 27
Heathfield. Ren 3E 126
Heathfield. Som
nr. Lydeard St Lawrence 3E 21
nr. Norton Fitzwarren 4E 21
Heath Green. Worc 3E 61
Heathhall. Dum 2A 112
Heath Hayes. Staf 4E 73
Heath Hill. Shrp 4B 72
Heath House. Som 2H 21
Heathrow Airport. G Lon **205** (3B 38)
Heathstock. Devn 2F 13
Heathton. Shrp 1C 60
Heathtop. Derbs 2G 73
Heath Town. W Mid 1D 60
Heatley. Staf 3E 73
Heatley. Warr 2B 84
Heaton. Lanc 3D 96
Heaton. Staf 4D 84
Heaton. Tyne 3F 115
Heaton. W Yor 1B 92
Heaton Moor. G Man 1C 84
Heaton's Bridge. Lanc 3C 90
Heaverham. Kent 5G 39
Heavitree. Devn 3C 12
Hebburn. Tyne 3G 115
Hebden. N Yor 3C 98
Hebden Bridge. W Yor 2H 91
Hebden Green. Ches W 4A 84
Hebing End. Herts 3D 52
Hebron. Carm 2F 43
Hebron. Nmbd 1E 115
Heck. Dum 1B 112
Heckdyke. Notts 1E 87
Heckfield. Hants 5F 37
Heckfield Green. Suff 3D 66
Heckfordbridge. Essx 3C 54
Heckington. Linc 1A 76
Heckmondwike. W Yor 2C 92
Heddington. Wilts 5E 35
Heddle. Orkn 6C 172
Heddon. Devn 4G 19
Heddon-on-the-Wall. Nmbd 3E 115
Hedenham. Norf 1F 67
Hedge End. Hants 1C 16
Hedgerley. Buck 2A 38
Hedging. Som 4G 21
Hedley on the Hill. Nmbd 4D 115
Hednesford. Staf 4E 73
Hedon. E Yor 2E 95
Hegdon Hill. Here 5H 59
Heglibister. Shet 6E 173
Heighington. Darl 2F 105
Heighington. Linc 4H 87
Heightington. Worc 3B 60
Heights of Brae. High 2H 157
Heights of Fodderty. High 2H 157
Heights of Kinlochewe. High 2C 156
Heiton. Bord 1B 120
Hele. Devn
nr. Exeter 2C 12
nr. Holsworthy 3D 10
nr. Ilfracombe 2F 19
Hele. Torb 2F 9
Helen's Bay. Ards 1J 179
Helensburgh. Arg 1D 126
Helford. Corn 4E 5
Helhoughton. Norf 3A 78
Helions Bumpstead. Essx 1G 53
Helland. Corn 5A 10
Helland. Som 4G 21
Hellandbridge. Corn 5A 10
Hellesdon. Norf 4E 78
Hellesveor. Corn 2C 4
Hellidon. Nptn 5C 62
Hellifield. N Yor 4A 98
Hellingly. E Sus 4G 27
Hellington. Norf 5F 79
Hellister. Shet 7E 173
Helmdon. Nptn 1D 50
Helmingham. Suff 5D 66
Helmington Row. Dur 1E 105
Helmsdale. High 2H 165
Helmshore. Lanc 2F 91
Helmsley. N Yor 1A 100
Helperby. N Yor 3G 99
Helperthorpe. N Yor 2D 100
Helpringham. Linc 1A 76
Helpston. Pet 5A 76
Helsby. Ches W 3G 83
Helsey. Linc 3E 89
Helston. Corn 4D 4
Helstone. Corn 4A 10
Helton. Cumb 2G 103
Helwith. N Yor 4D 105
Helwith Bridge. N Yor 3H 97
Helygain. Flin 3E 82
The Hem. Shrp 5B 72
Hemblington. Norf 4F 79
Hemel Hempstead. Herts 5A 52
Hemerdon. Devn 3B 8
Hemingbrough. N Yor 1G 93
Hemingby. Linc 3B 88
Hemingfield. S Yor 4D 93
Hemingford Abbots. Cambs 3B 64
Hemingford Grey. Cambs 3B 64
Hemingstone. Suff 5D 66
Hemington. Leics 3B 74
Hemington. Nptn 2H 63
Hemington. Som 1C 22
Hemley. Suff 1F 55
Hemlington. Midd 3B 106
Hempholme. E Yor 4E 101
Hempnall. Norf 1E 67
Hempnall Green. Norf 1E 67
Hempriggs. High 4F 169
Hemp's Green. Essx 3C 54
Hempstead. Essx 2G 53
Hempstead. Medw 4B 40
Hempstead. Norf
nr. Holt 2D 78
nr. Stalham 3G 79
Hempsted. Glos 4D 48
Hempton. Norf 3B 78
Hempton. Oxon 2C 50
Hemsby. Norf 4G 79
Hemswell. Linc 1G 87
Hemswell Cliff. Linc 2G 87
Hemsworth. Dors 2E 15
Hemsworth. W Yor 3E 93
Hemyock. Devn 1E 13
Henallt. Carm 3E 45
Henbury. Bris 4A 34
Henbury. Ches E 3C 84
Hendomen. Powy 1E 58
Hendon. G Lon 2D 38
Hendon. Tyne 4H 115
Hendra. Corn 3D 6
Hendre. B'end 3C 32
Hendreforgan. Rhon 3C 32
Hendy. Carm 5F 45
Heneglwys. IOA 3D 80
Henfeddau Fawr. Pemb 1G 43
Henfield. S Glo 4B 34
Henfield. W Sus 4D 26
Henford. Devn 3D 10
Hengoed. Cphy 2E 33
Hengoed. Shrp 2E 71
Hengrave. Suff 4H 65
Henham. Essx 3F 53
Henlade. Som 4F 21
Henley. Dors 2B 14
Henley. Shrp
nr. Church Stretton 2G 59
nr. Ludlow 3H 59
Henley. Som 3H 21
Henley. Suff 5D 66
Henley. W Sus 4G 25
Henley Down. E Sus 4B 28
Henley-in-Arden. Warw 4F 61
Henley-on-Thames. Oxon 3F 37
Henley Street. Kent 4A 40
Henllan. Cdgn 1D 44
Henllan. Den 4C 82
Henllan. Mon 3F 47
Henllan Amgoed. Carm 3F 43
Henllys. Torf 2F 33
Henlow. C Beds 2B 52
Hennock. Devn 4B 12
Henny Street. Essx 2B 54
Henryd. Cnwy 3G 81
Henry's Moat. Pemb 2E 43
Hensall. N Yor 2F 93
Henshaw. Nmbd 3A 114
Hensingham. Cumb 3A 102
Henstead. Suff 2G 67
Hensting. Hants 4C 24
Henstridge. Som 1C 14
Henstridge Ash. Som 4C 22
Henstridge Bowden. Som 4B 22
Henstridge Marsh. Som 4C 22
Henton. Oxon 5F 51
Henton. Som 2H 21
Henwood. Corn 5C 10
Heogan. Shet 7F 173
Heolgerrig. Mer T 5D 46
Heol Senni. Powy 3C 46
Heol-y-Cyw. B'end 3C 32

Hepburn—Howell

Hepburn. Nmbd 2E 121
Hepple. Nmbd 4D 121
Hepscott. Nmbd 1F 115
Heptonstall. W Yor 2H 91
Hepworth. Suff 3B 66
Hepworth. W Yor 4B 92
Herbrandston. Pemb 4C 42
Hereford. Here 2A 48
Heribusta. High 1D 154
Heriot. Bord 4H 129
Hermiston. Edin 2E 129
Hermitage. Dors 2B 14
Hermitage. Bord 5H 119
Hermitage. W Ber 4D 36
Hermitage. W Sus 2F 17
Hermon. Carm
nr. Llandeilo 3G 45
nr. Newcastle Emlyn 2D 44
Hermon. IOA 4C 80
Hermon. Pemb 1G 43
Herne. Kent 4F 41
Herne Bay. Kent 4F 41
Herne Common. Kent 4F 41
Herne Pound. Kent 5A 40
Herner. Devn 4F 19
Hernhill. Kent 4E 41
Herodsfoot. Corn 2G 7
Heronden. Kent 5G 41
Herongate. Essx 1H 39
Heronsford. S Ayr 1G 109
Heronsgate. Herts 1B 38
Heron's Ghyll. E Sus 3F 27
Herra. Shet 2H 173
Herriard. Hants 2E 25
Herringfleet. Suff 1G 67
Herringswell. Suff 4G 65
Herrington. Tyne 4G 115
Hersden. Kent 4G 41
Hersham. Corn 2C 10
Hersham. Surr 4C 38
Herstmonceux. E Sus 4H 27
Herston. Dors 5F 15
Herston. Orkn 8D 172
Hertford. Herts 4D 52
Hertford Heath. Herts 4D 52
Hertingfordbury. Herts 4D 52
Hesketh. Lanc 2C 90
Hesketh Bank. Lanc 2C 90
Hesketh Lane. Lanc 5F 97
Hesket Newmarket.
Cumb 1E 103
Heskin Green. Lanc 3D 90
Hesleden. Dur 1B 106
Hesleyside. Nmbd 1B 114
Heslington. York 4A 100
Hessay. York 4H 99
Hessenford. Corn 3H 7
Hessett. Suff 4B 66
Hessilhead. N Ayr 4E 127
Hessle. E Yor 2D 94
Hestaford. Shet 6D 173
Hest Bank. Lanc 3D 96
Hester's Way. Glos 3E 49
Hestinsetter. Shet 7D 173
Heston. G Lon 3C 38
Hestwall. Orkn 6B 172
Heswall. Mers 2E 83
Hethe. Oxon 3D 50
Hethelpit Cross. Glos 3C 48
Hethersett. Norf 5D 78
Hethersgill. Cumb 3F 113
Hetherside. Cumb 3F 113
Hethpool. Nmbd 2C 120
Hett. Dur 1F 105
Hetton. N Yor 4B 98
Hetton-le-Hole. Tyne 5G 115
Hetton Steads. Nmbd 1E 121
Heugh. Nmbd 2D 115
Heugh-head. Abers 2A 152
Heveningham. Suff 3F 67
Hever. Kent 1F 27
Heversham. Cumb 1D 97
Hevingham. Norf 3D 78
Hewas Water. Corn 4D 6
Hewelsfield. Glos 5A 48
Hewish. N Som 5H 33
Hewish. Som 2H 13
Hewood. Dors 2G 13
Heworth. York 4A 100
Hexham. Nmbd 3C 114
Hextable. Kent 3G 39
Hexton. Herts 2B 52
Hexworthy. Devn 5G 11
Heybridge. Essx
nr. Brentwood 1H 39
nr. Maldon 5B 54
Heybridge Basin. Essx 5B 54
Heybrook Bay. Devn 4A 8
Heydon. Cambs 1E 53
Heydon. Norf 3D 78
Heydour. Linc 2H 75
Heylipol. Arg 4A 138
Heyop. Powy 3E 59
Heysham. Lanc 3D 96
Heyshott. W Sus 1G 17
Heytesbury. Wilts 2E 23
Heythrop. Oxon 3B 50
Heywood. G Man 3G 91
Heywood. Wilts 1D 22
Hibaldstow. N Lin 4C 94
Hickleton. S Yor 4E 93
Hickling. Norf 3G 79
Hickling. Notts 3D 74
Hickling Green. Norf 3G 79
Hickling Heath. Norf 3G 79
Hickstead. W Sus 3D 26
Hidcote Bartrim. Glos 1G 49
Hidcote Boyce. Glos 1G 49
Higford. Shrp 5B 72
High Ackworth. W Yor 3E 93
Higham. Derbs 5A 86
Higham. Kent 3B 40
Higham. Lanc 1G 91
Higham. S Yor 4D 92
Higham. Suff
nr. Ipswich 2D 54
nr. Newmarket 4G 65
Higham Dykes. Nmbd 2E 115
Higham Ferrers. Nptn 4G 63
Higham Gobion. C Beds 2B 52
Higham on the Hill. Leics 1A 62
Highampton. Devn 2E 11
Higham Wood. Kent 1H 27
High Angerton. Nmbd 1D 115
High Auldgirth. Dum 1G 111
High Bankhill. Cumb 5G 113
High Banton. N Lan 1A 128
High Barnet. G Lon 1D 38
High Beech. Essx 1F 39
High Bentham. N Yor 3F 97
High Bickington. Devn 4G 19
High Biggins. Cumb 2E 97
High Birkwith. N Yor 2G 97
High Blantyre. S Lan 4H 127
High Bonnybridge. Falk 2B 128
High Borrans. Cumb 4F 103
High Bradfield. S Yor 1G 85
High Bray. Devn 3G 19
Highbridge. Cumb 5E 113
Highbridge. High 5E 148
Highbridge. Som 2G 21
Highbrook. W Sus 2E 27
High Brooms. Kent 1G 27
High Bullen. Devn 4F 19
Highburton. W Yor 3B 92
Highbury. Som 2B 22
High Buston. Nmbd 4G 121
High Callerton. Nmbd 2E 115
High Carlingill. Cumb 4H 103
High Catton. E Yor 4B 100
High Church. Nmbd 1E 115
Highclere. Hants 5C 36
Highcliffe. Dors 3H 15
High Cogges. Oxon 5B 50
High Common. Norf 5B 78
High Coniscliffe. Darl 3F 105
High Crosby. Cumb 4F 113
High Cross. Hants 4F 25
High Cross. Herts 4D 52
High Easter. Essx 4G 53
High Eggborough. N Yor 2F 93
High Ellington. N Yor 1D 98
Higher Alham. Som 2B 22
Higher Ansty. Dors 2C 14
Higher Ashton. Devn 4B 12
Higher Ballam. Lanc 1B 90
Higher Bartle. Lanc 1D 90
Higher Bockhampton.
Dors 3C 14
Higher Bojewyan. Corn 3A 4
Higher Ercall. Telf 4H 71
Higher Cheriton. Devn 2E 12
Higher Clovelly. Devn 4D 18
Higher Compton. Plym 3A 8
Higher Dean. Devn 2D 8
Higher Dinting. Derbs 1E 85
Higher Dunstone. Devn 5H 11
Higher End. G Man 4D 90
Higherford. Lanc 5A 98
Higher Gabwell. Devn 2F 9
Higher Halstock Leigh.
Dors 2A 14
Higher Heysham. Lanc 3D 96
Higher Hurdsfield. Ches E 3D 84
Higher Kingcombe. Dors 3A 14
Higher Kinnerton. Flin 4F 83
Higher Melcombe. Dors 2C 14
Higher Penwortham. Lanc 2D 90
Higher Porthpean. Corn 3E 7
Higher Poynton. Ches E 2D 84
Higher Shotton. Flin 4F 83
Higher Shurlach. Ches W 3A 84
Higher Slade. Devn 2F 19
Higher Tale. Devn 2D 12
Higher Town. IOS 1B 4
Higher Town. Som 2C 20
Highertown. Corn 4C 6
Higher Vexford. Som 3E 20
Higher Walton. Lanc 2D 90
Higher Walton. Warr 2H 83
Higher Whatcombe. Dors 2D 14
Higher Wheelton. Lanc 2E 90
Higher Whiteleigh. Corn 3C 10
Higher Whitley. Ches W 2A 84
Higher Wincham. Ches W 3A 84
Higher Wraxall. Dors 2A 14
Higher Wych. Ches W 1G 71
Higher Yalberton. Torb 3E 9
High Etherley. Dur 2E 105
High Ferry. Linc 1C 76
Highfield. E Yor 1H 93
Highfield. N Ayr 4E 126
Highfield. Tyne 4E 115
Highfields Caldecote.
Cambs 5C 64
High Gallowhill. E Dun 2H 127
High Garrett. Essx 3A 54
Highgate. G Lon 2D 39
Highgate. N Ayr 4E 127
Highgate. Powy 1D 58
High Grange. Dur 1E 105
High Green. Cumb 4F 103
High Green. Norf 5D 78
High Green. Shrp 2B 60
High Green. S Yor 1H 85
High Green. W Yor 3B 92
High Green. Worc 1D 49
Highgreen Manor. Nmbd 5C 120
High Halden. Kent 2C 28
High Halstow. Medw 3B 40
High Ham. Som 3H 21
High Harrington. Cumb 2B 102
High Haswell. Dur 5G 115
High Hatton. Shrp 3A 72
High Hawsker. N Yor 4G 107
High Hesket. Cumb 5F 113
High Hesleden. Dur 1B 106
High Hoyland. S Yor 3C 92
High Hunsley. E Yor 1C 94
High Hurstwood. E Sus 3F 27
High Hutton. N Yor 3B 100
High Ireby. Cumb 1D 102
High Keil. Arg 5A 122
High Kelling. Norf 2D 78
High Kilburn. N Yor 2H 99
High Knipe. Cumb 3G 103
High Lands. Dur 2E 105
The Highlands. Shrp 2A 60
High Lane. G Man 2D 84
High Lane. Worc 4A 60
Highlane. Ches E 4C 84
Highlane. Derbs 2B 86
High Laver. Essx 5F 53
Highlaws. Cumb 5C 112
Highleadon. Glos 3C 48
High Legh. Ches E 2B 84
Highleigh. W Sus 3G 17
High Leven. Stoc T 3B 106
Highley. Shrp 2B 60
High Littleton. Bath 1B 22
High Longthwaite. Cumb 5D 112
High Lorton. Cumb 2C 102
High Marishes. N Yor 2C 100
High Marnham. Notts 3F 87
High Melton. S Yor 4F 93
High Mickley. Nmbd 3D 115
High Moor. Lanc 3D 90
Highmoor. Cumb 5D 112
Highmoor. Oxon 3F 37
Highmoor Cross. Oxon 3F 37
Highmoor Hill. Mon 3H 33
Highnam. Glos 4C 48
High Newport. Tyne 4G 115
High Newton. Cumb 1D 96
High Newton-by-the-Sea.
Nmbd 2G 121
High Nibthwaite. Cumb 1B 96
High Offley. Staf 3B 72
High Ongar. Essx 5F 53
High Onn. Staf 4C 72
High Orchard. Glos 4D 48
High Park. Mers 3B 90
High Roding. Essx 4G 53
High Row. Cumb 1E 103
High Salvington. W Sus 5C 26
High Scales. Cumb 5C 112
High Shaw. N Yor 5B 104
High Shincliffe. Dur 5F 115
High Side. Cumb 1D 102
High Spen. Tyne 3E 115
Highsted. Kent 4D 40
High Stoop. Dur 5E 115
High Street. Corn 3D 6
High Street. Suff
nr. Aldeburgh 5G 67
nr. Bungay 2F 67
nr. Yoxford 3G 67
High Street Green. Suff 5C 66
Highstreet Green. Essx 2A 54
Highstreet Green. Surr 2A 26
Hightae. Dum 2B 112
High Throston. Hart 1B 106
High Town. Staf 4D 73
Hightown. Ches E 4C 84
Hightown. Mers 4A 90
Hightown Green. Suff 5B 66
High Toynton. Linc 4B 88
High Trewhitt. Nmbd 4E 121
High Valleyfield. Fife 1D 128
Highway. Here 1H 47
Highweek. Devn 5B 12
High Westwood. Dur 4E 115
Highwood. Staf 2E 73
Highwood. Worc 4A 60
High Worsall. N Yor 4A 106
Highworth. Swin 2H 35
High Wray. Cumb 5E 103
High Wych. Herts 4E 53
High Wycombe. Buck 2G 37
Hilborough. Norf 5H 77
Hilcott. Wilts 1G 23
Hildenborough. Kent 1G 27
Hildersham. Cambs 1F 53
Hilderstone. Staf 2D 72
Hilderthorpe. E Yor 3F 101
Hilfield. Dors 2B 14
Hilgay. Norf 1F 65
Hill. S Glo 2B 34
Hill. Warw 4B 62
Hill. Worc 1E 49
The Hill. Cumb 1A 96
Hillam. N Yor 2F 93
Hillbeck. Cumb 3A 104
Hillberry. IOM 4C 108
Hillborough. Kent 4G 41
Hillbourne. Pool 3F 15
Hillbrae. Abers
nr. Aberchirder 4D 160
nr. Inverurie 1E 153
nr. Methlick 5F 161
Hill Brow. Hants 4F 25
Hillbutts. Dors 2E 15
Hillclifflane. Derbs 1G 73
Hillcommon. Som 4E 21
Hill Deverill. Wilts 2D 22
Hilldyke. Linc 1C 76
Hill End. Dur 1D 104
Hill End. Fife 4C 136
Hill End. N Yor 4C 98
Hillend. Fife 1E 129
Hillend. N Lan 3B 128
Hillend. Shrp 1C 60
Hillend. Swan 3D 30
Hillersland. Glos 4A 48
Hillerton. Devn 3H 11
Hillesden. Buck 3E 51
Hillesley. Glos 3C 34
Hillfarrance. Som 4E 21
Hill Gate. Here 3H 47
Hill Green. Essx 2E 53
Hill Green. W Ber 4C 36
Hillhall. Lis 3G 179
Hill Head. Hants 2D 16
Hillhead. Abers 5C 160
Hillhead. Devn 3F 9
Hillhead. S Ayr 3D 116
Hillhead of Auchentumb.
Abers 3G 161
Hilliard's Cross. Staf 4F 73
Hilliclay. High 2D 168
Hillingdon. G Lon 2B 38
Hillington. Glas 3G 127
Hillington. Norf 3G 77
Hillmorton. Warw 3C 62
Hill of Beath. Fife 4D 136
Hill of Fearn. High 1C 158
Hill of Fiddes. Abers 1G 153
Hill of Keillor. Ang 4B 144
Hill of Overbrae. Abers 2F 161
Hill Ridware. Staf 4E 73
Hillsborough. Lis 4G 179
Hillsborough. S Yor 1H 85
Hill Side. W Yor 3B 92
Hillside. Abers 4G 153
Hillside. Ang 2G 145
Hillside. Devn 2D 8
Hillside. Mers 3B 90
Hillside. Orkn 5C 172
Hillside. Shet 5F 173
Hillside. Shrp 2A 60
Hillside. Worc 4B 60
Hillside of Prieston. Ang 5C 144
Hill Somersal. Derbs 2F 73
Hillstown. Derbs 4B 86
Hillstreet. Hants 1B 16
Hillswick. Shet 4D 173
Hill Top. Dur
nr. Barnard Castle 2C 104
nr. Durham 5F 115
nr. Stanley 4E 115
Hilltown. New M 7G 179
Hill View. Dors 3E 15
Hillwell. Shet 10E 173
Hill Wootton. Warw 4H 61
Hillyland. Per 1C 136
Hilmarton. Wilts 4F 35
Hilperton. Wilts 1D 22
Hilperton Marsh. Wilts 1D 22
Hilsea. Port 2E 17
Hilston. E Yor 1F 95
Hiltingbury. Hants 4C 24
Hilton. Cambs 4B 64
Hilton. Cumb 2A 104
Hilton. Derbs 2G 73
Hilton. Dors 2C 14
Hilton. Dur 2E 105
Hilton. High 5E 165
Hilton. Shrp 1B 60
Hilton. Staf 5E 73
Hilton. Stoc T 3B 106
Hilton of Cadboll. High 1C 158
Himbleton. Worc 5D 60
Himley. Staf 1C 60
Hincaster. Cumb 1E 97
Hinchwick. Glos 3G 49
Hinckley. Leics 1B 62
Hinderclay. Suff 3C 66
Hinderwell. N Yor 3E 107
Hindford. Shrp 2F 71
Hindhead. Surr 3G 25
Hindley. G Man 4E 90
Hindley. Nmbd 4D 114
Hindley Green. G Man 4E 91
Hindlip. Worc 5C 60
Hindolveston. Norf 3C 78
Hindon. Wilts 3E 23
Hindringham. Norf 2B 78
Hingham. Norf 5C 78
Hinksford. Staf 2C 60
Hinstock. Shrp 3A 72
Hintlesham. Suff 1D 54
Hinton. Hants 3H 15
Hinton. Here 2G 47
Hinton. Nptn 5C 62
Hinton. Shrp 5G 71
Hinton. S Glo 4C 34
Hinton Ampner. Hants 4D 24
Hinton Blewett. Bath 1A 22
Hinton Charterhouse.
Bath 1C 22
Hinton-in-the-Hedges.
Nptn 2D 50
Hinton Martell. Dors 2F 15
Hinton on the Green. Worc 1F 49
Hinton Parva. Swin 3H 35
Hinton St George. Som 1H 13
Hinton St Mary. Dors 1C 14
Hinton Waldrist. Oxon 2B 36
Hints. Shrp 3A 60
Hints. Staf 5F 73
Hinwick. Bed 4G 63
Hinxhill. Kent 1E 29
Hinxton. Cambs 1E 53
Hinxworth. Herts 1C 52
Hipley. Hants 1E 16
Hipperholme. W Yor 2B 92
Hipsburn. Nmbd 3G 121
Hipswell. N Yor 5E 105
Hiraeth. Carm 2F 43
Hirn. Abers 3E 153
Hirnant. Powy 3C 70
Hirst. N Lan 3B 128
Hirst. Nmbd 1F 115
Hirst Courtney. N Yor 2G 93
Hirwaen. Den 4D 82
Hirwaun. Rhon 5C 46
Hiscott. Devn 4F 19
Histon. Cambs 4D 64
Hitcham. Suff 5B 66
Hitchin. Herts 3B 52
Hittisleigh. Devn 3H 11
Hittisleigh Barton. Devn 3H 11
Hive. E Yor 1B 94
Hixon. Staf 3E 73
Hoaden. Kent 5G 41
Hoar Cross. Staf 3F 73
Hoarwithy. Here 3A 48
Hoath. Kent 4G 41
Yr Hôb. Flin 5F 83
Hobarris. Shrp 3F 59
Hobbister. Orkn 7C 172
Hobbles Green. Suff 5G 65
Hobbs Cross. Essx 1F 39
Hobkirk. Bord 3H 119
Hobson. Dur 4E 115
Hoby. Leics 4D 74
Hockering. Norf 4C 78
Hockering Heath. Norf 4C 78
Hockerton. Notts 5E 86
Hockley. Essx 1C 40
Hockley. Staf 5G 73
Hockley. W Mid 3G 61
Hockley Heath. W Mid 3F 61
Hockliffe. C Beds 3H 51
Hockwold cum Wilton.
Norf 2G 65
Hockworthy. Devn 1D 12
Hoddesdon. Herts 5D 52
Hoddlesden. Bkbn 2F 91
Hoddomcross. Dum 2C 112
Hodgeston. Pemb 5E 43
Hodley. Powy 1D 58
Hodnet. Shrp 3A 72
Hodsoll Street. Kent 4H 39
Hodson. Swin 3G 35
Hodthorpe. Derbs 3C 86
Hoe. Norf 4B 78
The Hoe. Plym 3A 8
Hoe Gate. Hants 1E 17
Hoff. Cumb 3H 103
Hoffleet Stow. Linc 2B 76
Hogaland. Shet 4E 173
Hogben's Hill. Kent 5E 41
Hoggard's Green. Suff 5A 66
Hoggeston. Buck 3G 51
Hoggrill's End. Warw 1G 61
Hogha Gearraidh. W Isl 1C 170
Hoghton. Lanc 2E 90
Hoghton Bottoms. Lanc 2E 91
Hognaston. Derbs 5G 85
Hogsthorpe. Linc 3E 89
Hogstock. Dors 2E 15
Holbeach. Linc 3C 76
Holbeach Bank. Linc 3C 76
Holbeach Clough. Linc 3C 76
Holbeach Drove. Linc 4C 76
Holbeach Hurn. Linc 3C 76
Holbeach St Johns. Linc 4C 76
Holbeach St Marks. Linc 2C 76
Holbeach St Matthew.
Linc 2D 76
Holbeck. Notts 3C 86
Holbeck. W Yor 1C 92
Holbeck Woodhouse.
Notts 3C 86
Holberrow Green. Worc 5E 61
Holbeton. Devn 3C 8
Holborn. G Lon 2E 39
Holbrook. Derbs 1A 74
Holbrook. S Yor 2B 86
Holbrook. Suff 2E 55
Holburn. Nmbd 1E 121
Holbury. Hants 2C 16
Holcombe. Devn 5C 12
Holcombe. G Man 3F 91
Holcombe. Som 2B 22
Holcombe Brook. G Man 3F 91
Holcombe Rogus. Devn 1D 12
Holcot. Nptn 4E 63
Holden. Lanc 5G 97
Holdenby. Nptn 4D 62
Holder's Green. Essx 3G 53
Holdgate. Shrp 2H 59
Holdingham. Linc 1H 75
Holditch. Dors 2G 13
Holemoor. Devn 2E 11
Hole Street. W Sus 4C 26
Holford. Som 2E 21
Holker. Cumb 2C 96
Holkham. Norf 1A 78
Hollacombe. Devn 2D 11
Holland. Orkn
on Papa Westray 2D 172
on Stronsay 5F 172
Holland Fen. Linc 1B 76
Holland Lees. Lanc 4D 90
Holland-on-Sea. Essx 4F 55
Holland Park. W Mid 5E 73
Hollandstoun. Orkn 2G 172
Hollesley. Suff 1G 55
Hollinfare. Warr 1A 84
Hollingbourne. Kent 5C 40
Hollingbury. Brig 5E 27
Hollingdon. Buck 3G 51
Hollingrove. E Sus 3A 28
Hollington. Derbs 2G 73
Hollington. E Sus 4B 28
Hollington. Staf 2E 73
Hollington Grove. Derbs 2G 73
Hollingworth. G Man 1E 85
Hollins. Derbs 3H 85
Hollins. G Man
nr. Bury 4G 91
nr. Middleton 4G 91
Hollinsclough. Staf 4E 85
Hollinswood. Telf 5B 72
Hollinthorpe. W Yor 1D 93
Hollinwood. G Man 4H 91
Hollinwood. Shrp 2H 71
Hollocombe. Devn 1G 11
Holloway. Derbs 5H 85
Hollowell. Nptn 3D 62
Hollow Meadows. S Yor 2G 85
Hollows. Dum 2E 113
Hollybush. Cphy 5E 47
Hollybush. E Ayr 3C 116
Hollybush. Worc 2C 48
Holly End. Norf 5D 77
Holly Hill. N Yor 4E 105
Hollyhurst. Shrp 1H 71
Hollym. E Yor 2G 95
Hollywood. Worc 3E 61
Holmacott. Devn 4F 19
Holmbridge. W Yor 4B 92
Holmbury St Mary. Surr 1C 26
Holmbush. Corn 3E 7
Holmcroft. Staf 3D 72
Holme. Cambs 2A 64
Holme. Cumb 2E 97
Holme. N Lin 4C 94
Holme. N Yor 1F 99
Holme. Notts 5F 87
Holme. W Yor 4B 92
Holmebridge. Dors 4D 15
Holme Chapel. Lanc 2G 91
Holme Hale. Norf 5A 78
Holme Lacy. Here 2A 48
Holme Marsh. Here 5F 59
Holmend. Dum 4C 118
Holme next the Sea. Norf 1G 77
Holme-on-Spalding-Moor.
E Yor 1B 94
Holme on the Wolds.
E Yor 5D 100
Holme Pierrepont. Notts 2D 74
Holmer. Here 1A 48
Holmer Green. Buck 1A 38
Holmes. Lanc 3C 90
Holme St Cuthbert. Cumb 5C 112
Holmes Chapel. Ches E 4B 84
Holmesfield. Derbs 3H 85
Holmeswood. Lanc 3C 90
Holmewood. Derbs 4B 86
Holmfirth. W Yor 4B 92
Holmhead. E Ayr 2E 117
Holmisdale. High 4A 154
Holm of Drumlanrig.
Dum 5H 117
Holmpton. E Yor 2G 95
Holmrook. Cumb 5B 102
Holmsgarth. Shet 7F 173
Holmside. Dur 5F 115
Holmwrangle. Cumb 5G 113
Holne. Devn 2D 8
Holsworthy. Devn 2D 10
Holsworthy Beacon. Devn 2D 10
Holt. Dors 2F 15
Holt. Norf 2C 78
Holt. Wilts 5D 34
Holt. Worc 4C 60
Holt. Wrex 5G 83
Holtby. York 4A 100
Holt End. Hants 3E 25
Holt End. Worc 4E 61
Holt Fleet. Worc 4C 60
Holt Green. Lanc 4B 90
Holt Heath. Dors 2F 15
Holt Heath. Worc 4C 60
Holton. Oxon 5D 50
Holton. Som 4B 22
Holton. Suff 3F 67
Holton cum Beckering.
Linc 2A 88
Holton Heath. Dors 3E 15
Holton le Clay. Linc 4F 95
Holton le Moor. Linc 1H 87
Holton St Mary. Suff 2D 54
Holt Pound. Hants 2G 25
Holtsmere End. Herts 4A 52
Holtye. E Sus 2F 27
Holwell. Dors 1C 14
Holwell. Herts 2B 52
Holwell. Leics 3E 75
Holwell. Oxon 5H 49
Holwell. Som 2C 22
Holwick. Dur 2C 104
Holworth. Dors 4C 14
Holybourne. Hants 2F 25
Holy City. Devn 2G 13
Holy Cross. Worc 3D 60
Holyfield. Essx 5D 53
Holyhead. IOA 2B 80
Holy Island. Nmbd 5H 131
Holymoorside. Derbs 4H 85
Holyport. Wind 4G 37
Holystone. Nmbd 4D 120
Holytown. N Lan 3A 128
Holywell. Cambs 3C 64
Holywell. Corn 3B 6
Holywell. Dors 2A 14
Holywell. Flin 3D 82
Holywell. Glos 2C 34
Holywell. Nmbd 2G 115
Holywell. Warw 4F 61
Holywell Green. W Yor 3A 92
Holywell Lake. Som 4E 20
Holywell Row. Suff 3G 65
Holywood. Ards 2J 179
Holywood. Dum 1G 111
Homer. Shrp 5A 72
Homer Green. Mers 4B 90
Homersfield. Suff 2E 67
Hom Green. Here 3A 48
Homington. Wilts 4G 23
Honeyborough. Pemb 4D 42
Honeybourne. Worc 1G 49
Honeychurch. Devn 2G 11
Honeydon. Bed 5A 64
Honey Hill. Kent 4F 41
Honey Street. Wilts 5G 35
Honey Tye. Suff 2C 54
Honeywick. C Beds 3H 51
Honiley. Warw 3G 61
Honing. Norf 3F 79
Honingham. Norf 4D 78
Honington. Linc 1G 75
Honington. Suff 3B 66
Honington. Warw 1A 50
Honiton. Devn 2E 13
Honley. W Yor 3B 92
Honnington. Telf 4B 72
Hoo. Suff 5E 67
Hoobrook. Worc 3C 60
Hood Green. S Yor 4D 92
Hooe. E Sus 5A 28
Hooe. Plym 3B 8
Hooe Common. E Sus 4A 28
Hoo Green. Ches E 2B 84
Hoohill. Bkpl 1B 90
Hook. Cambs 1D 64
Hook. E Yor 2A 94
Hook. G Lon 4C 38
Hook. Hants
nr. Basingstoke 1F 25
nr. Fareham 2D 16
Hook. Pemb 3D 43
Hook. Wilts 3F 35
Hook-a-Gate. Shrp 5G 71
Hook Bank. Worc 1D 48
Hooke. Dors 2A 14
Hooker Gate. Tyne 4E 115
Hookgate. Staf 2B 72
Hook Green. Kent
nr. Lamberhurst 2A 28
nr. Meopham 4H 39
nr. Southfleet 3H 39
Hook Norton. Oxon 2B 50
Hook's Cross. Herts 3C 52
Hook Street. Glos 2B 34
Hookway. Devn 3B 12
Hookwood. Surr 1D 26
Hoole. Ches W 4G 83
Hooley. Surr 5D 39
Hooley Bridge. G Man 3G 91
Hooley Brow. G Man 3G 91
Hoo St Werburgh. Medw 3B 40
Hooton. Ches W 3F 83
Hooton Levitt. S Yor 1C 86
Hooton Pagnell. S Yor 4E 93
Hooton Roberts. S Yor 1B 86
Hoove. Shet 7E 173
Hope. Derbs 2F 85
Hope. Flin 5F 83
Hope. High 2E 167
Hope. Powy 5E 71
Hope. Shrp 5F 71
Hope. Staf 5F 85
Hope Bagot. Shrp 3H 59
Hope Bowdler. Shrp 1G 59
Hopedale. Staf 5F 85
Hope Green. Ches E 2D 84
Hopeman. Mor 2F 159
Hope Mansell. Here 4B 48
Hopesay. Shrp 2F 59
Hope's Green. Essx 2B 40
Hopetown. W Yor 2D 93
Hope under Dinmore.
Here 5H 59
Hopley's Green. Here 5F 59
Hopperton. N Yor 4G 99
Hop Pole. Linc 4A 76
Hopstone. Shrp 1B 60
Hopton. Derbs 5G 85
Hopton. Powy 1E 59
Hopton. Shrp
nr. Oswestry 3F 71
nr. Wem 3H 71
Hopton. Staf 3D 72
Hopton. Suff 3B 66
Hopton Cangeford. Shrp 2H 59
Hopton Castle. Shrp 3F 59
Hopton Heath. Staf 3D 72
Hoptonheath. Shrp 3F 59
Hopton on Sea. Norf 5H 79
Hopton Wafers. Shrp 3A 60
Hopwas. Staf 5F 73
Hopwood. Worc 3E 61
Horam. E Sus 4G 27
Horbling. Linc 2A 76
Horbury. W Yor 3C 92
Horcott. Glos 5G 49
Horden. Dur 5H 115
Horderley. Shrp 2G 59
Hordle. Hants 3A 16
Hordley. Shrp 2F 71
Horeb. Carm
nr. Brechfa 3F 45
nr. Llanelli 5E 45
Horeb. Cdgn 1D 45
Horfield. Bris 4A 34
Horgabost. W Isl 8C 171
Horham. Suff 3E 66
Horkstow. N Lin 3C 94
Horley. Oxon 1C 50
Horley. Surr 1D 27
Horn Ash. Dors 2G 13
Hornblotton Green. Som 3A 22
Hornby. Lanc 3E 97
Hornby. N Yor
nr. Appleton Wiske 4A 106
nr. Catterick Garrison 5F 105
Horncastle. Linc 4B 88
Hornchurch. G Lon 2G 39
Horncliffe. Nmbd 5F 131
Horndean. Hants 1F 17
Horndean. Bord 5E 131
Horndon. Devn 4F 11
Horndon on the Hill. Thur 2A 40
Horne. Surr 1E 27
Horner. Som 2C 20
Horning. Norf 4F 79
Horninghold. Leics 1F 63
Horninglow. Staf 3G 73
Horningsea. Cambs 4D 65
Horningsham. Wilts 2D 22
Horningtoft. Norf 3B 78
Hornsbury. Som 1G 13
Hornsby. Cumb 4G 113
Hornsbygate. Cumb 4G 113
Horns Corner. Kent 3B 28
Horns Cross. Devn 4D 19
Hornsea. E Yor 5G 101
Hornsea Burton. E Yor 5G 101
Hornsey. G Lon 2E 39
Hornton. Oxon 1B 50
Horpit. Swin 3H 35
Horrabridge. Devn 2B 8
Horringer. Suff 4H 65
Horringford. IOW 4D 16
Horrocks Fold. G Man 3F 91
Horrocksford. Lanc 5G 97
Horsbrugh Ford. Bord 1E 119
Horsebridge. Devn 5E 11
Horsebridge. Hants 3B 24
Horsebrook. Staf 4C 72
Horsecastle. N Som 5H 33
Horsehay. Telf 5A 72
Horseheath. Cambs 1G 53
Horsehouse. N Yor 1C 98
Horsell. Surr 5A 38
Horseman's Green. Wrex 1G 71
Horsenden. Buck 5F 51
Horseway. Cambs 2D 64
Horsey. Norf 3G 79
Horsey. Som 3G 21
Horsford. Norf 4D 78
Horsforth. W Yor 1C 92
Horsham. W Sus 2C 26
Horsham. Worc 5B 60
Horsham St Faith. Norf 4E 78
Horsington. Linc 4A 88
Horsington. Som 4C 22
Horsley. Derbs 1A 74
Horsley. Glos 2D 34
Horsley. Nmbd
nr. Prudhoe 3D 115
nr. Rochester 5C 120
Horsley Cross. Essx 3E 54
Horsleycross Street. Essx 3E 54
Horsleyhill. Bord 3H 119
Horsleyhope. Dur 5D 114
Horsley Woodhouse.
Derbs 1A 74
Horsmonden. Kent 1A 28
Horspath. Oxon 5D 50
Horstead. Norf 4E 79
Horsted Keynes. W Sus 3E 27
Horton. Buck 4H 51
Horton. Dors 2F 15
Horton. Lanc 4A 98
Horton. Nptn 5F 63
Horton. Shrp 2G 71
Horton. Som 1G 13
Horton. S Glo 3C 34
Horton. Staf 5D 84
Horton. Swan 4D 30
Horton. Wilts 5F 35
Horton. Wind 3B 38
Horton Cross. Som 1G 13
Horton-cum-Studley.
Oxon 4D 50
Horton Grange. Nmbd 2F 115
Horton Green. Ches W 1G 71
Horton Heath. Hants 1C 16
Horton in Ribblesdale.
N Yor 2H 97
Horton Kirby. Kent 4G 39
Hortonwood. Telf 4A 72
Horwich. G Man 3E 91
Horwich End. Derbs 2E 85
Horwood. Devn 4F 19
Hoscar. Lanc 3C 90
Hose. Leics 3E 75
Hosh. Per 1A 136
Hosta. W Isl 1C 170
Hoswick. Shet 9F 173
Hotham. E Yor 1B 94
Hothfield. Kent 1D 28
Hoton. Leics 3C 74
Houbie. Shet 2H 173
Hough. Arg 4A 138
Hough. Ches E
nr. Crewe 5B 84
nr. Wilmslow 3C 84
Hougham. Linc 1F 75
Hough Green. Hal 2G 83
Hough-on-the-Hill. Linc 1G 75
Houghton. Cambs 3B 64
Houghton. Cumb 4F 113
Houghton. Hants 3B 24
Houghton. Nmbd 3E 115
Houghton. Pemb 4D 43
Houghton. W Sus 4B 26
Houghton Bank. Darl 2F 105
Houghton Conquest.
C Beds 1A 52
Houghton Green. E Sus 3D 28
Houghton-le-Side. Darl 2F 105
Houghton-le-Spring.
Tyne 4G 115
Houghton on the Hill.
Leics 5D 74
Houghton Regis. C Beds 3A 52
Houghton St Giles. Norf 2B 78
Houlland. Shet
on Mainland 6E 173
on Yell 4G 173
Houlsyke. N Yor 4E 107
Houlton. Warw 3C 62
Hound. Hants 2C 16
Hound Green. Hants 1F 25
Houndslow. Bord 5C 130
Houndsmoor. Som 4E 21
Houndwood. Bord 3E 131
Hounsdown. Hants 1B 16
Hounslow. G Lon 3C 38
Housabister. Shet 6F 173
Housay. Shet 4H 173
Househill. High 3C 158
Housetter. Shet 3E 173
Houss. Shet 8E 173
Houston. Ren 3F 127
Housty. High 5D 168
Houton. Orkn 7C 172
Hove. Brig 192 (5D 27)
Hoveringham. Notts 1D 74
Hoveton. Norf 4F 79
Hovingham. N Yor 2A 100
How. Cumb 4G 113
How Caple. Here 2B 48
Howden. E Yor 2H 93
Howden-le-Wear. Dur 1E 105
Howe. High 2F 169
Howe. Norf 5E 79
Howe. N Yor 1F 99
The Howe. Cumb 1D 96
The Howe. IOM 5A 108
Howe Green. Essx 5H 53
Howe Green. Warw 2H 61
Howegreen. Essx 5B 54
Howell. Linc 1A 76

How End—Kilmore

How End. C Beds 1A 52
Howe of Teuchar. Abers 4E 161
Howes. Dum 3C 112
Howe Street. Essx
nr. Chelmsford 4G 53
nr. Finchingfield 2G 53
Howey. Powy 5C 58
Howgate. Midl 4F 129
Howgill. Lanc 5H 97
Howgill. N Yor 4C 98
How Green. Kent 1F 27
How Hill. Norf 4F 79
Howick. Nmbd 3G 121
Howle. Telf 3A 72
Howle Hill. Here 3B 48
Howleigh. Som 1F 13
Howlett End. Essx 2F 53
Howley. Som 2F 13
Howley. Warr 2A 84
Hownam. Bord 3B 120
Howsham. N Lin 4D 94
Howsham. N Yor 3B 100
Howtel. Nmbd 1C 120
Howt Green. Kent 4C 40
Howton. Here 3H 47
Howwood. Ren 3E 127
Hoxne. Suff 3D 66
Hoylake. Mers 2E 82
Hoyland. S Yor 4D 92
Hoylandswaine. S Yor 4C 92
Hoyle. W Sus 4A 26
Hubberholme. N Yor 2B 98
Hubberston. Pemb 4C 42
Hubbert's Bridge. Linc 1B 76
Huby. N Yor
nr. Harrogate 5E 99
nr. York 3H 99
Hucclecote. Glos 4D 48
Hucking. Kent 5C 40
Hucknall. Notts 1C 74
Huddersfield. W Yor 3B 92
Huddington. Worc 5D 60
Huddlesford. Staf 5F 73
Hudswell. N Yor 4E 105
Huggate. E Yor 4C 100
Hugglescote. Leics 4B 74
Hughenden Valley. Buck 2G 37
Hughley. Shrp 1H 59
Hughton. High 4G 157
Hugh Town. IOS 1B 4
Hugus. Corn 4B 6
Huish. Devn 1F 11
Huish. Wilts 5G 35
Huish Champflower.
Som 4D 20
Huish Episcopi. Som 4H 21
Huisinis. W Isl 6B 171
Hulcote. Nptn 1F 51
Hulcott. Buck 4G 51
Hulham. Devn 4D 12
Hull. Hull 196 (2E 94)
Hulland. Derbs 1G 73
Hulland Moss. Derbs 1G 73
Hulland Ward. Derbs 1G 73
Hullavington. Wilts 3D 35
Hullbridge. Essx 1C 40
Hulme. G Man 1C 84
Hulme. Staf 1D 72
Hulme End. Staf 5F 85
Hulme Walfield. Ches E 4C 84
Hulverstone. IOW 4B 16
Hulver Street. Suff 2G 67
Humber. Devn 5C 12
Humber. Here 5H 59
Humber Bridge. N Lin 2D 94
Humberside Airport.
N Lin 3D 94
Humberston. NE Lin 4G 95
Humberstone. Leic 5D 74
Humbie. E Lot 3A 130
Humbleton. E Yor 1F 95
Humbleton. Nmbd 2D 121
Humby. Linc 2H 75
Hume. Bord 5D 130
Humshaugh. Nmbd 2C 114
Huna. High 1F 169
Huncoat. Lanc 1F 91
Huncote. Leics 1C 62
Hundall. Derbs 3A 86
Hunderthwaite. Dur 2C 104
Hundleby. Linc 4C 88
Hundle Houses. Linc 5B 88
Hundleton. Pemb 4D 42
Hundon. Suff 1H 53
The Hundred. Here 4H 59
Hundred Acres. Hants 1D 16
Hundred House. Powy 5D 58
Hungarton. Leics 5D 74
Hungerford. Hants 1G 15
Hungerford. Shrp 2H 59
Hungerford. Som 2D 20
Hungerford. W Ber 5B 36
Hungerford Newtown.
W Ber 4B 36
Hunger Hill. G Man 4E 91
Hungerton. Linc 2F 75
Hungladder. High 1C 154
Hungryhatton. Shrp 3A 72
Hunmanby. N Yor 2E 101
Hunmanby Sands. N Yor 2F 101
Hunningham. Warw 4A 62
Hunnington. Worc 2D 60
Hunny Hill. IOW 4C 16
Hunsdon. Herts 4E 53
Hunsdonbury. Herts 4E 53
Hunsingore. N Yor 4G 99
Hunslet. W Yor 1D 92
Hunslet Carr. W Yor 1D 92
Hunsonby. Cumb 1G 103
Hunspow. High 1E 169
Hunstanton. Norf 1F 77
Hunstanworth. Dur 5C 114
Hunston. Suff 4B 66
Hunston. W Sus 2G 17
Hunstrete. Bath 5B 34
Hunt End. Worc 4E 61
Hunterfield. Midl 3G 129
Hunters Forstal. Kent 4F 41
Hunter's Quay. Arg 2C 126
Huntham. Som 4G 21
Hunthill Lodge. Ang 1D 144
Huntingdon. Cambs 3B 64
Huntingfield. Suff 3F 67
Huntingford. Wilts 4D 22
Huntington. Ches W 4G 83
Huntington. E Lot 2A 130
Huntington. Here 5E 59
Huntington. Staf 4D 72
Huntington. Telf 5A 72
Huntington. York 4A 100
Huntingtower. Per 1C 136
Huntley. Glos 4C 48
Huntley. Staf 1E 73
Huntly. Abers 5C 160
Huntlywood. Bord 5C 130
Hunton. Hants 3C 24
Hunton. Kent 1B 28
Hunton. N Yor 5E 105
Hunton Bridge. Herts 1B 38
Hunt's Corner. Norf 2C 66
Huntscott. Som 2C 20
Hunt's Cross. Mers 2G 83
Hunts Green. Warw 1F 61
Huntsham. Devn 4D 20
Huntshaw. Devn 4F 19
Huntspill. Som 2G 21
Huntstile. Som 3F 21
Huntworth. Som 3G 21
Hunwick. Dur 1E 105
Hunworth. Norf 2C 78
Hurcott. Som
nr. Ilminster 1G 13
nr. Somerton 4A 22
Hurdcott. Wilts 3G 23
Hurdley. Powy 1E 59
Hurdsfield. Ches E 3D 84
Hurlet. Glas 3G 127
Hurley. Warw 1G 61
Hurley. Wind 3G 37
Hurlford. E Ayr 1D 116
Hurliness. Orkn 9B 172
Hurlston Green. Lanc 3C 90
Hurn. Dors 3G 15
Hursey. Dors 2H 13
Hursley. Hants 4C 24
Hurst. G Man 4H 91
Hurst. N Yor 4D 104
Hurst. Som 1H 13
Hurst. Wok 4F 37
Hurstbourne Priors.
Hants 2C 24
Hurstbourne Tarrant.
Hants 1B 24
Hurst Green. Ches E 1H 71
Hurst Green. E Sus 3B 28
Hurst Green. Essx 4D 54
Hurst Green. Lanc 1E 91
Hurst Green. Surr 5E 39
Hurstley. Here 1G 47
Hurstpierpoint. W Sus 4D 27
Hurstway Common. Here 1G 47
Hurst Wickham. W Sus 4D 27
Hurstwood. Lanc 1G 91
Hurtmore. Surr 1A 26
Hurworth-on-Tees. Darl 3A 106
Hurworth Place. Darl 4F 105
Hury. Dur 3C 104
Husbands Bosworth.
Leics 2D 62
Husborne Crawley.
C Beds 2H 51
Husthwaite. N Yor 2H 99
Hutcherleigh. Devn 3D 9
Hut Green. N Yor 2F 93
Huthwaite. Notts 5B 86
Huttoft. Linc 3E 89
Hutton. Cumb 2F 103
Hutton. E Yor 4E 101
Hutton. Essx 1H 39
Hutton. Lanc 2C 90
Hutton. N Som 1G 21
Hutton. Bord 4F 131
Hutton Bonville. N Yor 4A 106
Hutton Buscel. N Yor 1D 100
Hutton Conyers. N Yor 2F 99
Hutton Cranswick. E Yor 4E 101
Hutton End. Cumb 1F 103
Hutton Gate. Red C 3C 106
Hutton Henry. Dur 1B 106
Hutton-le-Hole. N Yor 1B 100
Hutton Magna. Dur 3E 105
Hutton Mulgrave. N Yor 4F 107
Hutton Roof. Cumb
nr. Kirkby Lonsdale 2E 97
nr. Penrith 1E 103
Hutton Rudby. N Yor 4B 106
Huttons Ambo. N Yor 3B 100
Hutton Sessay. N Yor 2G 99
Hutton Village. Red C 3D 106
Hutton Wandesley. N Yor 4H 99
Huxham. Devn 3C 12
Huxham Green. Som 3A 22
Huxley. Ches W 4H 83
Huxter. Shet
on Mainland 6C 173
on Whalsay 5G 173
Huyton. Mers 1G 83
Hwlffordd. Pemb 3D 42
Hycemoor. Cumb 1A 96
Hyde. Glos
nr. Stroud 5D 49
nr. Winchcombe 3F 49
Hyde. G Man 1D 84
Hyde Heath. Buck 5H 51
Hyde Lea. Staf 4D 72
Hyde Park. S Yor 4F 93
Hydestile. Surr 1A 26
Hyndford Bridge. S Lan 5C 128
Hynish. Arg 5A 138
Hyssington. Powy 1F 59
Hythe. Hants 2C 16
Hythe. Kent 2F 29
Hythe End. Wind 3B 38
Hythie. Abers 3H 161
Hyton. Cumb 1A 96

I

Ianstown. Mor 2B 160
Iarsiadar. W Isl 4D 171
Ibberton. Dors 2C 14
Ible. Derbs 5G 85
Ibrox. Glas 3G 127
Ibsley. Hants 2G 15
Ibstock. Leics 4B 74
Ibstone. Buck 2F 37
Ibthorpe. Hants 1B 24
Iburndale. N Yor 4F 107
Ibworth. Hants 1D 24
Icelton. N Som 5G 33
Ichrachan. Arg 5E 141
Ickburgh. Norf 1H 65
Ickenham. G Lon 2B 38
Ickenthwaite. Cumb 1C 96
Ickford. Buck 5E 51
Ickham. Kent 5G 41
Ickleford. Herts 2B 52
Icklesham. E Sus 4C 28
Ickleton. Cambs 1E 53
Icklingham. Suff 3G 65
Ickwell. C Beds 1B 52
Icomb. Glos 3H 49
Idbury. Oxon 4H 49
Iddesleigh. Devn 2F 11
Ide. Devn 3B 12
Ideford. Devn 5B 12
Ide Hill. Kent 5F 39
Iden. E Sus 3D 28
Iden Green. Kent
nr. Benenden 2C 28
nr. Goudhurst 2B 28
Idle. W Yor 1B 92
Idless. Corn 4C 6
Idlicote. Warw 1A 50
Idmiston. Wilts 3G 23
Idole. Carm 4E 45
Idridgehay. Derbs 1G 73
Idrigill. High 2C 154
Idstone. Oxon 3A 36
Iffley. Oxon 5D 50
Ifield. W Sus 2D 26
Ifieldwood. W Sus 2D 26
Ifold. W Sus 2B 26
Iford. E Sus 5F 27
Ifton Heath. Shrp 2F 71
Ightfield. Shrp 2H 71
Ightham. Kent 5G 39
Iken. Suff 5G 67
Ilam. Staf 5F 85
Ilchester. Som 4A 22
Ilderton. Nmbd 2E 121
Ilford. G Lon 2F 39
Ilford. Som 1G 13
Ilfracombe. Devn 2F 19
Ilkeston. Derbs 1B 74
Ilketshall St Andrew. Suff 2F 67
Ilketshall St Lawrence.
Suff 2F 67
Ilketshall St Margaret.
Suff 2F 67
Ilkley. W Yor 5D 98
Illand. Corn 5C 10
Illey. W Mid 2D 61
Illidge Green. Ches E 4B 84
Illington. Norf 2B 66
Illingworth. W Yor 2A 92
Illogan. Corn 4A 6
Illogan Highway. Corn 4A 6
Illston on the Hill. Leics 1E 62
Ilmer. Buck 5F 51
Ilmington. Warw 1H 49
Ilminster. Som 1G 13
Ilsington. Devn 5A 12
Ilsington. Dors 3C 14
Ilston. Swan 3E 31
Ilton. N Yor 2D 98
Ilton. Som 1G 13
Imachar. N Ayr 5G 125
Imber. Wilts 2E 23
Immingham. NE Lin 3E 95
Immingham Dock. NE Lin 3F 95
Impington. Cambs 4D 64
Ince. Ches W 3G 83
Ince Blundell. Mers 4B 90
Ince-in-Makerfield.
G Man 4D 90
Inchbae Lodge. High 2G 157
Inchbare. Ang 2F 145
Inchberry. Mor 3H 159
Inchbraoch. Ang 3G 145
Inchbrook. Glos 5D 48
Incheril. High 2C 156
Inchinnan. Ren 3F 127
Inchlaggan. High 3D 148
Inchmichael. Per 1E 137
Inchnadamph. High 1G 163
Inchree. High 2E 141
Inchture. Per 1E 137
Inchyra. Per 1D 136
Indian Queens. Corn 3D 6
Ingatestone. Essx 1H 39
Ingbirchworth. S Yor 4C 92
Ingestre. Staf 3D 73
Ingham. Linc 2G 87
Ingham. Norf 3F 79
Ingham. Suff 3A 66
Ingham Corner. Norf 3F 79
Ingleborough. Norf 4D 76
Ingleby. Derbs 3H 73
Ingleby Arncliffe. N Yor 4B 106
Ingleby Barwick. Stoc T 3B 106
Ingleby Greenhow.
N Yor 4C 106
Ingleigh Green. Devn 2G 11
Inglemire. Hull 1D 94
Inglesbatch. Bath 5C 34
Ingleton. Dur 2E 105
Ingleton. N Yor 2F 97
Inglewhite. Lanc 5E 97
Ingoe. Nmbd 2D 114
Ingol. Lanc 1D 90
Ingoldisthorpe. Norf 2F 77
Ingoldmells. Linc 4E 89
Ingoldsby. Linc 2H 75
Ingon. Warw 5G 61
Ingram. Nmbd 3E 121
Ingrave. Essx 1H 39
Ingrow. W Yor 1A 92
Ings. Cumb 5F 103
Ingst. S Glo 3A 34
Ingthorpe. Rut 5G 75
Ingworth. Norf 3D 78
Inishrush. M Ulst 6F 174
Inkberrow. Worc 5E 61
Inkford. Worc 3E 61
Inkpen. W Ber 5B 36
Inkstack. High 1E 169
Innellan. Arg 3C 126
Inner Hope. Devn 5C 8
Innerleith. Fife 2E 137
Innerleithen. Bord 1F 119
Innerleven. Fife 3F 137
Innermessan. Dum 3F 109
Innerwick. E Lot 2D 130
Innerwick. Per 4C 142
Innsworth. Glos 3D 48
Insch. Abers 1D 152
Insh. High 3C 150
Inshegra. High 3C 166
Inshore. High 1D 166
Inskip. Lanc 1C 90
Instow. Devn 3E 19
Intwood. Norf 5D 78
Inver. Abers 4G 151
Inver. High 5F 165
Inver. Per 4H 143
Inverailort. High 5F 147
Inveralligin. High 3H 155
Inverallochy. Abers 2H 161
Inveramsay. Abers 1E 153
Inveran. High 4C 164
Inveraray. Arg 3H 133
Inverarish. High 5E 155
Inverarity. Ang 4D 144
Inverarnan. Stir 2C 134
Inverarnie. High 5A 158
Inverbeg. Arg 4C 134
Inverbervie. Abers 1H 145
Inverboyndie. Abers 2D 160
Invercassley. High 3B 164
Invercharnan. High 4F 141
Inverchoran. High 3E 157
Invercreran. Arg 4E 141
Inverdruie. High 2D 150
Inverebrie. Abers 5G 161
Invereck. Arg 1C 126
Inveresk. E Lot 2G 129
Inveresragan. Arg 5D 141
Inverey. Abers 5E 151
Inverfarigaig. High 1H 149
Invergarry. High 3F 149
Invergeldie. Per 1G 135
Invergordon. High 2B 158
Invergowrie. Per 5C 144
Inverguseran. High 3F 147
Inverharroch. Mor 5A 160
Inverie. High 3F 147
Inverinan. Arg 2G 133
Inverinate. High 1B 148
Inverkeilor. Ang 4F 145
Inverkeithing. Fife 1E 129
Inverkeithny. Abers 4D 160
Inverkip. Inv 2D 126
Inverkirkaig. High 2E 163
Inverlael. High 5F 163
Inverliever Lodge. Arg 3F 133
Inverliver. Arg 5E 141
Inverlochlarig. Stir 2D 134
Inverlochy. High 1F 141
Inverlussa. Arg 1E 125
Inver Mallie. High 5D 148
Invermarkie. Abers 5B 160
Invermoriston. High 2G 149
Invernaver. High 2H 167
Inverneil House. Arg 1G 125
Inverness. High 196 (4A 158)
Inverness Airport. High 3B 158
Invernettie. Abers 4H 161
Inverpolly Lodge. High 2E 163
Inverquhomery. Abers 4H 161
Inverroy. High 5E 149
Inversanda. High 3D 140
Invershiel. High 2B 148
Invershin. High 4C 164
Invershore. High 5E 169
Inversnaid. Stir 3C 134
Inverugie. Abers 4H 161
Inveruglas. Arg 3C 134
Inverurie. Abers 1E 153
Invervar. Per 4D 142
Inverythan. Abers 4E 161
Inwardleigh. Devn 3F 11
Inworth. Essx 4B 54
Iochdar. W Isl 4C 170
Iping. W Sus 4G 25
Ipplepen. Devn 2E 9
Ipsden. Oxon 3E 37
Ipstones. Staf 1E 73
Ipswich. Suff 196 (1E 55)
Irby. Mers 2E 83
Irby in the Marsh. Linc 4D 88
Irby upon Humber.
NE Lin 4E 95
Irchester. Nptn 4G 63
Ireby. Cumb 1D 102
Ireby. Lanc 2F 97
Ireland. Shet 9E 173
Ireleth. Cumb 2B 96
Ireshopeburn. Dur 1B 104
Ireton Wood. Derbs 1G 73
Irlam. G Man 1B 84
Irnham. Linc 3H 75
Iron Acton. S Glo 3B 34
Iron Bridge. Cambs 1D 65
Ironbridge. Telf 5A 72
Iron Cross. Warw 5E 61
Ironville. Derbs 5B 86
Irstead. Norf 3F 79
Irthington. Cumb 3F 113
Irthlingborough. Nptn 3G 63
Irton. N Yor 1E 101
Irvine. N Ayr 1C 116
Irvine Mains. N Ayr 1C 116
Irvinestown. Ferm 7E 176
Isabella Pit. Nmbd 1G 115
Isauld. High 2B 168
Isbister. Orkn 6C 172
Isbister. Shet
on Mainland 2E 173
on Whalsay 5G 173
Isfield. E Sus 4F 27
Isham. Nptn 3F 63
Island Carr. N Lin 4C 94
Islay Airport. Arg 4B 124
Isle Abbotts. Som 4G 21
Isle Brewers. Som 4G 21
Isleham. Cambs 3F 65
Isle of Man Airport.
IOM 5B 108
Isle of Thanet. Kent 4H 41
Isle of Whithorn. Dum 5B 110
Isle of Wight. IOW 4C 16
Isleornsay. High 2F 147
Islesburgh. Shet 5E 173
Isles of Scilly Airport. IOS 1B 4
Islesteps. Dum 2A 112
Isleworth. G Lon 3C 38
Isley Walton. Leics 3B 74
Islibhig. W Isl 5B 171
Islington. G Lon 2E 39
Islington. Telf 3B 72
Islip. Nptn 3G 63
Islip. Oxon 4D 50
Isombridge. Telf 4A 72
Istead Rise. Kent 4H 39
Itchen. Sotn 1C 16
Itchen Abbas. Hants 3D 24
Itchenor. W Sus 2F 17
Itchen Stoke. Hants 3D 24
Itchingfield. W Sus 3C 26
Itchington. S Glo 3B 34
Itlaw. Abers 3D 160
Itteringham. Norf 2D 78
Itteringham Common.
Norf 3D 78
Itton. Devn 3G 11
Itton Common. Mon 2H 33
Ivegill. Cumb 5F 113
Ivelet. N Yor 5C 104
Iverchaolain. Arg 2B 126
Iver Heath. Buck 2B 38
Iveston. Dur 4E 115
Ivetsey Bank. Staf 4C 72
Ivinghoe. Buck 4H 51
Ivinghoe Aston. Buck 4H 51
Ivington. Here 5G 59
Ivington Green. Here 5G 59
Ivybridge. Devn 3C 8
Ivychurch. Kent 3E 29
Ivy Hatch. Kent 5G 39
Ivy Todd. Norf 5A 78
Iwade. Kent 4D 40
Iwerne Courtney. Dors 1D 14
Iwerne Minster. Dors 1D 14
Ixworth. Suff 3B 66
Ixworth Thorpe. Suff 3B 66

J

Jackfield. Shrp 5A 72
Jack Hill. N Yor 4D 98
Jacksdale. Notts 5B 86
Jackton. S Lan 4G 127
Jacobstow. Corn 3B 10
Jacobstowe. Devn 2F 11
Jacobs Well. Surr 5A 38
Jameston. Pemb 5E 43
Jamestown. Dum 5F 119
Jamestown. Fife 1E 129
Jamestown. High 3G 157
Jamestown. W Dun 1E 127
Janetstown. High
nr. Thurso 2C 168
nr. Wick 3F 169
Jarrow. Tyne 3G 115
Jarvis Brook. E Sus 3G 27
Jasper's Green. Essx 3H 53
Jaywick. Essx 4E 55
Jedburgh. Bord 2A 120
Jeffreyston. Pemb 4E 43
Jemimaville. High 2B 158
Jenkins Park. High 3F 149
Jersey Marine. Neat 3G 31
Jesmond. Tyne 3F 115
Jevington. E Sus 5G 27
Jingle Street. Mon 4H 47
Jockey End. Herts 4A 52
Jodrell Bank. Ches E 3B 84
Johnby. Cumb 1F 103
John O'Gaunts. W Yor 2D 92
John o' Groats. High 1F 169
John's Cross. E Sus 3B 28
Johnshaven. Abers 2G 145
Johnson Street. Norf 4F 79
Johnston. Pemb 3D 42
Johnstone. Ren 3F 127
Johnstonebridge. Dum 5C 118
Johnstown. Carm 4E 45
Johnstown. Wrex 1F 71
Jonesborough. New M 8E 178
Joppa. Edin 2G 129
Joppa. S Ayr 3D 116
Jordan Green. Norf 3C 78
Jordans. Buck 1A 38
Jordanston. Pemb 1D 42
Jump. S Yor 4D 93
Jumpers Common. Dors 3G 15
Juniper. Nmbd 4C 114
Juniper Green. Edin 3E 129
Jurby East. IOM 2C 108
Jurby West. IOM 2C 108
Jury's Gap. E Sus 4D 28

K

Kaber. Cumb 3A 104
Kaimend. S Lan 5C 128
Kaimes. Edin 3F 129
Kaimrig End. Bord 5D 129
Kames. Arg 2A 126
Kames. E Ayr 2F 117
Katesbridge. Arm 5G 179
Kea. Corn 4C 6
Keadby. N Lin 3B 94
Keady. Arm 6C 178
Keal Cotes. Linc 4C 88
Kearsley. G Man 4F 91
Kearsney. Kent 1G 29
Kearstwick. Cumb 1F 97
Kearton. N Yor 5C 104
Kearvaig. High 1C 166
Keasden. N Yor 3G 97
Keason. Corn 2H 7
Keckwick. Hal 2H 83
Keddington. Linc 2C 88
Keddington Corner. Linc 2C 88
Kedington. Suff 1H 53
Kedleston. Derbs 1H 73
Kedlock Feus. Fife 2F 137
Keekle. Cumb 3B 102
Keelby. Linc 3E 95
Keele. Staf 1C 72
Keeley Green. Bed 1A 52
Keeston. Pemb 3D 42
Keevil. Wilts 1E 23
Kegworth. Leics 3B 74
Kehelland. Corn 2D 4
Keig. Abers 2D 152
Keighley. W Yor 5C 98
Keilarsbrae. Clac 4A 136
Keillmore. Arg 1E 125
Keillor. Per 4B 144
Keillour. Per 1B 136
Keills. Arg 3C 124
Keiloch. Abers 4F 151
Keils. Arg 3D 124
Keinton Mandeville. Som 3A 22
Keir Mill. Dum 5A 118
Keirsleywell Row. Nmbd 4A 114
Keisby. Linc 3H 75
Keisley. Cumb 2A 104
Keiss. High 2F 169
Keith. Mor 3B 160
Keith Inch. Abers 4H 161
Kelbrook. Lanc 5B 98
Kelby. Linc 1H 75
Keld. Cumb 3G 103
Keld. N Yor 4B 104
Keldholme. N Yor 1B 100
Kelfield. N Lin 4B 94
Kelfield. N Yor 1F 93
Kelham. Notts 5E 87
Kellacott. Devn 4E 11
Kellan. Arg 4G 139
Kellas. Ang 5D 144
Kellas. Mor 3F 159
Kellaton. Devn 5E 9
Kelleth. Cumb 4H 103
Kelling. Norf 1C 78
Kellingley. N Yor 2F 93
Kellington. N Yor 2F 93
Kelloe. Dur 1A 106
Kelloholm. Dum 3G 117
Kells. Cumb 3A 102
Kells. ME Ant 7H 175
Kelly. Devn 4D 11
Kelly Bray. Corn 5D 10
Kelmarsh. Nptn 3E 63
Kelmscott. Oxon 2H 35
Kelsale. Suff 4F 67
Kelsall. Ches W 4H 83
Kelshall. Herts 2D 52
Kelsick. Cumb 4C 112
Kelso. Bord 1B 120
Kelstedge. Derbs 4H 85
Kelstern. Linc 1B 88
Kelsterton. Flin 3E 83
Kelston. Bath 5C 34
Keltneyburn. Per 4E 143
Kelton. Dum 2A 112
Kelton Hill. Dum 4E 111
Kelty. Fife 4D 136
Kelvedon. Essx 4B 54
Kelvedon Hatch. Essx 1G 39
Kelvinside. Glas 3G 127
Kelynack. Corn 3A 4
Kemback. Fife 2G 137
Kemberton. Shrp 5B 72
Kemble. Glos 2E 35
Kemerton. Worc 2E 49
Kemeys Commander.
Mon 5G 47
Kemnay. Abers 2E 153
Kempe's Corner. Kent 1E 29
Kempley. Glos 3B 48
Kempley Green. Glos 3B 48
Kempsey. Worc 1D 48
Kempsford. Glos 2G 35
Kemps Green. Warw 3F 61
Kempshott. Hants 2E 24
Kempston. Bed 1A 52
Kempston Hardwick. Bed 1A 52
Kempton. Shrp 2F 59
Kemp Town. Brig 5E 27
Kemsing. Kent 5G 39
Kemsley. Kent 4D 40
Kenardington. Kent 2D 28
Kenchester. Here 1H 47
Kencot. Oxon 5A 50
Kendal. Cumb 5G 103
Kendleshire. S Glo 4B 34
Kendray. S Yor 4D 92
Kenfig. B'end 3B 32
Kenfig Hill. B'end 3B 32
Kengharair. Arg 4F 139
Kenilworth. Warw 3G 61
Kenknock. Stir 5B 142
Kenley. G Lon 5E 39
Kenley. Shrp 5H 71
Kenmore. High 3G 155
Kenmore. Per 4E 143
Kenn. Devn 4C 12
Kenn. N Som 5H 33
Kennacraig. Arg 3G 125
Kenneggy Downs. Corn 4C 4
Kennerleigh. Devn 2B 12
Kennet. Clac 4B 136
Kennethmont. Abers 1C 152
Kennett. Cambs 4G 65
Kennford. Devn 4C 12
Kenninghall. Norf 2C 66
Kennington. Kent 1E 28
Kennington. Oxon 5D 50
Kennoway. Fife 3F 137
Kennyhill. Suff 3F 65
Kennythorpe. N Yor 3B 100
Kenovay. Arg 4A 138
Kensaleyre. High 3D 154
Kensington. G Lon 3D 38
Kenstone. Shrp 3H 71
Kensworth. C Beds 4A 52
Kensworth Common.
C Beds 4A 52
Kentallen. High 3E 141
Kentchurch. Here 3H 47
Kentford. Suff 4G 65
Kentisbeare. Devn 2D 12
Kentisbury. Devn 2G 19
Kentisbury Ford. Devn 2G 19
Kentmere. Cumb 4F 103
Kenton. Devn 4C 12
Kenton. G Lon 2C 38
Kenton. Suff 4D 66
Kenton Bankfoot. Tyne 3F 115
Kentra. High 2A 140
Kentrigg. Cumb 5G 103
Kents Bank. Cumb 2C 96
Kent's Green. Glos 3C 48
Kent's Oak. Hants 4B 24
Kent Street. E Sus 4B 28
Kent Street. Kent 5A 40
Kent Street. W Sus 3D 26
Kenwick. Shrp 2G 71
Kenwyn. Corn 4C 6
Kenyon. Warr 1A 84
Keoldale. High 2D 166
Keppoch. High 1B 148
Kepwick. N Yor 5B 106
Keresley. W Mid 2H 61
Keresley Newland. Warw 2H 61
Keristal. IOM 4C 108
Kerne Bridge. Here 4A 48
Kerridge. Ches E 3D 84
Kerris. Corn 4B 4
Kerrow. High 5F 157
Kerry. Powy 2D 58
Kerrycroy. Arg 3C 126
Kerry's Gate. Here 2G 47
Kersall. Notts 4E 86
Kersbrook. Devn 4D 12
Kerse. Ren 4E 127
Kersey. Suff 1D 54
Kershopefoot. Cumb 1F 113
Kersoe. Worc 1E 49
Kerswell. Devn 2D 12
Kerswell Green. Worc 1D 48
Kesgrave. Suff 1F 55
Kesh. Ferm 6D 176
Kessingland. Suff 2H 67
Kessingland Beach. Suff 2H 67
Kestle. Corn 4D 6
Kestle Mill. Corn 3C 6
Keston. G Lon 4F 39
Keswick. Cumb 2D 102
Keswick. Norf
nr. North Walsham 2F 79
nr. Norwich 5E 78
Ketsby. Linc 3C 88
Kettering. Nptn 3F 63
Ketteringham. Norf 5D 78
Kettins. Per 5B 144
Kettlebaston. Suff 5B 66
Kettlebridge. Fife 3F 137
Kettlebrook. Staf 5G 73
Kettleburgh. Suff 4E 67
Kettleholm. Dum 2C 112
Kettleness. N Yor 3F 107
Kettleshulme. Ches E 3D 85
Kettlesing. N Yor 4E 98
Kettlesing Bottom. N Yor 4E 99
Kettlestone. Norf 2B 78
Kettlethorpe. Linc 3F 87
Kettletoft. Orkn 4F 172
Kettlewell. N Yor 2B 98
Ketton. Rut 5G 75
Kew. G Lon 3C 38
Kewaigue. IOM 4C 108
Kewstoke. N Som 5G 33
Kexbrough. S Yor 4C 92
Kexby. Linc 2F 87
Kexby. York 4B 100
Keyford. Som 2C 22
Key Green. Ches E 4C 84
Key Green. N Yor 4F 107
Keyham. Leics 5D 74
Keyhaven. Hants 3B 16
Keyhead. Abers 3H 161
Keyingham. E Yor 2F 95
Keymer. W Sus 4E 27
Keynsham. Bath 5B 34
Keysoe. Bed 4H 63
Keysoe Row. Bed 4H 63
Key's Toft. Linc 5D 89
Keyston. Cambs 3H 63
Key Street. Kent 4C 40
Keyworth. Notts 2D 74
Kibblesworth. Tyne 4F 115
Kibworth Beauchamp.
Leics 1D 62
Kibworth Harcourt. Leics 1D 62
Kidbrooke. G Lon 3F 39
Kidburngill. Cumb 2B 102
Kiddemore Green. Staf 5C 72
Kidderminster. Worc 3C 60
Kiddington. Oxon 3C 50
Kidd's Moor. Norf 5D 78
Kidlington. Oxon 4C 50
Kidmore End. Oxon 4E 37
Kidnal. Ches W 1G 71
Kidsgrove. Staf 5C 84
Kidstones. N Yor 1B 98
Kidwelly. Carm 5E 45
Kiel Crofts. Arg 5D 140
Kielder. Nmbd 5A 120
Kilbagie. Fife 4B 136
Kilbarchan. Ren 3F 127
Kilbeg. High 3E 147
Kilberry. Arg 3F 125
Kilbirnie. N Ayr 4E 126
Kilbride. Arg 1F 133
Kilbride. High 1D 147
Kilbucho Place. Bord 1C 118
Kilburn. Derbs 1A 74
Kilburn. G Lon 2D 38
Kilburn. N Yor 2H 99
Kilby. Leics 1D 62
Kilchattan. Arg 4A 132
Kilchattan Bay. Arg 4C 126
Kilchenzie. Arg 3A 122
Kilcheran. Arg 5C 140
Kilchiaran. Arg 3A 124
Kilchoan. High
nr. Inverie 4F 147
nr. Tobermory 2F 139
Kilchoman. Arg 3A 124
Kilchrenan. Arg 1H 133
Kilclief. New M 5K 179
Kilconquhar. Fife 3G 137
Kilcoo. New M 6G 179
Kilcot. Glos 3B 48
Kilcoy. High 3H 157
Kilcreggan. Arg 1D 126
Kildale. N Yor 4D 106
Kildary. High 1B 158
Kildermorie Lodge. High 1H 157
Kildonan. Dum 4F 109
Kildonan. High
nr. Helmsdale 1G 165
on Isle of Skye 3C 154
Kildonan. N Ayr 3E 123
Kildonnan. High 5C 146
Kildrummy. Abers 2B 152
Kildwick. N Yor 5C 98
Kilfillan. Dum 4H 109
Kilfinan. Arg 2H 125
Kilfinnan. High 4E 149
Kilgetty. Pemb 4F 43
Kilgour. Fife 3E 136
Kilgrammie. S Ayr 4B 116
Kilham. E Yor 3E 101
Kilham. Nmbd 1C 120
Kilkeel. New M 8H 179
Kilkenneth. Arg 4A 138
Kilkhampton. Corn 1C 10
Killadeas. Ferm 7E 176
Killamarsh. Derbs 2B 86
Killandrist. Arg 4C 140
Killay. Swan 3F 31
Killean. Arg 5E 125
Killearn. Stir 1G 127
Killeen. M Ulst 3C 178
Killellan. Arg 4A 122
Killen. Derr 4E 176
Killen. High 3A 158
Killerby. Darl 3E 105
Killeter. Derr 4E 176
Killichonan. Per 3C 142
Killiechronan. Arg 4G 139
Killiecrankie. Per 2G 143
Killilan. High 5B 156
Killimster. High 3F 169
Killin. Stir 5C 142
Killinchy. Ards 3K 179
Killinghall. N Yor 4E 99
Killington. Cumb 1F 97
Killingworth. Tyne 2F 115
Killin Lodge. High 3H 149
Killinochonoch. Arg 4F 133
Killochyett. Bord 5A 130
Killough. New M 6K 179
Killowen. New M 8F 179
Killundine. High 4G 139
Killyleagh. New M 4K 179
Killyrammer. Caus 4F 175
Kilmacolm. Inv 3E 127
Kilmahog. Stir 3F 135
Kilmahumaig. Arg 4E 133
Kilmalieu. High 3C 140
Kilmaluag. High 1D 154
Kilmany. Fife 1F 137
Kilmarie. High 2D 146
Kilmarnock. E Ayr 196 (1D 116)
Kilmaron. Fife 2F 137
Kilmartin. Arg 4F 133
Kilmaurs. E Ayr 5F 127
Kilmelford. Arg 2F 133
Kilmeny. Arg 3B 124
Kilmersdon. Som 1B 22
Kilmeston. Hants 4D 24
Kilmichael Glassary. Arg 4F 133
Kilmichael of Inverlussa.
Arg 1F 125
Kilmington. Devn 3F 13
Kilmington. Wilts 3C 22
Kilmoluaig. Arg 4A 138
Kilmorack. High 4G 157
Kilmore. Arg 1F 133

Kilmore—Lea

Kilmore. Arm 4D 178
Kilmore. High 3E 147
Kilmore. New M 4J 179
Kilmory. Arg 2F 125
Kilmory. High
nr. Kilchoan 1G 139
on Rùm 3B 146
Kilmory. N Ayr 3D 122
Kilmory Lodge. Arg 3E 132
Kilmote. High 2G 165
Kilmuir. High
nr. Dunvegan 4B 154
nr. Invergordon 1B 158
nr. Inverness 4A 158
nr. Uig 1C 154
Kilmun. Arg 1C 126
Kilnave. Arg 2A 124
Kilncadzow. S Lan 5B 128
Kilndown. Kent 2B 28
Kiln Green. Here 4B 48
Kiln Green. Wok 4G 37
Kilnhill. Cumb 1D 102
Kilnhurst. S Yor 1B 86
Kilninian. Arg 4E 139
Kilninver. Arg 1F 133
Kiln Pit Hill. Nmbd 4D 114
Kilnsea. E Yor 3H 95
Kilnsey. N Yor 3B 98
Kilnwick. E Yor 5D 101
Kiloran. Arg 4A 132
Kilpatrick. N Ayr 3D 122
Kilpeck. Here 2H 47
Kilpin. E Yor 2A 94
Kilpin Pike. E Yor 2A 94
Kilrea. Caus 5F 174
Kilrenny. Fife 3H 137
Kilsby. Nptn 3C 62
Kilspindie. Per 1E 136
Kilsyth. N Lan 2A 128
Kiltarlity. High 4H 157
Kilton. Som 2E 21
Kilton Thorpe. Red C 3D 107
Kilvaxter. High 2C 154
Kilve. Som 2E 21
Kilvington. Notts 1F 75
Kilwinning. N Ayr 5D 126
Kimberley. Norf 5C 78
Kimberley. Notts 1B 74
Kimblesworth. Dur 5F 115
Kimble Wick. Buck 5G 51
Kimbolton. Cambs 4H 63
Kimbolton. Here 4H 59
Kimcote. Leics 2C 62
Kimmeridge. Dors 5E 15
Kimmerston. Nmbd 1D 120
Kimpton. Hants 2A 24
Kimpton. Herts 4B 52
Kinallen. Arm 5G 179
Kinawley. Ferm 6H 177
Kinbeachie. High 2A 158
Kinbrace. High 5A 168
Kinbuck. Stir 3G 135
Kincaple. Fife 2G 137
Kincardine. Fife 1C 128
Kincardine. High 5D 164
Kincardine Bridge. Falk 1C 128
Kincardine O'Neil. Abers 4C 152
Kinchrackine. Arg 1A 134
Kincorth. Aber 3G 153
Kincraig. High 3C 150
Kincraigie. Per 4G 143
Kindallachan. Per 3G 143
Kineton. Glos 3F 49
Kineton. Warw 5H 61
Kinfauns. Per 1D 136
Kingairloch. High 3C 140
Kingarth. Arg 4B 126
Kingcoed. Mon 5H 47
King Edward. Abers 3E 160
Kingerby. Linc 1H 87
Kingham. Oxon 3A 50
Kingholm Quay. Dum 2A 112
Kinghorn. Fife 1F 129
Kingie. High 3D 148
Kinglassie. Fife 4E 137
Kingledores. Bord 2D 118
King o' Muirs. Clac 4A 136
Kingoodie. Per 1F 137
King's Acre. Here 1H 47
Kingsand. Corn 3A 8
Kingsash. Buck 5G 51
Kingsbarns. Fife 2H 137
Kingsbridge. Devn 4D 8
Kingsbridge. Som 3C 20
King's Bromley. Staf 4F 73
Kingsburgh. High 3C 154
Kingsbury. G Lon 2C 38
Kingsbury. Warw 1G 61
Kingsbury Episcopi. Som 4H 21
Kings Caple. Here 3A 48
Kingscavil. W Lot 2D 128
Kingsclere. Hants 1D 24
King's Cliffe. Nptn 1H 63
Kings Clipstone. Notts 4D 86
Kingscote. Glos 2D 34
Kingscott. Devn 1F 11
Kings Coughton. Warw 5E 61
Kingscross. N Ayr 3E 123
Kingsdon. Som 4A 22
Kingsdown. Kent 1H 29
Kingsdown. Swin 3G 35
Kingsdown. Wilts 5D 34
Kingseat. Fife 4D 136
Kingsey. Buck 5F 51
Kingsfold. Lanc 2D 90
Kingsfold. W Sus 2C 26
Kingsford. E Ayr 5F 127
Kingsford. Worc 2C 60
Kingsforth. N Lin 3D 94
Kingsgate. Kent 3H 41
King's Green. Glos 2C 48
Kingshall Street. Suff 4B 66
Kingsheanton. Devn 3F 19
King's Heath. W Mid 2E 61
Kings Hill. Kent 5A 40
Kingsholm. Glos 4D 48
Kingshouse. High 3G 141
Kingshouse. Stir 1E 135
Kingshurst. W Mid 2F 61
Kingskerswell. Devn 2E 9
Kingskettle. Fife 3F 137
Kingsland. Here 4G 59
Kingsland. IOA 2B 80
Kings Langley. Herts 5A 52
Kingsley. Ches W 3H 83
Kingsley. Hants 3F 25
Kingsley. Staf 1E 73
Kingsley Green. W Sus 3G 25
Kingsley Holt. Staf 1E 73
King's Lynn. Norf 3F 77
King's Meaburn. Cumb 2H 103
Kings Moss. Mers 4D 90
Kings Muir. Bord 1E 119
Kingsmuir. Ang 4D 145
Kingsmuir. Fife 3H 137
King's Newnham. Warw 3B 62
King's Newton. Derbs 3A 74
Kingsnorth. Kent 2E 28
Kingsnorth. Medw 3C 40
King's Norton. Leics 5D 74
King's Norton. W Mid 3E 61
King's Nympton. Devn 1G 11
King's Pyon. Here 5G 59
Kings Ripton. Cambs 3B 64
King's Somborne. Hants 3B 24
King's Stag. Dors 1C 14
King's Stanley. Glos 5D 48
King's Sutton. Nptn 2C 50
Kingstanding. W Mid 1E 61
Kingsteignton. Devn 5B 12
Kingsteps. High 3D 158
King Sterndale. Derbs 3E 85
King's Thorn. Here 2A 48
Kingsthorpe. Nptn 4E 63
Kingston. Cambs 5C 64
Kingston. Devn 4C 8
Kingston. Dors
nr. Sturminster Newton 2C 14
nr. Swanage 5E 15
Kingston. E Lot 1B 130
Kingston. Hants 2G 15
Kingston. IOW 4C 16
Kingston. Kent 5F 41
Kingston. Mor 2H 159
Kingston. W Sus 5B 26
Kingston Bagpuize. Oxon 2C 36
Kingston Blount. Oxon 2F 37
Kingston by Sea. W Sus 5D 26
Kingston Deverill. Wilts 3D 22
Kingstone. Here 2H 47
Kingstone. Som 1G 13
Kingstone. Staf 3E 73
Kingston Lisle. Oxon 3B 36
Kingston Maurward. Dors 3C 14
Kingston near Lewes.
E Sus 5E 27
Kingston on Soar. Notts 3C 74
Kingston Russell. Dors 3A 14
Kingston St Mary. Som 4F 21
Kingston Seymour. N Som 5H 33
Kingston Stert. Oxon 5F 51
Kingston upon Hull.
Hull 196 (2E 94)
Kingston upon Thames.
G Lon 4C 38
King's Walden. Herts 3B 52
Kingswear. Devn 3E 9
Kingswells. Aber 3F 153
Kingswinford. W Mid 2C 60
Kingswood. Buck 4E 51
Kingswood. Glos 2C 34
Kingswood. Here 5E 59
Kingswood. Kent 5C 40
Kingswood. Per 5H 143
Kingswood. Powy 5E 71
Kingswood. Som 3E 20
Kingswood. S Glo 4B 34
Kingswood. Surr 5D 38
Kingswood. Warw 3F 61
Kingswood Common. Staf 5C 72
Kings Worthy. Hants 3C 24
Kingthorpe. Linc 3A 88
Kington. Here 5E 59
Kington. S Glo 2B 34
Kington. Worc 5D 61
Kington Langley. Wilts 4E 35
Kington Magna. Dors 4C 22
Kington St Michael. Wilts 4E 35
Kingussie. High 3B 150
Kingweston. Som 3A 22
Kinharrachie. Abers 5G 161
Kinhrive. High 1A 158
Kinkell Bridge. Per 2B 136
Kinknockie. Abers 4H 161
Kinkry Hill. Cumb 2G 113
Kinlet. Shrp 2B 60
Kinloch. High
nr. Lochaline 3A 140
nr. Loch More 5D 166
on Rùm 4B 146
Kinloch. Per 4A 144
Kinlochard. Stir 3D 134
Kinlochbervie. High 3C 166
Kinlocheil. High 1D 140
Kinlochewe. High 2C 156
Kinloch Hourn. High 3B 148
Kinloch Laggan. High 5H 149
Kinlochleven. High 2F 141
Kinloch Lodge. High 3F 167
Kinlochmoidart. High 1B 140
Kinlochmore. High 2F 141
Kinloch Rannoch. Per 3D 142
Kinlochspelve. Arg 1D 132
Kinloid. High 5E 147
Kinloss. Mor 2E 159
Kinmel Bay. Cnwy 2B 82
Kinmuck. Abers 2F 153
Kinnadie. Abers 4G 161
Kinnaird. Per 1E 137
Kinneff. Abers 1H 145
Kinnelhead. Dum 4C 118
Kinnell. Ang 3F 145
Kinnerley. Shrp 3F 71
Kinnernie. Abers 2E 152
Kinnersley. Here 1G 47
Kinnersley. Worc 1D 48
Kinnerton. Powy 4E 59
Kinnerton. Shrp 1F 59
Kinnesswood. Per 3D 136
Kinninvie. Dur 2D 104
Kinnordy. Ang 3C 144
Kinoulton. Notts 2D 74
Kinross. Per 3D 136
Kinrossie. Per 5A 144
Kinsbourne Green. Herts 4B 52
Kinsey Heath. Ches E 1A 72
Kinsham. Here 4F 59
Kinsham. Worc 2E 49
Kinsley. W Yor 3E 93
Kinson. Bour 3F 15
Kintbury. W Ber 5B 36
Kintessack. Mor 2E 159
Kintillo. Per 2D 136
Kinton. Here 3G 59
Kinton. Shrp 4F 71
Kintore. Abers 2E 153
Kintour. Arg 4C 124
Kintra. Arg 2B 132
Kintraw. Arg 3F 133
Kinveachy. High 2D 150
Kinver. Staf 2C 60
Kinwarton. Warw 5F 61
Kiplingcotes. E Yor 5D 100
Kippax. W Yor 1E 93
Kippen. Stir 4F 135
Kippford. Dum 4F 111
Kipping's Cross. Kent 1H 27
Kirbister. Orkn
nr. Hobbister 7C 172
nr. Quholm 6B 172
Kirbuster. Orkn 5F 172
Kirby Bedon. Norf 5E 79
Kirby Bellars. Leics 4E 74
Kirby Cane. Norf 1F 67
Kirby Cross. Essx 3F 55
Kirby Fields. Leics 5C 74
Kirby Green. Norf 1F 67
Kirby Grindalythe. N Yor 3D 100
Kirby Hill. N Yor
nr. Richmond 4E 105
nr. Ripon 3F 99
Kirby Knowle. N Yor 1G 99
Kirby-le-Soken. Essx 3F 55
Kirby Misperton. N Yor 2B 100
Kirby Muxloe. Leics 5C 74
Kirby Sigston. N Yor 5B 106
Kirby Underdale. E Yor 4C 100
Kirby Wiske. N Yor 1F 99
Kircubbin. Ards 3L 179
Kirdford. W Sus 3B 26
Kirk. High 3E 169
Kirkabister. Shet
on Bressay 8F 173
on Mainland 6F 173
Kirkandrews. Dum 5D 110
Kirkandrews-on-Eden.
Cumb 4E 113
Kirkapol. Arg 4B 138
Kirkbampton. Cumb 4E 112
Kirkbean. Dum 4A 112
Kirk Bramwith. S Yor 3G 93
Kirkbride. Cumb 4D 112
Kirkbridge. N Yor 5F 105
Kirkbuddo. Ang 4E 145
Kirkburn. E Yor 4D 101
Kirkburton. W Yor 3B 92
Kirkby. Linc 1H 87
Kirkby. Mers 1G 83
Kirkby. N Yor 4C 106
Kirkby Fenside. Linc 4C 88
Kirkby Fleetham. N Yor 5F 105
Kirkby Green. Linc 5H 87
Kirkby-in-Ashfield.
Notts 5C 86
Kirkby-in-Furness. Cumb 1B 96
Kirkby la Thorpe. Linc 1A 76
Kirkby Lonsdale. Cumb 2F 97
Kirkby Malham. N Yor 3A 98
Kirkby Mallory. Leics 5B 74
Kirkby Malzeard. N Yor 2E 99
Kirkby Mills. N Yor 1B 100
Kirkbymoorside. N Yor 1A 100
Kirkby on Bain. Linc 4B 88
Kirkby Overblow. N Yor 5F 99
Kirkby Stephen. Cumb 4A 104
Kirkby Thore. Cumb 2H 103
Kirkby Underwood. Linc 3H 75
Kirkby Wharfe. N Yor 5H 99
Kirkcaldy. Fife 4E 137
Kirkcambeck. Cumb 3G 113
Kirkcolm. Dum 3F 109
Kirkconnel. Dum 3G 117
Kirkconnell. Dum 3A 112
Kirkcowan. Dum 3A 110
Kirkcudbright. Dum 4D 111
Kirkdale. Mers 1F 83
Kirk Deighton. N Yor 4F 99
Kirk Ella. E Yor 2D 94
Kirkfieldbank. S Lan 5B 128
Kirkforthar Feus. Fife 3E 137
Kirkgunzeon. Dum 3F 111
Kirk Hallam. Derbs 1B 74
Kirkham. Lanc 1C 90
Kirkham. N Yor 3B 100
Kirkhamgate. W Yor 2C 92
Kirk Hammerton. N Yor 4G 99
Kirkharle. Nmbd 1D 114
Kirkheaton. Nmbd 2D 114
Kirkheaton. W Yor 3B 92
Kirkhill. Ang 2F 145
Kirkhill. High 4H 157
Kirkhope. S Lan 4B 118
Kirkhouse. Bord 1F 119
Kirkibost. High 2D 146
Kirkinch. Ang 4C 144
Kirkinner. Dum 4B 110
Kirkintilloch. E Dun 2H 127
Kirk Ireton. Derbs 5G 85
Kirkland. Cumb
nr. Cleator Moor 3B 102
nr. Penrith 1H 103
nr. Wigton 5D 112
Kirkland. Dum
nr. Kirkconnel 3G 117
nr. Moniaive 5H 117
Kirkland Guards. Cumb 5C 112
Kirk Langley. Derbs 2G 73
Kirklauchline. Dum 4F 109
Kirkleatham. Red C 2C 106
Kirklevington. Stoc T 4B 106
Kirkley. Suff 1H 67
Kirklington. N Yor 1F 99
Kirklington. Notts 5D 86
Kirklinton. Cumb 3F 113
Kirkliston. Edin 2E 129
Kirkmabreck. Dum 4B 110
Kirkmaiden. Dum 5E 109
Kirk Merrington. Dur 1F 105
Kirk Michael. IOM 2C 108
Kirkmichael. Per 2H 143
Kirkmichael. S Ayr 4C 116
Kirkmuirhill. S Lan 5A 128
Kirknewton. Nmbd 1D 120
Kirknewton. W Lot 3E 129
Kirkney. Abers 5C 160
Kirk of Shotts. N Lan 3B 128
Kirkoswald. Cumb 5G 113
Kirkoswald. S Ayr 4B 116
Kirkpatrick. Dum 5B 118
Kirkpatrick Durham.
Dum 2E 111
Kirkpatrick-Fleming.
Dum 2D 112
Kirk Sandall. S Yor 4G 93
Kirksanton. Cumb 1A 96
Kirk Smeaton. N Yor 3F 93
Kirkstall. W Yor 1C 92
Kirkstile. Dum 5F 119
Kirkstyle. High 1F 169
Kirkthorpe. W Yor 2D 92
Kirkton. Abers
nr. Alford 2D 152
nr. Insch 1D 152
nr. Turriff 4F 161
Kirkton. Ang
nr. Dundee 5D 144
nr. Forfar 4D 144
nr. Tarfside 5B 152
Kirkton. Dum 1A 112
Kirkton. Fife 1F 137
Kirkton. High
nr. Golspie 4E 165
nr. Kyle of Lochalsh 1G 147
nr. Lochcarron 4B 156
Kirkton. Bord 3H 119
Kirkton. S Lan 2B 118
Kirktonhill. W Dun 2E 127
Kirkton Manor. Bord 1E 118
Kirkton of Airlie. Ang 3C 144
Kirkton of Auchterhouse.
Ang 5C 144
Kirkton of Bourtie. Abers 1F 153
Kirkton of Collace. Per 5A 144
Kirkton of Craig. Ang 3G 145
Kirkton of Culsalmond.
Abers 5D 160
Kirkton of Durris. Abers 4E 153
Kirkton of Glenbuchat.
Abers 2A 152
Kirkton of Glenisla. Ang 2B 144
Kirkton of Kingoldrum.
Ang 3C 144
Kirkton of Largo. Fife 3G 137
Kirkton of Lethendy. Per 4A 144
Kirkton of Logie Buchan.
Abers 1G 153
Kirkton of Maryculter.
Abers 4F 153
Kirkton of Menmuir. Ang 2E 145
Kirkton of Monikie. Ang 5E 145
Kirkton of Oyne. Abers 1D 152
Kirkton of Rayne. Abers 5D 160
Kirkton of Skene. Abers 3F 153
Kirktown. Abers
nr. Fraserburgh 2G 161
nr. Peterhead 3H 161
Kirktown of Alvah. Abers 2D 160
Kirktown of Auchterless.
Abers 4E 160
Kirktown of Deskford.
Mor 2C 160
Kirktown of Fetteresso.
Abers 5F 153
Kirktown of Mortlach.
Mor 5H 159
Kirktown of Slains.
Abers 1H 153
Kirkurd. Bord 5E 129
Kirkwall. Orkn 6D 172
Kirkwall Airport. Orkn 7D 172
Kirkwhelpington. Nmbd 1C 114
Kirk Yetholm. Bord 2C 120
Kirmington. N Lin 3E 94
Kirmond le Mire. Linc 1A 88
Kirn. Arg 2C 126
Kirriemuir. Ang 3C 144
Kirstead Green. Norf 1E 67
Kirtlebridge. Dum 2D 112
Kirtleton. Dum 2D 112
Kirtling. Cambs 5F 65
Kirtling Green. Cambs 5F 65
Kirtlington. Oxon 4D 50
Kirtomy. High 2H 167
Kirton. Linc 2C 76
Kirton. Notts 4D 86
Kirton. Suff 2F 55
Kirton End. Linc 1B 76
Kirton Holme. Linc 1B 76
Kirton in Lindsey. N Lin 1G 87
Kishorn. High 4H 155
Kislingbury. Nptn 5D 62
Kites Hardwick. Warw 4B 62
Kittisford. Som 4D 20
Kittle. Swan 4E 31
Kittybrewster. Aber 3G 153
Kitwood. Hants 3E 25
Kivernoll. Here 2H 47
Kiveton Park. S Yor 2B 86
Knaith. Linc 2F 87
Knaith Park. Linc 2F 87
Knaphill. Surr 5A 38
Knapp. Hants 4C 24
Knapp. Per 5B 144
Knapp. Som 4G 21
Knapperfield. High 3E 169
Knapton. Norf 2F 79
Knapton. York 4H 99
Knapton Green. Here 5G 59
Knapwell. Cambs 4C 64
Knaresborough. N Yor 4F 99
Knarsdale. Nmbd 4H 113
Knatts Valley. Kent 4G 39
Knaven. Abers 4F 161
Knayton. N Yor 1G 99
Knebworth. Herts 3C 52
Knedlington. E Yor 2H 93
Kneesall. Notts 4E 86
Kneesworth. Cambs 1D 52
Kneeton. Notts 1E 74
Knelston. Swan 4D 30
Knenhall. Staf 2D 72
Knightacott. Devn 3G 19
Knightcote. Warw 5B 62
Knightcott. N Som 1G 21
Knightley. Staf 3C 72
Knightley Dale. Staf 3C 72
Knightlow Hill. Warw 3B 62
Knighton. Devn 4B 8
Knighton. Dors 1B 14
Knighton. Leic 5C 74
Knighton. Powy 3E 59
Knighton. Som 2E 21
Knighton. Staf
nr. Eccleshall 3B 72
nr. Woore 1B 72
Knighton. Wilts 4A 36
Knighton. Worc 5E 61
Knighton Common.
Worc 3A 60
Knight's End. Cambs 1D 64
Knightswood. Glas 3G 127
Knightwick. Worc 5B 60
Knill. Here 4E 59
Knipton. Leics 2F 75
Knitsley. Dur 5E 115
Kniveton. Derbs 5G 85
Knock. Arg 5G 139
Knock. Cumb 2H 103
Knock. Mor 3C 160
Knockally. High 5D 168
Knockan. Arg 1B 132
Knockan. High 2G 163
Knockandhu. Mor 1G 151
Knockando. Mor 4F 159
Knockarthur. High 3E 165
Knockbain. High 3A 158
Knockbreck. High 2B 154
Knockcloghrim. M Ulst 7E 174
Knockdee. High 2D 168
Knockdolian. S Ayr 1G 109
Knockdon. S Ayr 3C 116
Knockdown. Glos 3D 34
Knockenbaird. Abers 1D 152
Knockenkelly. N Ayr 3E 123
Knockentiber. E Ayr 1C 116
Knockfarrel. High 3H 157
Knockglass. High 2C 168
Knockholt. Kent 5F 39
Knockholt Pound. Kent 5F 39
Knockie Lodge. High 2G 149
Knockin. Shrp 3F 71
Knockinlaw. E Ayr 1D 116
Knockinnon. High 5D 169
Knocknacarry. Caus 3J 175
Knockrome. Arg 2D 124
Knocksharry. IOM 3B 108
Knockshinnoch. E Ayr 3D 116
Knockvennie. Dum 2E 111
Knockvologan. Arg 3B 132
Knodishall. Suff 4G 67
Knole. Som 4H 21
Knollbury. Mon 3H 33
Knolls Green. Ches E 3C 84
Knolton. Wrex 2F 71
Knook. Wilts 2E 23
Knossington. Leics 5F 75
Knott. High 3C 154
Knott End-on-Sea. Lanc 5C 96
Knotting. Bed 4H 63
Knotting Green. Bed 4H 63
Knottingley. W Yor 2E 93
Knotts. Cumb 2F 103
Knotty Ash. Mers 1G 83
Knotty Green. Buck 1A 38
Knowbury. Shrp 3H 59
Knowe. Dum 2A 110
Knowefield. Cumb 4F 113
Knowehead. Dum 5F 117
Knowes. E Lot 2C 130
Knowesgate. Nmbd 1C 114
Knoweside. S Ayr 3B 116
Knowes of Elrick. Abers 3D 160
Knowle. Bris 4B 34
Knowle. Devn
nr. Braunton 3E 19
nr. Budleigh Salterton 4D 12
nr. Crediton 2A 12
Knowle. Shrp 3H 59
Knowle. W Mid 3F 61
Knowle Green. Lanc 1E 91
Knowle St Giles. Som 1G 13
Knowlesands. Shrp 1B 60
Knowle Village. Hants 2D 16
Knowl Hill. Wind 4G 37
Knowlton. Kent 5G 41
Knowsley. Mers 1G 83
Knowstone. Devn 4B 20
Knucklas. Powy 3E 59
Knuston. Nptn 4G 63
Knutsford. Ches E 3B 84
Knypersley. Staf 5C 84
Krumlin. W Yor 3A 92
Kuggar. Corn 5E 5
Kyleakin. High 1F 147
Kyle of Lochalsh. High 1F 147
Kylerhea. High 1F 147
Kylesku. High 5C 166
Kyles Lodge. W Isl 1E 170
Kylesmorar. High 4G 147
Kylestrome. High 5C 166
Kymin. Mon 4A 48
Kynaston. Here 2B 48
Kynaston. Shrp 3F 71
Kynnersley. Telf 4A 72
Kyre Green. Worc 4A 60
Kyre Park. Worc 4A 60
Kyrewood. Worc 4A 60

L

Labost. W Isl 3E 171
Lacasaidh. W Isl 5F 171
Lacasdail. W Isl 4G 171
Laceby. NE Lin 4F 95
Lacey Green. Buck 5G 51
Lach Dennis. Ches W 3B 84
Lache. Ches W 4F 83
Lack. Ferm 6E 176
Lackagh. Caus 5C 174
Lackford. Suff 3G 65
Lacock. Wilts 5E 35
Ladbroke. Warw 5B 62
Laddingford. Kent 1A 28
Lade Bank. Linc 5C 88
Ladock. Corn 3C 6
Lady. Orkn 3F 172
Ladybank. Fife 2F 137
Ladycross. Corn 4D 10
Lady Green. Mers 4B 90
Lady Hall. Cumb 1A 96
Ladykirk. Bord 5E 131
Ladysford. Abers 2G 161
Ladywood. W Mid 2E 61
Ladywood. Worc 4C 60
Laga. High 2A 140
Lagavulin. Arg 5C 124
Lagg. Arg 2D 125
Lagg. N Ayr 3D 122
Laggan. Arg 4A 124
Laggan. High
nr. Fort Augustus 4E 149
nr. Newtonmore 4A 150
Laggan. Mor 5H 159
Lagganlia. High 3C 150
Lagganulva. Arg 4F 139
Laghey Corner. M Ulst 3C 178
Laglingarten. Arg 3A 134
Lagness. W Sus 2G 17
Laid. High 3E 166
Laide. High 4C 162
Laigh Fenwick. E Ayr 5F 127
Laindon. Essx 2A 40
Lairg. High 3C 164
Lairg Muir. High 3C 164
Laithes. Cumb 1F 103
Laithkirk. Dur 2C 104
Lake. Devn 3F 19
Lake. IOW 4D 16
Lake. Wilts 3G 23
Lakenham. Norf 5E 79
Lakenheath. Suff 2G 65
Lakesend. Norf 1E 65
Lakeside. Cumb 1C 96
Laleham. Surr 4B 38
Laleston. B'end 3B 32
Lamancha. Bord 4F 129
Lamarsh. Essx 2B 54
Lamas. Norf 3E 79
Lamb Corner. Essx 2D 54
Lambden. Bord 5D 130
Lamberhead Green.
G Man 4D 90
Lamberhurst. Kent 2A 28
Lamberhurst Quarter.
Kent 2A 28
Lamberton. Bord 4F 131
Lambeth. G Lon 3E 39
Lambfell Moar. IOM 3B 108
Lambhill. Glas 3G 127
Lambley. Nmbd 4H 113
Lambley. Notts 1D 74
Lambourn. W Ber 4B 36
Lambourne End. Essx 1F 39
Lambourn Woodlands.
W Ber 4B 36
Lambs Green. Dors 3E 15
Lambs Green. W Sus 2D 26
Lambston. Pemb 3D 42
Lamellion. Corn 2G 7
Lamerton. Devn 5E 11
Lamesley. Tyne 4F 115
Laminess. Orkn 4F 172
Lamington. High 1B 158
Lamington. S Lan 1B 118
Lamlash. N Ayr 2E 123
Lamonby. Cumb 1F 103
Lamorick. Corn 2E 7
Lamorna. Corn 4B 4
Lamorran. Corn 4C 6
Lampeter. Cdgn 1F 45
Lampeter Velfrey. Pemb 3F 43
Lamphey. Pemb 4E 43
Lamplugh. Cumb 2B 102
Lamport. Nptn 3E 63
Lamyatt. Som 3B 22
Lana. Devn
nr. Ashwater 3D 10
nr. Holsworthy 2D 10
Lanark. S Lan 5B 128
Lanarth. Corn 4E 5
Lancaster. Lanc 3D 97
Lanchester. Dur 5E 115
Lancing. W Sus 5C 26
Landbeach. Cambs 4D 65
Landcross. Devn 4E 19
Landerberry. Abers 3E 153
Landford. Wilts 1A 16
Land Gate. G Man 4D 90
Landhallow. High 5D 169
Landimore. Swan 3D 30
Landkey. Devn 3F 19
Landkey Newland. Devn 3F 19
Landore. Swan 3F 31
Landport. Port 2E 17
Landrake. Corn 2H 7
Landscove. Devn 2D 9
Land's End Airport. Corn 4A 4
Landshipping. Pemb 3E 43
Landulph. Corn 2A 8
Landywood. Staf 5D 73
Lane. Corn 2C 6
Laneast. Corn 4C 10
Lane Bottom. Lanc 1G 91
Lane End. Buck 2G 37
Lane End. Hants 4D 24
Lane End. IOW 4E 17
Lane End. Wilts 2D 22
Lane Ends. Derbs 2G 73
Lane Ends. Dur 1E 105
Lane Ends. Lanc 4G 97
Laneham. Notts 3F 87
Lane Head. Dur
nr. Hutton Magna 3E 105
nr. Woodland 2D 105
Lane Head. G Man 1A 84
Lane Head. W Yor 4B 92
Lanehead. Dur 5B 114
Lanehead. Nmbd 1A 114
Lane Heads. Lanc 1C 90
Lanercost. Cumb 3G 113
Laneshaw Bridge. Lanc 5B 98
Laney Green. Staf 5D 72
Langais. W Isl 2D 170
Langal. High 2B 140
Langar. Notts 2E 74
Langbank. Ren 2E 127
Langbar. N Yor 4C 98
Langburnshiels. Bord 4H 119
Langcliffe. N Yor 3H 97
Langdale End. N Yor 5G 107
Langdon. Corn 3C 10
Langdon Beck. Dur 1B 104
Langdon Cross. Corn 4D 10
Langdon Hills. Essx 2A 40
Langdown. Hants 2C 16
Langdyke. Fife 3F 137
Langenhoe. Essx 4D 54
Langford. C Beds 1B 52
Langford. Devn 2D 12
Langford. Essx 5B 54
Langford. Notts 5F 87
Langford. Oxon 5H 49
Langford. Som 4F 21
Langford Budville. Som 4E 20
Langham. Dors 4C 22
Langham. Essx 2D 54
Langham. Norf 1C 78
Langham. Rut 4F 75
Langham. Suff 4B 66
Langho. Lanc 1F 91
Langholm. Dum 1E 113
Langland. Swan 4F 31
Langleeford. Nmbd 2D 120
Langley. Ches E 3D 84
Langley. Derbs 1B 74
Langley. Essx 2E 53
Langley. Glos 3F 49
Langley. Hants 2C 16
Langley. Herts 3C 52
Langley. Kent 5C 40
Langley. Nmbd 3B 114
Langley. Slo 3B 38
Langley. Som 4D 20
Langley. Warw 4F 61
Langley. W Sus 4G 25
Langley Burrell. Wilts 4E 35
Langleybury. Herts 5A 52
Langley Common. Derbs 2G 73
Langley Green. Derbs 2G 73
Langley Green. Norf 5F 79
Langley Green. Warw 4F 61
Langley Green. W Sus 2D 26
Langley Heath. Kent 5C 40
Langley Marsh. Som 4D 20
Langley Moor. Dur 5F 115
Langley Park. Dur 5F 115
Langley Street. Norf 5F 79
Langney. E Sus 5H 27
Langold. Notts 2C 86
Langore. Corn 4C 10
Langport. Som 4H 21
Langrick. Linc 1B 76
Langridge. Bath 5C 34
Langridgeford. Devn 4F 19
Langrigg. Cumb 5C 112
Langrish. Hants 4F 25
Langsett. S Yor 4C 92
Langshaw. Bord 1H 119
Langstone. Hants 2F 17
Langthorne. N Yor 5F 105
Langthorpe. N Yor 3F 99
Langthwaite. N Yor 4D 104
Langtoft. E Yor 3E 101
Langtoft. Linc 4A 76
Langton. Dur 3E 105
Langton. Linc
nr. Horncastle 4B 88
nr. Spilsby 3C 88
Langton. N Yor 3B 100
Langton by Wragby.
Linc 3A 88
Langton Green. Kent 2G 27
Langton Herring. Dors 4B 14
Langton Long Blandford.
Dors 2D 15
Langton Matravers. Dors 5E 15
Langtree. Devn 1E 11
Langwathby. Cumb 1G 103
Langwith. Derbs 3C 86
Langworth. Linc 3H 87
Lanivet. Corn 2E 7
Lanjeth. Corn 3D 6
Lank. Corn 5A 10
Lanlivery. Corn 3E 7
Lanner. Corn 5B 6
Lanreath. Corn 3F 7
Lansallos. Corn 3F 7
Lansdown. Bath 5C 34
Lansdown. Glos 3E 49
Lanteglos Highway. Corn 3F 7
Lanton. Nmbd 1D 120
Lanton. Bord 2A 120
Lapford. Devn 2H 11
Lapford Cross. Devn 2H 11
Laphroaig. Arg 5B 124
Lapley. Staf 4C 72
Lapworth. Warw 3F 61
Larachbeg. High 4A 140
Larbert. Falk 1B 128
Larden Green. Ches E 5H 83
Largie. Abers 5D 160
Largiemore. Arg 1H 125
Largoward. Fife 3G 137
Largs. N Ayr 4D 126
Largue. Abers 4D 160
Largybeg. N Ayr 3E 123
Largymeanoch. N Ayr 3E 123
Largymore. N Ayr 3E 123
Larkfield. Inv 2D 126
Larkfield. Kent 5B 40
Larkhall. Bath 5C 34
Larkhall. S Lan 4A 128
Larkhill. Wilts 2G 23
Larling. Norf 2B 66
Larne. ME Ant 6L 175
Larport. Here 2A 48
Lartington. Dur 3D 104
Lary. Abers 3H 151
Lasham. Hants 2E 25
Lashenden. Kent 1C 28
Lasswade. Midl 3G 129
Lastingham. N Yor 5E 107
Latchford. Herts 3D 53
Latchford. Oxon 5E 51
Latchingdon. Essx 5B 54
Latchley. Corn 5E 11
Latchmere Green. Hants 1E 25
Lathbury. Mil 1G 51
Latheron. High 5D 169
Latheronwheel. High 5D 169
Lathom. Lanc 4C 90
Lathones. Fife 3G 137
Latimer. Buck 1B 38
Latteridge. S Glo 3B 34
Lattiford. Som 4B 22
Latton. Wilts 2F 35
Laudale House. High 3B 140
Lauder. Bord 5B 130
Laugharne. Carm 3H 43
Laughterton. Linc 3F 87
Laughton. E Sus 4G 27
Laughton. Leics 2D 62
Laughton. Linc
nr. Gainsborough 1F 87
nr. Grantham 2H 75
Laughton Common.
S Yor 2C 86
Laughton en le Morthen.
S Yor 2C 86
Launcells. Corn 2C 10
Launceston. Corn 4D 10
Launcherley. Som 2A 22
Launton. Oxon 3E 50
Laurelvale. Arm 5E 178
Laurencekirk. Abers 1G 145
Laurieston. Dum 3D 111
Laurieston. Falk 2C 128
Lavendon. Mil 5G 63
Lavenham. Suff 1C 54
Laverhay. Dum 5D 118
Laversdale. Cumb 3F 113
Laverstock. Wilts 3G 23
Laverstoke. Hants 2C 24
Laverton. Glos 2F 49
Laverton. N Yor 2E 99
Laverton. Som 1C 22
Lavister. Wrex 5F 83
Law. S Lan 4B 128
Lawers. Per 5D 142
Lawford. Essx 2D 54
Lawhitton. Corn 4D 10
Lawkland. N Yor 3G 97
Lawley. Telf 5A 72
Lawnhead. Staf 3C 72
Lawrencetown. Arm 5E 178
Lawrenny. Pemb 4E 43
Lawshall. Suff 5A 66
Lawton. Here 5G 59
Laxey. IOM 3D 108
Laxfield. Suff 3E 67
Laxfirth. Shet 6F 173
Laxo. Shet 5F 173
Laxton. E Yor 2A 94
Laxton. Nptn 1G 63
Laxton. Notts 4E 86
Laycock. W Yor 5C 98
Layer Breton. Essx 4C 54
Layer-de-la-Haye. Essx 3C 54
Layer Marney. Essx 4C 54
Laymore. Dors 2G 13
Laysters Pole. Here 4H 59
Layter's Green. Buck 1A 38
Laytham. E Yor 1H 93
Lazenby. Red C 3C 106
Lazonby. Cumb 1G 103
Lea. Derbs 5H 85
Lea. Here 3B 48
Lea. Linc 2F 87

Lea—Llanfihangel-y-Creuddyn

Lea. Shrp
nr. Bishop's Castle 2F 59
nr. Shrewsbury 5G 71
Lea. Wilts 3E 35
Leabrooks. Derbs 5B 86
Leac a Li. W Isl 8D 171
Leachd. Arg 4H 133
Leachkin. High 4A 158
Leachpool. Pemb 3D 42
Leadburn. Midl 4F 129
Leadenham. Linc 5G 87
Leaden Roding. Essx 4F 53
Leaderfoot. Bord 1H 119
Leadgate. Cumb 5A 114
Leadgate. Dur 4E 115
Leadgate. Nmbd 4E 115
Leadhills. S Lan 3A 118
Leadingcross Green. Kent 5C 40
Lea End. Worc 3E 61
Leafield. Oxon 4B 50
Leagrave. Lutn 3A 52
Lea Hall. W Mid 2F 61
Lea Heath. Staf 3E 73
Leake. N Yor 5B 106
Leake Common Side. Linc 5C 88
Leake Fold Hill. Linc 5D 88
Leake Hurn's End. Linc 1D 76
Lealholm. N Yor 4E 107
Lealt. Arg 4D 132
Lealt. High 2E 155
Leam. Derbs 3G 85
Lea Marston. Warw 1G 61
Leamington Hastings.
Warw 4B 62
Leamington Spa, Royal.
Warw 4H 61
Leamonsley. Staf 5F 73
Leamside. Dur 5G 115
Leargybreck. Arg 2D 124
Lease Rigg. N Yor 4F 107
Leasgill. Cumb 1D 97
Leasingham. Linc 1H 75
Leasingthorne. Dur 1F 105
Leasowe. Mers 1E 83
Leatherhead. Surr 5C 38
Leathley. N Yor 5E 99
Leaths. Dum 3E 111
Leaton. Shrp 4G 71
Leaton. Telf 4A 72
Lea Town. Lanc 1C 90
Leaveland. Kent 5E 40
Leavenheath. Suff 2C 54
Leavening. N Yor 3B 100
Leaves Green. G Lon 4F 39
Lea Yeat. Cumb 1G 97
Leazes. Dur 4E 115
Lebberston. N Yor 1E 101
Lechlade on Thames.
Glos 2H 35
Leck. Lanc 2F 97
Leckford. Hants 3B 24
Leckfurin. High 3H 167
Leckgruinart. Arg 3A 124
Leckhampstead. Buck 2F 51
Leckhampstead. W Ber 4C 36
Leckhampton. Glos 4E 49
Leckmelm. High 4F 163
Leckwith. V Glam 4E 33
Leconfield. E Yor 5E 101
Ledaig. Arg 5D 140
Ledburn. Buck 3H 51
Ledbury. Here 2C 48
Ledgemoor. Here 5G 59
Ledgowan. High 3D 156
Ledicot. Here 4G 59
Ledmore. High 2G 163
Lednabirichen. High 4E 165
Lednagullin. High 2A 168
Ledsham. Ches W 3F 83
Ledsham. W Yor 2E 93
Ledston. W Yor 2E 93
Ledstone. Devn 4D 8
Ledwell. Oxon 3C 50
Lee. Devn
nr. Ilfracombe 2E 19
nr. South Molton 4B 20
Lee. G Lon 3E 39
Lee. Hants 1B 16
Lee. Lanc 4E 97
Lee. Shrp 2G 71
The Lee. Buck 5H 51
Leeans. Shet 7E 173
Leebotten. Shet 9F 173
Leebotwood. Shrp 1G 59
Lee Brockhurst. Shrp 3H 71
Leece. Cumb 3B 96
Leechpool. Mon 3A 34
Lee Clump. Buck 5H 51
Leeds. Kent 5C 40
Leeds. W Yor 196 (1C 92)
Leeds Bradford Airport.
W Yor 5E 99
Leedstown. Corn 3D 4
Leegomery. Telf 4A 72
Lee Head. Derbs 1E 85
Leek. Staf 5D 85
Leekbrook. Staf 5D 85
Leek Wootton. Warw 4G 61
Lee Mill. Devn 3B 8
Leeming. N Yor 1E 99
Leeming Bar. N Yor 5F 105
Lee Moor. Devn 2B 8
Lee Moor. W Yor 2D 92
Lee-on-the-Solent. Hants 2D 16
Lees. Derbs 2G 73
Lees. G Man 4H 91
Lees. W Yor 1A 92
The Lees. Kent 5E 40
Leeswood. Flin 4E 83
Leetown. Per 1E 136
Leftwich. Ches W 3A 84
Legbourne. Linc 2C 88
Legburthwaite. Cumb 3E 102
Legerwood. Bord 5B 130
Legsby. Linc 2A 88
Leicester. Leic 196 (5C 74)
Leicester Forest East.
Leics 5C 74
Leigh. Dors 2B 14
Leigh. G Man 4E 91
Leigh. Kent 1G 27
Leigh. Shrp 5F 71
Leigh. Surr 1D 26
Leigh. Wilts 2F 35
Leigh. Worc 5B 60
The Leigh. Glos 3D 48
Leigham. Plym 3B 8
Leigh Beck. Essx 2C 40
Leigh Common. Som 4C 22
Leigh Delamere. Wilts 4D 35
Leigh Green. Kent 2D 28
Leighland Chapel. Som 3D 20
Leigh-on-Sea. S'end 2C 40
Leigh Park. Hants 2F 17
Leigh Sinton. Worc 5B 60
Leighterton. Glos 2D 34
Leighton. N Yor 2D 98
Leighton. Powy 5E 71
Leighton. Shrp 5A 72
Leighton. Som 2C 22
Leighton Bromswold.
Cambs 3A 64
Leighton Buzzard. C Beds 3H 51
Leigh-upon-Mendip. Som 2B 22
Leinthall Earls. Here 4G 59
Leinthall Starkes. Here 4G 59
Leintwardine. Here 3G 59
Leire. Leics 1C 62
Leirinmore. High 2E 166
Leishmore. High 4G 157
Leiston. Suff 4G 67
Leitfie. Per 4B 144
Leith. Edin 2F 129
Leitholm. Bord 5D 130
Leitrim. New M 6H 179
Lelant. Corn 3C 4
Lelant Downs. Corn 3C 4
Lelley. E Yor 1F 95
Lem Hill. Shrp 3B 60
Lemington. Tyne 3E 115
Lempitlaw. Bord 1B 120
Lemsford. Herts 4C 52
Lenacre. Cumb 1F 97
Lenchie. Abers 5C 160
Lenchwick. Worc 1F 49
Lendalfoot. S Ayr 1G 109
Lendrick. Stir 3E 135
Lenham. Kent 5C 40
Lenham Heath. Kent 1D 28
Lenimore. N Ayr 5G 125
Lennel. Bord 5E 131
Lennoxtown. E Dun 2H 127
Lenton. Linc 2H 75
Lentran. High 4H 157
Lenwade. Norf 4C 78
Lenzie. E Dun 2H 127
Leochel Cushnie. Abers 2C 152
Leogh. Shet 1B 172
Leominster. Here 5G 59
Leonard Stanley. Glos 5D 48
Lepe. Hants 3C 16
Lephenstrath. Arg 5A 122
Lephin. High 4A 154
Lephinchapel. Arg 4G 133
Lephinmore. Arg 4G 133
Leppington. N Yor 3B 100
Lepton. W Yor 3C 92
Lerryn. Corn 3F 7
Lerwick. Shet 7F 173
Lerwick (Tingwall) Airport.
Shet 7F 173
Lesbury. Nmbd 3G 121
Leslie. Abers 1C 152
Leslie. Fife 3E 137
Lesmahagow. S Lan 1H 117
Lesnewth. Corn 3B 10
Lessingham. Norf 3F 79
Lessonhall. Cumb 4D 112
Leswalt. Dum 3F 109
Letchmore Heath. Herts 1C 38
Letchworth Garden City.
Herts 2C 52
Letcombe Bassett. Oxon 3B 36
Letcombe Regis. Oxon 3B 36
Letham. Ang 4E 145
Letham. Falk 1B 128
Letham. Fife 2F 137
Lethanhill. E Ayr 3D 116
Lethenty. Abers 4F 161
Letheringham. Suff 5E 67
Letheringsett. Norf 2C 78
Lettaford. Devn 4H 11
Lettan. Orkn 3G 172
Letter. Abers 2E 153
Letterewe. High 1B 156
Letterfearn. High 1A 148
Lettermore. Arg 4F 139
Letters. High 5F 163
Lettershendoney. Derr 5B 174
Letterston. Pemb 2D 42
Letton. Here
nr. Kington 1G 47
nr. Leintwardine 3F 59
Letty Green. Herts 4C 52
Letwell. S Yor 2C 86
Leuchars. Fife 1G 137
Leumrabhagh. W Isl 6F 171
Leusdon. Devn 5H 11
Levaneap. Shet 5F 173
Levedale. Staf 4C 72
Leven. E Yor 5F 101
Leven. Fife 3F 137
Levencorroch. N Ayr 3E 123
Levenhall. E Lot 2G 129
Levens. Cumb 1D 97
Levens Green. Herts 3D 52
Levenshulme. G Man 1C 84
Levenwick. Shet 9F 173
Leverburgh. W Isl 9C 171
Leverington. Cambs 4D 76
Leverton. Linc 1C 76
Leverton. W Ber 4B 36
Leverton Lucasgate. Linc 1D 76
Leverton Outgate. Linc 1D 76
Levington. Suff 2F 55
Levisham. N Yor 5F 107
Levishie. High 2G 149
Lew. Oxon 5B 50
Lewaigue. IOM 2D 108
Lewannick. Corn 4C 10
Lewdown. Devn 4E 11
Lewes. E Sus 4F 27
Leweston. Pemb 2D 42
Lewisham. G Lon 3E 39
Lewiston. High 1H 149
Lewistown. B'end 3C 32
Lewknor. Oxon 2F 37
Leworthy. Devn
nr. Barnstaple 3G 19
nr. Holsworthy 2D 10
Lewson Street. Kent 4D 40
Lewthorn Cross. Devn 5A 12
Lewtrenchard. Devn 4E 11
Ley. Corn 2F 7
Leybourne. Kent 5A 40
Leyburn. N Yor 5E 105
Leycett. Staf 1B 72
Leyfields. Staf 5G 73
Ley Green. Herts 3B 52
Ley Hill. Buck 5H 51
Leyland. Lanc 2D 90
Leylodge. Abers 2E 153
Leymoor. W Yor 3B 92
Leys. Per 5B 144
Leysdown-on-Sea. Kent 3E 41
Leysmill. Ang 4F 145
Leyton. G Lon 2E 39
Leytonstone. G Lon 2F 39
Lezant. Corn 5D 10
Leziate. Norf 4F 77
Lhanbryde. Mor 2G 159
The Lhen. IOM 1C 108
Liatrie. High 5E 157
Libanus. Powy 3C 46
Libberton. S Lan 5C 128
Libbery. Worc 5D 60
Liberton. Edin 3F 129
Liceasto. W Isl 8D 171
Lichfield. Staf 5F 73
Lickey. Worc 3D 61
Lickey End. Worc 3D 60
Lickfold. W Sus 3A 26
Liddaton. Devn 4E 11
Liddington. Swin 3H 35
Liddle. Orkn 9D 172
Lidgate. Suff 5G 65
Lidgett. Notts 4D 86
Lidham Hill. E Sus 4C 28
Lidlington. C Beds 2H 51
Lidsey. W Sus 5A 26
Lidstone. Oxon 3B 50
Lienassie. High 1B 148
Liff. Ang 5C 144
Lifford. W Mid 2E 61
Lifton. Devn 4D 11
Liftondown. Devn 4D 10
Lighthorne. Warw 5H 61
Light Oaks. Stoke 5D 84
Lightwater. Surr 4A 38
Lightwood. Staf 1E 73
Lightwood. Stoke 1D 72
Lightwood Green. Ches E 1A 72
Lightwood Green. Wrex 1F 71
Lilbourne. Nptn 3C 62
Lilburn Tower. Nmbd 2E 121
Lillesdon. Som 4G 21
Lilleshall. Telf 4B 72
Lilley. Herts 3B 52
Lilliesleaf. Bord 2H 119
Lillingstone Dayrell. Buck 2F 51
Lillingstone Lovell. Buck 1F 51
Lillington. Dors 1B 14
Lilstock. Som 2E 21
Lilybank. Inv 2E 126
Lilyhurst. Shrp 4B 72
Limavady. Caus 4C 174
Limbrick. Lanc 3E 90
Limbury. Lutn 3A 52
Limekilnburn. S Lan 4A 128
Limekilns. Fife 1D 129
Limerigg. Falk 2B 128
Limestone Brae. Nmbd 5A 114
Lime Street. Worc 2D 48
Limington. Som 4A 22
Limpenhoe. Norf 5F 79
Limpley Stoke. Wilts 5C 34
Limpsfield. Surr 5F 39
Limpsfield Chart. Surr 5F 39
Linburn. W Lot 3E 129
Linby. Notts 5C 86
Linchmere. W Sus 3G 25
Lincluden. Dum 2A 112
Lincoln. Linc 197 (3G 87)
Lincomb. Worc 4C 60
Lindale. Cumb 1D 96
Lindal in Furness. Cumb 2B 96
Lindean. Bord 1G 119
Linden. Glos 4D 48
Lindfield. W Sus 3E 27
Lindford. Hants 3G 25
Lindores. Fife 2E 137
Lindridge. Worc 4A 60
Lindsell. Essx 3G 53
Lindsey. Suff 1C 54
Lindsey Tye. Suff 1C 54
Linford. Hants 2G 15
Linford. Thur 3A 40
Lingague. IOM 4B 108
Lingdale. Red C 3D 106
Lingen. Here 4F 59
Lingfield. Surr 1E 27
Lingreabhagh. W Isl 9C 171
Lingwood. Norf 5F 79
Lingy Close. Cumb 4E 113
Linicro. High 2C 154
Linkend. Worc 2D 48
Linkenholt. Hants 1B 24
Linkinhorne. Corn 5D 10
Linklater. Orkn 9D 172
Linksness. Orkn 6E 172
Linktown. Fife 4E 137
Linkwood. Mor 2G 159
Linley. Shrp
nr. Bishop's Castle 1F 59
nr. Bridgnorth 1A 60
Linley Green. Here 5A 60
Linlithgow. W Lot 2C 128
Linlithgow Bridge. Falk 2C 128
Linneraineach. High 3F 163
Linshiels. Nmbd 4C 120
Linsiadar. W Isl 4E 171
Linsidemore. High 4C 164
Linslade. C Beds 3H 51
Linstead Parva. Suff 3F 67
Linstock. Cumb 4F 113
Linthwaite. W Yor 3B 92
Lintlaw. Bord 4E 131
Lintmill. Mor 2C 160
Linton. Cambs 1F 53
Linton. Derbs 4G 73
Linton. Here 3B 48
Linton. Kent 5B 40
Linton. N Yor 3B 98
Linton. Bord 2B 120
Linton. W Yor 5F 99
Linton Colliery. Nmbd 5G 121
Linton Hill. Here 3B 48
Linton-on-Ouse. N Yor 3G 99
Lintzford. Dur 4E 115
Lintzgarth. Dur 5C 114
Linwood. Hants 2G 15
Linwood. Linc 2A 88
Linwood. Ren 3F 127
Lionacleit. W Isl 4C 170
Lionacro. High 2C 154
Lionacuidhe. W Isl 4C 170
Lional. W Isl 1H 171
Liphook. Hants 3G 25
Lipley. Shrp 2B 72
Lipyeate. Som 1B 22
Liquo. N Lan 4B 128
Lisbane. Ards 3J 179
Lisbellaw. Ferm 8F 176
Lisburn. Lis 3G 179
Liscard. Mers 1F 83
Liscolman. Caus 3F 175
Liscombe. Som 3B 20
Lishahawley. Derr 4A 174
Liskeard. Corn 2G 7
Lislea. New M 7E 178
Lisle Court. Hants 3B 16
Lisnarick. Ferm 7D 176
Lisnaskea. Ferm 6J 177
Liss. Hants 4F 25
Lissett. E Yor 4F 101
Liss Forest. Hants 4F 25
Lissington. Linc 2A 88
Liston. Essx 1B 54
Listooder. New M 4J 179
Lisvane. Card 3E 33
Liswerry. Newp 3G 33
Litcham. Norf 4A 78
Litchard. B'end 3C 32
Litchborough. Nptn 5D 62
Litchfield. Hants 1C 24
Litherland. Mers 1F 83
Litlington. Cambs 1D 52
Litlington. E Sus 5G 27
Littemill. Nmbd 3G 121
Litterty. Abers 3E 161
Little Abington. Cambs 1F 53
Little Addington. Nptn 3G 63
Little Airmyn. N Yor 2H 93
Little Alne. Warw 4F 61
Little Ardo. Abers 5F 161
Little Asby. Cumb 4H 103
Little Aston. Staf 5E 73
Little Atherfield. IOW 4C 16
Little Ayton. N Yor 3C 106
Little Baddow. Essx 5A 54
Little Badminton. S Glo 3D 34
Little Ballinluig. Per 3G 143
Little Bampton. Cumb 4D 112
Little Bardfield. Essx 2G 53
Little Barford. Bed 5A 64
Little Barningham. Norf 2D 78
Little Barrington. Glos 4H 49
Little Barrow. Ches W 4G 83
Little Barugh. N Yor 2B 100
Little Bavington. Nmbd 2C 114
Little Bealings. Suff 1F 55
Littlebeck. Cumb 3H 103
Little Bedwyn. Wilts 5A 36
Little Bentley. Essx 3E 54
Little Berkhamsted. Herts 5C 52
Little Billing. Nptn 4F 63
Little Billington. C Beds 3H 51
Little Birch. Here 2A 48
Little Bispham. Bkpl 5C 96
Little Blakenham. Suff 1E 54
Little Blencow. Cumb 1F 103
Little Bognor. W Sus 3B 26
Little Bolas. Shrp 3A 72
Little Bollington. Ches E 2B 84
Little Bookham. Surr 5C 38
Littleborough. Devn 1B 12
Littleborough. G Man 3H 91
Littleborough. Notts 2F 87
Littlebourne. Kent 5G 41
Little Bourton. Oxon 1C 50
Little Bowden. Leics 2E 63
Little Bradley. Suff 5F 65
Little Brampton. Shrp 2F 59
Little Brechin. Ang 2E 145
Littlebredy. Dors 4A 14
Little Brickhill. Mil 2H 51
Little Bridgeford. Staf 3C 72
Little Brington. Nptn 4D 62
Little Bromley. Essx 3D 54
Little Broughton. Cumb 1B 102
Little Budworth. Ches W 4H 83
Little Burstead. Essx 1A 40
Little Burton. E Yor 5F 101
Littlebury. Essx 2F 53
Littlebury Green. Essx 2E 53
Little Bytham. Linc 4H 75
Little Canfield. Essx 3F 53
Little Canford. Dors 3F 15
Little Carlton. Linc 2C 88
Little Carlton. Notts 5E 87
Little Casterton. Rut 5H 75
Little Catwick. E Yor 5F 101
Little Catworth. Cambs 3A 64
Little Cawthorpe. Linc 2C 88
Little Chalfont. Buck 1A 38
Little Chart. Kent 1D 28
Little Chesterford. Essx 1F 53
Little Cheverell. Wilts 1E 23
Little Chishill. Cambs 2E 53
Little Clacton. Essx 4E 55
Little Clanfield. Oxon 5A 50
Little Clifton. Cumb 2B 102
Little Coates. NE Lin 4F 95
Little Comberton. Worc 1E 49
Little Common. E Sus 5B 28
Little Compton. Warw 2A 50
Little Cornard. Suff 2B 54
Littlecote. Buck 3G 51
Littlecott. Wilts 1G 23
Little Cowarne. Here 5A 60
Little Coxwell. Oxon 2A 36
Little Crakehall. N Yor 5F 105
Little Crawley. Mil 1H 51
Little Creich. High 5D 164
Little Cressingham. Norf 5A 78
Little Crosby. Mers 4B 90
Little Crosthwaite. Cumb 2D 102
Little Cubley. Derbs 2F 73
Little Dalby. Leics 4E 75
Little Dawley. Telf 5A 72
Littledean. Glos 4B 48
Little Dens. Abers 4H 161
Little Dewchurch. Here 2A 48
Little Ditton. Cambs 5F 65
Little Down. Hants 1B 24
Little Downham. Cambs 2E 65
Little Drayton. Shrp 2A 72
Little Driffield. E Yor 4E 101
Little Dunham. Norf 4A 78
Little Dunkeld. Per 4H 143
Little Dunmow. Essx 3G 53
Little Easton. Essx 3G 53
Little Eaton. Derbs 1A 74
Little Eccleston. Lanc 5D 96
Little Ellingham. Norf 1C 66
Little End. Essx 5F 53
Little Everdon. Nptn 5C 62
Little Eversden. Cambs 5C 64
Little Faringdon. Oxon 5H 49
Little Fencote. N Yor 5F 105
Little Fenton. N Yor 1F 93
Littleferry. High 4F 165
Little Fransham. Norf 4B 78
Little Gaddesden. Herts 4H 51
Little Garway. Here 3H 47
Little Gidding. Cambs 2A 64
Little Glemham. Suff 5F 67
Little Glenshee. Per 5G 143
Little Gransden. Cambs 5B 64
Little Green. Suff 3C 66
Little Green. Wrex 1G 71
Little Grimsby. Linc 1C 88
Little Habton. N Yor 2B 100
Little Hadham. Herts 3E 53
Little Hale. Linc 1A 76
Little Hallingbury. Essx 4E 53
Littleham. Devn
nr. Bideford 4E 19
nr. Exmouth 4D 12
Little Hampden. Buck 5G 51
Littlehampton. W Sus 5B 26
Little Haresfield. Glos 5D 48
Little Harrowden. Nptn 3F 63
Little Haseley. Oxon 5E 51
Little Hatfield. E Yor 5F 101
Little Hautbois. Norf 3E 79
Little Haven. Pemb 3C 42
Little Hay. Staf 5F 73
Little Hayfield. Derbs 2E 85
Little Haywood. Staf 3E 73
Little Heath. W Mid 2H 61
Little Heck. N Yor 2F 93
Littlehempston. Devn 2E 9
Little Herbert's. Glos 4E 49
Little Hereford. Here 4H 59
Little Horkesley. Essx 2C 54
Little Hormead. Herts 3D 53
Little Horsted. E Sus 4F 27
Little Horton. W Yor 1B 92
Little Horwood. Buck 2F 51
Little Houghton. Nptn 5F 63
Little Houghton. S Yor 4E 93
Littlehoughton. Nmbd 3G 121
Little Hucklow. Derbs 3F 85
Little Hulton. G Man 4F 91
Little Irchester. Nptn 4G 63
Little Kelk. E Yor 3E 101
Little Kimble. Buck 5G 51
Little Kineton. Warw 5H 61
Little Kingshill. Buck 2G 37
Little Langdale. Cumb 4E 102
Little Langford. Wilts 3F 23
Little Laver. Essx 5F 53
Little Lawford. Warw 3B 62
Little Leigh. Ches W 3A 84
Little Leighs. Essx 4H 53
Little Leven. E Yor 5E 101
Little Lever. G Man 4F 91
Little Linford. Mil 1G 51
Little London. Buck 4E 51
Little London. E Sus 4G 27
Little London. Hants
nr. Andover 2B 24
nr. Basingstoke 1E 24
Little London. Linc
nr. Long Sutton 3D 76
nr. Spalding 3B 76
Little London. Norf
nr. North Walsham 2E 79
nr. Northwold 1G 65
nr. Saxthorpe 2D 78
nr. Southery 1F 65
Little London. Powy 2C 58
Little Longstone. Derbs 3F 85
Little Malvern. Worc 1C 48
Little Maplestead. Essx 2B 54
Little Marcle. Here 2B 48
Little Marlow. Buck 3G 37
Little Massingham. Norf 3G 77
Little Melton. Norf 5D 78
Little Mill. Mon 5G 47
Littlemill. Abers 4H 151
Littlemill. E Ayr 3D 116
Littlemill. High 4D 158
Little Milton. Oxon 5E 50
Little Missenden. Buck 1A 38
Littlemoor. Derbs 4A 86
Littlemoor. Dors 4B 14
Littlemore. Oxon 5D 50
Little Mountain. Flin 4E 83
Little Musgrave. Cumb 3A 104
Little Ness. Shrp 4G 71
Little Neston. Ches W 3E 83
Little Newcastle. Pemb 2D 43
Little Newsham. Dur 3E 105
Little Oakley. Essx 3F 55
Little Oakley. Nptn 2F 63
Little Onn. Staf 4C 72
Little Ormside. Cumb 3A 104
Little Orton. Cumb 4E 113
Little Orton. Leics 5H 73
Little Ouse. Cambs 2F 65
Little Ouseburn. N Yor 3G 99
Littleover. Derb 2H 73
Little Packington. Warw 2G 61
Little Paxton. Cambs 4A 64
Little Petherick. Corn 1D 6
Little Plumpton. Lanc 1B 90
Little Plumstead. Norf 4F 79
Little Ponton. Linc 2G 75
Littleport. Cambs 2E 65
Little Posbrook. Hants 2D 16
Little Potheridge. Devn 1F 11
Little Preston. Nptn 5C 62
Little Raveley. Cambs 3B 64
Little Reynoldston. Swan 4D 31
Little Ribston. N Yor 4F 99
Little Rissington. Glos 4G 49
Little Rogart. High 3E 165
Little Rollright. Oxon 2A 50
Little Ryburgh. Norf 3B 78
Little Ryle. Nmbd 3E 121
Little Ryton. Shrp 5G 71
Little Salkeld. Cumb 1G 103
Little Sampford. Essx 2G 53
Little Sandhurst. Brac 5G 37
Little Saredon. Staf 5D 72
Little Saxham. Suff 4G 65
Little Scatwell. High 3F 157
Little Shelford. Cambs 5D 64
Little Shoddesden. Hants 2A 24
Little Singleton. Lanc 1B 90
Little Smeaton. N Yor 3F 93
Little Snoring. Norf 2B 78
Little Sodbury. S Glo 3C 34
Little Somborne. Hants 3B 24
Little Somerford. Wilts 3E 35
Little Soudley. Shrp 3B 72
Little Stainforth. N Yor 3H 97
Little Stainton. Darl 3A 106
Little Stanney. Ches W 3G 83
Little Staughton. Bed 4A 64
Little Steeping. Linc 4D 88
Littlester. Shet 3G 173
Little Stoke. Staf 2D 72
Littlestone-on-Sea. Kent 3E 29
Little Stonham. Suff 4D 66
Little Stretton. Leics 5D 74
Little Stretton. Shrp 1G 59
Little Strickland. Cumb 3G 103
Little Stukeley. Cambs 3B 64
Little Sugnall. Staf 2C 72
Little Sutton. Ches W 3F 83
Little Sutton. Linc 3D 76
Little Swinburne. Nmbd 2C 114
Little Tew. Oxon 3B 50
Little Tey. Essx 3B 54
Little Thetford. Cambs 3E 65
Little Thirkleby. N Yor 2G 99
Little Thornage. Norf 2C 78
Little Thornton. Lanc 5C 96
Little Thorpe. W Yor 2B 92
Littlethorpe. Leics 1C 62
Littlethorpe. N Yor 3F 99
Little Thurlow. Suff 5F 65
Little Thurrock. Thur 3H 39
Littleton. Ches W 4G 83
Littleton. Hants 3C 24
Littleton. Som 3H 21
Littleton. Surr
nr. Guildford 1A 26
nr. Staines 4B 38
Littleton Drew. Wilts 3D 34
Littleton Pannell. Wilts 1F 23
Littleton-upon-Severn.
S Glo 3A 34
Little Torboll. High 4E 165
Little Torrington. Devn 1E 11
Little Totham. Essx 4B 54
Little Town. Cumb 3D 102
Little Town. Lanc 1E 91
Littletown. Dur 5G 115
Littletown. High 5E 165
Little Twycross. Leics 5H 73
Little Urswick. Cumb 2B 96
Little Wakering. Essx 2D 40
Little Walden. Essx 1F 53
Little Waldingfield. Suff 1C 54
Little Walsingham. Norf 2B 78
Little Waltham. Essx 4H 53
Little Warley. Essx 1H 39
Little Weighton. E Yor 1C 94
Little Wenham. Suff 2D 54
Little Wenlock. Telf 5A 72
Little Whelnetham. Suff 4A 66
Little Whittingham Green.
Suff 3E 67
Littlewick Green. Wind 4G 37
Little Wilbraham. Cambs 5E 65
Littlewindsor. Dors 2H 13
Little Wisbeach. Linc 2A 76
Little Witcombe. Glos 4E 49
Little Witley. Worc 4B 60
Little Wittenham. Oxon 2D 36
Little Wolford. Warw 2A 50
Littleworth. Bed 1A 52
Littleworth. Glos 2G 49
Littleworth. Oxon 2B 36
Littleworth. Staf
nr. Cannock 4E 73
nr. Eccleshall 3B 72
nr. Stafford 3D 72
Littleworth. W Sus 3C 26
Littleworth. Worc
nr. Redditch 4D 61
nr. Worcester 5C 60
Little Wratting. Suff 1G 53
Little Wymondley. Herts 3C 52
Little Wyrley. Staf 5E 73
Little Yeldham. Essx 2A 54
Littley Green. Essx 4G 53
Litton. Derbs 3F 85
Litton. N Yor 2B 98
Litton. Som 1A 22
Litton Cheney. Dors 3A 14
Liurbost. W Isl 5F 171
Liverpool. Mers 197 (1F 83)
Liverpool John Lennon Airport.
Mers 2G 83
Liversedge. W Yor 2B 92
Liverton. Devn 5B 12
Liverton. Red C 3E 107
Liverton Mines. Red C 3E 107
Livingston. W Lot 3D 128
Livingston Village. W Lot 3D 128
Lixwm. Flin 3D 82
Lizard. Corn 5E 5
Llaingoch. IOA 2B 80
Llaithddu. Powy 2C 58
Llampha. V Glam 4C 32
Llan. Powy 5A 70
Llanaber. Gwyn 4F 69
Llanaelhaearn. Gwyn 1C 68
Llanaeron. Cdgn 4D 57
Llanafan. Cdgn 3F 57
Llanafan-fawr. Powy 5B 58
Llanafan-fechan. Powy 5B 58
Llanallgo. IOA 2D 81
Llanandras. Powy 4F 59
Llananno. Powy 3C 58
Llanarmon. Gwyn 2D 68
Llanarmon Dyffryn Ceiriog.
Wrex 2D 70
Llanarmon-yn-Ial. Den 5D 82
Llanarth. Cdgn 5D 56
Llanarth. Mon 4G 47
Llanarthne. Carm 3F 45
Llanasa. Flin 2D 82
Llanbabo. IOA 2C 80
Llanbadarn Fawr. Cdgn 2F 57
Llanbadarn Fynydd. Powy 3D 58
Llanbadarn-y-garreg.
Powy 1E 46
Llanbadoc. Mon 5G 47
Llanbadrig. IOA 1C 80
Llanbeder. Newp 2G 33
Llanbedr. Gwyn 3E 69
Llanbedr. Powy
nr. Crickhowell 3F 47
nr. Hay-on-Wye 1E 47
Llanbedr-Dyffryn-Clwyd.
Den 5D 82
Llanbedrgoch. IOA 2E 81
Llanbedrog. Gwyn 2C 68
Llanbedr Pont Steffan.
Cdgn 1F 45
Llanbedr-y-cennin. Cnwy 4G 81
Llanberis. Gwyn 4E 81
Llanbethery. V Glam 5D 32
Llanbister. Powy 3D 58
Llanblethian. V Glam 4C 32
Llanboidy. Carm 2G 43
Llanbradach. Cphy 2E 33
Llanbrynmair. Powy 5A 70
Llanbydderi. V Glam 5D 32
Llancadle. V Glam 5D 32
Llancarfan. V Glam 4D 32
Llancatal. V Glam 5D 32
Llancayo. Mon 5G 47
Llancloudy. Here 3H 47
Llancoch. Powy 3E 58
Llancynfelyn. Cdgn 1F 57
Llandaff. Card 4E 33
Llandanwg. Gwyn 3E 69
Llandarcy. Neat 3G 31
Llandawke. Carm 3G 43
Llanddaniel Fab. IOA 3D 81
Llanddarog. Carm 4F 45
Llanddeiniol. Cdgn 3E 57
Llanddeiniolen. Gwyn 4E 81
Llandderfel. Gwyn 2B 70
Llanddeusant. Carm 3A 46
Llanddeusant. IOA 2C 80
Llanddew. Powy 2D 46
Llanddewi. Swan 4D 30
Llanddewi Brefi. Cdgn 5F 57
Llanddewi'r Cwm. Powy 1D 46
Llanddewi Rhydderch.
Mon 4G 47
Llanddewi Velfrey. Pemb 3F 43
Llanddewi Ystradenni.
Powy 4D 58
Llanddoged. Cnwy 4H 81
Llanddona. IOA 3E 81
Llanddowror. Carm 3G 43
Llanddulas. Cnwy 3B 82
Llanddwywe. Gwyn 3E 69
Llanddyfnan. IOA 3E 81
Llandecwyn. Gwyn 2F 69
Llandefaelog Fach. Powy 2D 46
Llandefaelog-tre'r-graig.
Powy 2E 47
Llandefalle. Powy 2E 46
Llandegfan. IOA 3E 81
Llandegla. Den 5D 82
Llandegley. Powy 4D 58
Llandegveth. Mon 2G 33
Llandeilo. Carm 3G 45
Llandeilo Graban. Powy 1D 46
Llandeilo'r Fan. Powy 2B 46
Llandeloy. Pemb 2C 42
Llandenny. Mon 5H 47
Llandevaud. Newp 2H 33
Llandevenny. Mon 3H 33
Llandilo. Pemb 2F 43
Llandinabo. Here 3A 48
Llandinam. Powy 2C 58
Llandissilio. Pemb 2F 43
Llandogo. Mon 5A 48
Llandough. V Glam
nr. Cowbridge 4C 32
nr. Penarth 4E 33
Llandovery. Carm 2A 46
Llandow. V Glam 4C 32
Llandre. Cdgn 2F 57
Llandrillo. Den 2C 70
Llandrillo-yn-Rhos. Cnwy 2H 81
Llandrindod. Powy 4C 58
Llandrindod Wells. Powy 4C 58
Llandrinio. Powy 4E 71
Llandudno. Cnwy 2G 81
Llandudno Junction.
Cnwy 3G 81
Llandudoch. Pemb 1B 44
Llandw. V Glam 4C 32
Llandwrog. Gwyn 5D 80
Llandybie. Carm 4G 45
Llandyfaelog. Carm 4E 45
Llandyfan. Carm 4G 45
Llandyfriog. Cdgn 1D 44
Llandyfrydog. IOA 2D 80
Llandygai. Gwyn 3F 81
Llandygwydd. Cdgn 1C 44
Llandynan. Den 1D 70
Llandyrnog. Den 4D 82
Llandysilio. Powy 4E 71
Llandyssil. Powy 1D 58
Llandysul. Cdgn 1E 45
Llanedeyrn. Card 3F 33
Llaneglwys. Powy 2D 46
Llanegryn. Gwyn 5F 69
Llanegwad. Carm 3F 45
Llaneilian. IOA 1D 80
Llanelian-yn-Rhos. Cnwy 3A 82
Llanelidan. Den 5D 82
Llanelieu. Powy 2E 47
Llanellen. Mon 4G 47
Llanelli. Carm 3E 31
Llanelltyd. Gwyn 4G 69
Llanelly. Mon 4F 47
Llanelly Hill. Mon 4F 47
Llanelwedd. Powy 5C 58
Llan-Elwy. Den 3C 82
Llanenddwyn. Gwyn 3E 69
Llanengan. Gwyn 3B 68
Llanerch. Powy 1F 59
Llanerchymedd. IOA 2D 80
Llanerfyl. Powy 5C 70
Llaneuddog. IOA 2D 80
Llanfachraeth. IOA 2C 80
Llanfachreth. Gwyn 3G 69
Llanfaelog. IOA 3C 80
Llanfaelrhys. Gwyn 3B 68
Llanfaenor. Mon 4H 47
Llanfaes. IOA 3F 81
Llanfaes. Powy 3D 46
Llanfaethlu. IOA 2C 80
Llanfaglan. Gwyn 4D 80
Llanfair. Gwyn 3E 69
Llanfair. Here 1F 47
Llanfair Caereinion. Powy 5D 70
Llanfair Clydogau. Cdgn 5F 57
Llanfair Dyffryn Clwyd.
Den 5D 82
Llanfairfechan. Cnwy 3F 81
Llanfair-Nant-Gwyn. Pemb 1F 43
Llanfair Pwllgwyngyll. IOA 3E 81
Llanfair Talhaiarn. Cnwy 3B 82
Llanfair Waterdine. Shrp 3E 59
Llanfair-ym-Muallt. Powy 5C 58
Llanfairyneubwll. IOA 3C 80
Llanfairynghornwy. IOA 1C 80
Llanfallteg. Carm 3F 43
Llanfallteg West. Carm 3F 43
Llanfaredd. Powy 5C 58
Llanfarian. Cdgn 3E 57
Llanfechain. Powy 3D 70
Llanfechell. IOA 1C 80
Llanfendigaid. Gwyn 5E 69
Llanferres. Den 4D 82
Llan Ffestiniog. Gwyn 1G 69
Llanfflewyn. IOA 2C 80
Llanfihangel-ar-Arth.
Carm 2E 45
Llanfihangel Glyn Myfyr.
Cnwy 1B 70
Llanfihangel Nant Bran.
Powy 2C 46
Llanfihangel-Nant-Melan.
Powy 5D 58
Llanfihangel near Rogiet.
Mon 3H 33
Llanfihangel Rhydithon.
Powy 4D 58
Llanfihangel Tal-y-llyn.
Powy 3E 46
Llanfihangel-uwch-Gwili.
Carm 3E 45
Llanfihangel-y-Creuddyn.
Cdgn 3F 57

Llanfihangel-yng-Ngwynfa—Lynemouth

Llanfihangel-yng-Ngwynfa. *Powy* 4C **70**
Llanfihangel yn Nhowyn. *IOA* 3C **80**
Llanfihangel-y-pennant. *Gwyn*
nr. Golan 1E **69**
nr. Tywyn 5F **69**
Llanfihangel-y-traethau. *Gwyn* 2E **69**
Llanfilo. *Powy* 2E **46**
Llanfleiddan. *V Glam* 4C **32**
Llanfoist. *Mon* 4F **47**
Llanfor. *Gwyn* 2B **70**
Llanfrechfa. *Torf* 2G **33**
Llanfrothen. *Gwyn* 1F **69**
Llanfrynach. *Powy* 3D **46**
Llanfwrog. *Den* 5D **82**
Llanfwrog. *IOA* 2C **80**
Llanfyllin. *Powy* 4D **70**
Llanfynydd. *Carm* 3F **45**
Llanfynydd. *Flin* 5E **83**
Llanfyrnach. *Pemb* 1G **43**
Llangadfan. *Powy* 4C **70**
Llangadog. *Carm*
nr. Llandovery 3H **45**
nr. Llanelli 5E **45**
Llangadwaladr. *IOA* 4C **80**
Llangadwaladr. *Powy* 2D **70**
Llangaffo. *IOA* 4D **80**
Llangain. *Carm* 4D **45**
Llangammarch Wells. *Powy* 1C **46**
Llangan. *V Glam* 4C **32**
Llangarron. *Here* 3A **48**
Llangasty-Talyllyn. *Powy* 3E **47**
Llangathen. *Carm* 3F **45**
Llangattock. *Powy* 4F **47**
Llangattock Lingoed. *Mon* 3G **47**
Llangattock-Vibon-Avel. *Mon* 4H **47**
Llangedwyn. *Powy* 3D **70**
Llangefni. *IOA* 3D **80**
Llangeinor. *B'end* 3C **32**
Llangeitho. *Cdgn* 5F **57**
Llangeler. *Carm* 2D **44**
Llangelynin. *Gwyn* 5E **69**
Llangendeirne. *Carm* 4E **45**
Llangennech. *Carm* 5F **45**
Llangennith. *Swan* 3D **30**
Llangenny. *Powy* 4F **47**
Llangernyw. *Cnwy* 4A **82**
Llangian. *Gwyn* 3B **68**
Llangiwg. *Neat* 5H **45**
Llangloffan. *Pemb* 1D **42**
Llanglydwen. *Carm* 2F **43**
Llangoed. *IOA* 3F **81**
Llangoedmor. *Cdgn* 1B **44**
Llangollen. *Den* 1E **70**
Llangolman. *Pemb* 2F **43**
Llangorse. *Powy* 3E **47**
Llangorwen. *Cdgn* 2F **57**
Llangovan. *Mon* 5H **47**
Llangower. *Gwyn* 2B **70**
Llangranog. *Cdgn* 5C **56**
Llangristiolus. *IOA* 3D **80**
Llangrove. *Here* 4A **48**
Llangua. *Mon* 3G **47**
Llangunllo. *Powy* 3E **58**
Llangunnor. *Carm* 3E **45**
Llangurig. *Powy* 3B **58**
Llangwm. *Cnwy* 1B **70**
Llangwm. *Mon* 5H **47**
Llangwm. *Pemb* 4D **43**
Llangwm-isaf. *Mon* 5H **47**
Llangwnnadl. *Gwyn* 2B **68**
Llangwyfan. *Den* 4D **82**
Llangwyfan-isaf. *IOA* 4C **80**
Llangwyllog. *IOA* 3D **80**
Llangwyryfon. *Cdgn* 3E **57**
Llangybi. *Cdgn* 5F **57**
Llangybi. *Gwyn* 1D **68**
Llangybi. *Mon* 2G **33**
Llangyfelach. *Swan* 3F **31**
Llangynhafal. *Den* 4D **82**
Llangynidr. *Powy* 4E **47**
Llangynin. *Carm* 3G **43**
Llangynog. *Carm* 3H **43**
Llangynog. *Powy* 3C **70**
Llangynwyd. *B'end* 3B **32**
Llanhamlach. *Powy* 3D **46**
Llanharan. *Rhon* 3D **32**
Llanharry. *Rhon* 3D **32**
Llanhennock. *Mon* 2G **33**
Llanhilleth. *Blae* 5F **47**
Llanidloes. *Powy* 2B **58**
Llaniestyn. *Gwyn* 2B **68**
Llanigon. *Powy* 1F **47**
Llanilar. *Cdgn* 3F **57**
Llanilid. *Rhon* 3C **32**
Llanilltud Fawr. *V Glam* 5C **32**
Llanishen. *Card* 3E **33**
Llanishen. *Mon* 5H **47**
Llanllawddog. *Carm* 3E **45**
Llanllechid. *Gwyn* 4F **81**
Llanllowell. *Mon* 2G **33**
Llanllugan. *Powy* 5C **70**
Llanllwch. *Carm* 4D **45**
Llanllwchaiarn. *Powy* 1D **58**
Llanllwni. *Carm* 2E **45**
Llanllyfni. *Gwyn* 5D **80**
Llanmadoc. *Swan* 3D **30**
Llanmaes. *V Glam* 5C **32**
Llanmartin. *Newp* 3G **33**
Llanmerwig. *Powy* 1D **58**
Llanmihangel. *V Glam* 4C **32**
Llan-mill. *Pemb* 3F **43**
Llanmiloe. *Carm* 4G **43**
Llanmorlais. *Swan* 3E **31**
Llannefydd. *Cnwy* 3B **82**
Llan-non. *Cdgn* 4E **57**
Llannon. *Carm* 5F **45**
Llannor. *Gwyn* 2C **68**
Llanover. *Mon* 5G **47**
Llanpumsaint. *Carm* 3E **45**
Llanrhaeadr. *Den* 4C **82**
Llanrhaeadr-ym-Mochnant. *Powy* 3D **70**
Llanrhian. *Pemb* 1C **42**
Llanrhidian. *Swan* 3D **31**
Llanrhos. *Cnwy* 2G **81**
Llanrhyddlad. *IOA* 2C **80**
Llanrhystud. *Cdgn* 4E **57**
Llanrothal. *Here* 4H **47**
Llanrug. *Gwyn* 4E **81**
Llanrumney. *Card* 3F **33**
Llanrwst. *Cnwy* 4G **81**
Llansadurnen. *Carm* 3G **43**
Llansadwrn. *Carm* 2G **45**
Llansadwrn. *IOA* 3E **81**
Llansaint. *Carm* 5D **45**
Llansamlet. *Swan* 3F **31**
Llansanffraid Glan Conwy. *Cnwy* 3H **81**
Llansannan. *Cnwy* 4B **82**
Llansannor. *V Glam* 4C **32**
Llansantffraed. *Cdgn* 4E **57**
Llansantffraed. *Powy* 3E **46**
Llansantffraed Cwmdeuddwr. *Powy* 4B **58**
Llansantffraed-in-Elwel. *Powy* 5C **58**
Llansantffraid-ym-Mechain. *Powy* 3E **70**
Llansawel. *Carm* 2G **45**
Llansawel. *Neat* 3G **31**
Llansilin. *Powy* 3E **70**
Llansoy. *Mon* 5H **47**
Llanspyddid. *Powy* 3D **46**
Llanstadwell. *Pemb* 4D **42**
Llansteffan. *Carm* 4D **44**
Llanstephan. *Powy* 1E **46**
Llantarnam. *Torf* 2G **33**
Llanteg. *Pemb* 3F **43**
Llanthony. *Mon* 3F **47**
Llantilio Crossenny. *Mon* 4G **47**
Llantilio Pertholey. *Mon* 4G **47**
Llantood. *Pemb* 1B **44**
Llantrisant. *Mon* 2G **33**
Llantrisant. *Rhon* 3D **32**
Llantrithyd. *V Glam* 4D **32**
Llantwit Fardre. *Rhon* 3D **32**
Llantwit Major. *V Glam* 5C **32**
Llanuwchllyn. *Gwyn* 2A **70**
Llanvaches. *Newp* 2H **33**
Llanvair Discoed. *Mon* 2H **33**
Llanvapley. *Mon* 4G **47**
Llanvetherine. *Mon* 4G **47**
Llanveynoe. *Here* 2G **47**
Llanvihangel Crucorney. *Mon* 3G **47**
Llanvihangel Gobion. *Mon* 5G **47**
Llanvihangel Ystern-Llewern. *Mon* 4H **47**
Llanwarne. *Here* 3A **48**
Llanwddyn. *Powy* 4C **70**
Llanwenarth. *Mon* 4F **47**
Llanwenog. *Cdgn* 1E **45**
Llanwern. *Newp* 3G **33**
Llanwinio. *Carm* 2G **43**
Llanwnda. *Gwyn* 5D **80**
Llanwnda. *Pemb* 1D **42**
Llanwnnen. *Cdgn* 1F **45**
Llanwnog. *Powy* 1C **58**
Llanwrda. *Carm* 2H **45**
Llanwrin. *Powy* 5G **69**
Llanwrthwl. *Powy* 4B **58**
Llanwrtud. *Powy* 1B **46**
Llanwrtyd. *Powy* 1B **46**
Llanwrtyd Wells. *Powy* 1B **46**
Llanwyddelan. *Powy* 5C **70**
Llanyblodwel. *Shrp* 3E **71**
Llanybri. *Carm* 3H **43**
Llanybydder. *Carm* 1F **45**
Llanycefn. *Pemb* 2E **43**
Llanychaer. *Pemb* 1D **43**
Llanycil. *Gwyn* 2B **70**
Llanymawddwy. *Gwyn* 4B **70**
Llanymddyfri. *Carm* 2A **46**
Llanymynech. *Powy* 3E **71**
Llanynghenedl. *IOA* 2C **80**
Llanynys. *Den* 4D **82**
Llan-y-pwll. *Wrex* 5F **83**
Llanyrafon. *Torf* 2G **33**
Llanyre. *Powy* 4C **58**
Llanystumdwy. *Gwyn* 2D **68**
Llanywern. *Powy* 3E **46**
Llawhaden. *Pemb* 3E **43**
Llawndy. *Flin* 2D **82**
Llawnt. *Shrp* 2E **71**
Llawr Dref. *Gwyn* 3B **68**
Llawryglyn. *Powy* 1B **58**
Llay. *Wrex* 5F **83**
Llechfaen. *Powy* 3D **46**
Llechryd. *Cphy* 5E **46**
Llechryd. *Cdgn* 1C **44**
Llechrydau. *Wrex* 2E **71**
Lledrod. *Cdgn* 3F **57**
Llethrid. *Swan* 3E **31**
Llidiad-Nenog. *Carm* 2F **45**
Llidiardau. *Gwyn* 2A **70**
Llidiart y Parc. *Den* 1D **70**
Llithfaen. *Gwyn* 1C **68**
Lloc. *Flin* 3D **82**
Llong. *Flin* 4E **83**
Llowes. *Powy* 1E **47**
Lloyney. *Powy* 3E **59**
Llundain-fach. *Cdgn* 5E **57**
Llwydcoed. *Rhon* 5C **46**
Llwyncelyn. *Cdgn* 5D **56**
Llwyncelyn. *Swan* 5G **45**
Llwyndafydd. *Cdgn* 5C **56**
Llwynderw. *Powy* 5E **70**
Llwyn-du. *Mon* 4F **47**
Llwyngwril. *Gwyn* 5E **69**
Llwynhendy. *Carm* 3E **31**
Llwynmawr. *Wrex* 2E **71**
Llwyn-on Village. *Mer T* 4D **46**
Llwyn-têg. *Carm* 5F **45**
Llwyn-y-brain. *Carm* 3F **43**
Llwynygog. *Powy* 1A **58**
Llwyn-y-groes. *Cdgn* 5E **57**
Llwynypia. *Rhon* 2C **32**
Llynclys. *Shrp* 3E **71**
Llynfaes. *IOA* 3D **80**
Llysfaen. *Cnwy* 3A **82**
Llyswen. *Powy* 2E **47**
Llysworney. *V Glam* 4C **32**
Llys-y-fran. *Pemb* 2E **43**
Llywel. *Powy* 2B **46**
Llywernog. *Cdgn* 2G **57**
Loan. *Falk* 2C **128**
Loanend. *Nmbd* 4F **131**
Loanhead. *Midl* 3F **129**
Loaningfoot. *Dum* 4A **112**
Loanreoch. *High* 1A **158**
Loans. *S Ayr* 1C **116**
Loansdean. *Nmbd* 1E **115**
Lobb. *Devn* 3E **19**
Lobhillcross. *Devn* 4E **11**
Lochaber. *Mor* 3E **159**
Loch a Charnain. *W Isl* 4D **170**
Loch a Ghainmhich. *W Isl* 5E **171**
Lochailort. *High* 5F **147**
Lochaline. *High* 4A **140**
Lochans. *Dum* 4F **109**
Locharbriggs. *Dum* 1A **112**
Lochardil. *High* 4A **158**
Lochassynt Lodge. *High* 1F **163**
Lochavich. *Arg* 2G **133**
Lochawe. *Arg* 1A **134**
Loch Baghasdail. *W Isl* 7C **170**
Lochboisdale. *W Isl* 7C **170**
Lochbuie. *Arg* 1D **132**
Lochcarron. *High* 5A **156**
Loch Choire Lodge. *High* 5G **167**
Lochdochart House. *Stir* 1D **134**
Lochdon. *Arg* 5B **140**
Lochearnhead. *Stir* 1E **135**
Lochee. *D'dee* 5C **144**
Lochend. *High*
nr. Inverness 5H **157**
nr. Thurso 2E **169**
Locherben. *Dum* 5B **118**
Loch Euphort. *W Isl* 2D **170**
Lochfoot. *Dum* 2F **111**
Lochgair. *Arg* 4G **133**
Lochgarthside. *High* 2H **149**
Lochgelly. *Fife* 4D **136**
Lochgilphead. *Arg* 1G **125**
Lochgoilhead. *Arg* 3A **134**
Loch Head. *Dum* 5A **110**
Lochhill. *Mor* 2G **159**
Lochindorb Lodge. *High* 5D **158**
Lochinver. *High* 1E **163**
Lochlane. *Per* 1H **135**
Loch Lomond. *Arg* 3C **134**
Loch Loyal Lodge. *High* 4G **167**
Lochluichart. *High* 2F **157**
Lochmaben. *Dum* 1B **112**
Lochmaddy. *W Isl* 2E **170**
Loch nam Madadh. *W Isl* 2E **170**
Lochore. *Fife* 4D **136**
Lochportain. *W Isl* 1E **170**
Lochranza. *N Ayr* 4H **125**
Loch Sgioport. *W Isl* 5D **170**
Lochside. *Abers* 2G **145**
Lochside. *High*
nr. Achentoul 5A **168**
nr. Nairn 3C **158**
Lochslin. *High* 5F **165**
Lochstack Lodge. *High* 4C **166**
Lochton. *Abers* 4E **153**
Lochty. *Fife* 3H **137**
Lochuisge. *High* 3B **140**
Lochussie. *High* 3G **157**
Lochwinnoch. *Ren* 4E **127**
Lochyside. *High* 1F **141**
Lockengate. *Corn* 2E **7**
Lockerbie. *Dum* 1C **112**
Lockeridge. *Wilts* 5G **35**
Lockerley. *Hants* 4A **24**
Lockhills. *Cumb* 5G **113**
Locking. *N Som* 1G **21**
Lockington. *E Yor* 5D **101**
Lockington. *Leics* 3B **74**
Lockleywood. *Shrp* 3A **72**
Locksgreen. *IOW* 3C **16**
Locks Heath. *Hants* 2D **16**
Lockton. *N Yor* 5F **107**
Loddington. *Leics* 5E **75**
Loddington. *Nptn* 3F **63**
Loddiswell. *Devn* 4D **8**
Loddon. *Norf* 1F **67**
Lode. *Cambs* 4E **65**
Loders. *Dors* 3H **13**
Lodsworth. *W Sus* 3A **26**
Lofthouse. *N Yor* 2D **98**
Lofthouse. *W Yor* 2D **92**
Lofthouse Gate. *W Yor* 2D **92**
Loftus. *Red C* 3E **107**
Logan. *E Ayr* 2E **117**
Loganlea. *W Lot* 3C **128**
Logaston. *Here* 5F **59**
Loggerheads. *Den* 4D **82**
Loggerheads. *Staf* 2B **72**
Loggie. *High* 4F **163**
Logie. *Ang* 2F **145**
Logie. *Fife* 1G **137**
Logie. *Mor* 3E **159**
Logie Coldstone. *Abers* 3B **152**
Logie Pert. *Ang* 2F **145**
Logierait. *Per* 3G **143**
Login. *Carm* 2F **43**
Lolworth. *Cambs* 4C **64**
Lonbain. *High* 3F **155**
Londesborough. *E Yor* 5C **100**
London. *G Lon* **198-199** (2E **39**)
London Apprentice. *Corn* 3E **6**
London Ashford Airport. *Kent* 3E **29**
London City Airport. *G Lon* 2F **39**
London Colney. *Herts* 5B **52**
Londonderry. *Derr* 5A **174**
Londonderry. *N Yor* 1F **99**
London Gatwick Airport. *W Sus* **205** (1D **26**)
London Heathrow Airport. *G Lon* **205** (3B **38**)
London Luton Airport. *Lutn* **205** (3B **52**)
London Southend Airport. *Essx* 2C **40**
London Stansted Airport. *Essx* **205** (3F **53**)
Londonthorpe. *Linc* 2G **75**
Londubh. *High* 5C **162**
Lone. *High* 4D **166**
Lonemore. *High*
nr. Dornoch 5E **165**
nr. Gairloch 1G **155**
Long Ashton. *N Som* 4A **34**
Long Bank. *Worc* 3B **60**
Longbar. *N Ayr* 4E **127**
Long Bennington. *Linc* 1F **75**
Longbenton. *Tyne* 3F **115**
Longborough. *Glos* 3G **49**
Long Bredy. *Dors* 3A **14**
Longbridge. *Warw* 4G **61**
Longbridge. *W Mid* 3E **61**
Longbridge Deverill. *Wilts* 2D **22**
Long Buckby. *Nptn* 4D **62**
Long Buckby Wharf. *Nptn* 4D **62**
Longburgh. *Cumb* 4E **112**
Longburton. *Dors* 1B **14**
Long Clawson. *Leics* 3E **74**
Longcliffe. *Derbs* 5G **85**
Long Common. *Hants* 1D **16**
Long Compton. *Staf* 3C **72**
Long Compton. *Warw* 2A **50**
Longcot. *Oxon* 2A **36**
Long Crendon. *Buck* 5E **51**
Long Crichel. *Dors* 1E **15**
Longcroft. *Cumb* 4D **112**
Longcroft. *Falk* 2A **128**
Longcross. *Surr* 4A **38**
Longdale. *Cumb* 4H **103**
Longdales. *Cumb* 5G **113**
Longden. *Shrp* 5G **71**
Longden Common. *Shrp* 5G **71**
Long Ditton. *Surr* 4C **38**
Longdon. *Staf* 4E **73**
Longdon. *Worc* 2D **48**
Longdon Green. *Staf* 4E **73**
Longdon on Tern. *Telf* 4A **72**
Longdown. *Devn* 3B **12**
Longdowns. *Corn* 5B **6**
Long Drax. *N Yor* 2G **93**
Long Duckmanton. *Derbs* 3B **86**
Long Eaton. *Derbs* 2B **74**
Longfield. *Kent* 4H **39**
Longfield. *Shet* 10E **173**
Longfield Hill. *Kent* 4H **39**
Longford. *Derbs* 2G **73**
Longford. *Glos* 3D **48**
Longford. *G Lon* 3B **38**
Longford. *Shrp* 2A **72**
Longford. *Telf* 4B **72**
Longford. *W Mid* 2A **62**
Longforgan. *Per* 5C **144**
Longformacus. *Bord* 4C **130**
Longframlington. *Nmbd* 4F **121**
Long Gardens. *Essx* 2B **54**
Long Green. *Ches W* 3G **83**
Long Green. *Worc* 2D **48**
Longham. *Dors* 3F **15**
Longham. *Norf* 4B **78**
Long Hanborough. *Oxon* 4C **50**
Longhedge. *Wilts* 2D **22**
Longhill. *Abers* 3H **161**
Longhirst. *Nmbd* 1F **115**
Longhope. *Glos* 4B **48**
Longhope. *Orkn* 8C **172**
Longhorsley. *Nmbd* 5F **121**
Longhoughton. *Nmbd* 3G **121**
Long Itchington. *Warw* 4B **62**
Longlands. *Cumb* 1D **102**
Long Lane. *Telf* 4A **72**
Longlane. *Derbs* 2G **73**
Longlane. *W Ber* 4C **36**
Long Lawford. *Warw* 3B **62**
Long Lease. *N Yor* 4G **107**
Longley Green. *Worc* 5B **60**
Long Load. *Som* 4H **21**
Longmanhill. *Abers* 2E **161**
Long Marston. *Herts* 4G **51**
Long Marston. *N Yor* 4H **99**
Long Marston. *Warw* 1G **49**
Long Marton. *Cumb* 2H **103**
Long Meadow. *Cambs* 4E **65**
Long Meadowend. *Shrp* 2G **59**
Long Melford. *Suff* 1B **54**
Longmoor Camp. *Hants* 3F **25**
Longmorn. *Mor* 3G **159**
Longmoss. *Ches E* 3C **84**
Long Newnton. *Glos* 2E **35**
Long Newton. *Stoc T* 3A **106**
Longnewton. *Bord* 2H **119**
Longney. *Glos* 4C **48**
Longniddry. *E Lot* 2H **129**
Longnor. *Shrp* 5G **71**
Longnor. *Staf*
nr. Leek 4E **85**
nr. Stafford 4C **72**
Longparish. *Hants* 2C **24**
Longpark. *Cumb* 3F **113**
Long Preston. *N Yor* 4H **97**
Longridge. *Lanc* 1E **90**
Longridge. *Staf* 4D **72**
Longridge. *W Lot* 3C **128**
Longriggend. *N Lan* 2B **128**
Long Riston. *E Yor* 5F **101**
Longrock. *Corn* 3C **4**
Longsdon. *Staf* 5D **84**
Longshaw. *G Man* 4D **90**
Longshaw. *Staf* 1E **73**
Longside. *Abers* 4H **161**
Longslow. *Shrp* 2A **72**
Longstanton. *Cambs* 4C **64**
Longstock. *Hants* 3B **24**
Longstowe. *Cambs* 5C **64**
Long Stratton. *Norf* 1D **66**
Long Street. *Mil* 1F **51**
Longstreet. *Wilts* 1G **23**
Long Sutton. *Hants* 2F **25**
Long Sutton. *Linc* 3D **76**
Long Sutton. *Som* 4H **21**
Longthorpe. *Pet* 1A **64**
Long Thurlow. *Suff* 4C **66**
Longthwaite. *Cumb* 2F **103**
Longton. *Lanc* 2C **90**
Longton. *Stoke* 1D **72**
Longtown. *Cumb* 3E **113**
Longtown. *Here* 3G **47**
Longville in the Dale. *Shrp* 1H **59**
Long Whatton. *Leics* 3B **74**
Longwick. *Buck* 5F **51**
Long Wittenham. *Oxon* 2D **36**
Longwitton. *Nmbd* 1D **115**
Longworth. *Oxon* 2B **36**
Longyester. *E Lot* 3B **130**
Lonmore. *High* 4B **154**
Looe. *Corn* 3G **7**
Loose. *Kent* 5B **40**
Loosegate. *Linc* 3C **76**
Loosley Row. *Buck* 5G **51**
Lopcombe Corner. *Wilts* 3A **24**
Lopen. *Som* 1H **13**
Loppington. *Shrp* 3G **71**
Lorbottle. *Nmbd* 4E **121**
Lordington. *W Sus* 2F **17**
Loscoe. *Derbs* 1B **74**
Loscombe. *Dors* 3A **14**
Losgaintir. *W Isl* 8C **171**
Lossiemouth. *Mor* 2G **159**
Lossit. *Arg* 4A **124**
Lostock Gralam. *Ches W* 3A **84**
Lostock Green. *Ches W* 3A **84**
Lostock Hall. *Lanc* 2D **90**
Lostock Junction. *G Man* 4E **91**
Lostwithiel. *Corn* 3F **7**
Lothbeg. *High* 2G **165**
Lothersdale. *N Yor* 5B **98**
Lothianbridge. *Midl* 3G **129**
Lothianburn. *Midl* 3F **129**
Lothmore. *High* 2G **165**
Lottisham. *Som* 3A **22**
Loudwater. *Buck* 1A **38**
Loughborough. *Leics* 4C **74**
Loughbrickland. *Arm* 5F **178**
Loughgall. *Arm* 4D **178**
Loughguile. *Caus* 4G **175**
Loughinisland. *New M* 5J **179**
Loughmacrory. *Ferm* 2L **177**
Loughor. *Swan* 3E **31**
Loughries. *Ards* 2K **179**
Loughton. *Essx* 1F **39**
Loughton. *Mil* 2G **51**
Loughton. *Shrp* 2A **60**
Lound. *Linc* 4H **75**
Lound. *Notts* 2D **86**
Lound. *Suff* 1H **67**
Lount. *Leics* 4A **74**
The Loup. *M Ulst* 1D **178**
Louth. *Linc* 2C **88**
Love Clough. *Lanc* 2G **91**
Lovedean. *Hants* 1E **17**
Lover. *Wilts* 4H **23**
Loversall. *S Yor* 1C **86**
Loves Green. *Essx* 5G **53**
Loveston. *Pemb* 4E **43**
Lovington. *Som* 3A **22**
Low Ackworth. *W Yor* 3E **93**
Low Angerton. *Nmbd* 1D **115**
Low Ardwell. *Dum* 5F **109**
Low Ballochdowan. *S Ayr* 2F **109**
Lowbands. *Glos* 2C **48**
Low Barlings. *Linc* 3H **87**
Low Bell End. *N Yor* 5E **107**
Low Bentham. *N Yor* 3F **97**
Low Borrowbridge. *Cumb* 4H **103**
Low Bradfield. *S Yor* 1G **85**
Low Bradley. *N Yor* 5C **98**
Low Braithwaite. *Cumb* 5F **113**
Low Brunton. *Nmbd* 2C **114**
Low Burnham. *N Lin* 4A **94**
Lowca. *Cumb* 2A **102**
Low Catton. *E Yor* 4B **100**
Low Coniscliffe. *Darl* 3F **105**
Low Coylton. *S Ayr* 3D **116**
Low Crosby. *Cumb* 4F **113**
Low Dalby. *N Yor* 1C **100**
Lowdham. *Notts* 1D **74**
Low Dinsdale. *Darl* 3A **106**
Lowe. *Shrp* 2H **71**
Low Ellington. *N Yor* 1E **98**
Lower Amble. *Corn* 1D **6**
Lower Ansty. *Dors* 2C **14**
Lower Arboll. *High* 5F **165**
Lower Arncott. *Oxon* 4E **50**
Lower Ashton. *Devn* 4B **12**
Lower Assendon. *Oxon* 3F **37**
Lower Auchenreath. *Mor* 2A **160**
Lower Badcall. *High* 4B **166**
Lower Ballam. *Lanc* 1B **90**
Lower Ballinderry. *Lis* 3F **178**
Lower Basildon. *W Ber* 4E **36**
Lower Beeding. *W Sus* 3D **26**
Lower Benefield. *Nptn* 2G **63**
Lower Bentley. *Worc* 4D **61**
Lower Beobridge. *Shrp* 1B **60**
Lower Bockhampton. *Dors* 3C **14**
Lower Boddington. *Nptn* 5B **62**
Lower Bordean. *Hants* 4E **25**
Lower Brailes. *Warw* 2B **50**
Lower Breakish. *High* 1E **147**
Lower Broadheath. *Worc* 5C **60**
Lower Brynamman. *Neat* 4H **45**
Lower Bullingham. *Here* 2A **48**
Lower Bullington. *Hants* 2C **24**
Lower Burgate. *Hants* 1G **15**
Lower Cam. *Glos* 5C **48**
Lower Catesby. *Nptn* 5C **62**
Lower Chapel. *Powy* 2D **46**
Lower Cheriton. *Devn* 2E **12**
Lower Chicksgrove. *Wilts* 3E **23**
Lower Chute. *Wilts* 1B **24**
Lower Clopton. *Warw* 5F **61**
Lower Common. *Hants* 2E **25**
Lower Crossings. *Derbs* 2E **85**
Lower Cumberworth. *W Yor* 4C **92**
Lower Darwen. *Bkbn* 2E **91**
Lower Dean. *Bed* 4H **63**
Lower Dean. *Devn* 2D **8**
Lower Diabaig. *High* 2G **155**
Lower Dicker. *E Sus* 4G **27**
Lower Dounreay. *High* 2B **168**
Lower Down. *Shrp* 2F **59**
Lower Dunsforth. *N Yor* 3G **99**
Lower East Carleton. *Norf* 5D **78**
Lower Egleton. *Here* 1B **48**
Lower Ellastone. *Staf* 1F **73**
Lower End. *Nptn* 4F **63**
Lower Everleigh. *Wilts* 1G **23**
Lower Eype. *Dors* 3H **13**
Lower Failand. *N Som* 4A **34**
Lower Faintree. *Shrp* 2A **60**
Lower Farringdon. *Hants* 3F **25**
Lower Foxdale. *IOM* 4B **108**
Lower Frankton. *Shrp* 2F **71**
Lower Froyle. *Hants* 2F **25**
Lower Gabwell. *Devn* 2F **9**
Lower Gledfield. *High* 4C **164**
Lower Godney. *Som* 2H **21**
Lower Gravenhurst. *C Beds* 2B **52**
Lower Green. *Essx* 2E **53**
Lower Green. *Norf* 2B **78**
Lower Green. *W Ber* 5B **36**
Lower Halstow. *Kent* 4C **40**
Lower Hardres. *Kent* 5F **41**
Lower Hardwick. *Here* 5G **59**
Lower Hartshay. *Derbs* 5A **86**
Lower Hawthwaite. *Cumb* 1B **96**
Lower Haysden. *Kent* 1G **27**
Lower Hayton. *Shrp* 2H **59**
Lower Hergest. *Here* 5E **59**
Lower Heyford. *Oxon* 3C **50**
Lower Heysham. *Lanc* 3D **96**
Lower Higham. *Kent* 3B **40**
Lower Holbrook. *Suff* 2E **55**
Lower Holditch. *Dors* 2G **13**
Lower Hordley. *Shrp* 3F **71**
Lower Horncroft. *W Sus* 4B **26**
Lower Horsebridge. *E Sus* 4G **27**
Lower Kilcott. *Glos* 3C **34**
Lower Killeyan. *Arg* 5A **124**
Lower Kingcombe. *Dors* 3A **14**
Lower Kingswood. *Surr* 5D **38**
Lower Kinnerton. *Ches W* 4F **83**
Lower Langford. *N Som* 5H **33**
Lower Largo. *Fife* 3G **137**
Lower Layham. *Suff* 1D **54**
Lower Ledwyche. *Shrp* 3H **59**
Lower Leigh. *Staf* 2E **73**
Lower Lemington. *Glos* 2H **49**
Lower Lenie. *High* 1H **149**
Lower Ley. *Glos* 4C **48**
Lower Llanfadog. *Powy* 4B **58**
Lower Lode. *Glos* 2D **49**
Lower Lovacott. *Devn* 4F **19**
Lower Loxhore. *Devn* 3G **19**
Lower Loxley. *Staf* 2E **73**
Lower Lydbrook. *Glos* 4A **48**
Lower Lye. *Here* 4G **59**
Lower Machen. *Newp* 3F **33**
Lower Maes-coed. *Here* 2G **47**
Lower Meend. *Glos* 5A **48**
Lower Midway. *Derbs* 3H **73**
Lower Milovaig. *High* 3A **154**
Lower Moor. *Worc* 1E **49**
Lower Morton. *S Glo* 2B **34**
Lower Mountain. *Flin* 5F **83**
Lower Nazeing. *Essx* 5D **53**
Lower Netchwood. *Shrp* 1A **60**
Lower Nyland. *Dors* 4C **22**
Lower Oakfield. *Fife* 4D **136**
Lower Oddington. *Glos* 3H **49**
Lower Ollach. *High* 5E **155**
Lower Penarth. *V Glam* 5E **33**
Lower Penn. *Staf* 1C **60**
Lower Pennington. *Hants* 3B **16**
Lower Peover. *Ches W* 3B **84**
Lower Pilsley. *Derbs* 4B **86**
Lower Pitkerrie. *High* 1C **158**
Lower Place. *G Man* 3H **91**
Lower Quinton. *Warw* 1G **49**
Lower Rainham. *Medw* 4C **40**
Lower Raydon. *Suff* 2D **54**
Lower Seagry. *Wilts* 3E **35**
Lower Shelton. *C Beds* 1H **51**
Lower Shiplake. *Oxon* 4F **37**
Lower Shuckburgh. *Warw* 4B **62**
Lower Sketty. *Swan* 3F **31**
Lower Slade. *Devn* 2F **19**
Lower Slaughter. *Glos* 3G **49**
Lower Soudley. *Glos* 4B **48**
Lower Stanton St Quintin. *Wilts* 3E **35**
Lower Stoke. *Medw* 3C **40**
Lower Stondon. *C Beds* 2B **52**
Lower Stonnall. *Staf* 5E **73**
Lower Stow Bedon. *Norf* 1B **66**
Lower Street. *Norf* 2E **79**
Lower Strensham. *Worc* 1E **49**
Lower Sundon. *C Beds* 3A **52**
Lower Swanwick. *Hants* 2C **16**
Lower Swell. *Glos* 3G **49**
Lower Tale. *Devn* 2D **12**
Lower Tean. *Staf* 2E **73**
Lower Thurlton. *Norf* 1G **67**
Lower Thurnham. *Lanc* 4D **96**
Lower Thurvaston. *Derbs* 2G **73**
Lower Town. *Here* 1B **48**
Lower Town. *IOS* 1B **4**
Lower Town. *Pemb* 1D **42**
Lowertown. *Corn* 4D **4**
Lowertown. *Orkn* 8D **172**
Lower Tysoe. *Warw* 1B **50**
Lower Upham. *Hants* 1D **16**
Lower Upnor. *Medw* 3B **40**
Lower Vexford. *Som* 3E **20**
Lower Walton. *Warr* 2A **84**
Lower Wear. *Devn* 4C **12**
Lower Weare. *Som* 1H **21**
Lower Welson. *Here* 5E **59**
Lower Whatcombe. *Dors* 2D **14**
Lower Whitley. *Ches W* 3A **84**
Lower Wield. *Hants* 2E **25**
Lower Withington. *Ches E* 4C **84**
Lower Woodend. *Buck* 3G **37**
Lower Woodford. *Wilts* 3G **23**
Lower Wraxall. *Dors* 2A **14**
Lower Wych. *Ches W* 1G **71**
Lower Wyche. *Worc* 1C **48**
Lowesby. *Leics* 5E **74**
Lowestoft. *Suff* 1H **67**
Loweswater. *Cumb* 2C **102**
Low Etherley. *Dur* 2E **105**
Lowfield Heath. *W Sus* 1D **26**
Lowford. *Hants* 1C **16**
Low Fulney. *Linc* 3B **76**
Low Gate. *Nmbd* 3C **114**
Lowgill. *Cumb* 5H **103**
Lowgill. *Lanc* 3F **97**
Low Grantley. *N Yor* 2E **99**
Low Green. *N Yor* 4E **98**
Low Habberley. *Worc* 3C **60**
Low Ham. *Som* 4H **21**
Low Hameringham. *Linc* 4C **88**
Low Hawsker. *N Yor* 4G **107**
Low Hesket. *Cumb* 5F **113**
Low Hesleyhurst. *Nmbd* 5E **121**
Lowick. *Cumb* 1B **96**
Lowick. *Nptn* 2G **63**
Lowick. *Nmbd* 1E **121**
Lowick Bridge. *Cumb* 1B **96**
Lowick Green. *Cumb* 1B **96**
Low Knipe. *Cumb* 2G **103**
Low Leighton. *Derbs* 2E **85**
Low Lorton. *Cumb* 2C **102**
Low Marishes. *N Yor* 2C **100**
Low Marnham. *Notts* 4F **87**
Low Mill. *N Yor* 5D **106**
Low Moor. *Lanc* 5G **97**
Low Moor. *W Yor* 2B **92**
Low Moorsley. *Tyne* 5G **115**
Low Newton-by-the-Sea. *Nmbd* 2G **121**
Lownie Moor. *Ang* 4D **145**
Lowood. *Bord* 1H **119**
Low Row. *Cumb*
nr. Brampton 3G **113**
nr. Wigton 5C **112**
Low Row. *N Yor* 5C **104**
Lowsonford. *Warw* 4F **61**
Low Street. *Norf* 5C **78**
Lowther. *Cumb* 2G **103**
Lowthorpe. *E Yor* 3E **101**
Lowton. *Devn* 2G **11**
Lowton. *G Man* 1A **84**
Lowton. *Som* 1E **13**
Lowton Common. *G Man* 1A **84**
Low Torry. *Fife* 1D **128**
Low Toynton. *Linc* 3B **88**
Low Valleyfield. *Fife* 1C **128**
Low Westwood. *Dur* 4E **115**
Low Whinnow. *Cumb* 4E **112**
Low Wood. *Cumb* 1C **96**
Low Worsall. *N Yor* 4A **106**
Low Wray. *Cumb* 4E **103**
Loxbeare. *Devn* 1C **12**
Loxhill. *Surr* 2B **26**
Loxhore. *Devn* 3G **19**
Loxley. *S Yor* 2H **85**
Loxley. *Warw* 5G **61**
Loxley Green. *Staf* 2E **73**
Loxton. *N Som* 1G **21**
Loxwood. *W Sus* 2B **26**
Lubcroy. *High* 3A **164**
Lubenham. *Leics* 2E **62**
Lubinvullin. *High* 2F **167**
Luccombe. *Som* 2C **20**
Luccombe Village. *IOW* 4D **16**
Lucker. *Nmbd* 1F **121**
Luckett. *Corn* 5D **11**
Luckington. *Wilts* 3D **34**
Lucklawhill. *Fife* 1G **137**
Luckwell Bridge. *Som* 3C **20**
Lucton. *Here* 4G **59**
Ludag. *W Isl* 7C **170**
Ludborough. *Linc* 1B **88**
Ludchurch. *Pemb* 3F **43**
Luddenden. *W Yor* 2A **92**
Luddenden Foot. *W Yor* 2A **92**
Luddenham. *Kent* 4D **40**
Ludderburn. *Cumb* 5F **103**
Luddesdown. *Kent* 4A **40**
Luddington. *N Lin* 3B **94**
Luddington. *Warw* 5F **61**
Luddington in the Brook. *Nptn* 2A **64**
Ludford. *Linc* 2A **88**
Ludford. *Shrp* 3H **59**
Ludgershall. *Buck* 4E **51**
Ludgershall. *Wilts* 1A **24**
Ludgvan. *Corn* 3C **4**
Ludham. *Norf* 4F **79**
Ludlow. *Shrp* 3H **59**
Ludstone. *Shrp* 1C **60**
Ludwell. *Wilts* 4E **23**
Ludworth. *Dur* 5G **115**
Luffenhall. *Herts* 3C **52**
Luffincott. *Devn* 3D **10**
Lugar. *E Ayr* 2E **117**
Luggate Burn. *E Lot* 2C **130**
Lugg Green. *Here* 4G **59**
Luggiebank. *N Lan* 2A **128**
Lugton. *E Ayr* 4F **127**
Lugwardine. *Here* 1A **48**
Luib. *High* 1D **146**
Luib. *Stir* 1D **135**
Lulham. *Here* 1H **47**
Lullington. *Derbs* 4G **73**
Lullington. *E Sus* 5G **27**
Lullington. *Som* 1C **22**
Lulsgate Bottom. *N Som* 5A **34**
Lulsley. *Worc* 5B **60**
Lulworth Camp. *Dors* 4D **14**
Lumb. *Lanc* 2G **91**
Lumby. *N Yor* 1E **93**
Lumphanan. *Abers* 3C **152**
Lumphinnans. *Fife* 4D **136**
Lumsdaine. *Bord* 3E **131**
Lumsden. *Abers* 1B **152**
Lunan. *Ang* 3F **145**
Lunanhead. *Ang* 3D **145**
Luncarty. *Per* 1C **136**
Lund. *E Yor* 5D **100**
Lund. *N Yor* 1G **93**
Lundie. *Ang* 5B **144**
Lundin Links. *Fife* 3G **137**
Lundy Green. *Norf* 1E **67**
Lunna. *Shet* 5F **173**
Lunning. *Shet* 5G **173**
Lunnon. *Swan* 4E **31**
Lunsford. *Kent* 5A **40**
Lunsford's Cross. *E Sus* 4B **28**
Lunt. *Mers* 4B **90**
Luppitt. *Devn* 2E **13**
Lupridge. *Devn* 3D **8**
Lupset. *W Yor* 3D **92**
Lupton. *Cumb* 1E **97**
Lurgan. *Arm* 4E **178**
Lurganare. *New M* 6E **178**
Lurgashall. *W Sus* 3A **26**
Lurley. *Devn* 1C **12**
Lusby. *Linc* 4C **88**
Luscombe. *Devn* 3D **9**
Luson. *Devn* 4C **8**
Luss. *Arg* 4C **134**
Lussagiven. *Arg* 1E **125**
Lusta. *High* 3B **154**
Lustleigh. *Devn* 4A **12**
Luston. *Here* 4G **59**
Luthermuir. *Abers* 2F **145**
Luthrie. *Fife* 2F **137**
Lutley. *Staf* 2C **60**
Luton. *Devn*
nr. Honiton 2D **12**
nr. Teignmouth 5C **12**
Luton. *Lutn* 3A **52**
Luton Airport. *Lutn* **205** (3B **52**)
Lutterworth. *Leics* 2C **62**
Lutton. *Devn*
nr. Ivybridge 3B **8**
nr. South Brent 2C **8**
Lutton. *Linc* 3D **76**
Lutton. *Nptn* 2A **64**
Lutton Gowts. *Linc* 3D **76**
Lutworthy. *Devn* 1A **12**
Luxborough. *Som* 3C **20**
Luxley. *Glos* 3B **48**
Luxulyan. *Corn* 3E **7**
Lybster. *High* 5E **169**
Lydbury North. *Shrp* 2F **59**
Lydcott. *Devn* 3G **19**
Lydd. *Kent* 3E **29**
Lydd Airport. *Kent* 3E **29**
Lydden. *Kent*
nr. Dover 1G **29**
nr. Margate 4H **41**
Lyddington. *Rut* 1F **63**
Lydd-on-Sea. *Kent* 3E **29**
Lydeard St Lawrence. *Som* 3E **21**
Lyde Green. *Hants* 1F **25**
Lydford. *Devn* 4F **11**
Lydford Fair Place. *Som* 3A **22**
Lydgate. *G Man* 4H **91**
Lydgate. *W Yor* 2H **91**
Lydham. *Shrp* 1F **59**
Lydiard Millicent. *Wilts* 3F **35**
Lydiate. *Mers* 4B **90**
Lydiate Ash. *Worc* 3D **61**
Lydlinch. *Dors* 1C **14**
Lydmarsh. *Som* 2G **13**
Lydney. *Glos* 5B **48**
Lydstep. *Pemb* 5E **43**
Lye. *W Mid* 2D **60**
The Lye. *Shrp* 1A **60**
Lye Green. *Buck* 5H **51**
Lye Green. *E Sus* 2G **27**
Lye Head. *Worc* 3B **60**
Lyford. *Oxon* 2B **36**
Lyham. *Nmbd* 1E **121**
Lylestone. *N Ayr* 5E **127**
Lymbridge Green. *Kent* 1F **29**
Lyme Regis. *Dors* 3G **13**
Lyminge. *Kent* 1F **29**
Lymington. *Hants* 3B **16**
Lyminster. *W Sus* 5B **26**
Lymm. *Warr* 2A **84**
Lymore. *Hants* 3A **16**
Lympne. *Kent* 2F **29**
Lympsham. *Som* 1G **21**
Lympstone. *Devn* 4C **12**
Lynaberack Lodge. *High* 4B **150**
Lynbridge. *Devn* 2H **19**
Lynch. *Som* 2C **20**
Lynchat. *High* 3B **150**
Lynch Green. *Norf* 5D **78**
Lyndhurst. *Hants* 2B **16**
Lyndon. *Rut* 5G **75**
Lyne. *Bord* 5F **129**
Lyne. *Surr* 4B **38**
Lyneal. *Shrp* 2G **71**
Lyne Down. *Here* 2B **48**
Lyneham. *Oxon* 3A **50**
Lyneham. *Wilts* 4F **35**
Lyneholmeford. *Cumb* 2G **113**
Lynemouth. *Nmbd* 5G **121**

Millgate—New Bewick

Millgate. Lanc 3G 91
Mill Green. Essx 5G 53
Mill Green. Norf 2D 66
Mill Green. Shrp 3A 72
Mill Green. Staf 3E 73
Mill Green. Suff 1C 54
Millhalf. Here 1F 47
Millhall. E Ren 4G 127
Millhayes. Devn
nr. Honiton 2F 13
nr. Wellington 1E 13
Millhead. Lanc 2D 97
Millheugh. S Lan 4A 128
Mill Hill. Bkbn 2E 91
Mill Hill. G Lon 1D 38
Millholme. Cumb 5G 103
Millhouse. Arg 2A 126
Millhouse. Cumb 1E 103
Millhousebridge. Dum 1C 112
Millhouses. S Yor 2H 85
Millikenpark. Ren 3F 127
Millington. E Yor 4C 100
Millington Green. Derbs 1G 73
Millisle. Ards 2K 179
Mill Knowe. Arg 3B 122
Mill Lane. Hants 1F 25
Millmeece. Staf 2C 72
Mill of Craigievar. Abers 2C 152
Mill of Fintray. Abers 2F 153
Mill of Haldane. W Dun 1F 127
Millom. Cumb 1A 96
Millow. C Beds 1C 52
Millpool. Corn 5B 10
Millport. N Ayr 4C 126
Mill Side. Cumb 1D 96
Mill Street. Norf
nr. Lyng 4C 78
nr. Swanton Morley 4C 78
Millthorpe. Derbs 3H 85
Millthorpe. Linc 2A 76
Millthrop. Cumb 5H 103
Milltimber. Aber 3F 153
Mill Town. Ant 8H 175
Milltown. Abers
nr. Corgarff 3G 151
nr. Lumsden 2B 152
Milltown. Ant 7G 175
Milltown. Arm
nr. Banbridge 5F 178
nr. Coalisland 3D 178
nr. Richhill 5D 178
Milltown. Corn 3F 7
Milltown. Derbs 4A 86
Milltown. Devn 3F 19
Milltown. Dum 2E 113
Milltown of Aberdalgie.
Per 1C 136
Milltown of Auchindoun.
Mor 4A 160
Milltown of Campfield.
Abers 3D 152
Milltown of Edinvillie.
Mor 4G 159
Milltown of Rothiemay.
Mor 4C 160
Milltown of Towie. Abers 2B 152
Milnacraig. Ang 3B 144
Milnathort. Per 3D 136
Milngavie. E Dun 2G 127
Milnholm. Stir 1A 128
Milnrow. G Man 3H 91
Milnthorpe. Cumb 1D 97
Milnthorpe. W Yor 3D 92
Milson. Shrp 3A 60
Milstead. Kent 5D 40
Milston. Wilts 2G 23
Milthorpe. Nptn 1D 50
Milton. Ang 4C 144
Milton. Cambs 4D 65
Milton. Cumb
nr. Brampton 3G 113
nr. Crooklands 1E 97
Milton. Derbs 3H 73
Milton. Dum
nr. Crocketford 2F 111
nr. Glenluce 4H 109
Milton. Glas 3G 127
Milton. High
nr. Achnasheen 3F 157
nr. Applecross 4G 155
nr. Drumnadrochit 5G 157
nr. Invergordon 1B 158
nr. Inverness 4H 157
nr. Wick 3F 169
Milton. Mor
nr. Cullen 2C 160
nr. Tomintoul 2F 151
Milton. N Som 5G 33
Milton. Notts 3E 86
Milton. Oxon
nr. Bloxham 2C 50
nr. Didcot 2C 36
Milton. Pemb 4E 43
Milton. Port 3E 17
Milton. Som 4H 21
Milton. S Ayr 2D 116
Milton. Stir
nr. Aberfoyle 3E 135
nr. Drymen 4D 134
Milton. Stoke 5D 84
Milton. W Dun 2F 127
Milton Abbas. Dors 2D 14
Milton Abbot. Devn 5E 11
Milton Auchlossan.
Abers 3C 152
Milton Bridge. Midl 3F 129
Milton Bryan. C Beds 2H 51
Milton Clevedon. Som 3B 22
Milton Coldwells. Abers 5G 161
Milton Combe. Devn 2A 8
Milton Common. Oxon 5E 51
Milton Damerel. Devn 1D 11
Miltonduff. Mor 2F 159
Milton End. Glos 5G 49
Milton Ernest. Bed 5H 63
Milton Green. Ches W 5G 83
Milton Hill. Devn 5C 12
Milton Hill. Oxon 2C 36
Milton Keynes. Mil 200 (2G 51)
Milton Keynes Village. Mil 2G 51
Milton Lilbourne. Wilts 5G 35
Milton Malsor. Nptn 5E 63
Milton Morenish. Per 5D 142
Milton of Auchinhove.
Abers 3C 152
Milton of Balgonie. Fife 3F 137
Milton of Barras. Abers 1H 145
Milton of Campsie.
E Dun 2H 127
Milton of Cultoquhey.
Per 1A 136
Milton of Cushnie. Abers 2C 152
Milton of Finavon. Ang 3D 145
Milton of Gollanfield.
High 3B 158
Milton of Lesmore.
Abers 1B 152
Milton of Leys. High 4A 158
Milton of Tullich. Abers 4A 152
Milton on Stour. Dors 4C 22
Milton Regis. Kent 4C 40
Milton Street. E Sus 5G 27
Milton-under-Wychwood.
Oxon 4A 50
Milverton. Som 4E 20
Milverton. Warw 4H 61
Milwich. Staf 2D 72
Mimbridge. Surr 4A 38
Minard. Arg 4G 133
Minchington. Dors 1E 15
Minchinhampton. Glos 5D 48
Mindrum. Nmbd 1C 120
Minehead. Som 2C 20
Minera. Wrex 5E 83
Minerstown. New M 6J 179
Minety. Wilts 2F 35
Minffordd. Gwyn 2E 69
Mingarrypark. High 2A 140
Mingary. High 2G 139
Mingearraidh. W Isl 6C 170
Miningsby. Linc 4C 88
Minions. Corn 5C 10
Minishant. S Ayr 3C 116
Minllyn. Gwyn 4A 70
Minnigaff. Dum 3B 110
Minorca. IOM 3D 108
Minskip. N Yor 3F 99
Minstead. Hants 1A 16
Minsted. W Sus 4G 25
Minster. Kent
nr. Ramsgate 4H 41
Minster. Kent
nr. Sheerness 3D 40
Minsteracres. Nmbd 4D 114
Minsterley. Shrp 5F 71
Minster Lovell. Oxon 4B 50
Minsterworth. Glos 4C 48
Minterne Magna. Dors 2B 14
Minterne Parva. Dors 2B 14
Minting. Linc 3A 88
Mintlaw. Abers 4H 161
Minto. Bord 2H 119
Minton. Shrp 1G 59
Minwear. Pemb 3E 43
Minworth. W Mid 1F 61
Miodar. Arg 4B 138
Mirbister. Orkn 5C 172
Mirehouse. Cumb 3A 102
Mireland. High 2F 169
Mirfield. W Yor 3C 92
Miserden. Glos 5E 49
Miskin. Rhon 3D 32
Misson. Notts 1D 86
Misterton. Leics 2C 62
Misterton. Notts 1E 87
Misterton. Som 2H 13
Mistley. Essx 2E 54
Mistley Heath. Essx 2E 55
Mitcham. G Lon 4D 39
Mitcheldean. Glos 4B 48
Mitchell. Corn 3C 6
Mitchel Troy. Mon 4H 47
Mitcheltroy Common.
Mon 5H 47
Mitford. Nmbd 1E 115
Mithian. Corn 3B 6
Mitton. Staf 4C 72
Mixbury. Oxon 2E 50
Mixenden. W Yor 2A 92
Mixon. Staf 5E 85
Moaness. Orkn 7B 172
Moarfield. Shet 1G 173
Moat. Cumb 2F 113
Moats Tye. Suff 5C 66
Mobberley. Ches E 3B 84
Mobberley. Staf 1E 73
Moccas. Here 1G 47
Mochdre. Cnwy 3H 81
Mochdre. Powy 2C 58
Mochrum. Dum 5A 110
Mockbeggar. Hants 2G 15
Mockerkin. Cumb 2B 102
Modbury. Devn 3C 8
Moddershall. Staf 2D 72
Modsarie. High 2G 167
Moelfre. Cnwy 3B 82
Moelfre. IOA 2E 81
Moelfre. Powy 3D 70
Moffat. Dum 4C 118
Moggerhanger. C Beds 1B 52
Mogworthy. Devn 1B 12
Moira. Leics 4H 73
Moira. Lis 3F 178
Molash. Kent 5E 41
Mol-chlach. High 2C 146
Mold. Flin 4E 83
Molehill Green. Essx 3F 53
Molescroft. E Yor 5E 101
Molesden. Nmbd 1E 115
Molesworth. Cambs 3H 63
Moll. High 1D 146
Molland. Devn 4B 20
Mollington. Ches W 3F 83
Mollington. Oxon 1C 50
Mollinsburn. N Lan 2A 128
Monachty. Cdgn 4E 57
Monachyle. Stir 2D 135
Monar Lodge. High 4E 156
Monaughty. Powy 4E 59
Monea. Ferm 7D 176
Monewden. Suff 5E 67
Moneydie. Per 1C 136
Moneyglass. Ant 7G 175
Moneymore. M Ulst 1C 178
Moneyneany. M Ulst 7C 174
Moneyreagh. Lis 3J 179
Moneyrow Green. Wind 4G 37
Moneyslane. Arm 6G 179
Moniaive. Dum 5G 117
Monifieth. Ang 5E 145
Monikie. Ang 5E 145
Monimail. Fife 2E 137
Monington. Pemb 1B 44
Monk Bretton. S Yor 4D 92
Monken Hadley. G Lon 1D 38
Monk Fryston. N Yor 2F 93
Monk Hesleden. Dur 1B 106
Monkhide. Here 1B 48
Monkhill. Cumb 4E 113
Monkhopton. Shrp 1A 60
Monkland. Here 5G 59
Monkleigh. Devn 4E 19
Monknash. V Glam 4C 32
Monkokehampton. Devn 2F 11
Monkseaton. Tyne 2G 115
Monks Eleigh. Suff 1C 54
Monk's Gate. W Sus 3D 26
Monk's Heath. Ches E 3C 84
Monk Sherborne. Hants 1E 24
Monkshill. Abers 4E 161
Monksilver. Som 3D 20
Monks Kirby. Warw 2B 62
Monk Soham. Suff 4E 66
Monk Soham Green. Suff 4E 66
Monkspath. W Mid 3F 61
Monks Risborough. Buck 5G 51
Monksthorpe. Linc 4D 88
Monkstown. Ant 1H 179
Monk Street. Essx 3G 53
Monkswood. Mon 5G 47
Monkton. Devn 2E 13
Monkton. Kent 4G 41
Monkton. Pemb 4D 42
Monkton. S Ayr 2C 116
Monkton Combe. Bath 5C 34
Monkton Deverill. Wilts 3D 22
Monkton Farleigh. Wilts 5D 34
Monkton Heathfield. Som 4F 21
Monktonhill. S Ayr 2C 116
Monkton Up Wimborne.
Dors 1F 15
Monkton Wyld. Dors 3G 13
Monkwearmouth. Tyne 4G 115
Monkwood. Dors 3H 13
Monkwood. Hants 3E 25
Monmarsh. Here 1A 48
Monmouth. Mon 4A 48
Monnington on Wye.
Here 1G 47
Monreith. Dum 5A 110
Montacute. Som 1H 13
Monteith. Arm 5F 179
Montford. Arg 3C 126
Montford. Shrp 4G 71
Montford Bridge. Shrp 4G 71
Montgarrie. Abers 2C 152
Montgarswood. E Ayr 2E 117
Montgomery. Powy 1E 58
Montgreenan. N Ayr 5E 127
Montrave. Fife 3F 137
Montrose. Ang 3G 145
Monxton. Hants 2B 24
Monyash. Derbs 4F 85
Monymusk. Abers 2D 152
Monzie. Per 1A 136
Moodiesburn. N Lan 2H 127
Moon's Green. Kent 3C 28
Moonzie. Fife 2F 137
Moor. Som 1H 13
The Moor. Kent 3B 28
Moor Allerton. W Yor 1C 92
Moorbath. Dors 3H 13
Moorbrae. Shet 3F 173
Moorby. Linc 4B 88
Moorcot. Here 5F 59
Moor Crichel. Dors 2E 15
Moor Cross. Devn 3C 8
Moordown. Bour 3F 15
Moore. Hal 2H 83
Moor End. E Yor 1B 94
Moorend. Dum 2D 112
Moorend. Glos
nr. Dursley 5C 48
nr. Gloucester 4D 48
Moorends. S Yor 3G 93
Moorfields. ME Ant 7H 175
Moorgate. S Yor 1B 86
Moor Green. Wilts 5D 34
Moorgreen. Hants 1C 16
Moorgreen. Notts 1B 74
Moorhaigh. Notts 4C 86
Moorhall. Derbs 3H 85
Moorhampton. Here 1G 47
Moorhouse. Cumb
nr. Carlisle 4E 113
nr. Wigton 4D 112
Moorhouse. Notts 4E 87
Moorhouse. Surr 5F 39
Moorhouses. Linc 5B 88
Moorland. Som 3G 21
Moorlinch. Som 3H 21
Moor Monkton. N Yor 4H 99
Moor of Granary. Mor 3E 159
Moor Row. Cumb
nr. Whitehaven 3B 102
nr. Wigton 5D 112
Moorsholm. Red C 3D 107
Moorside. Dors 1C 14
Moorside. G Man 4H 91
Moortown. Devn 3D 10
Moortown. Hants 2G 15
Moortown. IOW 4C 16
Moortown. Linc 1H 87
Moortown. M Ulst 2D 178
Moortown. Telf 4A 72
Moortown. W Yor 1D 92
Morangie. High 5E 165
Morar. High 4E 147
Morborne. Cambs 1A 64
Morchard Bishop. Devn 2A 12
Morcombelake. Dors 3H 13
Morcott. Rut 5G 75
Morda. Shrp 3E 71
Morden. G Lon 4D 38
Mordiford. Here 2A 48
Mordon. Dur 2A 106
More. Shrp 1F 59
Morebath. Devn 4C 20
Morebattle. Bord 2B 120
Morecambe. Lanc 3D 96
Morefield. High 4F 163
Moreleigh. Devn 3D 8
Morenish. Per 5C 142
Moresby Parks. Cumb 3A 102
Morestead. Hants 4D 24
Moreton. Dors 4D 14
Moreton. Essx 5F 53
Moreton. Here 4H 59
Moreton. Mers 1E 83
Moreton. Oxon 5E 51
Moreton. Staf 4B 72
Moreton Corbet. Shrp 3H 71
Moretonhampstead.
Devn 4A 12
Moreton-in-Marsh. Glos 2H 49
Moreton Jeffries. Here 1B 48
Moreton Morrell. Warw 5H 61
Moreton on Lugg. Here 1A 48
Moreton Pinkney. Nptn 1D 50
Moreton Say. Shrp 2A 72
Moreton Valence. Glos 5C 48
Morfa. Cdgn 5C 56
Morfa Bach. Carm 4D 44
Morfa Bychan. Gwyn 2E 69
Morfa Glas. Neat 5B 46
Morfa Nefyn. Gwyn 1B 68
Morganstown. Card 3E 33
Morgan's Vale. Wilts 4G 23
Morham. E Lot 2B 130
Moriah. Cdgn 3F 57
Morland. Cumb 2G 103
Morley. Ches E 2C 84
Morley. Derbs 1A 74
Morley. Dur 2E 105
Morley. W Yor 2C 92
Morley St Botolph. Norf 1C 66
Morningside. Edin 2F 129
Morningside. N Lan 4B 128
Morningthorpe. Norf 1E 67
Morpeth. Nmbd 1F 115
Morrey. Staf 4F 73
Morridge Side. Staf 5E 85
Morridge Top. Staf 4E 85
Morrington. Dum 1F 111
Morris Green. Essx 2H 53
Morriston. Swan 3F 31
Morston. Norf 1C 78
Mortehoe. Devn 2E 19
Morthen. S Yor 2B 86
Mortimer. W Ber 5E 37
Mortimer's Cross. Here 4G 59
Mortimer West End.
Hants 5E 37
Mortomley. S Yor 1H 85
Morton. Cumb
nr. Calthwaite 1F 103
nr. Carlisle 4E 113
Morton. Derbs 4B 86
Morton. Linc
nr. Bourne 3H 75
nr. Gainsborough 1F 87
nr. Lincoln 4F 87
Morton. Norf 4D 78
Morton. Notts 5E 87
Morton. Shrp 3E 71
Morton. S Glo 2B 34
Morton Bagot. Warw 4F 61
Morton Mill. Shrp 3H 71
Morton-on-Swale. N Yor 5A 106
Morton Tinmouth. Dur 2E 105
Morvah. Corn 3B 4
Morval. Corn 3G 7
Morvich. High
nr. Golspie 3E 165
nr. Shiel Bridge 1B 148
Morvil. Pemb 1E 43
Morville. Shrp 1A 60
Morwenstow. Corn 1C 10
Morwick. Nmbd 4G 121
Mosborough. S Yor 2B 86
Moscow. E Ayr 5F 127
Mose. Shrp 1B 60
Mosedale. Cumb 1E 103
Moseley. W Mid
nr. Birmingham 2E 61
nr. Wolverhampton 5D 72
Moseley. Worc 5C 60
Moss. Arg 4A 138
Moss. High 2A 140
Moss. S Yor 3F 93
Moss. Wrex 5F 83
Mossatt. Abers 2B 152
Moss Bank. Mers 1H 83
Mossbank. Shet 4F 173
Mossblown. S Ayr 2D 116
Mossbrow. G Man 2B 84
Mossburnford. Bord 3A 120
Mossdale. Dum 2D 110
Mossedge. Cumb 3F 113
Mossend. N Lan 3A 128
Mossgate. Staf 2D 72
Moss Lane. Ches E 3D 84
Mossley. Ant 1H 179
Mossley. Ches E 4C 84
Mossley. G Man 4H 91
Mossley Hill. Mers 2F 83
Moss of Barmuckity.
Mor 2G 159
Mosspark. Glas 3G 127
Mosspaul. Bord 5G 119
Moss Side. Cumb 4C 112
Moss Side. G Man 1C 84
Moss Side. Lanc
nr. Blackpool 1B 90
nr. Preston 2D 90
Moss Side. Mers 4B 90
Moss-side. Caus 3G 175
Moss-side. High 3C 158
Moss-side of Cairness.
Abers 2H 161
Mosstodloch. Mor 2H 159
Mosswood. Nmbd 4D 114
Mossy Lea. Lanc 3D 90
Mosterton. Dors 2H 13
Moston. Shrp 3H 71
Moston Green. Ches E 4B 84
Mostyn. Flin 2D 82
Mostyn Quay. Flin 2D 82
Motcombe. Dors 4D 22
Mothecombe. Devn 4C 8
Motherby. Cumb 2F 103
Motherwell. N Lan 4A 128
Mottingham. G Lon 3F 39
Mottisfont. Hants 4B 24
Mottistone. IOW 4C 16
Mottram in Longdendale.
G Man 1D 85
Mottram St Andrew.
Ches E 3C 84
Mott's Mill. E Sus 2G 27
Mouldsworth. Ches W 3H 83
Moulin. Per 3G 143
Moulsecoomb. Brig 5E 27
Moulsford. Oxon 3D 36
Moulsoe. Mil 1H 51
Moulton. Ches W 4A 84
Moulton. Linc 3C 76
Moulton. Nptn 4E 63
Moulton. N Yor 4F 105
Moulton. Suff 4F 65
Moulton. V Glam 4D 32
Moulton Chapel. Linc 4B 76
Moulton Eaugate. Linc 4C 76
Moulton St Mary. Norf 5F 79
Moulton Seas End. Linc 3C 76
Mount. Corn
nr. Bodmin 2F 7
nr. Newquay 3B 6
Mountain Ash. Rhon 2D 32
Mountain Cross. Bord 5E 129
Mountain Street. Kent 5E 41
Mountain Water. Pemb 2D 42
Mount Ambrose. Corn 4B 6
Mountbenger. Bord 2F 119
Mountblow. W Dun 2F 127
Mount Bures. Essx 2C 54
Mountfield. E Sus 3B 28
Mountfield. Ferm 2L 177
Mountgerald. High 2H 157
Mount Hawke. Corn 4B 6
Mount High. High 2A 158
Mountjoy. Corn 2C 6
Mountjoy. Ferm 2K 177
Mount Lothian. Midl 4F 129
Mountnessing. Essx 1H 39
Mountnorris. Arm 6D 178
Mounton. Mon 2A 34
Mount Pleasant. Buck 2E 51
Mount Pleasant. Ches E 5C 84
Mount Pleasant. Derbs
nr. Derby 1H 73
nr. Swadlincote 4G 73
Mount Pleasant. E Sus 4F 27
Mount Pleasant. Hants 3A 16
Mount Pleasant. Norf 1B 66
Mount Skippett. Oxon 4B 50
Mountsorrel. Leics 4C 74
Mount Stuart. Arg 4C 126
Mousehole. Corn 4B 4
Mouswald. Dum 2B 112
Mow Cop. Ches E 5C 84
Mowden. Darl 3F 105
Mowhaugh. Bord 2C 120
Mowmacre Hill. Leic 5C 74
Mowsley. Leics 2D 62
Moy. High 5B 158
Moy. M Ulst 4C 178
Moygashel. M Ulst 3C 178
Moylgrove. Pemb 1B 44
Moy Lodge. High 5G 149
Muasdale. Arg 5E 125
Muchalls. Abers 4G 153
Much Birch. Here 2A 48
Much Cowarne. Here 1B 48
Much Dewchurch. Here 2H 47
Muchelney. Som 4H 21
Muchelney Ham. Som 4H 21
Much Hadham. Herts 4E 53
Much Hoole. Lanc 2C 90
Muchlarnick. Corn 3G 7
Much Marcle. Here 2B 48
Muchrachd. High 5E 157
Much Wenlock. Shrp 5A 72
Mucking. Thur 2A 40
Muckle Breck. Shet 5G 173
Muckleford. Dors 3B 14
Mucklestone. Staf 2B 72
Muckleton. Norf 2H 77
Muckleton. Shrp 3H 71
Muckley. Shrp 1A 60
Muckley Corner. Staf 5E 73
Muckton. Linc 2C 88
Mudale. High 5F 167
Muddiford. Devn 3F 19
Mudeford. Dors 3G 15
Mudford. Som 1A 14
Mudgley. Som 2H 21
Mugdock. Stir 2G 127
Mugeary. High 5D 154
Mugginton. Derbs 1G 73
Muggintonlane End.
Derbs 1G 73
Muggleswick. Dur 4D 114
Mugswell. Surr 5D 38
Muie. High 3D 164
Muirden. Abers 3E 160
Muirdrum. Ang 5E 145
Muiredge. Per 1E 137
Muirend. Glas 3G 127
Muirhead. Ang 5C 144
Muirhead. Fife 3E 137
Muirhead. N Lan 3H 127
Muirhouses. Falk 1D 128
Muirkirk. E Ayr 2F 117
Muir of Alford. Abers 2C 152
Muir of Fairburn. High 3G 157
Muir of Fowlis. Abers 2C 152
Muir of Miltonduff. Mor 3F 159
Muir of Ord. High 3H 157
Muir of Tarradale. High 3H 157
Muirshearlich. High 5D 148
Muirtack. Abers 5G 161
Muirton. High 2B 158
Muirton. Per 1D 136
Muirton of Ardblair. Per 4A 144
Muirtown. Per 2B 136
Muiryfold. Abers 3E 161
Muker. N Yor 5C 104
Mulbarton. Norf 5D 78
Mulben. Mor 3A 160
Mulindry. Arg 4B 124
Mulla. Shet 5F 173
Mullach Charlabhaigh.
W Isl 3E 171
Mullacott. Devn 2F 19
Mullaghbane. New M 8D 178
Mullaghboy. ME Ant 6L 175
Mullaghglass. New M 7E 178
Mullion. Corn 5D 5
Mullion Cove. Corn 5D 4
Mumbles. Swan 4F 31
Mumby. Linc 3E 89
Munderfield Row. Here 5A 60
Munderfield Stocks. Here 5A 60
Mundesley. Norf 2F 79
Mundford. Norf 1H 65
Mundham. Norf 1F 67
Mundon. Essx 5B 54
Munerigie. High 3E 149
Muness. Shet 1H 173
Mungasdale. High 4D 162
Mungrisdale. Cumb 1E 103
Munlochy. High 3A 158
Munsley. Here 1B 48
Munslow. Shrp 2H 59
Murchington. Devn 4G 11
Murcot. Worc 1F 49
Murcott. Oxon 4D 50
Murdishaw. Hal 2H 83
Murieston. W Lot 3D 128
Murkle. High 2D 168
Murlaggan. High 4C 148
Murra. Orkn 7B 172
The Murray. S Lan 4H 127
Murrayfield. Edin 2F 129
Murrell Green. Hants 1F 25
Murroes. Ang 5D 144
Murrow. Cambs 5C 76
Mursley. Buck 3G 51
Murthly. Per 5H 143
Murton. Cumb 2A 104
Murton. Dur 5G 115
Murton. Nmbd 5F 131
Murton. Swan 4E 31
Murton. York 4A 100
Musbury. Devn 3F 13
Muscoates. N Yor 1A 100
Muscott. Nptn 4D 62
Musselburgh. E Lot 2G 129
Muston. Leics 2F 75
Muston. N Yor 2E 101
Mustow Green. Worc 3C 60
Muswell Hill. G Lon 2D 39
Mutehill. Dum 5D 111
Mutford. Suff 2G 67
Muthill. Per 2A 136
Mutterton. Devn 2D 12
Muxton. Telf 4B 72
Mwmbwls. Swan 4F 31
Mybster. High 3D 168
Myddfai. Carm 2A 46
Myddle. Shrp 3G 71
Mydroilyn. Cdgn 5D 56
Myerscough. Lanc 1C 90
Mylor Bridge. Corn 5C 6
Mylor Churchtown. Corn 5C 6
Mynachlog-ddu. Pemb 1F 43
Mynydd-bach. Mon 2H 33
Mynydd Isa. Flin 4E 83
Mynyddislwyn. Cphy 2E 33
Mynydd Llandegai. Gwyn 4F 81
Mynydd Mechell. IOA 1C 80
Mynydd-y-briw. Powy 3D 70
Mynyddygarreg. Carm 5E 45
Mynytho. Gwyn 2C 68
Myrebird. Abers 4E 153
Myrelandhorn. High 3E 169
Mytchett. Surr 1G 25
The Mythe. Glos 2D 49
Mytholmroyd. W Yor 2A 92
Myton-on-Swale. N Yor 3G 99
Mytton. Shrp 4G 71

N

Naast. High 5C 162
Na Buirgh. W Isl 8C 171
Naburn. York 5H 99
Nab Wood. W Yor 1B 92
Nackington. Kent 5F 41
Nacton. Suff 1F 55
Nafferton. E Yor 4E 101
Na Gearrannan. W Isl 3D 171
Nailbridge. Glos 4B 48
Nailsbourne. Som 4F 21
Nailsea. N Som 4H 33
Nailstone. Leics 5B 74
Nailsworth. Glos 2D 34
Nairn. High 3C 158
Nalderswood. Surr 1D 26
Nancegollan. Corn 3D 4
Nancledra. Corn 3B 4
Nangreaves. G Man 3G 91
Nanhyfer. Pemb 1E 43
Nannerch. Flin 4D 82
Nanpantan. Leics 4C 74
Nanpean. Corn 3D 6
Nanstallon. Corn 2E 7
Nant-ddu. Powy 4D 46
Nanternis. Cdgn 5C 56
Nantgaredig. Carm 3E 45
Nantgarw. Rhon 3E 33
Nant Glas. Powy 4B 58
Nantglyn. Den 4C 82
Nantgwyn. Powy 3B 58
Nantlle. Gwyn 5E 81
Nantmawr. Shrp 3E 71
Nantmel. Powy 4C 58
Nantmor. Gwyn 1F 69
Nant Peris. Gwyn 5F 81
Nantwich. Ches E 5A 84
Nant-y-bai. Carm 1A 46
Nant-y-bwch. Blae 4E 47
Nant-y-Derry. Mon 5G 47
Nant-y-dugoed. Powy 4B 70
Nant-y-felin. Cnwy 3F 81
Nantyffyllon. B'end 2B 32
Nantyglo. Blae 4E 47
Nant-y-meichiaid. Powy 4D 70
Nant-y-moel. B'end 2C 32
Nant-y-pandy. Cnwy 3F 81
Naphill. Buck 2G 37
Nappa. N Yor 4A 98
Napton on the Hill. Warw 4B 62
Narberth. Pemb 3F 43
Narberth Bridge. Pemb 3F 43
Narborough. Leics 1C 62
Narborough. Norf 4G 77
Narkurs. Corn 3H 7
The Narth. Mon 5A 48
Narthwaite. Cumb 5A 104
Nasareth. Gwyn 5D 80
Naseby. Nptn 3D 62
Nash. Buck 2F 51
Nash. Here 4F 59
Nash. Kent 5G 41
Nash. Newp 3G 33
Nash. Shrp 3A 60
Nash Lee. Buck 5G 51
Nassington. Nptn 1H 63
Nasty. Herts 3D 52
Natcott. Devn 4C 18
Nateby. Cumb 4A 104
Nateby. Lanc 5D 96
Nately Scures. Hants 1F 25
Natland. Cumb 1E 97
Naughton. Suff 1D 54
Naunton. Glos 3G 49
Naunton. Worc 2D 49
Naunton Beauchamp.
Worc 5D 60
Navenby. Linc 5G 87
Navestock. Essx 1G 39
Navestock Side. Essx 1G 39
Navidale. High 2H 165
Nawton. N Yor 1A 100
Nayland. Suff 2C 54
Nazeing. Essx 5E 53
Neacroft. Hants 3G 15
Nealhouse. Cumb 4E 113
Neal's Green. Warw 2H 61
Near Sawrey. Cumb 5E 103
Neasden. G Lon 2D 38
Neasham. Darl 3A 106
Neath. Neat 2A 32
Neath Abbey. Neat 3G 31
Neatishead. Norf 3F 79
Neaton. Norf 5B 78
Nebo. Cdgn 4E 57
Nebo. Cnwy 5H 81
Nebo. Gwyn 5D 81
Nebo. IOA 1D 80
Necton. Norf 5A 78
Nedd. High 5B 166
Nedderton. Nmbd 1F 115
Nedging. Suff 1D 54
Nedging Tye. Suff 1D 54
Needham. Norf 2E 67
Needham Market. Suff 5C 66
Needham Street. Suff 4G 65
Needingworth. Cambs 3C 64
Needwood. Staf 3F 73
Neen Savage. Shrp 3A 60
Neen Sollars. Shrp 3A 60
Neenton. Shrp 2A 60
Nefyn. Gwyn 1C 68
Neilston. E Ren 4F 127
Neithrop. Oxon 1C 50
Nelly Andrews Green.
Powy 5E 71
Nelson. Cphy 2E 32
Nelson. Lanc 1G 91
Nelson Village. Nmbd 2F 115
Nemphlar. S Lan 5B 128
Nempnett Thrubwell.
Bath 5A 34
Nene Terrace. Linc 5B 76
Nenthall. Cumb 5A 114
Nenthead. Cumb 5A 114
Nenthorn. Bord 1A 120
Nercwys. Flin 4E 83
Neribus. Arg 4A 124
Nerston. S Lan 4H 127
Nesbit. Nmbd 1D 121
Nesfield. N Yor 5C 98
Ness. Ches W 3F 83
Nesscliffe. Shrp 4F 71
Ness of Tenston. Orkn 6B 172
Neston. Ches W 3E 83
Neston. Wilts 5D 34
Nethanfoot. S Lan 5B 128
Nether Alderley. Ches E 3C 84
Netheravon. Wilts 2G 23
Nether Blainslie. Bord 5B 130
Netherbrae. Abers 3E 161
Netherbrough. Orkn 6C 172
Nether Broughton. Leics 3D 74
Netherburn. S Lan 5B 128
Nether Burrow. Lanc 2F 97
Netherbury. Dors 3H 13
Netherby. Cumb 2E 113
Nether Careston. Ang 3E 145
Nether Cerne. Dors 3B 14
Nether Compton. Dors 1A 14
Nethercote. Glos 3G 49
Nethercote. Warw 4C 62
Nethercott. Devn 3E 19
Nethercott. Oxon 3C 50
Nether Dallachy. Mor 2A 160
Nether Durdie. Per 1E 136
Nether End. Derbs 3G 85
Netherend. Glos 5A 48
Nether Exe. Devn 2C 12
Netherfield. E Sus 4B 28
Netherfield. Notts 1D 74
Nethergate. Norf 3C 78
Netherhampton. Wilts 4G 23
Nether Handley. Derbs 3B 86
Nether Haugh. S Yor 1B 86
Nether Heage. Derbs 5A 86
Nether Heyford. Nptn 5D 62
Netherhouses. Cumb 1B 96
Nether Howcleugh.
S Lan 3C 118
Nether Kellet. Lanc 3E 97
Nether Kinmundy. Abers 4H 161
Netherland Green. Staf 2F 73
Nether Langwith. Notts 3C 86
Netherlaw. Dum 5E 111
Netherley. Abers 4F 153
Nethermill. Dum 1B 112
Nethermills. Mor 3C 160
Nether Moor. Derbs 4A 86
Nether Padley. Derbs 3G 85
Netherplace. E Ren 4G 127
Nether Poppleton. York 4H 99
Netherseal. Derbs 4G 73
Nether Silton. N Yor 5B 106
Nether Stowey. Som 3E 21
Nether Street. Essx 4F 53
Netherstreet. Wilts 5E 35
Netherthird. E Ayr 3E 117
Netherthong. W Yor 4B 92
Netherton. Ang 3E 145
Netherton. Cumb 1B 102
Netherton. Devn 5B 12
Netherton. Hants 1B 24
Netherton. Here 3A 48
Netherton. Mers 1F 83
Netherton. N Lan 4A 128
Netherton. Nmbd 4D 121
Netherton. Per 3A 144
Netherton. Shrp 2B 60
Netherton. Stir 2G 127
Netherton. W Mid 2D 60
Netherton. W Yor
nr. Armitage Bridge 3B 92
nr. Horbury 3C 92
Netherton. Worc 1E 49
Nethertown. Cumb 4A 102
Nethertown. High 1F 169
Nethertown. Staf 4F 73
Nether Urquhart. Fife 3D 136
Nether Wallop. Hants 3B 24
Nether Wasdale. Cumb 4C 102
Nether Welton. Cumb 5E 113
Nether Westcote. Glos 3H 49
Nether Whitacre. Warw 1G 61
Nether Winchendon. Buck 4F 51
Netherwitton. Nmbd 5F 121
Nether Worton. Oxon 2C 50
Nethy Bridge. High 1E 151
Netley. Shrp 5G 71
Netley Abbey. Hants 2C 16
Netley Marsh. Hants 1B 16
Nettlebed. Oxon 3F 37
Nettlebridge. Som 2B 22
Nettlecombe. Dors 3A 14
Nettlecombe. IOW 5D 16
Nettleden. Herts 4A 52
Nettleham. Linc 3H 87
Nettlestead. Kent 5A 40
Nettlestead Green. Kent 5A 40
Nettlestone. IOW 3E 16
Nettlesworth. Dur 5F 115
Nettleton. Linc 4E 94
Nettleton. Wilts 4D 34
Netton. Devn 4B 8
Netton. Wilts 3G 23
Neuadd. Powy 5C 70
The Neuk. Abers 4E 153
Nevendon. Essx 1B 40
Nevern. Pemb 1E 43
New Abbey. Dum 3A 112
New Aberdour. Abers 2F 161
New Addington. G Lon 4E 39
Newall. W Yor 5E 98
New Alresford. Hants 3D 24
New Alyth. Per 4B 144
Newark. Orkn 3G 172
Newark. Pet 5B 76
Newark-on-Trent. Notts 5E 87
New Arley. Warw 2G 61
Newarthill. N Lan 4A 128
New Ash Green. Kent 4H 39
New Balderton. Notts 5F 87
New Barn. Kent 4H 39
New Barnetby. N Lin 3D 94
Newbattle. Midl 3G 129
New Bewick. Nmbd 2E 121

Newbie—Oake

Newbie. Dum 3C 112
Newbiggin. Cumb
nr. Appleby 2H 103
nr. Barrow-in-Furness 3B 96
nr. Cumrew 5G 113
nr. Penrith 2F 103
nr. Seascale 5B 102
Newbiggin. Dur
nr. Consett 5E 115
nr. Holwick 2C 104
Newbiggin. Nmbd 5C 114
Newbiggin. N Yor
nr. Askrigg 5C 104
nr. Filey 1F 101
nr. Thoralby 1B 98
Newbiggin-by-the-Sea.
Nmbd 1G 115
Newbigging. Ang
nr. Monikie 5D 145
nr. Newtyle 4B 144
nr. Tealing 5D 144
Newbigging. Edin 2E 129
Newbigging. S Lan 5D 128
Newbiggin-on-Lune.
Cumb 4A 104
Newbold. Derbs 3A 86
Newbold. Leics 4B 74
Newbold on Avon. Warw 3B 62
Newbold on Stour. Warw 1H 49
Newbold Pacey. Warw 5G 61
Newbold Verdon. Leics 5B 74
New Bolingbroke. Linc 5C 88
Newborough. IOA 4D 80
Newborough. Pet 5B 76
Newborough. Staf 3F 73
Newbottle. Nptn 2D 50
Newbottle. Tyne 4G 115
New Boultham. Linc 3G 87
Newbourne. Suff 1F 55
New Brancepeth. Dur 5F 115
New Bridge. Dum 2G 111
Newbridge. Cphy 2F 33
Newbridge. Cdgn 5E 57
Newbridge. Corn 3B 4
Newbridge. Edin 2E 129
Newbridge. Hants 1A 16
Newbridge. IOW 4C 16
Newbridge. N Yor 1C 100
Newbridge. Pemb 1D 42
Newbridge. Wrex 1E 71
Newbridge Green. Worc 2D 48
Newbridge-on-Usk. Mon 2G 33
Newbridge on Wye. Powy 5C 58
New Brighton. Flin 4E 83
New Brighton. Hants 2F 17
New Brighton. Mers 1F 83
New Brinsley. Notts 5B 86
Newbrough. Nmbd 3B 114
New Broughton. Wrex 5F 83
New Buckenham. Norf 1C 66
New Buildings. Derr 5A 174
Newbuildings. Devn 2A 12
Newburgh. Abers 1G 153
Newburgh. Fife 2E 137
Newburgh. Lanc 3C 90
Newburn. Tyne 3E 115
Newbury. W Ber 5C 36
Newbury. Wilts 2D 22
Newby. Cumb 2G 103
Newby. N Yor
nr. Ingleton 2G 97
nr. Scarborough 1E 101
nr. Stokesley 3C 106
Newby Bridge. Cumb 1C 96
Newby Cote. N Yor 2G 97
Newby East. Cumb 4F 113
Newby Head. Cumb 2G 103
New Byth. Abers 3F 161
Newby West. Cumb 4E 113
Newby Wiske. N Yor 1F 99
Newcastle. Ards 4L 179
Newcastle. B'end 3B 32
Newcastle. Mon 4H 47
Newcastle. New M 6H 179
Newcastle. Shrp 2E 59
Newcastle Emlyn. Carm 1D 44
Newcastle International Airport.
Tyne 2E 115
Newcastleton. Bord 1F 113
Newcastle-under-Lyme.
Staf 1C 72
Newcastle upon Tyne.
Tyne 197 (3F 115)
Newchapel. Pemb 1G 43
Newchapel. Powy 2B 58
Newchapel. Staf 5C 84
Newchapel. Surr 1E 27
New Cheriton. Hants 4D 24
Newchurch. Carm 3D 45
Newchurch. Here 5F 59
Newchurch. IOW 4D 16
Newchurch. Kent 2E 29
Newchurch. Lanc 2G 91
Newchurch. Mon 2H 33
Newchurch. Powy 5E 58
Newchurch. Staf 3F 73
Newchurch in Pendle.
Lanc 1G 91
New Costessey. Norf 4D 78
Newcott. Devn 2F 13
New Cowper. Cumb 5C 112
Newcraighall. Edin 2G 129
New Crofton. W Yor 3D 93
New Cross. Cdgn 3F 57
New Cross. Som 1H 13
New Cumnock. E Ayr 3F 117
New Deer. Abers 4F 161
New Denham. Buck 2B 38
Newdigate. Surr 1C 26
New Duston. Nptn 4E 62
New Earswick. York 4A 100
New Edlington. S Yor 1C 86
New Elgin. Mor 2G 159
New Ellerby. E Yor 1E 95
Newell Green. Brac 4G 37
New Eltham. G Lon 3F 39
New End. Warw 4F 61
New End. Worc 5E 61
Newenden. Kent 3C 28
New England. Essx 1H 53
New England. Pet 5A 76
Newent. Glos 3C 48
New Ferry. Mers 2F 83
Newfield. Dur
nr. Chester-le-Street 4F 115
nr. Willington 1F 105
Newfound. Hants 1D 24
New Fryston. W Yor 2E 93
Newgale. Pemb 2C 42
New Galloway. Dum 2D 110
Newgate. Norf 1C 78
Newgate Street. Herts 5D 52
New Greens. Herts 5B 52
New Grimsby. IOS 1A 4
New Hainford. Norf 4E 78
Newhall. Ches E 1A 72
Newhall. Derbs 3G 73
Newham. Nmbd 2F 121
New Hartley. Nmbd 2G 115
Newhaven. E Sus 204 (5F 27)
Newhaven. Edin 2F 129
New Haw. Surr 4B 38
New Hedges. Pemb 4F 43
New Herrington. Tyne 4G 115
Newhey. G Man 3H 91
New Holkham. Norf 2A 78
New Holland. N Lin 2D 94
Newholm. N Yor 3F 107
New Houghton. Derbs 4C 86
New Houghton. Norf 3G 77
Newhouse. N Lan 3A 128
New Houses. N Yor 2H 97
New Hutton. Cumb 5G 103
New Hythe. Kent 5B 40
Newick. E Sus 3F 27
Newingreen. Kent 2F 29
Newington. Edin 2F 129
Newington. Kent
nr. Folkestone 2F 29
nr. Sittingbourne 4C 40
Newington. Notts 1D 86
Newington. Oxon 2E 36
Newington Bagpath. Glos 2D 34
New Inn. Carm 2E 45
New Inn. Mon 5H 47
New Inn. N Yor 2H 97
New Inn. Torf 2G 33
New Invention. Shrp 3E 59
New Kelso. High 4B 156
New Lanark. S Lan 5B 128
Newland. Glos 5A 48
Newland. Hull 1D 94
Newland. N Yor 2G 93
Newland. Som 3B 20
Newland. Worc 1C 48
Newlandrig. Midl 3G 129
Newlands. Cumb 1E 103
Newlands. High 4B 158
Newlands. Nmbd 4D 115
Newlands. Staf 3E 73
Newlands of Geise. High 2C 168
Newlands of Tynet. Mor 2A 160
Newlands Park. IOA 2B 80
New Lane. Lanc 3C 90
New Lane End. Warr 1A 84
New Langholm. Dum 1E 113
New Leake. Linc 5D 88
New Leeds. Abers 3G 161
New Lenton. Nott 2C 74
New Longton. Lanc 2D 90
Newlot. Orkn 6E 172
New Luce. Dum 3G 109
Newlyn. Corn 4B 4
Newmachar. Abers 2F 153
Newmains. N Lan 4B 128
New Mains of Ury. Abers 5F 153
New Malden. G Lon 4D 38
Newman's Green. Suff 1B 54
Newmarket. Suff 4F 65
Newmarket. W Isl 4G 171
New Marske. Red C 2D 106
New Marton. Shrp 2F 71
New Micklefield. W Yor 1E 93
New Mill. Abers 4E 160
New Mill. Corn 3B 4
New Mill. Herts 4H 51
New Mill. W Yor 4B 92
New Mill. Wilts 5G 35
Newmill. Ant 8J 175
Newmill. Mor 3B 160
Newmill. Bord 3G 119
Newmillerdam. W Yor 3D 92
New Mills. Corn 3C 6
New Mills. Derbs 2E 85
New Mills. Mon 5A 48
New Mills. Powy 5C 70
Newmills. Arm 4E 178
Newmills. Fife 1D 128
Newmills. High 2A 158
Newmills. M Ulst 3C 178
Newmiln. Per 5A 144
Newmilns. E Ayr 1E 117
New Milton. Hants 3H 15
New Mistley. Essx 2E 54
New Moat. Pemb 2E 43
Newmore. High
nr. Dingwall 3H 157
nr. Invergordon 1A 158
Newnham. Cambs 5D 64
Newnham. Glos 4B 48
Newnham. Hants 1F 25
Newnham. Herts 2C 52
Newnham. Kent 5D 40
Newnham. Nptn 5C 62
Newnham. Warw 4F 61
Newnham Bridge. Worc 4A 60
New Ollerton. Notts 4D 86
New Oscott. W Mid 1E 61
New Park. N Yor 4E 99
Newpark. Fife 2G 137
New Pitsligo. Abers 3F 161
New Polzeath. Corn 1D 6
Newport. Corn 4D 10
Newport. Devn 3F 19
Newport. E Yor 1B 94
Newport. Essx 2F 53
Newport. Glos 2B 34
Newport. High 1H 165
Newport. IOW 4D 16
Newport. Newp 200 (3G 33)
Newport. Norf 4H 79
Newport. Pemb 1E 43
Newport. Som 4G 21
Newport. Telf 4B 72
Newport-on-Tay. Fife 1G 137
Newport Pagnell. Mil 1G 51
Newpound Common.
W Sus 3B 26
New Prestwick. S Ayr 2C 116
New Quay. Cdgn 5C 56
Newquay. Corn 2C 6
Newquay Cornwall Airport.
Corn 2C 6
New Rackheath. Norf 4E 79
New Radnor. Powy 4E 58
New Rent. Cumb 1F 103
New Ridley. Nmbd 4D 114
New Romney. Kent 3E 29
New Rossington. S Yor 1D 86
New Row. Cdgn 3G 57
Newry. New M 7E 178
New Sauchie. Clac 4A 136
Newsbank. Ches E 4C 84
Newseat. Abers 5E 160
Newsham. Lanc 1D 90
Newsham. Nmbd 2G 115
Newsham. N Yor
nr. Richmond 3E 105
nr. Thirsk 1F 99
New Sharlston. W Yor 2D 93
Newsholme. E Yor 2H 93
Newsholme. Lanc 4H 97
New Shoreston. Nmbd 1F 121
New Springs. G Man 4D 90
Newstead. Notts 5C 86
Newstead. Bord 1H 119
New Stevenston. N Lan 4A 128
New Street. Here 5F 59
Newstreet Lane. Shrp 2A 72
New Swanage. Dors 4F 15
New Swannington. Leics 4B 74
Newthorpe. N Yor 1E 93
Newthorpe. Notts 1B 74
Newton. Arg 4H 133
Newton. B'end 4B 32
Newton. Cambs
nr. Cambridge 1E 53
nr. Wisbech 4D 76
Newton. Ches W
nr. Chester 4G 83
nr. Tattenhall 5H 83
Newton. Cumb 2B 96
Newton. Derbs 5B 86
Newton. Dors 1C 14
Newton. Dum
nr. Annan 2D 112
nr. Moffat 5D 118
Newton. G Man 1D 84
Newton. Here
nr. Ewyas Harold 2G 47
nr. Leominster 5H 59
Newton. High
nr. Cromarty 2B 158
nr. Inverness 4B 158
nr. Kylestrome 5C 166
nr. Wick 4F 169
Newton. Lanc
nr. Blackpool 1B 90
nr. Carnforth 2E 97
nr. Clitheroe 4F 97
Newton. Linc 2H 75
Newton. Mers 2E 83
Newton. Mor 2F 159
Newton. Norf 4H 77
Newton. Nptn 2F 63
Newton. Nmbd 3D 114
Newton. Notts 1D 74
Newton. Bord 2A 120
Newton. Shet 8E 173
Newton. Shrp
nr. Bridgnorth 1B 60
nr. Wem 2G 71
Newton. Som 3E 20
Newton. S Lan
nr. Glasgow 3H 127
nr. Lanark 1B 118
Newton. Staf 3E 73
Newton. Suff 1C 54
Newton. Swan 4F 31
Newton. Warw 3C 62
Newton. W Lot 2D 129
Newton. Wilts 4H 23
Newton Abbot. Devn 5B 12
Newtonairds. Dum 1F 111
Newton Arlosh. Cumb 4D 112
Newton Aycliffe. Dur 2F 105
Newton Bewley. Hart 2B 106
Newton Blossomville. Mil 5G 63
Newton Bromswold.
Nptn 4G 63
Newton Burgoland. Leics 5A 74
Newton by Toft. Linc 2H 87
Newton Ferrers. Devn 4B 8
Newton Flotman. Norf 1E 66
Newtongrange. Midl 3G 129
Newton Green. Mon 2A 34
Newton Hall. Dur 5F 115
Newton Hall. Nmbd 3D 114
Newton Harcourt. Leics 1D 62
Newton Heath. G Man 4G 91
Newton Hill. W Yor 2D 92
Newtonhill. Abers 4G 153
Newtonhill. High 4H 157
Newton Ketton. Darl 2A 106
Newton Kyme. N Yor 5G 99
Newton-le-Willows.
Mers 1H 83
Newton-le-Willows. N Yor 1E 98
Newton Longville. Buck 2G 51
Newton Mearns. E Ren 4G 127
Newtonmore. High 4B 150
Newton Morrell. N Yor 4F 105
Newton Mulgrave. N Yor 3E 107
Newton of Ardtoe. High 1A 140
Newton of Balcanquhal.
Per 2D 136
Newton of Beltrees. Ren 4E 127
Newton of Falkland. Fife 3E 137
Newton of Mountblairy.
Abers 3D 160
Newton of Pitcairns. Per 2C 136
Newton-on-Ouse. N Yor 4H 99
Newton-on-Rawcliffe.
N Yor 5F 107
Newton on the Hill. Shrp 3G 71
Newton-on-the-Moor.
Nmbd 4F 121
Newton on Trent. Linc 3F 87
Newton Poppleford. Devn 4D 12
Newton Purcell. Oxon 2E 51
Newton Regis. Warw 5G 73
Newton Reigny. Cumb 1F 103
Newton Rigg. Cumb 1F 103
Newton St Cyres. Devn 3B 12
Newton St Faith. Norf 4E 78
Newton St Loe. Bath 5C 34
Newton St Petrock. Devn 1E 11
Newton Solney. Derbs 3G 73
Newton Stacey. Hants 2C 24
Newton Stewart. Dum 3B 110
Newton Toney. Wilts 2H 23
Newton Tony. Wilts 2H 23
Newton Tracey. Devn 4F 19
Newton under Roseberry.
Red C 3C 106
Newton upon Ayr. S Ayr 2C 116
Newton upon Derwent.
E Yor 5B 100
Newton Valence. Hants 3F 25
Newton-with-Scales.
Lanc 1C 90
New Town. Dors 1E 15
New Town. E Lot 2H 129
New Town. Lutn 3A 52
New Town. W Yor 2E 93
Newtown. Abers 2E 160
Newtown. Cambs 4H 63
Newtown. Corn 5C 10
Newtown. Cumb
nr. Aspatria 5B 112
nr. Brampton 3G 113
nr. Penrith 2G 103
Newtown. Derbs 2D 85
Newtown. Devn 4A 20
Newtown. Dors 2H 13
Newtown. Falk 1C 128
Newtown. Glos
nr. Lydney 5B 48
nr. Tewkesbury 2E 49
Newtown. Hants
nr. Bishop's Waltham 1D 16
nr. Liphook 3G 25
nr. Lyndhurst 1A 16
nr. Newbury 5C 36
nr. Romsey 4B 24
nr. Warsash 2C 16
nr. Wickham 1E 16
Newtown. Here
nr. Little Dewchurch 2A 48
nr. Stretton Grandison 1B 48
Newtown. High 3F 149
Newtown. IOM 4C 108
Newtown. IOW 3C 16
Newtown. Lanc 3D 90
Newtown. Nmbd
nr. Rothbury 4E 121
nr. Wooler 2E 121
Newtown. Pool 3F 15
Newtown. Powy 1D 58
Newtown. Rhon 2D 32
Newtown. Shet 3F 173
Newtown. Shrp 2G 71
Newtown. Som 1F 13
Newtown. Staf
nr. Biddulph 4D 84
nr. Cannock 5D 73
nr. Longnor 4E 85
Newtown. Wilts 4E 23
Newtownabbey. Ant 1H 179
Newtownards. Ards 2J 179
Newtownbutler. Ferm 7K 177
Newtown-Crommelin.
ME Ant 5H 175
Newtownhamilton.
New M 7D 178
Newtown-in-St Martin.
Corn 4E 5
Newtown Linford. Leics 5C 74
Newtown St Boswells.
Bord 1H 119
Newtownstewart. Derr 8A 174
Newtown Unthank. Leics 5B 74
New Tredegar. Cphy 5E 47
Newtyle. Ang 4B 144
New Village. E Yor 1D 94
New Village. S Yor 4F 93
New Walsoken. Cambs 5D 76
New Waltham. NE Lin 4F 95
New Winton. E Lot 2H 129
New World. Cambs 1C 64
New Yatt. Oxon 4B 50
Newyears Green. G Lon 2B 38
New York. Linc 5B 88
New York. Tyne 2G 115
Nextend. Here 5F 59
Neyland. Pemb 4D 42
Nib Heath. Shrp 4G 71
Nicholashayne. Devn 1E 12
Nicholaston. Swan 4E 31
Nidd. N Yor 3F 99
Niddrie. Edin 2G 129
Niddry. W Lot 2D 129
Nigg. Aber 3G 153
Nigg. High 1C 158
Nigg Ferry. High 2B 158
Nightcott. Som 4B 20
Nimmer. Som 1G 13
Nine Ashes. Essx 5F 53
Ninebanks. Nmbd 4A 114
Nine Elms. Swin 3G 35
Ninemile Bar. Dum 2F 111
Nine Mile Burn. Midl 4E 129
Ninfield. E Sus 4B 28
Ningwood. IOW 4C 16
Nisbet. Bord 2A 120
Nisbet Hill. Bord 4D 130
Niton. IOW 5D 16
Nitshill. Glas 3G 127
Niwbwrch. IOA 4D 80
Nixon's Corner. Derr 5A 174
Noak Hill. G Lon 1G 39
Nobold. Shrp 4G 71
Nobottle. Nptn 4D 62
Nocton. Linc 4H 87
Nogdam End. Norf 5F 79
Noke. Oxon 4D 50
Nolton. Pemb 3C 42
Nolton Haven. Pemb 3C 42
No Man's Heath. Ches W 1H 71
No Man's Heath. Warw 5G 73
Nomansland. Devn 1B 12
Nomansland. Wilts 1A 16
Noneley. Shrp 3G 71
Noness. Shet 9F 173
Nonikiln. High 1A 158
Nonington. Kent 5G 41
Nook. Cumb
nr. Longtown 2F 113
nr. Milnthorpe 1E 97
Noranside. Ang 2D 144
Norbreck. Bkpl 5C 96
Norbridge. Here 1C 48
Norbury. Ches E 1H 71
Norbury. Derbs 1F 73
Norbury. Shrp 1F 59
Norbury. Staf 3B 72
Norby. N Yor 1G 99
Norby. Shet 6C 173
Norcross. Lanc 5C 96
Nordelph. Norf 5E 77
Norden. G Man 3G 91
Nordley. Shrp 1A 60
Norham. Nmbd 5F 131
Norland Town. W Yor 2A 92
Norley. Ches W 3H 83
Norleywood. Hants 3B 16
Normanby. N Lin 3B 94
Normanby. N Yor 1B 100
Normanby. Red C 3C 106
Normanby-by-Spital. Linc 2H 87
Normanby le Wold. Linc 1A 88
Norman Cross. Cambs 1A 64
Normandy. Surr 5A 38
Norman's Bay. E Sus 5A 28
Norman's Green. Devn 2D 12
Normanton. Derb 2H 73
Normanton. Leics 1F 75
Normanton. Notts 5E 86
Normanton. W Yor 2D 93
Normanton le Heath.
Leics 4A 74
Normanton-on-Cliffe. Linc 1G 75
Normanton on Soar.
Notts 3C 74
Normanton-on-the-Wolds.
Notts 2D 74
Normanton on Trent. Notts 4E 87
Normoss. Lanc 1B 90
Norrington Common.
Wilts 5D 35
Norris Green. Mers 1F 83
Norris Hill. Leics 4H 73
Norristhorpe. W Yor 2C 92
Northacre. Norf 1B 66
Northall. Buck 3H 51
Northallerton. N Yor 5A 106
Northam. Devn 4E 19
Northam. Sotn 1C 16
Northampton. Nptn 200 (4E 63)
North Anston. S Yor 2C 86
North Ascot. Brac 4A 38
North Aston. Oxon 3C 50
Northaw. Herts 5C 52
Northay. Som 1F 13
North Baddesley. Hants 4B 24
North Balfern. Dum 4B 110
North Ballachulish. High 2E 141
North Barrow. Som 4B 22
North Barsham. Norf 2B 78
Northbeck. Linc 1H 75
North Benfleet. Essx 2B 40
North Bersted. W Sus 5A 26
North Berwick. E Lot 1B 130
North Bitchburn. Dur 1E 105
North Blyth. Nmbd 1G 115
North Boarhunt. Hants 1E 16
North Bockhampton. Dors 3G 15
Northborough. Pet 5A 76
Northbourne. Kent 5H 41
Northbourne. Oxon 3D 36
North Bovey. Devn 4H 11
North Bowood. Dors 3H 13
North Bradley. Wilts 1D 22
North Brentor. Devn 4E 11
North Brewham. Som 3C 22
Northbrook. Oxon 3C 50
North Brook End. Cambs 1C 52
North Broomhill. Nmbd 4G 121
North Buckland. Devn 2E 19
North Burlingham. Norf 4F 79
North Cadbury. Som 4B 22
North Carlton. Linc 3G 87
North Cave. E Yor 1B 94
North Cerney. Glos 5F 49
North Chailey. E Sus 3E 27
Northchapel. W Sus 3A 26
North Charford. Hants 1G 15
North Charlton. Nmbd 2F 121
North Cheriton. Som 4B 22
North Chideock. Dors 3H 13
Northchurch. Herts 5H 51
North Cliffe. E Yor 1B 94
North Clifton. Notts 3F 87
North Close. Dur 1F 105
North Cockerington. Linc 1C 88
North Coker. Som 1A 14
North Collafirth. Shet 3E 173
North Common. E Sus 3E 27
North Commonty. Abers 4F 161
North Coombe. Devn 1B 12
North Cornelly. B'end 3B 32
North Cotes. Linc 4G 95
Northcott. Devn
nr. Boyton 3D 10
nr. Culmstock 1D 12
Northcourt. Oxon 2D 36
North Cove. Suff 2G 67
North Cowton. N Yor 4F 105
North Craigo. Ang 2F 145
North Crawley. Mil 1H 51
North Cray. G Lon 3F 39
North Creake. Norf 2A 78
North Curry. Som 4G 21
North Dalton. E Yor 4D 100
North Deighton. N Yor 4F 99
North Dronley. Ang 5C 144
North Duffield. N Yor 1G 93
Northdyke. Orkn 5B 172
Northedge. Derbs 4A 86
North Elkington. Linc 1B 88
North Elmham. Norf 3B 78
North Elmsall. W Yor 3E 93
North End. E Yor 1F 95
North End. Essx
nr. Great Dunmow 4G 53
nr. Great Yeldham 2A 54
North End. Hants 5C 36
North End. Leics 4C 74
North End. Linc 1B 76
North End. Norf 1B 66
North End. N Som 5H 33
North End. Port 2E 17
North End. W Sus 5C 26
North End. Wilts 2F 35
Northend. Buck 2F 37
Northend. Warw 5A 62
North Erradale. High 5B 162
North Evington. Leic 5D 74
North Fambridge. Essx 1C 40
North Fearns. High 5E 155
North Featherstone.
W Yor 2E 93
North Feorline. N Ayr 3D 122
North Ferriby. E Yor 2C 94
Northfield. Aber 3F 153
Northfield. E Yor 2D 94
Northfield. Som 3F 21
Northfield. W Mid 3E 61
Northfleet. Kent 3H 39
North Frodingham. E Yor 4F 101
Northgate. Linc 3A 76
North Gluss. Shet 4E 173
North Gorley. Hants 1G 15
North Green. Norf 2E 66
North Green. Suff
nr. Framlingham 4F 67
nr. Halesworth 3F 67
nr. Saxmundham 4F 67
North Greetwell. Linc 3H 87
North Grimston. N Yor 3C 100
North Halling. Medw 4B 40
North Hayling. Hants 2F 17
North Hazelrigg. Nmbd 1E 121
North Heasley. Devn 3H 19
North Heath. W Sus 3B 26
North Hill. Corn 5C 10
North Holmwood. Surr 1C 26
North Huish. Devn 3D 8
North Hykeham. Linc 4G 87
Northiam. E Sus 3C 28
Northill. C Beds 1B 52
Northington. Hants 3D 24
North Kelsey. Linc 4D 94
North Kelsey Moor. Linc 4D 94
North Kessock. High 4A 158
North Killingholme. N Lin 3E 95
North Kilvington. N Yor 1G 99
North Kilworth. Leics 2D 62
North Kyme. Linc 5A 88
North Lancing. W Sus 5C 26
Northlands. Linc 5C 88
Northleach. Glos 4G 49
North Lee. Buck 5G 51
North Lees. N Yor 2E 99
North Leigh. Kent 1F 29
North Leigh. Oxon 4B 50
Northleigh. Devn
nr. Barnstaple 3G 19
nr. Honiton 3E 13
North Leverton. Notts 2E 87
Northlew. Devn 3F 11
North Littleton. Worc 1F 49
North Lopham. Norf 2C 66
North Luffenham. Rut 5G 75
North Marden. W Sus 1G 17
North Marston. Buck 3F 51
North Middleton. Midl 4G 129
North Middleton. Nmbd 2E 121
North Molton. Devn 4H 19
North Moor. N Yor 1D 100
Northmoor. Oxon 5C 50
Northmoor Green. Som 3G 21
North Moreton. Oxon 3D 36
Northmuir. Ang 3C 144
North Mundham. W Sus 2G 17
North Murie. Per 1E 137
North Muskham. Notts 5E 87
North Ness. Orkn 8C 172
North Newbald. E Yor 1C 94
North Newington. Oxon 2C 50
North Newnton. Wilts 1G 23
North Newton. Som 3F 21
Northney. Hants 2F 17
North Nibley. Glos 2C 34
North Oakley. Hants 1D 24
North Ockendon. G Lon 2G 39
Northolt. G Lon 2C 38
Northop. Flin 4E 83
Northop Hall. Flin 4E 83
North Ormesby. Midd 3C 106
North Ormsby. Linc 1B 88
Northorpe. Linc
nr. Bourne 4H 75
nr. Donington 2B 76
nr. Gainsborough 1F 87
North Otterington. N Yor 1F 99
Northover. Som
nr. Glastonbury 3H 21
nr. Yeovil 4A 22
North Owersby. Linc 1H 87
Northowram. W Yor 2B 92
North Perrott. Som 2H 13
North Petherton. Som 3F 21
North Petherwin. Corn 4C 10
North Pickenham. Norf 5A 78
North Piddle. Worc 5D 60
North Poorton. Dors 3A 14
North Port. Arg 1H 133
Northport. Dors 4E 15
North Queensferry. Fife 1E 129
North Radworthy. Devn 3A 20
North Rauceby. Linc 1H 75
Northrepps. Norf 2E 79
North Rigton. N Yor 5E 99
North Rode. Ches E 4C 84
North Roe. Shet 3E 173
North Ronaldsay Airport.
Orkn 2G 172
North Row. Cumb 1D 102
North Runcton. Norf 4F 77
North Sannox. N Ayr 5B 126
North Scale. Cumb 2A 96
North Scarle. Linc 4F 87
North Seaton. Nmbd 1F 115
North Seaton Colliery.
Nmbd 1F 115
North Sheen. G Lon 3C 38
North Shian. Arg 4D 140
North Shields. Tyne 3G 115
North Shoebury. S'end 2D 40
North Shore. Bkpl 1B 90
North Side. Cumb 2B 102
North Skelton. Red C 3D 106
North Somercotes. Linc 1D 88
North Stainley. N Yor 2E 99
North Stainmore. Cumb 3B 104
North Stifford. Thur 2H 39
North Stoke. Bath 5C 34
North Stoke. Oxon 3E 36
North Stoke. W Sus 4B 26
Northstowe. Cambs 4D 64
North Street. Hants 3E 25
North Street. Kent 5E 40
North Street. Medw 3C 40
North Street. W Ber 4E 37
North Sunderland.
Nmbd 1G 121
North Tamerton. Corn 3D 10
North Tawton. Devn 2G 11
North Thoresby. Linc 1B 88
North Tidworth. Wilts 2H 23
North Town. Devn 2F 11
North Town. Shet 10E 173
Northtown. Orkn 8D 172
North Tuddenham. Norf 4C 78
North Walbottle. Tyne 3E 115
Northwall. Orkn 3G 172
North Walney. Cumb 3A 96
North Walsham. Norf 2E 79
North Waltham. Hants 2D 24
North Warnborough.
Hants 1F 25
North Water Bridge. Ang 2F 145
North Watten. High 3E 169
Northway. Glos 2E 49
Northway. Swan 4E 31
North Weald Bassett. Essx 5F 53
North Weston. N Som 4H 33
North Weston. Oxon 5E 51
North Wheatley. Notts 2E 87
North Whilborough. Devn 2E 9
Northwich. Ches W 3A 84
North Wick. Bath 5A 34
Northwick. Som 2G 21
Northwick. S Glo 3A 34
North Widcombe. Bath 1A 22
North Willingham. Linc 2A 88
North Wingfield. Derbs 4B 86
North Witham. Linc 3G 75
Northwold. Norf 1G 65
Northwood. Derbs 4G 85
Northwood. G Lon 1B 38
Northwood. IOW 3C 16
Northwood. Kent 4H 41
Northwood. Shrp 2G 71
Northwood. Stoke 1C 72
Northwood Green. Glos 4C 48
North Wootton. Dors 1B 14
North Wootton. Norf 3F 77
North Wootton. Som 2A 22
North Wraxall. Wilts 4D 34
North Wroughton. Swin 3G 35
North Yardhope. Nmbd 4D 120
Norton. Devn 3E 9
Norton. Glos 3D 48
Norton. Hal 2H 83
Norton. Herts 2C 52
Norton. IOW 4B 16
Norton. Mon 3H 47
Norton. Nptn 4D 62
Norton. Notts 3C 86
Norton. Powy 4F 59
Norton. Shrp
nr. Ludlow 2G 59
nr. Madeley 5B 72
nr. Shrewsbury 5H 71
Norton. S Yor
nr. Askern 3F 93
nr. Sheffield 2A 86
Norton. Stoc T 2B 106
Norton. Suff 4B 66
Norton. Swan 4F 31
Norton. W Sus
nr. Selsey 3G 17
nr. Westergate 5A 26
Norton. Wilts 3D 35
Norton. Worc
nr. Evesham 1F 49
nr. Worcester 5C 60
Norton Bavant. Wilts 2E 23
Norton Bridge. Staf 2C 72
Norton Canes. Staf 5E 73
Norton Canon. Here 1G 47
Norton Corner. Norf 3C 78
Norton Disney. Linc 5F 87
Norton East. Staf 5E 73
Norton Ferris. Wilts 3C 22
Norton Fitzwarren. Som 4F 21
Norton Green. IOW 4B 16
Norton Green. Stoke 5D 84
Norton Hawkfield. Bath 5A 34
Norton Heath. Essx 5F 53
Norton in Hales. Shrp 2B 72
Norton in the Moors.
Stoke 5C 84
Norton-Juxta-Twycross.
Leics 5H 73
Norton-le-Clay. N Yor 2G 99
Norton Lindsey. Warw 4G 61
Norton Little Green. Suff 4B 66
Norton Malreward. Bath 5B 34
Norton Mandeville. Essx 5F 53
Norton-on-Derwent.
N Yor 2B 100
Norton St Philip. Som 1C 22
Norton Subcourse. Norf 1G 67
Norton sub Hamdon.
Som 1H 13
Norton Woodseats. S Yor 2A 86
Norwell. Notts 4E 87
Norwell Woodhouse.
Notts 4E 87
Norwich. Norf 200 (5E 79)
Norwich Airport. Norf 4E 79
Norwick. Shet 1H 173
Norwood. Derbs 2B 86
Norwood Green. W Yor 2B 92
Norwood Hill. Surr 1D 26
Norwood Park. Som 3A 22
Norwoodside. Cambs 1D 64
Noseley. Leics 1E 63
Noss. Shet 10E 173
Noss Mayo. Devn 4B 8
Nosterfield. N Yor 1E 99
Nostie. High 1A 148
Notgrove. Glos 3G 49
Nottage. B'end 4B 32
Nottingham. Nott 200 (1C 74)
Nottington. Dors 4B 14
Notton. Dors 3B 14
Notton. W Yor 3D 92
Notton. Wilts 5E 35
Nounsley. Essx 4A 54
Noutard's Green. Worc 4B 60
Nox. Shrp 4G 71
Noyadd Trefawr. Cdgn 1C 44
Nuffield. Oxon 3E 37
Nunburnholme. E Yor 5C 100
Nuncargate. Notts 5C 86
Nunclose. Cumb 5F 113
Nuneaton. Warw 1A 62
Nuneham Courtenay.
Oxon 2D 36
Nun Monkton. N Yor 4H 99
Nunnerie. S Lan 3B 118
Nunney. Som 2C 22
Nunnington. N Yor 2A 100
Nunnykirk. Nmbd 5E 121
Nunsthorpe. NE Lin 4F 95
Nunthorpe. Midd 3C 106
Nunthorpe. York 4H 99
Nunton. Wilts 4G 23
Nunwick. Nmbd 2B 114
Nunwick. N Yor 2F 99
Nupend. Glos 5C 48
Nursling. Hants 1B 16
Nursted. Hants 4F 25
Nursteed. Wilts 5F 35
Nurston. V Glam 5D 32
Nutbourne. W Sus
nr. Chichester 2F 17
nr. Pulborough 4B 26
Nutfield. Surr 5E 39
Nuthall. Notts 1C 74
Nuthampstead. Herts 2E 53
Nuthurst. Warw 3F 61
Nuthurst. W Sus 3C 26
Nutley. E Sus 3F 27
Nuttall. G Man 3F 91
Nutwell. S Yor 4G 93
Nybster. High 2F 169
Nyetimber. W Sus 3G 17
Nyewood. W Sus 4G 25
Nymet Rowland. Devn 2H 11
Nymet Tracey. Devn 2H 11
Nympsfield. Glos 5D 48
Nynehead. Som 4E 21
Nyton. W Sus 5A 26

O

Oadby. Leics 5D 74
Oad Street. Kent 4C 40
Oakamoor. Staf 1E 73
Oakbank. Arg 5B 140
Oakbank. W Lot 3D 129
Oakdale. Cphy 2E 33
Oakdale. Pool 3F 15
Oake. Som 4E 21

Oaken—Pentewan

Oaken. Staf 5C 72
Oakenclough. Lanc 5E 97
Oakengates. Telf 4A 72
Oakenholt. Flin 3E 83
Oakenshaw. Dur 1F 105
Oakenshaw. W Yor 2B 92
Oakerthorpe. Derbs 5A 86
Oakford. Cdgn 5D 56
Oakford. Devn 4C 20
Oakfordbridge. Devn 4C 20
Oakgrove. Ches E 4D 84
Oakham. Rut 5F 75
Oakhanger. Ches E 5B 84
Oakhanger. Hants 3F 25
Oakhill. Som 2B 22
Oakington. Cambs 4D 64
Oaklands. Powy 5C 58
Oakle Street. Glos 4C 48
Oakley. Bed 5H 63
Oakley. Buck 4E 51
Oakley. Fife 1D 128
Oakley. Hants 1D 24
Oakley. Suff 3D 66
Oakley Green. Wind 3A 38
Oakley Park. Powy 2B 58
Oakmere. Ches W 4H 83
Oakridge Lynch. Glos 5E 49
Oaks. Shrp 5G 71
Oaksey. Wilts 2E 35
Oaks Green. Derbs 2F 73
Oakshaw Ford. Cumb 2G 113
Oakshott. Hants 4F 25
Oakthorpe. Leics 4H 73
Oak Tree. Darl 3A 106
Oakwood. Derb 2A 74
Oakwood. W Yor 1D 92
Oakwoodhill. Surr 2C 26
Oakworth. W Yor 1A 92
Oape. High 3B 164
Oare. Kent 4E 40
Oare. Som 2B 20
Oare. W Ber 4D 36
Oare. Wilts 5G 35
Oareford. Som 2B 20
Oasby. Linc 2H 75
Oath. Som 4G 21
Oathlaw. Ang 3D 145
Oatlands. N Yor 4F 99
Oban. Arg 201 (1F 133)
Oban. W Isl 7D 171
Oborne. Dors 1B 14
Obsdale. High 2A 158
Obthorpe. Linc 4H 75
Occlestone Green.
Ches W 4A 84
Occold. Suff 3D 66
Ochiltree. E Ayr 2E 117
Ochtermuthill. Per 2H 135
Ochtertyre. Per 1H 135
Ockbrook. Derbs 2B 74
Ockeridge. Worc 4B 60
Ockham. Surr 5B 38
Ockle. High 1G 139
Ockley. Surr 1C 26
Ocle Pychard. Here 1A 48
Octofad. Arg 4A 124
Octomore. Arg 4A 124
Octon. E Yor 3E 101
Odcombe. Som 1A 14
Odd Down. Bath 5C 34
Oddingley. Worc 5D 60
Oddington. Oxon 4D 50
Oddsta. Shet 2G 173
Odell. Bed 5G 63
Odie. Orkn 5F 172
Odiham. Hants 1F 25
Odsey. Cambs 2C 52
Odstock. Wilts 4G 23
Odstone. Leics 5A 74
Offchurch. Warw 4A 62
Offenham. Worc 1F 49
Offenham Cross. Worc 1F 49
Offerton. G Man 2D 84
Offerton. Tyne 4G 115
Offham. E Sus 4E 27
Offham. Kent 5A 40
Offham. W Sus 5B 26
Offleyhay. Staf 3C 72
Offley Hoo. Herts 3B 52
Offleymarsh. Staf 3B 72
Offord Cluny. Cambs 4B 64
Offord D'Arcy. Cambs 4B 64
Offton. Suff 1D 54
Offwell. Devn 3E 13
Ogbourne Maizey. Wilts 4G 35
Ogbourne St Andrew.
Wilts 4G 35
Ogbourne St George.
Wilts 4H 35
Ogden. G Man 3H 91
Ogle. Nmbd 2E 115
Ogmore. V Glam 4B 32
Ogmore-by-Sea. V Glam 4B 32
Ogmore Vale. B'end 2C 32
Okeford Fitzpaine. Dors 1D 14
Okehampton. Devn 3F 11
Okehampton Camp. Devn 3F 11
Okraquoy. Shet 8F 173
Okus. Swin 3G 35
Old. Nptn 3E 63
Old Aberdeen. Aber 3G 153
Old Alresford. Hants 3D 24
Oldany. High 5B 166
Old Arley. Warw 1G 61
Old Basford. Nott 1C 74
Old Basing. Hants 1E 25
Oldberrow. Warw 4F 61
Old Bewick. Nmbd 2E 121
Old Bexley. G Lon 3F 39
Old Blair. Per 2F 143
Old Bolingbroke. Linc 4C 88
Oldborough. Devn 2A 12
Old Brampton. Derbs 3H 85
Old Bridge of Tilt. Per 2F 143
Old Bridge of Urr. Dum 3E 111
Old Brumby. N Lin 4B 94
Old Buckenham. Norf 1C 66
Old Burghclere. Hants 1C 24
Oldbury. Shrp 1B 60
Oldbury. Warw 1H 61
Oldbury. W Mid 2D 61
Oldbury-on-Severn. S Glo 2B 34
Oldbury on the Hill. Glos 3D 34
Old Byland. N Yor 1H 99
Old Cassop. Dur 1A 106
Oldcastle. Mon 3G 47
Oldcastle Heath. Ches W 1G 71
Old Catton. Norf 4E 79
Old Clee. NE Lin 4F 95
Old Cleeve. Som 2D 20
Old Colwyn. Cnwy 3A 82
Oldcotes. Notts 2C 86
Old Coulsdon. G Lon 5E 39
Old Dailly. S Ayr 5B 116
Old Dalby. Leics 3D 74
Old Dam. Derbs 3F 85
Old Deer. Abers 4G 161
Old Dilton. Wilts 2D 22
Old Down. S Glo 3B 34
Oldeamere. Cambs 1C 64
Old Edlington. S Yor 1C 86
Old Eldon. Dur 2F 105
Old Ellerby. E Yor 1E 95
Old Fallings. W Mid 5D 72
Oldfallow. Staf 4D 73
Old Felixstowe. Suff 2G 55
Oldfield. Shrp 2A 60
Oldfield. Worc 4C 60
Old Fletton. Pet 1A 64
Oldford. Som 1C 22
Old Forge. Here 4A 48
Old Glossop. Derbs 1E 85
Old Goole. E Yor 2H 93
Old Gore. Here 3B 48
Old Graitney. Dum 3E 112
Old Grimsby. IOS 1A 4
Oldhall. High 3E 169
Old Hall Street. Norf 2F 79
Oldham. G Man 4H 91
Oldhamstocks. E Lot 2D 130
Old Heathfield. E Sus 3G 27
Old Hill. W Mid 2D 60
Old Hunstanton. Norf 1F 77
Oldhurst. Cambs 3B 64
Old Hutton. Cumb 1E 97
Old Kea. Corn 4C 6
Old Kilpatrick. W Dun 2F 127
Old Kinnernie. Abers 3E 152
Old Knebworth. Herts 3C 52
Oldland. S Glo 4B 34
Old Laxey. IOM 3D 108
Old Leake. Linc 5D 88
Old Lenton. Nott 2C 74
Old Llanberis. Gwyn 5F 81
Old Malton. N Yor 2B 100
Oldmeldrum. Abers 1F 153
Old Micklefield. W Yor 1E 93
Old Mill. Corn 5D 10
Oldmixon. N Som 1G 21
Old Monkland. N Lan 3A 128
Old Newton. Suff 4C 66
Old Park. Telf 5A 72
Old Pentland. Midl 3F 129
Old Philpstoun. W Lot 2D 128
Old Quarrington. Dur 1A 106
Old Radnor. Powy 5E 59
Old Rayne. Abers 1D 152
Oldridge. Devn 3B 12
Old Romney. Kent 3E 29
Old Scone. Per 1D 136
Oldshore Beg. High 3B 166
Oldshoremore. High 3C 166
Old Snydale. W Yor 2E 93
Old Sodbury. S Glo 3C 34
Old Somerby. Linc 2G 75
Old Spital. Dur 3C 104
Oldstead. N Yor 1H 99
Old Stratford. Nptn 1F 51
Old Swan. Mers 1F 83
Old Swarland. Nmbd 4F 121
Old Tebay. Cumb 4H 103
Old Town. Cumb 5F 113
Old Town. E Sus 5G 27
Old Town. IOS 1B 4
Old Town. Nmbd 5C 120
Oldtown. High 5C 164
Old Trafford. G Man 1C 84
Old Tupton. Derbs 4A 86
Oldwall. Cumb 3F 113
Oldwalls. Swan 3D 31
Old Warden. C Beds 1B 52
Oldways End. Som 4B 20
Old Westhall. Abers 1D 152
Old Weston. Cambs 3H 63
Oldwhat. Abers 3F 161
Old Windsor. Wind 3A 38
Old Wives Lees. Kent 5E 41
Old Woking. Surr 5B 38
Oldwood Common. Worc 4H 59
Old Woodstock. Oxon 4C 50
Olgrinmore. High 3C 168
Oliver's Battery. Hants 4C 24
Ollaberry. Shet 3E 173
Ollerton. Ches E 3B 84
Ollerton. Notts 4D 86
Ollerton. Shrp 3A 72
Olmarch. Cdgn 5F 57
Olmstead Green. Cambs 1G 53
Olney. Mil 5F 63
Olrig. High 2D 169
Olton. W Mid 2F 61
Olveston. S Glo 3B 34
Omagh. Ferm 2K 177
Ombersley. Worc 4C 60
Ompton. Notts 4D 86
Omunsgarth. Shet 7E 173
Onchan. IOM 4D 108
Onecote. Staf 5E 85
Onehouse. Suff 5C 66
Onen. Mon 4H 47
Ongar Hill. Norf 3E 77
Ongar Street. Here 4F 59
Onibury. Shrp 3G 59
Onich. High 2E 141
Onllwyn. Neat 4B 46
Onneley. Staf 1B 72
Onslow Green. Essx 4G 53
Onslow Village. Surr 1A 26
Onthank. E Ayr 1D 116
Openwoodgate. Derbs 1A 74
Opinan. High
nr. Gairloch 1G 155
nr. Laide 4C 162
Orasaigh. W Isl 6F 171
Orbost. High 4B 154
Orby. Linc 4D 89
Orchard Hill. Devn 4E 19
Orchard Portman. Som 4F 21
Orcheston. Wilts 2F 23
Orcop. Here 3H 47
Orcop Hill. Here 3H 47
Ord. High 2E 147
Ordale. Shet 1H 173
Ordhead. Abers 2D 152
Ordie. Abers 3B 152
Ordiquish. Mor 3H 159
Ordley. Nmbd 4C 114
Ordsall. Notts 3E 86
Ore. E Sus 4C 28
Oreton. Shrp 2A 60
Orford. Suff 1H 55
Orford. Warr 1A 84
Organford. Dors 3E 15
Orgil. Orkn 7B 172
Orgreave. Staf 4F 73
Oridge Street. Glos 3C 48
Orlestone. Kent 2D 28
Orleton. Here 4G 59
Orleton. Worc 4A 60
Orleton Common. Here 4G 59
Orlingbury. Nptn 3F 63
Ormacleit. W Isl 5C 170
Ormathwaite. Cumb 2D 102
Ormesby. Red C 3C 106
Ormesby St Margaret.
Norf 4G 79
Ormesby St Michael. Norf 4G 79
Ormiscaig. High 4C 162
Ormiston. E Lot 3H 129
Ormsaigbeg. High 2F 139
Ormsaigmore. High 2F 139
Ormsary. Arg 2F 125
Ormsgill. Cumb 2A 96
Ormskirk. Lanc 4C 90
Orphir. Orkn 7C 172
Orpington. G Lon 4F 39
Orrell. G Man 4D 90
Orrell. Mers 1F 83
Orrisdale. IOM 2C 108
Orsett. Thur 2H 39
Orslow. Staf 4C 72
Orston. Notts 1E 75
Orthwaite. Cumb 1D 102
Orton. Cumb 4H 103
Orton. Mor 3H 159
Orton. Nptn 3F 63
Orton. Staf 1C 60
Orton Longueville. Pet 1A 64
Orton-on-the-Hill. Leics 5H 73
Orton Waterville. Pet 1A 64
Orton Wistow. Pet 1A 64
Orwell. Cambs 5C 64
Osbaldeston. Lanc 1E 91
Osbaldwick. York 4A 100
Osbaston. Leics 5B 74
Osbaston. Shrp 3F 71
Osbournby. Linc 2H 75
Osclay. High 5E 169
Oscroft. Ches W 4H 83
Ose. High 4C 154
Osgathorpe. Leics 4B 74
Osgodby. Linc 1H 87
Osgodby. N Yor
nr. Scarborough 1E 101
nr. Selby 1G 93
Oskaig. High 5E 155
Oskamull. Arg 5F 139
Osleston. Derbs 2G 73
Osmaston. Derb 2A 74
Osmaston. Derbs 1G 73
Osmington. Dors 4C 14
Osmington Mills. Dors 4C 14
Osmondthorpe. W Yor 1D 92
Osmondwall. Orkn 9C 172
Osmotherley. N Yor 5B 106
Osnaburgh. Fife 2G 137
Ospisdale. High 5E 164
Ospringe. Kent 4E 40
Ossett. W Yor 2C 92
Ossington. Notts 4E 87
Ostend. Essx 1D 40
Ostend. Norf 2F 79
Osterley. G Lon 3C 38
Oswaldkirk. N Yor 2A 100
Oswaldtwistle. Lanc 2F 91
Oswestry. Shrp 3E 71
Otby. Linc 1A 88
Otford. Kent 5G 39
Otham. Kent 5B 40
Otherton. Staf 4D 72
Othery. Som 3G 21
Otley. Suff 5E 66
Otley. W Yor 5E 98
Otterbourne. Hants 4C 24
Otterburn. Nmbd 5C 120
Otterburn. N Yor 4A 98
Otterburn Camp. Nmbd 5C 120
Otterburn Hall. Nmbd 5C 120
Otter Ferry. Arg 1H 125
Otterford. Som 1F 13
Otterham. Corn 3B 10
Otterhampton. Som 2F 21
Otterham Quay. Medw 4C 40
Ottershaw. Surr 4B 38
Otterspool. Mers 2F 83
Otterswick. Shet 3G 173
Otterton. Devn 4D 12
Otterwood. Hants 2C 16
Ottery St Mary. Devn 3E 12
Ottinge. Kent 1F 29
Ottringham. E Yor 2F 95
Oughterby. Cumb 4D 112
Oughtershaw. N Yor 1A 98
Oughterside. Cumb 5C 112
Oughtibridge. S Yor 1H 85
Oughtrington. Warr 2A 84
Oulston. N Yor 2H 99
Oulton. Cumb 4D 112
Oulton. Norf 3D 78
Oulton. Staf
nr. Gnosall Heath 3B 72
nr. Stone 2D 72
Oulton. Suff 1H 67
Oulton. W Yor 2D 92
Oulton Broad. Suff 1H 67
Oulton Street. Norf 3D 78
Oundle. Nptn 2H 63
Ousby. Cumb 1H 103
Ousdale. High 2H 165
Ousden. Suff 5G 65
Ousefleet. E Yor 2B 94
Ouston. Dur 4F 115
Ouston. Nmbd
nr. Bearsbridge 4A 114
nr. Stamfordham 2D 114
Outer Hope. Devn 4C 8
Outertown. Orkn 6B 172
Outgate. Cumb 5E 103
Outhgill. Cumb 4A 104
Outlands. Staf 2B 72
Outlane. W Yor 3A 92
Out Newton. E Yor 2G 95
Out Rawcliffe. Lanc 5D 96
Outwell. Norf 5E 77
Outwick. Hants 1G 15
Outwood. Surr 1E 27
Outwood. W Yor 2D 92
Outwood. Worc 3D 60
Outwoods. Leics 4B 74
Outwoods. Staf 4B 72
Ouzlewell Green. W Yor 2D 92
Ovenden. W Yor 2A 92
Over. Cambs 3C 64
Over. Ches W 4A 84
Over. Glos 4D 48
Over. S Glo 3A 34
Overbister. Orkn 3F 172
Over Burrows. Derbs 2G 73
Overbury. Worc 2E 49
Overcombe. Dors 4B 14
Over Compton. Dors 1A 14
Over End. Cambs 1H 63
Over Finlarg. Ang 4D 144
Over Green. Warw 1F 61
Overgreen. Derbs 3H 85
Over Haddon. Derbs 4G 85
Over Hulton. G Man 4E 91
Over Kellet. Lanc 2E 97
Over Kiddington. Oxon 3C 50
Overleigh. Som 3H 21
Overley. Staf 4F 73
Over Monnow. Mon 4A 48
Over Norton. Oxon 3B 50
Over Peover. Ches E 3B 84
Overpool. Ches W 3F 83
Overscaig. High 1B 164
Overseal. Derbs 4G 73
Over Silton. N Yor 5B 106
Oversland. Kent 5E 41
Overstone. Nptn 4F 63
Over Stowey. Som 3E 21
Overstrand. Norf 1E 79
Over Stratton. Som 1H 13
Over Street. Wilts 3F 23
Overthorpe. Nptn 1C 50
Overton. Aber 2F 153
Overton. Ches W 3H 83
Overton. Hants 2D 24
Overton. High 5E 169
Overton. Lanc 4D 96
Overton. N Yor 4H 99
Overton. Shrp
nr. Bridgnorth 2A 60
nr. Ludlow 3H 59
Overton. Swan 4D 30
Overton. W Yor 3C 92
Overton. Wrex 1F 71
Overtown. Lanc 2F 97
Overtown. N Lan 4B 128
Overtown. Swin 4G 35
Over Wallop. Hants 3A 24
Over Whitacre. Warw 1G 61
Over Worton. Oxon 3C 50
Oving. Buck 3F 51
Oving. W Sus 5A 26
Ovingdean. Brig 5E 27
Ovingham. Nmbd 3D 115
Ovington. Dur 3E 105
Ovington. Essx 1A 54
Ovington. Hants 3D 24
Ovington. Norf 5B 78
Ovington. Nmbd 3D 114
Owen's Bank. Staf 3G 73
Ower. Hants
nr. Holbury 2C 16
nr. Totton 1B 16
Owermoigne. Dors 4C 14
Owlbury. Shrp 1F 59
Owler Bar. Derbs 3G 85
Owlerton. S Yor 1H 85
Owlsmoor. Brac 5G 37
Owlswick. Buck 5F 51
Owmby. Linc 4D 94
Owmby-by-Spital. Linc 2H 87
Ownham. W Ber 4C 36
Owrytn. Wrex 1F 71
Owslebury. Hants 4D 24
Owston. Leics 5E 75
Owston. S Yor 3F 93
Owston Ferry. N Lin 4B 94
Owstwick. E Yor 1F 95
Owthorne. E Yor 2G 95
Owthorpe. Notts 2D 74
Owton Manor. Hart 2B 106
Oxborough. Norf 5G 77
Oxbridge. Dors 3H 13
Oxcombe. Linc 3C 88
Oxen End. Essx 3G 53
Oxenhall. Glos 3C 48
Oxenholme. Cumb 5G 103
Oxenhope. W Yor 1A 92
Oxen Park. Cumb 1C 96
Oxenpill. Som 2H 21
Oxenton. Glos 2E 49
Oxenwood. Wilts 1B 24
Oxford. Oxon 200 (5D 50)
Oxgangs. Edin 3F 129
Oxhey. Herts 1C 38
Oxhill. Warw 1B 50
Oxley. W Mid 5D 72
Oxley Green. Essx 4C 54
Oxley's Green. E Sus 3A 28
Oxlode. Cambs 2D 65
Oxnam. Bord 3B 120
Oxshott. Surr 4C 38
Oxspring. S Yor 4C 92
Oxted. Surr 5E 39
Oxton. Mers 2F 83
Oxton. N Yor 5H 99
Oxton. Notts 5D 86
Oxton. Bord 4A 130
Oxwich. Swan 4D 31
Oxwich Green. Swan 4D 31
Oxwick. Norf 3B 78
Oykel Bridge. High 3A 164
Oyne. Abers 1D 152
Oystermouth. Swan 4F 31
Ozleworth. Glos 2C 34

P

Pabail Iarach. W Isl 4H 171
Pabail Uarach. W Isl 4H 171
Pachesham Park. Surr 5C 38
Packers Hill. Dors 1C 14
Packington. Leics 4A 74
Packmoor. Stoke 5C 84
Packmores. Warw 4G 61
Packwood. W Mid 3F 61
Packwood Gullet.
W Mid 3F 61
Padanaram. Ang 3D 144
Padbury. Buck 2F 51
Paddington. G Lon 2D 38
Paddington. Warr 2A 84
Paddlesworth. Kent 2F 29
Paddock. Kent 5D 40
Paddockhole. Dum 1D 112
Paddock Wood. Kent 1A 28
Paddolgreen. Shrp 2H 71
Padeswood. Flin 4E 83
Padiham. Lanc 1F 91
Padside. N Yor 4D 98
Padson. Devn 3F 11
Padstow. Corn 1D 6
Padworth. W Ber 5E 36
Page Bank. Dur 1F 105
Pagham. W Sus 3G 17
Paglesham Churchend.
Essx 1D 40
Paglesham Eastend. Essx 1D 40
Paibeil. W Isl
on North Uist 2C 170
on Taransay 8C 171
Paiblesgearraidh. W Isl 2C 170
Paignton. Torb 2E 9
Pailton. Warw 2B 62
Paine's Corner. E Sus 3H 27
Painleyhill. Staf 2E 73
Painscastle. Powy 1E 47
Painshawfield. Nmbd 3D 114
Painsthorpe. E Yor 4C 100
Painswick. Glos 5D 48
Painter's Forstal. Kent 5D 40
Painthorpe. W Yor 3D 92
Pairc Shiaboist. W Isl 3E 171
Paisley. Ren 3F 127
Pakefield. Suff 1H 67
Pakenham. Suff 4B 66
Pale. Gwyn 2B 70
Palehouse Common.
E Sus 4F 27
Palestine. Hants 2A 24
Paley Street. Wind 4G 37
Palgowan. Dum 1A 110
Palgrave. Suff 3D 66
Pallington. Dors 3C 14
Palmarsh. Kent 2F 29
Palmer Moor. Derbs 2F 73
Palmers Cross. W Mid 5C 72
Palmerstown. V Glam 5E 33
Palnackie. Dum 4F 111
Palnure. Dum 3B 110
Palterton. Derbs 4B 86
Pamber End. Hants 1E 24
Pamber Green. Hants 1E 24
Pamber Heath. Hants 5E 36
Pamington. Glos 2E 49
Pamphill. Dors 2E 15
Pampisford. Cambs 1E 53
Panborough. Som 2H 21
Panbride. Ang 5E 145
Pancrasweek. Devn 2C 10
Pandy. Gwyn
nr. Bala 2A 70
nr. Tywyn 5F 69
Pandy. Mon 3G 47
Pandy. Powy 5B 70
Pandy. Wrex 2D 70
Pandy Tudur. Cnwy 4A 82
Panfield. Essx 3H 53
Pangbourne. W Ber 4E 37
Pannal. N Yor 4F 99
Pannal Ash. N Yor 4E 99
Pannanich. Abers 4A 152
Pant. Shrp 3E 71
Pant. Wrex 1E 71
Pantasaph. Flin 3D 82
Pant Glas. Gwyn 1D 68
Pant-glas. Shrp 2E 71
Pantgwyn. Carm 3F 45
Pantgwyn. Cdgn 1C 44
Pant-lasau. Swan 5G 45
Panton. Linc 3A 88
Pant-pastynog. Den 4C 82
Pantperthog. Gwyn 5G 69
Pant-teg. Carm 3E 45
Pant-y-Caws. Carm 2F 43
Pant-y-dwr. Powy 3B 58
Pant-y-ffridd. Powy 5D 70
Pantyffynnon. Carm 4G 45
Pantygasseg. Torf 5F 47
Pant-y-llyn. Carm 4G 45
Pant-yr-awel. B'end 3C 32
Pant y Wacco. Flin 3D 82
Panxworth. Norf 4F 79
Papa Stour Airport. Shet 6C 173
Papa Westray Airport.
Orkn 2D 172
Papcastle. Cumb 1C 102
Papigoe. High 3F 169
Papil. Shet 8E 173
Papple. E Lot 2B 130
Papplewick. Notts 5C 86
Papworth Everard. Cambs 4B 64
Papworth St Agnes.
Cambs 4B 64
Par. Corn 3E 7
Paramour Street. Kent 4G 41
Parbold. Lanc 3C 90
Parbrook. Som 3A 22
Parbrook. W Sus 3B 26
Parc. Gwyn 2A 70
Parcllyn. Cdgn 5B 56
Parc-Seymour. Newp 2H 33
Pardown. Hants 2D 24
Pardshaw. Cumb 2B 102
Parham. Suff 4F 67
Park. Abers 4E 153
Park. Arg 4D 140
Park. Derr 6B 174
Park. Dum 5B 118
Park Bottom. Corn 4A 6
Parkburn. Abers 5E 161
Park Corner. E Sus 2G 27
Park Corner. Oxon 3E 37
Park End. Nmbd 2B 114
Parkend. Glos 5B 48
Parkeston. Essx 2F 55
Parkfield. Corn 2H 7
Park Gate. Hants 2D 16
Park Gate. Worc 3D 60
Parkgate. Ches W 3E 83
Parkgate. Cumb 5D 112
Parkgate. Dum 1B 112
Parkgate. Surr 1D 26
Parkhall. W Dun 2F 127
Parkham. Devn 4D 19
Parkham Ash. Devn 4D 18
Parkhead. Cumb 5E 113
Parkhead. Glas 3H 127
Park Hill. Mers 4C 90
Parkhouse. Mon 5A 48
Parkhurst. IOW 3C 16
Park Lane. G Man 4F 91
Park Lane. Staf 5C 72
Park Mill. W Yor 3C 92
Parkmill. Swan 4E 31
Parkneuk. Abers 1G 145
Parkside. N Lan 4B 128
Parkstone. Pool 3F 15
Park Street. Herts 5B 52
Park Street. W Sus 2C 26
Park Town. Oxon 5D 50
Park Village. Nmbd 3H 113
Parkway. Here 2C 48
Parley Cross. Dors 3F 15
Parmoor. Buck 3F 37
Parr. Mers 1H 83
Parracombe. Devn 2G 19
Parrog. Pemb 1E 43
Parsonage Green. Essx 4H 53
Parsonby. Cumb 1C 102
Parson Cross. S Yor 1H 85
Parson Drove. Cambs 5C 76
Partick. Glas 3G 127
Partington. G Man 1B 84
Partney. Linc 4D 88
Parton. Cumb
nr. Whitehaven 2A 102
nr. Wigton 4D 112
Parton. Dum 2D 111
Partridge Green. W Sus 4C 26
Parwich. Derbs 5F 85
Passenham. Nptn 2F 51
Passfield. Hants 3G 25
Passingford Bridge. Essx 1G 39
Paston. Norf 2F 79
Pasturefields. Staf 3D 73
Patchacott. Devn 3E 11
Patcham. Brig 5E 27
Patchetts Green. Herts 1C 38
Patching. W Sus 5B 26
Patchole. Devn 2G 19
Patchway. S Glo 3B 34
Pateley Bridge. N Yor 3D 98
Pathe. Som 3G 21
Pathfinder Village. Devn 3B 12
Pathhead. Abers 2G 145
Pathhead. E Ayr 3F 117
Pathhead. Fife 4E 137
Pathhead. Midl 3G 129
Pathlow. Warw 5F 61
Path of Condie. Per 2C 136
Pathstruie. Per 2C 136
Patmore Heath. Herts 3E 53
Patna. E Ayr 3D 116
Patney. Wilts 1F 23
Patrick. IOM 3B 108
Patrick Brompton. N Yor 5F 105
Patrington. E Yor 2G 95
Patrington Haven. E Yor 2G 95
Patrixbourne. Kent 5F 41
Patterdale. Cumb 3E 103
Pattiesmuir. Fife 1D 129
Pattingham. Staf 1C 60
Pattishall. Nptn 5D 62
Pattiswick. Essx 3B 54
Patton Bridge. Cumb 5G 103
Paul. Corn 4B 4
Paulerspury. Nptn 1F 51
Paull. E Yor 2E 95
Paulton. Bath 1B 22
Pauperhaugh. Nmbd 5F 121
Pave Lane. Telf 4B 72
Pavenham. Bed 5G 63
Pawlett. Som 2G 21
Pawston. Nmbd 1C 120
Paxford. Glos 2G 49
Paxton. Bord 4F 131
Payhembury. Devn 2D 12
Paythorne. Lanc 4H 97
Payton. Som 4E 20
Peacehaven. E Sus 5F 27
Peak Dale. Derbs 3E 85
Peak Forest. Derbs 3F 85
Peak Hill. Linc 4B 76
Peakirk. Pet 5A 76
Pearsie. Ang 3C 144
Peasedown St John. Bath 1C 22
Peaseland Green. Norf 4C 78
Peasemore. W Ber 4C 36
Peasenhall. Suff 4F 67
Pease Pottage. W Sus 2D 26
Peaslake. Surr 1B 26
Peasley Cross. Mers 1H 83
Peasmarsh. E Sus 3C 28
Peasmarsh. Som 1G 13
Peasmarsh. Surr 1A 26
Peaston. E Lot 3H 129
Peastonbank. E Lot 3H 129
Peathill. Abers 2G 161
Peat Inn. Fife 3G 137
Peatling Magna. Leics 1C 62
Peatling Parva. Leics 2C 62
Peaton. Arg 1D 126
Peaton. Shrp 2H 59
Peats Corner. Suff 4D 66
Pebmarsh. Essx 2B 54
Pebworth. Worc 1G 49
Pecket Well. W Yor 2H 91
Peckforton. Ches E 5H 83
Peckham Bush. Kent 5A 40
Peckleton. Leics 5B 74
Pedair-ffordd. Powy 3D 70
Pedham. Norf 4F 79
Pedlinge. Kent 2F 29
Pedmore. W Mid 2D 60
Pedwell. Som 3H 21
Peebles. Bord 5F 129
Peel. IOM 3B 108
Peel. Bord 1G 119
Peel Common. Hants 2D 16
Peening Quarter. Kent 3C 28
Peggs Green. Leics 4B 74
Pegsdon. C Beds 2B 52
Pegswood. Nmbd 1F 115
Peinchorran. High 5E 155
Peinlich. High 3D 154
Pelaw. Tyne 3F 115
Pelcomb Bridge. Pemb 3D 42
Pelcomb Cross. Pemb 3D 42
Peldon. Essx 4C 54
Pelsall. W Mid 5E 73
Pelton. Dur 4F 115
Pelutho. Cumb 5C 112
Pelynt. Corn 3G 7
Pemberton. Carm 5F 45
Pembrey. Carm 5E 45
Pembridge. Here 5F 59
Pembroke. Pemb 4D 43
Pembroke Dock.
Pemb 204 (4D 42)
Pembroke Ferry. Pemb 4D 42
Pembury. Kent 1H 27
Penallt. Mon 4A 48
Penally. Pemb 5F 43
Penalt. Here 3A 48
Penalum. Pemb 5F 43
Penare. Corn 4D 6
Penarth. V Glam 4E 33
Penbeagle. Corn 3C 4
Penberth. Corn 4B 4
Pen-bont Rhydybeddau.
Cdgn 2F 57
Penbryn. Cdgn 5B 56
Pencader. Carm 2E 45
Pen-cae. Cdgn 5D 56
Pencaenewydd. Gwyn 1D 68
Pencaerau. Neat 3G 31
Pencaitland. E Lot 3H 129
Pencarnisiog. IOA 3C 80
Pencarreg. Carm 1F 45
Pencarrow. Corn 4B 10
Pencelli. Powy 3D 46
Pen-clawdd. Swan 3E 31
Pencoed. B'end 3C 32
Pencombe. Here 5H 59
Pencraig. Here 3A 48
Pencraig. Powy 3C 70
Pendeen. Corn 3A 4
Pendeford. W Mid 5C 72
Penderyn. Rhon 5C 46
Pendine. Carm 4G 43
Pendlebury. G Man 4F 91
Pendleton. G Man 1C 84
Pendleton. Lanc 1F 91
Pendock. Worc 2C 48
Pendoggett. Corn 5A 10
Pendomer. Som 1A 14
Pendoylan. V Glam 4D 32
Pendre. B'end 3C 32
Penegoes. Powy 5G 69
Penelewey. Corn 4C 6
Penffordd. Pemb 2E 43
Penffordd-Lâs. Powy 1A 58
Penfro. Pemb 4D 43
Pengam. Cphy 2E 33
Pengam. Card 4F 33
Penge. G Lon 4E 39
Pengelly. Corn 4A 10
Pengenffordd. Powy 2E 47
Pengersick. Corn 4C 4
Pengorffwysfa. IOA 1D 80
Pengover Green. Corn 2G 7
Pengwern. Den 3C 82
Penhale. Corn
nr. Mullion 5D 5
nr. St Austell 3D 6
Penhale Camp. Corn 3B 6
Penhallow. Corn 3B 6
Penhalvean. Corn 5B 6
Penhelig. Gwyn 1F 57
Penhill. Swin 3G 35
Penhow. Newp 2H 33
Penhurst. E Sus 4A 28
Peniarth. Gwyn 5F 69
Penicuik. Midl 3F 129
Peniel. Carm 3E 45
Penifiler. High 4D 155
Peninver. Arg 3B 122
Penisa'r Waun. Gwyn 4E 81
Penistone. S Yor 4C 92
Penketh. Warr 2H 83
Penkill. S Ayr 5B 116
Penkridge. Staf 4D 72
Penley. Wrex 2G 71
Penllech. Gwyn 2B 68
Penllergaer. Swan 3F 31
Pen-llyn. IOA 2C 80
Penmachno. Cnwy 5G 81
Penmaen. Swan 4E 31
Penmaenmawr. Cnwy 3G 81
Penmaenpool. Gwyn 4F 69
Penmaen Rhos. Cnwy 3A 82
Pen-marc. V Glam 5D 32
Penmark. V Glam 5D 32
Penmarth. Corn 5B 6
Penmon. IOA 2F 81
Penmorfa. Gwyn 1E 69
Penmynydd. IOA 3E 81
Penn. Buck 1A 38
Penn. Dors 3G 13
Penn. W Mid 1C 60
Pennal. Gwyn 5G 69
Pennan. Abers 2F 161
Pennant. Cdgn 4E 57
Pennant. Den 2C 70
Pennant. Gwyn 3B 70
Pennant. Powy 1A 58
Pennant Melangell. Powy 3C 70
Pennar. Pemb 4D 42
Pennard. Swan 4E 31
Pennerley. Shrp 1F 59
Pennington. Cumb 2B 96
Pennington. G Man 1A 84
Pennington. Hants 3B 16
Pennorth. Powy 3E 46
Penn Street. Buck 1A 38
Pennsylvania. Devn 3C 12
Pennsylvania. S Glo 4C 34
Penny Bridge. Cumb 1C 96
Pennycross. Plym 3A 8
Pennygate. Norf 3F 79
Pennyghael. Arg 1C 132
Penny Hill. Linc 3C 76
Pennylands. Lanc 4C 90
Pennymoor. Devn 1B 12
Pennyvenie. E Ayr 4D 117
Pennywell. Tyne 4G 115
Penparc. Cdgn 1C 44
Penparcau. Cdgn 2E 57
Pen-pedair-heol. Cphy 2E 33
Penperlleni. Mon 5G 47
Penpillick. Corn 3E 7
Penpol. Corn 5C 6
Penpoll. Corn 3F 7
Penponds. Corn 3D 4
Penpont. Corn 5A 10
Penpont. Dum 5H 117
Penpont. Powy 3C 46
Penprysg. B'end 3C 32
Penquit. Devn 3C 8
Penrherber. Carm 1G 43
Penrhiw. Pemb 1C 44
Penrhiwceiber. Rhon 2D 32
Pen-Rhiw-fawr. Neat 4H 45
Penrhiw-llan. Cdgn 1D 44
Penrhiw-pal. Cdgn 1D 44
Penrhos. Gwyn 2C 68
Penrhos. Here 5F 59
Penrhos. IOA 2B 80
Penrhos. Mon 4H 47
Penrhos. Powy 4B 46
Penrhos Garnedd. Gwyn 3E 81
Penrhyn. IOA 1C 80
Penrhyn Bay. Cnwy 2H 81
Penrhyn-coch. Cdgn 2F 57
Penrhyndeudraeth. Gwyn 2F 69
Penrhyn-side. Cnwy 2H 81
Penrice. Swan 4D 31
Penrith. Cumb 2G 103
Penrose. Corn 1C 6
Penruddock. Cumb 2F 103
Penryn. Corn 5B 6
Pen-sarn. Carm 4E 45
Pen-sarn. Gwyn 3E 69
Pensax. Worc 4B 60
Pensby. Mers 2E 83
Penselwood. Som 3C 22
Pensford. Bath 5B 34
Pensham. Worc 1E 49
Penshaw. Tyne 4G 115
Penshurst. Kent 1G 27
Pensilva. Corn 2G 7
Pensnett. W Mid 2D 60
Penston. E Lot 2H 129
Penstone. Devn 2A 12
Pentewan. Corn 4E 6

Queensferry—Rudley Green

Queensferry. Flin 4F 83
Queensferry Crossing.
Edin 2E 129
Queenstown. Bkpl 1B 90
Queen Street. Kent 1A 28
Queenzieburn. N Lan 2H 127
Quemerford. Wilts 5F 35
Quendale. Shet 10E 173
Quendon. Essx 2F 53
Queniborough. Leics 4D 74
Quenington. Glos 5G 49
Quernmore. Lanc 3E 97
Quethiock. Corn 2H 7
Quholm. Orkn 6B 172
Quick's Green. W Ber 4D 36
Quidenham. Norf 2C 66
Quidhampton. Hants 1D 24
Quidhampton. Wilts 3G 23
Quilquox. Abers 5G 161
Quina Brook. Shrp 2H 71
Quindry. Orkn 8D 172
Quine's Hill. IOM 4C 108
Quinton. Nptn 5E 63
Quinton. W Mid 2D 61
Quintrell Downs. Corn 2C 6
Quixhill. Staf 1F 73
Quoditch. Devn 3E 11
Quorn. Leics 4C 74
Quorndon. Leics 4C 74
Quothquan. S Lan 1B 118
Quoyloo. Orkn 5B 172
Quoyness. Orkn 7B 172
Quoys. Shet
on Mainland 5F 173
on Unst 1H 173

R

Rableyheath. Herts 4C 52
Raby. Cumb 4C 112
Raby. Mers 3F 83
Rachan Mill. Bord 1D 118
Rachub. Gwyn 4F 81
Rack End. Oxon 5C 50
Rackenford. Devn 1B 12
Rackham. W Sus 4B 26
Rackheath. Norf 4E 79
Racks. Dum 2B 112
Rackwick. Orkn
on Hoy 8B 172
on Westray 3D 172
Radbourne. Derbs 2G 73
Radcliffe. G Man 4F 91
Radcliffe. Nmbd 4G 121
Radcliffe on Trent. Notts 2D 74
Radclive. Buck 2E 51
Radernie. Fife 3G 137
Radfall. Kent 4F 41
Radford. Bath 1B 22
Radford. Nott 1C 74
Radford. Oxon 3C 50
Radford. W Mid 2H 61
Radford. Worc 5E 61
Radford Semele. Warw 4H 61
Radipole. Dors 4B 14
Radlett. Herts 1C 38
Radley. Oxon 2D 36
Radnage. Buck 2F 37
Radstock. Bath 1B 22
Radstone. Nptn 1D 50
Radway. Warw 1B 50
Radway Green. Ches E 5B 84
Radwell. Bed 5H 63
Radwell. Herts 2C 52
Radwinter. Essx 2G 53
Radyr. Card 3E 33
RAF Coltishall. Norf 3E 79
Rafford. Mor 3E 159
Raffrey. New M 4J 179
Ragdale. Leics 4D 74
Ragdon. Shrp 1G 59
Ragged Appleshaw. Hants 2B 24
Raggra. High 4F 169
Raglan. Mon 5H 47
Ragnall. Notts 3F 87
Raholp. New M 5K 179
Raigbeg. High 1C 150
Rainford. Mers 4C 90
Rainford Junction. Mers 4C 90
Rainham. G Lon 2G 39
Rainham. Medw 4C 40
Rainhill. Mers 1G 83
Rainow. Ches E 3D 84
Rainton. N Yor 2F 99
Rainworth. Notts 5C 86
Raisbeck. Cumb 4H 103
Raise. Cumb 5A 114
Rait. Per 1E 137
Raithby. Linc 2C 88
Raithby by Spilsby. Linc 4C 88
Raithwaite. N Yor 3F 107
Rake. W Sus 4G 25
Rake End. Staf 4E 73
Rakeway. Staf 1E 73
Rakewood. G Man 3H 91
Ralia. High 4B 150
Ram Alley. Wilts 5H 35
Ramasaig. High 4A 154
Rame. Corn
nr. Millbrook 4A 8
nr. Penryn 5B 6
Ram Lane. Kent 1D 28
Ramnageo. Shet 1H 173
Rampisham. Dors 2A 14
Rampside. Cumb 3B 96
Rampton. Cambs 4D 64
Rampton. Notts 3E 87
Ramsbottom. G Man 3F 91
Ramsburn. Mor 3C 160
Ramsbury. Wilts 4A 36
Ramscraigs. High 1H 165
Ramsdean. Hants 4F 25
Ramsdell. Hants 1D 24
Ramsden. Oxon 4B 50
Ramsden. Worc 1E 49
Ramsden Bellhouse. Essx 1B 40
Ramsden Heath. Essx 1B 40
Ramsey. Cambs 2B 64
Ramsey. Essx 2F 55
Ramsey. IOM 2D 108
Ramsey Forty Foot.
Cambs 2C 64
Ramsey Heights. Cambs 2B 64
Ramsey Island. Essx 5C 54
Ramsey Mereside. Cambs 2B 64
Ramsey St Mary's. Cambs 2B 64
Ramsgate. Kent 4H 41
Ramsgill. N Yor 2D 98
Ramshaw. Dur 5C 114
Ramshorn. Staf 1E 73
Ramsley. Devn 3G 11
Ramsnest Common. Surr 2A 26
Ramstone. Abers 2D 152
Ranais. W Isl 5G 171
Ranby. Linc 3B 88
Ranby. Notts 2D 86
Rand. Linc 3A 88
Randalstown. Ant 7G 175
Randwick. Glos 5D 48
Ranfurly. Ren 3E 127
Rangag. High 4D 169
Rangemore. Staf 3F 73
Rangeworthy. S Glo 3B 34
Rankinston. E Ayr 3D 116
Rank's Green. Essx 4H 53
Ranmore Common. Surr 5C 38
Rannoch Station. Per 3B 142
Ranochan. High 5G 147
Ranskill. Notts 2D 86
Ranton. Staf 3C 72
Ranton Green. Staf 3C 72
Ranworth. Norf 4F 79
Raploch. Stir 4G 135
Rapness. Orkn 3E 172
Rapps. Som 1G 13
Rascal Moor. E Yor 1B 94
Rascarrel. Dum 5E 111
Rasharkin. Caus 5F 175
Rashfield. Arg 1C 126
Rashwood. Worc 4D 60
Raskelf. N Yor 2G 99
Rassau. Blae 4E 47
Rastrick. W Yor 2B 92
Ratagan. High 2B 148
Ratby. Leics 5C 74
Ratcliffe Culey. Leics 1H 61
Ratcliffe on Soar. Notts 3B 74
Ratcliffe on the Wreake.
Leics 4D 74
Rathen. Abers 2H 161
Rathfriland. Arm 6F 179
Rathillet. Fife 1F 137
Rathmell. N Yor 3H 97
Ratho. Edin 2E 129
Ratho Station. Edin 2E 129
Rathven. Mor 2B 160
Ratley. Hants 4B 24
Ratley. Warw 1B 50
Ratlinghope. Shrp 1G 59
Rattar. High 1E 169
Ratten Row. Cumb 5E 113
Ratten Row. Lanc 5D 96
Rattery. Devn 2D 8
Rattlesden. Suff 5B 66
Ratton Village. E Sus 5G 27
Rattray. Abers 3H 161
Rattray. Per 4A 144
Raughton. Cumb 5E 113
Raughton Head. Cumb 5E 113
Raunds. Nptn 3G 63
Ravenfield. S Yor 1B 86
Ravenfield Common.
S Yor 1B 86
Ravenglass. Cumb 5B 102
Ravenhills Green. Worc 5B 60
Raveningham. Norf 1F 67
Ravenscar. N Yor 4G 107
Ravensdale. IOM 2C 108
Ravensden. Bed 5H 63
Ravenseat. N Yor 4B 104
Ravenshead. Notts 5C 86
Ravensmoor. Ches E 5A 84
Ravensthorpe. Nptn 3D 62
Ravensthorpe. W Yor 2C 92
Ravenstone. Leics 4B 74
Ravenstone. Mil 5F 63
Ravenstonedale. Cumb 4A 104
Ravenstown. Cumb 2C 96
Ravenstruther. S Lan 5C 128
Ravensworth. N Yor 4E 105
Ravernet. Lis 3G 179
Raw. N Yor 4G 107
Rawcliffe. E Yor 2G 93
Rawcliffe. York 4H 99
Rawcliffe Bridge. E Yor 2G 93
Rawdon. W Yor 1C 92
Rawgreen. Nmbd 4C 114
Rawmarsh. S Yor 1B 86
Rawnsley. Staf 4E 73
Rawreth. Essx 1B 40
Rawridge. Devn 2F 13
Rawson Green. Derbs 1A 74
Rawtenstall. Lanc 2G 91
Raydon. Suff 2D 54
Raylees. Nmbd 5D 120
Rayleigh. Essx 1C 40
Raymond's Hill. Devn 3G 13
Rayne. Essx 3H 53
Rayners Lane. G Lon 2C 38
Reach. Cambs 4E 65
Read. Lanc 1F 91
Reading. Read 201 (4F 37)
Reading Green. Suff 3D 66
Reading Street. Kent 2D 28
Readymoney. Corn 3F 7
Reagill. Cumb 3H 103
Rearquhar. High 4E 165
Rearsby. Leics 4D 74
Reasby. Linc 3H 87
Reaseheath. Ches E 5A 84
Reaster. High 2E 169
Reawick. Shet 7E 173
Reay. High 2B 168
Rechullin. High 3A 156
Reculver. Kent 4G 41
Redberth. Pemb 4E 43
Redbourn. Herts 4B 52
Redbourne. N Lin 4C 94
Redbrook. Glos 5A 48
Redbrook. Wrex 1H 71
Redburn. High 4D 158
Redburn. Nmbd 3A 114
Redcar. Red C 2D 106
Redcastle. High 4H 157
Redcliffe Bay. N Som 4H 33
Red Dial. Cumb 5D 112
Redding. Falk 2C 128
Reddingmuirhead. Falk 2C 128
The Reddings. Glos 3E 49
Reddish. G Man 1C 84
Redditch. Worc 4E 61
Rede. Suff 5H 65
Redenhall. Norf 2E 67
Redesdale Camp. Nmbd 5C 120
Redesmouth. Nmbd 1B 114
Redford. Ang 4E 145
Redford. Dur 1D 105
Redford. W Sus 4G 25
Redfordgreen. Bord 3F 119
Redgate. Corn 2G 7
Redgrave. Suff 3C 66
Red Hill. Warw 5F 61
Red Hill. W Yor 2E 93
Redhill. Abers 3E 153
Redhill. Herts 2C 52
Redhill. N Som 5A 34
Redhill. Shrp 4B 72
Redhill. Surr 5D 39
Redhouses. Arg 3B 124
Redisham. Suff 2G 67
Redland. Bris 4A 34
Redland. Orkn 5C 172
Redlingfield. Suff 3D 66
Red Lodge. Suff 3F 65
Redlynch. Som 3C 22
Redlynch. Wilts 4H 23
Redmain. Cumb 1C 102
Redmarley. Worc 4B 60
Redmarley D'Abitot. Glos 2C 48
Redmarshall. Stoc T 2A 106
Redmile. Leics 2E 75
Redmire. N Yor 5D 104
Rednal. Shrp 3F 71
Redpath. Bord 1H 119
Redpoint. High 2G 155
Red Post. Corn 2C 10
Red Rock. G Man 4D 90
Red Roses. Carm 3G 43
Red Row. Nmbd 5G 121
Redruth. Corn 4B 6
Red Street. Staf 5C 84
Redvales. G Man 4G 91
Red Wharf Bay. IOA 2E 81
Redwick. Newp 3H 33
Redwick. S Glo 3A 34
Redworth. Darl 2F 105
Reed. Herts 2D 52
Reed End. Herts 2D 52
Reedham. Linc 5B 88
Reedham. Norf 5G 79
Reedness. E Yor 2B 94
Reeds Beck. Linc 4B 88
Reemshill. Abers 4E 161
Reepham. Linc 3H 87
Reepham. Norf 3C 78
Reeth. N Yor 5D 104
Regaby. IOM 2D 108
Regil. N Som 5A 34
Regoul. High 3C 158
Reiff. High 2D 162
Reigate. Surr 5D 38
Reighton. N Yor 2F 101
Reilth. Shrp 2E 59
Reinigeadal. W Isl 7E 171
Reisque. Abers 2F 153
Reiss. High 3F 169
Rejerrah. Corn 3B 6
Releath. Corn 5A 6
Relubbus. Corn 3C 4
Relugas. Mor 4D 159
Remenham. Wok 3F 37
Remenham Hill. Wok 3F 37
Rempstone. Notts 3C 74
Rendcomb. Glos 5F 49
Rendham. Suff 4F 67
Rendlesham. Suff 5F 67
Renfrew. Ren 3G 127
Renhold. Bed 5H 63
Renishaw. Derbs 3B 86
Rennington. Nmbd 3G 121
Renton. W Dun 2E 127
Renwick. Cumb 5G 113
Repps. Norf 4G 79
Repton. Derbs 3H 73
Rescassa. Corn 4D 6
Rescobie. Ang 3E 145
Rescorla. Corn
nr. Penwithick 3E 7
nr. Sticker 4D 6
Resipole. High 2B 140
Resolfen. Neat 5B 46
Resolis. High 2A 158
Resolven. Neat 5B 46
Rest and be thankful.
Arg 3B 134
Reston. Bord 3E 131
Restrop. Wilts 3F 35
Retford. Notts 2E 86
Retire. Corn 2E 6
Rettendon. Essx 1B 40
Revesby. Linc 4B 88
Rew. Devn 5D 8
Rewe. Devn 3C 12
Rew Street. IOW 3C 16
Rexon. Devn 4E 11
Reybridge. Wilts 5E 35
Reydon. Suff 3H 67
Reymerston. Norf 5C 78
Reynalton. Pemb 4E 43
Reynoldston. Swan 4D 31
Rezare. Corn 5D 10
Rhadyr. Mon 5G 47
Rhaeadr Gwy. Powy 4B 58
Rhandirmwyn. Carm 1A 46
Rhayader. Powy 4B 58
Rheindown. High 4H 157
Rhemore. High 3G 139
Rhenetra. High 3D 154
Rhewl. Den
nr. Llangollen 1D 70
nr. Ruthin 4D 82
Rhewl. Shrp 2F 71
Rhewl-Mostyn. Flin 2D 82
Rhian. High 2C 164
Rhian Breck. High 3C 164
Rhicarn. High 1E 163
Rhiconich. High 3C 166
Rhicullen. High 1A 158
Rhidorroch. High 4F 163
Rhifail. High 4H 167
Rhigos. Rhon 5C 46
Rhilochan. High 3E 165
Rhiroy. High 5F 163
Rhitongue. High 3G 167
Rhiw. Gwyn 3B 68
Rhiwabon. Wrex 1F 71
Rhiwbina. Card 3E 33
Rhiwbryfdir. Gwyn 1F 69
Rhiwderin. Newp 3F 33
Rhiwlas. Gwyn
nr. Bala 2B 70
nr. Bangor 4E 81
Rhiwlas. Powy 2D 70
Rhodes. G Man 4G 91
Rhodesia. Notts 2C 86
Rhodes Minnis. Kent 1F 29
Rhodiad-y-Brenin. Pemb 2B 42
Rhondda. Rhon 2C 32
Rhonehouse. Dum 4E 111
Rhoose. V Glam 5D 32
Rhos. Carm 2D 45
Rhos. Neat 5H 45
The Rhos. Pemb 3E 43
Rhosaman. Carm 4H 45
Rhoscefnhir. IOA 3E 81
Rhoscolyn. IOA 3B 80
Rhos Common. Powy 4E 71
Rhoscrowther. Pemb 4D 42
Rhos-ddu. Gwyn 2B 68
Rhosdylluan. Gwyn 3A 70
Rhosesmor. Flin 4E 82
Rhos-fawr. Gwyn 2C 68
Rhosgadfan. Gwyn 5E 81
Rhosgoch. IOA 2D 80
Rhosgoch. Powy 1E 47
Rhos Haminiog. Cdgn 4E 57
Rhos-hill. Pemb 1B 44
Rhoshirwaun. Gwyn 3A 68
Rhoslan. Gwyn 1D 69
Rhoslefain. Gwyn 5E 69
Rhosllanerchrugog.
Wrex 1E 71
Rhôs Lligwy. IOA 2D 81
Rhosmaen. Carm 3G 45
Rhosmeirch. IOA 3D 80
Rhosneigr. IOA 3C 80
Rhôs-on-Sea. Cnwy 2H 81
Rhossili. Swan 4D 30
Rhosson. Pemb 2B 42
Rhostrenwfa. IOA 3D 80
Rhostryfan. Gwyn 5D 81
Rhostyllen. Wrex 1F 71
Rhoswiel. Shrp 2E 71
Rhosybol. IOA 2D 80
Rhos-y-brithdir. Powy 3D 70
Rhos-y-garth. Cdgn 3F 57
Rhos-y-gwaliau. Gwyn 2B 70
Rhos-y-llan. Gwyn 2B 68
Rhos-y-meirch. Powy 4E 59
Rhu. Arg 1D 126
Rhualt. Den 3C 82
Rhubha Stoer. High 1E 163
Rhubodach. Arg 2B 126
Rhuddall Heath. Ches W 4H 83
Rhuddlan. Cdgn 1E 45
Rhuddlan. Den 3C 82
Rhue. High 4E 163
Rhulen. Powy 1E 47
Rhunahaorine. Arg 5F 125
Rhuthun. Den 5D 82
Rhuvoult. High 3C 166
Y Rhws. V Glam 5D 32
Rhyd. Gwyn 1F 69
Rhydaman. Carm 4G 45
Rhydargaeau. Carm 3E 45
Rhydcymerau. Carm 2F 45
Rhydd. Worc 1D 48
Rhyd-Ddu. Gwyn 5E 81
Rhydding. Neat 3G 31
Rhydfudr. Cdgn 4E 57
Rhydlanfair. Cnwy 5H 81
Rhydlewis. Cdgn 1D 44
Rhydlios. Gwyn 2A 68
Rhydlydan. Cnwy 5A 82
Rhyd-meirionydd. Cdgn 2F 57
Rhydowen. Cdgn 1E 45
Rhyd-Rosser. Cdgn 4E 57
Rhydspence. Here 1F 47
Rhydtalog. Flin 5E 83
Rhyd-uchaf. Gwyn 2B 70
Rhydwyn. IOA 2C 80
Rhyd-y-clafdy. Gwyn 2C 68
Rhydycroesau. Powy 2E 71
Rhydyfelin. Cdgn 3E 57
Rhydyfelin. Rhon 3D 32
Rhyd-y-foel. Cnwy 3B 82
Rhyd-y-fro. Neat 5H 45
Rhydymain. Gwyn 3H 69
Rhyd-y-meudwy. Den 5D 82
Rhydymwyn. Flin 4E 82
Rhyd-yr-onen. Gwyn 5F 69
Rhyd-y-sarn. Gwyn 1F 69
Rhyl. Den 2C 82
Rhymney. Cphy 5E 46
Rhymni. Cphy 5E 46
Rhynd. Per 1D 136
Rhynie. Abers 1B 152
Ribbesford. Worc 3B 60
Ribbleton. Lanc 1D 90
Ribby. Lanc 1C 90
Ribchester. Lanc 1E 91
Riber. Derbs 5H 85
Ribigill. High 3F 167
Riby. Linc 4E 95
Riccall. N Yor 1G 93
Riccarton. E Ayr 1D 116
Richards Castle. Here 4G 59
Richborough Port. Kent 4H 41
Richhill. Arm 5D 178
Richings Park. Buck 3B 38
Richmond. G Lon 3C 38
Richmond. N Yor 4E 105
Rickarton. Abers 5F 153
Rickerby. Cumb 4F 113
Rickerscote. Staf 3D 72
Rickford. N Som 1H 21
Rickham. Devn 5D 8
Rickinghall. Suff 3C 66
Rickleton. Tyne 4F 115
Rickling. Essx 2E 53
Rickling Green. Essx 3F 53
Rickmansworth. Herts 1B 38
Riddings. Derbs 5B 86
Riddlecombe. Devn 1G 11
Riddlesden. W Yor 5C 98
Ridge. Dors 4E 15
Ridge. Herts 5C 52
Ridge. Wilts 3E 23
Ridgebourne. Powy 4C 58
Ridge Lane. Warw 1G 61
Ridgeway. Derbs
nr. Alfreton 5A 86
nr. Sheffield 2B 86
Ridgeway. Staf 5C 84
Ridgeway Cross. Here 1C 48
Ridgeway Moor. Derbs 2B 86
Ridgewell. Essx 1H 53
Ridgewood. E Sus 3F 27
Ridgmont. C Beds 2H 51
Ridgwardine. Shrp 2A 72
Riding Mill. Nmbd 3D 114
Ridley. Kent 4H 39
Ridley. Nmbd 3A 114
Ridlington. Norf 2F 79
Ridlington. Rut 5F 75
Ridsdale. Nmbd 1C 114
Riemore Lodge. Per 4H 143
Rievaulx. N Yor 1H 99
Rift House. Hart 1B 106
Rigg. Dum 3D 112
Riggend. N Lan 2A 128
Rigsby. Linc 3D 88
Rigside. S Lan 1A 118
Riley Green. Lanc 2E 90
Rileyhill. Staf 4F 73
Rilla Mill. Corn 5C 10
Rillington. N Yor 2C 100
Rimington. Lanc 5H 97
Rimpton. Som 4B 22
Rimsdale. High 4H 167
Rimswell. E Yor 2G 95
Ringasta. Shet 10E 173
Ringford. Dum 4D 111
Ringing Hill. Leics 4B 74
Ringinglow. S Yor 2G 85
Ringland. Norf 4D 78
Ringlestone. Kent 5C 40
Ringmer. E Sus 4F 27
Ringmore. Devn
nr. Kingsbridge 4C 8
nr. Teignmouth 5C 12
Ring o' Bells. Lanc 3C 90
Ring's End. Cambs 5C 76
Ringsfield. Suff 2G 67
Ringsfield Corner. Suff 2G 67
Ringshall. Buck 4H 51
Ringshall. Suff 5C 66
Ringshall Stocks. Suff 5C 66
Ringstead. Norf 1G 77
Ringstead. Nptn 3G 63
Ringwood. Hants 2G 15
Ringwould. Kent 1H 29
Rinmore. Abers 2B 152
Rinnigill. Orkn 8C 172
Rinsey. Corn 4C 4
Riof. W Isl 4D 171
Ripe. E Sus 4G 27
Ripley. Derbs 5B 86
Ripley. Hants 3G 15
Ripley. N Yor 3E 99
Ripley. Surr 5B 38
Riplingham. E Yor 1C 94
Ripon. N Yor 2F 99
Rippingale. Linc 3H 75
Ripple. Kent 1H 29
Ripple. Worc 2D 48
Ripponden. W Yor 3A 92
Rireavach. High 4E 163
Risabus. Arg 5B 124
Risbury. Here 5H 59
Risby. E Yor 1D 94
Risby. N Lin 3C 94
Risby. Suff 4G 65
Risca. Cphy 2F 33
Rise. E Yor 5F 101
Riseden. E Sus 2H 27
Riseden. Kent 2B 28
Rise End. Derbs 5G 85
Risegate. Linc 3B 76
Riseholme. Linc 3G 87
Riseley. Bed 4H 63
Riseley. Wok 5F 37
Rishangles. Suff 4D 66
Rishton. Lanc 1F 91
Rishworth. W Yor 3A 92
Risley. Derbs 2B 74
Risley. Warr 1A 84
Risplith. N Yor 3E 99
Rispond. High 2E 167
Rivar. Wilts 5B 36
Rivenhall. Essx 4B 54
Rivenhall End. Essx 4B 54
River. Kent 1G 29
River. W Sus 3A 26
River Bank. Cambs 4E 65
Riverhead. Kent 5G 39
Rivington. Lanc 3E 91
Roach Bridge. Lanc 2D 90
Roachill. Devn 4B 20
Roade. Nptn 5E 63
Road Green. Norf 1E 67
Roadhead. Cumb 2G 113
Roadmeetings. S Lan 5B 128
Roadside. High 2D 168
Roadside of Catterline.
Abers 1H 145
Roadside of Kinneff.
Abers 1H 145
Roadwater. Som 3D 20
Road Weedon. Nptn 5D 62
Roag. High 4B 154
Roa Island. Cumb 3B 96
Roath. Card 4E 33
Roberton. Bord 3G 119
Roberton. S Lan 2B 118
Robertsbridge. E Sus 3B 28
Robertstown. Mor 4G 159
Robertstown. Rhon 5C 46
Roberttown. W Yor 2B 92
Robeston Back. Pemb 3E 43
Robeston Wathen. Pemb 3E 43
Robeston West. Pemb 4C 42
Robin Hood. Lanc 3D 90
Robin Hood. W Yor 2D 92
Robinhood End. Essx 2H 53
Robin Hood's Bay. N Yor 4G 107
Roborough. Devn
nr. Great Torrington 1F 11
nr. Plymouth 2B 8
Rob Roy's House. Arg 2A 134
Roby Mill. Lanc 4D 90
Rocester. Staf 2F 73
Roch. Pemb 2C 42
Rochdale. G Man 3G 91
Roche. Corn 2D 6
Rochester. Medw
. . Medway Towns 197 (4B 40)
Rochester. Nmbd 5C 120
Rochford. Essx 1C 40
Rock. Corn 1D 6
Rock. Nmbd 2G 121
Rock. W Sus 4C 26
Rock. Worc 3B 60
The Rock. M Ulst 2B 178
Rockbeare. Devn 3D 12
Rockbourne. Hants 1G 15
Rockcliffe. Cumb 3E 113
Rockcliffe. Dum 4F 111
Rockcliffe Cross. Cumb 3E 113
Rock Ferry. Mers 2F 83
Rockfield. High 5G 165
Rockfield. Mon 4H 47
Rockford. Hants 2G 15
Rockgreen. Shrp 3H 59
Rockhampton. S Glo 2B 34
Rockhead. Corn 4A 10
Rockingham. Nptn 1F 63
Rockland All Saints. Norf 1B 66
Rockland St Mary. Norf 5F 79
Rockland St Peter. Norf 1B 66
Rockley. Wilts 4G 35
Rockwell End. Buck 3F 37
Rockwell Green. Som 1E 13
Rodborough. Glos 5D 48
Rodbourne. Wilts 3E 35
Rodd. Here 4F 59
Roddam. Nmbd 2E 121
Rodden. Dors 4B 14
Roddenloft. E Ayr 2D 117
Roddymoor. Dur 1E 105
Rode. Som 1D 22
Rode Heath. Ches E 5C 84
Rodeheath. Ches E 4C 84
Rodel. W Isl 9C 171
Roden. Telf 4H 71
Rodhuish. Som 3D 20
Rodington. Telf 4H 71
Rodington Heath. Telf 4H 71
Rodley. Glos 4C 48
Rodmarton. Glos 2E 35
Rodmell. E Sus 5F 27
Rodmersham. Kent 4D 40
Rodmersham Green. Kent 4D 40
Rodney Stoke. Som 2H 21
Rodsley. Derbs 1G 73
Rodway. Som 3F 21
Rodway. Telf 4A 72
Rodwell. Dors 5B 14
Roecliffe. N Yor 3F 99
Roe Green. Herts 2D 52
Roehampton. G Lon 3D 38
Roesound. Shet 5E 173
Roffey. W Sus 2C 26
Rogart. High 3E 165
Rogate. W Sus 4G 25
Roger Ground. Cumb 5E 103
Rogerstone. Newp 3F 33
Roget. Mon 3H 33
Rogue's Alley. Cambs 5C 76
Roke. Oxon 2E 37
Rokemarsh. Oxon 2E 36
Roker. Tyne 4H 115
Rollesby. Norf 4G 79
Rolleston. Leics 5E 75
Rolleston. Notts 5E 87
Rolleston on Dove. Staf 3G 73
Rolston. E Yor 5G 101
Rolvenden. Kent 2C 28
Rolvenden Layne. Kent 2C 28
Romaldkirk. Dur 2C 104
Roman Bank. Shrp 1H 59
Romanby. N Yor 5A 106
Romannobridge. Bord 5E 129
Romansleigh. Devn 4H 19
Romers Common. Worc 4H 59
Romesdal. High 3D 154
Romford. G Lon 2G 39
Romiley. G Man 1D 84
Romsey. Hants 4B 24
Romsley. Shrp 2B 60
Romsley. Worc 3D 60
Ronague. IOM 4B 108
Ronaldsvoe. Orkn 8D 172
Rookby. Cumb 3B 104
Rookhope. Dur 5C 114
Rooking. Cumb 3F 103
Rookley. IOW 4D 16
Rooks Bridge. Som 1G 21
Rooksey Green. Suff 5B 66
Rook's Nest. Som 3D 20
Rookwood. W Sus 3F 17
Roos. E Yor 1F 95
Roosebeck. Cumb 3B 96
Roosecote. Cumb 3B 96
Rootfield. High 3H 157
Rootham's Green. Bed 5A 64
Rootpark. S Lan 4C 128
Ropley. Hants 3E 25
Ropley Dean. Hants 3E 25
Ropsley. Linc 2G 75
Rora. Abers 3H 161
Rorandle. Abers 2D 152
Rorrington. Shrp 5F 71
Rose. Corn 3B 6
Roseacre. Lanc 1C 90
Rose Ash. Devn 4A 20
Rosebank. S Lan 5B 128
Rosebush. Pemb 2E 43
Rosedale Abbey. N Yor 5E 107
Roseden. Nmbd 2E 121
Rose Green. Essx 3B 54
Rose Green. Suff 1C 54
Rosehall. High 3B 164
Rosehearty. Abers 2G 161
Rose Hill. E Sus 4F 27
Rose Hill. Lanc 1G 91
Rosehill. Shrp
nr. Market Drayton 2A 72
nr. Shrewsbury 4G 71
Roseisle. Mor 2F 159
Rosemarket. Pemb 4D 42
Rosemarkie. High 3B 158
Rosemary Lane. Devn 1E 13
Rosemount. Per 4A 144
Rosenannon. Corn 2D 6
Roser's Cross. E Sus 3G 27
Rosevean. Corn 3E 6
Rosewell. Midl 3F 129
Roseworth. Stoc T 2B 106
Roseworthy. Corn 3D 4
Rosgill. Cumb 3G 103
Roshven. High 1B 140
Roskhill. High 4B 154
Roskorwell. Corn 4E 5
Rosley. Cumb 5E 112
Roslin. Midl 3F 129
Rosliston. Derbs 4G 73
Rosneath. Arg 1D 126
Ross. Dum 5D 110
Ross. Nmbd 1F 121
Ross. Per 1G 135
Ross. Bord 3F 131
Rossendale. Lanc 2F 91
Rossett. Wrex 5F 83
Rossington. S Yor 1D 86
Rosskeen. High 2A 158
Rossland. Ren 2F 127
Rosslea. Ferm 6L 177
Ross-on-Wye. Here 3B 48
Roster. High 5E 169
Rostherne. Ches E 2B 84
Rostholme. S Yor 4F 93
Rosthwaite. Cumb 3D 102
Roston. Derbs 1F 73
Rostrevor. New M 8F 179
Rosudgeon. Corn 4C 4
Rosyth. Fife 1E 129
Rothbury. Nmbd 4E 121
Rotherby. Leics 4D 74
Rotherfield. E Sus 3G 27
Rotherfield Greys. Oxon 3F 37
Rotherfield Peppard. Oxon 3F 37
Rotherham. S Yor 1B 86
Rothersthorpe. Nptn 5E 62
Rotherwick. Hants 1F 25
Rothes. Mor 4G 159
Rothesay. Arg 3B 126
Rothienorman. Abers 5E 160
Rothiesholm. Orkn 5F 172
Rothley. Leics 4C 74
Rothley. Nmbd 1D 114
Rothwell. Linc 1A 88
Rothwell. Nptn 2F 63
Rothwell. W Yor 2D 92
Rotsea. E Yor 4E 101
Rottal. Ang 2C 144
Rotten End. Suff 4F 67
Rotten Row. Norf 4C 78
Rotten Row. W Ber 4D 36
Rotten Row. W Mid 3F 61
Rottingdean. Brig 5E 27
Rottington. Cumb 3A 102
Roud. IOW 4D 16
Rougham. Norf 3H 77
Rougham. Suff 4B 66
Rough Close. Staf 2D 72
Rough Common. Kent 5F 41
Roughcote. Staf 1D 72
Roughfort. Ant 1G 179
Rough Haugh. High 4H 167
Rough Hay. Staf 3G 73
Roughlee. Lanc 5H 97
Roughley. W Mid 1F 61
Roughsike. Cumb 2G 113
Roughton. Linc 4B 88
Roughton. Norf 2E 78
Roughton. Shrp 1B 60
Roundbush Green. Essx 4F 53
Roundham. Som 2H 13
Roundhay. W Yor 1D 92
Round Hill. Torb 2E 9
Roundhurst. W Sus 2A 26
Round Maple. Suff 1C 54
Round Oak. Shrp 2F 59
Roundstreet Common.
W Sus 3B 26
Roundthwaite. Cumb 4H 103
Roundway. Wilts 5F 35
Roundyhill. Ang 3C 144
Rousdon. Devn 3F 13
Rousham. Oxon 3C 50
Rousky. Ferm 8B 174
Rous Lench. Worc 5E 61
Routh. E Yor 5E 101
Rout's Green. Buck 2F 37
Row. Corn 5A 10
Row. Cumb
nr. Kendal 1D 96
nr. Penrith 1H 103
The Row. Lanc 2D 96
Rowanburn. Dum 2F 113
Rowanhill. Abers 3H 161
Rowardennan. Stir 4C 134
Rowarth. Derbs 2E 85
Row Ash. Hants 1D 16
Rowberrow. Som 1H 21
Rowde. Wilts 5E 35
Rowden. Devn 3G 11
Rowen. Cnwy 3G 81
Rowfoot. Nmbd 3H 113
Row Green. Essx 3H 53
Row Heath. Essx 4E 55
Rowhedge. Essx 3D 54
Rowhook. W Sus 2C 26
Rowington. Warw 4G 61
Rowland. Derbs 3G 85
Rowlands Castle. Hants 1F 17
Rowlands Gill. Tyne 4E 115
Rowledge. Hants 2G 25
Rowley. Dur 5D 115
Rowley. E Yor 1C 94
Rowley. Shrp 5F 71
Rowley Hill. W Yor 3B 92
Rowley Regis. W Mid 2D 60
Rowlstone. Here 3G 47
Rowly. Surr 1B 26
Rowner. Hants 2D 16
Rowney Green. Worc 3E 61
Rownhams. Hants 1B 16
Rowrah. Cumb 3B 102
Rowsham. Buck 4G 51
Rowsley. Derbs 4G 85
Rowstock. Oxon 3C 36
Rowston. Linc 5H 87
Rowthorne. Derbs 4B 86
Rowton. Ches W 4G 83
Rowton. Shrp
nr. Ludlow 2G 59
nr. Shrewsbury 4F 71
Rowton. Telf 4A 72
Row Town. Surr 4B 38
Roxburgh. Bord 1B 120
Roxby. N Lin 3C 94
Roxby. N Yor 3E 107
Roxhill. Ant 7G 175
Roxton. Bed 5A 64
Roxwell. Essx 5G 53
Royal Leamington Spa.
Warw 4H 61
Royal Oak. Darl 2F 105
Royal Oak. Lanc 4C 90
Royal Oak. N Yor 2F 101
Royal's Green. Ches E 1A 72
Royal Sutton Coldfield.
W Mid 1F 61
Royal Tunbridge Wells.
Kent 2G 27
Royal Wootton Bassett.
Wilts 3F 35
Roybridge. High 5E 149
Roydon. Essx 4E 53
Roydon. Norf
nr. Diss 2C 66
nr. King's Lynn 3G 77
Roydon Hamlet. Essx 5E 53
Royston. Herts 1D 52
Royston. S Yor 3D 92
Royston Water. Som 1F 13
Royton. G Man 4H 91
Ruabon. Wrex 1F 71
Ruaig. Arg 4B 138
Ruan High Lanes. Corn 5D 6
Ruan Lanihorne. Corn 4C 6
Ruan Major. Corn 5E 5
Ruan Minor. Corn 5E 5
Ruarach. High 1B 148
Ruardean. Glos 4B 48
Ruardean Hill. Glos 4B 48
Ruardean Woodside. Glos 4B 48
Rubane. Ards 3L 179
Rubery. Worc 3D 61
Ruchazie. Glas 3H 127
Ruckcroft. Cumb 5G 113
Ruckinge. Kent 2E 29
Ruckland. Linc 3C 88
Rucklers Lane. Herts 5A 52
Ruckley. Shrp 5H 71
Rudbaxton. Pemb 2D 42
Rudby. N Yor 4B 106
Ruddington. Notts 2C 74
Rudford. Glos 3C 48
Rudge. Shrp 1C 60
Rudge. Wilts 1D 22
Rudge Heath. Shrp 1B 60
Rudgeway. S Glo 3B 34
Rudgwick. W Sus 2B 26
Rudhall. Here 3B 48
Rudheath. Ches W 3A 84
Rudley Green. Essx 5B 54

Rudloe—Shawford

Rudloe. Wilts 4D 34
Rudry. Cphy 3F 33
Rudston. E Yor 3E 101
Rudyard. Staf 5D 84
Rufford. Lanc 3C 90
Rufforth. York 4H 99
Rugby. Warw 3C 62
Rugeley. Staf 4E 73
Ruglen. S Ayr 4B 116
Ruilick. High 4H 157
Ruisaurie. High 4G 157
Ruishton. Som 4F 21
Ruisigearraidh. W Isl 1E 170
Ruislip. G Lon 2B 38
Ruislip Common. G Lon 2B 38
Rumbling Bridge. Per 4C 136
Rumburgh. Suff 2F 67
Rumford. Corn 1C 6
Rumford. Falk 2C 128
Rumney. Card 4F 33
Rumwell. Som 4E 21
Runcorn. Hal 2H 83
Runcton. W Sus 2G 17
Runcton Holme. Norf 5F 77
Rundlestone. Devn 5F 11
Runfold. Surr 2G 25
Runhall. Norf 5C 78
Runham. Norf 4G 79
Runnington. Som 4E 20
Runshaw Moor. Lanc 3D 90
Runswick. N Yor 3F 107
Runtaleave. Ang 2B 144
Runwell. Essx 1B 40
Ruscombe. Wok 4F 37
Rushall. Here 2B 48
Rushall. Norf 2D 66
Rushall. W Mid 5E 73
Rushall. Wilts 1G 23
Rushbrooke. Suff 4A 66
Rushbury. Shrp 1H 59
Rushden. Herts 2D 52
Rushden. Nptn 4G 63
Rushenden. Kent 3D 40
Rushford. Devn 5E 11
Rushford. Suff 2B 66
Rush Green. Herts 3C 52
Rushlake Green. E Sus 4H 27
Rushmere. Suff 2G 67
Rushmere St Andrew.
Suff 1F 55
Rushmoor. Surr 2G 25
Rushock. Worc 3C 60
Rusholme. G Man 1C 84
Rushton. Ches W 4H 83
Rushton. Nptn 2F 63
Rushton. Shrp 5A 72
Rushton Spencer. Staf 4D 84
Rushwick. Worc 5C 60
Rushyford. Dur 2F 105
Ruskie. Stir 3F 135
Ruskington. Linc 5H 87
Rusland. Cumb 1C 96
Rusper. W Sus 2D 26
Ruspidge. Glos 4B 48
Russell's Water. Oxon 3F 37
Russel's Green. Suff 3E 67
Russ Hill. Surr 1D 26
Russland. Orkn 6C 172
Rusthall. Kent 2G 27
Rustington. W Sus 5B 26
Ruston. N Yor 1D 100
Ruston Parva. E Yor 3E 101
Ruswarp. N Yor 4F 107
Rutherglen. S Lan 3H 127
Ruthernbridge. Corn 2E 6
Ruthin. Den 5D 82
Ruthin. V Glam 4C 32
Ruthrieston. Aber 3G 153
Ruthven. Abers 4C 160
Ruthven. Ang 4B 144
Ruthven. High
nr. Inverness 5C 158
nr. Kingussie 4B 150
Ruthvoes. Corn 2D 6
Ruthwaite. Cumb 1D 102
Ruthwell. Dum 3C 112
Ruxton Green. Here 4A 48
Ruyton-XI-Towns. Shrp 3F 71
Ryal. Nmbd 2D 114
Ryall. Dors 3H 13
Ryall. Worc 1D 48
Ryarsh. Kent 5A 40
Rychraggan. High 5G 157
Rydal. Cumb 4E 103
Ryde. IOW 3D 16
Rye. E Sus 3D 28
Ryecroft Gate. Staf 4D 84
Ryeford. Here 3B 48
Rye Foreign. E Sus 3D 28
Rye Harbour. E Sus 4D 28
Ryehill. E Yor 2F 95
Rye Street. Worc 2C 48
Ryhall. Rut 4H 75
Ryhill. W Yor 3D 93
Ryhope. Tyne 4H 115
Ryhope Colliery. Tyne 4H 115
Rylands. Notts 2C 74
Rylstone. N Yor 4B 98
Ryme Intrinseca. Dors 1A 14
Ryther. N Yor 1F 93
Ryton. Glos 2C 48
Ryton. N Yor 2B 100
Ryton. Shrp 5B 72
Ryton. Tyne 3E 115
Ryton. Warw 2B 62
Ryton-on-Dunsmore.
Warw 3A 62
Ryton Woodside. Tyne 3E 115

S

Saasaig. High 3E 147
Sabden. Lanc 1F 91
Sacombe. Herts 4D 52
Sacriston. Dur 5F 115
Sadberge. Darl 3A 106
Saddell. Arg 2B 122
Saddington. Leics 1D 62
Saddle Bow. Norf 4F 77
Saddlescombe. W Sus 4D 26
Saddleworth. G Man 4H 91
Sadgill. Cumb 4F 103
Saffron Walden. Essx 2F 53
Sageston. Pemb 4E 43
Saham Hills. Norf 5B 78
Saham Toney. Norf 5A 78
Saighdinis. W Isl 2D 170
Saighton. Ches W 4G 83
Sain Dunwyd. V Glam 5C 32
Sain Hilari. V Glam 4D 32
St Abbs. Bord 3F 131
St Agnes. Corn 3B 6
St Albans. Herts 5B 52
St Allen. Corn 3C 6
St Andrews. Fife 2H 137
St Andrews Major. V Glam 4E 33
St Anne's. Lanc 2B 90
St Ann's. Dum 5C 118
St Ann's Chapel. Corn 5E 11
St Ann's Chapel. Devn 4C 8
St Anthony. Corn 5C 6
St Anthony-in-Meneage.
Corn 4E 5
St Arvans. Mon 2A 34
St Asaph. Den 3C 82
Sain Tathan. V Glam 5D 32
St Athan. V Glam 5D 32
St Austell. Corn 3E 6
St Bartholomew's Hill.
Wilts 4E 23
St Bees. Cumb 3A 102
St Blazey. Corn 3E 7
St Blazey Gate. Corn 3E 7
St Boswells. Bord 1H 119
St Breock. Corn 1D 6
St Breward. Corn 5A 10
St Briavels. Glos 5A 48
St Brides. Pemb 3B 42
St Brides Major. V Glam 4B 32
St Bride's Netherwent.
Mon 3H 33
St Bride's-super-Ely.
V Glam 4D 32
St Brides Wentlooge.
Newp 3F 33
St Budeaux. Plym 3A 8
Saintbury. Glos 2G 49
St Buryan. Corn 4B 4
St Catherine. Bath 4C 34
St Catherines. Arg 3A 134
St Clears. Carm 3G 43
St Cleer. Corn 2G 7
St Clement. Corn 4C 6
St Clether. Corn 4C 10
St Colmac. Arg 3B 126
St Columb Major. Corn 2D 6
St Columb Minor. Corn 2C 6
St Columb Road. Corn 3D 6
St Combs. Abers 2H 161
St Cross. Hants 4C 24
St Cross South Elmham.
Suff 2E 67
St Cyrus. Abers 2G 145
St David's. Per 1B 136
St Davids. Pemb 2B 42
St Day. Corn 4B 6
St Dennis. Corn 3D 6
St Dogmaels. Pemb 1B 44
St Dominick. Corn 2H 7
St Donat's. V Glam 5C 32
St Edith's Marsh. Wilts 5E 35
St Endellion. Corn 1D 6
St Enoder. Corn 3C 6
St Erme. Corn 4C 6
St Erney. Corn 3H 7
St Erth. Corn 3C 4
St Erth Praze. Corn 3C 4
St Ervan. Corn 1C 6
St Eval. Corn 2C 6
St Ewe. Corn 4D 6
St Fagans. Card 4E 32
St Fergus. Abers 3H 161
Saintfield. New M 4J 179
St Fillans. Per 1F 135
St Florence. Pemb 4E 43
St Gennys. Corn 3B 10
St George. Cnwy 3B 82
St George's. N Som 5G 33
St Georges. V Glam 4D 32
St George's Hill. Surr 4B 38
St Germans. Corn 3H 7
St Giles in the Wood.
Devn 1F 11
St Giles on the Heath.
Devn 3D 10
St Giles's Hill. Hants 4C 24
St Gluvias. Corn 5B 6
St Harmon. Powy 3B 58
St Helena. Warw 5G 73
St Helen Auckland. Dur 2E 105
St Helen's. E Sus 4C 28
St Helens. Cumb 1B 102
St Helens. IOW 4E 17
St Helens. Mers 1H 83
St Hilary. Corn 3C 4
St Hilary. V Glam 4D 32
Saint Hill. Devn 2D 12
Saint Hill. W Sus 2E 27
St Illtyd. Blae 5F 47
St Ippolyts. Herts 3B 52
St Ishmael. Carm 5D 44
St Ishmael's. Pemb 4C 42
St Issey. Corn 1D 6
St Ive. Corn 2H 7
St Ives. Cambs 3C 64
St Ives. Corn 2C 4
St Ives. Dors 2G 15
St James' End. Nptn 4E 63
St James South Elmham.
Suff 2F 67
St Jidgey. Corn 2D 6
St John. Corn 3A 8
St John's. IOM 3B 108
St John's. Worc 5C 60
St John's Chapel. Devn 4F 19
St John's Chapel. Dur 1B 104
St John's Fen End. Norf 4E 77
St John's Town of Dalry.
Dum 1D 110
St Judes. IOM 2C 108
St Just. Corn 3A 4
St Just in Roseland. Corn 5C 6
St Katherines. Abers 5E 161
St Keverne. Corn 4E 5
St Kew. Corn 5A 10
St Kew Highway. Corn 5A 10
St Keyne. Corn 2G 7
St Lawrence. Corn 2E 7
St Lawrence. Essx 5C 54
St Lawrence. IOW 5D 16
St Leonards. Buck 5H 51
St Leonards. Dors 2G 15
St Leonards. E Sus 5B 28
St Levan. Corn 4A 4
St Lythans. V Glam 4E 32
St Mabyn. Corn 5A 10
St Madoes. Per 1D 136
St Margaret's. Herts 4A 52
St Margaret's. Wilts 5H 35
St Margarets. Here 2G 47
St Margarets. Herts 4D 53
St Margaret's at Cliffe.
Kent 1H 29
St Margaret's Hope.
Orkn 8D 172
St Margaret South Elmham.
Suff 2F 67
St Mark's. IOM 4B 108
St Martin. Corn
nr. Helston 4E 5
nr. Looe 3G 7
St Martin's. Shrp 2F 71
St Martins. Per 5A 144
St Mary Bourne. Hants 1C 24
St Mary Church. V Glam 4D 32
St Marychurch. Torb 2F 9
St Mary Cray. G Lon 4F 39
St Mary Hill. V Glam 4C 32
St Mary Hoo. Medw 3C 40
St Mary in the Marsh.
Kent 3E 29
St Mary's. Orkn 7D 172
St Mary's Airport. IOS 1B 4
St Mary's Bay. Kent 3E 29
St Marys Platt. Kent 5H 39
St Maughan's Green. Mon 4H 47
St Mawes. Corn 5C 6
St Mawgan. Corn 2C 6
St Mellion. Corn 2H 7
St Mellons. Card 3F 33
St Merryn. Corn 1C 6
St Mewan. Corn 3D 6
St Michael Caerhays. Corn 4D 6
St Michael Penkevil. Corn 4C 6
St Michaels. Kent 2C 28
St Michaels. Torb 3E 9
St Michaels. Worc 4H 59
St Michael's on Wyre.
Lanc 5D 96
St Michael South Elmham.
Suff 2F 67
St Minver. Corn 1D 6
St Monans. Fife 3H 137
St Neot. Corn 2F 7
St Neots. Cambs 4A 64
St Newlyn East. Corn 3C 6
St Nicholas. Pemb 1C 42
St Nicholas. V Glam 4D 32
St Nicholas at Wade. Kent 4G 41
St Nicholas South Elmham.
Suff 2F 67
St Ninians. Stir 4G 135
St Olaves. Norf 1G 67
St Osyth. Essx 4E 54
St Osyth Heath. Essx 4E 55
St Owen's Cross. Here 3A 48
St Paul's Cray. G Lon 4F 39
St Paul's Walden. Herts 3B 52
St Peter's. Kent 4H 41
St Peter The Great. Worc 5C 60
St Petrox. Pemb 5D 42
St Pinnock. Corn 2G 7
St Quivox. S Ayr 2C 116
St Ruan. Corn 5E 5
St Stephen. Corn 3D 6
St Stephens. Corn
nr. Launceston 4D 10
nr. Saltash 3A 8
St Teath. Corn 4A 10
St Thomas. Devn 3C 12
St Thomas. Swan 3F 31
St Tudy. Corn 5A 10
St Twynnells. Pemb 5D 42
St Veep. Corn 3F 7
St Vigeans. Ang 4F 145
St Wenn. Corn 2D 6
St Weonards. Here 3H 47
St Winnolls. Corn 3H 7
St Winnow. Corn 3F 7
Salcombe. Devn 5D 8
Salcombe Regis. Devn 4E 13
Salcott. Essx 4C 54
Sale. G Man 1B 84
Saleby. Linc 3D 88
Sale Green. Worc 5D 60
Salehurst. E Sus 3B 28
Salem. Carm 3G 45
Salem. Cdgn 2F 57
Salen. Arg 4G 139
Salen. High 2A 140
Salesbury. Lanc 1E 91
Saleway. Worc 5D 60
Salford. C Beds 2H 51
Salford. G Man
...... **Manchester 197** (1C 84)
Salford. Oxon 3A 50
Salford Priors. Warw 5E 61
Salfords. Surr 1D 27
Salhouse. Norf 4F 79
Saligo. Arg 3A 124
Saline. Fife 4C 136
Salisbury. Wilts **201** (3G 23)
Salkeld Dykes. Cumb 1G 103
Sallachan. High 2D 141
Sallachy. High
nr. Lairg 3C 164
nr. Stromeferry 5B 156
Salle. Norf 3D 78
Salmonby. Linc 3C 88
Salmond's Muir. Ang 5E 145
Salperton. Glos 3F 49
Salph End. Bed 5H 63
Salsburgh. N Lan 3B 128
Salt. Staf 3D 72
Salta. Cumb 5B 112
Saltaire. W Yor 1B 92
Saltash. Corn 3A 8
Saltburn. High 2B 158
Saltburn-by-the-Sea.
Red C 2D 106
Saltby. Leics 3F 75
Saltcoats. Cumb 5B 102
Saltcoats. N Ayr 5D 126
Saltdean. Brig 5E 27
Salt End. E Yor 2E 95
Salter. Lanc 3F 97
Salterforth. Lanc 5A 98
Salters Lode. Norf 5E 77
Salterswall. Ches W 4A 84
Salterton. Wilts 3G 23
Saltfleet. Linc 1D 88
Saltfleetby All Saints.
Linc 1D 88
Saltfleetby St Clements.
Linc 1D 88
Saltfleetby St Peter. Linc 2D 88
Saltford. Bath 5B 34
Salthouse. Norf 1C 78
Saltmarshe. E Yor 2A 94
Saltness. Orkn 9B 172
Saltness. Shet 7D 173
Saltney. Flin 4F 83
Salton. N Yor 2B 100
Saltrens. Devn 4E 19
Saltwick. Nmbd 2E 115
Saltwood. Kent 2F 29
Salum. Arg 4B 138
Salwarpe. Worc 4C 60
Salwayash. Dors 3H 13
Samalaman. High 1A 140
Sambourne. Warw 4E 61
Sambourne. Wilts 2D 22
Sambrook. Telf 3B 72
Samhia. W Isl 2C 170
Samlesbury. Lanc 1D 90
Samlesbury Bottoms.
Lanc 2E 90
Sampford Arundel. Som 1E 12
Sampford Brett. Som 2D 20
Sampford Courtenay.
Devn 2G 11
Sampford Peverell. Devn 1D 12
Sampford Spiney. Devn 5F 11
Samsonslane. Orkn 5F 172
Samuelston. E Lot 2A 130
Sanaigmore. Arg 2A 124
Sancreed. Corn 4B 4
Sancton. E Yor 1C 94
Sand. High 4D 162
Sand. Shet 7E 173
Sand. Som 2H 21
Sandaig. Arg 4A 138
Sandaig. High 3F 147
Sandale. Cumb 5D 112
Sandal Magna. W Yor 3D 92
Sandavore. High 5C 146
Sanday Airport. Orkn 3F 172
Sandbach. Ches E 4B 84
Sandbank. Arg 1C 126
Sandbanks. Pool 4F 15
Sandend. Abers 2C 160
Sanderstead. G Lon 4E 39
Sandfields. Neat 3G 31
Sandford. Cumb 3A 104
Sandford. Devn 2B 12
Sandford. Dors 4E 15
Sandford. Hants 2G 15
Sandford. IOW 4D 16
Sandford. N Som 1H 21
Sandford. Shrp
nr. Oswestry 3F 71
nr. Whitchurch 2H 71
Sandford. S Lan 5A 128
Sandfordhill. Abers 4H 161
Sandford-on-Thames.
Oxon 5D 50
Sandford Orcas. Dors 4B 22
Sandford St Martin. Oxon 3C 50
Sandgate. Kent 2G 29
Sandgreen. Dum 4C 110
Sandhaven. Abers 2G 161
Sandhead. Dum 4F 109
Sandhill. Cambs 2E 65
Sandhills. Dors 1B 14
Sandhills. Oxon 5D 50
Sandhills. Surr 2A 26
Sandhoe. Nmbd 3C 114
Sand Hole. E Yor 1B 94
Sandholes. M Ulst 2B 178
Sandholme. E Yor 1B 94
Sandholme. Linc 2C 76
Sandhurst. Brac 5G 37
Sandhurst. Glos 3D 48
Sandhurst. Kent 3B 28
Sandhurst Cross. Kent 3B 28
Sand Hutton. N Yor 4A 100
Sandhutton. N Yor 1F 99
Sandiacre. Derbs 2B 74
Sandilands. Linc 2E 89
Sandiway. Ches W 3A 84
Sandleheath. Hants 1G 15
Sandling. Kent 5B 40
Sandlow Green. Ches E 4B 84
Sandness. Shet 6C 173
Sandon. Essx 5H 53
Sandon. Herts 2D 52
Sandon. Staf 3D 72
Sandonbank. Staf 3D 72
Sandown. IOW 4D 16
Sandplace. Corn 3G 7
Sandridge. Herts 4B 52
Sandringham. Norf 3F 77
The Sands. Surr 2G 25
Sandsend. N Yor 3F 107
Sandside. Cumb 2C 96
Sandsound. Shet 7E 173
Sandtoft. N Lin 4H 93
Sandvoe. Shet 2E 173
Sandway. Kent 5C 40
Sandwich. Kent 5H 41
Sandwick. Cumb 3F 103
Sandwick. Orkn
on Mainland 6B 172
on South Ronaldsay 9D 172
Sandwick. Shet
on Mainland 9F 173
on Whalsay 5G 173
Sandwith. Cumb 3A 102
Sandy. Carm 5E 45
Sandy. C Beds 1B 52
Sandy Bank. Linc 5B 88
Sandycroft. Flin 4F 83
Sandy Cross. Here 5A 60
Sandygate. Devn 5B 12
Sandygate. IOM 2C 108
Sandy Haven. Pemb 4C 42
Sandyhills. Dum 4F 111
Sandylands. Lanc 3D 96
Sandy Lane. Wilts 5E 35
Sandylane. Swan 4E 31
Sandystones. Bord 2H 119
Sandyway. Here 3H 47
Sangobeg. High 2E 167
Sangomore. High 2E 166
Sankyn's Green. Worc 4B 60
Sanna. High 2F 139
Sanndabhaig. W Isl
on Isle of Lewis 4G 171
on South Uist 4D 170
Sannox. N Ayr 5B 126
Sanquhar. Dum 3G 117
Santon. Cumb 4B 102
Santon Bridge. Cumb 4C 102
Santon Downham. Suff 2H 65
Sapcote. Leics 1B 62
Sapey Common. Here 4B 60
Sapiston. Suff 3B 66
Sapley. Cambs 3B 64
Sapperton. Derbs 2F 73
Sapperton. Glos 5E 49
Sapperton. Linc 2H 75
Saracen's Head. Linc 3C 76
Sarclet. High 4F 169
Sardis. Carm 5F 45
Sardis. Pemb
nr. Milford Haven 4D 42
nr. Tenby 4F 43
Sarisbury Green. Hants 2D 16
Sarn. B'end 3C 32
Sarn. Powy 1E 58
Sarnau. Carm 3E 45
Sarnau. Cdgn 5C 56
Sarnau. Gwyn 2B 70
Sarnau. Powy
nr. Brecon 2D 46
nr. Welshpool 4E 71
Sarn Bach. Gwyn 3C 68
Sarnesfield. Here 5F 59
Sarn Meyllteyrn. Gwyn 2B 68
Saron. Carm
nr. Ammanford 4G 45
nr. Newcastle Emlyn 2D 45
Saron. Gwyn
nr. Bethel 4E 81
nr. Bontnewydd 5D 80
Sarratt. Herts 1B 38
Sarre. Kent 4G 41
Sarsden. Oxon 3A 50
Satley. Dur 5E 115
Satron. N Yor 5C 104
Satterleigh. Devn 4G 19
Satterthwaite. Cumb 5E 103
Satwell. Oxon 3F 37
Sauchen. Abers 2D 152
Saucher. Per 5A 144
Saughall. Ches W 3F 83
Saughtree. Bord 5H 119
Saul. Glos 5C 48
Saul. New M 5K 179
Saundby. Notts 2E 87
Saundersfoot. Pemb 4F 43
Saunderton. Buck 5F 51
Saunderton Lee. Buck 2G 37
Saunton. Devn 3E 19
Sausthorpe. Linc 4C 88
Saval. High 3C 164
Saverley Green. Staf 2D 72
Sawbridge. Warw 4C 62
Sawbridgeworth. Herts 4E 53
Sawdon. N Yor 1D 100
Sawley. Derbs 2B 74
Sawley. Lanc 5G 97
Sawley. N Yor 3E 99
Sawston. Cambs 1E 53
Sawtry. Cambs 2A 64
Saxby. Leics 3F 75
Saxby. Linc 2H 87
Saxby All Saints. N Lin 3C 94
Saxelbye. Leics 3D 74
Saxham Street. Suff 4C 66
Saxilby. Linc 3F 87
Saxlingham. Norf 2C 78
Saxlingham Green. Norf 1E 67
Saxlingham Nethergate.
Norf 1E 67
Saxlingham Thorpe. Norf 1E 66
Saxmundham. Suff 4F 67
Saxondale. Notts 1D 74
Saxon Street. Cambs 5F 65
Saxtead. Suff 4E 67
Saxtead Green. Suff 4E 67
Saxthorpe. Norf 2D 78
Saxton. N Yor 1E 93
Sayers Common. W Sus 4D 26
Scackleton. N Yor 2A 100
Scadabhagh. W Isl 8D 171
Scaddy. New M 5J 179
Scaftworth. Notts 1D 86
Scagglethorpe. N Yor 2C 100
Scaitcliffe. Lanc 2F 91
Scaladal. W Isl 6D 171
Scalasaig. Arg 4A 132
Scalby. E Yor 2B 94
Scalby. N Yor 5H 107
Scalby Mills. N Yor 5H 107
Scaldwell. Nptn 3E 63
Scaleby. Cumb 3F 113
Scaleby Hill. Cumb 3F 113
Scale Houses. Cumb 5G 113
Scales. Cumb
nr. Barrow-in-Furness 2B 96
nr. Keswick 2E 103
Scalford. Leics 3E 75
Scaling. N Yor 3E 107
Scaling Dam. Red C 3E 107
Scalloway. Shet 8F 173
Scalpaigh. W Isl 8E 171
Scalpay House. High 1E 147
Scamblesby. Linc 3B 88
Scamodale. High 1C 140
Scampston. N Yor 2C 100
Scampton. Linc 3G 87
Scaniport. High 5A 158
Scapa. Orkn 7D 172
Scapegoat Hill. W Yor 3A 92
Scar. Orkn 3F 172
Scarasta. W Isl 8C 171
Scarborough. N Yor 1E 101
Scarcliffe. Derbs 4B 86
Scarcroft. W Yor 5F 99
Scardroy. High 3E 156
Scarfskerry. High 1E 169
Scargill. Dur 3D 104
Scarinish. Arg 4B 138
Scarisbrick. Lanc 3B 90
Scarning. Norf 4B 78
Scarrington. Notts 1E 75
Scarth Hill. Lanc 4C 90
Scartho. NE Lin 4F 95
Scarva. Arm 5E 178
Scarvister. Shet 7E 173
Scatness. Shet 10E 173
Scatwell. High 3F 157
Scaur. Dum 4F 111
Scawby. N Lin 4C 94
Scawby Brook. N Lin 4C 94
Scawsby. S Yor 4F 93
Scawton. N Yor 1H 99
Scaynes Hill. W Sus 3E 27
Scethrog. Powy 3E 46
Scholar Green. Ches E 5C 84
Scholes. G Man 4D 90
Scholes. W Yor
nr. Bradford 2B 92
nr. Holmfirth 4B 92
nr. Leeds 1D 93
Scholey Hill. W Yor 2D 93
School Aycliffe. Darl 2F 105
School Green. Ches W 4A 84
School Green. Essx 2H 53
Scissett. W Yor 3C 92
Scleddau. Pemb 1D 42
Scofton. Notts 2D 86
Scole. Norf 3D 66
Scollogstown. New M 6J 179
Scolpaig. W Isl 1C 170
Scolton. Pemb 2D 43
Scone. Per 1D 136
Sconser. High 5E 155
Scoonie. Fife 3F 137
Scopwick. Linc 5H 87
Scoraig. High 4E 163
Scorborough. E Yor 5E 101
Scorrier. Corn 4B 6
Scorriton. Devn 2D 8
Scorton. Lanc 5E 97
Scorton. N Yor 4F 105
Sco Ruston. Norf 3E 79
Scotbheinn. W Isl 3D 170
Scotby. Cumb 4F 113
Scotch Corner. N Yor 4F 105
Scotch Street. Arm 4D 178
Scotforth. Lanc 3D 97
Scot Hay. Staf 1C 72
Scothern. Linc 3H 87
Scotland End. Oxon 2B 50
Scotlandwell. Per 3D 136
Scot Lane End. G Man 4E 91
Scotsburn. High 1B 158
Scotsburn. Mor 2G 159
Scotsdike. Cumb 2E 113
Scot's Gap. Nmbd 1D 114
Scotstoun. Glas 3G 127
Scotstown. High 2C 140
Scotswood. Tyne 3F 115
Scottas. High 3F 147
Scotter. Linc 4B 94
Scotterthorpe. Linc 4B 94
Scottlethorpe. Linc 3H 75
Scotton. Linc 1F 87
Scotton. N Yor
nr. Catterick Garrison 5E 105
nr. Harrogate 4F 99
Scottow. Norf 3E 79
Scoulton. Norf 5B 78
Scounslow Green. Staf 3E 73
Scourie. High 4B 166
Scourie More. High 4B 166
Scousburgh. Shet 10E 173
Scout Green. Cumb 4G 103
Scouthead. G Man 4H 91
Scrabster. High 1C 168
Scrafield. Linc 4C 88
Scrainwood. Nmbd 4D 121
Scrane End. Linc 1C 76
Scraptoft. Leics 5D 74
Scratby. Norf 4H 79
Scrayingham. N Yor 3B 100
Scredington. Linc 1H 75
Scremby. Linc 4D 88
Scremerston. Nmbd 5G 131
Screveton. Notts 1E 75
Scrivelsby. Linc 4B 88
Scriven. N Yor 4F 99
Scronkey. Lanc 5D 96
Scrooby. Notts 1D 86
Scropton. Derbs 2F 73
Scrub Hill. Linc 5B 88
Scruton. N Yor 5F 105
Scuggate. Cumb 2F 113
Sculamus. High 1E 147
Sculcoates. Hull 1D 94
Sculthorpe. Norf 2B 78
Scunthorpe. N Lin 3B 94
Scurlage. Swan 4D 30
Sea. Som 1G 13
Seaborough. Dors 2H 13
Seabridge. Staf 1C 72
Seabrook. Kent 2F 29
Seaburn. Tyne 3H 115
Seacombe. Mers 1F 83
Seacroft. Linc 4E 89
Seacroft. W Yor 1D 92
Seadyke. Linc 2C 76
Seafield. High 5G 165
Seafield. Midl 3F 129
Seafield. S Ayr 2C 116
Seafield. W Lot 3D 128
Seaford. E Sus 5F 27
Seaforde. New M 5J 179
Seaforth. Mers 1F 83
Seagrave. Leics 4D 74
Seaham. Dur 5H 115
Seahouses. Nmbd 1G 121
Seal. Kent 5G 39
Sealand. Flin 4F 83
Seale. Surr 2G 25
Seamer. N Yor
nr. Scarborough 1E 101
nr. Stokesley 3B 106
Seamill. N Ayr 5D 126
Sea Mills. Bris 4A 34
Sea Palling. Norf 3G 79
Seapatrick. Arm 5F 178
Searby. Linc 4D 94
Seasalter. Kent 4E 41
Seascale. Cumb 4B 102
Seaside. Per 1E 137
Seater. High 1F 169
Seathorne. Linc 4E 89
Seathwaite. Cumb
nr. Buttermere 3D 102
nr. Ulpha 5D 102
Seatle. Cumb 1C 96
Seatoller. Cumb 3D 102
Seaton. Corn 3H 7
Seaton. Cumb 1B 102
Seaton. Devn 3F 13
Seaton. Dur 4G 115
Seaton. E Yor 5F 101
Seaton. Nmbd 2G 115
Seaton. Rut 1G 63
Seaton Burn. Tyne 2F 115
Seaton Carew. Hart 2C 106
Seaton Delaval. Nmbd 2G 115
Seaton Junction. Devn 3F 13
Seaton Ross. E Yor 5B 100
Seaton Sluice. Nmbd 2G 115
Seatown. Abers 2C 160
Seatown. Dors 3H 13
Seatown. Mor
nr. Cullen 2C 160
nr. Lossiemouth 1G 159
Seave Green. N Yor 4C 106
Seaview. IOW 3E 17
Seaville. Cumb 4C 112
Seavington St Mary. Som 1H 13
Seavington St Michael.
Som 1H 13
Seawick. Essx 4E 55
Sebastopol. Torf 2F 33
Sebergham. Cumb 5E 113
Seckington. Warw 5G 73
Second Coast. High 4D 162
Sedbergh. Cumb 5H 103
Sedbury. Glos 2A 34
Sedbusk. N Yor 5B 104
Sedgeberrow. Worc 2F 49
Sedgebrook. Linc 2F 75
Sedgefield. Dur 2A 106
Sedgeford. Norf 2G 77
Sedgehill. Wilts 4D 22
Sedgley. W Mid 1D 60
Sedgwick. Cumb 1E 97
Sedlescombe. E Sus 4B 28
Seend. Wilts 5E 35
Seend Cleeve. Wilts 5E 35
Seer Green. Buck 1A 38
Seething. Norf 1F 67
Sefster. Shet 6E 173
Sefton. Mers 4B 90
Sefton Park. Mers 2F 83
Segensworth. Hants 2D 16
Seggat. Abers 4E 161
Seghill. Nmbd 2F 115
Seifton. Shrp 2G 59
Seighford. Staf 3C 72
Seilebost. W Isl 8C 171
Seisdon. Staf 1C 60
Seisiadar. W Isl 4H 171
Selattyn. Shrp 2E 71
Selborne. Hants 3F 25
Selby. N Yor 1G 93
Selham. W Sus 3A 26
Selkirk. Bord 2G 119
Sellack. Here 3A 48
Sellafirth. Shet 2G 173
Sellick's Green. Som 1F 13
Sellindge. Kent 2F 29
Selling. Kent 5E 41
Sells Green. Wilts 5E 35
Selly Oak. W Mid 2E 61
Selmeston. E Sus 5G 27
Selsdon. G Lon 4E 39
Selsey. W Sus 3G 17
Selsfield Common. W Sus 2E 27
Selside. Cumb 5G 103
Selside. N Yor 2G 97
Selsley. Glos 5D 48
Selsted. Kent 1G 29
Selston. Notts 5B 86
Selworthy. Som 2C 20
Semblister. Shet 6E 173
Semer. Suff 1D 54
Semington. Wilts 5D 35
Semley. Wilts 4D 23
Sempringham. Linc 2A 76
Send. Surr 5B 38
Send Marsh. Surr 5B 38
Senghenydd. Cphy 2E 32
Sennen. Corn 4A 4
Sennen Cove. Corn 4A 4
Sennybridge. Powy 3C 46
Serlby. Notts 2D 86
Seskinore. Ferm 3K 177
Sessay. N Yor 2G 99
Setchey. Norf 4F 77
Setley. Hants 2B 16
Setter. Shet 3F 173
Settiscarth. Orkn 6C 172
Settle. N Yor 3H 97
Settrington. N Yor 2C 100
Seven Ash. Som 3E 21
Sevenhampton. Glos 3F 49
Sevenhampton. Swin 2H 35
Sevenoaks. Kent 5G 39
Sevenoaks Weald. Kent 5G 39
Seven Sisters. Neat 5B 46
Seven Springs. Glos 4E 49
Severn Beach. S Glo 3A 34
Severn Stoke. Worc 1D 48
Sevington. Kent 1E 29
Sewards End. Essx 2F 53
Sewardstone. Essx 1E 39
Sewell. C Beds 3H 51
Sewerby. E Yor 3G 101
Seworgan. Corn 5B 6
Sewstern. Leics 3F 75
Sgallairidh. W Isl 9B 170
Sgarasta Mhor. W Isl 8C 171
Sgiogarstaigh. W Isl 1H 171
Sgreadan. Arg 4A 132
Shabbington. Buck 5E 51
Shackerley. Shrp 5C 72
Shackerstone. Leics 5A 74
Shackleford. Surr 1A 26
Shadforth. Dur 5G 115
Shadingfield. Suff 2G 67
Shadoxhurst. Kent 2D 28
Shadsworth. Bkbn 2F 91
Shadwell. Norf 2B 66
Shadwell. W Yor 1D 92
Shaftesbury. Dors 4D 22
Shafton. S Yor 3D 93
Shafton Two Gates. S Yor 3D 93
Shaggs. Dors 4D 14
Shakesfield. Glos 2B 48
Shalbourne. Wilts 5B 36
Shalcombe. IOW 4B 16
Shalden. Hants 2E 25
Shaldon. Devn 5C 12
Shalfleet. IOW 4C 16
Shalford. Essx 3H 53
Shalford. Surr 1B 26
Shalford Green. Essx 3H 53
Shallowford. Devn 2H 19
Shallowford. Staf 3C 72
Shalmsford Street. Kent 5E 41
Shalstone. Buck 2E 51
Shamley Green. Surr 1B 26
Shandon. Arg 1D 126
Shandwick. High 1C 158
Shangton. Leics 1E 62
Shankhouse. Nmbd 2F 115
Shanklin. IOW 4D 16
Shannochie. N Ayr 3D 123
Shap. Cumb 3G 103
Shapwick. Dors 2E 15
Shapwick. Som 3H 21
Sharcott. Wilts 1G 23
Shardlow. Derbs 2B 74
Shareshill. Staf 5D 72
Sharlston. W Yor 3D 93
Sharlston Common.
W Yor 3D 93
Sharnal Street. Medw 3B 40
Sharnbrook. Bed 5G 63
Sharneyford. Lanc 2G 91
Sharnford. Leics 1B 62
Sharnhill Green. Dors 2C 14
Sharoe Green. Lanc 1D 90
Sharow. N Yor 2F 99
Sharpenhoe. C Beds 2A 52
Sharperton. Nmbd 4D 120
Sharpness. Glos 5B 48
Sharp Street. Norf 3F 79
Sharpthorne. W Sus 2E 27
Sharrington. Norf 2C 78
Shatterford. Worc 2B 60
Shatton. Derbs 2F 85
Shaugh Prior. Devn 2B 8
Shavington. Ches E 5B 84
Shaw. G Man 4H 91
Shaw. W Ber 5C 36
Shaw. Wilts 5D 35
Shawbirch. Telf 4A 72
Shawbury. Shrp 3H 71
Shawell. Leics 2C 62
Shawford. Hants 4C 24

Shawforth—Sower Carr

Shawforth. Lanc 2G 91
Shaw Green. Lanc 3D 90
Shawhead. Dum 2F 111
Shaw Mills. N Yor 3E 99
Shawwood. E Ayr 2E 117
Shearington. Dum 3B 112
Shearsby. Leics 1D 62
Shearston. Som 3F 21
Shebbear. Devn 2E 11
Shebdon. Staf 3B 72
Shebster. High 2C 168
Sheddocksley. Aber 3F 153
Shedfield. Hants 1D 16
Shedog. N Ayr 2D 122
Sheen. Staf 4F 85
Sheepbridge. Derbs 3A 86
Sheep Hill. Dur 4E 115
Sheepscar. W Yor 1D 92
Sheepscombe. Glos 4D 49
Sheepstor. Devn 2B 8
Sheepwash. Devn 2E 11
Sheepwash. Nmbd 1F 115
Sheepway. N Som 4H 33
Sheepy Magna. Leics 5H 73
Sheepy Parva. Leics 5H 73
Sheering. Essx 4F 53
Sheerness. Kent 3D 40
Sheerwater. Surr 4B 38
Sheet. Hants 4F 25
Sheffield. S Yor 202 (2A 86)
Sheffield Bottom. W Ber 5E 37
Sheffield Green. E Sus 3F 27
Shefford. C Beds 2B 52
Shefford Woodlands.
W Ber 4B 36
Sheigra. High 2B 166
Sheinton. Shrp 5A 72
Shelderton. Shrp 3G 59
Sheldon. Derbs 4F 85
Sheldon. Devn 2E 12
Sheldon. W Mid 2F 61
Sheldwich. Kent 5E 40
Sheldwich Lees. Kent 5E 40
Shelf. W Yor 2B 92
Shelfanger. Norf 2D 66
Shelfield. Warw 4F 61
Shelfield. W Mid 5E 73
Shelford. Notts 1D 74
Shelford. Warw 2B 62
Shell. Worc 5D 60
Shelley. Suff 2D 54
Shelley. W Yor 3C 92
Shell Green. Hal 2H 83
Shellingford. Oxon 2B 36
Shellow Bowells. Essx 5G 53
Shelsley Beauchamp.
Worc 4B 60
Shelsley Walsh. Worc 4B 60
Shelthorpe. Leics 4C 74
Shelton. Bed 4H 63
Shelton. Norf 1E 67
Shelton. Notts 1E 75
Shelton. Shrp 4G 71
Shelton Green. Norf 1E 67
Shelton Lock. Derb 2A 74
Shelve. Shrp 1F 59
Shelwick. Here 1A 48
Shelwick Green. Here 1A 48
Shenfield. Essx 1H 39
Shenington. Oxon 1B 50
Shenley. Herts 5B 52
Shenley Brook End. Mil 2G 51
Shenleybury. Herts 5B 52
Shenley Church End. Mil 2G 51
Shenmore. Here 2G 47
Shennanton. Dum 3A 110
Shenstone. Staf 5F 73
Shenstone. Worc 3C 60
Shenstone Woodend. Staf 5F 73
Shenton. Leics 5A 74
Shenval. Mor 1G 151
Shepeau Stow. Linc 4C 76
Shephall. Herts 3C 52
Shepherd's Bush. G Lon 2D 38
Shepherd's Gate. Norf 4E 77
Shepherd's Green. Oxon 3F 37
Shepherd's Port. Norf 2F 77
Shepherdswell. Kent 1G 29
Shepley. W Yor 4B 92
Sheppardstown. High 4D 169
Shepperdine. S Glo 2B 34
Shepperton. Surr 4B 38
Shepreth. Cambs 1D 53
Shepshed. Leics 4B 74
Shepton Beauchamp.
Som 1H 13
Shepton Mallet. Som 2B 22
Shepton Montague. Som 3B 22
Shepway. Kent 5B 40
Sheraton. Dur 1B 106
Sherborne. Dors 1B 14
Sherborne. Glos 4G 49
Sherborne. Som 1A 22
Sherborne Causeway.
Dors 4D 22
Sherborne St John. Hants 1E 24
Sherbourne. Warw 4G 61
Sherburn. Dur 5G 115
Sherburn. N Yor 2D 100
Sherburn Hill. Dur 5G 115
Sherburn in Elmet. N Yor 1E 93
Shere. Surr 1B 26
Shereford. Norf 3A 78
Sherfield English. Hants 4A 24
Sherfield on Loddon.
Hants 1E 25
Sherford. Devn 4D 9
Sherford. Dors 3E 15
Sheriffhales. Shrp 4B 72
Sheriff Hutton. N Yor 3A 100
Sheriffston. Mor 2G 159
Sheringham. Norf 1D 78
Sherington. Mil 1G 51
Shermanbury. W Sus 4D 26
Shernal Green. Worc 4D 60
Shernborne. Norf 2G 77
Sherrington. Wilts 3E 23
Sherston. Wilts 3D 34
Sherwood. Nott 1C 74
Sherwood Green. Devn 4F 19
Shettleston. Glas 3H 127
Shevington. G Man 4D 90
Shevington Moor. G Man 3D 90
Shevington Vale. G Man 4D 90
Sheviock. Corn 3H 7
Shide. IOW 4C 16
Shiel Bridge. High 2B 148
Shieldaig. High
nr. Charlestown 1H 155
nr. Torridon 3H 155
Shieldhill. Dum 1B 112
Shieldhill. Falk 2B 128
Shieldhill. S Lan 5D 128
Shieldmuir. N Lan 4A 128
Shielfoot. High 1A 140
Shielhill. Abers 3H 161
Shielhill. Ang 3D 144
Shifnal. Shrp 5B 72
Shilbottle. Nmbd 4F 121
Shilbottle Grange. Nmbd 4G 121
Shildon. Dur 2F 105
Shillford. E Ren 4F 127
Shillingford. Devn 4C 20
Shillingford. Oxon 2D 36
Shillingford St George.
Devn 4C 12
Shillingstone. Dors 1D 14
Shillington. C Beds 2B 52
Shillmoor. Nmbd 4C 120
Shilton. Oxon 5A 50
Shilton. Warw 2B 62
Shilvinghampton. Dors 4B 14
Shilvington. Nmbd 1E 115
Shimpling. Norf 2D 66
Shimpling. Suff 5A 66
Shimpling Street. Suff 5A 66
Shincliffe. Dur 5F 115
Shiney Row. Tyne 4G 115
Shinfield. Wok 5F 37
Shingay. Cambs 1D 52
Shingham. Norf 5G 77
Shingle Street. Suff 1G 55
Shinner's Bridge. Devn 2D 9
Shinness. High 2C 164
Shipbourne. Kent 5G 39
Shipdham. Norf 5B 78
Shipham. Som 1H 21
Shiphay. Torb 2E 9
Shiplake. Oxon 4F 37
Shipley. Derbs 1B 74
Shipley. Nmbd 3F 121
Shipley. Shrp 1C 60
Shipley. W Sus 3C 26
Shipley. W Yor 1B 92
Shipley Bridge. Surr 1E 27
Shipmeadow. Suff 2F 67
Shippon. Oxon 2C 36
Shipston-on-Stour. Warw 1A 50
Shipton. Buck 3F 51
Shipton. Glos 4F 49
Shipton. N Yor 4H 99
Shipton. Shrp 1H 59
Shipton Bellinger. Hants 2H 23
Shipton Gorge. Dors 3H 13
Shipton Green. W Sus 3G 17
Shipton Moyne. Glos 3D 35
Shipton-on-Cherwell.
Oxon 4C 50
Shiptonthorpe. E Yor 5C 100
Shipton-under-Wychwood.
Oxon 4A 50
Shirburn. Oxon 2E 37
Shirdley Hill. Lanc 3B 90
Shire. Cumb 1H 103
Shirebrook. Derbs 4C 86
Shiregreen. S Yor 1A 86
Shirehampton. Bris 4A 34
Shiremoor. Tyne 2G 115
Shirenewton. Mon 2H 33
Shireoaks. Notts 2C 86
Shires Mill. Fife 1D 128
Shirkoak. Kent 2D 28
Shirland. Derbs 5A 86
Shirley. Derbs 1G 73
Shirley. Sotn 1B 16
Shirley. W Mid 3F 61
Shirleywich. Staf 3D 73
Shirl Heath. Here 5G 59
Shirrell Heath. Hants 1D 16
Shirwell. Devn 3F 19
Shiskine. N Ayr 3D 122
Shobdon. Here 4F 59
Shobnall. Staf 3G 73
Shobrooke. Devn 2B 12
Shoby. Leics 3D 74
Shocklach. Ches W 1G 71
Shoeburyness. S'end 2D 40
Sholden. Kent 5H 41
Sholing. Sotn 1C 16
Sholver. G Man 4H 91
Shoot Hill. Shrp 4G 71
Shop. Corn
nr. Bude 1C 10
nr. Padstow 1C 6
Shop. Devn 1D 11
Shopford. Cumb 2G 113
Shoreditch. G Lon 2E 39
Shoreditch. Som 4F 21
Shoregill. Cumb 4A 104
Shoreham. Kent 4G 39
Shoreham-by-Sea.
W Sus 5D 26
Shoresdean. Nmbd 5F 131
Shoreswood. Nmbd 5F 131
Shorncote. Glos 2F 35
Shorne. Kent 3A 40
Shorne Ridgeway. Kent 3A 40
Shortacombe. Devn 4F 11
Shortbridge. E Sus 3F 27
Shortgate. E Sus 4F 27
Short Green. Norf 2C 66
Shorthampton. Oxon 3B 50
Short Heath. Derbs 4H 73
Short Heath. W Mid
nr. Erdington 1E 61
nr. Wednesfield 5D 73
Shortlanesend. Corn 4C 6
Shorton. Torb 2E 9
Shortstown. Bed 1A 52
Shortwood. S Glo 4B 34
Shorwell. IOW 4C 16
Shoscombe. Bath 1C 22
Shotesham. Norf 1E 67
Shotgate. Essx 1B 40
Shotley. Suff 2F 55
Shotley Bridge. Dur 4D 115
Shotleyfield. Nmbd 4D 114
Shotley Gate. Suff 2F 55
Shottenden. Kent 5E 41
Shottermill. Surr 3G 25
Shottery. Warw 5F 61
Shotteswell. Warw 1C 50
Shottisham. Suff 1G 55
Shottle. Derbs 1H 73
Shotton. Dur
nr. Peterlee 1B 106
nr. Sedgefield 2A 106
Shotton. Flin 4F 83
Shotton. Nmbd
nr. Morpeth 2F 115
nr. Town Yetholm 1C 120
Shotton Colliery. Dur 5G 115
Shotts. N Lan 3B 128
Shotwick. Ches W 3F 83
Shouldham. Norf 5F 77
Shouldham Thorpe. Norf 5F 77
Shoulton. Worc 5C 60
Shrawardine. Shrp 4G 71
Shrawley. Worc 4C 60
Shreding Green. Buck 2B 38
Shrewley. Warw 4G 61
Shrewsbury. Shrp 202 (4G 71)
Shrewton. Wilts 2F 23
Shrigley. New M 4K 179
Shripney. W Sus 5A 26
Shrivenham. Oxon 3H 35
Shropham. Norf 1B 66
Shroton. Dors 1D 14
Shrub End. Essx 3C 54
Shucknall. Here 1A 48
Shudy Camps. Cambs 1G 53
Shulishadermor. High 4D 155
Shulista. High 1D 154
Shurdington. Glos 4E 49
Shurlock Row. Wind 4G 37
Shurrery. High 3C 168
Shurton. Som 2F 21
Shustoke. Warw 1G 61
Shute. Devn
nr. Axminster 3F 13
nr. Crediton 2B 12
Shutford. Oxon 1B 50
Shut Heath. Staf 3C 72
Shuthonger. Glos 2D 49
Shutlanehead. Staf 1C 72
Shutlanger. Nptn 1F 51
Shutt Green. Staf 5C 72
Shuttington. Warw 5G 73
Shuttlewood. Derbs 3B 86
Shuttleworth. G Man 3G 91
Siabost. W Isl 3E 171
Siabost bho Dheas. W Isl 3E 171
Siabost bho Thuath.
W Isl 3E 171
Siadar. W Isl 2F 171
Siadar Uarach. W Isl 2F 171
Sibbaldbie. Dum 1C 112
Sibbertoft. Nptn 2D 62
Sibdon Carwood. Shrp 2G 59
Sibertswold. Kent 1G 29
Sibford Ferris. Oxon 2B 50
Sibford Gower. Oxon 2B 50
Sible Hedingham. Essx 2A 54
Sibsey. Linc 5C 88
Sibsey Fen Side. Linc 5C 88
Sibson. Cambs 1H 63
Sibson. Leics 5A 74
Sibster. High 3F 169
Sibthorpe. Notts 1E 75
Sibton. Suff 4F 67
Sicklesmere. Suff 4A 66
Sicklinghall. N Yor 5F 99
Sid. Devn 4E 13
Sidbury. Devn 3E 13
Sidbury. Shrp 2A 60
Sidcot. N Som 1H 21
Sidcup. G Lon 3F 39
Siddick. Cumb 1B 102
Siddington. Ches E 3C 84
Siddington. Glos 2F 35
Side of the Moor. G Man 3F 91
Sidestrand. Norf 2E 79
Sidford. Devn 3E 13
Sidlesham. W Sus 3G 17
Sidley. E Sus 5B 28
Sidlow. Surr 1D 26
Sidmouth. Devn 4E 13
Sigford. Devn 5A 12
Sigglesthorne. E Yor 5F 101
Sighthill. Edin 2E 129
Sigingstone. V Glam 4C 32
Signet. Oxon 4H 49
Silchester. Hants 5E 37
Sildinis. W Isl 6E 171
Sileby. Leics 4D 74
Silecroft. Cumb 1A 96
Silfield. Norf 1D 66
Silian. Cdgn 5E 57
Silkstone. S Yor 4C 92
Silkstone Common. S Yor 4C 92
Silksworth. Tyne 4G 115
Silk Willoughby. Linc 1H 75
Silloth. Cumb 4C 112
Sills. Nmbd 4C 120
Sillyearn. Mor 3C 160
Silpho. N Yor 5G 107
Silsden. W Yor 5C 98
Silsoe. C Beds 2A 52
Silverbank. Abers 4E 152
Silverbridge. New M 8D 178
Silverburn. Midl 3F 129
Silverdale. Lanc 2D 96
Silverdale. Staf 1C 72
Silverdale Green. Lanc 2D 96
Silver End. Essx 4B 54
Silver End. W Mid 2D 60
Silvergate. Norf 3D 78
Silver Green. Norf 1E 67
Silverhillocks. Abers 2E 161
Silverley's Green. Suff 3E 67
Silverstone. Nptn 1E 51
Silverton. Devn 2C 12
Silverton. W Dun 2F 127
Simm's Cross. Hal 2H 83
Simm's Lane End. Mers 4D 90
Simonburn. Nmbd 2B 114
Simonsbath. Som 3A 20
Simonstone. Lanc 1F 91
Simprim. Bord 5E 131
Simpson. Pemb 3C 42
Simpson Cross. Pemb 3C 42
Sinclairston. E Ayr 3D 116
Sinclairtown. Fife 4E 137
Sinderby. N Yor 1F 99
Sinderhope. Nmbd 4B 114
Sindlesham. Wok 5F 37
Sinfin. Derb 2H 73
Singleborough. Buck 2F 51
Singleton. Kent 1D 28
Singleton. Lanc 1B 90
Singleton. W Sus 1G 17
Singlewell. Kent 3A 40
Sinkhurst Green. Kent 1C 28
Sinnahard. Abers 2B 152
Sinnington. N Yor 1B 100
Sinton Green. Worc 4C 60
Sion Mills. Derr 3F 176
Sipson. G Lon 3B 38
Sirhowy. Blae 4E 47
Sisland. Norf 1F 67
Sissinghurst. Kent 2B 28
Siston. S Glo 4B 34
Sithney. Corn 4D 4
Sittingbourne. Kent 4D 40
Six Ashes. Staf 2B 60
Six Bells. Blae 5F 47
Six Hills. Leics 3D 74
Sixhills. Linc 2A 88
Six Mile Bottom. Cambs 5E 65
Sixmilecross. Ferm 3L 177
Sixpenny Handley. Dors 1E 15
Sizewell. Suff 4G 67
Skail. High 4H 167
Skaill. Orkn 6B 172
Skaills. Orkn 7E 172
Skares. E Ayr 3E 117
Skateraw. E Lot 2D 130
Skaw. Shet 5G 173
Skeabost. High 4D 154
Skeabrae. Orkn 5B 172
Skeeby. N Yor 4E 105
Skeffington. Leics 5E 75
Skeffling. E Yor 3G 95
Skegby. Notts
nr. Mansfield 4B 86
nr. Tuxford 3E 87
Skegness. Linc 4E 89
Skelberry. Shet
nr. Boddam 10E 173
nr. Housetter 3E 173
Skelbo. High 4E 165
Skelbo Street. High 4E 165
Skelbrooke. S Yor 3F 93
Skeldyke. Linc 2C 76
Skelfhill. Bord 4G 119
Skellingthorpe. Linc 3G 87
Skellister. Shet 6F 173
Skellorn Green. Ches E 2D 84
Skellow. S Yor 3F 93
Skelmanthorpe. W Yor 3C 92
Skelmersdale. Lanc 4C 90
Skelmorlie. N Ayr 3C 126
Skelpick. High 3H 167
Skelton. Cumb 1F 103
Skelton. E Yor 2A 94
Skelton. N Yor
nr. Richmond 4D 105
nr. Ripon 3F 99
Skelton. Red C 3D 106
Skelton. York 4H 99
Skelton Green. Red C 3D 106
Skelwick. Orkn 3D 172
Skelwith Bridge. Cumb 4E 103
Skendleby. Linc 4D 88
Skendleby Psalter. Linc 3D 88
Skenfrith. Mon 3H 47
Skerne. E Yor 4E 101
Skeroblingarry. Arg 3B 122
Skerray. High 2G 167
Skerricha. High 3C 166
Skerries Airport. Shet 4H 173
Skerton. Lanc 3D 97
Sketchley. Leics 1B 62
Sketty. Swan 3F 31
Skewen. Neat 3G 31
Skewsby. N Yor 2A 100
Skeyton. Norf 3E 79
Skeyton Corner. Norf 3E 79
Skiall. High 2C 168
Skidbrooke. Linc 1D 88
Skidbrooke North End.
Linc 1D 88
Skidby. E Yor 1D 94
Skilgate. Som 4C 20
Skillington. Linc 3F 75
Skinburness. Cumb 4C 112
Skinflats. Falk 1C 128
Skinidin. High 4B 154
Skinnet. High 2F 167
Skinningrove. Red C 3E 107
Skipness. Arg 4G 125
Skippool. Lanc 5C 96
Skiprigg. Cumb 5E 113
Skipsea. E Yor 4F 101
Skipsea Brough. E Yor 4F 101
Skipton. N Yor 4B 98
Skipton-on-Swale. N Yor 2F 99
Skipwith. N Yor 1G 93
Skirbeck. Linc 1C 76
Skirbeck Quarter. Linc 1C 76
Skirlaugh. E Yor 1E 95
Skirling. Bord 1C 118
Skirmett. Buck 2F 37
Skirpenbeck. E Yor 4B 100
Skirwith. Cumb 1H 103
Skirwith. N Yor 2G 97
Skirza. High 2F 169
Skitby. Cumb 3F 113
Skitham. Lanc 5D 96
Skittle Green. Buck 5F 51
Skroo. Shet 1B 172
Skulamus. High 1E 147
Skullomie. High 2G 167
Skyborry Green. Shrp 3E 59
Skye Green. Essx 3B 54
Skye of Curr. High 1D 151
Slack. W Yor 2H 91
The Slack. Dur 2E 105
Slackhall. Derbs 2E 85
Slack Head. Cumb 2D 97
Slackhead. Mor 2B 160
Slackholme End. Linc 3E 89
Slacks of Cairnbanno.
Abers 4F 161
Slad. Glos 5D 48
Slade. Swan 4D 31
The Slade. W Ber 5D 36
Slade End. Oxon 2D 36
Slade Field. Cambs 2C 64
Slade Green. G Lon 3G 39
Slade Heath. Staf 5D 72
Slade Hooton. S Yor 2C 86
Sladesbridge. Corn 5A 10
Slaggyford. Nmbd 4H 113
Slaidburn. Lanc 4G 97
Slaid Hill. W Yor 5F 99
Slaithwaite. W Yor 3A 92
Slaley. Derbs 5G 85
Slaley. Nmbd 4C 114
Slamannan. Falk 2B 128
Slapton. Buck 3H 51
Slapton. Devn 4E 9
Slapton. Nptn 1E 51
Slattocks. G Man 4G 91
Slaugham. W Sus 3D 26
Slaughterbridge. Corn 4B 10
Slaughterford. Wilts 4D 34
Slawston. Leics 1E 63
Sleaford. Hants 3G 25
Sleaford. Linc 1H 75
Sleagill. Cumb 3G 103
Sleap. Shrp 3G 71
Sledmere. E Yor 3D 100
Sleightholme. Dur 3C 104
Sleights. N Yor 4F 107
Slepe. Dors 3E 15
Slickly. High 2E 169
Sliddery. N Ayr 3D 122
Sligachan. High 1C 146
Slimbridge. Glos 5C 48
Slindon. Staf 2C 72
Slindon. W Sus 5A 26
Slinfold. W Sus 2C 26
Slingsby. N Yor 2A 100
Slip End. C Beds 4A 52
Slipton. Nptn 3G 63
Slitting Mill. Staf 4E 73
Slochd. High 1C 150
Slockavullin. Arg 4F 133
Sloley. Norf 3E 79
Sloncombe. Devn 4H 11
Sloothby. Linc 3D 89
Slough. Slo 3A 38
Slough Green. Som 4F 21
Slough Green. W Sus 3D 27
Sluggan. High 1C 150
Slyne. Lanc 3D 97
Smailholm. Bord 1A 120
Smallbridge. G Man 3H 91
Smallbrook. Devn 3B 12
Smallburgh. Norf 3F 79
Smallburn. E Ayr 2F 117
Smalldale. Derbs 3E 85
Small Dole. W Sus 4D 26
Smalley. Derbs 1B 74
Smallfield. Surr 1E 27
Small Heath. W Mid 2E 61
Smallholm. Dum 2C 112
Small Hythe. Kent 2C 28
Smallrice. Staf 2D 72
Smallridge. Devn 2G 13
Smallwood Hey. Lanc 5C 96
Smallworth. Norf 2C 66
Smannell. Hants 2B 24
Smardale. Cumb 4A 104
Smarden. Kent 1C 28
Smarden Bell. Kent 1C 28
Smart's Hill. Kent 1G 27
Smeatharpe. Devn 1F 13
Smeeth. Kent 2E 29
The Smeeth. Norf 4E 77
Smeeton Westerby. Leics 1D 62
Smeircleit. W Isl 7C 170
Smerral. High 5D 168
Smestow. Staf 1C 60
Smethwick. W Mid 2E 61
Smirisary. High 1A 140
Smisby. Derbs 4H 73
Smitham Hill. Bath 1A 22
Smith End Green. Worc 5B 60
Smithfield. Cumb 3F 113
Smith Green. Lanc 4D 97
The Smithies. Shrp 1A 60
Smithincott. Devn 1D 12
Smith's Green. Essx 3F 53
Smithstown. High 1G 155
Smithton. High 4B 158
Smithwood Green. Suff 5B 66
Smithy Bridge. G Man 3H 91
Smithy Green. Ches E 3B 84
Smithy Lane Ends. Lanc 3C 90
Smockington. Leics 2B 62
Smoogro. Orkn 7C 172
Smythe's Green. Essx 4C 54
Snaigow House. Per 4H 143
Snailbeach. Shrp 5F 71
Snailwell. Cambs 4F 65
Snainton. N Yor 1D 100
Snaith. E Yor 2G 93
Snape. N Yor 1E 99
Snape. Suff 5F 67
Snape Green. Lanc 3B 90
Snapper. Devn 3F 19
Snarestone. Leics 5H 73
Snarford. Linc 2H 87
Snargate. Kent 3D 28
Snave. Kent 3E 28
Sneachill. Worc 5D 60
Snead. Powy 1F 59
Snead Common. Worc 4B 60
Sneaton. N Yor 4F 107
Sneatonthorpe. N Yor 4G 107
Snelland. Linc 2H 87
Snelston. Derbs 1F 73
Snetterton. Norf 1B 66
Snettisham. Norf 2F 77
Snibston. Leics 4B 74
Sniseabhal. W Isl 5C 170
Snitter. Nmbd 4E 121
Snitterby. Linc 1G 87
Snitterfield. Warw 5G 61
Snitton. Shrp 3H 59
Snodhill. Here 1G 47
Snodland. Kent 4B 40
Snods Edge. Nmbd 4D 114
Snowshill. Glos 2F 49
Snow Street. Norf 2C 66
Snydale. W Yor 3E 93
Soake. Hants 1E 17
Soar. Carm 3G 45
Soar. Gwyn 2F 69
Soar. IOA 3C 80
Soar. Powy 2C 46
Soberton. Hants 1E 16
Soberton Heath. Hants 1E 16
Sockbridge. Cumb 2G 103
Sockburn. Darl 4A 106
Sodom. Den 3C 82
Sodom. Shet 5G 173
Soham. Cambs 3E 65
Soham Cotes. Cambs 3E 65
Solas. W Isl 1D 170
Soldon Cross. Devn 1D 10
Soldridge. Hants 3E 25
Solent Breezes. Hants 2D 16
Sole Street. Kent
nr. Meopham 4A 40
nr. Waltham 1E 29
Solihull. W Mid 3F 61
Sollers Dilwyn. Here 5G 59
Sollers Hope. Here 2B 48
Sollom. Lanc 3C 90
Solva. Pemb 2B 42
Somerby. Leics 4E 75
Somerby. Linc 4D 94
Somercotes. Derbs 5B 86
Somerford. Dors 3G 15
Somerford. Staf 5C 72
Somerford Keynes. Glos 2F 35
Somerley. W Sus 3G 17
Somerleyton. Suff 1G 67
Somersal Herbert. Derbs 2F 73
Somersby. Linc 3C 88
Somersham. Cambs 3C 64
Somersham. Suff 1D 54
Somerton. Oxon 3C 50
Somerton. Som 4H 21
Somerton. Suff 5H 65
Sompting. W Sus 5C 26
Sonning. Wok 4F 37
Sonning Common. Oxon 3F 37
Sonning Eye. Oxon 4F 37
Sookholme. Notts 4C 86
Sopley. Hants 3G 15
Sopworth. Wilts 3D 34
Sorbie. Dum 5B 110
Sordale. High 2D 168
Sorisdale. Arg 2D 138
Sorn. E Ayr 2E 117
Sornhill. E Ayr 1E 117
Sortat. High 2E 169
Sotby. Linc 3B 88
Sots Hole. Linc 4A 88
Sotterley. Suff 2G 67
Soudley. Shrp
nr. Church Stretton 1G 59
nr. Market Drayton 3B 72
Soughton. Flin 4E 83
Soulbury. Buck 3G 51
Soulby. Cumb
nr. Appleby 3A 104
nr. Penrith 2F 103
Souldern. Oxon 2D 50
Souldrop. Bed 4G 63
Sound. Ches E 1A 72
Sound. Shet
nr. Lerwick 7F 173
nr. Tresta 6E 173
Soundwell. S Glo 4B 34
Sourhope. Bord 2C 120
Sourin. Orkn 4D 172
Sour Nook. Cumb 5E 113
Sourton. Devn 3F 11
Soutergate. Cumb 1B 96
South Acre. Norf 4H 77
Southall. G Lon 3C 38
South Allington. Devn 5D 9
South Alloa. Falk 4A 136
Southam. Glos 3E 49
Southam. Warw 4B 62
South Ambersham.
W Sus 3A 26
Southampton.
Sotn 202 (1C 16)
Southampton Airport.
Hants 1C 16
Southannan. N Ayr 4D 126
South Anston. S Yor 2C 86
South Ascot. Wind 4A 38
South Baddesley. Hants 3B 16
South Balfern. Dum 4B 110
South Ballachulish. High 3E 141
South Bank. Red C 2C 106
South Barrow. Som 4B 22
South Benfleet. Essx 2B 40
South Bents. Tyne 3H 115
South Bersted. W Sus 5A 26
Southborough. Kent 1G 27
Southbourne. Bour 3G 15
Southbourne. W Sus 2F 17
South Bowood. Dors 3H 13
South Brent. Devn 3C 8
South Brewham. Som 3C 22
South Broomage. Falk 1B 128
South Broomhill. Nmbd 5G 121
Southburgh. Norf 5B 78
South Burlingham. Norf 5F 79
Southburn. E Yor 4D 101
South Cadbury. Som 4B 22
South Carlton. Linc 3G 87
South Cave. E Yor 1C 94
South Cerney. Glos 2F 35
South Chailey. E Sus 4E 27
South Chard. Som 2G 13
South Charlton. Nmbd 2F 121
South Cheriton. Som 4B 22
South Church. Dur 2F 105
Southchurch. S'end 2D 40
South Cleatlam. Dur 3E 105
South Cliffe. E Yor 1B 94
South Clifton. Notts 3F 87
South Clunes. High 4H 157
South Cockerington. Linc 2C 88
South Common. Devn 2G 13
South Cornelly. B'end 3B 32
Southcott. Devn
nr. Great Torrington 1E 11
nr. Okehampton 3F 11
Southcott. Wilts 1G 23
Southcourt. Buck 4G 51
South Cove. Suff 2G 67
South Creagan. Arg 4D 141
South Creake. Norf 2A 78
South Crosland. W Yor 3B 92
South Croxton. Leics 4D 74
South Dalton. E Yor 5D 100
South Darenth. Kent 4G 39
Southdean. Bord 4A 120
Southdown. Bath 5C 34
South Duffield. N Yor 1G 93
Southease. E Sus 5F 27
South Elkington. Linc 2B 88
South Elmsall. W Yor 3E 93
South End. Cumb 3B 96
South End. N Lin 2E 94
Southend. Arg 5A 122
Southend. Glos 2C 34
Southend. W Ber 4D 36
Southend Airport. Essx 2C 40
Southend-on-Sea. S'end 2C 40
Southerfield. Cumb 5C 112
Southerhouse. Shet 8E 173
Southerly. Devn 4F 11
Southernden. Kent 1C 28
Southerndown. V Glam 4B 32
Southerness. Dum 4A 112
South Erradale. High 1G 155
Southerton. Devn 3D 12
Southery. Norf 1F 65
Southey Green. Essx 2A 54
South Fambridge. Essx 1C 40
South Fawley. W Ber 3B 36
South Feorline. N Ayr 3D 122
South Ferriby. N Lin 2C 94
South Field. E Yor 2D 94
Southfleet. Kent 3H 39
South Garvan. High 1D 141
Southgate. Cdgn 2E 57
Southgate. G Lon 1E 39
Southgate. Norf
nr. Aylsham 3D 78
nr. Fakenham 2A 78
Southgate. Swan 4E 31
South Gluss. Shet 4E 173
South Godstone. Surr 1E 27
South Gorley. Hants 1G 15
South Green. Essx
nr. Billericay 1A 40
nr. Colchester 4D 54
South Green. Kent 4C 40
South Hanningfield. Essx 1B 40
South Harting. W Sus 1F 17
South Hayling. Hants 3F 17
South Hazelrigg. Nmbd 1E 121
South Heath. Buck 5H 51
South Heath. Essx 4E 55
South Heighton. E Sus 5F 27
South Hetton. Dur 5G 115
South Hiendley. W Yor 3D 93
South Hill. Corn 5D 10
South Hill. Som 4H 21
South Hinksey. Oxon 5D 50
South Hole. Devn 4C 18
South Holme. N Yor 2B 100
South Holmwood. Surr 1C 26
South Hornchurch. G Lon 2G 39
South Huish. Devn 4C 8
South Hykeham. Linc 4G 87
South Hylton. Tyne 4G 115
Southill. C Beds 1B 52
Southington. Hants 2D 24
South Kelsey. Linc 1H 87
South Kessock. High 4A 158
South Killingholme. N Lin 3E 95
South Kilvington. N Yor 1G 99
South Kilworth. Leics 2D 62
South Kirkby. W Yor 3E 93
South Kirkton. Abers 3E 153
South Knighton. Devn 5B 12
South Kyme. Linc 1A 76
South Lancing. W Sus 5C 26
South Ledaig. Arg 5D 140
South Leigh. Oxon 5B 50
Southleigh. Devn 3F 13
South Leverton. Notts 2E 87
South Littleton. Worc 1F 49
South Lopham. Norf 2C 66
South Luffenham. Rut 5G 75
South Malling. E Sus 4F 27
South Marston. Swin 3G 35
South Middleton. Nmbd 2D 121
South Milford. N Yor 1E 93
South Milton. Devn 4D 8
South Mimms. Herts 5C 52
Southminster. Essx 1D 40
South Molton. Devn 4H 19
South Moor. Dur 4E 115
Southmoor. Oxon 2B 36
South Moreton. Oxon 3D 36
South Mundham. W Sus 2G 17
South Muskham. Notts 5E 87
South Newbald. E Yor 1C 94
South Newington. Oxon 2C 50
South Newsham. Nmbd 2G 115
South Newton. N Ayr 4H 125
South Newton. Wilts 3F 23
South Normanton. Derbs 5B 86
South Norwood. G Lon 4E 39
South Nutfield. Surr 1E 27
South Ockendon. Thur 2G 39
Southoe. Cambs 4A 64
Southolt. Suff 4D 66
South Ormsby. Linc 3C 88
Southorpe. Pet 5H 75
South Otterington. N Yor 1F 99
South Owersby. Linc 1H 87
Southowram. W Yor 2B 92
South Oxhey. Herts 1C 38
South Perrott. Dors 2H 13
South Petherton. Som 1H 13
South Petherwin. Corn 4D 10
South Pickenham. Norf 5A 78
South Pool. Devn 4D 9
South Poorton. Dors 3A 14
Southport. Mers 3B 90
Southpunds. Shet 10F 173
South Queensferry. Edin 2E 129
South Radworthy. Devn 3A 20
South Rauceby. Linc 1H 75
South Raynham. Norf 3A 78
Southrepps. Norf 2E 79
South Reston. Linc 2D 88
Southrey. Linc 4A 88
Southrop. Glos 5G 49
Southrope. Hants 2E 25
South Runcton. Norf 5F 77
South Scarle. Notts 4F 87
Southsea. Port 3E 17
South Shields. Tyne 3G 115
South Shore. Bkpl 1B 90
Southside. Orkn 5E 172
South Somercotes. Linc 1D 88
South Stainley. N Yor 3F 99
South Stainmore. Cumb 3B 104
South Stifford. Thur 3G 39
South Stoke. Bath 5C 34
South Stoke. Oxon 3D 36
South Stoke. W Sus 5B 26
South Street. E Sus 4E 27
South Street. Kent
nr. Faversham 5E 41
nr. Whitstable 4F 41
South Tawton. Devn 3G 11
South Thoresby. Linc 3D 88
South Tidworth. Wilts 2H 23
South Town. Devn 4C 12
South Town. Hants 3E 25
Southtown. Norf 5H 79
Southtown. Orkn 8D 172
South View. Shet 7E 173
Southwaite. Cumb 5F 113
South Walsham. Norf 4F 79
South Warnborough.
Hants 2F 25
Southwater. W Sus 3C 26
Southwater Street. W Sus 3C 26
Southway. Som 2A 22
South Weald. Essx 1G 39
South Weirs. Hants 2A 16
Southwell. Dors 5B 14
Southwell. Notts 5E 86
South Weston. Oxon 2F 37
South Wheatley. Corn 3C 10
South Wheatley. Notts 2E 87
Southwick. Hants 2E 17
Southwick. Nptn 1H 63
Southwick. Tyne 4G 115
Southwick. W Sus 5D 26
Southwick. Wilts 1D 22
South Widcombe. Bath 1A 22
South Wigston. Leics 1C 62
South Willingham. Linc 2A 88
South Wingfield. Derbs 5A 86
South Witham. Linc 4G 75
Southwold. Suff 3H 67
South Wonston. Hants 3C 24
Southwood. Norf 5F 79
Southwood. Som 3A 22
South Woodham Ferrers.
Essx 1C 40
South Wootton. Norf 3F 77
South Wraxall. Wilts 5D 34
South Zeal. Devn 3G 11
Soval Lodge. W Isl 5F 171
Sowerby. N Yor 1G 99
Sowerby. W Yor 2A 92
Sowerby Bridge. W Yor 2A 92
Sowerby Row. Cumb 5E 113
Sower Carr. Lanc 5C 96

Sowley Green—Surfleet Seas End

Sowley Green. *Suff* 5G 65
Sowood. *W Yor* 3A 92
Sowton. *Devn* 3C 12
Soyal. *High* 4C 164
Soyland Town. *W Yor* 2A 92
The Spa. *New M* 5H 179
Spacey Houses. *N Yor* 4F 99
Spa Common. *Norf* 2E 79
Spalding. *Linc* 3B 76
Spaldington. *E Yor* 1A 94
Spaldwick. *Cambs* 3A 64
Spalford. *Notts* 4F 87
Spamount. *Derr* 4E 176
Spanby. *Linc* 2H 75
Sparham. *Norf* 4C 78
Sparhamhill. *Norf* 4C 78
Spark Bridge. *Cumb* 1C 96
Sparket. *Cumb* 2F 103
Sparkford. *Som* 4B 22
Sparkwell. *Devn* 3B 8
Sparrow Green. *Norf* 4B 78
Sparrowpit. *Derbs* 2E 85
Sparrow's Green. *E Sus* 2H 27
Sparsholt. *Hants* 3C 24
Sparsholt. *Oxon* 3B 36
Spartylea. *Nmbd* 5B 114
Spath. *Staf* 2E 73
Spaunton. *N Yor* 1B 100
Spaxton. *Som* 3F 21
Spean Bridge. *High* 5E 149
Spear Hill. *W Sus* 4C 26
Speen. *Buck* 2G 37
Speen. *W Ber* 5C 36
Speeton. *N Yor* 2F 101
Speke. *Mers* 2G 83
Speldhurst. *Kent* 1G 27
Spellbrook. *Herts* 4E 53
Spelsbury. *Oxon* 3B 50
Spencers Wood. *Wok* 5F 37
Spennithorne. *N Yor* 1D 98
Spennymoor. *Dur* 1F 105
Spernall. *Warw* 4E 61
Sperrin. *Derr* 7C 174
Spetchley. *Worc* 5C 60
Spetisbury. *Dors* 2E 15
Spexhall. *Suff* 2F 67
Speybank. *High* 3C 150
Spey Bay. *Mor* 2A 160
Speybridge. *High* 1E 151
Speyview. *Mor* 4G 159
Spilsby. *Linc* 4D 88
Spindlestone. *Nmbd* 1F 121
Spinkhill. *Derbs* 3B 86
Spinney Hills. *Leic* 5D 74
Spinningdale. *High* 5D 164
Spital. *Mers* 2F 83
Spitalhill. *Derbs* 1F 73
Spital in the Street. *Linc* 1G 87
Spithurst. *E Sus* 4F 27
Spittal. *Dum* 4A 110
Spittal. *E Lot* 2A 130
Spittal. *High* 3D 168
Spittal. *Nmbd* 4G 131
Spittal. *Pemb* 2D 43
Spittalfield. *Per* 4A 144
Spittal of Glenmuick.
Abers 5H 151
Spittal of Glenshee. *Per* 1A 144
Spittal-on-Rule. *Bord* 2H 119
Spixworth. *Norf* 4E 79
Splatt. *Corn* 4C 10
Spofforth. *N Yor* 4F 99
Spondon. *Derb* 2B 74
Spon End. *W Mid* 3H 61
Spooner Row. *Norf* 1C 66
Sporle. *Norf* 4H 77
Spott. *E Lot* 2C 130
Spratton. *Nptn* 3E 62
Spreakley. *Surr* 2G 25
Spreyton. *Devn* 3H 11
Spridlington. *Linc* 2H 87
Springburn. *Glas* 3H 127
Springfield. *Dum* 3E 113
Springfield. *Ferm* 8D 176
Springfield. *Fife* 2F 137
Springfield. *High* 2A 158
Springfield. *W Mid* 2E 61
Spring Hill. *W Mid* 1C 60
Springhill. *Staf* 5D 73
Springholm. *Dum* 3F 111
Springside. *N Ayr* 1C 116
Springthorpe. *Linc* 2F 87
Spring Vale. *IOW* 3E 16
Spring Valley. *IOM* 4C 108
Springwell. *Tyne* 4F 115
Sproatley. *E Yor* 1E 95
Sproston Green. *Ches W* 4B 84
Sprotbrough. *S Yor* 4F 93
Sproughton. *Suff* 1E 54
Sprouston. *Bord* 1B 120
Sprowston. *Norf* 4E 79
Sproxton. *Leics* 3F 75
Sproxton. *N Yor* 1A 100
Sprunston. *Cumb* 5E 113
Spurstow. *Ches E* 5H 83
Squires Gate. *Bkpl* 1B 90
Sraid Ruadh. *Arg* 4A 138
Srannda. *W Isl* 9C 171
Sron an t-Sithein. *High* 2C 140
Sronphadruig Lodge. *Per* 1E 142
Sruth Mor. *W Isl* 2E 170
Stableford. *Shrp* 1B 60
Stackhouse. *N Yor* 3H 97
Stackpole. *Pemb* 5D 43
Stackpole Elidor. *Pemb* 5D 43
Stacksford. *Norf* 1C 66
Stacksteads. *Lanc* 2G 91
Staddiscombe. *Plym* 3B 8
Staddlethorpe. *E Yor* 2B 94
Staddon. *Devn* 2D 10
Stadhampton. *Oxon* 2E 36
Stadhlaigearraidh. *W Isl* 5C 170
Stafainn. *High* 2D 155
Staffield. *Cumb* 5G 113
Staffin. *High* 2D 155
Stafford. *Staf* 3D 72
Stafford Park. *Telf* 5B 72
Stagden Cross. *Essx* 4G 53
Stagsden. *Bed* 1H 51
Stag's Head. *Devn* 4G 19
Stainburn. *Cumb* 2B 102
Stainburn. *N Yor* 5E 99
Stainby. *Linc* 3G 75
Staincliffe. *W Yor* 2C 92
Staincross. *S Yor* 3D 92
Staindrop. *Dur* 2E 105
Staines-upon-Thames.
Surr 3B 38
Stainfield. *Linc*
nr. Bourne 3H 75
nr. Lincoln 3A 88
Stainforth. *N Yor* 3H 97
Stainforth. *S Yor* 3G 93
Staining. *Lanc* 1B 90
Stainland. *W Yor* 3A 92
Stainsacre. *N Yor* 4G 107
Stainton. *Cumb*
nr. Carlisle 4E 113
nr. Kendal 1E 97
nr. Penrith 2F 103
Stainton. *Dur* 3D 104
Stainton. *Midd* 3B 106
Stainton. *N Yor* 5E 105
Stainton. *S Yor* 1C 86
Stainton by Langworth.
Linc 3H 87
Staintondale. *N Yor* 5G 107
Stainton le Vale. *Linc* 1A 88
Stainton with Adgarley.
Cumb 2B 96
Stair. *Cumb* 2D 102
Stair. *E Ayr* 2D 116
Stairhaven. *Dum* 4H 109
Staithes. *N Yor* 3E 107
Stakeford. *Nmbd* 1F 115
Stake Pool. *Lanc* 5D 96
Stakes. *Hants* 2E 17
Stalbridge. *Dors* 1C 14
Stalbridge Weston. *Dors* 1C 14
Stalham. *Norf* 3F 79
Stalham Green. *Norf* 3F 79
Stalisfield Green. *Kent* 5D 40
Stallen. *Dors* 1B 14
Stallingborough. *NE Lin* 3F 95
Stalling Busk. *N Yor* 1B 98
Stallington. *Staf* 2D 72
Stalmine. *Lanc* 5C 96
Stalybridge. *G Man* 1D 84
Stambourne. *Essx* 2H 53
Stamford. *Linc* 5H 75
Stamford. *Nmbd* 3G 121
Stamford Bridge. *Ches W* 4G 83
Stamford Bridge. *E Yor* 4B 100
Stamfordham. *Nmbd* 2D 115
Stamperland. *E Ren* 4G 127
Stanah. *Lanc* 5C 96
Stanborough. *Herts* 4C 52
Stanbridge. *C Beds* 3H 51
Stanbridge. *Dors* 2F 15
Stanbury. *W Yor* 1A 92
Stand. *N Lan* 3A 128
Standburn. *Falk* 2C 128
Standeford. *Staf* 5D 72
Standen. *Kent* 1C 28
Standen Street. *Kent* 2C 28
Standerwick. *Som* 1D 22
Standford. *Hants* 3G 25
Standford Bridge. *Telf* 3B 72
Standingstone. *Cumb* 5D 112
Standish. *Glos* 5D 48
Standish. *G Man* 3D 90
Standish Lower Ground.
G Man 4D 90
Standlake. *Oxon* 5B 50
Standon. *Hants* 4C 24
Standon. *Herts* 3D 53
Standon. *Staf* 2C 72
Standon Green End.
Herts 4D 52
Stane. *N Lan* 4B 128
Stanecastle. *N Ayr* 1C 116
Stanfield. *Norf* 3B 78
Stanfield. *Suff* 5G 65
Stanford. *C Beds* 1B 52
Stanford. *Kent* 2F 29
Stanford Bishop. *Here* 5A 60
Stanford Bridge. *Worc* 4B 60
Stanford Dingley. *W Ber* 4D 36
Stanford in the Vale.
Oxon 2B 36
Stanford-le-Hope. *Thur* 2A 40
Stanford on Avon. *Nptn* 3C 62
Stanford on Soar. *Notts* 3C 74
Stanford on Teme. *Worc* 4B 60
Stanford Rivers. *Essx* 5F 53
Stanfree. *Derbs* 3B 86
Stanghow. *Red C* 3D 107
Stanground. *Pet* 1B 64
Stanhoe. *Norf* 2H 77
Stanhope. *Dur* 1C 104
Stanhope. *Bord* 2D 118
Stanion. *Nptn* 2G 63
Stanley. *Derbs* 1B 74
Stanley. *Dur* 4E 115
Stanley. *Per* 5A 144
Stanley. *Shrp* 2B 60
Stanley. *Staf* 5D 84
Stanley. *W Yor* 2D 92
Stanley Common. *Derbs* 1B 74
Stanley Crook. *Dur* 1E 105
Stanley Hill. *Here* 1B 48
Stanlow. *Ches W* 3G 83
Stanmer. *Brig* 5E 27
Stanmore. *G Lon* 1C 38
Stanmore. *Hants* 4C 24
Stanmore. *W Ber* 4C 36
Stannersburn. *Nmbd* 1A 114
Stanningfield. *Suff* 5A 66
Stannington. *Nmbd* 2F 115
Stannington. *S Yor* 2H 85
Stansbatch. *Here* 4F 59
Stanshope. *Staf* 5F 85
Stanstead. *Suff* 1B 54
Stanstead Abbotts. *Herts* 4D 53
Stansted. *Kent* 4H 39
Stansted Airport.
Essx 205 (3F 53)
Stansted Mountfitchet.
Essx 3F 53
Stanthorne. *Ches W* 4A 84
Stanton. *Derbs* 4G 73
Stanton. *Glos* 2F 49
Stanton. *Nmbd* 5F 121
Stanton. *Staf* 1F 73
Stanton. *Suff* 3B 66
Stanton by Bridge. *Derbs* 3A 74
Stanton-by-Dale. *Derbs* 2B 74
Stanton Chare. *Suff* 3B 66
Stanton Drew. *Bath* 5A 34
Stanton Fitzwarren. *Swin* 2G 35
Stanton Harcourt. *Oxon* 5C 50
Stanton Hill. *Notts* 4B 86
Stanton in Peak. *Derbs* 4G 85
Stanton Lacy. *Shrp* 3G 59
Stanton Long. *Shrp* 1H 59
Stanton-on-the-Wolds.
Notts 2D 74
Stanton Prior. *Bath* 5B 34
Stanton St Bernard. *Wilts* 5F 35
Stanton St John. *Oxon* 5D 50
Stanton St Quintin. *Wilts* 4E 35
Stanton Street. *Suff* 4B 66
Stanton under Bardon.
Leics 4B 74
Stanton upon Hine Heath.
Shrp 3H 71
Stanton Wick. *Bath* 5B 34
Stanwardine in the Fields.
Shrp 3G 71
Stanwardine in the Wood.
Shrp 3G 71
Stanway. *Essx* 3C 54
Stanway. *Glos* 2F 49
Stanwell. *Surr* 3B 38
Stanwell Green. *Suff* 3D 66
Stanwell Moor. *Surr* 3B 38
Stanwick. *Nptn* 3G 63
Stanydale. *Shet* 6D 173
Staoinebrig. *W Isl* 5C 170
Stape. *N Yor* 5E 107
Stapehill. *Dors* 2F 15
Stapeley. *Ches E* 1A 72
Stapenhill. *Staf* 3G 73
Staple. *Kent* 5G 41
Staple Cross. *Devn* 4D 20
Staplecross. *E Sus* 3B 28
Staplefield. *W Sus* 3D 27
Staple Fitzpaine. *Som* 1F 13
Stapleford. *Cambs* 5D 64
Stapleford. *Herts* 4D 52
Stapleford. *Leics* 4F 75
Stapleford. *Linc* 5F 87
Stapleford. *Notts* 2B 74
Stapleford. *Wilts* 3F 23
Stapleford Abbotts. *Essx* 1G 39
Stapleford Tawney. *Essx* 1G 39
Staplegrove. *Som* 4F 21
Staplehay. *Som* 4F 21
Staple Hill. *S Glo* 4B 34
Staplehurst. *Kent* 1B 28
Staplers. *IOW* 4D 16
Stapleton. *Bris* 4B 34
Stapleton. *Cumb* 2G 113
Stapleton. *Here* 4F 59
Stapleton. *Leics* 1B 62
Stapleton. *N Yor* 3F 105
Stapleton. *Shrp* 5G 71
Stapleton. *Som* 4H 21
Stapley. *Som* 1E 13
Staploe. *Bed* 4A 64
Staplow. *Here* 1B 48
Star. *Fife* 3F 137
Star. *Pemb* 1G 43
Starbeck. *N Yor* 4F 99
Starbotton. *N Yor* 2B 98
Starcross. *Devn* 4C 12
Stareton. *Warw* 3H 61
Starkholmes. *Derbs* 5H 85
Starling. *G Man* 3F 91
Starling's Green. *Essx* 2E 53
Starston. *Norf* 2E 67
Start. *Devn* 4E 9
Startforth. *Dur* 3D 104
Start Hill. *Essx* 3F 53
Startley. *Wilts* 3E 35
Stathe. *Som* 4G 21
Stathern. *Leics* 2E 75
Station Town. *Dur* 1B 106
Staughton Green. *Cambs* 4A 64
Staughton Highway.
Cambs 4A 64
Staunton. *Glos*
nr. Cheltenham 3C 48
nr. Monmouth 4A 48
Staunton in the Vale.
Notts 1F 75
Staunton on Arrow. *Here* 4F 59
Staunton on Wye. *Here* 1G 47
Staveley. *Cumb* 5F 103
Staveley. *Derbs* 3B 86
Staveley. *N Yor* 3F 99
Staveley-in-Cartmel.
Cumb 1C 96
Staverton. *Devn* 2D 9
Staverton. *Glos* 3D 49
Staverton. *Nptn* 4C 62
Staverton. *Wilts* 5D 34
Stawell. *Som* 3G 21
Stawley. *Som* 4D 20
Staxigoe. *High* 3F 169
Staxton. *N Yor* 2E 101
Staylittle. *Powy* 1A 58
Staynall. *Lanc* 5C 96
Staythorpe. *Notts* 5E 87
Stean. *N Yor* 2C 98
Stearsby. *N Yor* 2A 100
Steart. *Som* 2F 21
Stebbing. *Essx* 3G 53
Stebbing Green. *Essx* 3G 53
Stedham. *W Sus* 4G 25
Steel. *Nmbd* 4C 114
Steel Cross. *E Sus* 2G 27
Steelend. *Fife* 4C 136
Steele Road. *Bord* 5H 119
Steel Heath. *Shrp* 2H 71
Steen's Bridge. *Here* 5H 59
Steep. *Hants* 4F 25
Steep Lane. *W Yor* 2A 92
Steeple. *Dors* 4E 15
Steeple. *Essx* 5C 54
Steeple Ashton. *Wilts* 1E 23
Steeple Aston. *Oxon* 3C 50
Steeple Barton. *Oxon* 3C 50
Steeple Bumpstead. *Essx* 1G 53
Steeple Claydon. *Buck* 3E 51
Steeple Gidding. *Cambs* 2A 64
Steeple Langford. *Wilts* 3F 23
Steeple Morden. *Cambs* 1C 52
Steeton. *W Yor* 5C 98
Stein. *High* 3B 154
Steinmanhill. *Abers* 4E 161
Stelling Minnis. *Kent* 1F 29
Stembridge. *Som* 4H 21
Stemster. *High*
nr. Halkirk 2D 169
nr. Westfield 2C 168
Stenalees. *Corn* 3E 6
Stenhill. *Devn* 1D 12
Stenhouse. *Edin* 2F 129
Stenhousemuir. *Falk* 1B 128
Stenigot. *Linc* 2B 88
Stenscholl. *High* 2D 155
Stenso. *Orkn* 5C 172
Stenson. *Derbs* 3H 73
Stenson Fields. *Derbs* 2H 73
Stenton. *E Lot* 2C 130
Stenwith. *Linc* 2F 75
Steòrnabhagh. *W Isl* 4G 171
Stepaside. *Pemb* 4F 43
Stepford. *Dum* 1F 111
Stepney. *G Lon* 2E 39
Steppingley. *C Beds* 2A 52
Stepps. *N Lan* 3H 127
Sterndale Moor. *Derbs* 4F 85
Sternfield. *Suff* 4F 67
Stert. *Wilts* 1F 23
Stetchworth. *Cambs* 5F 65
Stevenage. *Herts* 3C 52
Stevenston. *N Ayr* 5D 126
Stevenstone. *Devn* 1F 11
Steventon. *Hants* 2D 24
Steventon. *Oxon* 2C 36
Steventon End. *Essx* 1F 53
Stevington. *Bed* 5G 63
Stewartby. *Bed* 1A 52
Stewarton. *Arg* 4A 122
Stewarton. *E Ayr* 5F 127
Stewartstown. *M Ulst* 2C 178
Stewkley. *Buck* 3G 51
Stewkley Dean. *Buck* 3G 51
Stewley. *Som* 1G 13
Stewton. *Linc* 2C 88
Steyning. *W Sus* 4C 26
Steynton. *Pemb* 4D 42
Stibb. *Corn* 1C 10
Stibbard. *Norf* 3B 78
Stibb Cross. *Devn* 1E 11
Stibb Green. *Wilts* 5H 35
Stibbington. *Cambs* 1H 63
Stichill. *Bord* 1B 120
Sticker. *Corn* 3D 6
Stickford. *Linc* 4C 88
Sticklepath. *Devn* 3G 11
Sticklinch. *Som* 3A 22
Stickling Green. *Essx* 2E 53
Stickney. *Linc* 5C 88
Stiffkey. *Norf* 1B 78
Stifford's Bridge. *Here* 1C 48
Stileway. *Som* 2H 21
Stillingfleet. *N Yor* 5H 99
Stillington. *N Yor* 3H 99
Stillington. *Stoc T* 2A 106
Stilton. *Cambs* 2A 64
Stinchcombe. *Glos* 2C 34
Stinsford. *Dors* 3C 14
Stiperstones. *Shrp* 5F 71
Stirchley. *Telf* 5B 72
Stirchley. *W Mid* 2E 61
Stirling. *Abers* 4H 161
Stirling. *Stir* 202 (4G 135)
Stirton. *N Yor* 4B 98
Stisted. *Essx* 3A 54
Stitchcombe. *Wilts* 5H 35
Stithians. *Corn* 5B 6
Stittenham. *High* 1A 158
Stivichall. *W Mid* 3H 61
Stixwould. *Linc* 4A 88
Stoak. *Ches W* 3G 83
Stobo. *Bord* 1D 118
Stobo Castle. *Bord* 1D 118
Stoborough. *Dors* 4E 15
Stoborough Green. *Dors* 4E 15
Stobs Castle. *Bord* 4H 119
Stobswood. *Nmbd* 5G 121
Stock. *Essx* 1A 40
Stockbridge. *Hants* 3B 24
Stockbridge. *W Yor* 5C 98
Stockbury. *Kent* 4C 40
Stockcross. *W Ber* 5C 36
Stockdalewath. *Cumb* 5E 113
Stocker's Head. *Kent* 5D 40
Stockerston. *Leics* 1F 63
Stock Green. *Worc* 5D 61
Stocking. *Here* 2B 48
Stockingford. *Warw* 1H 61
Stocking Green. *Essx* 2F 53
Stocking Pelham. *Herts* 3E 53
Stockland. *Devn* 2F 13
Stockland Bristol. *Som* 2F 21
Stockleigh English. *Devn* 2B 12
Stockleigh Pomeroy. *Devn* 2B 12
Stockley. *Wilts* 5F 35
Stocklinch. *Som* 1G 13
Stockport. *G Man* 2C 84
The Stocks. *Kent* 3D 28
Stocksbridge. *S Yor* 1G 85
Stocksfield. *Nmbd* 3D 114
Stockstreet. *Essx* 3B 54
Stockton. *Here* 4H 59
Stockton. *Norf* 1F 67
Stockton. *Shrp*
nr. Bridgnorth 1B 60
nr. Chirbury 5E 71
Stockton. *Telf* 4B 72
Stockton. *Warw* 4B 62
Stockton. *Wilts* 3E 23
Stockton Brook. *Staf* 5D 84
Stockton Cross. *Here* 4H 59
Stockton Heath. *Warr* 2A 84
Stockton-on-Tees.
Stoc T 3B 106
Stockton on Teme. *Worc* 4B 60
Stockton-on-the-Forest.
York 4A 100
Stockwell Heath. *Staf* 3E 73
Stock Wood. *Worc* 5E 61
Stockwood. *Bris* 5B 34
Stodmarsh. *Kent* 4G 41
Stody. *Norf* 2C 78
Stoer. *High* 1E 163
Stoford. *Som* 1A 14
Stoford. *Wilts* 3F 23
Stogumber. *Som* 3D 20
Stogursey. *Som* 2F 21
Stoke. *Devn* 4C 18
Stoke. *Hants*
nr. Andover 1C 24
nr. South Hayling 2F 17
Stoke. *Medw* 3C 40
Stoke. *W Mid* 3A 62
Stoke Abbott. *Dors* 2H 13
Stoke Albany. *Nptn* 2F 63
Stoke Ash. *Suff* 3D 66
Stoke Bardolph. *Notts* 1D 74
Stoke Bliss. *Worc* 4A 60
Stoke Bruerne. *Nptn* 1F 51
Stoke by Clare. *Suff* 1H 53
Stoke-by-Nayland. *Suff* 2C 54
Stoke Canon. *Devn* 3C 12
Stoke Charity. *Hants* 3C 24
Stoke Climsland. *Corn* 5D 10
Stoke Cross. *Here* 5A 60
Stoke D'Abernon. *Surr* 5C 38
Stoke Doyle. *Nptn* 2H 63
Stoke Dry. *Rut* 1F 63
Stoke Edith. *Here* 1B 48
Stoke Farthing. *Wilts* 4F 23
Stoke Ferry. *Norf* 5G 77
Stoke Fleming. *Devn* 4E 9
Stokeford. *Dors* 4D 14
Stoke Gabriel. *Devn* 3E 9
Stoke Gifford. *S Glo* 4B 34
Stoke Golding. *Leics* 1A 62
Stoke Goldington. *Mil* 1G 51
Stokeham. *Notts* 3E 87
Stoke Hammond. *Buck* 3G 51
Stoke Heath. *Shrp* 3A 72
Stoke Holy Cross. *Norf* 5E 79
Stokeinteignhead. *Devn* 5C 12
Stoke Lacy. *Here* 1B 48
Stoke Lyne. *Oxon* 3D 50
Stoke Mandeville. *Buck* 4G 51
Stokenchurch. *Buck* 2F 37
Stoke Newington. *G Lon* 2E 39
Stokenham. *Devn* 4E 9
Stoke on Tern. *Shrp* 3A 72
Stoke-on-Trent.
Stoke 202 (1C 72)
Stoke Orchard. *Glos* 3E 49
Stoke Pero. *Som* 2B 20
Stoke Poges. *Buck* 2A 38
Stoke Prior. *Here* 5H 59
Stoke Prior. *Worc* 4D 60
Stoke Rivers. *Devn* 3G 19
Stoke Rochford. *Linc* 3G 75
Stoke Row. *Oxon* 3E 37
Stoke St Gregory. *Som* 4G 21
Stoke St Mary. *Som* 4F 21
Stoke St Michael. *Som* 2B 22
Stoke St Milborough.
Shrp 2H 59
Stokesay. *Shrp* 2G 59
Stokesby. *Norf* 4G 79
Stokesley. *N Yor* 4C 106
Stoke sub Hamdon. *Som* 1H 13
Stoke Talmage. *Oxon* 2E 37
Stoke Town. *Stoke* 202 (1C 72)
Stoke Trister. *Som* 4C 22
Stoke Wake. *Dors* 2C 14
Stolford. *Som* 2F 21
Stondon Massey. *Essx* 5F 53
Stone. *Buck* 4F 51
Stone. *Glos* 2B 34
Stone. *Kent* 3G 39
Stone. *Som* 3A 22
Stone. *Staf* 2D 72
Stone. *Worc* 3C 60
Stonea. *Cambs* 1D 64
Stoneacton. *Shrp* 1H 59
Stone Allerton. *Som* 1H 21
Ston Easton. *Som* 1B 22
Stonebridge. *N Som* 1G 21
Stonebridge. *Surr* 1C 26
Stone Bridge Corner. *Pet* 5B 76
Stonebroom. *Derbs* 5B 86
Stonebyres Holdings.
S Lan 5B 128
Stone Chair. *W Yor* 2B 92
Stone Cross. *E Sus* 5H 27
Stone Cross. *Kent* 2G 27
Stone-edge Batch. *N Som* 4H 33
Stoneferry. *Hull* 1D 94
Stonefield. *Arg* 5D 140
Stonefield. *S Lan* 4H 127
Stonegate. *E Sus* 3A 28
Stonegate. *N Yor* 4E 107
Stonegrave. *N Yor* 2A 100
Stonehall. *Worc* 1D 49
Stonehaugh. *Nmbd* 2A 114
Stonehaven. *Abers* 5F 153
Stone Heath. *Staf* 2D 72
Stone Hill. *Kent* 2E 29
Stone House. *Cumb* 1G 97
Stonehouse. *Glos* 5D 48
Stonehouse. *Nmbd* 4H 113
Stonehouse. *S Lan* 5A 128
Stone in Oxney. *Kent* 3D 28
Stoneleigh. *Warw* 3H 61
Stoneley Green. *Ches E* 5A 84
Stonely. *Cambs* 4A 64
Stonepits. *Worc* 5E 61
Stoner Hill. *Hants* 4F 25
Stonesby. *Leics* 3F 75
Stonesfield. *Oxon* 4B 50
Stones Green. *Essx* 3E 55
Stone Street. *Kent* 5G 39
Stone Street. *Suff*
nr. Boxford 2C 54
nr. Halesworth 2F 67
Stonethwaite. *Cumb* 3D 102
Stoneyburn. *W Lot* 3C 128
Stoney Cross. *Hants* 1A 16
Stoneyford. *Devn* 2D 12
Stoneygate. *Leic* 5D 74
Stoneyhills. *Essx* 1D 40
Stoneykirk. *Dum* 4F 109
Stoney Middleton. *Derbs* 3G 85
Stoney Stanton. *Leics* 1B 62
Stoney Stoke. *Som* 3C 22
Stoney Stratton. *Som* 3B 22
Stoney Stretton. *Shrp* 5F 71
Stoneywood. *Aber* 2F 153
Stonham Aspal. *Suff* 5D 66
Stonnall. *Staf* 5E 73
Stonor. *Oxon* 3F 37
Stonton Wyville. *Leics* 1E 63
Stonybreck. *Shet* 1B 172
Stony Cross. *Devn* 4F 19
Stony Cross. *Here*
nr. Great Malvern 1C 48
nr. Leominster 4H 59
Stonyford. *Lis* 2G 179
Stony Houghton. *Derbs* 4B 86
Stony Stratford. *Mil* 1F 51
Stoodleigh. *Devn*
nr. Barnstaple 3G 19
nr. Tiverton 1C 12
Stopham. *W Sus* 4B 26
Stopsley. *Lutn* 3B 52
Stoptide. *Corn* 1D 6
Storeton. *Mers* 2F 83
Stormontfield. *Per* 1D 136
Stornoway. *W Isl* 4G 171
Stornoway Airport. *W Isl* 4G 171
Storridge. *Here* 1C 48
Storrington. *W Sus* 4B 26
Storrs. *Cumb* 5E 103
Storth. *Cumb* 1D 97
Storwood. *E Yor* 5B 100
Stotfield. *Mor* 1G 159
Stotfold. *C Beds* 2C 52
Stottesdon. *Shrp* 2A 60
Stoughton. *Leics* 5D 74
Stoughton. *Surr* 5A 38
Stoughton. *W Sus* 1G 17
Stoul. *High* 4F 147
Stoulton. *Worc* 1E 49
Stourbridge. *W Mid* 2C 60
Stourpaine. *Dors* 2D 14
Stourport-on-Severn.
Worc 3C 60
Stour Provost. *Dors* 4C 22
Stour Row. *Dors* 4D 22
Stourton. *Staf* 2C 60
Stourton. *Warw* 2A 50
Stourton. *W Yor* 1D 92
Stourton. *Wilts* 3C 22
Stourton Caundle. *Dors* 1C 14
Stove. *Orkn* 4F 172
Stove. *Shet* 9F 173
Stoven. *Suff* 2G 67
Stow. *Linc*
nr. Billingborough 2H 75
nr. Gainsborough 2F 87
Stow. *Bord* 5A 130
Stow Bardolph. *Norf* 5F 77
Stow Bedon. *Norf* 1B 66
Stowbridge. *Norf* 5F 77
Stow cum Quy. *Cambs* 4E 65
Stowe. *Glos* 5A 48
Stowe. *Shrp* 3F 59
Stowe. *Staf* 4F 73
Stowe-by-Chartley. *Staf* 3E 73
Stowell. *Som* 4B 22
Stowey. *Bath* 1A 22
Stowford. *Devn*
nr. Colaton Raleigh 4D 12
nr. Combe Martin 2G 19
nr. Tavistock 4E 11
Stowlangtoft. *Suff* 4B 66
Stow Longa. *Cambs* 3A 64
Stow Maries. *Essx* 1C 40
Stowmarket. *Suff* 5C 66
Stow-on-the-Wold. *Glos* 3G 49
Stowting. *Kent* 1F 29
Stowupland. *Suff* 5C 66
Straad. *Arg* 3B 126
Strabane. *Derr* 3F 176
Strachan. *Abers* 4D 152
Stradbroke. *Suff* 3E 67
Stradishall. *Suff* 5G 65
Stradsett. *Norf* 5F 77
Stragglethorpe. *Linc* 5G 87
Stragglethorpe. *Notts* 2D 74
Straid. *Ant* 7K 175
Straid. *ME Ant* 7G 175
Straid. *S Ayr* 5A 116
Straight Soley. *Wilts* 4B 36
Straiton. *Midl* 3F 129
Straiton. *S Ayr* 4C 116
Straloch. *Per* 2H 143
Stramshall. *Staf* 2E 73
Strang. *IOM* 4C 108
Strangford. *Here* 3A 48
Strangford. *New M* 5K 179
Stranocum. *Caus* 3G 175
Stranraer. *Dum* 3F 109
Strata Florida. *Cdgn* 4G 57
Stratfield Mortimer. *W Ber* 5E 37
Stratfield Saye. *Hants* 5E 37
Stratfield Turgis. *Hants* 1E 25
Stratford. *G Lon* 2E 39
Stratford. *Worc* 2D 49
Stratford St Andrew. *Suff* 4F 67
Stratford St Mary. *Suff* 2D 54
Stratford sub Castle.
Wilts 3G 23
Stratford Tony. *Wilts* 4F 23
Stratford-upon-Avon.
Warw 202 (5G 61)
Strath. *High*
nr. Gairloch 1G 155
nr. Wick 3E 169
Strathan. *High*
nr. Fort William 4B 148
nr. Lochinver 1E 163
nr. Tongue 2F 167
Strathan Skerray. *High* 2G 167
Strathaven. *S Lan* 5A 128
Strathblane. *Stir* 2G 127
Strathcanaird. *High* 3F 163
Strathcarron. *High* 4B 156
Strathcoil. *Arg* 5A 140
Strathdon. *Abers* 2A 152
Strathkinness. *Fife* 2G 137
Strathmashie House.
High 4H 149
Strathmiglo. *Fife* 2E 136
Strathmore Lodge. *High* 4D 168
Strathpeffer. *High* 3G 157
Strathrannoch. *High* 1F 157
Strathtay. *Per* 3G 143
Strathvaich Lodge. *High* 1F 157
Strathwhillan. *N Ayr* 2E 123
Strathy. *High*
nr. Invergordon 1A 158
nr. Melvich 2A 168
Strathyre. *Stir* 2E 135
Stratton. *Corn* 2C 10
Stratton. *Dors* 3B 14
Stratton. *Glos* 5F 49
Stratton Audley. *Oxon* 3E 50
Stratton-on-the-Fosse.
Som 1B 22
Stratton St Margaret.
Swin 3G 35
Stratton St Michael. *Norf* 1E 66
Stratton Strawless. *Norf* 3E 78
Stravithie. *Fife* 2H 137
Straw. *M Ulst* 7D 174
Stream. *Som* 3D 20
Streat. *E Sus* 4E 27
Streatham. *G Lon* 3E 39
Streatley. *C Beds* 3A 52
Streatley. *W Ber* 3D 36
Street. *Corn* 3C 10
Street. *Lanc* 4E 97
Street. *N Yor* 4E 107
Street. *Som*
nr. Chard 2G 13
Street. *Som*
nr. Glastonbury 3H 21
Street Ash. *Som* 1F 13
Street Dinas. *Shrp* 2F 71
Street End. *Kent* 5F 41
Street End. *W Sus* 3G 17
Streetgate. *Tyne* 4F 115
Streethay. *Staf* 4F 73
Streethouse. *W Yor* 2D 93
Streetlam. *N Yor* 5A 106
Street Lane. *Derbs* 1A 74
Streetly. *W Mid* 1E 61
Streetly End. *Cambs* 1G 53
Street on the Fosse. *Som* 3B 22
Strefford. *Shrp* 2G 59
Strelley. *Notts* 1C 74
Strensall. *York* 3A 100
Strensall Camp. *York* 4A 100
Stretcholt. *Som* 2F 21
Strete. *Devn* 4E 9
Stretford. *G Man* 1C 84
Stretford. *Here* 5H 59
Strethall. *Essx* 2E 53
Stretham. *Cambs* 3E 65
Stretton. *Ches W* 5G 83
Stretton. *Derbs* 4A 86
Stretton. *Rut* 4G 75
Stretton. *Staf*
nr. Brewood 4C 72
nr. Burton upon Trent 3G 73
Stretton. *Warr* 2A 84
Stretton en le Field. *Leics* 4H 73
Stretton Grandison. *Here* 1B 48
Stretton Heath. *Shrp* 4F 71
Stretton-on-Dunsmore.
Warw 3B 62
Stretton-on-Fosse. *Warw* 2H 49
Stretton Sugwas. *Here* 1H 47
Stretton under Fosse.
Warw 2B 62
Stretton Westwood. *Shrp* 1H 59
Strichen. *Abers* 3G 161
Strines. *G Man* 2D 84
Stringston. *Som* 2E 21
Strixton. *Nptn* 4G 63
Stroanfreggan. *Dum* 5F 117
Stroat. *Glos* 2A 34
Stromeferry. *High* 5A 156
Stromemore. *High* 5A 156
Stromness. *Orkn* 7B 172
Stronachie. *Per* 3C 136
Stronachlachar. *Stir* 2D 134
Stronchreggan. *High* 1E 141
Strone. *Arg* 1C 126
Strone. *High*
nr. Drumnadrochit 1H 149
nr. Kingussie 3B 150
Stronenaba. *High* 5E 148
Stronganess. *Shet* 1G 173
Stronmilchan. *Arg* 1A 134
Stronsay Airport. *Orkn* 5F 172
Strontian. *High* 2C 140
Strood. *Kent* 2C 28
Strood. *Medw* 4B 40
Strood Green. *Surr* 1D 26
Strood Green. *W Sus*
nr. Billingshurst 3B 26
nr. Horsham 2C 26
Strothers Dale. *Nmbd* 4C 114
Stroud. *Glos* 5D 48
Stroud. *Hants* 4F 25
Stroud Green. *Essx* 1C 40
Stroxton. *Linc* 2G 75
Struan. *High* 5C 154
Struan. *Per* 2F 143
Struanmore. *High* 5C 154
Strubby. *Linc* 2D 88
Strugg's Hill. *Linc* 2B 76
Strumpshaw. *Norf* 5F 79
Strutherhill. *S Lan* 4A 128
Struy. *High* 5G 157
Stryd. *IOA* 2B 80
Stryt-issa. *Wrex* 1E 71
Stuartfield. *Abers* 4G 161
Stubbington. *Hants* 2D 16
Stubbins. *Lanc* 3F 91
Stubble Green. *Cumb* 5B 102
Stubb's Cross. *Kent* 2D 28
Stubbs Green. *Norf* 1F 67
Stubhampton. *Dors* 1E 15
Stubton. *Linc* 1F 75
Stubwood. *Staf* 2E 73
Stuckton. *Hants* 1G 15
Studham. *C Beds* 4A 52
Studland. *Dors* 4F 15
Studley. *Warw* 4E 61
Studley. *Wilts* 4E 35
Studley Roger. *N Yor* 2E 99
Stuntney. *Cambs* 3E 65
Stunts Green. *E Sus* 4H 27
Sturbridge. *Staf* 2C 72
Sturgate. *Linc* 2F 87
Sturmer. *Essx* 1G 53
Sturminster Marshall.
Dors 2E 15
Sturminster Newton. *Dors* 1C 14
Sturry. *Kent* 4F 41
Sturton. *N Lin* 4C 94
Sturton by Stow. *Linc* 2F 87
Sturton le Steeple. *Notts* 2E 87
Stuston. *Suff* 3D 66
Stutton. *N Yor* 5G 99
Stutton. *Suff* 2E 55
Styal. *Ches E* 2C 84
Stydd. *Lanc* 1E 91
Styrrup. *Notts* 1D 86
Suainebost. *W Isl* 1H 171
Suardail. *W Isl* 4G 171
Succoth. *Abers* 5B 160
Succoth. *Arg* 3B 134
Suckley. *Worc* 5B 60
Suckley Knowl. *Worc* 5B 60
Sudborough. *Nptn* 2G 63
Sudbourne. *Suff* 5G 67
Sudbrook. *Linc* 1G 75
Sudbrook. *Mon* 3A 34
Sudbrooke. *Linc* 3H 87
Sudbury. *Derbs* 2F 73
Sudbury. *Suff* 1B 54
Sudgrove. *Glos* 5E 49
Suffield. *Norf* 2E 79
Suffield. *N Yor* 5G 107
Sugnall. *Staf* 2B 72
Sugwas Pool. *Here* 1H 47
Suisnish. *High* 5E 155
Sulaisiadar. *W Isl* 4H 171
Sùlaisiadar Mòr. *High* 4D 155
Sulby. *IOM* 2C 108
Sulgrave. *Nptn* 1D 50
Sulham. *W Ber* 4E 37
Sulhamstead. *W Ber* 5E 37
Sullington. *W Sus* 4B 26
Sullom. *Shet* 4E 173
Sully. *V Glam* 5E 33
Sumburgh. *Shet* 10F 173
Sumburgh Airport. *Shet* 10E 173
Summer Bridge. *N Yor* 3E 98
Summercourt. *Corn* 3C 6
Summergangs. *Hull* 1E 94
Summer Hill. *W Mid* 1D 60
Summerhill. *Aber* 3G 153
Summerhill. *Pemb* 4F 43
Summerhouse. *Darl* 3F 105
Summersdale. *W Sus* 2G 17
Summerseat. *G Man* 3F 91
Summit. *G Man* 3H 91
Sunbury. *Surr* 4C 38
Sunderland. *Cumb* 1C 102
Sunderland. *Lanc* 4D 96
Sunderland. *Tyne* 202 (4G 115)
Sunderland Bridge. *Dur* 1F 105
Sundon Park. *Lutn* 3A 52
Sundridge. *Kent* 5F 39
Sunk Island. *E Yor* 3F 95
Sunningdale. *Wind* 4A 38
Sunninghill. *Wind* 4A 38
Sunningwell. *Oxon* 5C 50
Sunniside. *Dur* 1E 105
Sunniside. *Tyne* 4F 115
Sunny Bank. *Cumb* 5D 102
Sunny Hill. *Derb* 2H 73
Sunnyhurst. *Bkbn* 2E 91
Sunnylaw. *Stir* 4G 135
Sunnymead. *Oxon* 5D 50
Sunnyside. *S Yor* 1B 86
Sunnyside. *W Sus* 2E 27
Sunton. *Wilts* 1H 23
Surbiton. *G Lon* 4C 38
Surby. *IOM* 4B 108
Surfleet. *Linc* 3B 76
Surfleet Seas End. *Linc* 3B 76

Surlingham—Tobha Beag

Surlingham. Norf 5F 79
Surrex. Essx 3B 54
Sustead. Norf 2D 78
Susworth. Linc 4B 94
Sutcombe. Devn 1D 10
Suton. Norf 1C 66
Sutors of Cromarty. High 2C 158
Sutterby. Linc 3C 88
Sutterton. Linc 2B 76
Sutterton Dowdyke. Linc 2B 76
Sutton. Buck 3B 38
Sutton. Cambs 3D 64
Sutton. C Beds 1C 52
Sutton. E Sus 5F 27
Sutton. G Lon 4D 38
Sutton. Kent 1H 29
Sutton. Norf 3F 79
Sutton. Notts 2E 75
Sutton. Oxon 5C 50
Sutton. Pemb 3D 42
Sutton. Pet 1H 63
Sutton. Shrp
 nr. Bridgnorth 2B 60
 nr. Market Drayton 2A 72
 nr. Oswestry 3F 71
 nr. Shrewsbury 4H 71
Sutton. Som 3B 22
Sutton. S Yor 3F 93
Sutton. Staf 3B 72
Sutton. Suff 1G 55
Sutton. W Sus 4A 26
Sutton. Worc 4A 60
Sutton Abinger. Surr 1C 26
Sutton at Hone. Kent 3G 39
Sutton Bassett. Nptn 1E 63
Sutton Benger. Wilts 4E 35
Sutton Bingham. Som 1A 14
Sutton Bonington. Notts 3C 74
Sutton Bridge. Linc 3D 76
Sutton Cheney. Leics 5B 74
Sutton Coldfield, Royal.
 W Mid 1F 61
Sutton Corner. Linc 3D 76
Sutton Courtenay. Oxon 2D 36
Sutton Crosses. Linc 3D 76
Sutton cum Lound. Notts 2D 86
Sutton Gault. Cambs 3D 64
Sutton Grange. N Yor 2E 99
Sutton Green. Surr 5B 38
Sutton Howgrave. N Yor 2F 99
Sutton in Ashfield. Notts 5B 86
Sutton-in-Craven. N Yor 5C 98
Sutton Ings. Hull 1E 94
Sutton in the Elms. Leics 1C 62
Sutton Lane Ends. Ches E 3D 84
Sutton Leach. Mers 1H 83
Sutton Maddock. Shrp 5B 72
Sutton Mallet. Som 3G 21
Sutton Mandeville. Wilts 4E 23
Sutton Montis. Som 4B 22
Sutton on Hull. Hull 1E 94
Sutton on Sea. Linc 2E 89
Sutton-on-the-Forest.
 N Yor 3H 99
Sutton on the Hill. Derbs 2G 73
Sutton on Trent. Notts 4E 87
Sutton Poyntz. Dors 4C 14
Sutton St Edmund. Linc 4C 76
Sutton St Edmund's Common.
 Linc 5C 76
Sutton St James. Linc 4C 76
Sutton St Michael. Here 1A 48
Sutton St Nicholas. Here 1A 48
Sutton Scarsdale. Derbs 4B 86
Sutton Scotney. Hants 3C 24
Sutton-under-Brailes.
 Warw 2B 50
Sutton-under-Whitestonecliffe.
 N Yor 1G 99
Sutton upon Derwent.
 E Yor 5B 100
Sutton Valence. Kent 1C 28
Sutton Veny. Wilts 2E 23
Sutton Waldron. Dors 1D 14
Sutton Weaver. Ches W 3H 83
Swaby. Linc 3C 88
Swadlincote. Derbs 4G 73
Swaffham. Norf 5H 77
Swaffham Bulbeck.
 Cambs 4E 65
Swaffham Prior. Cambs 4E 65
Swafield. Norf 2E 79
Swainby. N Yor 4B 106
Swainshill. Here 1H 47
Swainsthorpe. Norf 5E 78
Swainswick. Bath 5C 34
Swalcliffe. Oxon 2B 50
Swalecliffe. Kent 4F 41
Swallow. Linc 4E 95
Swallow Beck. Linc 4G 87
Swallowcliffe. Wilts 4E 23
Swallowfield. Wok 5F 37
Swallownest. S Yor 2B 86
Swampton. Hants 1C 24
Swanage. Dors 5F 15
Swanbister. Orkn 7C 172
Swanbourne. Buck 3G 51
Swanbridge. V Glam 5E 33
Swan Green. Ches W 3B 84
Swanland. E Yor 2C 94
Swanley. Kent 4G 39
Swanmore. Hants 1D 16
Swannington. Leics 4B 74
Swannington. Norf 4D 78
Swanpool. Linc 4G 87
Swanscombe. Kent 3H 39
Swansea. Swan 203 (3F 31)
Swan Street. Essx 3B 54
Swanton Abbott. Norf 3E 79
Swanton Morley. Norf 4C 78
Swanton Novers. Norf 2C 78
Swanton Street. Kent 5C 40
Swanwick. Derbs 5B 86
Swanwick. Hants 2D 16
Swanwick Green. Ches E 1H 71
Swarby. Linc 1H 75
Swardeston. Norf 5E 78
Swarister. Shet 3G 173
Swarkestone. Derbs 3A 74
Swarland. Nmbd 4F 121
Swarraton. Hants 3D 24
Swartha. W Yor 5C 98
Swarthmoor. Cumb 2B 96
Swaton. Linc 2A 76
Swatragh. M Ulst 6E 174
Swavesey. Cambs 4C 64
Sway. Hants 3A 16
Swayfield. Linc 3G 75
Swaythling. Sotn 1C 16
Sweet Green. Worc 4A 60
Sweetham. Devn 3B 12
Sweetholme. Cumb 3G 103
Sweets. Corn 3B 10
Sweetshouse. Corn 2E 7
Swefling. Suff 4F 67
Swell. Som 4G 21
Swepstone. Leics 4A 74
Swerford. Oxon 2B 50
Swettenham. Ches E 4C 84
Swetton. N Yor 2D 98
Swffryd. Blae 2F 33
Swiftsden. E Sus 3B 28
Swilland. Suff 5D 66
Swillington. W Yor 1D 93
Swimbridge. Devn 4G 19
Swimbridge Newland.
 Devn 3G 19
Swinbrook. Oxon 4A 50
Swincliffe. N Yor 4E 99
Swincliffe. W Yor 2C 92
Swinderby. Linc 4F 87
Swindon. Glos 3E 49
Swindon. Nmbd 5D 121
Swindon. Staf 1C 60
Swindon. Swin 203 (3G 35)
Swine. E Yor 1E 95
Swinefleet. E Yor 2A 94
Swineford. S Glo 5B 34
Swineshead. Bed 4H 63
Swineshead. Linc 1B 76
Swineshead Bridge. Linc 1B 76
Swiney. High 5E 169
Swinford. Leics 3C 62
Swinford. Oxon 5C 50
Swingate. Notts 1C 74
Swingbrow. Cambs 2C 64
Swingfield Minnis. Kent 1G 29
Swingfield Street. Kent 1G 29
Swingleton Green. Suff 1C 54
Swinhill. S Lan 5A 128
Swinhoe. Nmbd 2G 121
Swinhope. Linc 1B 88
Swinister. Shet 3E 173
Swinithwaite. N Yor 1C 98
Swinmore Common. Here 1B 48
Swinscoe. Staf 1F 73
Swinside Hall. Bord 3B 120
Swinstead. Linc 3H 75
Swinton. G Man 4F 91
Swinton. N Yor
 nr. Malton 2B 100
 nr. Masham 2E 98
Swinton. Bord 5E 131
Swinton. S Yor 1B 86
Swithland. Leics 4C 74
Swordale. High 2H 157
Swordly. High 2H 167
Sworton Heath. Ches E 2A 84
Swyddffynnon. Cdgn 4F 57
Swynnerton. Staf 2C 72
Swyre. Dors 4A 14
Sycharth. Powy 3E 70
Sychdyn. Flin 4E 83
Sychnant. Powy 3B 58
Sychtyn. Powy 5B 70
Syde. Glos 4E 49
Sydenham. G Lon 3E 39
Sydenham. Oxon 5F 51
Sydenham. Som 3G 21
Sydenham Damerel. Devn 5E 11
Syderstone. Norf 2H 77
Sydling St Nicholas. Dors 3B 14
Sydmonton. Hants 1C 24
Sydney. Ches E 5B 84
Syerston. Notts 1E 75
Syke. G Man 3G 91
Sykehouse. S Yor 3G 93
Sykes. Lanc 4F 97
Syleham. Suff 3E 66
Sylen. Carm 5F 45
Sylfaen. Powy 5D 70
Symbister. Shet 5G 173
Symington. S Ayr 1C 116
Symington. S Lan 1B 118
Symondsbury. Dors 3H 13
Symonds Yat. Here 4A 48
Synod Inn. Cdgn 5D 56
Syre. High 4G 167
Syreford. Glos 3F 49
Syresham. Nptn 1E 51
Syston. Leics 4D 74
Syston. Linc 1G 75
Sytchampton. Worc 4C 60
Sywell. Nptn 4F 63

T

Tabost. W Isl
 nr. Cearsiadar 6F 171
 nr. Suainebost 1H 171
Tachbrook Mallory. Warw 4H 61
Tackley. Oxon 3C 50
Tacleit. W Isl 4D 171
Tacolneston. Norf 1D 66
Tadcaster. N Yor 5G 99
Taddington. Derbs 3F 85
Taddington. Glos 2F 49
Taddiport. Devn 1E 11
Tadley. Hants 5E 36
Tadlow. Cambs 1C 52
Tadmarton. Oxon 2B 50
Tadwick. Bath 4C 34
Tadworth. Surr 5D 38
Tafarnaubach. Blae 4E 46
Tafarn-y-bwlch. Pemb 1E 43
Tafarn-y-Gelyn. Den 4D 82
Taff's Well. Rhon 3E 33
Tafolwern. Powy 5A 70
Tai-bach. Powy 3D 70
Taibach. Neat 3A 32
Taigh a Ghearraidh.
 W Isl 1C 170
Taigh Bhuirgh. W Isl 8C 171
Tain. High
 nr. Invergordon 5E 165
 nr. Thurso 2E 169
Tai-Nant. Wrex 1E 71
Tai'n Lon. Gwyn 5D 80
Tairbeart. W Isl 8D 171
Tairgwaith. Neat 4H 45
Takeley. Essx 3F 53
Takeley Street. Essx 3F 53
Talachddu. Powy 2D 46
Talacre. Flin 2D 82
Talardd. Gwyn 3A 70
Talaton. Devn 3D 12
Talbenny. Pemb 3C 42
Talbot Green. Rhon 3D 32
Taleford. Devn 3D 12
Talerddig. Powy 5B 70
Talgarreg. Cdgn 5D 56
Talgarth. Powy 2E 47
Talisker. High 5C 154
Talke. Staf 5C 84
Talkin. Cumb 4G 113
Talladale. High 1B 156
Talla Linnfoots. Bord 2D 118
Tallaminnock. S Ayr 5C 116
Tallarn Green. Wrex 1G 71
Tallentire. Cumb 1C 102
Talley. Carm 2G 45
Tallington. Linc 5H 75
Talmine. High 2F 167
Talog. Carm 2H 43
Talsarn. Carm 3A 46
Talsarn. Cdgn 5E 57
Talsarnau. Gwyn 2F 69
Talskiddy. Corn 2D 6
Talwrn. IOA 3D 81
Talwrn. Wrex 1E 71
Tal-y-bont. Cnwy 4G 81
Tal-y-bont. Cdgn 2F 57
Tal-y-bont. Gwyn
 nr. Bangor 3F 81
 nr. Barmouth 3E 69
Talybont-on-Usk. Powy 3E 46
Tal-y-cafn. Cnwy 3G 81
Tal-y-coed. Mon 4H 47
Tal-y-llyn. Gwyn 5G 69
Talyllyn. Powy 3E 46
Talysarn. Gwyn 5D 81
Tal-y-waenydd. Gwyn 1F 69
Talywain. Torf 5F 47
Tal-y-Wern. Powy 5H 69
Tamerton Foliot. Plym 2A 8
Tamlaght. Ferm 8E 176
Tamlaght O'Crilly. M Ulst 6E 174
Tamnamore. M Ulst 3C 178
Tamworth. Staf 5G 73
Tamworth Green. Linc 1C 76
Tandlehill. Ren 3F 127
Tandragee. Arm 5E 178
Tandridge. Surr 5E 39
Tanerdy. Carm 3E 45
Tanfield. Dur 4E 115
Tanfield Lea. Dur 4E 115
Tangasdal. W Isl 8B 170
Tang Hall. York 4A 100
Tangiers. Pemb 3D 42
Tangley. Hants 1B 24
Tangmere. W Sus 5A 26
Tangwick. Shet 4D 173
Tankerness. Orkn 7E 172
Tankersley. S Yor 1H 85
Tankerton. Kent 4F 41
Tan-lan. Cnwy 4G 81
Tan-lan. Gwyn 1F 69
Tannach. High 4F 169
Tannadice. Ang 3D 145
Tanner's Green. Worc 3E 61
Tannington. Suff 4E 67
Tannochside. N Lan 3A 128
Tan Office Green. Suff 5G 65
Tansley. Derbs 5H 85
Tansley Knoll. Derbs 4H 85
Tansor. Nptn 1H 63
Tantobie. Dur 4E 115
Tanton. N Yor 3C 106
Tanvats. Linc 4A 88
Tanworth-in-Arden. Warw 3F 61
Tan-y-bwlch. Gwyn 1F 69
Tan-y-fron. Cnwy 4B 82
Tanyfron. Wrex 5E 83
Tanygrisiau. Gwyn 1F 69
Tan-y-groes. Cdgn 1C 44
Tan-y-pistyll. Powy 3C 70
Tan-yr-allt. Den 2C 82
Taobh a Chaolais. W Isl 7C 170
Taobh a Deas Loch Aineort.
 W Isl 6C 170
Taobh a Ghlinne. W Isl 6F 171
Taobh a Tuath Loch Aineort.
 W Isl 6C 170
Taplow. Buck 2A 38
Tapton. Derbs 3A 86
Tarbert. Arg
 on Jura 1E 125
 on Kintyre 3G 125
Tarbert. W Isl 8D 171
Tarbet. Arg 3C 134
Tarbet. High
 nr. Mallaig 4F 147
 nr. Scourie 4B 166
Tarbock Green. Mers 2G 83
Tarbolton. S Ayr 2D 116
Tarbrax. S Lan 4D 128
Tardebigge. Worc 4D 61
Tarfside. Ang 1D 145
Tarland. Abers 3B 152
Tarleton. Lanc 2C 90
Tarlogie. High 5E 165
Tarlscough. Lanc 3C 90
Tarlton. Glos 2E 35
Tarnbrook. Lanc 4E 97
Tarnock. Som 1G 21
Tarns. Cumb 5C 112
Tarporley. Ches W 4H 83
Tarpots. Essx 2B 40
Tarr. Som 3E 20
Tarrant Crawford. Dors 2E 15
Tarrant Gunville. Dors 1E 15
Tarrant Hinton. Dors 1E 15
Tarrant Keyneston. Dors 2E 15
Tarrant Launceston. Dors 2E 15
Tarrant Monkton. Dors 2E 15
Tarrant Rawston. Dors 2E 15
Tarrant Rushton. Dors 2E 15
Tarrel. High 5F 165
Tarring Neville. E Sus 5F 27
Tarrington. Here 1B 48
Tarsappie. Per 1D 136
Tarscabhaig. High 3D 147
Tarskavaig. High 3D 147
Tarves. Abers 5F 161
Tarvie. High 3G 157
Tarvin. Ches W 4G 83
Tasburgh. Norf 1E 66
Tasley. Shrp 1A 60
Tassagh. Arm 6C 178
Taston. Oxon 3B 50
Tatenhill. Staf 3G 73
Tathall End. Mil 1G 51
Tatham. Lanc 3F 97
Tathwell. Linc 2C 88
Tatling End. Buck 2B 38
Tatsfield. Surr 5F 39
Tattenhall. Ches W 5G 83
Tatterford. Norf 3A 78
Tattersett. Norf 2H 77
Tattershall. Linc 5B 88
Tattershall Bridge. Linc 5A 88
Tattershall Thorpe. Linc 5B 88
Tattingstone. Suff 2E 55
Tattingstone White Horse.
 Suff 2E 55
Tattle Bank. Warw 4F 61
Tatworth. Som 2G 13
Taunton. Som 203 (4F 21)
Taverham. Norf 4D 78
Taverners Green. Essx 4F 53
Tavernspite. Pemb 3F 43
Tavistock. Devn 5E 11
Tavool House. Arg 1B 132
Taw Green. Devn 3G 11
Tawstock. Devn 4F 19
Taxal. Derbs 2E 85
Tayinloan. Arg 5E 125
Taynish. Arg 1F 125
Taynton. Glos 3C 48
Taynton. Oxon 4H 49
Taynuilt. Arg 5E 141
Tayport. Fife 1G 137
Tay Road Bridge. D'dee 1G 137
Tayvallich. Arg 1F 125
Tealby. Linc 1A 88
Tealing. Ang 5D 144
Teams. Tyne 3F 115
Teangue. High 3E 147
Teanna Mhachair. W Isl 2C 170
Tebay. Cumb 4H 103
Tebworth. C Beds 3H 51
Tedburn St Mary. Devn 3B 12
Teddington. Glos 2E 49
Teddington. G Lon 3C 38
Tedsmore. Shrp 3F 71
Tedstone Delamere. Here 5A 60
Tedstone Wafer. Here 5A 60
Teemore. Ferm 7J 177
Teesport. Red C 2C 106
Teesside. Stoc T 2C 106
Teeton. Nptn 3D 62
Teffont Evias. Wilts 3E 23
Teffont Magna. Wilts 3E 23
Tegryn. Pemb 1G 43
Teigh. Rut 4F 75
Teigncombe. Devn 4G 11
Teigngrace. Devn 5B 12
Teignmouth. Devn 5C 12
Telford. Telf 4A 72
Telham. E Sus 4B 28
Tellisford. Som 1D 22
Telscombe. E Sus 5F 27
Telscombe Cliffs. E Sus 5E 27
Tempar. Per 3D 142
Templand. Dum 1B 112
Temple. Corn 5B 10
Temple. Glas 3G 127
Temple. Midl 4G 129
Temple Balsall. W Mid 3G 61
Temple Bar. Carm 4F 45
Temple Bar. Cdgn 5E 57
Temple Cloud. Bath 1B 22
Templecombe. Som 4C 22
Temple Ewell. Kent 1G 29
Temple Grafton. Warw 5F 61
Temple Guiting. Glos 3F 49
Templehall. Fife 4E 137
Temple Hirst. N Yor 2G 93
Temple Normanton. Derbs 4B 86
Templepatrick. Ant 8J 175
Temple Sowerby. Cumb 2H 103
Templeton. Devn 1B 12
Templeton. Pemb 3F 43
Templeton. W Ber 5B 36
Templetown. Dur 5E 115
Tempo. Ferm 8F 176
Tempsford. C Beds 5A 64
Tenandry. Per 2G 143
Tenbury Wells. Worc 4H 59
Tenby. Pemb 4F 43
Tendring. Essx 3E 55
Tendring Green. Essx 3E 55
Tenga. Arg 4G 139
Ten Mile Bank. Norf 1F 65
Tenterden. Kent 2C 28
Terfyn. Cnwy 3B 82
Terhill. Som 3E 21
Terling. Essx 4A 54
Termon Rock. Ferm 2A 178
Ternhill. Shrp 2A 72
Terregles. Dum 2G 111
Terrick. Buck 5G 51
Terrington. N Yor 2A 100
Terrington St Clement.
 Norf 3E 77
Terrington St John. Norf 4E 77
Terry's Green. Warw 3F 61
Teston. Kent 5B 40
Testwood. Hants 1B 16
Tetbury. Glos 2D 35
Tetbury Upton. Glos 2D 35
Tetchill. Shrp 2F 71
Tetcott. Devn 3D 10
Tetford. Linc 3C 88
Tetney. Linc 4G 95
Tetney Lock. Linc 4G 95
Tetsworth. Oxon 5E 51
Tettenhall. W Mid 5C 72
Teversal. Notts 4B 86
Teversham. Cambs 5D 65
Teviothead. Bord 4G 119
Tewel. Abers 5F 153
Tewin. Herts 4C 52
Tewkesbury. Glos 2D 49
Teynham. Kent 4D 40
Teynham Street. Kent 4D 40
Thackthwaite. Cumb 2F 103
Thakeham. W Sus 4C 26
Thame. Oxon 5F 51
Thames Ditton. Surr 4C 38
Thames Haven. Thur 2B 40
Thamesmead. G Lon 2F 39
Thamesport. Medw 3C 40
Thanington Without. Kent 5F 41
Thankerton. S Lan 1B 118
Tharston. Norf 1D 66
Thatcham. W Ber 5D 36
Thatto Heath. Mers 1H 83
Thaxted. Essx 2G 53
Theakston. N Yor 1F 99
Thealby. N Lin 3B 94
Theale. Som 2H 21
Theale. W Ber 4E 37
Thearne. E Yor 1D 94
Theberton. Suff 4G 67
Theddingworth. Leics 2D 62
Theddlethorpe All Saints.
 Linc 2D 88
Theddlethorpe St Helen.
 Linc 2D 89
Thelbridge Barton. Devn 1A 12
Thelnetham. Suff 3C 66
Thelveton. Norf 2D 66
Thelwall. Warr 2A 84
Themelthorpe. Norf 3C 78
Thenford. Nptn 1D 50
Therfield. Herts 2D 52
Thetford. Linc 4A 76
Thetford. Norf 2A 66
Thethwaite. Cumb 5E 113
Theydon Bois. Essx 1F 39
Thick Hollins. W Yor 3B 92
Thickwood. Wilts 4D 34
Thimbleby. Linc 4B 88
Thimbleby. N Yor 5B 106
Thingwall. Mers 2E 83
Thirlby. N Yor 1G 99
Thirlestane. Bord 5B 130
Thirn. N Yor 1E 98
Thirsk. N Yor 1G 99
Thirtleby. E Yor 1E 95
Thistleton. Lanc 1C 90
Thistleton. Rut 4G 75
Thistley Green. Suff 3F 65
Thixendale. N Yor 3C 100
Thockrington. Nmbd 2C 114
Tholomas Drove. Cambs 5D 76
Tholthorpe. N Yor 3G 99
Thomas Chapel. Pemb 4F 43
Thomas Close. Cumb 5F 113
Thomastown. Abers 4E 160
Thomastown. Rhon 3D 32
Thompson. Norf 1B 66
Thomshill. Mor 3G 159
Thong. Kent 3A 40
Thongsbridge. W Yor 4B 92
Thoralby. N Yor 1C 98
Thoresby. Notts 3D 86
Thoresway. Linc 1A 88
Thorganby. Linc 1B 88
Thorganby. N Yor 5A 100
Thorgill. N Yor 5E 107
Thorington. Suff 3G 67
Thorington Street. Suff 2D 54
Thorlby. N Yor 4B 98
Thorley. Herts 4E 53
Thorley Street. Herts 4E 53
Thorley Street. IOW 4B 16
Thormanby. N Yor 2G 99
Thorn. Powy 4E 59
Thornaby-on-Tees.
 Stoc T 3B 106
Thornage. Norf 2C 78
Thornborough. Buck 2F 51
Thornborough. N Yor 2E 99
Thornbury. Devn 2E 11
Thornbury. Here 5A 60
Thornbury. S Glo 2B 34
Thornby. Cumb 4D 112
Thornby. Nptn 3D 62
Thorncliffe. Staf 5E 85
Thorncombe. Dors 2G 13
Thorncombe Street. Surr 1A 26
Thorncote Green. C Beds 1B 52
Thorndon. Suff 4D 66
Thorndon Cross. Devn 3F 11
Thorne. S Yor 3G 93
Thornehillhead. Devn 1E 11
Thorner. W Yor 5F 99
Thorne St Margaret. Som 4D 20
Thorney. Notts 3F 87
Thorney. Pet 5B 76
Thorney. Som 4H 21
Thorney Hill. Hants 3G 15
Thorney Toll. Cambs 5C 76
Thornfalcon. Som 4F 21
Thornford. Dors 1B 14
Thorngrafton. Nmbd 3A 114
Thorngrove. Som 3G 21
Thorngumbald. E Yor 2F 95
Thornham. Norf 1G 77
Thornham Magna. Suff 3D 66
Thornham Parva. Suff 3D 66
Thornhaugh. Pet 5H 75
Thornhill. Cphy 3E 33
Thornhill. Cumb 4B 102
Thornhill. Derbs 2F 85
Thornhill. Dum 5A 118
Thornhill. Sotn 1C 16
Thornhill. Stir 4F 135
Thornhill. W Yor 3C 92
Thornhill Lees. W Yor 3C 92
Thornhills. W Yor 2B 92
Thornholme. E Yor 3F 101
Thornicombe. Dors 2D 14
Thornington. Nmbd 1C 120
Thornley. Dur
 nr. Durham 1A 106
 nr. Tow Law 1E 105
Thornley Gate. Nmbd 4B 114
Thornliebank. E Ren 3G 127
Thornroan. Abers 5F 161
Thorns. Suff 5G 65
Thornsett. Derbs 2E 85
Thornthwaite. Cumb 2D 102
Thornthwaite. N Yor 4D 98
Thornton. Ang 4C 144
Thornton. Buck 2F 51
Thornton. E Yor 5B 100
Thornton. Fife 4E 137
Thornton. Lanc 5C 96
Thornton. Leics 5B 74
Thornton. Linc 4B 88
Thornton. Mers 4B 90
Thornton. Midd 3B 106
Thornton. Nmbd 5F 131
Thornton. Pemb 4D 42
Thornton. W Yor 1A 92
Thornton Curtis. N Lin 3D 94
Thorntonhall. S Lan 4G 127
Thornton Heath. G Lon 4E 39
Thornton Hough. Mers 2F 83
Thornton-in-Craven.
 N Yor 5B 98
Thornton in Lonsdale.
 N Yor 2F 97
Thornton-le-Beans.
 N Yor 5A 106
Thornton-le-Clay. N Yor 3A 100
Thornton-le-Dale. N Yor 1C 100
Thornton le Moor. Linc 1H 87
Thornton-le-Moor. N Yor 1F 99
Thornton-le-Moors.
 Ches W 3G 83
Thornton-le-Street. N Yor 1G 99
Thorntonloch. E Lot 2D 130
Thornton Rust. N Yor 1B 98
Thornton Steward. N Yor 1D 98
Thornton Watlass. N Yor 1E 99
Thornwood Common.
 Essx 5E 53
Thornythwaite. Cumb 2E 103
Thoroton. Notts 1E 75
Thorp Arch. W Yor 5G 99
Thorpe. Derbs 5F 85
Thorpe. E Yor 5D 101
Thorpe. Linc 2D 89
Thorpe. Norf 1G 67
Thorpe. N Yor 3C 98
Thorpe. Notts 1E 75
Thorpe. Surr 4B 38
Thorpe Abbotts. Norf 3D 66
Thorpe Acre. Leics 3C 74
Thorpe Arnold. Leics 3E 75
Thorpe Audlin. W Yor 3E 93
Thorpe Bassett. N Yor 2C 100
Thorpe Bay. S'end 2D 40
Thorpe by Water. Rut 1F 63
Thorpe Common. S Yor 1A 86
Thorpe Common. Suff 2F 55
Thorpe Constantine. Staf 5G 73
Thorpe End. Norf 4E 79
Thorpe Fendike. Linc 4D 88
Thorpe Green. Essx 3E 55
Thorpe Green. Suff 5B 66
Thorpe Hall. N Yor 2H 99
Thorpe Hamlet. Norf 5E 79
Thorpe Hesley. S Yor 1A 86
Thorpe in Balne. S Yor 3F 93
Thorpe in the Fallows.
 Linc 2G 87
Thorpe Langton. Leics 1E 63
Thorpe Larches. Dur 2A 106
Thorpe Latimer. Linc 1A 76
Thorpe-le-Soken. Essx 3E 55
Thorpe le Street. E Yor 5C 100
Thorpe Malsor. Nptn 3F 63
Thorpe Mandeville. Nptn 1D 50
Thorpe Market. Norf 2E 79
Thorpe Marriott. Norf 4D 78
Thorpe Morieux. Suff 5B 66
Thorpeness. Suff 5G 67
Thorpe on the Hill. Linc 4G 87
Thorpe on the Hill. W Yor 2D 92
Thorpe St Andrew. Norf 5E 79
Thorpe St Peter. Linc 4D 89
Thorpe Salvin. S Yor 2C 86
Thorpe Satchville. Leics 4E 75
Thorpe Thewles. Stoc T 2A 106
Thorpe Tilney. Linc 5A 88
Thorpe Underwood. N Yor 4G 99
Thorpe Waterville. Nptn 2H 63
Thorpe Willoughby. N Yor 1F 93
Thorpland. Norf 5F 77
Thorrington. Essx 3D 54
Thorverton. Devn 2C 12
Thrandeston. Suff 3D 66
Thrapston. Nptn 3G 63
Thrashbush. N Lan 3A 128
Threapland. Cumb 1C 102
Threapland. N Yor 3B 98
Threapwood. Ches W 1G 71
Threapwood. Staf 1E 73
Three Ashes. Here 3A 48
Three Bridges. Linc 2D 88
Three Bridges. W Sus 2D 27
Three Burrows. Corn 4B 6
Three Chimneys. Kent 2C 28
Three Cocks. Powy 2E 47
Three Crosses. Swan 3E 31
Three Cups Corner. E Sus 3H 27
Threehammer Common.
 Norf 3F 79
Three Holes. Norf 5E 77
Threekingham. Linc 2H 75
Three Leg Cross. E Sus 2A 28
Three Legged Cross. Dors 2F 15
Three Mile Cross. Wok 5F 37
Threemilestone. Corn 4B 6
Three Oaks. E Sus 4C 28
Threlkeld. Cumb 2E 102
Threshfield. N Yor 3B 98
Thrigby. Norf 4G 79
Thringarth. Dur 2C 104
Thringstone. Leics 4B 74
Thrintoft. N Yor 5A 106
Thriplow. Cambs 1E 53
Throckenholt. Linc 5C 76
Throcking. Herts 2D 52
Throckley. Tyne 3E 115
Throckmorton. Worc 1E 49
Throop. Bour 3G 15
Throphill. Nmbd 1E 115
Thropton. Nmbd 4E 121
Throsk. Stir 4A 136
Througham. Glos 5E 49
Throughgate. Dum 1F 111
Throwleigh. Devn 3G 11
Throwley. Kent 5D 40
Throwley Forstal. Kent 5D 40
Throxenby. N Yor 1E 101
Thrumpton. Notts 2C 74
Thrumster. High 4F 169
Thrunton. Nmbd 3E 121
Thrupp. Glos 5D 48
Thrupp. Oxon 4C 50
Thrushelton. Devn 4E 11
Thrushgill. Lanc 3F 97
Thrussington. Leics 4D 74
Thruxton. Hants 2A 24
Thruxton. Here 2H 47
Thrybergh. S Yor 1B 86
Thulston. Derbs 2B 74
Thundergay. N Ayr 5G 125
Thundersley. Essx 2B 40
Thundridge. Herts 4D 52
Thurcaston. Leics 4C 74
Thurcroft. S Yor 2B 86
Thurdon. Corn 1C 10
Thurgarton. Norf 2D 78
Thurgarton. Notts 1D 74
Thurgoland. S Yor 4C 92
Thurlaston. Leics 1C 62
Thurlaston. Warw 3B 62
Thurlbear. Som 4F 21
Thurlby. Linc
 nr. Alford 3D 89
 nr. Baston 4A 76
 nr. Lincoln 4G 87
Thurleigh. Bed 5H 63
Thurlestone. Devn 4C 8
Thurloxton. Som 3F 21
Thurlstone. S Yor 4C 92
Thurlton. Norf 1G 67
Thurmaston. Leics 5D 74
Thurnby. Leics 5D 74
Thurne. Norf 4G 79
Thurnham. Kent 5C 40
Thurning. Norf 3C 78
Thurning. Nptn 2H 63
Thurnscoe. S Yor 4E 93
Thursby. Cumb 4E 113
Thursford. Norf 2B 78
Thursford Green. Norf 2B 78
Thursley. Surr 2A 26
Thurso. High 2D 168
Thurso East. High 2D 168
Thurstaston. Mers 2E 83
Thurston. Suff 4B 66
Thurston End. Suff 5G 65
Thurstonfield. Cumb 4E 112
Thurstonland. W Yor 3B 92
Thurton. Norf 5F 79
Thurvaston. Derbs
 nr. Ashbourne 2F 73
 nr. Derby 2G 73
Thuxton. Norf 5C 78
Thwaite. Dur 3D 104
Thwaite. N Yor 5B 104
Thwaite. Suff 4D 66
Thwaite Head. Cumb 5E 103
Thwaites. W Yor 5C 98
Thwaite St Mary. Norf 1F 67
Thwing. E Yor 2E 101
Tibbermore. Per 1C 136
Tibberton. Glos 3C 48
Tibberton. Telf 3A 72
Tibberton. Worc 5D 60
Tibenham. Norf 2D 66
Tibshelf. Derbs 4B 86
Tibthorpe. E Yor 4D 100
Ticehurst. E Sus 2A 28
Tichborne. Hants 3D 24
Tickencote. Rut 5G 75
Tickenham. N Som 4H 33
Tickhill. S Yor 1C 86
Ticklerton. Shrp 1G 59
Ticknall. Derbs 3A 74
Tickton. E Yor 5E 101
Tidbury Green. W Mid 3F 61
Tidcombe. Wilts 1A 24
Tiddington. Oxon 5E 51
Tiddington. Warw 5G 61
Tiddleywink. Wilts 4D 34
Tidebrook. E Sus 3H 27
Tideford. Corn 3H 7
Tideford Cross. Corn 2H 7
Tidenham. Glos 2A 34
Tideswell. Derbs 3F 85
Tidmarsh. W Ber 4E 37
Tidmington. Warw 2A 50
Tidpit. Hants 1F 15
Tidworth. Wilts 2H 23
Tidworth Camp. Wilts 2H 23
Tiers Cross. Pemb 3D 42
Tiffield. Nptn 5D 62
Tifty. Abers 4E 161
Tigerton. Ang 2E 145
Tighnabruaich. Arg 2A 126
Tigley. Devn 2D 8
Tilbrook. Cambs 4H 63
Tilbury. Thur 3H 39
Tilbury Green. Essx 1H 53
Tilbury Juxta Clare. Essx 1A 54
Tile Hill. W Mid 3G 61
Tilehurst. Read 4E 37
Tilford. Surr 2G 25
Tilgate Forest Row.
 W Sus 2D 26
Tillathrowie. Abers 5B 160
Tillers Green. Glos 2B 48
Tillery. Abers 1G 153
Tilley. Shrp 3H 71
Tillicoultry. Clac 4B 136
Tillingham. Essx 5C 54
Tillington. Here 1H 47
Tillington. W Sus 3A 26
Tillington Common. Here 1H 47
Tillybirloch. Abers 3D 152
Tillyfourie. Abers 2D 152
Tilmanstone. Kent 5H 41
Tilney All Saints. Norf 4E 77
Tilney Fen End. Norf 4E 77
Tilney High End. Norf 4E 77
Tilney St Lawrence. Norf 4E 77
Tilshead. Wilts 2F 23
Tilstock. Shrp 2H 71
Tilston. Ches W 5G 83
Tilstone Fearnall. Ches W 4H 83
Tilsworth. C Beds 3H 51
Tilton on the Hill. Leics 5E 75
Tiltups End. Glos 2D 34
Timberland. Linc 5A 88
Timbersbrook. Ches E 4C 84
Timberscombe. Som 2C 20
Timble. N Yor 4D 98
Timperley. G Man 2B 84
Timsbury. Bath 1B 22
Timsbury. Hants 4B 24
Timsgearraidh. W Isl 4C 171
Timworth Green. Suff 4A 66
Tincleton. Dors 3C 14
Tindale. Cumb 4H 113
Tindale Crescent. Dur 2F 105
Tingewick. Buck 2E 51
Tingrith. C Beds 2A 52
Tingwall. Orkn 5D 172
Tinhay. Devn 4D 11
Tinshill. W Yor 1C 92
Tinsley. S Yor 1B 86
Tinsley Green. W Sus 2D 27
Tintagel. Corn 4A 10
Tintern. Mon 5A 48
Tintinhull. Som 1H 13
Tintwistle. Derbs 1E 85
Tinwald. Dum 1B 112
Tinwell. Rut 5H 75
Tippacott. Devn 2A 20
Tipperty. Abers 1G 153
Tipps End. Cambs 1E 65
Tiptoe. Hants 3A 16
Tipton. W Mid 1D 60
Tipton St John. Devn 3D 12
Tiptree. Essx 4B 54
Tiptree Heath. Essx 4B 54
Tirabad. Powy 1B 46
Tircoed Forest Village.
 Swan 5G 45
Tiree Airport. Arg 4B 138
Tirinie. Per 2F 143
Tirley. Glos 3D 48
Tiroran. Arg 1B 132
Tir-Phil. Cphy 5E 47
Tirril. Cumb 2G 103
Tirryside. High 2C 164
Tir-y-dail. Carm 4G 45
Tisbury. Wilts 4E 23
Tisman's Common.
 W Sus 2B 26
Tissington. Derbs 5F 85
Titchberry. Devn 4C 18
Titchfield. Hants 2D 16
Titchmarsh. Nptn 3H 63
Titchwell. Norf 1G 77
Tithby. Notts 2D 74
Titley. Here 5F 59
Titlington. Nmbd 3E 121
Titsey. Surr 5F 39
Titson. Corn 2C 10
Tittensor. Staf 2C 72
Tittleshall. Norf 3A 78
Titton. Worc 4C 60
Tiverton. Ches W 4H 83
Tiverton. Devn 1C 12
Tivetshall St Margaret.
 Norf 2D 66
Tivetshall St Mary. Norf 2D 66
Tivington. Som 2C 20
Tixall. Staf 3D 73
Tixover. Rut 5G 75
Toab. Orkn 7E 172
Toab. Shet 10E 173
Toadmoor. Derbs 5A 86
Tobermore. M Ulst 7E 174
Tobermory. Arg 3G 139
Toberonochy. Arg 3E 133
Tobha Beag. W Isl 5C 170

Tobha-Beag—Upper Sheringham

Tobha-Beag. W Isl 1E 170
Tobha Mor. W Isl 5C 170
Tobhtarol. W Isl 4D 171
Tobson. W Isl 4D 171
Tocabhaig. High 2E 147
Tocher. Abers 5D 160
Tockenham. Wilts 4F 35
Tockenham Wick.
Wilts 3F 35
Tockholes. Bkbn 2E 91
Tockington. S Glo 3B 34
Tockwith. N Yor 4G 99
Todber. Dors 4D 22
Todding. Here 3G 59
Toddington. C Beds 3A 52
Toddington. Glos 2F 49
Todenham. Glos 2H 49
Todhills. Cumb 3E 113
Todmorden. W Yor 2H 91
Todwick. S Yor 2B 86
Toft. Cambs 5C 64
Toft. Linc 4H 75
Toft Hill. Dur 2E 105
Toft Monks. Norf 1G 67
Toft next Newton. Linc 2H 87
Toftrees. Norf 3A 78
Tofts. High 2F 169
Toftwood. Norf 4B 78
Togston. Nmbd 4G 121
Tokavaig. High 2E 147
Tokers Green. Oxon 4F 37
Tolastadh a Chaolais.
W Isl 4D 171
Tolladine. Worc 5C 60
Tolland. Som 3E 20
Tollard Farnham. Dors 1E 15
Tollard Royal. Wilts 1E 15
Toll Bar. S Yor 4F 93
Toller Fratrum. Dors 3A 14
Toller Porcorum. Dors 3A 14
Tollerton. N Yor 3H 99
Tollerton. Notts 2D 74
Toller Whelme. Dors 2A 14
Tollesbury. Essx 4C 54
Tolleshunt D'Arcy. Essx 4C 54
Tolleshunt Knights.
Essx 4C 54
Tolleshunt Major. Essx 4C 54
Tollie. High 3H 157
Tollie Farm. High 1A 156
Tolm. W Isl 4G 171
Tolpuddle. Dors 3C 14
Tolstadh bho Thuath.
W Isl 3H 171
Tolworth. G Lon 4C 38
Tomachlaggan. Mor 1F 151
Tomaknock. Per 1A 136
Tomatin. High 1C 150
Tombuidhe. Arg 3H 133
Tomdoun. High 3D 148
Tomich. High
nr. Cannich 1F 149
nr. Invergordon 1B 158
nr. Lairg 3D 164
Tomintoul. Mor 2F 151
Tomnavoulin. Mor 1G 151
Tomsléibhe. Arg 5A 140
Ton. Mon 2G 33
Tonbridge. Kent 1G 27
Tondu. B'end 3B 32
Tonedale. Som 4E 21
Tonfanau. Gwyn 5E 69
Tong. Shrp 5B 72
Tonge. Leics 3B 74
Tong Forge. Shrp 5B 72
Tongham. Surr 2G 25
Tongland. Dum 4D 111
Tong Norton. Shrp 5B 72
Tongue. High 3F 167
Tongue End. Linc 4A 76
Tongwynlais. Card 3E 33
Tonmawr. Neat 2B 32
Tonna. Neat 2A 32
Tonnau. Neat 2A 32
Ton Pentre. Rhon 2C 32
Ton-Teg. Rhon 3D 32
Tonwell. Herts 4D 52
Tonypandy. Rhon 2C 32
Tonyrefail. Rhon 3D 32
Toome. Ant 7F 175
Toot Baldon. Oxon 5D 50
Toot Hill. Essx 5F 53
Toothill. Hants 1B 16
Topcliffe. N Yor 2G 99
Topcliffe. W Yor 2C 92
Topcroft. Norf 1E 67
Topcroft Street. Norf 1E 67
Toppesfield. Essx 2H 53
Toppings. G Man 3F 91
Toprow. Norf 1D 66
Topsham. Devn 4C 12
Torbay. Torb 2F 9
Torbeg. N Ayr 3C 122
Torbothie. N Lan 4B 128
Torbryan. Devn 2E 9
Torcross. Devn 4E 9
Tore. High 3A 158
Torgyle. High 2F 149
Torinturk. Arg 3G 125
Torksey. Linc 3F 87
Torlum. W Isl 3C 170
Torlundy. High 1F 141
Tormarton. S Glo 4C 34
Tormitchell. S Ayr 5B 116
Tormore. High 3E 147
Tormore. N Ayr 2C 122
Tornagrain. High 4B 158
Tornaveen. Abers 3D 152
Torness. High 1H 149
Toronto. Dur 1E 105
Torpenhow. Cumb 1D 102
Torphichen. W Lot 2C 128
Torphins. Abers 3D 152
Torpoint. Corn 3A 8
Torquay. Torb 2F 9
Torr. Devn 3B 8
Torra. Arg 4B 124
Torran. High 4E 155
Torrance. E Dun 2H 127
Torrans. Arg 1B 132
Torranyard. N Ayr 5E 127
Torre. Som 3D 20
Torre. Torb 2F 9
Torridon. High 3B 156
Torrin. High 1D 147
Torrisdale. Arg 2B 122
Torrisdale. High 2G 167
Torrish. High 2G 165
Torrisholme. Lanc 3D 96
Torroble. High 3C 164
Torroy. High 4C 164
Torry. Aber 3G 153
Torryburn. Fife 1D 128
Torthorwald. Dum 2B 112
Tortington. W Sus 5B 26
Tortworth. S Glo 2C 34
Torvaig. High 4D 155
Torver. Cumb 5D 102
Torwood. Falk 1B 128
Torworth. Notts 2D 86
Toscaig. High 5G 155
Toseland. Cambs 4B 64
Tosside. N Yor 4G 97
Tostock. Suff 4B 66
Totaig. High 3A 154
Totardor. High 5C 154
Tote. High 4D 154
Totegan. High 2A 168
Tothill. Linc 2D 88
Totland. IOW 4B 16
Totley. S Yor 3H 85
Totnell. Dors 2B 14
Totnes. Devn 2E 9
Toton. Notts 2B 74
Totronald. Arg 3C 138
Totscore. High 2C 154
Tottenham. G Lon 1E 39
Tottenhill. Norf 4F 77
Tottenhill Row. Norf 4F 77
Totteridge. G Lon 1D 38
Totternhoe. C Beds 3H 51
Tottington. G Man 3F 91
Totton. Hants 1B 16
Touchen-end. Wind 4G 37
Toulvaddie. High 5F 165
The Towans. Corn 3C 4
Toward. Arg 3C 126
Towcester. Nptn 1E 51
Towednack. Corn 3B 4
Tower End. Norf 4F 77
Tower Hill. Mers 4C 90
Tower Hill. W Sus 3C 26
Towersey. Oxon 5F 51
Towie. Abers 2B 152
Towiemore. Mor 4A 160
Tow Law. Dur 1E 105
The Town. IOS 1A 4
Town End. Cambs 1D 64
Town End. Cumb
nr. Ambleside 4F 103
nr. Kirkby Thore 2H 103
nr. Lindale 1D 96
nr. Newby Bridge 1C 96
Town End. Mers 2G 83
Townend. W Dun 2F 127
Townfield. Dur 5C 114
Towngate. Cumb 5G 113
Towngate. Linc 4A 76
Town Green. Lanc 4C 90
Town Head. Cumb
nr. Grasmere 4E 103
nr. Great Asby 3H 103
Townhead. Cumb
nr. Lazonby 1G 103
nr. Maryport 1B 102
nr. Ousby 1H 103
Townhead. Dum 5D 111
Townhead of Greenlaw.
Dum 3E 111
Townhill. Fife 1E 129
Townhill. Swan 3F 31
Town Kelloe. Dur 1A 106
Town Littleworth.
E Sus 4F 27
Town Row. E Sus 2G 27
Towns End. Hants 1D 24
Townsend. Herts 5B 52
Townshend. Corn 3C 4
Town Street. Suff 2G 65
Town Yetholm. Bord 2C 120
Towthorpe. E Yor 3D 100
Towthorpe. York 4A 100
Towton. N Yor 1E 93
Towyn. Cnwy 3B 82
Toxteth. Mers 2F 83
Toynton All Saints.
Linc 4C 88
Toynton Fen Side. Linc 4C 88
Toynton St Peter. Linc 4D 88
Toy's Hill. Kent 5F 39
Trabboch. E Ayr 2D 116
Traboe. Corn 4E 5
Tradespark. High 3C 158
Tradespark. Orkn 7D 172
Trafford Park.
G Man 1B 84
Trallong. Powy 3C 46
Y Trallwng. Powy 5E 70
Tranent. E Lot 2H 129
Tranmere. Mers 2F 83
Trantlebeg. High 3A 168
Trantlemore. High 3A 168
Tranwell. Nmbd 1E 115
Trapp. Carm 4G 45
Traquair. Bord 1F 119
Trash Green. W Ber 5E 37
Trawden. Lanc 1H 91
Trawscoed. Powy 2D 46
Trawsfynydd. Gwyn 2G 69
Trawsgoed. Cdgn 3F 57
Treaddow. Here 3A 48
Trealaw. Rhon 2D 32
Treales. Lanc 1C 90
Trearddur. IOA 3B 80
Treaslane. High 3C 154
Treator. Corn 1D 6
Trebanog. Rhon 2D 32
Trebanos. Neat 5H 45
Trebarber. Corn 2C 6
Trebartha. Corn 5C 10
Trebarwith. Corn 4A 10
Trebetherick. Corn 1D 6
Treborough. Som 3D 20
Trebudannon. Corn 2C 6
Trebullett. Corn 5D 10
Treburley. Corn 5D 10
Treburrick. Corn 1C 6
Trebyan. Corn 2E 7
Trecastle. Powy 3B 46
Trecenydd. Cphy 3E 33
Trecott. Devn 2G 11
Trecwn. Pemb 1D 42
Trecynon. Rhon 5C 46
Tredaule. Corn 4C 10
Tredavoe. Corn 4B 4
Tredegar. Blae 5E 47
Trederwen. Powy 4E 71
Tredington. Glos 3E 49
Tredington. Warw 1A 50
Tredinnick. Corn
nr. Bodmin 2F 7
nr. Looe 3G 7
nr. Padstow 1D 6
Tredogan. V Glam 5D 32
Tredomen. Powy 2E 46
Tredunnock. Mon 2G 33
Tredustan. Powy 2E 47
Treen. Corn
nr. Land's End 4A 4
nr. St Ives 3B 4
Treeton. S Yor 2B 86
Trefaldwyn. Powy 1E 58
Trefasser. Pemb 1C 42
Trefdraeth. IOA 3D 80
Trefdraeth. Pemb 1E 43
Trefecca. Powy 2E 47
Trefechan. Mer T 5D 46
Trefeglwys. Powy 1B 58
Trefenter. Cdgn 4F 57
Treffgarne. Pemb 2D 42
Treffynnon. Flin 3D 82
Treffynnon. Pemb 2C 42
Trefil. Blae 4E 46
Trefilan. Cdgn 5E 57
Trefin. Pemb 1C 42
Treflach. Shrp 3E 71
Trefnant. Den 3C 82
Trefonen. Shrp 3E 71
Trefor. Gwyn 1C 68
Trefor. IOA 2C 80
Treforest. Rhon 3D 32
Trefrew. Corn 4B 10
Trefriw. Cnwy 4G 81
Tref-y-Clawdd. Powy 3E 59
Trefynwy. Mon 4A 48
Tregada. Corn 4D 10
Tregadillett. Corn 4C 10
Tregare. Mon 4H 47
Tregarne. Corn 4E 5
Tregaron. Cdgn 5F 57
Tregarth. Gwyn 4F 81
Tregear. Corn 3C 6
Tregeare. Corn 4C 10
Tregeiriog. Wrex 2D 70
Tregele. IOA 1C 80
Tregeseal. Corn 3A 4
Tregiskey. Corn 4E 6
Tregole. Corn 3B 10
Tregolwyn. V Glam 4C 32
Tregonetha. Corn 2D 6
Tregonhawke. Corn 3A 8
Tregony. Corn 4D 6
Tregoodwell. Corn 4B 10
Tregorrick. Corn 3E 6
Tregoss. Corn 2D 6
Tregowris. Corn 4E 5
Tregoyd. Powy 2E 47
Tregrehan Mills. Corn 3E 7
Tre-groes. Cdgn 1E 45
Tregullon. Corn 2E 7
Tregurrian. Corn 2C 6
Tregynon. Powy 1C 58
Trehafod. Rhon 2D 32
Trehan. Corn 3A 8
Treharris. Mer T 2D 32
Treherbert. Rhon 2C 32
Trehunist. Corn 2H 7
Trekenner. Corn 5D 10
Trekenning. Corn 2D 6
Treknow. Corn 4A 10
Trelales. B'end 3B 32
Trelan. Corn 5E 5
Trelash. Corn 3B 10
Trelassick. Corn 3C 6
Trelawnyd. Flin 3C 82
Trelech. Carm 1G 43
Treleddyd-fawr. Pemb 2B 42
Trelewis. Mer T 2E 32
Treligga. Corn 4A 10
Trelights. Corn 1D 6
Trelill. Corn 5A 10
Trelissick. Corn 5C 6
Trellech. Mon 5A 48
Trelleck Grange. Mon 5H 47
Trelogan. Flin 2D 82
Trelystan. Powy 5E 71
Tremadog. Gwyn 1E 69
Tremail. Corn 4B 10
Tremain. Cdgn 1C 44
Tremaine. Corn 4C 10
Tremar. Corn 2G 7
Trematon. Corn 3H 7
Tremeirchion. Den 3C 82
Tremore. Corn 2E 6
Tremorfa. Card 4F 33
Trenance. Corn
nr. Newquay 2C 6
nr. Padstow 1D 6
Trenarren. Corn 4E 7
Trench. Telf 4A 72
Trencreek. Corn 2C 6
Trendeal. Corn 3C 6
Trenear. Corn 5A 6
Treneglos. Corn 4C 10
Trenewan. Corn 3F 7
Trengune. Corn 3B 10
Trent. Dors 1A 14
Trentham. Stoke 1C 72
Trentishoe. Devn 2G 19
Trentlock. Derbs 2B 74
Treoes. V Glam 4C 32
Treorchy. Rhon 2C 32
Treorci. Rhon 2C 32
Tre'r-ddol. Cdgn 1F 57
Tre'r llai. Powy 5E 71
Trerulefoot. Corn 3H 7
Tresaith. Cdgn 5B 56
Trescott. Staf 1C 60
Trescowe. Corn 3C 4
Tresham. Glos 2C 34
Tresigin. V Glam 4C 32
Tresillian. Corn 4C 6
Tresimwn. V Glam 4D 32
Tresinney. Corn 4B 10
Treskillard. Corn 5A 6
Treskinnick Cross. Corn 3C 10
Tresmeer. Corn 4C 10
Tresparrett. Corn 3B 10
Tresparrett Posts. Corn 3B 10
Tressady. High 3D 164
Tressait. Per 2F 143
Tresta. Shet
on Fetlar 2H 173
on Mainland 6E 173
Treswell. Notts 3E 87
Treswithian. Corn 3D 4
Tre Taliesin. Cdgn 1F 57
Trethomas. Cphy 3E 33
Trethosa. Corn 3D 6
Trethurgy. Corn 3E 7
Tretio. Pemb 2B 42
Tretire. Here 3A 48
Tretower. Powy 3E 47
Treuddyn. Flin 5E 83
Trevadlock. Corn 5C 10
Trevalga. Corn 4A 10
Trevalyn. Wrex 5F 83
Trevance. Corn 1D 6
Trevanger. Corn 1D 6
Trevanson. Corn 1D 6
Trevarrack. Corn 3B 4
Trevarren. Corn 2D 6
Trevarrian. Corn 2C 6
Trevarrick. Corn 4D 6
Trevaughan. Carm
nr. Carmarthen 3E 45
nr. Whitland 3F 43
Treveighan. Corn 5A 10
Trevellas. Corn 3B 6
Trevelmond. Corn 2G 7
Treverva. Corn 5B 6
Trevescan. Corn 4A 4
Trevethin. Torf 5F 47
Trevia. Corn 4A 10
Trevigro. Corn 2H 7
Trevilley. Corn 4A 4
Treviscoe. Corn 3D 6
Trevivian. Corn 4B 10
Trevone. Corn 1C 6
Trevor. Wrex 1E 71
Trevor Uchaf. Den 1E 71
Trew. Corn 4D 4
Trewalder. Corn 4A 10
Trewarlett. Corn 4D 10
Trewarmett. Corn 4A 10
Trewassa. Corn 4B 10
Treween. Corn 4C 10
Trewellard. Corn 3A 4
Trewen. Corn 4C 10
Trewennack. Corn 4D 5
Trewern. Powy 4E 71
Trewetha. Corn 5A 10
Trewidland. Corn 3G 7
Trewint. Corn 3B 10
Trewithian. Corn 5C 6
Trewoofe. Corn 4B 4
Trewoon. Corn 3D 6
Treworthal. Corn 5C 6
Trewyddel. Pemb 1B 44
Treyarnon. Corn 1C 6
Treyford. W Sus 1G 17
Triangle. Staf 5E 73
Triangle. W Yor 2A 92
Trickett's Cross. Dors 2F 15
Trillick. Ferm 7F 176
Trimdon. Dur 1A 106
Trimdon Colliery. Dur 1A 106
Trimdon Grange. Dur 1A 106
Trimingham. Norf 2E 79
Trimley Lower Street.
Suff 2F 55
Trimley St Martin. Suff 2F 55
Trimley St Mary. Suff 2F 55
Trimpley. Worc 3B 60
Trimsaran. Carm 5E 45
Trimstone. Devn 2F 19
Trinafour. Per 2E 143
Trinant. Cphy 2F 33
Tring. Herts 4H 51
Trinity. Ang 2F 145
Trinity. Edin 2F 129
Trisant. Cdgn 3G 57
Triscombe. Som 3E 21
Trislaig. High 1E 141
Trispen. Corn 3C 6
Tritlington. Nmbd 5G 121
Trochry. Per 4G 143
Troedrhiwdalar. Powy 5B 58
Troedrhiwfuwch. Cphy 5E 47
Troedrhiw-gwair. Blae 5E 47
Troedyraur. Cdgn 1D 44
Troedyrhiw. Mer T 5D 46
Trondavoe. Shet 4E 173
Troon. Corn 5A 6
Troon. S Ayr 1C 116
Troqueer. Dum 2A 112
Troston. Suff 3A 66
Trostrey. Mon 5G 47
Trotiscliffe. Kent 4H 39
Trotton. W Sus 4G 25
Troutbeck. Cumb
nr. Ambleside 4F 103
nr. Penrith 2E 103
Troutbeck Bridge. Cumb 4F 103
Troway. Derbs 3A 86
Trowbridge. Wilts 1D 22
Trowell. Notts 2B 74
Trowle Common. Wilts 1D 22
Trowley Bottom. Herts 4A 52
Trowse Newton. Norf 5E 79
Trudoxhill. Som 2C 22
Trull. Som 4F 21
Trumaisgearraidh.
W Isl 1D 170
Trumpan. High 2B 154
Trumpet. Here 2B 48
Trumpington. Cambs 5D 64
Trumps Green. Surr 4A 38
Trunch. Norf 2E 79
Trunnah. Lanc 5C 96
Truro. Corn 4C 6
Trusham. Devn 4B 12
Trusley. Derbs 2G 73
Trusthorpe. Linc 2E 89
Tryfil. IOA 2D 80
Trysull. Staf 1C 60
Tubney. Oxon 2C 36
Tuckenhay. Devn 3E 9
Tuckhill. Shrp 2B 60
Tuckingmill. Corn 4A 6
Tuckton. Bour 3G 15
Tuddenham. Suff 3G 65
Tuddenham St Martin.
Suff 1E 55
Tudeley. Kent 1H 27
Tudhoe. Dur 1F 105
Tudhoe Grange. Dur 1F 105
Tudorville. Here 3A 48
Tudweiliog. Gwyn 2B 68
Tuesley. Surr 1A 26
Tufton. Hants 2C 24
Tufton. Pemb 2E 43
Tugby. Leics 5E 75
Tugford. Shrp 2H 59
Tughall. Nmbd 2G 121
Tulchan. Per 1B 136
Tullibardine. Per 2B 136
Tullibody. Clac 4A 136
Tullich. Arg 2H 133
Tullich. High
nr. Lochcarron 4B 156
nr. Tain 1C 158
Tullich. Mor 4H 159
Tullich Muir. High 1B 158
Tulliemet. Per 3G 143
Tulloch. Abers 5F 161
Tulloch. High
nr. Bonar Bridge 4D 164
nr. Fort William 5F 149
nr. Grantown-on-Spey
2D 151
Tulloch. Per 1C 136
Tullochgorm. Arg 4G 133
Tullybeagles Lodge. Per 5H 143
Tullyhogue. M Ulst 2C 178
Tullymurdoch. Per 3B 144
Tullynessle. Abers 2C 152
Tumble. Carm 4F 45
Tumbler's Green. Essx 3B 54
Tumby. Linc 4B 88
Tumby Woodside. Linc 5B 88
Tummel Bridge. Per 3E 143
Tunbridge Wells, Royal.
Kent 2G 27
Tunga. W Isl 4G 171
Tungate. Norf 3E 79
Tunley. Bath 1B 22
Tunstall. E Yor 1G 95
Tunstall. Kent 4C 40
Tunstall. Lanc 2F 97
Tunstall. Norf 5G 79
Tunstall. N Yor 5F 105
Tunstall. Staf 3B 72
Tunstall. Stoke 5C 84
Tunstall. Suff 5F 67
Tunstall. Tyne 4G 115
Tunstead. Derbs 3F 85
Tunstead. Norf 3E 79
Tunstead Milton. Derbs 2E 85
Tunworth. Hants 2E 25
Tupsley. Here 1A 48
Tupton. Derbs 4A 86
Turfholm. S Lan 1H 117
Turfmoor. Devn 2F 13
Turgis Green. Hants 1E 25
Turkdean. Glos 4G 49
Turkey Island. Hants 1D 16
Tur Langton. Leics 1E 62
Turleigh. Wilts 5D 34
Turlin Moor. Pool 3E 15
Turnastone. Here 2G 47
Turnberry. S Ayr 4B 116
Turnchapel. Plym 3A 8
Turnditch. Derbs 1G 73
Turners Hill. W Sus 2E 27
Turners Puddle. Dors 3D 14
Turnford. Herts 5D 52
Turnhouse. Edin 2E 129
Turnworth. Dors 2D 14
Turriff. Abers 4E 161
Tursdale. Dur 1A 106
Turton Bottoms. Bkbn 3F 91
Turtory. Mor 4C 160
Turves Green. W Mid 3E 61
Turvey. Bed 5G 63
Turville. Buck 2F 37
Turville Heath. Buck 2F 37
Turweston. Buck 2E 50
Tushielaw. Bord 3F 119
Tutbury. Staf 3G 73
Tutnall. Worc 3D 61
Tutshill. Glos 2A 34
Tuttington. Norf 3E 79
Tutts Clump. W Ber 4D 36
Tutwell. Corn 5D 11
Tuxford. Notts 3E 87
Twatt. Orkn 5B 172
Twatt. Shet 6E 173
Twechar. E Dun 2H 127
Tweedale. Telf 5B 72
Tweedbank. Bord 1H 119
Tweedmouth. Nmbd 4F 131
Tweedsmuir. Bord 2C 118
Twelveheads. Corn 4B 6
Twemlow Green. Ches E 4B 84
Twenty. Linc 3A 76
Twerton. Bath 5C 34
Twickenham. G Lon 3C 38
Twigworth. Glos 3D 48
Twineham. W Sus 4D 26
Twinhoe. Bath 1C 22
Twinstead. Essx 2B 54
Twinstead Green. Essx 2B 54
Twiss Green. Warr 1A 84
Twiston. Lanc 5H 97
Twitchen. Devn 3A 20
Twitchen. Shrp 3F 59
Two Bridges. Devn 5G 11
Two Bridges. Glos 5B 48
Two Dales. Derbs 4G 85
Two Gates. Staf 5G 73
Two Mile Oak. Devn 2E 9
Twycross. Leics 5H 73
Twyford. Buck 3E 51
Twyford. Derbs 3H 73
Twyford. Dors 1D 14
Twyford. Hants 4C 24
Twyford. Leics 4E 75
Twyford. Norf 3C 78
Twyford. Wok 4F 37
Twyford Common. Here 2A 48
Twyncholm. Dum 4D 110
Twyning. Glos 2D 49
Twyning Green. Glos 2E 49
Twynllanan. Carm 3A 46
Twyn-y-Sheriff. Mon 5H 47
Twywell. Nptn 3G 63
Tyberton. Here 2G 47
Tyburn. W Mid 1F 61
Tyby. Norf 3C 78
Tycroes. Carm 4G 45
Tycrwyn. Powy 4D 70
Tyddewi. Pemb 2B 42
Tydd Gote. Linc 4D 76
Tydd St Giles. Cambs 4D 76
Tydd St Mary. Linc 4D 76
Tye. Hants 2F 17
Tye Green. Essx
nr. Bishop's Stortford 3F 53
nr. Braintree 3A 54
nr. Saffron Walden 2F 53
Tyersal. W Yor 1B 92
Ty Issa. Powy 2D 70
Tyldesley. G Man 4E 91
Tyler Hill. Kent 4F 41
Tyler's Green. Essx 5F 53
Tylers Green. Buck 2G 37
Tylorstown. Rhon 2D 32
Tylwch. Powy 2B 58
Y Tymbl. Carm 4F 45
Tynan. Arm 5B 178
Ty-nant. Cnwy 1B 70
Tyndrum. Stir 5H 141
Tyneham. Dors 4D 15
Tynehead. Midl 4G 129
Tynemouth. Tyne 3G 115
Tyneside. Tyne 3F 115
Tyne Tunnel. Tyne 3G 115
Tynewydd. Rhon 2C 32
Tyninghame. E Lot 2C 130
Tynron. Dum 5H 117
Ty'n-y-bryn. Rhon 3D 32
Tyn-y-celyn. Wrex 2D 70
Tyn-y-cwm. Swan 5G 45
Ty'n-y-ffridd. Powy 2D 70
Tynygongl. IOA 2E 81
Tynygraig. Cdgn 4F 57
Ty'n-y-groes. Cnwy 3G 81
Ty'n-yr-eithin. Cdgn 4F 57
Tyn-y-rhyd. Powy 4C 70
Tyn-y-wern. Powy 3C 70
Tyrie. Abers 2G 161
Tyringham. Mil 1G 51
Tythecott. Devn 1E 11
Tythegston. B'end 4B 32
Tytherington. Ches E 3D 84
Tytherington. Som 2C 22
Tytherington. S Glo 3B 34
Tytherington. Wilts 2E 23
Tytherleigh. Devn 2G 13
Tywardreath. Corn 3E 7
Tywardreath Highway. Corn 3E 7
Tywyn. Cnwy 3G 81
Tywyn. Gwyn 5E 69

U

Uachdar. W Isl 3D 170
Uags. High 5G 155
Ubbeston Green. Suff 3F 67
Ubley. Bath 1A 22
Uckerby. N Yor 4F 105
Uckfield. E Sus 3F 27
Uckinghall. Worc 2D 48
Uckington. Glos 3E 49
Uckington. Shrp 5H 71
Uddingston. S Lan 3H 127
Uddington. S Lan 1A 118
Udimore. E Sus 4C 28
Udny Green. Abers 1F 153
Udny Station. Abers 1G 153
Udston. S Lan 4H 127
Udstonhead. S Lan 5A 128
Uffcott. Wilts 4G 35
Uffculme. Devn 1D 12
Uffington. Linc 5H 75
Uffington. Oxon 3B 36
Uffington. Shrp 4H 71
Ufford. Pet 5H 75
Ufford. Suff 5E 67
Ufton. Warw 4A 62
Ufton Nervet. W Ber 5E 37
Ugadale. Arg 3B 122
Ugborough. Devn 3C 8
Ugford. Wilts 3F 23
Uggeshall. Suff 2G 67
Ugglebarnby. N Yor 4F 107
Ugley. Essx 3F 53
Ugley Green. Essx 3F 53
Ugthorpe. N Yor 3E 107
Uidh. W Isl 9B 170
Uig. Arg 3C 138
Uig. High
nr. Balgown 2C 154
nr. Dunvegan 3A 154
Uigshader. High 4D 154
Uisken. Arg 2A 132
Ulbster. High 4F 169
Ulcat Row. Cumb 2F 103
Ulceby. Linc 3D 88
Ulceby. N Lin 3E 94
Ulceby Skitter. N Lin 3E 94
Ulcombe. Kent 1C 28
Uldale. Cumb 1D 102
Uley. Glos 2C 34
Ulgham. Nmbd 5G 121
Ullapool. High 4F 163
Ullenhall. Warw 4F 61
Ulleskelf. N Yor 1F 93
Ullesthorpe. Leics 2C 62
Ulley. S Yor 2B 86
Ullingswick. Here 5H 59
Ullinish. High 5C 154
Ullock. Cumb 2B 102
Ulpha. Cumb 5C 102
Ulrome. E Yor 4F 101
Ulsta. Shet 3F 173
Ulting. Essx 5B 54
Ulva House. Arg 5F 139
Ulverston. Cumb 2B 96
Ulwell. Dors 4F 15
Umberleigh. Devn 4G 19
Unapool. High 5C 166
Underbarrow. Cumb 5F 103
Undercliffe. W Yor 1B 92
Underdale. Shrp 4H 71
Underhoull. Shet 1G 173
Underriver. Kent 5G 39
Under Tofts. S Yor 2H 85
Underton. Shrp 1A 60
Underwood. Newp 3G 33
Underwood. Notts 5B 86
Underwood. Plym 3B 8
Undley. Suff 2F 65
Undy. Mon 3H 33
Union Mills. IOM 4C 108
Union Street. E Sus 2B 28
Unstone. Derbs 3A 86
Unstone Green. Derbs 3A 86
Unthank. Cumb
nr. Carlisle 5E 113
nr. Gamblesby 5H 113
nr. Penrith 1F 103
Unthank End. Cumb 1F 103
Upavon. Wilts 1G 23
Up Cerne. Dors 2B 14
Upchurch. Kent 4C 40
Upcott. Devn 2F 11
Upcott. Here 5F 59
Upend. Cambs 5F 65
Up Exe. Devn 2C 12
Upgate. Norf 4D 78
Upgate Street. Norf 1C 66
Uphall. Dors 2A 14
Uphall. W Lot 2D 128
Uphall Station. W Lot 2D 128
Upham. Devn 2B 12
Upham. Hants 4D 24
Uphampton. Here 4F 59
Uphampton. Worc 4C 60
Up Hatherley. Glos 3E 49
Uphill. N Som 1G 21
Up Holland. Lanc 4D 90
Uplawmoor. E Ren 4F 127
Upleadon. Glos 3C 48
Upleatham. Red C 3D 106
Uplees. Kent 4D 40
Uploders. Dors 3A 14
Uplowman. Devn 1D 12
Uplyme. Devn 3G 13
Up Marden. W Sus 1F 17
Upminster. G Lon 2G 39
Up Nately. Hants 1E 25
Upottery. Devn 2F 13
Uppat. High 3F 165
Upper Affcot. Shrp 2G 59
Upper Arley. Worc 2B 60
Upper Armley. W Yor 1C 92
Upper Arncott. Oxon 4E 50
Upper Astrop. Nptn 2D 50
Upper Badcall. High 4B 166
Upper Ballinderry. Lis 3F 179
Upper Bangor. Gwyn 3E 81
Upper Basildon. W Ber 4D 36
Upper Batley. W Yor 2C 92
Upper Beeding. W Sus 4C 26
Upper Benefield. Nptn 2G 63
Upper Bentley. Worc 4D 61
Upper Bighouse. High 3A 168
Upper Boddam. Abers 5D 160
Upper Boddington. Nptn 5B 62
Upper Bogside. Mor 3G 159
Upper Booth. Derbs 2F 85
Upper Borth. Cdgn 2F 57
Upper Boyndlie. Abers 2G 161
Upper Brailes. Warw 1B 50
Upper Breinton. Here 1H 47
Upper Broughton. Notts 3D 74
Upper Brynamman. Carm 4H 45
Upper Bucklebury. W Ber 5D 36
Upper Bullington. Hants 2C 24
Upper Burgate. Hants 1G 15
Upper Caldecote. C Beds 1B 52
Upper Canterton. Hants 1A 16
Upper Catesby. Nptn 5C 62
Upper Chapel. Powy 1D 46
Upper Cheddon. Som 4F 21
Upper Chicksgrove. Wilts 4E 23
Upper Church Village.
Rhon 3D 32
Upper Chute. Wilts 1A 24
Upper Clatford. Hants 2B 24
Upper Coberley. Glos 4E 49
Upper Coedcae. Torf 5F 47
Upper Cound. Shrp 5H 71
Upper Cudworth. S Yor 4D 93
Upper Cumberworth.
W Yor 4C 92
Upper Cuttlehill. Abers 4B 160
Upper Cwmbran. Torf 2F 33
Upper Dallachy. Mor 2A 160
Upper Dean. Bed 4H 63
Upper Denby. W Yor 4C 92
Upper Derraid. High 5E 159
Upper Diabaig. High 2H 155
Upper Dicker. E Sus 5G 27
Upper Dinchope. Shrp 2G 59
Upper Dochcarty. High 2H 157
Upper Dounreay. High 2B 168
Upper Dovercourt. Essx 2F 55
Upper Dunsforth. N Yor 3G 99
Upper Dunsley. Herts 4H 51
Upper Eastern Green.
W Mid 2G 61
Upper Elkstone. Staf 5E 85
Upper Ellastone. Staf 1F 73
Upper End. Derbs 3E 85
Upper Enham. Hants 2B 24
Upper Farmcote. Shrp 1B 60
Upper Farringdon. Hants 3F 25
Upper Framilode. Glos 4C 48
Upper Froyle. Hants 2F 25
Upper Gills. High 1F 169
Upper Glenfintaig. High 5E 149
Upper Godney. Som 2H 21
Upper Gravenhurst.
C Beds 2B 52
Upper Green. Essx 2E 53
Upper Green. W Ber 5B 36
Upper Green. W Yor 2C 92
Upper Grove Common.
Here 3A 48
Upper Hackney. Derbs 4G 85
Upper Hale. Surr 2G 25
Upper Halliford. Surr 4B 38
Upper Halling. Medw 4A 40
Upper Hambleton. Rut 5G 75
Upper Hardres Court. Kent 5F 41
Upper Hardwick. Here 5G 59
Upper Hartfield. E Sus 2F 27
Upper Haugh. S Yor 1B 86
Upper Hayton. Shrp 2H 59
Upper Heath. Shrp 2H 59
Upper Hellesdon. Norf 4E 78
Upper Helmsley. N Yor 4A 100
Upper Hengoed. Shrp 2E 71
Upper Hergest. Here 5E 59
Upper Heyford. Nptn 5D 62
Upper Heyford. Oxon 3C 50
Upper Hill. Here 5G 59
Upper Hindhope. Bord 4B 120
Upper Hopton. W Yor 3B 92
Upper Howsell. Worc 1C 48
Upper Hulme. Staf 4E 85
Upper Inglesham. Swin 2H 35
Upper Kilcott. S Glo 3C 34
Upper Killay. Swan 3E 31
Upper Kirkton. Abers 5E 161
Upper Kirkton. N Ayr 4C 126
Upper Knockando. Mor 4F 159
Upper Knockchoilum.
High 2G 149
Upper Lambourn. W Ber 3B 36
Upperlands. M Ulst 6E 174
Upper Langford. N Som 1H 21
Upper Langwith. Derbs 4C 86
Upper Largo. Fife 3G 137
Upper Latheron. High 5D 169
Upper Layham. Suff 1D 54
Upper Leigh. Staf 2E 73
Upper Lenie. High 1H 149
Upper Lochton. Abers 4D 152
Upper Longdon. Staf 4E 73
Upper Longwood. Shrp 5A 72
Upper Lybster. High 5E 169
Upper Lydbrook. Glos 4B 48
Upper Lye. Here 4F 59
Upper Maes-coed. Here 2G 47
Upper Midway. Derbs 3G 73
Uppermill. G Man 4H 91
Upper Millichope. Shrp 2H 59
Upper Milovaig. High 4A 154
Upper Minety. Wilts 2F 35
Upper Mitton. Worc 3C 60
Upper Nash. Pemb 4E 43
Upper Neepaback. Shet 3G 173
Upper Netchwood. Shrp 1A 60
Upper Nobut. Staf 2E 73
Upper North Dean. Buck 2G 37
Upper Norwood. W Sus 4A 26
Upper Nyland. Dors 4C 22
Upper Oddington. Glos 3H 49
Upper Ollach. High 5E 155
Upper Outwoods. Staf 3G 73
Upper Padley. Derbs 3G 85
Upper Pennington. Hants 3B 16
Upper Poppleton. York 4H 99
Upper Quinton. Warw 1G 49
Upper Rissington. Glos 4H 49
Upper Rochford. Worc 4A 60
Upper Rusko. Dum 3C 110
Upper Sandaig. High 2F 147
Upper Sanday. Orkn 7E 172
Upper Sapey. Here 4A 60
Upper Seagry. Wilts 3E 35
Upper Shelton. C Beds 1H 51
Upper Sheringham. Norf 1D 78

Upper Skelmorlie—West Grafton

Upper Skelmorlie. N Ayr 3C 126
Upper Slaughter. Glos 3G 49
Upper Sonachan. Arg 1H 133
Upper Soudley. Glos 4B 48
Upper Staploe. Bed 5A 64
Upper Stoke. Norf 5E 79
Upper Stondon. C Beds 2B 52
Upper Stowe. Nptn 5D 62
Upper Street. Hants 1G 15
Upper Street. Norf
nr. Horning 4F 79
nr. Hoveton 4F 79
Upper Street. Suff 2E 55
Upper Strensham. Worc 2E 49
Upper Studley. Wilts 1D 22
Upper Sundon. C Beds 3A 52
Upper Swell. Glos 3G 49
Upper Tankersley. S Yor 1H 85
Upper Tean. Staf 2E 73
Upperthong. W Yor 4B 92
Upperthorpe. N Lin 4A 94
Upper Thurnham. Lanc 4D 96
Upper Tillyrie. Per 3D 136
Upperton. W Sus 3A 26
Upper Tooting. G Lon 3D 39
Upper Town. Derbs
nr. Bonsall 5G 85
nr. Hognaston 5G 85
Upper Town. Here 1A 48
Upper Town. N Som 5A 34
Uppertown. Derbs 4H 85
Uppertown. High 1F 169
Uppertown. Nmbd 2B 114
Uppertown. Orkn 8D 172
Upper Tysoe. Warw 1B 50
Upper Upham. Wilts 4H 35
Upper Upnor. Medw 3B 40
Upper Urquhart. Fife 3D 136
Upper Wardington. Oxon 1C 50
Upper Weald. Mil 2F 51
Upper Weedon. Nptn 5D 62
Upper Wellingham. E Sus 4F 27
Upper Whiston. S Yor 2B 86
Upper Wield. Hants 3E 25
Upper Winchendon. Buck 4F 51
Upperwood. Derbs 5G 85
Upper Woodford. Wilts 3G 23
Upper Wootton. Hants 1D 24
Upper Wraxall. Wilts 4D 34
Upper Wyche. Worc 1C 48
Uppincott. Devn 2B 12
Uppingham. Rut 1F 63
Uppington. Shrp 5A 72
Upsall. N Yor 1G 99
Upsettlington. Bord 5E 131
Upshire. Essx 5E 53
Up Somborne. Hants 3B 24
Upstreet. Kent 4G 41
Up Sydling. Dors 2B 14
Upthorpe. Suff 3B 66
Upton. Buck 4F 51
Upton. Cambs 3A 64
Upton. Ches W 4G 83
Upton. Corn
nr. Bude 2C 10
nr. Liskeard 5C 10
Upton. Cumb 1E 102
Upton. Devn
nr. Honiton 2D 12
nr. Kingsbridge 4D 8
Upton. Dors
nr. Poole 3E 15
nr. Weymouth 4C 14
Upton. E Yor 4F 101
Upton. Hants
nr. Andover 1B 24
nr. Southampton 1B 16
Upton. IOW 3D 16
Upton. Leics 1A 62
Upton. Linc 2F 87
Upton. Mers 2E 83
Upton. Norf 4F 79
Upton. Nptn 4E 62
Upton. Notts
nr. Retford 3E 87
nr. Southwell 5E 87
Upton. Oxon 3D 36
Upton. Pemb 4E 43
Upton. Pet 5A 76
Upton. Slo 3A 38
Upton. Som
nr. Somerton 4H 21
nr. Wiveliscombe 4C 20
Upton. Warw 5F 61
Upton. W Yor 3E 93
Upton. Wilts 3D 22
Upton Bishop. Here 3B 48
Upton Cheyney. S Glo 5B 34
Upton Cressett. Shrp 1A 60
Upton Crews. Here 3B 48
Upton Cross. Corn 5C 10
Upton End. C Beds 2B 52
Upton Grey. Hants 2E 25
Upton Heath. Ches W 4G 83
Upton Hellions. Devn 2B 12
Upton Lovell. Wilts 2E 23
Upton Magna. Shrp 4H 71
Upton Noble. Som 3C 22
Upton Pyne. Devn 3C 12
Upton St Leonards. Glos 4D 48
Upton Scudamore. Wilts 2D 22
Upton Snodsbury. Worc 5D 60
Upton upon Severn. Worc 1D 48
Upton Warren. Worc 4D 60
Upwaltham. W Sus 4A 26
Upware. Cambs 3E 65
Upwell. Norf 5E 77
Upwey. Dors 4B 14
Upwick Green. Herts 3E 53
Upwood. Cambs 2B 64
Urafirth. Shet 4E 173
Uragaig. Arg 4A 132
Urchany. High 4C 158
Urchfont. Wilts 1F 23
Urdimarsh. Here 1A 48
Ure. Shet 4D 173
Ure Bank. N Yor 2F 99
Urgha. W Isl 8D 171
Urlay Nook. Stoc T 3B 106
Urmston. G Man 1B 84
Urquhart. Mor 2G 159
Urra. N Yor 4C 106
Urray. High 3H 157
Usan. Ang 3G 145
Ushaw Moor. Dur 5F 115
Usk. Mon 5G 47
Usselby. Linc 1H 87
Usworth. Tyne 4G 115
Utkinton. Ches W 4H 83
Uton. Devn 3B 12
Utterby. Linc 1C 88
Uttoxeter. Staf 2E 73
Uwchmynydd. Gwyn 3A 68
Uxbridge. G Lon 2B 38
Uyeasound. Shet 1G 173
Uzmaston. Pemb 3D 42

V

Valley. IOA 3B 80
Valley End. Surr 4A 38
Valley Truckle. Corn 4B 10
Valsgarth. Shet 1H 173
Valtos. High 2E 155
Van. Powy 2B 58
Vange. Essx 2B 40
Varteg. Torf 5F 47
Vatsetter. Shet 3G 173
Vatten. High 4B 154
Vaul. Arg 4B 138
The Vauld. Here 1A 48
Vaynor. Mer T 4D 46
Veensgarth. Shet 7F 173
Velindre. Powy 2E 47
Vellow. Som 3D 20
Velly. Devn 4C 18
Veness. Orkn 5E 172
Venhay. Devn 1A 12
Venn. Devn 4D 8
Venngreen. Devn 1D 11
Vennington. Shrp 5F 71
Venn Ottery. Devn 3D 12
Venn's Green. Here 1A 48
Venny Tedburn. Devn 3B 12
Venterdon. Corn 5D 10
Ventnor. IOW 5D 16
Vernham Dean. Hants 1B 24
Vernham Street. Hants 1B 24
Vernolds Common. Shrp 2G 59
Verwood. Dors 2F 15
Veryan. Corn 5D 6
Veryan Green. Corn 5D 6
Vicarage. Devn 4F 13
Vickerstown. Cumb 3A 96
Victoria. Corn 2D 6
Victoria Bridge. Derr 3F 176
Vidlin. Shet 5F 173
Viewpark. N Lan 3A 128
Vigo. W Mid 5E 73
Vigo Village. Kent 4H 39
Vinehall Street. E Sus 3B 28
Vine's Cross. E Sus 4G 27
Viney Hill. Glos 5B 48
Virginia Water. Surr 4A 38
Virginstow. Devn 3D 11
Vobster. Som 2C 22
Voe. Shet
nr. Hillside 5F 173
nr. Swinister 3E 173
Vole. Som 2G 21
Vowchurch. Here 2G 47
Voxter. Shet 4E 173
Voy. Orkn 6B 172
Vulcan Village. Mers 1H 83

W

Waberthwaite. Cumb 5C 102
Wackerfield. Dur 2E 105
Wacton. Norf 1D 66
Wadbister. Shet 7F 173
Wadborough. Worc 1E 49
Wadbrook. Devn 2G 13
Waddesdon. Buck 4F 51
Waddeton. Devn 3E 9
Waddicar. Mers 1F 83
Waddingham. Linc 1G 87
Waddington. Lanc 5G 97
Waddington. Linc 4G 87
Waddon. Devn 5B 12
Wadebridge. Corn 1D 6
Wadeford. Som 1G 13
Wadenhoe. Nptn 2H 63
Wadesmill. Herts 4D 52
Wadhurst. E Sus 2H 27
Wadshelf. Derbs 3H 85
Wadsley. S Yor 1H 85
Wadsley Bridge. S Yor 1H 85
Wadswick. Wilts 5D 34
Wadwick. Hants 1C 24
Wadworth. S Yor 1C 86
Waen. Den
nr. Llandymog 4D 82
nr. Nantglyn 4B 82
Waen. Powy 1E 58
Waen Fach. Powy 4E 70
Waen Goleugoed. Den 3C 82
Wag. High 1H 165
Wainfleet All Saints. Linc 5D 89
Wainfleet Bank. Linc 5D 88
Wainfleet St Mary. Linc 5D 89
Wainhouse Corner. Corn 3B 10
Wainscott. Medw 3B 40
Wainstalls. W Yor 2A 92
Waitby. Cumb 4A 104
Waithe. Linc 4F 95
Wakefield. W Yor 2D 92
Wakerley. Nptn 1G 63
Wakes Colne. Essx 3B 54
Walberswick. Suff 3G 67
Walberton. W Sus 5A 26
Walbottle. Tyne 3E 115
Walby. Cumb 3F 113
Walcombe. Som 2A 22
Walcot. Linc 2H 75
Walcot. N Lin 2B 94
Walcot. Swin 3G 35
Walcot. Telf 4H 71
Walcot. Warw 5F 61
Walcote. Leics 2C 62
Walcot Green. Norf 2D 66
Walcott. Linc 5A 88
Walcott. Norf 2F 79
Walden. N Yor 1C 98
Walden Head. N Yor 1B 98
Walden Stubbs. N Yor 3F 93
Walderslade. Medw 4B 40
Walderton. W Sus 1F 17
Walditch. Dors 3H 13
Waldley. Derbs 2F 73
Waldridge. Dur 4F 115
Waldringfield. Suff 1F 55
Waldron. E Sus 4G 27
Wales. S Yor 2B 86
Walesby. Linc 1A 88
Walesby. Notts 3D 86
Walford. Here
nr. Leintwardine 3F 59
nr. Ross-on-Wye 3A 48
Walford. Shrp 3G 71
Walford. Staf 2C 72
Walford Heath. Shrp 4G 71
Walgherton. Ches E 1A 72
Walgrave. Nptn 3F 63
Walhampton. Hants 3B 16
Walkden. G Man 4F 91
Walker. Tyne 3F 115
Walkerburn. Bord 1F 119
Walker Fold. Lanc 5F 97
Walkeringham. Notts 1E 87
Walkerith. Linc 1E 87
Walkern. Herts 3C 52
Walker's Green. Here 1A 48
Walkerton. Fife 3E 137
Walkerville. N Yor 5F 105
Walkford. Dors 3H 15
Walkhampton. Devn 2B 8
Walkington. E Yor 1C 94
Walkley. S Yor 2H 85
Walk Mill. Lanc 1G 91
Wall. Corn 3D 4
Wall. Nmbd 3C 114
Wall. Staf 5F 73
Wallaceton. Dum 1F 111
Wallacetown. Shet 6E 173
Wallacetown. S Ayr
nr. Ayr 2C 116
nr. Dailly 4B 116
Wallands Park. E Sus 4F 27
Wallasey. Mers 1E 83
Wallaston Green. Pemb 4D 42
Wallbrook. W Mid 1D 60
Wallcrouch. E Sus 2A 28
Wall End. Cumb 1B 96
Wallend. Medw 3C 40
Wall Heath. W Mid 2C 60
Wallingford. Oxon 3E 36
Wallington. G Lon 4D 39
Wallington. Hants 2D 16
Wallington. Herts 2C 52
Wallis. Pemb 2E 43
Wallisdown. Bour 3F 15
Walliswood. Surr 2C 26
Wall Nook. Dur 5F 115
Walls. Shet 7D 173
Wallsend. Tyne 3G 115
Wallsworth. Glos 3D 48
Wall under Heywood.
Shrp 1H 59
Wallyford. E Lot 2G 129
Walmer. Kent 5H 41
Walmer Bridge. Lanc 2C 90
Walmersley. G Man 3G 91
Walmley. W Mid 1F 61
Walnut Grove. Per 1D 136
Walpole. Suff 3F 67
Walpole Cross Keys. Norf 4E 77
Walpole Gate. Norf 4E 77
Walpole Highway. Norf 4E 77
Walpole Marsh. Norf 4D 77
Walpole St Andrew. Norf 4E 77
Walpole St Peter. Norf 4E 77
Walsall. W Mid 1E 61
Walsall Wood. W Mid 5E 73
Walsden. W Yor 2H 91
Walsgrave on Sowe.
W Mid 2A 62
Walsham le Willows. Suff 3C 66
Walshaw. G Man 3F 91
Walshford. N Yor 4G 99
Walsoken. Norf 4D 76
Walston. S Lan 5D 128
Walsworth. Herts 2B 52
Walter's Ash. Buck 2G 37
Walterston. V Glam 4D 32
Walterstone. Here 3G 47
Waltham. Kent 1F 29
Waltham. NE Lin 4F 95
Waltham Abbey. Essx 5D 53
Waltham Chase. Hants 1D 16
Waltham Cross. Herts 5D 52
Waltham on the Wolds.
Leics 3F 75
Waltham St Lawrence.
Wind 4G 37
Waltham's Cross. Essx 2G 53
Walthamstow. G Lon 2E 39
Walton. Cumb 3G 113
Walton. Derbs 4A 86
Walton. Leics 2C 62
Walton. Mers 1F 83
Walton. Mil 2G 51
Walton. Pet 5A 76
Walton. Powy 5E 59
Walton. Som 3H 21
Walton. Staf
nr. Eccleshall 3C 72
nr. Stone 2C 72
Walton. Suff 2F 55
Walton. Telf 4H 71
Walton. Warw 5G 61
Walton. W Yor
nr. Wakefield 3D 92
nr. Wetherby 5G 99
Walton Cardiff. Glos 2E 49
Walton East. Pemb 2E 43
Walton Elm. Dors 1C 14
Walton Highway. Norf 4D 77
Walton in Gordano.
N Som 4H 33
Walton-le-Dale. Lanc 2D 90
Walton-on-Thames. Surr 4C 38
Walton on the Hill. Surr 5D 38
Walton-on-the-Hill. Staf 3D 72
Walton-on-the-Naze.
Essx 3F 55
Walton on the Wolds.
Leics 4C 74
Walton-on-Trent. Derbs 4G 73
Walton West. Pemb 3C 42
Walwick. Nmbd 2C 114
Walworth. Darl 3F 105
Walworth Gate. Darl 2F 105
Walwyn's Castle. Pemb 3C 42
Wambrook. Som 2F 13
Wampool. Cumb 4D 112
Wanborough. Surr 1A 26
Wanborough. Swin 3H 35
Wandel. S Lan 2B 118
Wandsworth. G Lon 3D 38
Wangford. Suff
nr. Lakenheath 2G 65
nr. Southwold 3G 67
Wanlip. Leics 4C 74
Wanlockhead. Dum 3A 118
Wannock. E Sus 5G 27
Wansford. E Yor 4E 101
Wansford. Pet 1H 63
Wanshurst Green. Kent 1B 28
Wanstead. G Lon 2F 39
Wanstrow. Som 2C 22
Wanswell. Glos 5B 48
Wantage. Oxon 3C 36
Wapley. S Glo 4C 34
Wappenbury. Warw 4A 62
Wappenham. Nptn 1E 51
Warbleton. E Sus 4H 27
Warblington. Hants 2F 17
Warborough. Oxon 2D 36
Warboys. Cambs 2C 64
Warbreck. Bkpl 1B 90
Warbstow. Corn 3C 10
Warburton. G Man 2B 84
Warcop. Cumb 3A 104
Warden. Kent 3E 40
Warden. Nmbd 3C 114
Ward End. W Mid 2F 61
Ward Green. Suff 4C 66
Ward Green Cross. Lanc 1E 91
Wardhedges. C Beds 2A 52
Wardhouse. Abers 5C 160
Wardington. Oxon 1C 50
Wardle. Ches E 5A 84
Wardle. G Man 3H 91
Wardley. Rut 5F 75
Wardley. W Sus 4G 25
Wardlow. Derbs 3F 85
Wardsend. Ches E 2D 84
Wardy Hill. Cambs 2D 64
Ware. Herts 4D 52
Ware. Kent 4G 41
Wareham. Dors 4E 15
Warehorne. Kent 2D 28
Warenford. Nmbd 2F 121
Waren Mill. Nmbd 1F 121
Warenton. Nmbd 1F 121
Wareside. Herts 4D 53
Waresley. Cambs 5B 64
Waresley. Worc 4C 60
Warfield. Brac 4G 37
Warfleet. Devn 3E 9
Wargate. Linc 2B 76
Wargrave. Wok 4F 37
Warham. Norf 1B 78
Waringsford. Arm 5G 179
Waringstown. Arm 4F 178
Wark. Nmbd
nr. Coldstream 1C 120
nr. Hexham 2B 114
Warkleigh. Devn 4G 19
Warkton. Nptn 3F 63
Warkworth. Nptn 1C 50
Warkworth. Nmbd 4G 121
Warlaby. N Yor 5A 106
Warland. W Yor 2H 91
Warleggan. Corn 2F 7
Warlingham. Surr 5E 39
Warmanbie. Dum 3C 112
Warmfield. W Yor 2D 93
Warmingham. Ches E 4B 84
Warminghurst. W Sus 4C 26
Warmington. Nptn 1H 63
Warmington. Warw 1C 50
Warminster. Wilts 2D 23
Warmley. S Glo 4B 34
Warmsworth. S Yor 4F 93
Warmwell. Dors 4C 14
Warndon. Worc 5C 60
Warners End. Herts 5A 52
Warnford. Hants 4E 24
Warnham. W Sus 2C 26
Warningcamp. W Sus 5B 26
Warninglid. W Sus 3D 26
Warren. Ches E 3C 84
Warren. Pemb 5D 42
Warrenby. Red C 2C 106
Warren Corner. Hants
nr. Aldershot 2G 25
nr. Petersfield 4F 25
Warrenpoint. New M 8F 178
Warren Row. Wind 3G 37
Warren Street. Kent 5D 40
Warrington. Mil 5F 63
Warrington. Warr 2A 84
Warsash. Hants 2C 16
Warse. High 1F 169
Warslow. Staf 5E 85
Warsop. Notts 4C 86
Warsop Vale. Notts 4C 86
Warter. E Yor 4C 100
Warthermarske. N Yor 2E 98
Warthill. N Yor 4A 100
Wartling. E Sus 5A 28
Wartnaby. Leics 3E 74
Warton. Lanc
nr. Carnforth 2D 97
nr. Freckleton 2C 90
Warton. Nmbd 4E 121
Warton. Warw 5G 73
Warwick. Warw 4G 61
Warwick Bridge. Cumb 4F 113
Warwick-on-Eden. Cumb 4F 113
Warwick Wold. Surr 5E 39
Wasbister. Orkn 4C 172
Wasdale Head. Cumb 4C 102
Wash. Derbs 2E 85
Washaway. Corn 2E 7
Washbourne. Devn 3D 9
Washbrook. Suff 1E 54
Wash Common. W Ber 5C 36
Washerwall. Staf 1D 72
Washfield. Devn 1C 12
Washfold. N Yor 4D 104
Washford. Som 2D 20
Washford Pyne. Devn 1B 12
Washingborough. Linc 3H 87
Washington. Tyne 4G 115
Washington. W Sus 4C 26
Washington Village.
Tyne 4G 115
Waskerley. Dur 5D 114
Wasperton. Warw 5G 61
Wasp Green. Surr 1E 27
Wasps Nest. Linc 4H 87
Wass. N Yor 2H 99
Watchet. Som 2D 20
Watchfield. Oxon 2H 35
Watchgate. Cumb 5G 103
Watchhill. Cumb 5C 112
Watcombe. Torb 2F 9
Watendlath. Cumb 3D 102
Water. Devn 4A 12
Water. Lanc 2G 91
Waterbeach. Cambs 4D 65
Waterbeach. W Sus 2G 17
Waterbeck. Dum 2D 112
Waterditch. Hants 3G 15
Water End. C Beds 2A 52
Water End. E Yor 1A 94
Water End. Essx 1F 53
Water End. Herts
nr. Hatfield 5C 52
nr. Hemel Hempstead 4A 52
Waterfall. Staf 5E 85
Waterfoot. Caus 4J 175
Waterfoot. E Ren 4G 127
Waterfoot. Lanc 2G 91
Waterford. Herts 4D 52
Water Fryston. W Yor 2E 93
Waterhead. Cumb 4E 103
Waterhead. E Ayr 3E 117
Waterhead. S Ayr 5C 116
Waterheads. Bord 4F 129
Waterhouses. Dur 5E 115
Waterhouses. Staf 5E 85
Wateringbury. Kent 5A 40
Waterlane. Glos 5E 49
Waterlip. Som 2B 22
Waterloo. Cphy 3E 33
Waterloo. Corn 5B 10
Waterloo. Here 1G 47
Waterloo. High 1E 147
Waterloo. Mers 1F 83
Waterloo. Norf 4E 78
Waterloo. N Lan 4B 128
Waterloo. Pemb 4D 42
Waterloo. Per 5H 143
Waterloo. Pool 3F 15
Waterloo. Shrp 2G 71
Waterlooville. Hants 2E 17
Watermead. Buck 4G 51
Watermillock. Cumb 2F 103
Water Newton. Cambs 1A 64
Water Orton. Warw 1F 61
Waterperry. Oxon 5E 51
Waterrow. Som 4D 20
Watersfield. W Sus 4B 26
Waterside. Buck 5H 51
Waterside. Cambs 3F 65
Waterside. Cumb 5D 112
Waterside. E Ayr
nr. Ayr 4D 116
nr. Kilmarnock 5F 127
Waterside. E Dun 2H 127
Waterstein. High 4A 154
Waterstock. Oxon 5E 51
Waterston. Pemb 4D 42
Water Stratford. Buck 2E 51
Waters Upton. Telf 4A 72
Water Yeat. Cumb 1B 96
Watford. Herts 1C 38
Watford. Nptn 4D 62
Wath. Cumb 4H 103
Wath. N Yor
nr. Pateley Bridge 3D 98
nr. Ripon 2F 99
Wath Brow. Cumb 3B 102
Wath upon Dearne. S Yor 4E 93
Watlington. Norf 4F 77
Watlington. Oxon 2E 37
Watten. High 3E 169
Wattisfield. Suff 3C 66
Wattisham. Suff 5C 66
Wattlesborough Heath.
Shrp 4F 71
Watton. Dors 3H 13
Watton. E Yor 4E 101
Watton. Norf 5B 78
Watton at Stone. Herts 4C 52
Wattston. N Lan 2A 128
Wattstown. Rhon 2D 32
Wattsville. Cphy 2F 33
Wauldby. E Yor 2C 94
Waulkmill. Abers 4D 152
Waun. Powy 4E 71
Y Waun. Wrex 2E 71
Waunarlwydd. Swan 3F 31
Waun Fawr. Cdgn 2F 57
Waunfawr. Gwyn 5E 81
Waungilwen. Carm 1H 43
Waun-Lwyd. Blae 5E 47
Waun y Clyn. Carm 5E 45
Wavendon. Mil 2H 51
Waverbridge. Cumb 5D 112
Waverley. Surr 2G 25
Waverton. Ches W 4G 83
Waverton. Cumb 5D 112
Wavertree. Mers 2F 83
Wawne. E Yor 1D 94
Waxham. Norf 3G 79
Waxholme. E Yor 2G 95
Wayford. Som 2H 13
Way Head. Cambs 2D 65
Waytown. Dors 3H 13
Way Village. Devn 1B 12
Wdig. Pemb 1D 42
Wealdstone. G Lon 2C 38
Weardley. W Yor 5E 99
Weare. Som 1H 21
Weare Giffard. Devn 4E 19
Wearhead. Dur 1B 104
Wearne. Som 4H 21
Weasdale. Cumb 4H 103
Weasenham All Saints.
Norf 3H 77
Weasenham St Peter.
Norf 3A 78
Weaverham. Ches W 3A 84
Weaverthorpe. N Yor 2D 100
Webheath. Worc 4E 61
Webton. Here 2H 47
Wedderlairs. Abers 5F 161
Weddington. Warw 1A 62
Wedhampton. Wilts 1F 23
Wedmore. Som 2H 21
Wednesbury. W Mid 1D 61
Wednesfield. W Mid 5D 72
Weecar. Notts 4F 87
Weedon. Buck 4G 51
Weedon Bec. Nptn 5D 62
Weedon Lois. Nptn 1E 50
Weeford. Staf 5F 73
Week. Devn
nr. Barnstaple 4F 19
nr. Okehampton 2G 11
nr. South Molton 1H 11
nr. Totnes 2D 9
Week. Som 3C 20
Weeke. Devn 2A 12
Weeke. Hants 3C 24
Week Green. Corn 3C 10
Weekley. Nptn 2F 63
Week St Mary. Corn 3C 10
Weel. E Yor 1D 94
Weeley. Essx 3E 55
Weeley Heath. Essx 3E 55
Weem. Per 4F 143
Weeping Cross. Staf 3D 72
Weethly. Warw 5E 61
Weeting. Norf 2G 65
Weeton. E Yor 2G 95
Weeton. Lanc 1B 90
Weeton. N Yor 5E 99
Weetwood Hall. Nmbd 2E 121
Weir. Lanc 2G 91
Welborne. Norf 4C 78
Welbourn. Linc 5G 87
Welburn. N Yor
nr. Kirkbymoorside 1A 100
nr. Malton 3B 100
Welbury. N Yor 4A 106
Welby. Linc 2G 75
Welches Dam. Cambs 2D 64
Welcombe. Devn 1C 10
Weld Bank. Lanc 3D 90
Weldon. Nptn 2G 63
Weldon. Nmbd 5F 121
Welford. Nptn 2D 62
Welford. W Ber 4C 36
Welford-on-Avon. Warw 5F 61
Welham. Leics 1E 63
Welham. Notts 2E 87
Welham Green. Herts 5C 52
Well. Hants 2F 25
Well. Linc 3D 88
Well. N Yor 1E 99
Welland. Worc 1C 48
Wellbank. Ang 5D 144
Well Bottom. Dors 1E 15
Welldale. Dum 3C 112
Wellesbourne. Warw 5G 61
Well Hill. Kent 4F 39
Wellhouse. W Ber 4D 36
Welling. G Lon 3F 39
Wellingborough. Nptn 4F 63
Wellingham. Norf 3A 78
Wellingore. Linc 5G 87
Wellington. Cumb 4B 102
Wellington. Here 1H 47
Wellington. Som 4E 21
Wellington. Telf 4A 72
Wellington Heath. Here 1C 48
Wellow. Bath 1C 22
Wellow. IOW 4B 16
Wellow. Notts 4D 86
Wellpond Green. Herts 3E 53
Wells. Som 2A 22
Wellsborough. Leics 5A 74
Wells Green. Ches E 5A 84
Wells-next-the-Sea. Norf 1B 78
Wellswood. Torb 2F 9
Wellwood. Fife 1D 129
Welney. Norf 1E 65
Welsford. Devn 4C 18
Welshampton. Shrp 2G 71
Welsh End. Shrp 2H 71
Welsh Frankton. Shrp 2F 71
Welsh Hook. Pemb 2D 42
Welsh Newton. Here 4H 47
Welsh Newton Common.
Here 4A 48
Welshpool. Powy 5E 70
Welsh St Donats. V Glam 4D 32
Welton. Bath 1B 22
Welton. Cumb 5E 113
Welton. E Yor 2C 94
Welton. Linc 2H 87
Welton. Nptn 4C 62
Welton Hill. Linc 2H 87
Welton le Marsh. Linc 4D 88
Welton le Wold. Linc 2B 88
Welwick. E Yor 2G 95
Welwyn. Herts 4C 52
Welwyn Garden City.
Herts 4C 52
Wem. Shrp 3H 71
Wembdon. Som 3F 21
Wembley. G Lon 2C 38
Wembury. Devn 4B 8
Wembworthy. Devn 2G 11
Wemyss Bay. Inv 2C 126
Wenallt. Cdgn 3F 57
Wenallt. Gwyn 1B 70
Wendens Ambo. Essx 2F 53
Wendlebury. Oxon 4D 50
Wendling. Norf 4B 78
Wendover. Buck 5G 51
Wendron. Corn 5A 6
Wendy. Cambs 1D 52
Wenfordbridge. Corn 5A 10
Wenhaston. Suff 3G 67
Wennington. Cambs 3B 64
Wennington. G Lon 2G 39
Wennington. Lanc 2F 97
Wensley. Derbs 4G 85
Wensley. N Yor 1C 98
Wentbridge. W Yor 3E 93
Wentnor. Shrp 1F 59
Wentworth. Cambs 3D 65
Wentworth. S Yor 1A 86
Wenvoe. V Glam 4E 32
Weobley. Here 5G 59
Weobley Marsh. Here 5G 59
Wepham. W Sus 5B 26
Wereham. Norf 5F 77
Wergs. W Mid 5C 72
Wern. Gwyn 1E 69
Wern. Powy
nr. Brecon 4E 46
nr. Guilsfield 4E 71
nr. Llangadfan 4B 70
nr. Llanymynech 3E 71
Wernffrwd. Swan 3E 31
Wernyrheolydd. Mon 4G 47
Werrington. Corn 4D 10
Werrington. Pet 5A 76
Werrington. Staf 1D 72
Wervin. Ches W 3G 83
Wesham. Lanc 1C 90
Wessington. Derbs 5A 86
West Aberthaw. V Glam 5D 32
West Acre. Norf 4G 77
West Allerdean. Nmbd 5F 131
West Alvington. Devn 4D 8
West Amesbury. Wilts 2G 23
West Anstey. Devn 4B 20
West Appleton. N Yor 5F 105
West Ardsley. W Yor 2C 92
West Arthurlie. E Ren 4F 127
West Ashby. Linc 3B 88
West Ashling. W Sus 2G 17
West Ashton. Wilts 1D 23
West Auckland. Dur 2E 105
West Ayton. N Yor 1D 101
West Bagborough. Som 3E 21
West Bank. Hal 2H 83
West Barkwith. Linc 2A 88
West Barnby. N Yor 3F 107
West Barns. E Lot 2C 130
West Barsham. Norf 2B 78
West Bay. Dors 3H 13
West Beckham. Norf 2D 78
West Bennan. N Ayr 3D 123
Westbere. Kent 4F 41
West Bergholt. Essx 3C 54
West Bexington. Dors 4A 14
West Bilney. Norf 4G 77
West Blackdene. Dur 1B 104
West Blatchington. Brig 5D 27
Westborough. Linc 1F 75
Westbourne. Bour 3F 15
Westbourne. W Sus 2F 17
West Bowling. W Yor 1B 92
West Brabourne. Kent 1E 29
West Bradford. Lanc 5G 97
West Bradley. Som 3A 22
West Bretton. W Yor 3C 92
West Bridgford. Notts 2C 74
West Briggs. Norf 4F 77
West Bromwich. W Mid 1E 61
Westbrook. Here 1F 47
Westbrook. Kent 3H 41
Westbrook. Wilts 5E 35
West Buckland. Devn
nr. Barnstaple 3G 19
nr. Thurlestone 4C 8
West Buckland. Som 4E 21
West Burnside. Abers 1G 145
West Burrafirth. Shet 6D 173
West Burton. N Yor 1C 98
West Burton. W Sus 4B 26
Westbury. Buck 2E 50
Westbury. Shrp 5F 71
Westbury. Wilts 1D 22
Westbury Leigh. Wilts 1D 22
Westbury-on-Severn.
Glos 4C 48
Westbury on Trym. Bris 4A 34
Westbury-sub-Mendip.
Som 2A 22
West Butsfield. Dur 5E 115
West Butterwick. N Lin 4B 94
Westby. Linc 3G 75
West Byfleet. Surr 4B 38
West Caister. Norf 4H 79
West Calder. W Lot 3D 128
West Camel. Som 4A 22
West Carr. N Lin 4H 93
West Chaldon. Dors 4C 14
West Challow. Oxon 3B 36
West Charleton. Devn 4D 8
West Chelborough. Dors 2A 14
West Chevington. Nmbd 5G 121
West Chiltington. W Sus 4B 26
West Chiltington Common.
W Sus 4B 26
West Chinnock. Som 1H 13
West Chisenbury. Wilts 1G 23
West Clandon. Surr 5B 38
West Cliffe. Kent 1H 29
Westcliff-on-Sea. S'end 2C 40
West Clyne. High 3F 165
West Coker. Som 1A 14
Westcombe. Som
nr. Evercreech 3B 22
nr. Somerton 4H 21
West Compton. Dors 3A 14
West Compton. Som 2A 22
West Cornforth. Dur 1A 106
Westcot. Oxon 3B 36
Westcott. Buck 4F 51
Westcott. Devn 2D 12
Westcott. Surr 1C 26
Westcott Barton. Oxon 3C 50
West Cowick. E Yor 2G 93
West Cranmore. Som 2B 22
West Croftmore. High 2D 150
West Cross. Swan 4F 31
West Cullerlie. Abers 3E 153
West Culvennan. Dum 3H 109
West Curry. Corn 3C 10
West Curthwaite. Cumb 5E 113
West Dean. W Sus 1G 17
West Dean. Wilts 4A 24
Westdean. E Sus 5G 27
West Deeping. Linc 5A 76
West Derby. Mers 1F 83
West Dereham. Norf 5F 77
West Down. Devn 2F 19
Westdowns. Corn 4A 10
West Drayton. G Lon 3B 38
West Drayton. Notts 3E 86
West Dunnet. High 1E 169
West Ella. E Yor 2D 94
West End. Bed 5G 63
West End. Cambs 1D 64
West End. Dors 2E 15
West End. E Yor
nr. Kilham 3E 101
nr. Preston 1E 95
nr. South Cove 1C 94
nr. Ulrome 4F 101
West End. G Lon 2D 39
West End. Hants 1C 16
West End. Herts 5C 52
West End. Kent 4F 41
West End. Lanc 3D 96
West End. Linc 1C 76
West End. Norf 4H 79
West End. N Som 5H 33
West End. N Yor 4D 98
West End. S Glo 3C 34
West End. S Lan 5C 128
West End. Surr 4A 38
West End. Wilts 4E 23
West End. Wind 4G 37
West End Green. Hants 5E 37
Westenhanger. Kent 2F 29
Wester Aberchalder.
High 2H 149
Wester Balgedie. Per 3D 136
Wester Brae. High 2A 158
Wester Culbeuchly.
Abers 2D 160
Westerdale. High 3D 168
Westerdale. N Yor 4D 106
Wester Dechmont.
W Lot 2D 128
Wester Fearn. High 5D 164
Westerfield. Suff 1E 55
Wester Galcantray. High 4C 158
Westergate. W Sus 5A 26
Wester Gruinards. High 4C 164
Westerham. Kent 5F 39
Westerleigh. S Glo 4C 34
Westerloch. High 3F 169
Wester Mandally. High 3E 149
Wester Quarff. Shet 8F 173
Wester Rarichie. High 1C 158
Wester Shian. Per 5F 143
Wester Skeld. Shet 7D 173
Westerton. Ang 3F 145
Westerton. Dur 1F 105
Westerton. W Sus 2G 17
Westerwick. Shet 7D 173
West Farleigh. Kent 5B 40
West Farndon. Nptn 5C 62
West Felton. Shrp 3F 71
Westfield. Cumb 2A 102
Westfield. E Sus 4C 28
Westfield. High 2C 168
Westfield. Norf 5B 78
Westfield. N Lan 2A 128
Westfield. W Lot 2C 128
Westfields. Dors 2C 14
Westfields of Rattray.
Per 4A 144
West Fleetham. Nmbd 2F 121
Westford. Som 4E 20
West Garforth. W Yor 1D 93
Westgate. Dur 1C 104
Westgate. Norf 1B 78
Westgate. N Lin 4A 94
Westgate on Sea. Kent 3H 41
West Ginge. Oxon 3C 36
West Grafton. Wilts 5H 35

West Green—Witcham

West Green. Hants 1F 25
West Grimstead. Wilts 4H 23
West Grinstead. W Sus 3C 26
West Haddlesey. N Yor 2F 93
West Haddon. Nptn 3D 62
West Hagbourne. Oxon 3D 36
West Hagley. Worc 2D 60
West Hall. Cumb 3G 113
Westhall. Suff 2G 67
West Hallam. Derbs 1B 74
Westhall Terrace. Ang 5D 144
West Halton. N Lin 2C 94
West Ham. G Lon 2E 39
Westham. Dors 5B 14
Westham. E Sus 5H 27
Westham. Som 2H 21
Westhampnett. W Sus 2G 17
West Handley. Derbs 3A 86
West Hanney. Oxon 2C 36
West Hanningfield. Essx 1B 40
West Hardwick. W Yor 3E 93
West Harptree. Bath 1A 22
West Harting. W Sus 4F 25
West Harton. Tyne 3G 115
West Hatch. Som 4F 21
Westhay. Som 2H 21
West Head. Norf 5E 77
Westhead. Lanc 4C 90
West Heath. Hants
nr. Basingstoke 1D 24
nr. Farnborough 1G 25
West Helmsdale. High 2H 165
West Hendred. Oxon 3C 36
West Heogaland. Shet 4D 173
West Heslerton. N Yor 2D 100
West Hewish. N Som 5G 33
Westhide. Here 1A 48
West Hill. Devn 3D 12
West Hill. E Yor 3F 101
West Hill. N Som 4H 33
West Hill. W Sus 2E 27
Westhill. Abers 3F 153
Westhill. High 4B 158
West Hoathly. W Sus 2E 27
West Holme. Dors 4D 15
Westhope. Here 5G 59
Westhope. Shrp 2G 59
West Horndon. Essx 2H 39
Westhorp. Nptn 5C 62
Westhorpe. Linc 2B 76
Westhorpe. Suff 4C 66
West Horrington. Som 2A 22
West Horsley. Surr 5B 38
West Horton. Nmbd 1E 121
West Hougham. Kent 1G 29
Westhoughton. G Man 4E 91
West Houlland. Shet 6D 173
Westhouse. N Yor 2F 97
Westhouses. Derbs 5B 86
West Howe. Bour 3F 15
Westhumble. Surr 5C 38
West Huntspill. Som 2G 21
West Hyde. Herts 1B 38
West Hynish. Arg 5A 138
West Hythe. Kent 2F 29
West Ilsley. W Ber 3C 36
Westing. Shet 1G 173
West Keal. Linc 4C 88
West Kennett. Wilts 5G 35
West Kilbride. N Ayr 5D 126
West Kingsdown. Kent 4G 39
West Kington. Wilts 4D 34
West Kirby. Mers 2E 82
West Knapton. N Yor 2C 100
West Knighton. Dors 4C 14
West Knoyle. Wilts 3D 22
West Kyloe. Nmbd 5G 131
Westlake. Devn 3C 8
West Lambrook. Som 1H 13
West Langdon. Kent 1H 29
West Langwell. High 3D 164
West Lavington. W Sus 4G 25
West Lavington. Wilts 1F 23
West Layton. N Yor 4E 105
West Leake. Notts 3C 74
West Learmouth. Nmbd 1C 120
West Leigh. Devn 2G 11
Westleigh. Devn
nr. Bideford 4E 19
nr. Tiverton 1D 12
Westleigh. G Man 4E 91
West Leith. Herts 4H 51
Westleton. Suff 4G 67
West Lexham. Norf 4H 77
Westley. Shrp 5F 71
Westley. Suff 4H 65
Westley Waterless. Cambs 5F 65
West Lilling. N Yor 3A 100
West Lingo. Fife 3G 137
Westlington. Buck 4F 51
West Linton. Bord 4E 129
Westlinton. Cumb 3E 113
West Littleton. S Glo 4C 34
West Looe. Corn 3G 7
West Lulworth. Dors 4D 14
West Lutton. N Yor 3D 100
West Lydford. Som 3A 22
West Lyng. Som 4G 21
West Lynn. Norf 4F 77
West Mains. Per 2B 136
West Malling. Kent 5A 40
West Malvern. Worc 1C 48
Westmancote. Worc 2E 49
West Marden. W Sus 1F 17
West Markham. Notts 3E 86
West Marsh. NE Lin 4F 95
Westmarsh. Kent 4G 41
West Marton. N Yor 4A 98
West Meon. Hants 4E 25
West Mersea. Essx 4D 54
Westmeston. E Sus 4E 27
Westmill. Herts
nr. Buntingford 3D 52
nr. Hitchin 2B 52
West Milton. Dors 3A 14
Westminster. G Lon 3D 39
West Molesey. Surr 4C 38
West Monkton. Som 4F 21
Westmoor End. Cumb 1B 102
West Moors. Dors 2F 15
West Morden. Dors 3E 15
West Muir. Ang 2E 145
Westmuir. Ang 3C 144
West Murkle. High 2D 168
West Ness. N Yor 2A 100
Westness. Orkn 5C 172
West Newton. E Yor 1E 95
West Newton. Norf 3F 77
West Newton. Som 4F 21
Westnewton. Cumb 5C 112
Westnewton. Nmbd 1D 120
West Norwood. G Lon 3E 39
Westoe. Tyne 3G 115
West Ogwell. Devn 2E 9
Weston. Bath 5C 34
Weston. Ches E
nr. Crewe 5B 84
nr. Macclesfield 3C 84
Weston. Devn
nr. Honiton 2E 13
nr. Sidmouth 4E 13
Weston. Dors
nr. Weymouth 5B 14
nr. Yeovil 2A 14
Weston. Hal 2H 83
Weston. Hants 4F 25
Weston. Here 5F 59
Weston. Herts 2C 52
Weston. Linc 3B 76
Weston. Nptn 1D 50
Weston. Notts 4E 87
Weston. Shrp
nr. Bridgnorth 1H 59
nr. Knighton 3F 59
nr. Wem 3H 71
Weston. S Lan 5D 128
Weston. Staf 3D 73
Weston. Suff 2G 67
Weston. W Ber 4B 36
Weston Bampfylde. Som 4B 22
Weston Beggard. Here 1A 48
Westonbirt. Glos 3D 34
Weston by Welland. Nptn 1E 63
Weston Colville. Cambs 5F 65
Westoncommon. Shrp 3G 71
Weston Coyney. Stoke 1D 72
Weston Ditch. Suff 3F 65
Weston Favell. Nptn 4E 63
Weston Green. Cambs 5F 65
Weston Green. Norf 4D 78
Weston Heath. Shrp 4B 72
Weston Hills. Linc 4B 76
Weston in Arden. Warw 2A 62
Westoning. C Beds 2A 52
Weston in Gordano.
N Som 4H 33
Weston Jones. Staf 3B 72
Weston Longville. Norf 4D 78
Weston Lullingfields.
Shrp 3G 71
Weston-on-Avon. Warw 5F 61
Weston-on-the-Green.
Oxon 4D 50
Weston-on-Trent. Derbs 3B 74
Weston Patrick. Hants 2E 25
Weston Rhyn. Shrp 2E 71
Weston-sub-Edge. Glos 1G 49
Weston-super-Mare.
N Som 5G 33
Weston Town. Som 2C 22
Weston Turville. Buck 4G 51
Weston under Lizard. Staf 4C 72
Weston under Penyard.
Here 3B 48
Weston under Wetherley.
Warw 4A 62
Weston Underwood.
Derbs 1G 73
Weston Underwood. Mil 5F 63
Westonzoyland. Som 3G 21
West Orchard. Dors 1D 14
West Overton. Wilts 5G 35
Westow. N Yor 3B 100
Westown. Per 1E 137
West Panson. Devn 3D 10
West Park. Hart 1B 106
West Parley. Dors 3F 15
West Peckham. Kent 5H 39
West Pelton. Dur 4F 115
West Pennard. Som 3A 22
West Pentire. Corn 2B 6
West Perry. Cambs 4A 64
West Pitcorthie. Fife 3H 137
West Plean. Stir 1B 128
West Poringland. Norf 5E 79
West Porlock. Som 2B 20
Westport. Som 1G 13
West Putford. Devn 1D 10
West Quantoxhead. Som 2E 20
Westra. V Glam 4E 33
West Rainton. Dur 5G 115
West Rasen. Linc 2H 87
West Ravendale. NE Lin 1B 88
Westray Airport. Orkn 2D 172
West Raynham. Norf 3A 78
Westrigg. W Lot 3C 128
West Rounton. N Yor 4B 106
West Row. Suff 3F 65
West Rudham. Norf 3H 77
West Runton. Norf 1D 78
Westruther. Bord 4C 130
Westry. Cambs 1C 64
West Saltoun. E Lot 3A 130
West Sandford. Devn 2B 12
West Sandwick. Shet 3F 173
West Scrafton. N Yor 1C 98
Westside. Orkn 5C 172
West Sleekburn. Nmbd 1F 115
West Somerton. Norf 4G 79
West Stafford. Dors 4C 14
West Stockwith. Notts 1E 87
West Stoke. W Sus 2G 17
West Stonesdale. N Yor 4B 104
West Stoughton. Som 2H 21
West Stour. Dors 4C 22
West Stourmouth. Kent 4G 41
West Stow. Suff 3H 65
West Stowell. Wilts 5G 35
West Strathan. High 2F 167
West Stratton. Hants 2D 24
West Street. Kent 5D 40
West Tanfield. N Yor 2E 99
West Taphouse. Corn 2F 7
West Tarbert. Arg 3G 125
West Thirston. Nmbd 4F 121
West Thorney. W Sus 2F 17
West Thurrock. Thur 3G 39
West Tilbury. Thur 3A 40
West Tisted. Hants 4E 25
West Tofts. Norf 1H 65
West Torrington. Linc 2A 88
West Town. Bath 5A 34
West Town. Hants 3F 17
West Town. N Som 5H 33
West Tytherley. Hants 4A 24
West Tytherton. Wilts 4E 35
West View. Hart 1B 106
Westville. Notts 1C 74
West Walton. Norf 4D 76
Westward. Cumb 5D 112
Westward Ho!. Devn 4E 19
Westwell. Kent 1D 28
Westwell. Oxon 5H 49
Westwell Leacon. Kent 1D 28
West Wellow. Hants 1A 16
West Wemyss. Fife 4F 137
Westwick. N Som 5G 33
Westwick. Cambs 4D 64
Westwick. Dur 3D 104
Westwick. Norf 3E 79
West Wickham. Cambs 1G 53
West Wickham. G Lon 4E 39
West Williamston. Pemb 4E 43
West Willoughby. Linc 1G 75
West Winch. Norf 4F 77
West Winterslow. Wilts 3H 23
West Wittering. W Sus 3F 17
West Witton. N Yor 1C 98
Westwood. Devn 3D 12
Westwood. Kent 4H 41
Westwood. Pet 5A 76
Westwood. S Lan 4H 127
Westwood. Wilts 1D 22
West Woodburn. Nmbd 1B 114
West Woodhay. W Ber 5B 36
West Woodlands. Som 2C 22
West Woodside. Cumb 5E 112
Westwoodside. N Lin 1E 87
West Worldham. Hants 3F 25
West Worlington. Devn 1A 12
West Worthing. W Sus 5C 26
West Wratting. Cambs 5F 65
West Wycombe. Buck 2G 37
West Wylam. Nmbd 3E 115
West Yatton. Wilts 4D 34
West Yell. Shet 3F 173
West Youlstone. Corn 1C 10
Wetheral. Cumb 4F 113
Wetherby. W Yor 5G 99
Wetherden. Suff 4C 66
Wetheringsett. Suff 4D 66
Wethersfield. Essx 2H 53
Wethersta. Shet 5E 173
Wetherup Street. Suff 4D 66
Wetley Rocks. Staf 1D 72
Wettenhall. Ches E 4A 84
Wetton. Staf 5F 85
Wetwang. E Yor 4D 100
Wetwood. Staf 2B 72
Wexcombe. Wilts 1A 24
Wexham Street. Buck 2A 38
Weybourne. Norf 1D 78
Weybourne. Surr 2G 25
Weybread. Suff 2E 67
Weybridge. Surr 4B 38
Weycroft. Devn 3G 13
Weydale. High 2D 168
Weyhill. Hants 2B 24
Weymouth. Dors 204 (5B 14)
Weythel. Powy 5E 59
Whaddon. Buck 2G 51
Whaddon. Cambs 1D 52
Whaddon. Glos 4D 48
Whaddon. Wilts 4G 23
Whale. Cumb 2G 103
Whaley. Derbs 3C 86
Whaley Bridge. Derbs 2E 85
Whaley Thorns. Derbs 3C 86
Whalley. Lanc 1F 91
Whalton. Nmbd 1E 115
Whaplode. Linc 3C 76
Whaplode Drove. Linc 4C 76
Whaplode St Catherine.
Linc 3C 76
Wharfe. N Yor 3G 97
Wharles. Lanc 1C 90
Wharley End. C Beds 1H 51
Wharncliffe Side. S Yor 1G 85
Wharram-le-Street.
N Yor 3C 100
Wharton. Ches W 4A 84
Wharton. Here 5H 59
Whashton. N Yor 4E 105
Whasset. Cumb 1E 97
Whatcote. Warw 1B 50
Whateley. Warw 1G 61
Whatfield. Suff 1D 54
Whatley. Som
nr. Chard 2G 13
nr. Frome 2C 22
Whatlington. E Sus 4B 28
Whatmore. Shrp 3A 60
Whatstandwell. Derbs 5H 85
Whatton. Notts 1E 75
Whauphill. Dum 5B 110
Whaw. N Yor 4C 104
Wheatacre. Norf 1G 67
Wheatcroft. Derbs 5A 86
Wheathampstead. Herts 4B 52
Wheathill. Shrp 2A 60
Wheatley. Devn 3B 12
Wheatley. Hants 2F 25
Wheatley. Oxon 5E 50
Wheatley. S Yor 4F 93
Wheatley. W Yor 2A 92
Wheatley Hill. Dur 1A 106
Wheatley Lane. Lanc 1G 91
Wheatley Park. S Yor 4F 93
Wheaton Aston. Staf 4C 72
Wheatstone Park. Staf 5C 72
Wheddon Cross. Som 3C 20
Wheelerstreet. Surr 1A 26
Wheelock. Ches E 5B 84
Wheelock Heath. Ches E 5B 84
Wheelton. Lanc 2E 90
Wheldrake. York 5A 100
Whelford. Glos 2G 35
Whelpley Hill. Buck 5H 51
Whelpo. Cumb 1E 102
Whelston. Flin 3E 82
Whenby. N Yor 3A 100
Whepstead. Suff 5H 65
Wherstead. Suff 1E 55
Wherwell. Hants 2B 24
Wheston. Derbs 3F 85
Whetsted. Kent 1A 28
Whetstone. G Lon 1D 38
Whetstone. Leics 1C 62
Whicham. Cumb 1A 96
Whichford. Warw 2B 50
Whickham. Tyne 3F 115
Whiddon. Devn 2E 11
Whiddon Down. Devn 3G 11
Whigstreet. Ang 4D 145
Whilton. Nptn 4D 62
Whimble. Devn 2D 10
Whimple. Devn 3D 12
Whimpwell Green. Norf 3F 79
Whinburgh. Norf 5C 78
Whin Lane End. Lanc 5C 96
Whinney Hill. Stoc T 3A 106
Whinnyfold. Abers 5H 161
Whippingham. IOW 3D 16
Whipsnade. C Beds 4A 52
Whipton. Devn 3C 12
Whirlow. S Yor 2H 85
Whisby. Linc 4G 87
Whissendine. Rut 4F 75
Whissonsett. Norf 3B 78
Whisterfield. Ches E 3C 84
Whistley Green. Wok 4F 37
Whiston. Mers 1G 83
Whiston. Nptn 4F 63
Whiston. S Yor 1B 86
Whiston. Staf
nr. Cheadle 1E 73
nr. Penkridge 4C 72
Whiston Cross. Shrp 5B 72
Whiston Eaves. Staf 1E 73
Whitacre Heath. Warw 1G 61
Whitbeck. Cumb 1A 96
Whitbourne. Here 5B 60
Whitburn. Tyne 3H 115
Whitburn. W Lot 3C 128
Whitburn Colliery. Tyne 3H 115
Whitby. Ches W 3F 83
Whitby. N Yor 3F 107
Whitbyheath. Ches W 3F 83
Whitchester. Bord 4D 130
Whitchurch. Bath 5B 34
Whitchurch. Buck 3F 51
Whitchurch. Card 4E 33
Whitchurch. Devn 5E 11
Whitchurch. Hants 2C 24
Whitchurch. Here 4A 48
Whitchurch. Pemb 2B 42
Whitchurch. Shrp 1H 71
Whitchurch Canonicorum.
Dors 3G 13
Whitchurch Hill. Oxon 4E 37
Whitchurch-on-Thames.
Oxon 4E 37
Whitcombe. Dors 4C 14
Whitcot. Shrp 1F 59
Whitcott Keysett. Shrp 2E 59
Whiteabbey. Ant 1H 179
Whiteash Green. Essx 2A 54
Whitebog. High 2B 158
Whitebridge. High 2G 149
Whitebrook. Mon 5A 48
Whitecairns. Abers 2G 153
Whitechapel. Lanc 5E 97
Whitechurch. Pemb 1F 43
White Colne. Essx 3B 54
White Coppice. Lanc 3E 90
White Corries. High 3G 141
Whitecraig. E Lot 2G 129
Whitecroft. Glos 5B 48
White Cross. Corn 4D 5
Whitecross. Corn 1D 6
Whitecross. Falk 2C 128
Whitecross. New M 6D 178
White End. Worc 2C 48
Whiteface. High 5E 164
Whitefarland. N Ayr 5G 125
Whitefaulds. S Ayr 4B 116
Whitefield. G Man 4G 91
Whitefield. Som 4D 20
Whiteford. Abers 1E 152
Whitegate. Ches W 4A 84
Whitehall. Devn 1E 12
Whitehall. Hants 1F 25
Whitehall. Orkn 5F 172
Whitehall. W Sus 3C 26
Whitehaven. Cumb 3A 102
Whitehaven. Shrp 3E 71
Whitehead. ME Ant 7L 175
Whitehill. Hants 3F 25
Whitehill. N Ayr 4D 126
Whitehills. Abers 2D 160
Whitehills. Ang 3D 144
White Horse Common.
Norf 3F 79
Whitehough. Derbs 2E 85
Whitehouse. Abers 2D 152
Whitehouse. Arg 3G 125
Whiteinch. Glas 3G 127
Whitekirk. E Lot 1B 130
White Kirkley. Dur 1D 104
White Lackington. Dors 3C 14
Whitelackington. Som 1G 13
White Ladies Aston. Worc 5D 60
White Lee. W Yor 2C 92
Whiteley. Hants 2D 16
Whiteley Bank. IOW 4D 16
Whiteley Village. Surr 4B 38
Whitemans Green. W Sus 3E 27
White Mill. Carm 3E 45
Whitemire. Mor 3D 159
Whitemoor. Corn 3D 6
Whitenap. Hants 4B 24
Whiteness. Shet 7F 173
White Notley. Essx 4A 54
Whiteoak Green. Oxon 4B 50
Whiteparish. Wilts 4H 23
White Pit. Linc 3C 88
Whiterashes. Abers 1F 153
Whiterock. Ards 3K 179
White Rocks. Here 3H 47
White Roding. Essx 4F 53
Whiterow. High 4F 169
Whiterow. Mor 3E 159
Whiteshill. Glos 5D 48
Whiteside. Nmbd 3A 114
Whiteside. W Lot 3C 128
Whitesmith. E Sus 4G 27
Whitestaunton. Som 1F 13
White Stone. Here 1A 48
Whitestone. Abers 4D 152
Whitestone. Devn 3B 12
Whitestones. Abers 3F 161
Whitestreet Green. Suff 2C 54
Whitewall Corner. N Yor 2B 100
White Waltham. Wind 4G 37
Whiteway. Glos 4E 49
Whitewell. Lanc 5F 97
Whitewell Bottom. Lanc 2G 91
Whiteworks. Devn 5G 11
Whitewreath. Mor 3G 159
Whitfield. D'dee 5D 144
Whitfield. Kent 1H 29
Whitfield. Nptn 2E 50
Whitfield. Nmbd 4A 114
Whitfield. S Glo 2B 34
Whitford. Devn 3F 13
Whitford. Flin 3D 82
Whitgift. E Yor 2B 94
Whitgreave. Staf 3C 72
Whithorn. Dum 5B 110
Whiting Bay. N Ayr 3E 123
Whitkirk. W Yor 1D 92
Whitland. Carm 3G 43
Whitleigh. Plym 3A 8
Whitletts. S Ayr 2C 116
Whitley. N Yor 2F 93
Whitley. Wilts 5D 35
Whitley Bay. Tyne 2G 115
Whitley Chapel. Nmbd 4C 114
Whitley Heath. Staf 3C 72
Whitley Lower. W Yor 3C 92
Whitley Thorpe. N Yor 2F 93
Whitlock's End. W Mid 3F 61
Whitminster. Glos 5C 48
Whitmore. Dors 2F 15
Whitmore. Staf 1C 72
Whitnage. Devn 1D 12
Whitnash. Warw 4H 61
Whitney. Here 1F 47
Whitrigg. Cumb
nr. Kirkbride 4D 112
nr. Torpenhow 1D 102
Whitsbury. Hants 1G 15
Whitsome. Bord 4E 131
Whitson. Newp 3G 33
Whitstable. Kent 4F 41
Whitstone. Corn 3C 10
Whittingham. Nmbd 3E 121
Whittingslow. Shrp 2G 59
Whittington. Derbs 3B 86
Whittington. Glos 3F 49
Whittington. Lanc 2F 97
Whittington. Norf 1G 65
Whittington. Shrp 2F 71
Whittington. Staf
nr. Kinver 2C 60
nr. Lichfield 5F 73
Whittington. Warw 1G 61
Whittington. Worc 5C 60
Whittington Barracks. Staf 5F 73
Whittlebury. Nptn 1E 51
Whittleford. Warw 1H 61
Whittle-le-Woods. Lanc 2D 90
Whittlesey. Cambs 1B 64
Whittlesford. Cambs 1E 53
Whittlestone Head. Bkbn 3F 91
Whitton. N Lin 2C 94
Whitton. Nmbd 4E 121
Whitton. Powy 4E 59
Whitton. Bord 2B 120
Whitton. Shrp 3H 59
Whitton. Stoc T 2A 106
Whittonditch. Wilts 4A 36
Whittonstall. Nmbd 4D 114
Whitway. Hants 1C 24
Whitwell. Derbs 3C 86
Whitwell. Herts 3B 52
Whitwell. IOW 5D 16
Whitwell. N Yor 5F 105
Whitwell. Rut 5G 75
Whitwell-on-the-Hill.
N Yor 3B 100
Whitwick. Leics 4B 74
Whitwood. W Yor 2E 93
Whitworth. Lanc 3G 91
Whixall. Shrp 2H 71
Whixley. N Yor 4G 99
Whoberley. W Mid 3H 61
Whorlton. Dur 3E 105
Whorlton. N Yor 4B 106
Whygate. Nmbd 2A 114
Whyle. Here 4H 59
Whyteleafe. Surr 5E 39
Wibdon. Glos 2A 34
Wibtoft. Warw 2B 62
Wichenford. Worc 4B 60
Wichling. Kent 5D 40
Wick. Bour 3G 15
Wick. Devn 2E 13
Wick. High 3F 169
Wick. Shet
on Mainland 8F 173
on Unst 1G 173
Wick. Som
nr. Bridgwater 2F 21
nr. Burnham-on-Sea 1G 21
nr. Somerton 4H 21
Wick. S Glo 4C 34
Wick. V Glam 4C 32
Wick. W Sus 5B 26
Wick. Wilts 4G 23
Wick. Worc 1E 49
Wick Airport. High 3F 169
Wicken. Cambs 3E 65
Wicken. Nptn 2F 51
Wicken Bonhunt. Essx 2E 53
Wickenby. Linc 2H 87
Wicken Green Village.
Norf 2H 77
Wickersley. S Yor 1B 86
Wicker Street Green. Suff 1C 54
Wickford. Essx 1B 40
Wickham. Hants 1D 16
Wickham. W Ber 4B 36
Wickham Bishops. Essx 4B 54
Wickhambreaux. Kent 5G 41
Wickhambrook. Suff 5G 65
Wickhamford. Worc 1F 49
Wickham Green. Suff 4C 66
Wickham Heath. W Ber 5C 36
Wickham Market. Suff 5F 67
Wickhampton. Norf 5G 79
Wickham St Paul. Essx 2B 54
Wickham Skeith. Suff 4C 66
Wickham Street. Suff 4C 66
Wick Hill. Wok 5F 37
Wicklewood. Norf 5C 78
Wickmere. Norf 2D 78
Wick St Lawrence. N Som 5G 33
Wickwar. S Glo 3C 34
Widdington. Essx 2F 53
Widdrington. Nmbd 5G 121
Widdrington Station.
Nmbd 5G 121
Widecombe in the Moor.
Devn 5H 11
Widegates. Corn 3G 7
Widemouth Bay. Corn 2C 10
Wide Open. Tyne 2F 115
Widewall. Orkn 8D 172
Widford. Essx 5G 53
Widford. Herts 4E 53
Widham. Wilts 3F 35
Widmer End. Buck 2G 37
Widmerpool. Notts 3D 74
Widnes. Hal 2H 83
Widworthy. Devn 3F 13
Wigan. G Man 4D 90
Wigbeth. Dors 2F 15
Wigborough. Som 1H 13
Wiggaton. Devn 3E 12
Wiggenhall St Germans.
Norf 4E 77
Wiggenhall St Mary Magdalen.
Norf 4E 77
Wiggenhall St Mary the Virgin.
Norf 4E 77
Wiggenhall St Peter. Norf 4F 77
Wiggens Green. Essx 1G 53
Wigginton. Herts 4H 51
Wigginton. Oxon 2B 50
Wigginton. Staf 5G 73
Wigginton. York 4H 99
Wigglesworth. N Yor 4H 97
Wiggonby. Cumb 4D 112
Wiggonholt. W Sus 4B 26
Wighill. N Yor 5G 99
Wighton. Norf 2B 78
Wightwick. W Mid 1C 60
Wigley. Hants 1B 16
Wigmore. Here 4G 59
Wigmore. Medw 4B 40
Wigsley. Notts 3F 87
Wigsthorpe. Nptn 2H 63
Wigston. Leics 1D 62
Wigtoft. Linc 2B 76
Wigton. Cumb 5D 112
Wigtown. Dum 4B 110
Wike. W Yor 5F 99
Wilbarston. Nptn 2F 63
Wilberfoss. E Yor 4B 100
Wilburton. Cambs 3D 65
Wilby. Norf 2C 66
Wilby. Nptn 4F 63
Wilby. Suff 3E 67
Wilcot. Wilts 5G 35
Wilcott. Shrp 4F 71
Wilcove. Corn 3A 8
Wildboarclough. Ches E 4D 85
Wilden. Bed 5H 63
Wilden. Worc 3C 60
Wildern. Hants 1C 16
Wilderspool. Warr 2A 84
Wilde Street. Suff 3G 65
Wildhern. Hants 1B 24
Wildmanbridge. S Lan 4B 128
Wildmoor. Worc 3D 60
Wildsworth. Linc 1F 87
Wildwood. Staf 3D 72
Wilford. Nott 2C 74
Wilkesley. Ches E 1A 72
Wilkhaven. High 5G 165
Wilkieston. W Lot 3E 129
Wilksby. Linc 4B 88
Willand. Devn 1D 12
Willaston. Ches E 5A 84
Willaston. Ches W 3F 83
Willaston. IOM 4C 108
Willen. Mil 1G 51
Willenhall. W Mid
nr. Coventry 3A 62
nr. Wolverhampton 1D 60
Willerby. E Yor 1D 94
Willerby. N Yor 2E 101
Willersey. Glos 2G 49
Willersley. Here 1G 47
Willesborough. Kent 1E 28
Willesborough Lees. Kent 1E 29
Willesden. G Lon 2D 38
Willesley. Wilts 3D 34
Willett. Som 3E 20
Willey. Shrp 1A 60
Willey. Warw 2B 62
Willey Green. Surr 5A 38
Williamscot. Oxon 1C 50
Williamsetter. Shet 9E 173
Willian. Herts 2C 52
Willingale. Essx 5F 53
Willingdon. E Sus 5G 27
Willingham. Cambs 3D 64
Willingham by Stow. Linc 2F 87
Willingham Green. Cambs 5F 65
Willington. Bed 1B 52
Willington. Derbs 3G 73
Willington. Dur 1E 105
Willington. Tyne 3G 115
Willington. Warw 2A 50
Willington Corner.
Ches W 4H 83
Willisham Tye. Suff 5C 66
Willitoft. E Yor 1H 93
Williton. Som 2D 20
Willoughbridge. Staf 1B 72
Willoughby. Linc 3D 88
Willoughby. Warw 4C 62
Willoughby-on-the-Wolds.
Notts 3D 74
Willoughby Waterleys.
Leics 1C 62
Willoughton. Linc 1G 87
Willow Green. Worc 5B 60
Willows Green. Essx 4H 53
Willsbridge. S Glo 4B 34
Willslock. Staf 2E 73
Wilmcote. Warw 5F 61
Wilmington. Bath 5B 34
Wilmington. Devn 3F 13
Wilmington. E Sus 5G 27
Wilmington. Kent 3G 39
Wilmslow. Ches E 2C 84
Wilnecote. Staf 5G 73
Wilney Green. Norf 2C 66
Wilpshire. Lanc 1E 91
Wilsden. W Yor 1A 92
Wilsford. Linc 1H 75
Wilsford. Wilts
nr. Amesbury 3G 23
nr. Devizes 1F 23
Wilsill. N Yor 3D 98
Wilsley Green. Kent 2B 28
Wilson. Here 3A 48
Wilson. Leics 3B 74
Wilsontown. S Lan 4C 128
Wilstead. Bed 1A 52
Wilsthorpe. E Yor 3F 101
Wilsthorpe. Linc 4H 75
Wilstone. Herts 4H 51
Wilton. Cumb 3B 102
Wilton. N Yor 1C 100
Wilton. Red C 3C 106
Wilton. Bord 3H 119
Wilton. Wilts
nr. Marlborough 5A 36
nr. Salisbury 3F 23
Wimbish. Essx 2F 53
Wimbish Green. Essx 2G 53
Wimblebury. Staf 4E 73
Wimbledon. G Lon 3D 38
Wimblington. Cambs 1D 64
Wimboldsley. Ches W 4A 84
Wimborne Minster. Dors 2F 15
Wimborne St Giles. Dors 1F 15
Wimbotsham. Norf 5F 77
Wimpole. Cambs 1D 52
Wimpstone. Warw 1H 49
Wincanton. Som 4C 22
Winceby. Linc 4C 88
Wincham. Ches W 3A 84
Winchburgh. W Lot 2D 129
Winchcombe. Glos 3F 49
Winchelsea. E Sus 4D 28
Winchelsea Beach. E Sus 4D 28
Winchester. Hants 203 (4C 24)
Winchet Hill. Kent 1B 28
Winchfield. Hants 1F 25
Winchmore Hill. Buck 1A 38
Winchmore Hill. G Lon 1E 39
Wincle. Ches E 4D 84
Windermere. Cumb 5F 103
Winderton. Warw 1B 50
Windhill. High 4H 157
Windle Hill. Ches W 3F 83
Windlesham. Surr 4A 38
Windley. Derbs 1H 73
Windmill. Derbs 3F 85
Windmill Hill. E Sus 4H 27
Windmill Hill. Som 1G 13
Windrush. Glos 4G 49
Windsor. Wind 203 (3A 38)
Windsor Green. Suff 5A 66
Windyedge. Abers 4F 153
Windygates. Fife 3F 137
Windyharbour. Ches E 3C 84
Windyknowe. W Lot 3C 128
Wineham. W Sus 3D 26
Winestead. E Yor 2G 95
Winfarthing. Norf 2D 66
Winford. IOW 4D 16
Winford. N Som 5A 34
Winforton. Here 1F 47
Winfrith Newburgh. Dors 4D 14
Wing. Buck 3G 51
Wing. Rut 5F 75
Wingate. Dur 1B 106
Wingates. G Man 4E 91
Wingates. Nmbd 5F 121
Wingerworth. Derbs 4A 86
Wingfield. C Beds 3A 52
Wingfield. Suff 3E 67
Wingfield. Wilts 1D 22
Wingfield Park. Derbs 5A 86
Wingham. Kent 5G 41
Wingmore. Kent 1F 29
Wingrave. Buck 4G 51
Winkburn. Notts 5E 86
Winkfield. Brac 3A 38
Winkfield Row. Brac 4G 37
Winkhill. Staf 5E 85
Winklebury. Hants 1E 24
Winkleigh. Devn 2G 11
Winksley. N Yor 2E 99
Winkton. Dors 3G 15
Winlaton. Tyne 3E 115
Winlaton Mill. Tyne 3E 115
Winless. High 3F 169
Winmarleigh. Lanc 5D 96
Winnal Common. Here 2H 47
Winnard's Perch. Corn 2D 6
Winnersh. Wok 4F 37
Winnington. Ches W 3A 84
Winnington. Staf 2B 72
Winnothdale. Staf 1E 73
Winscales. Cumb 2B 102
Winscombe. N Som 1H 21
Winsford. Ches W 4A 84
Winsford. Som 3C 20
Winsham. Devn 3E 19
Winsham. Som 2G 13
Winshill. Staf 3G 73
Winsh-wen. Swan 3F 31
Winskill. Cumb 1G 103
Winslade. Hants 2E 25
Winsley. Wilts 5D 34
Winslow. Buck 3F 51
Winson. Glos 5F 49
Winson Green. W Mid 2E 61
Winsor. Hants 1B 16
Winster. Cumb 5F 103
Winster. Derbs 4G 85
Winston. Dur 3E 105
Winston. Suff 4D 66
Winstone. Glos 5E 49
Winswell. Devn 1E 11
Winterborne Clenston.
Dors 2D 14
Winterborne Herringston.
Dors 4B 14
Winterborne Houghton.
Dors 2D 14
Winterborne Kingston.
Dors 3D 14
Winterborne Monkton.
Dors 4B 14
Winterborne St Martin.
Dors 4B 14
Winterborne Stickland.
Dors 2D 14
Winterborne Whitechurch.
Dors 2D 14
Winterborne Zelston.
Dors 3D 15
Winterbourne. S Glo 3B 34
Winterbourne. W Ber 4C 36
Winterbourne Abbas.
Dors 3B 14
Winterbourne Bassett.
Wilts 4G 35
Winterbourne Dauntsey.
Wilts 3G 23
Winterbourne Earls. Wilts 3G 23
Winterbourne Gunner.
Wilts 3G 23
Winterbourne Monkton.
Wilts 4G 35
Winterbourne Steepleton.
Dors 4B 14
Winterbourne Stoke. Wilts 2F 23
Winterbrook. Oxon 3E 36
Winterburn. N Yor 4B 98
Winter Gardens. Essx 2B 40
Winterhay Green. Som 1G 13
Winteringham. N Lin 2C 94
Winterley. Ches E 5B 84
Wintersett. W Yor 3D 93
Winterton. N Lin 3C 94
Winterton-on-Sea. Norf 4G 79
Winthorpe. Linc 4E 89
Winthorpe. Notts 5F 87
Winton. Bour 3F 15
Winton. Cumb 3A 104
Winton. E Sus 5G 27
Wintringham. N Yor 2C 100
Winwick. Cambs 2A 64
Winwick. Nptn 3D 62
Winwick. Warr 1A 84
Wirksworth. Derbs 5G 85
Wirswall. Ches E 1H 71
Wisbech. Cambs 4D 76
Wisbech St Mary. Cambs 5D 76
Wisborough Green.
W Sus 3B 26
Wiseton. Notts 2E 86
Wishaw. N Lan 4A 128
Wishaw. Warw 1F 61
Wisley. Surr 5B 38
Wispington. Linc 3B 88
Wissenden. Kent 1D 28
Wissett. Suff 3F 67
Wistanstow. Shrp 2G 59
Wistanswick. Shrp 3A 72
Wistaston. Ches E 5A 84
Wiston. Pemb 3E 43
Wiston. S Lan 1B 118
Wiston. W Sus 4C 26
Wistow. Cambs 2B 64
Wistow. N Yor 1F 93
Wiswell. Lanc 1F 91
Witcham. Cambs 2D 64

(1) A strict alphabetical order is used e.g. Benmore Botanic Gdn. follows Ben Macdui but precedes Ben Nevis.

(2) Places of Interest which fall on City and Town Centre maps are referenced first to the detailed map page, followed by the main map page if appropriate. The name of the map is included if it is not clear from the index entry.
e.g. Ashmolean Mus. of Art & Archaeology (OX1 2PH) .... **Oxford 200** (5D **50**)

(3) Entries in italics are not named on the map but are shown with a symbol only.
e.g. *Aberdour Castle (KY3 0XA)* 1E **129**

SAT NAV POSTCODES

Postcodes are shown to assist Sat Nav users and are included on this basis.
It should be noted that postcodes have been selected by their proximity to the Place of Interest and that they may not form part of the actual postal address. Drivers should follow the Tourist Brown Signs when available.

ABBREVIATIONS USED IN THIS INDEX

Centre : Cen.   Garden : Gdn.   Gardens : Gdns.   Museum : Mus.   National : Nat.   Park : Pk.

Lakeside & Haverthwaite Railway—Sainsbury Cen. for Visual Arts

Lakeside & Haverthwaite Railway (LA12 8AL) 1C **96**
Lamb House (TN31 7ES) 3D **28**
Lamphey Bishop's Palace (SA71 5NT) 4E **43**
Lamport Hall & Gdns. (NN6 9HD) 3E **63**
Lancaster Castle. (LA1 1YJ) 3D 96
Landmark Forest Adventure Pk. (PH23 3AJ) 1D **150**
Land's End (TR19 7AA) 4A **4**
Lanercost Priory (CA8 2HQ) 3G **113**
Langdale Pikes (LA22 9JY) 4D **102**
Langley Chapel (SY5 7HU) 1H **59**
Lanhydrock (PL30 5AD) 2E **7**
Lappa Valley Steam Railway (TR8 5LX) 3C **6**
Larmer Tree Gdns. (SP5 5PZ) 1E **15**
Laugharne Castle. (SA33 4SA) 3H 43
Launceston Castle. (PL15 7DR) 4D 10
Launceston Steam Railway (PL15 8DA) 4D **10**
Lauriston Castle (EH4 5QD) 2F **129**
Laxey Wheel (IM4 7NL) 3D **108**
Layer Marney Tower (CO5 9US) 4C **54**
Leeds Castle (ME17 1PL) 5C **40**
Leeds City Mus. (LS1 3AA) **196**
Legoland (SL4 4AY) 3A **38**
Leighton Buzzard Railway (LU7 4TN) 3H **51**
Leighton Hall (LA5 9ST) 2E **97**
Leiston Abbey (IP16 4TD) 4G **67**
Leith Hall (AB54 4NQ) 1C **152**
Leith Hill (RH5 6LX) 1C **26**
Lennoxlove House (EH41 4NZ) 2B **130**
Leonardslee Gdns. (RH13 6PP) 3D **26**
Levant Mine & Beam Engine (TR19 7SX) 3A **4**
Levens Hall (LA8 0PD) 1D **97**
Lewes Castle. (BN7 1YE) 4F 27
Lichfield Cathedral. (WS13 7LD) 4F 73
Life (NE1 4EP) **Newcastle upon Tyne 197**
Lightwater Valley (HG4 3HT) 2E **99**
Lilleshall Abbey (TF10 9HW) 4B **72**
Lincoln Castle (LN1 3AA) **197** (3G **87**)
Lincoln Cathedral (LN2 1PZ) **197** (3G **87**)
Lincolnshire Road Transport Mus. (LN6 3QT) 4G **87**
Lindisfarne (TD15 2SF) 5H **131**
Lindisfarne Castle (TD15 2SH) 5H **131**
Lindisfarne Priory (TD15 2RX) 5H **131**
Linlithgow Palace (EH49 7AL) 2D **128**
Linton Zoo (CB21 4XN) 1F **53**
Little Clarendon (SP3 5DZ) 3F **23**
Little Malvern Court (WR14 4JN) 1C **48**
Little Moreton Hall (CW12 4SD) 5C **84**
Liverpool Cathedral Church of Christ. (L1 7AZ) 2F 83
Liverpool Metropolitan RC Cathedral of Christ the King
(L3 5TQ) **197** (1F **83**)
Lizard Point (TR12 7NU) 5E **5**
Llanberis Lake Railway (LL55 3HB) 4E **81**
Llanerchaeron (SA48 8DG) 4D **57**
Llangollen Railway (LL20 7AJ) 1D **70**
Llansteffan Castle. (SA33 5JX) 4D 44
Llawhaden Castle. (SA67 8HL) 3E 43
Llechwedd Slate Caverns (LL41 3NB) 1G **69**
Llywernog Silver-Lead Mine (SY23 3AB) 2G **57**
Lochalsh Woodland Gdn. (IV40 8DN) 1F **147**
Loch Doon Castle (KA6 7QE) 5D **117**
Lochleven Castle (KY13 8ET) 3D **136**
Loch Lomond (G83 8PA) 4C **134**
Loch Lomond & The Trossachs Nat. Pk.
(FK8 3UA) 2D **134**
Lochmaben Castle. (DG11 1JE) 1B 112
Loch Ness Cen & Exhibition (IV63 6TU) 5H **157**
Locomotion (DL4 1PQ) 2F **105**
The Lodge Nature Reserve (SG19 2DL) 1B **52**
Lodge Pk. (GL54 3PP) 4G **49**
Logan Botanic Gdn. (DG9 9ND) 5F **109**
Logan Fish Pond & Marine Life Cen
(DG9 9NF) 5F **109**
London Dungeon (SE1 2SZ) **199**
London Eye (SE1 7PB) **199**
London Film Mus. (WC2E 7BN) **199**
London Zoo (NW1 4RY) **198** (2D **39**)
Long Cross Victorian Gdns. (PL29 3TF) 1D **6**
Longleat Safari & Adventure Pk.
(BA12 7NW) 2D **22**
Long Mynd (SY7 8BH) 1G **59**
Longthorpe Tower (PE3 6SU) 1A **64**
Longtown Castle. (HR2 0LE) 3G 47
Lord Leycester Hospital & The Master's Gdn.
(CV34 4BH) 4G 61
Loseley Pk. (GU3 1HS) 1A **26**
The Lost Gdns. of Heligan (PL26 6EN) 4D **6**
Lotherton Hall (LS25 3EB) 1E **93**
Lough Neagh Discovery Cen (BT66 6NJ) 3E **178**
Loughwood Meeting House (EX13 7DU) 3F **13**
Ludgershall Castle. (SP11 9QS) 1A 24
Ludlow Castle. (SY8 1AY) 3H 59
Lullingstone Castle & World Gdn.
(DA4 0JA) 4G **39**
Lullingstone Roman Villa (DA4 0JA) 4G **39**
Lulworth Castle & Pk. (BH20 5QS) 4D **14**
Lundy Island (EX39 2LY) 2B **18**
Lyddington Bede House (LE15 9LZ) 1F **63**
Lydford Castle & Saxon Town. (EX20 4BH) 4F 11
Lydford Gorge (EX20 4BH) 4F **11**
Lydiard House & Pk. (SN5 3PA) 3G **35**
Lydney Pk. Gdns. (GL15 6BU) 5B **48**
Lyme Pk. (SK12 2NX) 2D **84**
Lytes Cary Manor (TA11 7HU) 4A **22**
Lyveden New Bield (PE8 5AT) 2G **63**

M

Macclesfield Silk Mus. (SK11 6PD) 3D **84**
Macduff Marine Aquarium (AB44 1SL) 2E **160**
MacLellan's Castle (DG6 4JD) 4D **111**
Madame Tussaud's (NW1 5LR) **London 198**
Maeshowe Chambered Cairn (KW16 3HQ) 6C **172**
Magna Science Adventure Cen. (S60 1DX) 1B **86**
Maiden Castle (DT2 9PP) 4B **14**
The Major Oak, Sherwood Forest Country Pk.
(NG21 9HN) 4D **86**
Malham Cove (BD23 4DJ) 3A **98**
Malham Tarn (BD24 9PU) 3A **98**
Malleny Gdn. (EH14 7AF) 3E **129**
Malton Mus. (YO17 7LP) 2B 100
Malvern Hills (HR8 1EN) 2C **48**
Manchester Art Gallery (M2 3JL) **197**
Manderston (TD11 3PP) 4E **130**
Mannington Gdns. (NR11 7BB) 2D **78**
Manorbier Castle. (SA70 7SY) 5E 43
Manx Electric Railway (IM2 4NR) 2D **108**
Manx Mus. (IM1 3LY) 4C **108**
Mapledurham House (RG4 7TR) 4E **37**
Marble Arch Caves Global Geopark
(BT92 1EW) 6G **177**
Marble Hill House (TW1 2NL) 3C **38**
Markenfield Hall (HG4 3AD) 3E **99**
Mar Lodge Estate. (AB35 5YJ) 5E 151
Martin Mere Wetland Cen. (L40 0TA) 3C **90**
Marwell Wildlife (SO21 1JH) 4D **24**
Marwood Hill Gdns. (EX31 4EB) 3F **19**
Mary Arden's Farm (CV37 9UN) 5F **61**
Mary, Queen of Scots' Visitor Cen
(TD8 6EN) 2A **120**
Mary Rose Mus. (PO1 3LJ) **Portsmouth 201**
Max Gate (DT1 2AB) 3C **14**
M&D's Scotland Theme Pk. (ML1 3RT) 4A **128**
The Medieval Bishop's Palace
(LN2 1PU) **Lincoln 197**
Megginch Castle Gdns. (PH2 7SW) 1E **137**
Melbourne Hall & Gdns. (DE73 8EN) 3A **74**
Melford Hall (CO10 9AA) 1B **54**
Mellerstain House (TD3 6LG) 1A **120**
Melrose Abbey. (TD6 9LG) 1H 119
Menai Suspension Bridge (LL59 5HH) 3E **81**
Mendip Hills (BS40 7XS) 1H **21**
Merriments Gdns. (TN19 7RA) 3B **28**
Merseyside Maritime Mus.
(L3 4AQ) **Liverpool 197** (2F **83**)
Mertoun Gdns. (TD6 0EA) 1A **120**
Michelham Priory (BN27 3QS) 5G **27**
Middleham Castle, Middleham. (DL8 4QR) 1D 98
Midland Railway Cen (DE5 3QZ) 5B **86**
Mid-Norfolk Railway (NR19 1DF) 5C **78**
Millennium Coastal Pk. (SA15 2LG) 3D **31**
Milton Manor House (OX14 4EN) 2C **36**
Milton's Cottage (HP8 4JH) 1A **38**
Minack Theatre (TR19 6JU) 4A **4**
Minsmere (IP17 3BY) 4G **67**
Minterne House & Gdns. (DT2 7AU) 2B **14**
Mirehouse (CA12 4QE) 2D **102**
Misarden Pk. Gdns. (GL6 7JA) 5E **49**
Mr Straw's House (S81 0JG) 2C **86**
Mistley Towers (CO11 1ET) 2E **54**
Mompesson House (SP1 2EL) **Salisbury 201** (4G **23**)
Monk Bretton Priory (S71 5QE) 4D **93**
Monkey Forest at Trentham (ST4 8AY) 2C **72**
Monkey Sanctuary (PL13 1NZ) 3G **7**
Monkey World (BH20 6HH) 4D **14**
Monk's House (BN7 3HF) 5F **27**
Montacute House (TA15 6XP) 1H **13**
Monteviot House (TD8 6UH) 2A **120**
Montgomery Castle. (SY15 6HN) 1E 58
Moreton Corbet Castle. (SY4 4DW) 3H 71
Morwellham Quay (PL19 8JL) 2A **8**
Moseley Old Hall. (WV10 7HY) 5D 72
Mother Shipton's Cave (HG5 8DD) 4F **99**
Mottisfont (SO51 0LP) 4B **24**
Mount Edgcumbe House (PL10 1HZ) 3A **8**
Mount Ephraim Gdns. (ME13 9TX) 4E **41**
Mountfitchet Castle (CM24 8SP) 3F **53**
Mount Grace Priory (DL6 3JG) 5B **106**
Mount Stewart House & Gdns. (BT22 2AD) 2K **179**
Mount Stuart. (PA20 9LR) 4C 126
Muchelney Abbey (TA10 0DQ) 4H **21**
Muchelney Priest's House (TA10 0DQ) 4H **21**
Mull of Kintyre (PA28 6RU) 1K **175** (5A **122**)
Muncaster Castle (CA18 1RQ) 5C **102**
Murlough Nat. Nature Reserve (BT33 0NQ) 6J **179**
Mus. of Army Flying (SO20 8DY) 3B **24**
Mus. of East Anglian Life (IP14 1DL) 5C **66**
Mus. of Lakeland Life & Industry. (LA9 5AL) 5G 103
Mus. of Lincolnshire Life
(LN1 3LY) **Lincoln 197** (3G **87**)
Mus. of London (EC2Y 5HN) **199**
Mus. of Royal Worcester (WR1 2ND) **203** (5C **60**)
Mus. of Scottish Lighthouses
(AB43 9DU) 2G **161**
Mus. of The Gorge (TF8 7NH) 5A **72**
Mus. of the Isles (IV45 8RS) 3E **147**
Mus. of the Jewellery Quarter
(B18 6HA) **Birmingham 192**

N

National Botanic Gdn. of Wales (SA32 8HG) 4F **45**
National Coal Mining Mus. for England
(WF4 4RH) 3C **92**
National Coracle Cen (SA38 9JL) 1C **44**
National Exhibition Cen (NEC) (B40 1NT) 2F **61**
National Football Mus. (M4 3BG) **Manchester 197**
The National Forest (DE12 6HZ) 4H **73**
National Gallery (WC2N 5DN) **London 199**
National Glass Cen. (SR6 0GL) 4H **115**
National Heritage Cen. for Horseracing & Sporting Art
(CB8 8JL) 4F **65**
National Marine Aquarium (PL4 0LF) **Plymouth 201**
National Maritime Mus. (SE10 9NF) 3E 39
National Maritime Mus. Cornwall. (TR11 3QY) 5C 6
National Memorial Arboretum (DE13 7AR) 4F **73**
National Mining Mus. Scotland (EH22 4QN) 3G **129**
National Motorcycle Mus. (B92 0EJ) 2G **61**
The National Motor Mus. (SO42 7ZN) 2B **16**
National Mus. Cardiff (CF10 3NP) **193** (4E **33**)
National Mus. of Flight (EH39 5LF) 2B **130**
National Mus. of Rural Life Scotland
(G76 9HR) 4H **127**
National Mus. of Scotland
(EH1 1JF) **Edinburgh 195** (2F **129**)
National Mus. of the Royal Navy
(PO1 3NH) **Portsmouth 201**
National Portrait Gallery (WC2H 0HE) **London 199**
National Railway Mus., York
(YO26 4XJ) **203** (4H **99**)
National Roman Legion Mus. (NP18 1AE) 2G 33
National Science & Media Mus.
(BD1 1NQ) **Bradford 192** (1B **92**)
National Sea Life Cen. (B1 2HL) **Birmingham 192**
National Showcaves Cen for Wales
(SA9 1GJ) 4B **46**
National Slate Mus. (LL55 4TY) 4E **81**
National Space Cen. (LE4 5NS) 5C **74**
National Waterfront Mus.
(SA1 3RD) **Swansea 203** (3F **31**)
National Waterways Mus. (CH65 4FW) 3G **83**
National Wool Mus. (SA44 5UP) 2D **44**
Natural History Mus., London (SW7 5BD) **198**
Natural History Mus. at Tring (HP23 6AP) 4H **51**
Neath Abbey (SA10 7DW) 3G **31**
The Needles (PO39 0JH) 4A **16**
Nene Valley Railway (PE8 6LR) 1A **64**
Ness Botanic Gdns. (CH64 4AY) 3F **83**
Nessieland (IV63 6TU) 5H **157**
Nether Winchendon House (HP18 0DY) 4F **51**
Netley Abbey (SO31 5HB) 2C **16**
New Abbey Corn Mill (DG2 8DX) 3A **112**
Newark Air Mus. (NG24 2NY) 5F **87**
Newark Castle, Port Glasgow (PA14 5NG) 2E **127**
Newark Castle, Newark-on-Trent. (NG24 1BN) 5E 87
Newark Pk. (GL12 7PZ) 2C **34**
The New Art Gallery Walsall. (WS2 8LG) 1E 61
Newburgh Priory (YO61 4AS) 2H **99**
Newbury Racecourse (RG14 7NZ) 5C **36**
Newby Hall & Gdns. (HG4 5AE) 3F **99**
Newcastle Castle, Bridgend. (CF31 4JW) 3B 32
Newcastle Upon Tyne Castle Keep (NE1 1RQ) **197**
New Forest Nat. Pk. (SO43 7BD) 1H **15**
New Lanark World Heritage Site (ML11 9DB) 5B **128**
Newmarket Racecourse. (CB8 0TG) 4F 65
Newquay Zoo. (TR7 2LZ) 2C 6
Newstead Abbey (NG15 8NA) 5C **86**
Nine Ladies Stone Circle (DE4 2LF) 4G **85**
Norfolk Broads Nat. Pk. (NR3 1BJ) 5G **79**
Norfolk Lavender (PE31 7JE) 2F **77**
Norham Castle. (TD15 2LL) 5F 131
Normanby Hall Mus. (DN15 9HU) 3B **94**
North Downs (GU10 5QE) 5C **38**
North Norfolk Railway (NR26 8RA) 1D **78**
Northumberlandia, the Lady of the North
(NE23 8AU) 2F **115**
Northumberland Nat. Pk. (NE46 1BS) 5C **120**
North York Moors Nat. Pk. (YO18 8RN) 5D **107**
North Yorkshire Moors Railway (YO18 7AJ) 1C **100**
Norton Conyers (HG4 5EQ) 2F **99**
Norton Priory Mus. & Gdns. (WA7 1SX) 2H **83**
Norwich Castle Mus. & Art Gallery
(NR1 3JU) **200** (5E **79**)
Norwich Cathedral (NR1 4DH) **200** (5E **79**)
Nostell Priory (WF4 1QE) 3E **93**
Nuffield Place (RG9 5RX) 3E **37**
Nunney Castle. (BA11 4LN) 2C 22
Nunnington Hall (YO62 5UY) 2A **100**
Nymans (RH17 6EB) 3D **26**

O

Oakham Castle (LE15 6DR) 5F **75**
Oakwell Hall. (WF17 9LG) 2C 92
Oakwood Theme Pk. (SA67 8DE) 3E **43**
The Observatory Science Cen. (BN27 1RN) 4A **28**
Oceanarium (BH2 5AA) **Bournemouth 192**
Offa's Dyke, Brockweir (NP16 7NQ) 5A **48**
Okehampton Castle. (EX20 1JA) 3F 11
Old Beaupre Castle (CF71 7LT) 4D **32**
Old Gorhambury House (AL3 6AH) 5B **52**
Old Oswestry Hill Fort (SY10 7AA) 2E **71**
Old Sarum (SP1 3SD) 3G **23**
Old Wardour Castle (SP3 6RR) 4E **23**
Old Winchester Hill Hill Fort (GU32 1HN) 4E **25**
Orford Castle & Mus. (IP12 2NF) 1H 55
Orford Ness (IP12 2NU) 1H **55**
Ormesby Hall (TS7 9AS) 3C **106**
Osborne House (PO32 6JX) 3D **16**
Osterley Pk. & House. (TW7 4RB) 3C 38
Oulton Pk. Circuit (CW6 9BW) 4H **83**
Overbeck's (TQ8 8LW) 5D **8**
Owletts (DA12 3AP) 4A **40**
Oxburgh Hall (PE33 9PS) 5G **77**
Oxford Christ Church Cathedral
(OX1 4JF) **200** (5D **50**)
Oxford Island Nat. Nature Reserve
(BT66 6NJ) 3E **178**
Oxwich Castle. (SA3 1LU) 4D 31
Oystermouth Castle (SA3 5TA) 4F **31**

P

Packwood House (B94 6AT) 3F **61**
Paignton Zoo (TQ4 7EU) 3E **9**
Painshill Pk. (KT11 1JE) 5B **38**
Painswick Rococo Gdn. (GL6 6TH) 4D **48**
Palace of Holyroodhouse
(EH8 8DX) **Edinburgh 195** (2F **129**)
Papplewick Pumping Station (NG15 9AJ) 5C **86**
Paradise Pk. Wildlife Sanctuary (TR27 4HB) 3C **4**
Paradise Wildlife Pk. (EN10 7QZ) 5D **52**
Parcevall Hall Gdns. (BD23 6DE) 3C **98**
Parham (RH20 4HS) 4B **26**
Pashley Manor Gdns. (TN5 7HE) 3B **28**
Patterson's Spade Mill (BT39 0AP) 8J **175**
Paultons Pk. (SO51 6AL) 1B **16**
Paxton House. (TD15 1SZ) 4F 131
Paycocke's House & Gdn. (CO6 1NS) 3B **54**
Peak Cavern (S33 8WS) 2F **85**
Peak District Nat. Pk. (DE45 1AE) 2F **85**
Peak Rail (DE4 3NA) 4G **85**
Peckover House & Gdn. (PE13 1JR) 5D **76**
Peel Castle. (IM5 1AB) 3B 108
Pembroke Castle. (SA71 4LA) 4D 43
Pembrokeshire Coast Nat. Pk. (SA41 3XD) 4C **42**
Pencarrow (PL30 3AG) 5A **10**
Pendennis Castle (TR11 4LP) 5C **6**
Penrhyn Castle (LL57 4HN) 3F **81**
Penrith Castle. (CA11 7JB) 2G 103
Penshurst Place & Gdns. (TN11 8DG) 1G **27**
Peover Hall (WA16 9HW) 3B **84**
Perth Mus. & Art Gallery (PH1 5LB) **201**
Peterborough St Peter's Cathedral
(PE1 1XZ) **201** (1A **64**)
Petworth House & Pk. (GU28 0AE) 3A **26**
Pevensey Castle. (BN24 5LE) 5H 27
Peveril Castle (S33 8WQ) 2F **85**
Pickering Castle (YO18 7AX) 1C **100**
Picton Castle (SA62 4AS) 3E **43**
Piel Castle (LA13 0QN) 3B **96**
Pistyll Rhaeadr (SY10 0BZ) 3C **70**
Pitmedden Gdn. (AB41 7PD) 1F **153**
Pitt Rivers Mus. (OX1 3PP) **Oxford 200** (5D **50**)
Plantasia, Swansea (SA1 2AL) **203**
Plas Brondanw Gdns. (LL48 6SW) 1F **69**
Plas Newydd, Llangollen (LL20 8AW) 1E **70**
Plas Newydd, Llanfair Pwllgwyngyll
(LL61 6DQ) 4E **81**
Plas yn Rhiw (LL53 8AB) 3B **68**
Pleasurewood Hills (NR32 5DZ) 1H **67**
Poldark Mine (TR13 0ES) 5A **6**
Polesden Lacey (RH5 6BD) 5C **38**
Pollok House (G43 1AT) 3G **127**
Pontcysyllte Aqueduct (LL20 7YS) 1E **71**
Portchester Castle. (PO16 9QW) 2E 17
Portland Castle (DT5 1AZ) 5B **14**
Port Lympne Reserve (CT21 4PD) 2F **29**
Portsmouth Historic Dockyard
(PO1 3LJ) **201** (2E **17**)
The Potteries Mus. & Art Gallery (ST1 3DW) **202**
Powderham Castle. (EX6 8JQ) 4C 12
Powis Castle & Gdn. (SY21 8RF) 5E **70**
The Prebendal Manor House (PE8 6QG) 1H **63**
Prestongrange Mus. (EH32 9RX) 2G **129**
Preston Manor. (BN1 6SD) 5E 27
Preston Mill & Phantassie Doocot (EH40 3DS) 2B **130**
Preston Tower, Prestonpans (EH32 9NN) 2G **129**
Preston Tower, Chathill (NE67 5DH) 2F **121**
Prideaux Place (PL28 8RP) 1D **6**
Principality Stadium (CF10 1NS) **Cardiff 193**
Prior Pk. Landscape Gdn. (BA2 5AH) 5C **34**
Provan Hall (G34 9NJ) 3H **127**
Prudhoe Castle (NE42 6NA) 3D **115**

Q

Quantock Hills (TA4 4AP) 3E **21**
Quarry Bank Mill (SK9 4LA) 2C **84**
Quebec House (TN16 1TD) 5F **39**
Queen Elizabeth Country Pk. (PO8 0QE) 1F **17**
Queen Elizabeth Forest Pk. (FK8 3UZ) 4D **134**
Queen Elizabeth Olympic Pk. (E20 2ST) 2E **39**
Quex House & Gdns. (CT7 0BH) 4H **41**

R

Raby Castle (DL2 3AH) 2E **105**
RAF Holmpton (HU19 2RG) 2G **95**
RAF Mus. Cosford (TF11 8UP) 5B **72**
RAF Mus. London (NW9 5LL) 1D **38**
Raglan Castle (NP15 2BT) 5H **47**
Ragley (B49 5NJ) 5E **61**
Ramsey Island (SA62 6SA) 2A **42**
Ravenglass & Eskdale Railway (CA18 1SW) 5C **102**
Raveningham Gdns. (NR14 6NS) 1F **67**
Ravenscraig Castle (KY1 2AZ) 4E **137**
Reculver Towers (CT6 6SX) 4G **41**
Red House (DA6 8JF) 3F **39**
Renishaw Hall & Gdns. (S21 3WB) 3B **86**
Restoration House, Rochester
(ME1 1RF) **Medway Towns 197**
Restormel Castle (PL22 0HN) 2F **7**
Revolution House (S41 9LA) 3A **86**
Rheged Cen. (CA11 0DQ) 2F **103**
Rheidol Power Station (SY23 3NF) 3G **57**
Rhossili Bay (SA3 1PR) 4D **30**
RHS Gdn. Harlow Carr (HG3 1QB) 4E **99**
RHS Gdn. Hyde Hall (CM3 8ET) 1B **40**
RHS Gdn. Rosemoor (EX38 8PH) 1F **11**
RHS Gdn. Wisley (GU23 6QB) 5B **38**
Rhuddlan Castle. (LL18 5AD) 3C 82
Ribchester Roman Mus. (PR3 3XS) 1E **91**
Richmond Castle. (DL10 4QW) 4E 105
Rievaulx Abbey (YO62 5LB) 1H **99**
Rievaulx Terrace (YO62 5LJ) 1H **99**
Ripley Castle (HG3 3AY) 3E **99**
Ripon Cathedral. (HG4 1QT) 2F 99
River & Rowing Mus. (RG9 1BF) 3F **37**
Riverside Mus., Mus. of Transport & Travel.
(G3 8RS) 3G 127
Robert Burns Birthplace Mus. (KA7 4PY) 3C **116**
Robert Burns House
(DG1 2PS) **Dumfries 194** (2A **112**)
Roche Abbey (S66 8NW) 2C **86**
Rochester Castle
(ME1 1SW) **Medway Towns 197** (4B **40**)
Rochester Cathedral
(ME1 1SX) **Medway Towns 197** (4B **40**)
Rockbourne Roman Villa (SP6 3PG) 1G **15**
Rockingham Castle (LE16 8TH) 1F **63**
Rockingham Motor Speedway (NN17 5AF) 1G **63**
Rocks by Rail (LE15 7BX) 4F **75**
Rode Hall & Gdns. (ST7 3QP) 5C **84**
Rodmarton Manor (GL7 6PF) 2E **35**
Rokeby Pk. (DL12 9RZ) 3D **105**
Rollright Stones (OX7 5QB) 2A **50**
Roman Army Mus. (CA8 7JB) 3H **113**
Roman Baths (BA1 1LZ) **Bath 192** (5C **34**)
The Roman Painted House (CT17 9AJ) **Dover 194**
Roman Vindolanda (NE47 7JN) 3A **114**
Romney, Hythe & Dymchurch Railway
(TN28 8PL) 3E **29**
Roseberry Topping (TS9 6QX) 3C **106**
Rothesay Castle. (PA20 0DA) 3B 126
Rothiemurchus Cen (PH22 1QH) 2D **150**
Rousham House & Gdns. (OX25 4QX) 3C **50**
Rowallane Gdn. (BT24 7JA) 4J **179**
Royal Academy of Arts (Burlington House)
(W1J 0BD) **London 199**
Royal Albert Bridge. (PL12 4QT) 3A 8
The Royal Armouries Mus. (LS10 1LT) **Leeds 196**
Royal Botanic Gdn. (EH3 5LR) 2F **129**
Royal Botanic Gdns., Kew (TW9 3AB) 3C **38**
Royal Cornwall Mus. (TR1 2SJ) 4C **6**
Royal Crown Derby Mus. (DE23 8JZ) **194** (2A **74**)
Royal Mint Mus. (CF72 8YT) 3D **32**
Royal Navy Submarine Mus. (PO12 2AS) 3E **16**
Royal Pavilion
(BN1 1EE) **Brighton & Hove 192** (5E **27**)
Royal Pump Room Mus.
(HG1 2RY) **Harrogate 196** (4E **99**)
Royal Yacht Britannia (EH6 6JJ) 2F **129**
Ruddington Framework Knitters Mus.
(NG11 6HE) 2C **74**
Rufford Abbey (NG22 9DF) 4D **86**
Rufford Old Hall (L40 1SG) 3C **90**
Rufus Stone (SO43 7HN) 1A **16**
Rushton Triangular Lodge (NN14 1RP) 2F **63**
Russell-Cotes Art Gallery & Mus.
(BH1 3AA) **Bournemouth 192** (3F **15**)
Rutland County Mus. (LE15 6HW) 5F **75**
Rydal Mount & Gdns. (LA22 9LU) 4E **103**
Ryedale Folk Mus. (YO62 6UA) 5E **107**
Ryton Gdns. (CV8 3LG) 3B **62**

S

Saatchi Gallery (SW3 4RY) **London 198**
Sainsbury Cen. for Visual Arts (NR4 7TJ) 5D **78**

Limited Interchange Motorway Junctions

Limited Interchange Motorway Junctions are shown on the mapping pages by red junction indicators **2**

M1

Junction	Direction	Restriction
2	Northbound	No exit, access from A1 only
	Southbound	No access, exit to A1 only
4	Northbound	No exit, access from A41 only
	Southbound	No access, exit to A41 only
6a	Northbound	No exit, access from M25 only
	Southbound	No access, exit to M25 only
17	Northbound	No access, exit to M45 only
	Southbound	No exit, access from M45 only
19	Northbound	Exit to M6 only, access from A14 only
	Southbound	Access from M6 only, exit to A14 only
21a	Northbound	No access, exit to A46 only
	Southbound	No exit, access from A46 only
24a	Northbound	No exit
	Southbound	Access from A50 only
35a	Northbound	No access, exit to A616 only
	Southbound	No exit, access from A616 only
43	Northbound	Exit to M621 only
	Southbound	Access from M621 only
48	Eastbound	Exit to A1(M) northbound only
	Westbound	Access from A1(M) southbound only

M2

Junction	Direction	Restriction
1	Eastbound	Access from A2 eastbound only
	Westbound	Exit to A2 westbound only

M3

Junction	Direction	Restriction
8	Eastbound	No exit, access from A303 only
	Westbound	No access, exit to A303 only
10	Northbound	No access from A31
	Southbound	No exit to A31
13	Southbound	No access from A335 to M3 leading to M27 Eastbound

M4

Junction	Direction	Restriction
1	Eastbound	Exit to A4 eastbound only
	Westbound	Access from A4 westbound only
21	Eastbound	No exit to M48
	Westbound	No access from M48
23	Eastbound	No access from M48
	Westbound	No exit to M48
25	Eastbound	No exit
	Westbound	No access
25a	Eastbound	No exit
	Westbound	No access
29	Eastbound	No exit, access from A48(M) only
	Westbound	No access, exit to A48(M) only
38	Westbound	No access, exit to A48 only
39	Eastbound	No access or exit
	Westbound	No exit, access from A48 only
42	Eastbound	No access from A48
	Westbound	No exit to A48

M5

Junction	Direction	Restriction
10	Northbound	No exit, access from A4019 only
	Southbound	No access, exit to A4019 only
11a	Southbound	No exit to A417 westbound
18a	Northbound	No access from M49
	Southbound	No exit to M49

M6

Junction	Direction	Restriction
3a	Eastbound	No exit to M6 Toll
	Westbound	No access from M6 Toll
4	Northbound	No exit to M42 northbound No access from M42 southbound
	Southbound	No exit to M42 No access from M42 southbound
4a	Northbound	No exit, access from M42 southbound only
	Southbound	No access, exit to M42 only
5	Northbound	No access, exit to A452 only
	Southbound	No exit, access from A452 only
10a	Northbound	No access, exit to M54 only
	Southbound	No exit, access from M54 only
11a	Northbound	No exit to M6 Toll
	Southbound	No access from M6 Toll
20	Northbound	No exit to M56 eastbound
	Southbound	No access from M56 westbound
24	Northbound	No exit, access from A58 only
	Southbound	No access, exit to A58 only
25	Northbound	No access, exit to A49 only
	Southbound	No exit, access from A49 only
30	Northbound	No exit, access from M61 northbound only
	Southbound	No access, exit to M61 southbound only
31a	Northbound	No access, exit to B6242 only
	Southbound	No exit, access from B6242 only
45	Northbound	No access onto A74(M)
	Southbound	No exit from A74(M)

M6 Toll

Junction	Direction	Restriction
T1	Northbound	No exit
	Southbound	No access
T2	Northbound	No access or exit
	Southbound	No access
T5	Northbound	No exit
	Southbound	No access
T7	Northbound	No access from A5
	Southbound	No exit
T8	Northbound	No exit to A460 northbound
	Southbound	No exit

M8

Junction	Direction	Restriction
6	Eastbound	No exit, access only
	Westbound	No access, exit only
6a	Eastbound	No access, exit only
	Westbound	No exit, access only
7	Eastbound	No access, exit only
	Westbound	No exit, access only
7a	Eastbound	No exit, access from A725 Northbound only
	Westbound	No access, exit to A725 Southbound only
8	Eastbound	No exit to M73 northbound
	Westbound	No access from M73 southbound
9	Eastbound	No access, exit only
	Westbound	No exit, access only
13	Eastbound	No access from M80 southbound
	Westbound	No exit to M80 northbound
14	Eastbound	No access, exit only
	Westbound	No exit, access only
16	Eastbound	No exit, access only
	Westbound	No access, exit only
17	Eastbound	No exit, access from A82 only
	Westbound	No access, exit to A82 only
18	Westbound	No exit, access only
19	Eastbound	No exit to A814 eastbound
	Westbound	No access from A814 westbound
20	Eastbound	No exit, access only
	Westbound	No access, exit only
21	Eastbound	No access, exit only
	Westbound	No exit, access only
22	Eastbound	No exit, access from M77 only
	Westbound	No access, exit to M77 only
23	Eastbound	No exit, access from B768 only
	Westbound	No access, exit to B768 only
25	Eastbound & Westbound	Access from A739 southbound only Exit to A739 northbound only
25a	Eastbound	Access only
	Westbound	Exit only
28	Eastbound	No exit, access from airport only
	Westbound	No access, exit to airport only
29a	Eastbound	No exit, access only
	Westbound	No access, exit only

M9

Junction	Direction	Restriction
2	Northbound	No exit, access from B8046 only
	Southbound	No access, exit to B8046 only
3	Northbound	No access, exit to A803 only
	Southbound	No exit, access from A803 only
6	Northbound	No exit, access only
	Southbound	No access, exit to A905 only
8	Northbound	No access, exit to M876 only
	Southbound	No exit, access from M876 only

M11

Junction	Direction	Restriction
4	Northbound	No exit, access from A406 eastbound only
	Southbound	No access, exit to A406 westbound only
5	Northbound	No access, exit to A1168 only
	Southbound	No exit, access from A1168 only
8a	Northbound	No access, exit only
	Southbound	No exit, access only
9	Northbound	No access, exit only
	Southbound	No exit, access only
13	Northbound	No access, exit only
	Southbound	No exit, access only
14	Northbound	No access from A428 eastbound No exit to A428 westbound
	Southbound	No exit, access from A428 southbound only

M20

Junction	Direction	Restriction
2	Eastbound	No access, exit to A20 only (access via M26 Junction 2a)
	Westbound	No exit, access only (exit via M26 Jun.2a)
3	Eastbound	No exit, access from M26 eastbound only
	Westbound	No access, exit to M26 westbound only
10	Eastbound	No access, exit only
	Westbound	No exit, access only
11a	Eastbound	No access from Channel Tunnel
	Westbound	No exit to Channel Tunnel

M23

Junction	Direction	Restriction
7	Northbound	No exit to A23 southbound
	Southbound	No access from A23 northbound

M25

Junction	Direction	Restriction
5	Clockwise	No exit to M26 eastbound
	Anti-clockwise	No access from M26 westbound
Spur to A21	Northbound	No exit to M26 eastbound
	Southbound	No access from M26 westbound
19	Clockwise	No access, exit only
	Anti-clockwise	No exit, access only
21	Clockwise & Anti-clockwise	No exit to M1 southbound No access from M1 northbound
31	Northbound	No access, exit only (access via Jun.30)
	Southbound	No exit, access only (exit via Jun.30)

M26

Junction	Direction	Restriction
Junction with M25 (M25 Jun.5)	Eastbound	No access from M25 clockwise or spur from A21 northbound
	Westbound	No exit to M25 anti-clockwise or spur to A21 southbound
Junction with M20 (M20 Jun.3)	Eastbound	No exit to M20 westbound
	Westbound	No access from M20 eastbound

M27

Junction	Direction	Restriction
4	Eastbound & Westbound	No exit to A33 southbound (Southampton) No access from A33 northbound
10	Eastbound	No exit, access from A32 only
	Westbound	No access, exit to A32 only

M40

Junction	Direction	Restriction
3	North-Westbound	No access, exit to A40 only
	South-Eastbound	No exit, access from A40 only
7	N.W bound	No access, exit only
	S.E bound	No exit, access only
13	N.W bound	No access, exit only
	S.E bound	No exit, access only
14	N.W bound	No exit, access only
	S.E bound	No access, exit only
16	N.W bound	No exit, access only
	S.E bound	No access, exit only

M42

Junction	Direction	Restriction
1	Eastbound	No exit
	Westbound	No access
7	Northbound	No access, exit to M6 only
	Southbound	No exit, access from M6 northbound only
8	Northbound	No exit, access from M6 southbound only
	Southbound	Exit to M6 nothbound only Access from M6 southbound only

M45

Junction	Direction	Restriction
Junction with M1 (M1 Jun.17)	Eastbound	No exit to M1 northbound
	Westbound	No access from M1 southbound
Junction with A45 east of Dunchurch	Eastbound	No access, exit to A45 only
	Westbound	No exit, access from A45 northbound only

M48

Junction	Direction	Restriction
Junction with M4 (M4 Jun.21)	Eastbound	No exit to M4 westbound
	Westbound	No access from M4 eastbound
Junction with M4 (M4 Jun.23)	Eastbound	No access from M4 westbound
	Westbound	No exit to M4 eastbound

M53

Junction	Direction	Restriction
11	Northbound & Southbound	No access from M56 eastbound, no exit to M56 westbound

M56

Junction	Direction	Restriction
1	Eastbound	No exit to M60 N.W bound No exit to A34 southbound
	S.E bound	No access from A34 northbound
	Westbound	No access from M60
2	Eastbound	No exit, access from A560 only
	Westbound	No access, exit to A560 only
3	Eastbound	No access, exit only
	Westbound	No exit, access only
4	Eastbound	No exit, access only
	Westbound	No access, exit only
7	Westbound	No access, exit only
8	Eastbound	No access or exit
	Westbound	No exit, access from A556 only
9	Eastbound	No access from M6 northbound
	Westbound	No exit to M60 southbound
10a	Northbound	No exit, access only
	Southbound	No access, exit only
15	Eastbound	No exit to M53
	Westbound	No access from M53

M57

Junction	Direction	Restriction
3	Northbound	No exit, access only
	Southbound	No access, exit only
5	Northbound	No exit, access from A580 westbound only
	Southbound	No access, exit to A580 eastbound only

M60

Junction	Direction	Restriction
2	N.E bound	No access, exit to A560 only
	S.W bound	No exit, access from A560 only
3	Eastbound	No access from A34 southbound
	Westbound	No exit to A34 northbound
4	Eastbound	No exit to M56 S.W bound No exit to A34 northbound
	Westbound	No access from A34 southbound No access from M56 eastbound
5	N.W bound	No access from or exit to A5103 southbound
	S.E bound	No access from or exit to A5103 northbound
14	Eastbound	No exit to A580 No access from A580 westbound
	Westbound	No exit to A580 eastbound No access from A580
16	Eastbound	No exit, access from A666 only
	Westbound	No access, exit to A666 only
20	Eastbound	No access from A664
	Westbound	No exit to A664
22	Westbound	No access from A62
25	S.W bound	No access from A560 / A6017
26	N.E bound	No access or exit
27	N.E bound	No access, exit only
	S.W bound	No exit, access only

M61

Junction	Direction	Restriction
2&3	N.W bound	No access from A580 eastbound
	S.E bound	No exit to A580 westbound
Junction with M6 (M6 Jun.30)	N.W bound	No exit to M6 southbound
	S.E bound	No access from M6 northbound

M62

Junction	Direction	Restriction
23	Eastbound	No access, exit to A640 only
	Westbound	No exit, access from A640 only

M65

Junction	Direction	Restriction
9	N.E bound	No access, exit to A679 only
	S.W bound	No exit, access from A679 only
11	N.E bound	No exit, access only
	S.W bound	No access, exit only

M66

Junction	Direction	Restriction
1	Northbound	No access, exit to A56 only
	Southbound	No exit, access from A56 only

M67

Junction	Direction	Restriction
1	Eastbound	Access from A57 eastbound only
	Westbound	Exit to A57 westbound only
1a	Eastbound	No access, exit to A6017 only
	Westbound	No exit, access from A6017 only
2	Eastbound	No exit, access from A57 only
	Westbound	No access, exit to A57 only

M69

Junction	Direction	Restriction
2	N.E bound	No exit, access from B4669 only
	S.W bound	No access, exit to B4669 only

M73

Junction	Direction	Restriction
1	Southbound	No exit to A721 eastbound
2	Northbound	No access from M8 eastbound No exit to A89 eastbound
	Southbound	No exit to M8 westbound No access from A89 westbound
3	Northbound	No exit to A80 S.W bound
	Southbound	No access from A80 N.E bound

M74

Junction	Direction	Restriction
1	Eastbound	No access from M8 Westbound
	Westbound	No exit to M8 Westbound
3	Eastbound	No exit
	Westbound	No access
7	Northbound	No exit, access from A72 only
	Southbound	No access, exit to A72 only
9	Northbound	No access or exit
	Southbound	No access, exit to B7078 only
10	Southbound	No exit, access from B7078 only
11	Northbound	No exit, access from B7078 only
	Southbound	No access, exit to B7078 only
12	Northbound	No access, exit to A70 only
	Southbound	No exit, access from A70 only

M77

Junction	Direction	Restriction
Junction with M8 (M8 Jun.22)	Northbound	No exit to M8 westbound
	Southbound	No access from M8 eastbound
4	Northbound	No exit
	Southbound	No access
6	Northbound	No exit to A77
	Southbound	No access from A77
7	Northbound	No access from A77 No exit to A77

M80

Junction	Direction	Restriction
1	Northbound	No access from M8 westbound
	Southbound	No exit to M8 eastbound
4a	Northbound	No access
	Southbound	No exit
6a	Northbound	No exit
	Southbound	No access
8	Northbound	No access from M876
	Southbound	No exit to M876

M90

Junction	Direction	Restriction
1	Northbound	No exit
	Southbound	No Access from A90
2a	Northbound	No access, exit to A92 only
	Southbound	No exit, access from A92 only
7	Northbound	No exit, access from A91 only
	Southbound	No access, exit to A91 only
8	Northbound	No access, exit to A91 only
	Southbound	No exit, access from A91 only
10	Northbound	No access from A912 Exit to A912 northbound only
	Southbound	No exit to A912 Access from A912 southbound only

M180

Junction	Direction	Restriction
1	Eastbound	No access, exit only
	Westbound	No exit, access from A18 only

M606

Junction	Direction	Restriction
2	Northbound	No access, exit only

M621

Junction	Direction	Restriction
2a	Eastbound	No exit, access only
	Westbound	No access, exit only
4	Southbound	No exit
5	Northbound	No access, exit to A61 only
	Southbound	No exit, access from A61 only
6	Northbound	No exit, access only
	Southbound	No access, exit only
7	Eastbound	No access, exit only
	Westbound	No exit, access only
8	Northbound	No access, exit only
	Southbound	No exit, access only

M876

Junction	Direction	Restriction
Junction with M80 (M80 Jun.5)	N.E bound	No access from M80 southbound
	S.W bound	No exit to M80 northbound
Junction with M9 (M9 Jun.8)	N.E bound	No exit to M9 northbound
	S.W bound	No access from M9 southbound

A1(M)

Junction	Direction	Restriction
Hertfordshire Section		
2	Northbound	No access, exit only
	Southbound	No exit, access from A1001 only
3	Southbound	No access, exit only
5	Northbound	No exit, access only
	Southbound	No access or exit
Cambridgeshire Section		
14	Northbound	No exit, access only
	Southbound	No access, exit only
Leeds Section		
40	Southbound	Exit to A1 southbound only
43	Northbound	Access from M1 eastbound only
	Southbound	Exit to M1 westbound only
Durham Section		
57	Northbound	No access, exit to A66(M) only
	Southbound	No exit, access from A66(M)
65	Northbound	Exit to A1 N.W bound and to A194(M) only
	Southbound	Access from A1 S.E bound and from A194(M) only

A3(M)

Junction	Direction	Restriction
4	Northbound	No access, exit only
	Southbound	No exit, access only

Aston Expressway A38(M)

Junction	Direction	Restriction
Junction with Victoria Road, Aston	Northbound	No exit, access only
	Southbound	No access, exit only

A48(M)

Junction	Direction	Restriction
Junction with M4 (M4 Jun.29)	N.E bound	Exit to M4 eastbound only
	S.W bound	Access from M4 westbound only
29a	N.E bound	Access from A48 eastbound only
	S.W bound	Exit to A48 westbound only

Mancunian Way A57(M)

Junction	Direction	Restriction
Junction with A34 Brook Street, Manchester	Eastbound	No access, exit to A34 Brook Street, southbound only
	Westbound	No exit, access only

Leeds Inner Ring Road A58(M)

Junction	Direction	Restriction
Junction with Park Lane / Westgate	Southbound	No access, exit only

Leeds Inner Ring Road A64(M) (continuation of A58(M))

Junction	Direction	Restriction
Junction with A58 Clay Pit Lane	Eastbound	No access
	Westbound	No exit

A66(M)

Junction	Direction	Restriction
Junction with A1(M) (A1(M) Jun.57)	N.E bound	Access from A1(M) northbound only
	S.W bound	Exit to A1(M) southbound only

A74(M)

Junction	Direction	Restriction
18	Northbound	No access
	Southbound	No exit

Newcastle Central Motorway A167(M)

Junction	Direction	Restriction
Junction with Camden Street	Northbound	No exit, access only
	Southbound	No access or exit

A194(M)

Junction	Direction	Restriction
Junction with A1(M) (A1(M) Jun.65) and A1 Gateshead Western By-Pass	Northbound	Access from A1(M) only
	Southbound	Exit to A1(M) only

Northern Ireland

M1

Junction	Direction	Restriction
3	Northbound	No exit, access only
	Southbound	No access, exit only
7	Westbound	No access, exit only

M2

Junction	Direction	Restriction
2	Eastbound	No access to M5 northbound
	Westbound	No exit to M5 southbound

M5

Junction	Direction	Restriction
2	Northbound	No access from M2 eastbound
	Southbound	No exit to M2 westbound

customised **MAP** products

Customised Wall Maps

- Any area and size, designed to your specification. Perfect for display in your office.
- Add logos, company information or have the map in your corporate colours.
- Additional information can be overlaid, such as postcode boundaries or radius rings.
- Choose from a range of mounting types such as Acrylic, Foamex board, wallpaper and many more.

Digital Mapping

- High resolution map data available in a range of scales – road, street and large scale.
- Perfect for use within GIS applications.
- Ideal for large format printing, within brochures or in presentations.
- Mapping can be supplied in full colour, black and white or corporate colours.
- A separate gazetteer of street names and grid references can be supplied to accompany a custom map image.

Additional Products

- Posters,which can be framed, covering a range of cities and in a variety of colours.
- Wallpaper: all major cities across the UK are available. Our set size, set area wallpaper makes the perfect feature wall that you won't get bored of.
  For more personalised areas, maybe centred on a location of your choice, please contact us.
- Gifts that are perfect for those special occasions.
- Customised Location and Route Planning maps.

Cartographic Services

Our highly skilled and experienced cartographic services team can modify and interpret geographical data to create products for your business. Working with you on map design and bespoke cartographic projects including advertising material, walking and cycle guides, transport maps, major event publications and information panels.

To discuss your specific map requirements please call us on: 01732 783413 or contact us via our online enquiry form on www.azdigital.co.uk

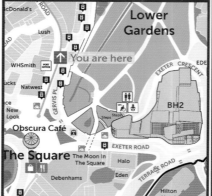

www./az.co.uk